——second edition——

DISPLAYS

fundamentals & Applications

second edition

DISPLAYS

fundamentals & Applications

Rolf R. Hainich • **Oliver Bimber**

Foreword by Henry Fuchs

CRC Press
Taylor & Francis Group
Boca Raton London New York

CRC Press is an imprint of the
Taylor & Francis Group, an **informa** business

AN A K PETERS BOOK

CRC Press
Taylor & Francis Group
6000 Broken Sound Parkway NW, Suite 300
Boca Raton, FL 33487-2742

First issued in paperback 2020

© 2017 by Taylor & Francis Group, LLC
CRC Press is an imprint of Taylor & Francis Group, an Informa business

No claim to original U.S. Government works

ISBN-13: 978-1-4987-6568-8 (hbk)
ISBN-13: 978-0-367-65817-5 (pbk)

Visit the Taylor & Francis Web site at
http://www.taylorandfrancis.com

and the CRC Press Web site at
http://www.crcpress.com

Contents

List of Tables

Foreword to the Second Edition

I N MY FOREWORD TO THE FIRST EDITION OF THIS EXCELLENT BOOK (see below), I wrote "If there is a better text on this topic, I have yet to see it." Well, here it is – Hainich and Bimber took the best book and made it even better! For details on just how they made it better, see the section "The Second Edition" starting on page xxxii. Here I'll just highlight two areas that are particularly important: multi-viewer auto stereoscopic displays and near-eye displays. In the five years since the first edition of this book, these two areas have developed rapidly.

Generations of researchers (and users!) have dreamt of multi-viewer auto stereoscopic displays. In the past five years, new designs have been presented that may overcome the prohibitive cost, space, and quality issues that have plagued all previous such displays. In addition to the new advances in design, the second edition also expands the section on methods of recording for 3D displays.

As for near-eye displays, interest in them has exploded in the past five years. This second edition expands the first edition's already extended treatment of this important topic, including explanations of a wide variety of latest designs, including waveguides, diffractive optics, pinlights, and contact lenses. The included designs range from basic concepts to early prototype demonstrations to new commercial offerings.

All-in-all, the best single book on displays, made even better.

Henry Fuchs
Chapel Hill, North Carolina

Foreword to the First Edition

I AM PLEASED AND HONORED TO BE INVITED TO WRITE THE FOREWORD to this excellent book. In fact, it is not merely excellent; it may well be the best ever comprehensive overview of computer display technology. If there is a better text on this topic, I have yet to see it.

Display technology is of increasing importance to all of us. We humans are acutely visual beings, and in todays' world displays are truly ubiquitous. Of course, twenty years ago we would already have said that they were "ubiquitous", but today they're even more so – with mobile devices in every pocket, digital displays on every automobile dashboard, laptops and tablets with every student and adult, and large flat panel displays in every home and workplace. Stereo feature films are now commonplace and consumer televisions displays are increasingly 3D ready. And there is more to come–and soon. For those who wish to understand these technologies of today and tomorrow, this is the book to have and to study.

The authors wisely start the book by first whetting our appetites with a short history of display technology, starting around the Renaissance. Having captured our interest, they transition to an overview of the serious parts of this book.

Chapter 2 starts with the fundamentals of light, light generation, color gamut, plasma lamps, phosphor, electroluminescence, and radiometry. Next, the fundamentals of the physics of light are discussed, including classic experiments about uncertainty and quantum effects – surprising, but welcome topics in a book on computer display technology. Next, polarization and polarizing filters are described–ideas central to many computer displays.

Chapter 3 is a tutorial on the principles of optics, starting with wavefronts and diffraction, moving to reflective and refractive optics, including examples of concave and convex mirrors, and converging and diverging lenses, and also fresnel lenses. Also described are exciting new technologies such as varifocal "liquid lenses", which are applicable not only to miniature cameras in today's mobile devices but perhaps in the future, the authors point out, also to novel steerable autostereo displays (a topic treated in detail in Chapter 9).

Chapter 4 introduces visual perception. The authors include this topic in order to educate the reader to understand that display technologies always work through the human visual system; understanding that coupling is essential for the designer of any display system. Spatial and temporal and colorimetric response of the human visual system are covered in some detail. Stereo, depth perception, depth cues, and visual field effects are also explained, as are motion parallax and motion dynamics.

Holographic principles are covered in chapter 5. After presentation of basic principles, other topics are also described, such as holographic optical elements (HOE). These optical emulations of lenses, mirrors, and prisms are sometime used in display systems whose promoters label them "holographic". A variety of other holographic optical systems are also discussed.

Chapter 6 focuses on displays basics, with discussions of resolution, brightness, contrast, Gamma, color gamut, as well as wide-color gamut displays and luminescent and light valve displays. The chapter also includes a discussion of signal and image processing issues such as sampling, antialiasing, image compression, noise reduction; electronic issues such as passive and active matrix displays; and assembly issues such as touch sensing and tactile feedback.

Spatial light modulation is the topic of chapter 7, including LCDs, LCoS, DMDs and esoteric technologies such as PISTON-type micro-mirror displays and electronic paper. Projection displays are also covered, including projection optics and the various image-forming technologies: CRT, LCD, DLP, and others. Chapter 8 discusses camera-projector systems.

Chapter 9 describes a wide variety of three-dimensional displays. All these chapters are solid, serious, sober. They cover material that is well-documented in the research literature and well understood from commercial products. The same characterization applies to the long (nearly 30-page) Appendix on image processing for displays, one that includes a discussion about GPUs and GPU-based algorithms for common raster graphics operations such as color space conversions and image distortion correction– and much more.

The book's last two chapters are decidedly more colorful, wide-ranging, and speculative. The book's final chapter, on Discussion and Outlook, includes such "far out" possibilities as brain-computer interface, and retinal and neural implants. These ideas are casually tossed about in the general culture and in science fiction films, so if for no other reason, it is useful for the student of display technology to have some exposure to them from a more serious source.

The penultimate chapter, Chapter 10, on Near-Eye Displays, what many call head-mounted displays (HMD), is perhaps the most colorful and wide-ranging portion of the book, veering between sober discussion of current HMDs and their optical designs to "theoretical" discussion about holographic scanners and microprojectors implanted in the eyeball.

Right in the introduction to the chapter, the authors forewarn the reader that after more than 40 years of research, a head-mounted display that's effective for widespread consumer applications still does not exist. The rest of the chapter is a study of the complex design issues and plethora of the conflicting constraints. A selection of optical designs used in commercial and research systems are described and illustrated.

Sections on these are followed by several design studies developed by the authors. Designs to solve different problems are sketched out. The authors admirably include various caveats such as "The usefulness of most of these concepts has not been tested in practice thus far." An entire somewhat-speculative section is devoted to "Holographic image generation for NED". However, a following section, on NEDs that use of Holographic Optical Elements, brings the reader back to real, working, commercial display systems.

The very next section (10.11), on contact lens displays, is among the most vivid in the book. The authors flatly state "some recent reports about actual 'contact lens displays' were greatly exaggerated". They then describe what has actually been demonstrated (very little) and speculate on paths toward realizing certain necessary developments. They consider several possible developments paths, including including miniature moving mirrors inside a thick contact lens, and even microprojectors implanted in the eyeball(!). None of these seem very feasible. They therefore conclude that "contact lens displays up to now are just mere speculation". However, our optimistic authors don't give up on finding some solutions to NEDs; they go on to describe various designs and technologies for adaptive displays (e.g., micro piezo motors) and eye tracking methods needed to control them. There is also a short section on video see-through displays (a topic that would benefit from more extensive coverage), and a section on the design of an optical see-through HMD that can mask out any parts of the real world that are occluded by pixels of virtual objects that are closer to the user.

The authors end the chapter with a combination of sober conclusions (effective NEDs are "far off") and enthusiastic speculation about smart phones driving sophisticated NEDs with eye-tracking and eye-steering, of web pages "floating in space, hardly occluding the real environment. With a plastic front mirror and a totally integrated eye-tracker chip, this could all be affordable and simple". How can you resist such enthusiasm?

As with any comprehensive introductory text, the interested reader often yearns for more detail in many sections. The overwhelming reaction, however, is one of gratitude to the authors for compiling, distilling, and integrating such a large body of useful knowledge into a single volume and then enhancing it so substantially with ideas and designs of their own. They have produced a fascinating book, one that will be valued by serious students of the field for many years to come.

Henry Fuchs
Chapel Hill, North Carolina

Preface

SINCE ITS INVENTION IN THE LATE TWENTIES, TELEVISION HAS RADICALLY SHAPED the 20th century. Today, most of our visual entertainment and daily technological tasks are viewed on new and innovative displays. Bulky cathode-ray tubes, for instance, have almost completely disappeared from our desks and have been widely replaced by flat panels. The form-factor and style of home-entertainment displays is evolving from small cubes to large planes. The maximum size of flat-panel devices is constrained by technological and applicability issues. If limits of size are reached, advanced video projectors may be an option in order to continue this trend.

Small displays are continuously carried around by most of us, as in the form of mobile phones, personal digital assistants, navigation systems, or laptops. What will come next? What will TVs be like in another 30 years? Will pixels be passed over in favor of voxels or hogels? Will interactive three-dimensional experiences rule out passive two-dimensional ones? Will printed displays be sold by the square yard and be glued to the wall? Will disposable displays with built-in storage chips talk to us from the corn flakes box, powered by printed batteries? Or will we all be wearing display glasses, simulating for us any kind and any number of virtual displays we ever need? Or will we all wear chip implants that directly interface to our brains, eliminating any need for displays at all? These and other questions are of particular interest – especially considering that many of us will likely witness this evolution. Display technology will certainly be going through many interesting changes, and perhaps some unexpected revolutions as well. Currently, new displays are being developed at an ever-increasing pace. In the end, price and usability will determine which of these numerous developments will prevail. Concurrently, new possibilities such as flexible displays, electronic paper and display glasses will change usage habits and lead to new and entirely unexpected applications. These complex interdependencies make the future of display technology quite unpredictable.

The purpose of our work is to address many of the recent and current developments, and to offer technical insights into the present and the foreseeable future of display technologies and techniques. In spite of the overwhelming complexity of the field, the following pages will provide information so that interested students and professionals may make qualified evaluations of existing and soon-to-appear displays. We also present some innovative ideas of our own that we hope will stimulate further research and development.

WHO SHOULD READ THIS BOOK

This self-contained book is written for students and professionals in computer science, engineering, media, and arts who have an interest in present and future graphical displays. With about 500 illustrations, it explains fundamentals that help to understand how particular types of displays work on a level that does not require a PhD in optics.

In particular, this book will discuss the following constructive topics: basics of wave optics and geometric optics, fundamentals of light modulation, principles of holography, visual perception and display measures and calibration methods, basic display technologies, projection displays, projector-camera systems and techniques (including calibration and image correction), essence of stereoscopic and auto-stereoscopic displays (including parallax displays, light-field displays and volumetric displays), functioning of computer-generated holography, near-eye displays and computer vision aspects that enable the visualization of graphical 2D and 3D content with such displays, as well as applications.

Supplementary material (including all images used in this book) can be found at http://www.displaysbook.info.

THE SECOND EDITION

The first edition of this book was published in 2011, 5 years ago. Given the dynamic developments in display technology, this is a long time and several recent developments were calling for an update.

In this period, flat-panel displays completed their replacement of nearly any screen at least in the more developed parts of the planet. LED technology conquered many applications, not only for displays but also for about any kind of electric lighting. Plasma displays vanished (making our extended treatment of them historic already), 3D became hype and then normal again, OLED screens became current with mobile phones while still struggling to conquer TV sets (not so unexpected, as reaching a competitive price level with a new technology always takes time), and an exotic technology like quantum dots is now present in almost any better TV.

Some of these news are adequately treated with small remarks, but others also called for additions in the fundamentals, like in the optics or the visual perception chapters. Topics concerned, for example, are mirror optics, index lenses, or depth perception. We also took up the opportunity to include many little improvements in the explanatory text and illustrations throughout the entire book.

Temporal resolution with 2D as well as 3D displays is a topic that deserved and received even more attention. Another new topic is smart displays, both for spatial and near-eye displays.

The chapter on three-dimensional displays received more on 3D recording and multi-viewer autostereoscopic displays, and several new topics such as compressive displays and focus synthesis.

The most dynamic field has been near-eye displays; it right out exploded since the last edition, with almost any major company investing hundreds of millions of dollars in development and acquisitions. We include an extended treatment of mirror optics and many new approaches such as on-axis displays, smart displays, lightfield near-eye displays, various types of waveguide displays, and diffractive optics, pinlight, and contact lens-supported near-eye displays.

We also include a new appendix, written by Rafał K. Mantiuk. The CUDA algorithms in the former appendix are now common knowledge. But a new topic with increasing display quality is calibration, as this enables an optimal reproduction of color and the best possible image, and we think this deserves increased attention. The appendix should therefore be a useful and timely guide to best practice in calibration, even more so as it concentrates on perceptual calibration techniques, requiring no measuring equipment.

Finally, we decided to make this book more affordable, by printing it in black and white, except for those illustrations essentially requiring color. We will still provide all figures (in color) and materials for download – for academic use – on the book's web page. This also includes supplemental materials to the book content originating from sources of our own, such as a Blender model for a comprehensive simulation of NED with mirror optics.

ADDITIONAL READINGS

For additional and in-depth information on individual topics, the following literature is recommended to complement the chapters this book:

- *The History of the Discovery of Cinematography*, Paul Burns, http://www. precinemahistory.net, is an extensive online collection of facts, covering the history of lenses, cameras, displays, and more. It complements our review in Chapter 1.

- *Light and Matter: Electromagnetism, Optics, Spectroscopy and Lasers*, Yehuda B. Band, Wiley & Sons, 2006, provides more mathematical background on the nature of light than is presented in Chapter 2.

- *Optics*, 4th edition, Eugene Hecht, Addison-Wesley, 2001, is a frequently used textbook on physical optics for undergraduate courses and completes our discussions in Chapter 3.

- *Field Guide to Geometrical Optics*, John E. Greivenkamp, SPIE Publications, 2003, is a textbook on geometric optics. It is also suitable for undergraduate students and complements Chapter 3.

- *Vision Science: Photons to Phenomenology*, Stephen E. Palmer, MIT Press, 1999, covers all of the details on visual perception that are not included in Chapter 4.

- *Seeing in Depth, Volume 1: Basic Mechanics; Volume 2: Depth Perception*, Ian P. Howard and Brian J. Rogers, Oxford University Press, 2008, is a superb two-volume edition on binocular vision that goes beyond the scope of our discussion in Chapter 4.

- *Practical Holography*, Graham Saxby, 3rd edition, IoP Publishing, 2004, is the classical book on optical holography and includes many practical examples. It complements Chapter 5.

- *Holographic Imaging*, Stephen Benton and V. Michael Bove, Wiley & Sons, 2008, is an excellent book by a pioneer of white-light and computer-generated holography and the inventor of rainbow holography. It provides additional information to that found in our Chapters 5 and 9.

- The SID-Wiley series on display technology (http://www.sid.org/publications/bookswiley.html) is an excellent book series of the Society of Information Displays (SID, http://www.sid.org) that covers more in-depth discussions on individual topics (such as backlight, liquid-crystal, and flat-panel technology; mobile and micro displays; as well as color engineering and display measurements). These books offer thorough discussion of the display basics explained in Chapter 6 and the presentation of spatial light modulators in Chapter 7.

- *Electrical Measurement, Signal Processing, and Displays*, John G. Webster, CRC Press, 2003, offers further details on the display-related signal processing discussions in Chapter 6.

- *Projection Displays*, Edward Stupp and Matthew Brennesholtz, 2nd edition, Wiley & Sons, 2008, complements the discussion on basic projection technology in Chapter 7. It is part of the SID-Wiley series in display technology (http://www.sid.org/publications/bookswiley.html).

- *High Dynamic Range Imaging: Acquisition, Display, and Image-Based Lighting*, 2nd edition, Erik Reinhard, Greg Ward, Sumanta Pattanaik, Paul Debevec, Wolfgang Heidrich, and Karol Myszkowski, Morgan Kaufman, 2010, is a comprehensive book that covers HDR fully. It provides all the details that have not been discussed in Chapter 7.

- *Practical Multi-Projector Display Design*, Aditi Majumder and Michael S. Brown, A K Peters, 2007, provides details on multiprojector calibration in addition to what is discussed in Chapter 8.

- *Three-Dimensional Television: Capture, Transmission, Display*, Haldun M. Ozaktas and Levent Onural, Springer, 2007, is a book written by more than 60 authors that provides a collection of different topics related to 3DTV. It also provides additional examples on concrete projects in the context of the 3D display technology that are explained in Chapter 9.

- *The End of Hardware: Augmented Reality and Beyond*, 3rd edition, Rolf R. Hainich, BookSurge Publishing, 2009, is the basis for Chapter 10 and parts of several others, and provides much additional detail on near-eye displays.

- *Spatial Augmented Reality: A Modern Approach to Augmented Reality*, Oliver Bimber and Ramesh Raskar, A K Peters, 2005, gives a different spin on augmented reality by using spatial display technology. It is complementary to Chapters 10 and 8.

- *The Other Brain*, R. D. Fields, Simon & Schuster, 2009, gives a very well-written overview on the state and latest discoveries in brain science, recommendable for anyone interested in more background on issues discussed in Chapter 11.

- *Color Imaging: Fundamentals and Applications*, Erik Reinhard, Erum Arif Khan, Ahmet Oguz Akyüz, and Garrett M. Johnson, A K Peters, 2008. Although it focuses less on display technology, it is complementary to this book because it gives an excellent and detailed overview over the entire digital imaging pipeline – including capturing and image processing. It also shares many basic considerations on fundamentals of physics, optics, and perception.

- *Color Appearance Models*, 2nd edition, Mark D. Fairchild, John Wiley & Sons, 2005. The essential resource for readers needing to understand visual perception and for those trying to produce, reproduce, and measure color appearance. It is complementary to Chapters 4 and 6 and the Appendix.

- *Information Display Measurement Standard*, Society for Information Display, 2012. The IDMS is the "go-to" document for standard measurement procedures to quantify electronic display characteristics and qualities. It is complementary to Chapters 2, 4, and 6 and the Appendix.

- *Contrast Sensitivity of the Human Eye and Its Effects on Image Quality*, Peter G. J. Barten, SPIE Press, 1999, provides equations for determining various aspects of contrast sensitivity, in addition to models (mathematical expressions) that can easily be adapted for practical applications. It is complementary to Chapter 4 and the Appendix.

- High Dynamic Range Imaging, Rafał K. Mantiuk, Karol Myszkowski, and Hans-Peter Seidel. In: *Wiley Encyclopedia of Electrical and Electronics Engineering*. This 81-page article offers a broad review of the HDR methods and technologies with an introduction on fundamental concepts behind the perception of HDR imagery. The preprint is available at http://www.cl.cam.ac.uk/rkm38/hdri_book.html. It is complementary to Chapters 4 and 7 and the Appendix.

ABOUT THE COVER

The illustration on the front cover is an artist impression about a near-eye display. The rings symbolize displayed data – in this case, the chapter structure of the book, similar to Figure 1.5 on page 10. Near-eye displays for augmented or virtual reality are an ultimate objective for display technology, and the more advanced the technology, the less visible will be the display itself – just as in the cover illustration.

ACKNOWLEDGMENTS

The idea for this book grew from courses on the subject of Information Displays taught by Oliver Bimber at different universities since 2006. He has taught these classes at the Bauhaus-University Weimar, the Technical University Munich, the University of Applied Sciences Hagenberg, the Brandenburg University of Technology Cottbus, and the Johannes Kepler University Linz. We thank the many students who have contributed to the book indirectly by asking pertinent and insightful questions. We have attempted to answer some of them in the following pages.

We are grateful to our reviewers who provided us with valuable feedback, suggestions, critics, and discussions (in alphabetical order):

- Mark Billinghurst, Human Interface Technology Laboratory New Zealand (HIT Lab NZ), Christchurch, NZ (now at University of South Australia)

- Nelson Chang, Hewlett-Packard Laboratories, Palo Alto, USA

- Neil Dodgson, Computer Laboratory, Cambridge University, UK (now at Victoria University of Wellington, NZ)

- Tim Frieb, Laservision, Germany

- Wolfgang Heidrich, Department of Computer Science, University of British Columbia, CA (now at King Abdullah University of Science and Technology)

- Hong Hua, College of Optical Sciences, University of Arizona, USA

- Daisuke Iwai, Graduate School of Engineering Science, Osaka University, JP

- Kiyoshi Kiyokawa, Cybermedia Center, Osaka University, JP

- Aditi Majumder, Department of Computer Science, University of California Irvine, USA

- Kari Pulli, Visual Computing and Ubiquitous Imaging, Nokia (now at Intel Corporation)

- Jannick Rolland, Institute of Optics, University of Rochester, USA

- Hideo Saito, Department of Information and Computer Science, Keio University, Japan

- Andrei State, Department of Computer Science, University of North Carolina at Chapel Hill, USA

They and our copyeditors, Eileen Worthley, Alice Peters, and Sarah Cutler for the first edition, and Karthick Parthasarathy for the second edition, helped to put the finishing touches on this book. Thank you very much!

Figures in Chapters 3, 4, 5, 6, 7, 9, and 10 are partly adapted from [116]. Chapter 8 (Projector-Camera Systems) is largely based on a previous state-of-the-art report, published at EUROGRAPHICS [31,32] (with friendly permission of the EUROGRAPHICS association). We thank the original co-authors Daisuke Iwai (Osaka University), Gordon Wetzstein (University of British Columbia, Stanford University) and Anselm Grundhöfer (Bauhaus-University Weimar, Disney Research, ETH Zürich). We thank Rafał K. Mantiuk for providing the appendix, Perceptual Display Calibration.

We also want to thank all colleagues, companies and institutions who provided additional image material (in alphabetical order):

Arrington Research, Mark Ashdown, Edwin P. Berlin (LightSail Energy), Fred Brooks (Univ. of N.C. at Chapel Hill), BAE Systens, Burton Inc., CAE Elektronik GmbH, Nelson Chang (Hewlett-Packard Laboratories), Paul Debevec (University of Southern California; Los Angeles), Elizabeth Downing (3DTL Inc.), Gregg Favalora, FogScreen Inc., FhG-IPMS (Fraunhofer Institute for Photonic Micro-systems), Markus Gross (Computer Graphics Laboratory, ETH Zurich), Wolfgang Heidrich (University of British Columbia; KAUST), HOLOEYE Photonics AG, Infitec GmbH, IMI Intelligent Medical Implants GmbH, Kent Displays Inc., Masahiko Kitamura (NTT Network Innovation Labs), Yoshifumi Kitamura (Tohoku University), Kiyoshi Kiyokawa (Osaka University), Sebastian Knorr (Technical University of Berlin), Franz Kreupl (Sandisk, citations from work at Infineon), Yuichi Kusakabe (NHK Science and Technical Research Laboratories), Knut Langhans (Gymnasium Staade), Leibniz-Rechenzentrum (Technical University Munich), LG Philips LCD, Light Blue Optics, LightSpace Technologies, Inc., Lumus Inc., Max Planck Institute of Biochemistry, Microsoft, Microvision Inc., Shree Nayar (Columbia University), New Scale Technologies, Richard A. Normann (University of Utah), NTERA, Oculus VR LLC, Hanhoon Park (NHK Science and Technology Research Laboratories Tokyo), Pixel Qi Corp., PolyIC, RAFI GmbH, Imso Rakkolainen (Tampere University of Technology), Retina Implant AG, Sax3d GmbH, Hideo Saito (Keio University), John Rogers (University of Illinois), SeeReal Technologies GmbH, Stefan Seipel (Uppsala University), Alfred Stett (NMI, Universität Tübingen), Dennis J. Solomon (Holoverse, Inc.), Gordon Wetzstein (University of British Columbia; Stanford University), U.S. Air Force 403rd Wing, VIOSO GmbH, WRSYSTEMS, Vusix Corporation, Walter Wrobel (Universitäts-Augenklinik Tübingen), Tomohiro Yendo (Nagoya University), Chongwu Zhou (University of Southern California), Eberhart Zrenner (Center for Ophthalmology, University of Tübingen).

CHAPTER 1

Introduction

M ANKIND HAS A FASCINATION FOR DISTANT PLACES and different times and a desire to observe such experiences without actually being there.

The paradigm of displays has been to provide a virtual window to a remote scene. In achieving this, the recording and the transmission of images are challenges that are as difficult to master as their presentation. Displays are at the forefront of this visual information link, and their requirements are restricted by the capabilities of our human visual system.

Fortunately, we can use our imaginations to get realistic visual impressions from flat images. We can imagine real scenes even if color is missing, we can approximate depth if the displayed scene is moving, and we can perceive images up to a maximum spatial and temporal resolution.

One of the simplest display implementation requires nothing more than a matrix of dots (also called *picture elements*, or short *pixels*) of varying brightness. If these pixels are small enough and dense enough, they will blend into an image for us. If these images are exchanged fast enough, they will merge into a moving scene.

Display technology has evolved tremendously within the past 50 years. The rapid development of semiconductor technology enabled entire circuits to be built directly on glass panels, making many kinds of light-generation principles accessible for display use. New methods of light modulation seem to be discovered every year. The explosive pace of information technology demands the correspondingly rapid development of innovative displays.

If we speak of displays today, we are most likely considering spatial flat panels, but there are many more forms. Projection displays, for example, have made considerable progress; they are so small now that they can be inserted into mobile phones. Microdisplays integrated into glasses may provide an alternative for many existing display concepts, because they can provide the impression of large or small screens without their weight or energy consumption. While some displays provide a fully immersive experience, others have become as flat as paper.

As a result of these developments, the simple "flat" window view that we have been accustomed to for so many years may be relinquished to new display principles providing a truly *three-dimensional* (3D) experience. These displays may be holographic, they may produce light fields or points in space, or they may simply deceive stereo vision. They may provide images for a singe user or many, and they may provide images dynamically adjusted for the viewer's perspective or location.

The evolution of displays and accompanying technologies with regard to the recording and transmission of images, has been strongly driven by consumer applications, such as television. Much of it has been enabled by the invention of the raster display, and the basic principle of scanning an image, transmitting it in serial form, and reassembling it at the receiver. In this book we will cover only the display link of this signal chain, with mention of the others where necessary.

The simple serializing principle, for example, may soon be replaced by the transformation of scenes into object descriptions. Presently, this requires a formidable amount of image processing, because object separation may be natural for the human eye but it is still difficult for machines. Yet, it will allow the application of virtual cameras to virtual scenes for synthesizing novel views, as is currently done for computer game scenes. The advantage of this process is a perfect 3D impression for any display size and type. Synthetic and real content can be merged more efficiently, allowing for a wide variety of production maneuvers and visual effects in a very easy way.

Regardless of the recording and transmission chain, displays themselves will be *two-dimensional* (2D) or 3D in any of the numerous scenarios that are possible today or tomorrow, until –some day– we may bypass the visual system entirely and send images directly to the brain. We will consider the possibilities of brain-computer interfaces in the last chapter of this book, but first we explore the richness of displays, their fundamentals, their applications, and the outlook for this technology.

1.1 DISPLAYS: BIRD'S-EYE VIEW

An electronic display can be considered a converter that translates time sequential electrical signals (analog or digital) into spatially and temporally configured visible light signals (i.e., images). The key component for this conversion is a device that is generally referred to as a *spatial light modulator*, or *SLM*.

With respect to the applied SLM technology, displays can be categorized into two main classes: self-luminous displays and light valve displays.

Light-valve displays require additional photon sources (i.e., external light sources) which are modulated spatially and temporally on the basis of either refraction, diffraction, reflection, transmission, polarization or phase changes. Self-luminous displays do not apply external light sources, but generate photons on their own from electrical excitations. A CRT TV is an example of a self-luminous display because it applies an electron beam to excite phosphor to emit visible photons; an LCD monitor is a light-valve display because it filters white back-light sources through polarization changes.

Electronics has always been closely related to display technologies, for signal processing as well as for display driving. From the earliest tube circuits, development has propelled toward highly integrated digital circuits, as well as large-scale semiconductor circuits coated directly onto display panels. An ever-growing number of technologies offer new possibilities. Latest developments, for example, are transparent circuits, organic semiconductors, compounds with carbon nanotubes, or quantum dots. This will be discussed more completely in a later chapter.

1.2 MILESTONES OF DISPLAY TECHNOLOGY

The evolution of display technology has been influenced primarily by the public desire for entertainment, with movie theaters and television being the two drawing cards of the last century, and 3D versions of film becoming increasingly popular at the moment.

Displays have evolved tremendously in the past 250 years, and even 3D became of interest several years ago. Beginning with purely optical experiments, the first real displays were mechanical and electromechanical, then transitioned to electronics, and are now complex digital structures. This evolution was clearly driven by the scientific advances of the corresponding eras. Therefore, it is interesting to consider the major scientific advances that are currently being made in order to hypothesize a potential future continuation of this evolution. Quantum mechanics, for example, will be one of these major scientific advancements.

In searching for the earliest examples of display technology, we first ought to know what we are looking for. The key question is, what is considered display, and what is not. A key property of a display for our purpose is its ability to modulate light into variable images that are not immutable. Thus, we are not looking for static drawings or paintings. We could consider Chinese shadow theaters, but we wish to begin our search with early traces of a technology that changed all of our lives. And here we are: film projection.

1.2.1 Early 1400s to Late 1800s: The Optical Era

Possibly, the very first depiction of a projector was in a drawing by Johannes de Fontana in 1420, showing a candle lantern with a small painted window that projected an image of the devil onto a wall (Figure 1.1(left)). Without a lens, such a projector would be very blurry, and the drawing does not show the details of the lantern very precisely. Therefore, some historians argue that the drawing could also depict a camera obscura rather than a projector. The first notion of lenses is said to date from an Egyptian source in 600 B.C., Archimedes reportedly experimented with lenses (Chrysippos, before 212 B.C.), and spectacles emerged in Europe before 1300 A.D. It is unclear when lenses may actually have been first used in projection systems.

In the 15th and 16th centuries, several people introduced the idea of projecting images, but it was probably not before 1515 that Leonardo Da Vinci presented a drawing of a lantern showing a condensing lens and a candle, unfortunately without giving any hint of actually projecting an image (Figure 1.1(center)).

It is believed that, sometime between 1640 and 1644, Athansius Kirchner showed a device that passed light from a lamp (or sunlight reflected by a mirror) through a painted window that was focused on a wall by a lens. But Kirchner's first official publication about this device was made in his 1671 book Ars Magna Lucis et Umbrae (The Great Art of Light and Shadow), where he called it a *magic lantern*. In 1659, Christian Huygens presented a similar device, and today it remains fuzzy who the true inventor of the magic lantern really is. The illustration of

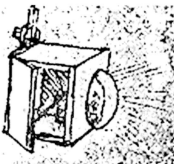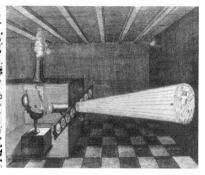

FIGURE 1.1   Historic drawings of early projectors (from left to right): Fontana's 1420 projecting lantern without lens (possibly a camera obscura), Da Vinci's 1515 lantern with lens (but without indication of projecting an image), and Kirchner's 1640-1671 magic lantern (with lens on wrong side).

the magic lantern in Kirchner's 1671 Ars Magna (Figure 1.1(right)) is also flawed – showing the lens on the wrong side (between lamp and slide). But this might well have been a misunderstanding by the artist who has drawn the sketch, rather than a mistake by Kirchner. The magic lantern concept was used and refined by various individuals, and Thomas Rasmusser Walgenstein, who coined the term Laterna Magica, toured with it through various cities in Europe. One focus of science in the first half of the 19th century was on light, and it was the time when many relevant achievements were made, including public gas light and the first electrical light (years before Edison invented the first practical light bulb). It was also the time when the lighting of the magic lantern was improved.

The limelight effect –basically an oxyhydrogen flame heating a cylinder of quicklime (calcium oxide), emitting a bright and brilliant light– that was discovered by Goldsworthy Gurney in 1820 was used not only for stage lighting in theaters, but also in the magic lantern. It was replaced by electrical lighting in the late 19th century. The step toward the first digital projectors followed several years later. Several other inventions had to be made before this, and we will return to this subject in later pages.

Clearly, the era of display technology was driven by the possibilities that simple optics offered at that time.

1.2.2   Late 1800s to Early 1900s: The Electromechanical Era

The late 1800s brought not only the evolution of early projectors, but also the first experiments with what became television. Constantin Perskyi coined the term "television" in 1900, and the first devices were mainly electromechanical. In 1884, Paul Gottlieb Nipkow first described his scanning disk, known as the *Nipkow disk*, Figure 1.2); John Logie Baird demonstrated moving images on it in 1926, and it remained in use until about 1939.

The Nipkow disk is basically a spinning disk with holes at varying lengths from the disk center. For recording, a lens is used to focus the scene on only one segment of the disk. Spinning it causes every hole to slice through an individual line of the projected image, leading to a pattern of bright and dark intensities behind the holes that can be picked up by a sensor (the photoconductivity of selenium had already been discovered by Willoughby Smith in 1873). Conversely, the Nipkow disk can also be used as a display by modulating a light

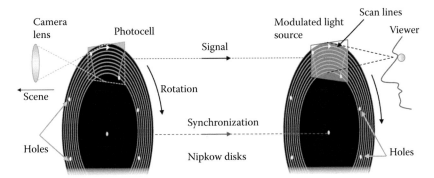

FIGURE 1.2 Image recording, transmission and display with Nipkow disks, the very first approach to television.

source behind it in synchronization with the recorded light pulses. Thus, the Nipkow disk represents an image rasterizer for recording and display. Since the scan lines are not straight, relatively large disk diameters are required.

In the first half of the 20th century, many improvements to the various factors involved in the concept of electromechanical television had been achieved, including recording, signal transmission and display. Note that the first color and stereoscopic variations using additional lenses, disks and filters had been demonstrated by John Logie Baird. But the Nipkow disk would soon be replaced.

1.2.3 Early and mid-1900s: The Electronic Era

In 1897, Ferdinand Braun invented an initial version of the Braun tube, which is better known as the *Cathode Ray Tube* (CRT) (see Section 7.6.1 at page 264). Boris Rosing was the first to use the CRT, in 1907, for displaying a received video signal. It became a commercial product in 1922, and soon replaced the Nipkow disk. The CRT revolutionized television and was a major component of the medium until the early 21st century. Like the Nipkow disk, the CRT could be used as a transmitting or receiving device and marked the beginning of the electronic television era. Camera tubes, display tubes and transmission technology continued to improve and were used all over the world. The first fully electronic color picture tube was demonstrated by John Logie Baird in 1944, with early TV standards also evolving in the mid-1900s. For almost half a century, TV technology relied on tube technology and analog signals (Figure 1.3). Broadcasting was done with *amplitude modulation* (AM), with one side band largely suppressed (*vestigial sideband transmission*, VST) for better bandwidth utilization. Even with this, only a few of the available radio frequencies could be used at one location, because AM TV transmission is very sensitive to interferences, even from very distant stations. This limited the number of available TV programs, until cable and satellite TV were introduced. Terrestrial TV transmission now has switched to digital in many countries, with an order of magnitude better bandwidth utilization. The CRT not only influenced television, but also improved projector technology. The first CRT projectors enabled the presentation of electronically encoded images to larger audiences. In computer technology, CRT monitors dominated for many decades.

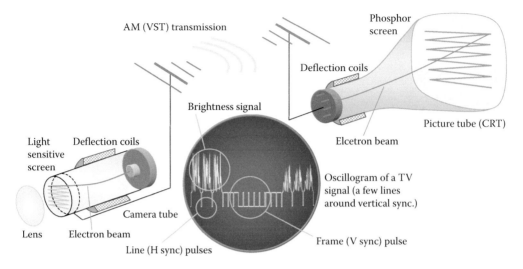

FIGURE 1.3 For half a century, TV technology involved taking pictures with a camera tube, sending them as an analog signal with synchronizing pulses carefully designed to work with simple tube circuits, and finally displaying the images with a cathode ray tube.

1.2.4 Late 1900s to Early 2000s: The Digital Era

A discovery made by Friedrich Reinitzer in 1888 revolutionized consumer display technology (i.e., television, computer screens, and projectors) again, a century later. Reinitzer investigated the physicochemical properties of various derivatives of cholesterol, known as *cholesteric liquid crystals*. Of course, he was unaware of the impact that his discovery would have on today's digital era of television; several other discoveries had to be made before this happened.

Semiconductor technology first enabled sophisticated signal processing in the beginning of the 1970s, and with it the development of flat-panel displays. These were first introduced for portable computers in the 1990s and came to be used for TVs after 2000 – fifty years after the color CRT went into mass production. The first large, flat-panel TVs, however, were based on plasma displays, before *liquid crystal displays* (LCD) started to dominate the market a few years later. Donald Bitzer and Gene Slottow invented the first plasma display in 1964, decades before it became a commercial product.

The worldwide sales of LCD television surpassed the sale of CRT-based TVs by the year 2008; now we are expecting *organic light emitting diodes* (OLED) to dominate in a few years.

It was not only TV and monitors that were influenced by new forms of spatial light modulation, but also projectors. In 1968, Gene Dolgoff started to develop a projection technology with the aim of achieving a result that would be brighter than CRT projectors could display. Not until 1984 did he succeed in applying an addressable LCD panel in a projector. He also coined the term "light valve", which we will learn more about in a later chapter. In 1977, Larry Hornbeck of Texas Instruments began exploring the principles of reflection (rather than transmission) to modulate light, and he presented the first *digital micromirror device* (DMD) in 1987 – a big step for projectors and other applications that require spatial light modulation. The technology was named *digital light processing* (DLP) in 1993.

An invention made in the 1970s by Nick Sheridon is just now beginning to influence one particular aspect of consumer displays – electronic paper. Sheridon's first electronic paper was called *Gyricon* and consisted of polyethylene spheres, each with a black and a white face, embedded in a transparent silicone sheet. By applying a voltage, the polarity decides which face (i.e., which color) is rotated toward the display surface. In the 1990s, Joseph Jacobson replaced the two-colored spheres with microcapsules that contained electrically charged white particles that floated in a dark oil inside the capsules. These particles could be moved to the display surface by applying an electric field. Such displays are called *electrophoretic*. Today, electrophoretic electronic-paper displays are most common in ebook readers.

LCD, CRT, OLED, plasma, electronic paper, and many other spatial light modulation technologies will be discussed in great detail later in this book.

Today, LCD, plasma, and DLP technologies have widely replaced CRT systems, and have brought us large flat-panel screens, TVs, and projectors that are also entirely digital. Not only have displays become digital, but also recording and transmission technologies. In many countries around the world, the transition from analog to digital television has already been completed. Advanced computer animation, digital broadcasting, digital video capture, displays and projectors, digital media formats and storage have created new opportunities for 3D movies in theaters and for television.

1.2.5 The Fascination of Three Dimensions

Throughout the development of display technology, and throughout the centuries, three-dimensional displays have always held particular fascination – up until today. The fact that the brain fuses the two images of both eyes to a 3D image was recognized by Charles Wheatstone as early as 1838. Wheatstone also produced some of the first stereographs which were drawings rather than photographs. Stereographs are basically two side-by-side perspective images that can be viewed either directly, or with the help of a stereoscope –a device invented by Sir William Brewster in 1850– that ensures the correct separation of both images (Figure 1.4).

The first stereoscopic photographs were taken by capturing two single photographs while shifting the camera slightly between them. Later, cameras with multiple lenses were used. Stereograms and stereoscopes were very popular until the 1930s, when they were increasingly replaced by moving pictures and the first electromechanical displays, such as stereoscopic versions of the Nipkow disk. Around 1850, the anaglyph stereoscopic process (first, using red-green filters in glasses) had also been discovered, and the boom of stereoscopy reached one of its peaks in the 1890s, because of the first anaglyphic stereoscopic 3D movies (all black and white). Polarization filters have been used instead of color filters to record and display stereoscopic movies since the 1950s, enabling color. Technological problems and the cost of 3D movie production limited the 3D hype in movie theaters at that time.

Together with the development of the CRT, monitors and projectors became fast enough to support time-sequential display for image separation. Active liquid crystal shutter glasses were invented by Stephen McAllister in the mid-1970s, and commercial versions were

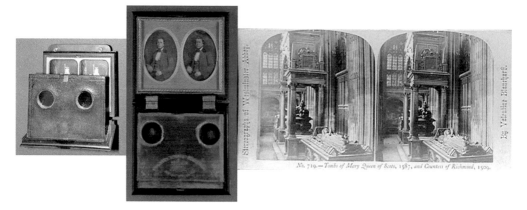

FIGURE 1.4 The Mascher Stereoscopic Viewer was a foldable stereoscope that already used two lenses (John Frederick Mascher, 1852) (left). Stereograph of two tombs within Westminster Abbey (London Stereoscopic Company, 1858) (right).

available in the mid-1980s. Today, DLP and LCD also process fast enough for active stereoscopy, using shutter glasses.

Active (shutter glasses) and passive (color or polarization glasses) stereoscopy are still very common in movie theaters and for professional applications, such as *virtual reality* (VR). Especially for virtual reality, a large variety of non-immersive, semi-immersive and immersive stereoscopic displays of all shapes (walls, tables, rooms, cylinders, spheres, etc.) have been developed. Today, stereoscopy is not only experiencing a revival in movie theaters, but is also entering the TV market.

In addition to spatial stereoscopic screens, VR has always been connected with personal, head-mounted displays. *Head-mounted displays* (HMDs) are very similar to stereoscopes, except that they provide a microdisplay instead of a photograph, for each eye. Ivan Sutherland was the first to experiment with HMDs, and he presented the first functional system in 1968. With additional optics, HMDs can support a direct view to the surrounding environment, by allowing a view through the displayed images. These see-through versions of HMDs inspired a new community for many years to build "the ultimate display" for general human-computer interaction. Sutherland's invention gave birth to *augmented reality* (AR).

The evolution of VR and AR was strongly influenced by the development of personal computers and is still very much driven by such independent technological advances. This becomes obvious considering the recent direction of AR with regard to mobile phones at a time when these devices have been tremendously improved because of their explosive increase in popularity.

Unfortunately, both AR and VR remain niche applications and have not profited from many of the recent advances in display electronics and optics, so the displays of any kind available for them (spatial and especially near-eye displays), leave a lot to be desired. We will treat this topic extensively in the near-eye displays chapter.

With spatial 3D displays, new developments can be anticipated. Autostereoscopic display approaches have the advantage that they do not require the observer to wear any glasses for stereo separation. French painter Bois-Clair, in 1692, was the first to use physical barriers in front of a painting, causing changes to become visible as a viewer walked by. In 1896, Jacobson and Berthier used this principle with photographs, and it was also applied in 1903 by Frederick E. Ives, who coined the term "parallax stereogram". The barriers were essentially an aid for stereoscopic separation and were placed on the picture itself instead of in front of the eyes. One problem with barriers for stereoscopic separation is the loss of light (i.e., the light of the image being blocked by the barriers). In 1908, Gabriel M. Lippmann used a series of lenses instead of barriers in order to increase the light output. He was awarded the Nobel Prize for his invention of "La Photographie Integral" (Integral Photography). It represents the basis for many modern photography- and display-related principles, such as autostereoscopic displays, and light field recording and display. In the 1920s, Frederick Ives' son, Herbert, and others simplified Lippmann's idea by using lenticular lens arrays instead of spherical lenses (omitting vertical parallax). Lenticular lenses were first used in photography, but are most common in today's autostereoscopic displays.

We should mention another Nobel Prize winner at this point; Dennis Gabor, who received the prize in 1971 for his discovery of the basic principles of holography in 1947. As you are reading this book, it will become clear how essential these principles are for display technology in general, and not only for upcoming *computer-generated holographic displays* (CGHs). Practical holography did not become feasible before the invention of the laser in the 1960s. It certainly opened a door that allows a new view on three-dimensional displays and imaging that goes far beyond stereoscopy and autostereoscopy. The first algorithms for wavefront computation to support CGHs were reported by Brown and Lohmann in 1966. The first CGHs could reconstruct only 2D images; 3D images were first generated in 1969. The development of CGHs is still ongoing, because they are much more challenging than any other display technology. Not only display-related problems have to be solved, but also challenges with respect to recording and transmission – as has always been the case in the history of displays. Although not quite visible on the market at the moment, we can consider holography (in one or the other form) as one potential technology that will lead to true 3D TV.

We will extensively discuss many different possibilities for 3D displays in this book, including a thorough introduction to holographic principles and several other fundamentals of optics and light modulation.

1.3 ORGANIZATION OF THE BOOK

Display technology is a truly interdisciplinary field. To develop an understanding of various display principles that goes beyond a simple application perspective, several technological and non-technological threads have to be followed in many cases. Some of them lead us across fundamental principles of optics and physics to the quite modern findings in the realm of quantum mechanics. Others involve visual perception, computer graphics and vision, signal processing, material sciences, mechanics, electronics, and electromechanics.

This book will not, and cannot, replace any of the textbooks that are individually dedicated to any one of these fields. Instead, we have culled the most important aspects from each discipline in order to explain how displays work, and why some don't.

For example, to understand why particular 3D display approaches are better than others (not only technologically, but also from the point of view of 3D perception), one might want to compare them with the ultimate method for presenting 3D images. This is certainly holography, and several CGH displays follow exactly this principle. But to understand CGHs for the purpose of identifying limitations of other 3D displays, one has to understand the principles of holography. To grasp these principles, however, one must have an understanding of wave optics. Furthermore, the basis for wave optics lies deeply in the fundamental physical nature of light. Finally, one needs to have a fair understanding of human visual perception (in particular, depth perception) in order to find explanations and to draw appropriate conclusions.

This simple rationale explains that there are interdisciplinary dependencies among different fields that we need to understand. This book discusses and correlates these fields within nine main chapters. In these chapters we intersperse some innovative ideas of our own that may potentially stimulate further research-and-development activities.

Figure 1.5 illustrates the organization of this book and the relations of its nine main chapters as a sunburst diagram. Every adjacent discipline is highly correlated.

For CGHs as one type of 3D displays, for instance, not only holographic principles are essential, but also the various ways spatial light modulation forms appropriate wavefronts. Both require a fair comprehension of optical principles that is based on knowledge of the fundamentals of light. When perception properties of CGHs are considered in addition to the opto-electronics, then laws of visual perception are as essential as display basics that explain how the anatomical findings of human visual perception are finally applied to spatial light modulators.

This book is organized as follows: Chapter 2 begins with a discussion of the fundamentals of light. It introduces electromagnetic radiation, explains how light is generated and

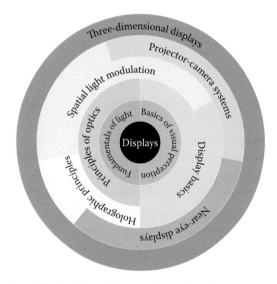

FIGURE 1.5 Organization of the book and chapter dependencies.

how it can be measured, and concludes with a short glimpse at the discipline of quantum mechanics.

Chapter 3 applies the previously discussed fundamentals to describe principles of optics. It will review wave optics as well as geometric optics, and present principles of lasers and image formation. Chapter 4 summarizes the basics of visual perception by outlining the human visual system and its essential sensory properties.

Though radiometry and photometry are considered in Chapter 2, Chapter 4 continues this discussion with colorimetry and some insights on depth perception.

Holographic principles are outlined in Chapter 5. An introductory summary on holography is followed by a detailed discussion on the fundamental wave-optical elements of holography. Holographic optical elements and display holograms are the two considered applications of holography at this point.

Display basics are treated in Chapter 6, and with these we want to correlate the optical and perception principles that have been presented to that point with the electronic signal and image processing of displays. Fundamental display measures are explained as well as general possibilities of color and intensity production, basic electronic-signal processing, and component assembly of common displays.

Since displays involve light modulation, Chapter 7 is dedicated to the rich pool of *spatial light modulation* (SLM) optics and electronics. Transmissive, reflective, and emissive SLM technologies are reviewed, and *high-dynamic range* (HDR) and bi-directional displays that apply such SLMs are explained. Projection displays and their components are also covered.

After reviewing projector optics, Chapter 8 explains several software calibration techniques for projector-camera systems. Automatic geometric and radiometric calibration methods for various surface types (from planar to geometrically complex, and from uniform to color textured) are presented. These individual approaches are finally brought together by measuring and processing inverse light transport. Also presented are several future options for projectors, such as high speed, high-dynamic range, large depth of field and super resolution.

Chapter 9 concerns spatial (mostly nonmobile) 3D displays. The chapter begins with a general discussion of basic considerations for 3D displays and a comparison of 3D TV and 3D cinema. It continues with reviews of single-viewer and multi-viewer stereoscopic display technologies, and classical autostereoscopic approaches – such as parallax and volumetric displays, light field displays, and CGH displays. Chapter 9 closes with a discussion of 3D media encoding for light field and hologram displays, as well as with a comparison of the various 3D display technologies.

Chapter 10 outlines near-eye displays, which are believed to be, in many respects, more efficient than spatial displays in the future. Our discussion explains current examples for near-eye displays that are on the market today, but focuses on an optimal design for future devices. Modern micro and laser display technology, holography and other advanced optics, eye tracking, and techniques for effective integration of images into the visual field are considered.

Finally, this book is concluded with a discussion and an outlook to the foreseeable future of display technology in Chapter 11. Yet, we will also venture to risk a glance into the far future of displays that cannot reliably be predicted today. The decline of display technology as we know it might happen with the rise of advanced brain-computer interfaces. We will provide a glimpse into the areas of retinal and neural implants.

The attached appendix complements the main chapters by providing more insights into how perceptual models can be incorporated into display design. First, it introduces displays models, required to convert the digital signals driving a display into photometric and colorimetric units, in which perceptual models operate. Then, several visual display calibration methods, which do not require measuring instruments, are described. This is followed by a discussion of a contrast sensitivity function (CSF), which is one of the most commonly used perceptual models. The last section of the appendix demonstrates how the CSF can be used to test for and reduce banding artifacts due to limited color channel bit depth.

CHAPTER 2

Fundamentals of Light

2.1 INTRODUCTION

Successful displays depend on modulating light effectively so images can be perceived. In this chapter we will examine the properties and physical effects of light that can be useful for display technology.

We are familiar with light. Our experiences have taught us what its effects will be under most circumstances.

Yet, upon closer examination, we discover that light is still a mystery. Many experiments have concluded with most peculiar results, contradicting our everyday experiences and our belief in causality.

We can think of light in a simple way, considering only its common effects such as refraction or color dispersion. Many sophisticated optical designs that are useful for displays and imaging devices can be derived from this approach.

Further consideration, however, leads us to the creation of special effects related to wave optics, such as interference, which is essential for holography. Holography is so important for displays that we dedicate an entire chapter to it (Chapter 5).

If we continue to contemplate, we have to admit that we still don't know what light really is: particles, waves, or something in between? Quantum mechanics delivers the models and the calculus necessary for the treatment of light at molecular and particle levels. This is important for many new findings, such as quantum dots. However, quantum mechanics is also essential for the in-depth understanding of almost anything that is involved with the creation and the modulation of light. Even familiar things, such as the polarization of light, turn out to be stranger than we thought, and require quantum mechanics for a proper explanation.

This chapter begins with a short introduction to electromagnetic radiation (Section 2.2), and then gives answers on how light is generated (Section 2.3).

We will see that almost any form of light generation (including thermal) can be related to moving electrical charges (which is quite logical indeed, because light is an electromagnetic wave), and we will present several forms of light generation that are effective for displays.

In Section 2.4 at page 29, we continue to explain how light is measured, the physical entities related to light and their definitions.

We will offer a short introduction to quantum mechanics (Section 2.5 at page 35) and will attempt to present this largely counterintuitive material as intuitively as possible. Also in this chapter, we will discuss basics of light behavior relative to its quantum nature.

We will conclude this chapter with a discourse on polarization (Section 2.5.7 at page 48), because this effect relates more to quantum principles than to geometric or wave optics, which are then treated in the chapters that follow.

2.2 ELECTROMAGNETIC RADIATION

Light is an electromagnetic wave. Imagine electromagnetic waves to be self-propagating waves of intermittent electric and magnetic fields, wherein the energy is cyclically exchanged between the electric and magnetic components. Both field vectors are perpendicular to each other and perpendicular to the propagation direction (Figure 2.21). Electromagnetic waves were first investigated by Michael Faraday and then were mathematically described by James Clerk Maxwell, in the 19th century.

Maxwell's electromagnetic field equations delivered the important result that fluctuating electromagnetic fields must travel at a speed equaling that of light ($c \approx 3 * 10^8$ m/s, in a vacuum), which in turn led to the conclusion that light is electromagnetic radiation.

Electromagnetic waves cover a frequency range of more than 30 decades.

Frequency ν and wavelength λ are related by (in vacuum)

$$\nu = c/\lambda \tag{2.1}$$

A range of frequencies is called a *spectrum* (Figure 2.1). In the range of visible light (wavelengths 380 nm … 780 nm, frequencies in the 10^{15} Hz range), wavelength and amplitude correspond to perceived color and intensity. For example, a wavelength of about 400 nm is perceived as blue (about 700 nm is perceived as red, and approximately 550 nm is perceived as green).

2.3 PRINCIPLES OF LIGHT GENERATION

The straightforward way to generate electromagnetic waves is moving electric charges, causing an electrical field to change quickly. Radio waves, for example, are generated exactly in this manner. Generating light waves works in a quite similar way, but the principle of

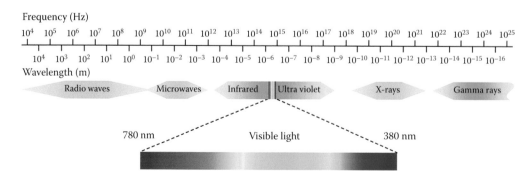

FIGURE 2.1 Spectrum of electromagnetic radiation and visible spectrum.

single charges (e.g., electrons) giving birth to single light quanta (photons) bears closer examination.

A principle often found in modern light sources is that of electrons changing orbits in an atom, releasing the energy difference (if positive) as a photon.

A quite similar process occurs in semiconductors (light emitting diodes) only that the energy levels (bands) between which the electrons are changing are caused by the properties of the entire material rather than the single atoms.

These principles are very selective with regard to the wavelengths emitted.

Another principle is thermal emission, caused by the motion of entire atoms either oscillating in a solid piece of matter, or moving and colliding in a gas or a liquid. This is the basis of tungsten lamps, for example. Thermal emission may contain photons of almost any energy and we can again attribute the emission itself to moving charges (the electron hulls of the atoms).

An emission method that most clearly illustrates the general principle is *Bremsstrahlung*, which occurs when a free-flying electron is accelerated by a magnetic field, for example. If an electron is forced to change its flight direction without changing its speed, the energy applied causes a random emission of photons over a wide energy range (*synchrotron radiation*).

While a simple linear acceleration of electrons (as in an electron tube) does not generate visually perceivable photons, suddenly stopping a fast moving electron at a solid obstacle releases most of its motion energy into high-energy photons matching that energy difference. X-rays are generated in this manner.

Inverse principles exist for all of the processes described: photons can lift electrons to higher orbits in atoms and can likewise lift electrons to higher energy levels in semiconductors (e.g., solar cells); they can accelerate atoms (causing heat) and can accelerate single electrons. We will introduce many of these principles in this chapter.

Thermal radiation is closely related to the temperatures of bodies and to energy dissipation. Because an understanding of thermal radiation processes is crucial to understanding most principles of light distribution and absorption relevant for display technology, we will explore them in some detail.

The consideration of quantum mechanics is important to all of the preceding fundamentals. Very early findings about light (the Planck laws for thermal radiation) gave rise to the quantum theory because the formulae worked only if a certain constant, the Planck constant *h*, was introduced. Max Planck hypothesized that under certain conditions, the energy must be a multiple of a very small quantity, later named a *quantum*.

Polarization and many other effects cannot be properly understood without understanding quantum mechanics as well, so we have dedicated a section in this chapter to it.

It the course of our considerations, we will often encounter some commonly known symbols for physical constants and parameters. For your convenience we have listed them in Table 2.1.

2.3.1 Thermal Radiation

Thermal emission is an important kind of light generation. Any matter emits electromagnetic radiation relative to its temperature, also called *thermal radiation*. A part of this

TABLE 2.1   Frequently Encountered Physical Entities and Their Meanings

Symbol	Meaning	Approximate Value	Units
K	Boltzmann constant	$1{,}3806504 \cdot 10^{-23}$	J/K
b	Wien's displacement constant	$2.8977685 \cdot 10^{3}$	m · K
h	Planck constant	$6.6260693 \cdot 10^{-34}$	J · s
h	Planck constant	$4.1356673 \cdot 10^{-15}$	eV · s
$\hbar$	Reduced Planck constant ($h/2\pi$)	$1.0545716 \cdot 10^{-34}$	J · s
c	Speed of light	299792458	m/s
e	Electron charge	$1.6021765 \cdot 10^{-19}$	A · s
eV	1 Electron Volt	$1.6021765 \cdot 10^{-19}$	J or W · s
E	Energy	—	W · s
ν	Frequency	—	1/s or Hz
λ	Wavelength	—	m
m	Mass	—	kg

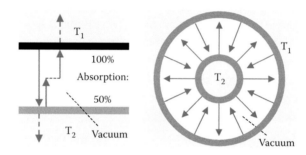

FIGURE 2.2   The radiation absorption of a gray surface, here approximately 50%, (left), is smaller but its emittance is less as well, by the same fraction. If no energy is transported by other means, opposing surfaces must settle at the same temperature in this manner (T_1 and T_2 converge). A body inside a cavity must acquire the temperature of the cavity walls (right).

radiation can also be seen, or felt as heat. Examples are glowing metal, a hot stove, or the sun, a thermal emitter at very high temperature (approximately 6000 K).

The fundamentals of thermal radiation were explored in the 19th century. It was found that bodies of the same temperature emitted different amounts of thermal radiation if they were of different colors, black bodies, for instance, emitted higher degrees of thermal radiation than gray or white bodies (Figure 2.2).

2.3.1.1 Radiation, Absorption and Efficiency

Any piece of matter will not only emit radiation, it will also absorb it. The absorption and emission coefficients of a surface were found to be identical. Figure 2.2 illustrates the reason: opposing walls as well as objects inside a cavity all tend to align their temperatures because of the emission and absorption of thermal radiation, even if no heat transport by matter is involved (i.e., in a vacuum). The emission and absorption coefficients combine to conduct thermal energy between the opposing surfaces. If there is no external heat transport (cooling), the opposing surfaces will align to the same temperature after a finite period of time. Otherwise, more energy would be transported in one direction and less in the other, violating energy conservation laws.

If the surface of the body inside the cavity absorbs more radiation than it emits, its temperature would rise indefinitely. So absorption and emission must come to a balance.

Because white or gray surfaces emit and absorb less thermal radiation than black surfaces (Figure 2.2), the thermal equilibrium is reached more slowly. With a highly reflective (e.g., silver) surface, balance is achieved very slowly, which is the principle of a vacuum flask.

An important finding was that regardless of surface color or reflectivity, the spectrum of the thermal radiation emitted is dictated almost entirely by the temperature of the matter.

The time it takes for temperatures to align depends on the thermal conductivity of the assembly and the thermal capacities of the bodies connected with the surfaces.

The thermal conductivity caused by radiation is temperature dependent, because the energy emitted (or absorbed) by a surface through radiation rises with the 4th power of the temperature in Kelvin, a finding also experimentally established in the 19th century and subsequently theorized.

These facts were first described by Gustav Kirchhoff in context with thermodynamics.

To simplify things, in physics we consider "black bodies" with regard to thermal behavior. Most natural objects are more absorbing than they appear to the eye[*]. Moreover, many surfaces that appear to be white in visible light are almost "black" in the thermal infrared.

For an exact experimental analysis, a perfect standard body was needed. An ideal black body was defined for this purpose. As no real body is perfectly black, one had to be created: a cavity that was all black inside, with a hole at one side (Figure 2.3). Radiation going into the hole is reflected many times inside, and each time most of it is absorbed by the walls of the cavity. Literally none of it can return to the outside, hence the hole itself can be considered an ideal black surface. The reciprocity is like that of a real body: thermal radiation exactly matching that of an ideally black surface with the temperature of the cavity walls is emitted. Such ideal black bodies were used to explore thermal radiation with great accuracy.

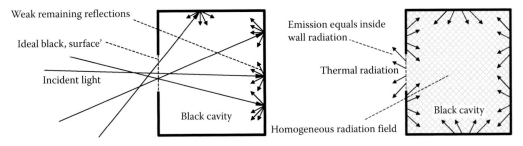

FIGURE 2.3 Ideal black body equivalent. Incident radiation is absorbed totally in the black cavity, due to multiple reflections or absorptions (left). Thermal radiation leaves the opening, matching the average emission at the inside walls, improved to a perfect black body spectrum by the multiple reflections (absorptions), (right).

---

[*] Note that apparently bright objects may still absorb a lot of light. Because it sees nonlinearly, the human eye perceives an area remitting only about 20% of the light as middle gray, or half as bright as a white surface (this is a common definition in painting and in photography). Many natural objects emit comparably little radiation.

Electricity, as well as thermodynamics, had already been discovered at this time, and it was assumed that light is an electromagnetic wave.

Ludwig Boltzmann had developed his theory of *statistical mechanics*, describing the thermodynamic behavior of large numbers of particles, which could be charged. One hypothesis was that moving particles (in solid matter, oscillating particles) could be the cause of thermal radiation; by a statistical process they release radiation at random but according to certain, yet unknown, laws.

Wilhelm Wien experimentally established that the spectra of bodies at any temperature were similar, but of different wavelengths. In 1893, Wien formulated his empirical *displacement law*, describing the wavelength of maximum emission as:

$$\lambda_{max} = b/T \tag{2.2}$$

with the temperature T (in Kelvin) of a black body and Wien's displacement constant b (see Table 2.1 on page 16).

Energy emission was also found to depend on temperature, as formulated by its fourth power. Hence, a hot body like the sun violently radiates while objects at room temperature radiate but a little.

A formula deriving these spectra (e.g., from statistical mechanics, which was one favored option for an explanation of radiation laws), remained unresolved until Max Planck finally succeeded by introducing a certain smallest entity, the Planck constant h, later dubbed the Planck quantum [228].

The formulas Planck found for the black body spectrum are (by frequency and by wavelength):

$$I(\nu) = \frac{2h\nu^3}{c^2} \frac{1}{e^{\frac{h\nu}{kT}} - 1} \qquad I(\lambda) = \frac{2hc^2}{\lambda^5} \frac{1}{e^{\frac{hc}{\lambda kT}} - 1} \tag{2.3}$$

$$M(\nu) = \frac{2\pi h\nu^3}{c^2} \frac{1}{e^{\frac{h\nu}{kT}} - 1} \qquad M(\lambda) = \frac{2\pi c^3}{\lambda^5} \frac{1}{e^{\frac{hc}{\lambda kT}} - 1} \tag{2.4}$$

The spectral emission curves for bodies of various temperatures as given by Planck's formula (and by experiments as well) are shown in Figures 2.4 and 2.5.

In conclusion, thermal radiation originates from probabilistic processes involving moving electrical charges. Atoms may randomly emit radiation because of accelerations related to thermal agitation. The energy of the radiation emitted depends on temperature, hence on the velocity of the atoms.

The idea of photons as particles, however, was not developed until after Planck introduced his constant.

In 1905, Albert Einstein found that Planck's constant would explain why ultra violet photons of a minimum energy were required to beat electrons out of a metal surface (photoelectric effect). His revolutionary idea was to use Planck's constant h as more than just a mathematical construct; so he interpreted photons not only as waves but also as particles. This was the birth of quantum physics (more in section 2.5.2 at page 35).

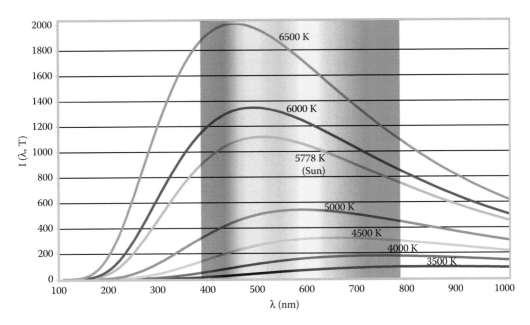

FIGURE 2.4   Black body spectra (linear scale).

The energy of a photon of a frequency v is hence given by $E = hv$.

Note that a photon can have any energy and that a black body can emit photons of any wavelength. This spectrum is not discrete. Quantum physics tells us only that a photon can be interpreted as a particle and that certain energy levels relate to certain wavelengths, by the Planck quantum.

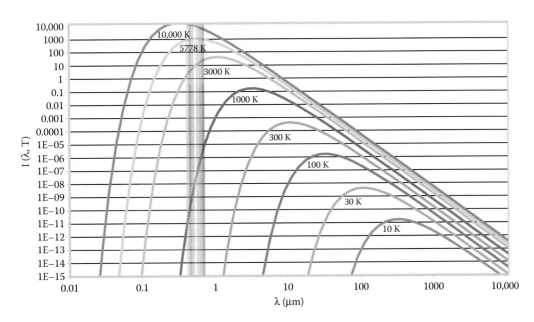

FIGURE 2.5   Black body spectra (logarithmic scale).

Electrons in an atom however, can occupy only certain "orbits" (quantum physics regards an electron as a standing wave around an atom core). We will see that this has implications for other forms of light generation, allowing only certain energy levels for emitted photons.

2.3.2 Applications of Thermal Radiation Laws

Black body physics can tell us the spectrum of a tungsten lamp, but also things apparently as extraordinary as the temperature of the earth.

Even though the intensity of the emission depends on the surface reflectance of the body, the spectrum alone allows the measurement of the temperature of the body to a fairly high precision. This fact is the basis for radiation thermometers and thermal cameras. According to Wien's displacement law, the emission maximum of a body at room temperature is approximately $10\,\mu$m.

Infrared motion sensors are sensitive in this range, for example; they have plastic lenses that disperse directional sensitivity into many separate rays, causing intensity fluctuations when bodies are moving.

Because thermal emission spectra are very reliable measures of a body's temperature, regardless of its actual emission coefficient, this allows the measurement of temperatures over large distances (even for distant planets and stars), by simply receiving the radiation via an (infrared transmissive) lens and analyzing it.

An excellent example of a practical application of radiation laws is the calculation of the temperature of the earth according to the radiation of the sun.

We need to know only the temperature of the sun, and that energy is proportional to the 4th power of temperature (in Kelvin). The radiation (energy) density of the sun at the Earth's orbit is given by the ratio between the diameter of the Earth's orbit and the sun's diameter squared (as all radiation from the sun is distributed over a globe with the diameter of the Earth's orbit).

The earth is hit by radiation from a section of this globe as large as its cross section (Figure 2.6). Concurrently, it can emit radiation from all of its surface, which, for a sphere, is four times its cross section. Hence, the earth will acquire the temperature of the virtual orbit-sized globe divided by the 4th root of four. With a sun radius = 0.697 million km, earth orbit radius = 149.6 million km, sun temperature = 5778 K, we can immediately calculate that the earth would have an average surface temperature of 279 K (6°C) if it was an ideal black body $(((0.697/149.6)^2/4)^{1/4} * 5778 = 278.9\,[\text{K}])$. Without any radiation from the sun, the earth would cool to the temperature of the vacuum, mainly given by the 3 Kelvin thermal cosmic background radiation left over from the *big bang*, because outgoing thermal radiation is not balanced by any other incident radiation. A 3 K radiation, however, is negligible in our above calculation because of its very low energy given by the E^4 law.

2.3.3 Open Systems and the Greenhouse Effect

The average temperature of the Earth's surface actually being somewhat different from the black body model (15°C instead of 6°C) results from other influences. For one, clouds can prevent some of the sun's radiation from reaching the surface and heating it, while thermal radiation would still be dispersed in all directions according to the surface (clouds and soil)

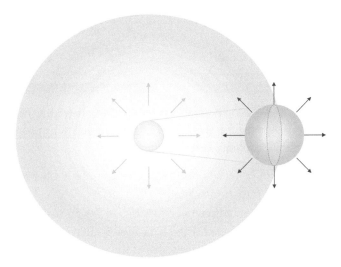

FIGURE 2.6 Solar heating of the earth (extremely out of scale: the sun is 100 × the Earth's size, and its distance is over 100 × larger).

temperatures. This would seem to lead to a cooler earth, but actually it is warmer. Here the *greenhouse effect* comes into place. Greenhouse effects occur when the sun's radiation in the visible spectrum (representing most of the energy) passes through Earth's atmosphere and heats Earth's surface, while the thermal radiation emitted from Earth's surface is partially absorbed by a gas layer, usually gaseous water vapor (moisture) or carbon dioxide (Figure 2.7), very similar to the effect of a glass window.

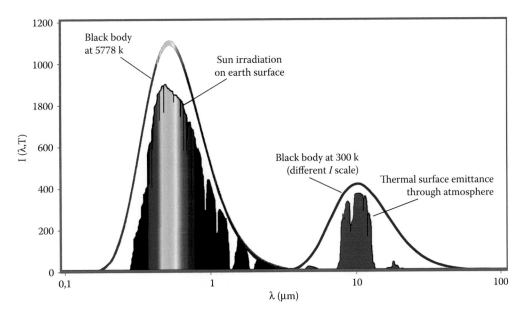

FIGURE 2.7 Sun irradiation on earth: black body and actual spectrum curves, irradiation (left) and thermal emission from the surface after atmospheric absorption (right).

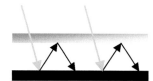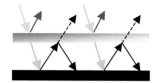

FIGURE 2.8 Normal glass (left) and thermal protection glass, reflecting near infrared (right). Thermal radiation is kept under the glass (black rays). An additional transmissivity for the thermal spectrum could further improve cooling (dashed rays).

Clouds really have a two-fold effect: cooling (reflecting sunlight back to space) at day and reducing heat loss by thermal radiation at night.

Note that due to the absorption of thermal emissions in the atmosphere, the surface temperature of the earth can't be measured using a radiation thermometer from outer space, through which we would see only the temperature of the upper atmosphere layers. Because of this fact, for example, nobody knew that the surface of Venus is over 400°C hot, until a probe landed there.

We will now consider the practical implications of these effects. We will base our discussion on radiation only and will not include heat transport inside bodies or convection effects.

Visible light usually passes through a glass window with little loss, but most glass varieties absorb or reflect thermal radiation, which at room temperature is very far into the infrared range. The light is absorbed by objects behind the window, heating them, but thermal radiation is kept withheld the window, destroying radiation balance with the outside. For example, this effect causes interiors of cars to heat excessively when exposed to the sun. It is also used in some types of solar-thermal power cells. Because most of sun's radiation is in the visible spectrum, or near infrared, its effects are not sufficiently described by the thermal processes we have considered so far.

Thermal protection glass reflects at near infrared and, in most cases, also part of the visible light, therefore reducing heating by the visible as well as the invisible part of the sun spectrum (Figure 2.8). Ideally, it should also be transparent for far infrared, allowing the thermal radiation from the heated inside to escape.

Different absorption factors also cause black objects to heat when exposed to the sun, while white objects stay relatively cool. This results from the fact that these surfaces usually aren't insulated, and are in thermal contact with the surrounding air and also with the bodies they belong to. The black surface absorbs a good deal more of the incident radiation, but is not cooled through thermal conduction by the same amount. Thus, the effect is especially strong for thin objects (car body, manhole cover).

2.3.4 Color Temperature

Depending on the temperature of an ideal black-body radiator, the emitted spectrum can reach its maximum in the infrared range or below, in the visible range, or in the ultra-violet range or above. For visible light emission, temperature gives emitted light a certain color, which can range from red over yellow to white and blue (green is not observed because a thermal spectrum is not sufficiently selective).

Thermally generated light is attributed to a certain *color temperature* that corresponds to the temperature of the emitting body. Any light generated in other ways is also classified by its color temperature, comparing it to an equivalent thermal source, even if its spectrum is not continuous (fluorescent lamps for example). Tungsten lamps, for instance, always have a color temperature in the 3300 K range, ("warm" light), while daylight has about 6000 K. Because our color perception changes a bit with brightness, 6000 K for normal room lighting would be perceived as excessively "cold". Fluorescent lamps are available in warm (3300 K) or cooler varieties (4000 . . . >5000 K). Generally, because of the characteristics of our eye's sensitivity curve (see Figure 2.15 on page 32), "warm" lamps are a bit brighter than "cold" lamps at the same radiation energy.

Color temperature is also important for image recording. Though our eyes easily adapt to different colored lighting, cameras record vastly different colors under different light conditions. They have to be adjusted to "indoor" or "outdoor" conditions by calibrating them with a white sheet (white balance).

Displays are also sensitive to color temperature. As our eyes adapt to environmental lighting conditions, a display has to conform to these or its color would not be accurate in comparison.

2.3.5 Bremsstrahlung

Any charged particle that is accelerated emits photons. This is not only a prerequisite for thermal radiation, the phenomenon also occurs when electrons are stopped at an obstacle.

This effect was first discovered by Conrad Roentgen in 1895, when he experimented with vacuum tubes at high voltages. He accidentally found that radiation was produced which blackened films in their packages. He further discovered that this radiation also transgresses human flesh and produces an image of the bones on photographic film. He named this radiation X-rays.

X-rays are produced by the electrons in the tube, which travel from the negative electrode (cathode) to the positive one (anode), hitting the latter with an energy given by the voltage between cathode and anode. Photons are produced at this point, and their energy corresponds to the kinetic energy of the suddenly stopped electrons.

The wavelength of the radiation emitted from an X-ray tube with operating voltage V is given by its operating voltage:

$$\lambda_{min} = \frac{hc}{eV} \tag{2.5}$$

Because a portion of the energy also goes into heating the anode, this should be considered the minimum wavelength (maximum frequency or energy).

Basically, the photon energy, or frequency, is given by a *motion energy difference*. This principle is generally referred to as *Bremsstrahlung*, a German word combined from "bremsen" (to brake) and "Strahlung" (radiation), however it is not used as a synonym for X-rays.

If only the *direction* of motion is changed (electrons running in circles), obviously there is no motion energy difference to the particle itself. The energy applied, however, has to

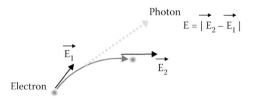

FIGURE 2.9 Photon emission by acceleration of an electron.

go somewhere, it could accelerate the apparatus applying the energy, or it may actually be emitted as photons originating from the particle.

Generally, we can calculate the energy of the photon from the change of motion energy vectors $\vec{E}_1$ to $\vec{E}_2$ of the electron (Figure 2.9):

$$\nu = \frac{\left|\vec{E}_2 - \vec{E}_1\right|}{h} \tag{2.6}$$

A very strong acceleration of the electrons is required to produce useful amounts of light with this effect. Instruments able to achieve this, for example, are specialized particle accelerators, called *synchrotrons*. The radiation produced from forcing electrons to move in a circle is therefore dubbed synchrotron radiation.

With synchrotron radiation, the emission occurs statistically in a very wide, continuous spectrum that may go from far infrared to very far ultra-violet or even hard gamma radiation, depending on the acceleration energies applied. It is a valuable light source for many physical experiments.

The angular characteristics to this radiation are basically similar to the radio wave emissions of a dipole antenna, but the angle gets very narrow when electrons approach the speed of light and relativistic effects begin.

Protons can also emit Bremsstrahlung or synchrotron radiation, but their efficiency is about 13 orders of magnitude lower because their higher mass makes other forms of energy dissipation more likely.

2.3.6 Photon Energies

Photon energies can be expressed directly in electron volts (eV, the energy an electron picks up when accelerated by an electric-field-strength increase or voltage in a conductor, of just 1 V).

With Planck's formula $e = h\nu$, the energy of a "red" photon is about $1.7\,eV$, of a 'green' photon, $2.2\,eV$, and of a "blue" photon, $3.2\,eV$.

Light emitting diodes for example, require operating voltages corresponding to the energies of the photons produced (see Section 2.3.9.1 at page 28).

Though visible light has only a few eV, X-rays typically have photon energies between 50 and $>200\,keV$, hence the tubes to produce them work with 50 to $>200\,kV$ between cathode and anode. *Cathode ray tubes* (CRT, TV picture tubes) and high-energy, high-frequency generator tubes used in radar systems also emit X-rays. Though the about $25\,kV$ of a color CRT are comparably weak and are usually well shielded by a lead-glass front screen, radar tubes working with several hundred kV are known to be dangerous; their strong X-rays may cause cancer.

2.3.7 Electron Excitation

Atoms consist of a nucleus made from protons (electrically positive) and neutrons. Electrons circling the nucleus are held in orbit by electrical force, but can also move from atom to atom, allowing electrical current (= electrons) to flow in a material. Atoms attached together by shared electrons form molecules.

As circling electrons would normally always emit Bremsstrahlung, special conditions must exist allowing them to circle around an atomic nucleus forever.

According to the atomic model of Niels Bohr, this is the case if the wave equivalent of the electron forms a standing wave around the orbit, so orbit lengths must equal a whole number of wavelengths (see Section 2.5.2 at page 35).

This may be plausible regarding the fact that the wave packet representing the electron cannot be arbitrarily short according to the argument in Section 2.5.2.4 at page 42, Figure 2.18, and a long wave packet whose wavelength is not an integer fraction of the orbit circumference would interfere with itself in the orbit.

The level at which an electron orbits the nucleus is called *energy state*. By default, electrons exist at the lowest energy state (lowest orbit) possible.

If excited by an external energy (e.g., heat or a photon, see Figure 2.10, top), an electron can move from a lower to a higher energy state with a move called *quantum leap*. Note that

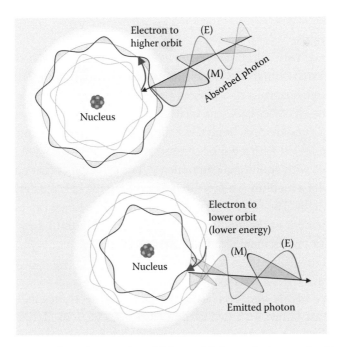

FIGURE 2.10 Excitation of an electron into higher orbit by a photon, and release of energy as a photon.

an exciting photon may not necessarily have the same energy as an emitted photon. It cannot have less energy, of course, but if it has more, the excess energy becomes into heat.

Electrons cannot remain in an excited energy state forever. There is a half-life time for any particular energy level during which half of the electrons will decay to a lower energy state (Figure 2.10, bottom). Energy is never lost but it may be converted. When electrons drop back to lower states, their energy is emitted in packages of either *photons* ($E_2 - E_1 = E = h\nu$) or *phonons* (mechanical quantum units essentially translating to heat in this case). The energy of the photons released is equal to the energy difference between the electron states. This random emission of photons is called *luminescence*.

Because of various effects such as the *Doppler effect*[*], caused by the temperature of the medium (agitation of its atoms), the energy will vary and the spectral line of the light emitted will have a certain distribution.

2.3.8 Gas Discharge

In an ionized gas, free electrons can transport a current and will frequently collide with atoms in the gas. This will cause energy-level transition emissions. In neon lamps, frequently used for advertising signs, mixtures of different noble gases (neon, argon, krypton or xenon) with sulfur, sodium, or metal halides may produce almost any color desired.

2.3.8.1 Neon Lamps

In neon lamps, frequently used for advertising signs, mixtures of different noble gases (neon, argon, krypton or xenon) with sulfur, sodium, or metal halides may produce almost any color desired. They work with cold cathodes and need a high ignition voltage.

2.3.8.2 Plasma Lamps

Plasma lamps operate with a high-frequency voltage. Nikola Tesla discovered this principle through his research of high-frequencies between 1888 and 1897. *Radio frequency* (RF) power accelerates free electrons of a plasma (ionized gas) enclosed in a transparent bulb. These lamps need no electrodes and can have an extremely long life expectancy.

For example, e^3 *lamps* are slim (typically 3 mm wide) RF operated lamps. The insides of their glass tubes are coated with a doped ceramic material and the low-to medium-pressure gas filling is enriched with additional components. The principle is that noble gas and phosphor molecules under a medium-voltage RF field of some 100 kHz cluster together to emit a broad spectrum of light. The color temperature in the visible range can be widely adjusted, to resemble incandescent or daylight spectra for example. Up until now, these lamps have been used mainly for professional illumination projects.

2.3.8.3 Arc Lamps

An electrical arc is a highly ionized plasma between two electrodes that are close to each other. Historically, arc lamps with two carbon electrodes were used, operating in air. The

---

[*] Compressing waves of an approaching source to shorter wavelength and expanding those from a departing source to longer wavelength.

ionization of the plasma was maintained by constantly burning off carbon particles, which also amplified the light emission by emitting excitation photons.

Today, arc lamps enclosed in quartz bulbs filled with xenon gas are widely used for video projectors and for high-end car headlamps. Their advantages are very high efficiency and high radiation temperature (i.e., very "white" light).

The latest development are *Ultra High Performance* (UHP) lamps, which work with mercury vapor. They also have a very high color temperature (above 7000 K). Higher pressure and temperature not only improve efficiency, but also lead to a smoother spectral curve. Arc lamps are discussed in greater detail in Section 7.10.3 at page 287.

2.3.8.4 Phosphors

Some inorganic materials ("phosphors", not to be confused with the element phosphorus) generate light with excitation electrons that have been impacted by either photons or free electrons, or by a current flowing through them (e.g., causing electron-atom collisions). Such effects are generally called *luminescence*, in the case of phosphors they are also known as *phosphorescence* (indicating luminescence with a long afterglow).

If photons cause the excitation, we refer to it as *photoluminescence*. If electrons are the cause, the term is *electroluminescence*.

Photoluminescence is also referred to as *fluorescence* if the exciting photons have a shorter wavelength (higher energy) than the emitted ones.

Typical phosphors may contain oxides, nitrides, sulfides, selenides, halides or silicates of zinc, cadmium, manganese, aluminum, silicon, or various rare earth metals.

In CRT, the phosphor material forms the display screen and emits light when hit by an electron beam produced in the vacuum tube behind it.

Phosphors can exhibit an incredible amount of luminous flux:

- In white-light emitting diodes (see Section 2.3.9.1), a phosphor layer converts blue light into yellowish white, with radiation densities matching those of a halogen lamp filament.

- In recently introduced high-power projector light sources, a green phosphor dot converts the light of a laser diode (green semiconductor lasers are still problematic to build).

Note that no phosphor releases photons instantly, there is always a certain time after the excitation during which photons are emitted. This *relaxation time* can range from nanoseconds to hours, depending on the materials involved.

Slow relaxation time is related to "forbidden" quantum energy-state transitions. As these transitions occur very infrequently in some materials, radiation may be re-emitted at low intensity and over a long time. Common applications are "glow-in-the-dark" toys or the glowing numbers on mechanical wristwatches. A typical material here is copper-activated zinc sulfide. This principle historically had important applications in "afterglowing" oscilloscopes or radar screen tubes.

2.3.8.5 Fluorescent Lamps

Fluorescent lamps work on the principle of very low pressure gas discharges within a glass enclosure. Mercury (vapor) added to the gas emits UV light, which is converted to visual light by a phosphor layer on the inside of the glass.

These lamps are the most common for commercial indoor lighting and are also gaining popularity as energy-saving lamps to replace tungsten bulbs. With display technology, their main use is for panel backlighting. Most LCD screens currently work with a fluorescent light source. These special fluorescent lamps use cold cathodes and are driven by dedicated high-voltage converters. LC displays are discussed in Section 6.6.2 at page 225.

The spectral characteristics of fluorescent lamps are a cause of concern in terms of color reproduction, because their spectral characteristics depend on materials available and so cannot be perfectly designed. Together with the problem of obtaining ideal filter dyes, this explains why most current LCD panels render color inaccurately at times.

2.3.8.6 Other Forms of Luminescence

Light can be generated by many forms of electron excitation. For example, *chemilumines-cence* is based on electrons being excited by chemical reactions within a material. Some types of emergency lights, for example, employ this phenomenon. It has little relation to display technology. Another example, *mechanoluminescence*, is based on mechanical stress in materials.

The purpose of this work is to examine and discuss display technology, and though there are various other light-effecting principles, we will not list all of them here.

2.3.9 Electroluminescence

Electroluminescent (EL) devices are based on thin films of organic or inorganic semiconduct-ing materials (see Section 6.5.1 at page 215). A semiconducting layer (the anode) provides holes in an attached electroluminescent emission layer that determines the color emitted. From the other side of the emission layer, a conducting layer (the cathode) provides elec-trons that recombine with the holes inside the emission layer, causing photon generation. The layers used allow for the light to pass outside. A typical inorganic thin film EL material is ZnS:Mn, emitting orange light; another well known material is *gallium arsenide* (GaAs).

2.3.9.1 LED

Light emitting diodes (LED) are semiconductor chips (see Section 6.5.1 at page 215) doped with other elements, creating a p-n junction, with current that flows from the p-side to the n-side only. Electrons and electron holes then flow into the junction. Other than with silicon or germanium, materials used for LED such as gallium arsenide have a direct band gap. When an electron meets a hole in these materials, it falls into a lower energy level, and releases energy in the form of a photon.

According to Planck's Law, the energy of a red photon is about $1.7\,eV$, that of a green photon is $2.2\,eV$, and that of a blue photon is $3.2\,eV$, and these are the typical band gaps or threshold voltages of the corresponding LED devices. White LEDs are obtained by covering a blue LED with a fluorescent material (similar to fluorescent lamps), that adds a yellow component to the emitted light.

LEDs are used for displays both as backlights (e.g., for LCD screens), or directly either in matrix displays with separate LED pixels for display sizes up to many meters, or as integrated LED-on-silicon devices for micro displays. The efficiency of LEDs is very high, making them a prime choice not only for displays but also for illumination, such as car headlamps.

2.3.9.2 OLED

Organic electroluminescence devices are most commonly referred to as *OLED* (*organic light-emitting diodes*). There are a large variety of OLED and related devices.

Current OLEDs are proving to be as efficient as LEDs already. Life expectancy is still inferior, especially with blue OLEDs, but rapid improvements can be expected to be made, which will allow for a variety of display applications. Many mobile phones and cameras use OLED displays already.

Because some types of OLEDs can be manufactured by silk-screen or ink-jet printing, they are expected to become very inexpensive. Active organic driver circuits for larger displays have been demonstrated and are expected to be manufactured by the same printing techniques.

2.3.9.3 Laser

Lasers are characterized by light amplification because of the laser effect (*light amplification by stimulated emission of radiation*). But this is not only amplification of light, it is generic light generation caused by an energy (pumping energy), which can, for example, be light or electric current, to name just two of the many possibilities. Lasers (laser diodes, for example) are an important light source for various kinds of displays. We treat lasers in more detail in Section 3.5 at page 81).

2.4 MEASURING LIGHT

When measuring light, we distinguish between *photometry* and *radiometry*. Photometric units are based on perceived brightness, while radiometric units are based on energy. All radiometric units have photometric counterparts, and can be converted into photometric units by spectrally integrating the product of their spectral power (W/Hz) with the eye sensitivity curve $V(\lambda)$ (Figure 2.15 on page 32).

2.4.1 Radiometry

Radiometric units correspond to the radiation power leaving a light source, hitting a surface, etc. We distinguish radiant emittance (outgoing) and irradiance (incident) radiation.

Radiometric units can be measured with a variety of instruments, usually converting light intensities into electrical units. Almost all instruments today use semiconductor diodes, directly transforming light energy into a proportional current. Former approaches, such as light dependent resistors or electron tubes, have been widely abandoned, with the exception of photomultipliers, which are still used for extremely low light conditions, down to single photon detection.

Silicon photo diodes in conjunction with *Complimentary Metal-Oxide Semiconductor* (CMOS) operational amplifiers can deliver an illumination-proportional current for over nine orders of magnitude, equaling intensities from starlight to bright sunlight.

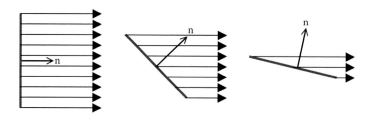

FIGURE 2.11 Angular behavior of a Lambert emitter, light beams, and area normal vectors.

2.4.1.1 Angular Range

A light source that originates from an entire (transparent) volume, for example, a gas where photons are produced by discharge, is called a *volumetric emitter*. Such a source emits omnidirectionally. A solid, ball-shaped source also displays this angular behavior.

2.4.1.2 Lambert Emitters

Many light sources are surface emitters; the measured radiation density is a function of the angle at which the surface is observed.

Even when a surface emits light in all directions equally, the apparent size of the surface degrades with an angle that increases to its normal by the cosine function (Figures 2.11, 2.12). This is called *Lambert's cosine law*, and emitters of this type are called *Lambert emitters*.

2.4.1.3 Solid Angle and Angular Density

Radiation originating from a source in three-dimensional space occupies an angular range that is two-dimensional. This can be characterized by the solid angle, Ω. The solid angle is equal to an area on the unit sphere (sphere with radius 1), entirely analogous to the definition of a simple angle which equals the length of a segment on the unit circle (Figure 2.13).

The unit of solid angle is *steradian* (sr). The simple angle is measured in radians, the full circle (360°) being equal to the circumference of the unit circle, 2π. Hence, the natural definition for steradian, "full sphere" is equal to the surface of the unit sphere, 4π.

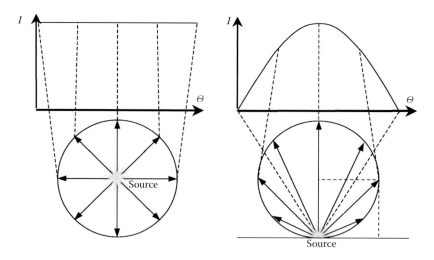

FIGURE 2.12 Directional intensity of volumetric (left) and Lambert emitter (right).

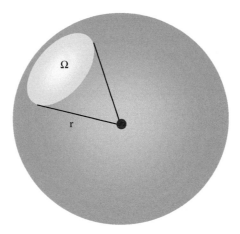

FIGURE 2.13 Definition of the solid angle.

Other than the simple angle, the solid angle is an area and so it can take arbitrary shapes (a circular or rectangular delimited area on the unit sphere, for example, see Figure 2.13). The solid angle can be measured by measuring the area transgressed by radiation at a source distance r (the *subtended area*, defined by the light cone cutting through a sphere at r) and dividing it by r^2.

If the radiation is not perfectly confined to a certain area, a solid angle for it can also be determined by an integral of its density in polar coordinates.

The angular density of radiation is the amount of radiation going through a small solid angle at a given point, divided by that solid angle.

2.4.1.4 The Ulbricht Sphere

An important device for measuring the total output of light sources is the Ulbricht sphere (Figure 2.14). This is a sphere usually of about one to three ft. in size, with an all-white inside

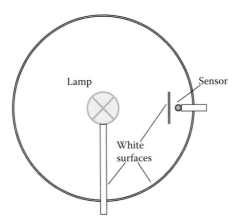

FIGURE 2.14 The Ulbricht sphere: Multiple reflections in a white cavity result in an even light distribution. The sensor, shielded from direct light, delivers a signal proportional to the total radiation output of the lamp.

TABLE 2.2   Radiometric Units

Quantity	Symbol	SI Unit	Comments
Radiant flux	Φ	W	Radiant power
Radiant intensity	I	W/sr	Per solid angle
Radiance	L	$W/sr/m^2$	Intensity
Irradiance	I	W/m^2	Incident power
Radiant emittance	M	W/m^2	Emitted power
Radiosity	J	W/m^2	Reflected+emitted
Spectral radiance	L_λ	$W/sr/m^3$	Per wavelength
Spectral radiance	L_ν	$W/sr/m^2/Hz$	Per frequency
Spectral irradiance	E_λ	W/m^3	Per wavelength
Spectral irradiance	E_ν	$W/m^2/Hz$	Per frequency

coating (e.g., magnesium oxide) scattering any light as often as necessary to produce a totally even light distribution in all directions everywhere inside the sphere. Small holes are used to insert lamp holders or cables or photometric sensors, so the effect is disturbed as little as possible.

Without the Ulbricht sphere, measuring the total output of a light source would require scanning the entire angular range around it with a sensor and integrating the results.

Given the large variety of radiometric emitters and receivers, as well as the requirements in different fields of application, a variety of radiometric units have been defined (Table 2.2). The spectral parameters vary in wavelength or in frequency. We have given them corresponding indices (ν, λ) to distinguish them.

2.4.2 Photometry

Photometry is entirely similar to radiometry, the sole difference being that all light is not measured in total spectral power but in the relative intensity perceived by the human eye. Hence, photometric units are color dependent and valid for the visual range only.

The human eye's sensitivity to light is a function of wavelength, with a maximum of approximately 555 nm. The curve in Figure 2.15 is valid for bright light (photopic vision).

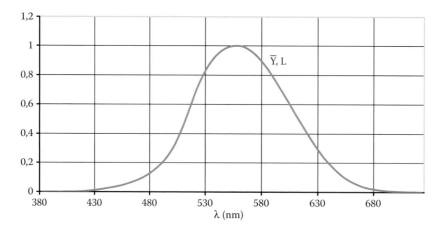

FIGURE 2.15   Perceived brightness: eye sensitivity curve.

TABLE 2.3   Photometric Units

Quantity	Symbol	Definition	SI Unit	Comments
Luminous energy	Q	$lm \cdot s$	lm s	
Luminous flux	F	$cd \cdot sr$	lm	Luminous power
Luminous intensity	I_V	lm/sr	cd	SI base unit
Luminance	L_V	cd/m^2	cd/m^2	Also *nit* (US)
Illuminance	E_V	lm/m^2	lx	Incident light
Luminous emittance	M_V	lm/m^2	lx	Emitted light
Luminous efficacy	η	lm/W	lm/W	

At low light levels (scotopic vision), the curve and its maximum shift to the left. This is not considered for our purposes because displays are supposed to deliver bright images.

The perceived brightness of a light source depends on its spectral characteristics. Luminous efficacy for example, a measure for the visual efficiency of a light source, is limited by this spectral response. Only a pure green light source at 555 nm can reach the theoretical optimum of about 683 lm/W. The luminous efficiency (radiant flux per watt), in this case, would have to be 100%. For a lamp with a spectrum similar to the sun, luminous efficacy only can reach about 251 lm/W in the best theoretical case.

The table of photometric units (Table 2.3) is quite similar to that shown for radiometric units (Table 2.2). Note that because of the relative meaning of these units, it is still appropriate to call one unit a *candela* (cd), the term derived from –what else– the light output of a candle.

Because some units are denoted with letters similar to their radiometric counterparts, we have given them an index V for better distinction.

The luminous flux is the radiation going through a solid angle, as expressed in *candela·steradian* (cd·sr) or *lumen* (lm).

Also of practical importance is the illuminance or *luminous emittance* of a surface, (i.e., its brightness regardless if illuminated or self-luminous), which is usually expressed in *lux* (lx). Bright sunlight is between 110,000 and 120,000 lux, and a radiometric irradiance between 1300 and 1400 W/m^2. Under overcast sky, approximately 1000 . . . 10,000 lux are measured.

Indoor lighting usually ranges from between 500 lux (bright office light) and 20 lux (cozy living room light). Moonlight is about 0.3 . . . 1 lux (full moon) and starlight is about 0.002 lux.

The light emission of display surfaces is usually expressed in cd/m^2, which indicates the perceived brightness if calculated for a specific viewing angle. Comparing this to illuminance (the brightness of the environment) requires some convention:

Consider an opaque white surface of 1 m^2 illuminated by 1 lux. This can be compared to a display surface as an ideal Lambert emitter. Integrating the surface radiance over the solid angle 2π of the half-sphere and considering the cos Θ law for the Lambert emitter (see Section 2.4.1.2 at page 30), we get a factor π. Therefore, the surface illuminated by 1 lux will resemble a display surface emitting $1/\pi$ cd/m^2 in the normal direction. Note that this perceived brightness value will be valid for any viewing angle; the radiation density per solid angle will change with cos Θ, but the perceived size of the surface will accordingly be smaller, so it appears equally bright.

2.4.3 Luminous Efficiency of Light Sources

The output of a light source is measured in lumen. This parameter takes into account the spectral sensitivity curve of the eye, therefore it depends on the color of the light source. It is a practical means of comparing light sources for displays and also for illumination (many lamps have their lumen output printed on the sales package).

Obviously, a luminous efficiency of 100% (this equals a luminous efficacy of 683 lm/W, for 555 nm green light) is practically impossible except for unusual applications, because pure green light would not be a useful illumination in most cases. In practice, even a light source converting 100% of the energy into photons is limited to 37% luminous efficiency, because of the spectral characteristics of the human eye. Table 2.4 lists the luminous efficacy of various common light sources. The highest practical luminous efficiency known is from low pressure sodium lamps (almost 30%), which have a yellow light and are sometimes used for road illumination.

LEDs and OLEDs also are among the most efficient light sources; both deliver about the same level of performance.

2.4.4 Durability of Light Sources

For practical applications, the life expectancy of light sources can be of major concern, and different types vary greatly. Tungsten lamps usually achieve 1000–2000 hours. Gas discharge and fluorescent lamps usually last five times longer, and e^3 lamps exceed 50000 hours. Xenon arc lamps are quite durable as well; their life expectancy in car headlamps approaches that of the car. For displays, many factors may affect life expectancy. CRT tubes and fluorescent lamps usually degrade because their cathodes burn out, while their phosphors degrade very slowly. CRT tubes can last for decades of normal use, if not tuned too bright. LCD displays can fail due to water vapor diffusion, if they are not sealed with glass solder; their light source is limiting life expectancy as well. OLED displays have a limited life expectancy because their organic materials suffer from chemical changes.

In display technology, a very important consideration is *duty time*, (i.e., the length of time a display is really used during a certain period). The viewfinder display of a digital camera, for example, has a short duty time, so OLED displays can be used without disadvantage. With an office computer, however, we have to expect eight hours of use per day, requiring a very durable display technology. Most video projectors have lamps that may extinguish after

TABLE 2.4 Luminous Efficiency and (Visual) Efficacy of Different Light Sources

Source Type	Luminous Efficiency (%)	Luminous Efficacy (lm/W)
Candle	0.04	0.3
Tungsten	2.5	17
Tungsten halogen	3	20
White LED/OLED	1.5–22	10–150
Xenon arc lamp	6	40
Fluorescent lamp	8–11	45–70
Max. for Sun spectrum	37	251
Max. for 555 nm green	100	683

a few thousand hours; they can be replaced but are very expensive. A projector is usually not used as a replacement for a normal TV set, but if it was, lamp costs would become a concern. So, durability is quite a complex matter. In any case, complete technical information should be acquired about all contributing factors when considering illumination or display technologies for specific applications.

2.5 PHYSICS OF LIGHT

We will now discuss light in more detail, and will examine its wave and quantum nature, explaining such matters as interference, tunneling, and polarization. Most of the topics can be difficult to understand without a certain background in quantum physics, so we will describe the basics, as comprehensibly as possible.

2.5.1 Interference

In the early 1800s, Thomas Young demonstrated that light waves interfere with each other. They can superimpose, and depending on their phase, the amplitudes of multiple waves can increase or decrease (Figure 2.16). When in phase (or with a phase shift being a multiple of 360° or 2π), they interfere constructively, in other words they increase. With a phase-shift being a multiple of 180° or π, they interfere destructively, resulting in an amplitude of zero.

2.5.2 Quantum Effects

Light is not simply electromagnetic waves. We must also consider its quantum nature; we will discuss this now (for a comprehensive introduction to quantum physics, refer to [85]).

A proper formula for black-body radiation was derived subsequently by Max Planck to the principle that described light as consisting of discrete packets of energy. He found that the theoretical problems to explain it could be solved by introducing a constant h (the famous Planck constant), with photon energies given by $E = h\nu$ (ν being the frequency).

It was Albert Einstein, however, who seriously considered Planck's particle interpretation as a physical fact. In 1905, Einstein explained the photoelectric effect using the particle description:

When a metal target is illuminated by a light source in vacuum, one can detect that under certain conditions, electrons are emitted from the metal ("beaten" out of the surface). The effect, however, occurs only with ultraviolet light. Above a certain wavelength, no light is

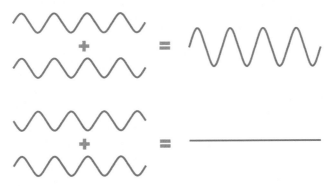

FIGURE 2.16 Constructive (top) and destructive (bottom) interference of waves.

emitted, and below that wavelength, the emission is proportional to the light's intensity. Hence, the effect cannot depend only on total intensity, but must require a minimum energy that can be attributed to light particles.

If waves can be described as particles as well, then the question arises whether particles can, conversely, also be described as waves, and indeed, experiments with electron beams produced wave interference that demonstrates this phenomenon.

Light particles have a wavelength of $\lambda = hc/E$ ($E = h\nu = hc/\lambda$).

In 1924, Louis de Broglie derived for massive particles the formula:

$$\lambda = \frac{h}{mv} = \frac{h}{p} \tag{2.7}$$

with p being the momentum of the particle. This implies $mv = E/c$ or, with $v = c$ (as is always the case for photons), $E = mc^2$. Hence, Einstein's famous mass-energy relation (that he published in 1905 in a short note after his paper on special relativity) was a precursor of de Broglie's wavelength relation for particles, but it took until 1924 to realize that even massive objects can be interpreted as waves.

The next riddle leading to the evolution of quantum physics was the discreteness of spectral emissions from gases. Hydrogen, for example, emits only certain wavelengths corresponding to energies of

$$E_n = 13.6 \, eV/n^2 \quad \text{with } n = 1, 2, \ldots,$$

where the photons emitted have energies of $E_j - E_i$ with $i > j$, as if the atoms were switching between energy levels E_n.

This could be interpreted as electrons bound to atoms by certain discrete energy levels. Niels Bohr provided a model to explain this in 1913. First, he assumed that electrons circling the nucleus are bound by an electrostatic force equal to the centrifugal force:

$$m\frac{v^2}{r} = \frac{q^2}{4\pi \varepsilon_0 r^2} \tag{2.8}$$

Yet, this would still allow for any radius r to occur. So Bohr introduced the hypothesis that the circumference of the orbit should equal an integer multiple of a certain constant. Later on, this turned out to be the de Broglie wavelength of the electron:

$$2\pi r = n\lambda \tag{2.9}$$

The electron can then be interpreted as a standing electromagnetic wave around the nucleus, the energy levels as different modes of that wave (see Figure 2.10 on page 25).

We will see a further explanation for this requirement in Section 2.5.2.4 at page 42.

Solving this with the above two formulas and the de Broglie wavelength formula, one finds the Bohr radius values a_0:

$$a_0 = \frac{\varepsilon_0 h^2 n^2}{\pi m_0 q^2} \tag{2.10}$$

The energy levels can be calculated by adding the kinetic and the potential energies of the electron. The potential energy is given by the electrostatic potential of the proton:

$$V(r) = -\frac{q^2}{4\pi\varepsilon_0 r} \tag{2.11}$$

With this, the total electron energy levels are:

$$E_n = \frac{m_0 q^4}{8\varepsilon_0^2 h^2 n^2}, \quad \text{with } n = 1, 2, \ldots \tag{2.12}$$

An important addition to Bohr's model is the *exclusion principle* of Wolfgang Pauli. According to Pauli, no two electrons can occupy the same energy level corresponding to a unique set of quantum numbers. A limited number of electrons can be in the same "orbit", given that they are distinct from other quantum properties whose discussion would exceed the scope of our topic. For photons, such an exclusion does not exist. Virtually any number of photons can occupy an arbitrary small space without influencing each other (except for nonlinear optical media).

It is important to recall at this point (because this is often intermixed), that thermal radiation is *not* generated by electron transitions, but by spontaneous emission due to the thermal motion of atoms, and that thermal radiation has a *continuous* spectrum, because in $E = h\nu$, h is a constant, but ν can take *any* value.

The Bohr model explained the electron energy levels, but it did not yet provide a general solution to quantum mechanical problems. The reason were experimental results exposing very strange, random, and even nonlocal quantum effects.

2.5.2.1 The Double-Slit Experiment

With thermal radiation, we already introduced the concept of probabilistic effects.

Remarkably, Planck, in his 1900 paper [228], preempted the uncertainty element in quantum physics. He stated that "entropy needs disorder; if amplitude and phase of the oscillators would be absolutely constant, their energy could completely be converted into work". (Oscillators back then were a working hypothesis preempting the existence of thermally moving atoms.)

Abandoning determinism seems to be a nightmare to many physicists even today, but it is by far not the most formidable aspect of quantum physics.

Let us consider one of the more worrying experiments. It consists of an electron source, a wall with two parallel slits, and a screen –or an array of sensors– detecting electrons (this works with photons as well, but with electrons, isolating single particles is a bit easier).

If the electron source emits many electrons hitting the entire surface of the wall, we may see evenly spaced parallel lines on the screen (Figure 2.17). This could be a phosphor screen, for example, and the whole setup could be built as a modified cathode ray tube.

The result appears to be logical if we already know Einstein's duality hypothesis, seeing particles also as waves. Simply, the electrons passing the slits form two cylindrical wavefronts interfering at the screen, thereby causing the pattern.

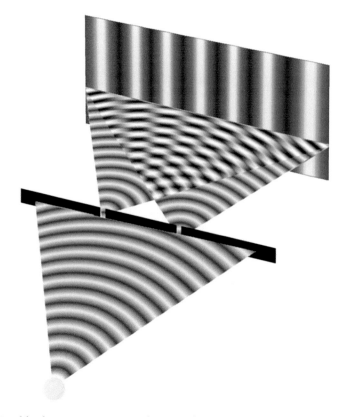

FIGURE 2.17 Double slit experiment: Interference of particles?

This was acceptable, however, some nitpicky physicists tuned down the electron source until only single electrons were trickling through, one after another. Then they counted the (single) electrons hitting the screen (this experiment was first conducted by Claus Jönsson [142]). To their surprise, the statistics of many electrons continued to show the interference pattern. But how could a single electron interfere with another that came seconds after or before it?

The answer as it is partially understood today: the electron is not a solid particle, it only appears so at the moment it is measured.

What is leaving the electron source is a probability wave with a specific opening angle and duration, describing a probability field for the likeliness of a particle at a certain place, and also for some other properties it may have, such as its phase.

Such a wave is defined by the Schrödinger equation (see Section 2.5.2.2).

2.5.2.2 The Schrödinger Equation
An interpretation of the double-slit and other quantum physical experiments involves equations originally proposed by Erwin Schrödinger in 1924. Starting from the classical formula for total (kinetic + potential) energy:

$$E = \frac{p^2}{2m} + V(x) \tag{2.13}$$

and

$$E = h\nu = \hbar\omega \tag{2.14}$$

$$\hbar = h/2\pi, \quad \omega = 2\pi\nu \tag{2.15}$$

$$p = h/\lambda = \hbar k \text{ resp. } \vec{p} = \hbar\vec{k} \text{ (de Broglie particle 1924)} \tag{2.16}$$

where k is introduced as the space-like equivalent of ω.

Schrödinger postulated a wave function as a complex plane wave (remember that $e^{ix} = \cos(x) + i\sin(x)$ describes a sine wave with a certain phase):

$$\psi(x,t) = Ae^{i(\vec{k}\vec{x}-\omega t)} \tag{2.17}$$

Together with Heisenberg's uncertainty principle developed shortly after (see Section 2.5.2.4 at page 42), this expression turned out to be even more appropriate, because it has the properties of a wave, but also a probability $|\psi|^2$ that is not oscillating.

The t-derivative of this function is $\frac{\partial\psi}{\partial t} = -i\omega\psi$, hence

$$E\psi = \hbar\omega\psi = i\hbar\frac{\partial\psi}{\partial t} \quad \text{(time dependent Schrödinger equation)} \tag{2.18}$$

and likewise with the x-derivatives $\frac{\partial\psi}{\partial x} = ik_x\psi$ and $\frac{\partial^2\psi}{\partial x^2} = -k_x^2\psi$ we can write

$$p_x^2\psi = (\hbar k_x)^2\psi = -\hbar^2\frac{\partial^2\psi}{\partial x^2} \tag{2.19}$$

Hence, together with with Equuation2.13:

$$E\psi = V\psi - \frac{\hbar^2}{2m}\frac{\partial^2\psi}{\partial x^2} \quad \text{(time independent Schrödinger equation)} \tag{2.20}$$

Finally if we look at a plane wave in three dimensions we can write:

$$p^2\psi = (p_x^2 + p_y^2 + p_z^2)\psi = -\hbar^2\left(\frac{\partial^2}{\partial x^2} + \frac{\partial^2}{\partial y^2} + \frac{\partial^2}{\partial z^2}\right)\psi = -\hbar^2\nabla^2\psi \tag{2.21}$$

and inserting this energy and momentum into Equation 2.13, we get the renowned Schrödinger equation for a particle in $\mathbb{R}^3$ in presence of a potential V:

$$E\psi = V\psi - \frac{\hbar^2}{2m}\nabla^2\psi \tag{2.22}$$

This equation is commonly called the *wave function*. Now, let us come back to the double-slit experiment and see how it can be interpreted by these formulas.

2.5.2.3 Interpretation

To simplify, we will regard the Schrödinger equation in one dimension (x), where it reduces to

$$E\psi(x) = -\frac{\hbar^2}{2m}\frac{d^2\psi(x)}{dx^2} + V(x)\psi(x) \tag{2.23}$$

Quantum theory postulates that the product of the wavefunction $\psi(x)$ with its complex conjugate $\psi^*(x)$ (which is mathematically identical to the absolute square $|\psi|^2$) results in a probability function $P(x)$ associated with the described particle:

$$P(x) = \psi(x)\psi^*(x) = |\psi|^2 \tag{2.24}$$

The probability density function when integrated provides the probability that the particle is within the integral range. The probability function is normalized to account for the fact that its integral over the entire range must be 100%:

$$\int_{-\infty}^{\infty} P(x)dx = 1 \tag{2.25}$$

So what actually occurs in the double slit experiments is like this: at the slits, the wave does what any wave would do: because there are only two point sources, the wave forms two interfering, cylindrical (probability) waves, resulting in overlaying probability distributions at the screen.

Any electron may appear anywhere at the wall or the screen, according to the probabilities. When this happens, the probability wave disappears, instantly, because it is not possible that the electron can appear anywhere else, so all probabilities become zero. And indeed, it has been shown that this happens; the phenomenon is usually referred to as *breakdown of the wavefuntion*, or as *decoherence*.

Because of the probabilities, the numbers of electrons appearing at a certain place on the screen have the same distribution as the formerly measured interference pattern. Though the probability function of a single wave is not oscillating, the complex phase values of two different waves indeed result in an interference pattern of probabilities exactly matching the interference pattern of two "macroscopic" electromagnetic waves.

The statistical distribution of electrons measured at the wall generates the interference pattern measured. This is always the case, even if we regard not single, but many, concurrent electrons. Any "normal life" experience is the sum of many quantum events, and electromagnetic waves approximate an application for large systems. Evidently, an electron is likely to appear anywhere in its wave, before it is measured.

Moreover, as has been demonstrated in other experiments, this location is not determined in any way before *measurement* occurs accidentally somewhere, with a probability exactly described by the probabilities of the wavefunctions of the two particles involved.

The probability wave of an electron could spread over half of the universe and, a billion years later, someone (or something) may "measure" it and the electron would *appear* at that point, while its probability wave would instantly disappear for all space and related time, past and future even, if relativity is considered.

The same phenomenon occurs for any photon that reaches our eye from a distant star.

The breakdown of the wavefront, or *decoherence*, is a disturbingly nonlocal effect and seems to violate anything we know from experience; but it is not the only nonlocality in quantum physics.

There are certain processes by which, for example, two photons are emitted in different directions, and it is known that they must have, e.g., perpendicular (or opposite) polarizations. Interpreting the photons as probability waves, however, implies that the polarization angles are not fixed before at least one of the photons is measured. The other one should –afterward– show a polarization determined by the measurement of the first one. Particles related in such a manner for their quantum properties are called 'entangled'.

Most physicists first believed that there would have to be some *hidden variables* determining the result beforehand. But in 1964, John S. Bell [16] designed an experiment that would decide the matter by a sophisticated statistical analysis. When the experiment was performed years later, it proved that nonlocality is a fact. Numerous increasingly sophisticated experiments have been carried out since, all of them supporting nonlocality as well as randomness (e.g., [99]). Still, most physicists do not really accept the full consequence of this, however.

It really appears as if we are not seeing the world as it really is. Space may be a phenomenon emerging from myriads of quantum processes, continuously establishing and re-establishing relationships between objects. Seeing it as a kind of background fabric ruled by geometry laws may be a convenient hypothesis that breaks down in some cases. We could, for example, assume that single quanta or pairs of entangled quanta occupy an arbitrary, private extra dimension in an infinite dimensional *nothing*, with their distance or probability wave extension remaining zero in that dimension (faintly analogous to worm holes). The geometric complications of such an approach, however, are formidable, and they literally explode with the myriad of quanta existing. Classical geometries that attempt to explain quantum nonlocality may therefore be very unusual or even impossible. We may need new concepts. Perhaps, could what we perceive as distance, be related to some kind of *information distance*?

Another conclusion that has to be considered is that particles primarily exist as wavefunctions. Indeed, the particle metaphor describes only the short moment of interaction with other "particles" and apparent trajectories of particles are nothing but an illusion, an imaginary line between two places and two events. This is true also for light "rays". They are not the result of straight flying photons but of spherically symmetric, propagating probability waves.

The physical world that we experience is a result, a history, of quantum events. Because the outcome of any of these events incurs randomness, inverting the time vector would result in a totally different past (so much for time travel).

Nevertheless, complex quantum systems can be held in a superposition state as long as their state is not measured (which can be avoided only at near zero temperatures). In this state, possible quantum events can be considered to be continually occurring forward and backward (sometimes one reads that time reversal is possible in quantum mechanics, which is, however, not true as soon as any measurement occurs, i.e., practically anytime). Although at a first glance such superposition experiments appear to deliver nothing but random noise, it has been shown that they can be exploited for solving very difficult mathematical problems, such as the factorization of large numbers. The discipline evolving from this is known as *quantum computing* [211].

We may conclude with the common assumption that the "correct" physical theory always is the one that describes matters in the most elegant and "simple" way. But with quanta, maybe the most elegant theory also is the most incomprehensible. Because comprehending something means being able to perform a quick and easy simulation of it, we may have to add an appropriate simulation machine to our brain functions in order to "understand" these matters as easy as we now deal with (three-dimensional) geometry.

2.5.2.4 The Uncertainty Principle

Another quantum principle, probably more important to display technology, is Werner Heisenberg's *uncertainty principle*, discovered in 1927. It states that both impulse and location of an electron and likewise frequency and location of a photon, cannot concurrently be measured with accuracy:

$$\Delta x \Delta p \geq \frac{\hbar}{2} \tag{2.26}$$

The uncertainty principle delivers a more fundamental explanation of why random events such as those mentioned above have to occur. One possible interpretation we may derive from information theory: a quantum can hold only a few bits of information (one quantum bit or *qubit*, resembling a few binary bits in complexity), and more accurate information on one quantum can be encoded only in a large number of other quanta relating to it.

If we regard a space with point-like particles, we can describe it entirely by mapping distances and other relations between any two particles in a two-dimensional matrix (just like the distance table on an ordinary roadmap, cf. [113]). This is a simple argument indicating that the complexity of any quantum system is just two dimensional. In a rigorous version, this has been derived from black-hole physics and is known as the "holographic principle," introduced by Gerardus 't Hooft, Leonard Susskind, and others.

This also imposes a straight limit on the maximum amount of information that can be encoded in a closed system. Indeed, no system can contain complete information about itself. This is a general principle implying uncertainty.

Uncertainty as a general philosophical principle may also be indicated when we regard a photon as a wave and consider that the spatial extension of this wave in propagation direction must of course be very limited (Figure 2.18). Such a wave burst, however, would have no exact frequency, its bandwidth grows proportionally larger the shorter the burst is, as a simple Fourier analysis shows (more on Fourier in Section 2.5.3 at page 43). Trying to measure the wavelength accurately, we must extend (i.e., spread) the wave over a considerable amount of time, so the location of the photon can no longer be determined.

Note that although the left image in Figure 2.18 appears to show only one frequency, this is not really the case. A simple demonstration apart from Fourier transformation goes like this:

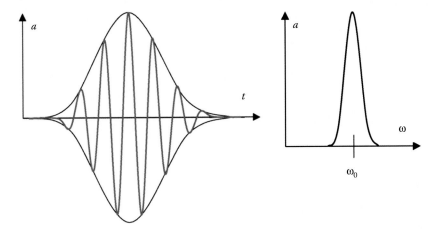

FIGURE 2.18 Wave packet of a photon (left) and the corresponding frequency distribution around the mean frequency ω_0 (right).

The frequency spread of an originally pure sine wave is simply calculated if we regard a sine wave of frequency ω_0 and amplitude 1, being multiplied (modulated) by another sine wave of frequency ω_m and amplitude a. We add a constant to the modulating wave in order to keep it positive. We assume that $a \leq 1$ and $\omega_m \leq \omega_0$.

$$\left(\frac{1}{2} + \frac{a}{2} \sin(\omega_m t) \right) \sin(\omega_0 t) = \sin(\omega_0 t) - \frac{a}{2} \cos(\omega_0 t + \omega_m t) + \frac{a}{2} \cos(\omega_0 t - \omega_m t)$$

(2.27)

Therefore, we get the original frequency plus two side frequencies at distance $\pm \omega_m$. Replacing the modulating sine wave by any sum of sine waves, or any spectrum, we get the same spectrum repeated left and right of the "carrier frequency" ω_0. What we have shown here is nothing but amplitude modulation as used in AM radio. If we want to know the frequency distribution caused by any pulse shaping of a wave packet, we may use the Fourier analysis of the shaping function.

What we have shown here, is known as the "mathematical uncertainty principle" (explained in more detail in [226]), and it just reflects the fundamental properties of waves.

Revisiting the Bohr atom model, we can now argue that the wavefunction of an electron needs to have a certain extension (as for and arbitrarily short wave packet, the energy would become more and more undefined), and if it were not an integer fraction of the orbit circumference, it could destructively interfere with itself in the orbit.

2.5.3 Fourier Spectrum

Given an arbitrary function $f(x)$ defined in the x-range $-\pi \ldots + \pi$, this function can be approximated by a sum of sine and cosine waves as follows (Figure 2.19):

$$f_N(x) = \frac{a_0}{2} + \sum_{n=1}^{N} [a_n \cos(nx) + b_n \sin(nx)] \quad \text{with } N \geq 0$$

(2.28)

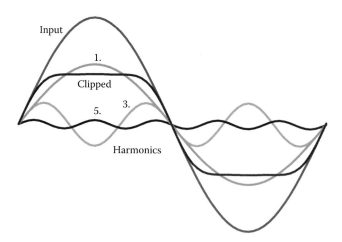

FIGURE 2.19 Example of a Fourier series: constructing a partly clipped sine wave from the base frequency plus the 3rd and 5th harmonic.

where the coefficients a_n and b_n can be derived by the following formulas:

$$a_n = \frac{1}{\pi} \int_{-\pi}^{\pi} f(x) \cos(nx) dx \quad \text{with } n \geq 0 \tag{2.29}$$

$$b_n = \frac{1}{\pi} \int_{-\pi}^{\pi} f(x) \sin(nx) dx \quad \text{with } n \geq 1 \tag{2.30}$$

The Fourier series is only one of many possible ways of dissecting arbitrary functions, but it is most commonly used as it is well suited for periodic oscillations. Joseph Fourier found this formula in 1807. A more general variety is the Fourier transform, converting arbitrary functions of time into functions of frequency, yielding a detailed spectrum analysis:

$$F(v) = \int_{-\infty}^{\infty} f(t) e^{-2\pi i t v} dt \tag{2.31}$$

The inverse of the Fourier transform is quite similar given by:

$$f(t) = \int_{-\infty}^{\infty} F(v) e^{-2\pi i t v} dv \tag{2.32}$$

With the Fourier transform, the above-mentioned similarity between the Heisenberg uncertainty principle and the uncertainty in frequency and location of a wave packet (*mathematical uncertainty principle*) can be shown to be mathematically perfect.

There are many other useful applications of the general Fourier transform. For example, clipping frequency ranges from the spectrum presentation and transforming it back into the time domain yields a so-called *Fourier filter*.

Fourier transforms are convenient to compute, because an especially efficient algorithm has been developed for it: the *Fast Fourier Transform* (FFT).

Another variety of time-frequency (or wave-spectrum) transforms is the *Discrete Cosine Transform* (DCT), mainly used for image compression, there in a two-dimensional extension (see Section 6.4.8 at page 210).

Let us add a few remarks that explain why and how the Fourier transform equations work.

What we see in the Fourier transform equations is basically a product of a signal $f(x)$ with sine waves (cosine just being a phase-shifted sine). Now consider the product of two sine waves (assuming that $f(x)$ is also a simple sine wave). If they have the same frequency and phase, we get an integral value that is proportional to integration time of the signal (because negative portions, when multiplied, always yield positive values). If they don't share the same frequency and phase, then we get an integral value that becomes successively smaller. This is due to the fact that the relative phase of both signals changes permanently, resulting in an equal number of positive and negative contributions.

Note that integrating the product of two functions (of which this is one example) is also known as *cross-correlation*. It delivers a measure for similarities of these functions.

Now consider a signal $f(x)$ mixed from a composition of many sine waves, and that we integrate its product with one certain sample sine wave (remember that $a \sum b_i = \sum ab_i$). If a component that is similar (frequency and phase) to that sample wave is contained in $f(x)$, then we get an integral value that is proportional to the sample wave's amplitude and the integration time. All other components of the signal yield zero in comparison.

Hence we "probe" the signal for the presence of our sample frequency. So far, this would require that $f(x)$ and the sample wave have the same phase. Nevertheless, we can probe for any phase if sine and cosine functions are both considered, because

$$\sin(x + \varphi) = \cos \varphi \sin x + \sin \varphi \cos x \tag{2.33}$$

Therefore, any sine wave with a phase shift φ can be represented with a combination of sine and cosine.

If we repeat this for many frequencies, we receive the entire spectrum (i.e., the integral values being the magnitudes) of the entire signal $f(x)$ (including phase). This is what the Fourier transform equations represent.

2.5.4 Radiation Processes Revisited

We have seen that considering physical objects as waves naturally leads to uncertainty. Uncertainty in turn implies the Planck quantum. This doesn't mean we could calculate h from Heisenberg's formula, as h itself is fundamental (e.g., if bricks were the smallest entity possible, and we measure the height of a building in bricks, we would never be able to tell how high a brick actually is, except for expressing it as a fraction of the building's height).

A particle wave (including, but not restricted to, electrons) is electromagnetic in essence; it appears quite natural that even small changes in the wavefront may also give rise to another electromagnetic wave, like a photon. Such an emission, of course, has to occur in packets of $e = h\nu$.

With thermal radiation, we have to consider multiple molecule collisions in a gas, or atoms oscillating in a body, for example. Gas molecule collisions are difficult to approach because they are mainly elastic, and only a small portion of the energy at each collision is emitted as thermal photons. What was studied originally were oscillating atoms. Although little was known about atoms at the time, this was exactly what Planck did (discussing *electro magnetic oscillators*), using Boltzmann's statistical mechanics, and he found the correct formulas for the thermal-emission spectrum.

There is no necessity to reassess this with quantum physics as a consideration, as Planck has already done exactly this, by introducing the Planck quantum h. Note that h does not contradict the fact that thermal spectra are continuous, because ν can take *any* value.

2.5.5 Tunneling

Uncertainty has more implications, and these are indeed of major importance in technology. If the location or energy of a quantum is somewhat uncertain (i.e., it can obtain any value within a certain probability range), an electron could well be measured at a place where it wasn't expected, for example behind a thin wall it otherwise couldn't transgress. Likewise, it could also pass an energetic barrier, such as a voltage threshold, that in principle would be too "high" for it (Figure 2.20).

The number of particles doing so may be minute, but implications for everyday life are formidable. For example, the temperature and pressure even at the heart of the sun would normally be too low to start nuclear fusion. Only tunneling allows a few hydrogen atoms to merge. So without tunneling, the sun wouldn't shine. And if its core had enough pressure for fusion without tunneling, probably all hydrogen would turn into helium almost at once and the sun would explode. Tunneling indeed allows certain processes to run smoothly.

In technology, tunneling appears as a working principle of certain semiconductors (tunnel diodes), but in general it has implications for the characteristics of many others.

Calculating the tunneling behavior of even a simple potential well is a lengthy endeavor, and does not suit the purposes of this text. Results such as those in (Figure 2.20) are

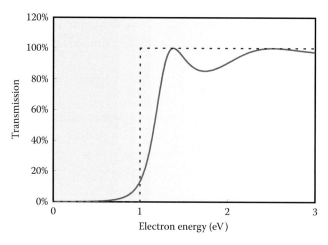

FIGURE 2.20 Passing probability of an electron through a 1 V barrier, 1 nm wide. Note that the probability above 1 V is not immediately 1.

resembling the pulse response of an electrical amplifier, or the frequency response of an electrical filter, because they are derived from the behavior of the particle wavefunction facing a sudden change of voltage in an electrical field. Again, we see that much of peculiar quantum behavior can just be explained by the inherent nature of a wave.

2.5.6 Quantum Dots

A quantum dot is a microscopic assembly of usually ten thousand or more atoms, usually of semiconductor material, where the electrons and holes are confined in all three spatial dimensions. Their energy in this case can only have discrete levels, comparable to the behavior of electrons in atoms. The size, shape and other parameters of a quantum dot can be chosen in a wide range, and a large variety of custom properties can be generated. The size of typical quantum dots is a multiple of the de Broglie wavelength of an electron at room temperature, about 7 . . . 8 nm, allowing for standing waves to emerge. Usual sizes are between 5 and 100 nm. Typical semiconductor atoms are in the range of 0.3 nm, so 10^4 or more atoms may form a quantum dot.

While quantum dots confine electrons in three dimensions, structures confining them to two or one dimensions exhibit resonances as well. These are known as *quantum wires* or *quantum wells*. Carbon nanotubes (see Section 6.6.6.3 at page 236) for example exhibit properties of quantum wires.

Quantum dots can be manufactured in several ways:

- in a chemical solution, where atoms can agglomerate under controlled conditions,
- by molecular beam epitaxy, producing dot structures under certain conditions,
- photo lithographic, as in semiconductor manufacturing.

Quantum dots are especially interesting for their photon emitting and absorbing characteristics that can be achieved in the visible range. They can, for example, be custom tailored for fluorescence at any desired wavelength. Likewise, quantum dots can be used as photon receptors, injecting electrons into semiconductors. Their advantages are increased efficiency, with displays as well as with photoreceptors. Practical applications are:

- LEDs, displays
- Quantum dot lasers
- Single photon sources
- Quantum computing
- Camera sensors
- Improved solar cells

Quantum dots are already used in TV technology, transforming the light of LEDs into narrow-banded spectral emissions, improving the accuracy of the primary colors and hence the color gamut of the display.

2.5.7 Polarization

Polarization is the orientation of the field vectors of light waves (by definition, the electric field vector). Natural light is widely nonpolarized: all orientations have equal probabilities. Linear polarization is given if the orientation of the electrical field is in one direction only for all photons involved (Figure 2.21).

Linear-polarized light can be produced with linear polarizer filters, absorbing half of incident nonpolarized light. These usually work like a microscopic lattice (Figure 2.22), shortcutting the electrical field in one direction; waves with an electric field vector that is perpendicular to the lattice may pass through.

2.5.7.1 Polarizer Filters
Typical polarizer filters could be

- *iodine-based:* cast *polyvinyl alcohol* (PVA) film stained with iodine, stretched so the PVA molecules and the iodine are aligned in one direction. The film is laminated between *triacetate* (TAC) films. This type has up to 99.99% efficiency.

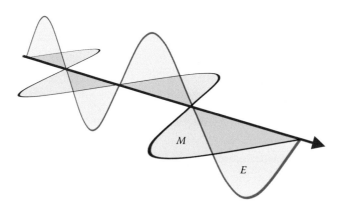

FIGURE 2.21 Polarized light wave (E-field:red M-Field:blue).

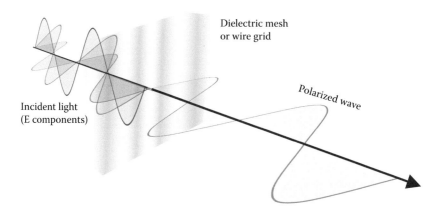

FIGURE 2.22 Principle of a linear polarizer filter.

- *dyestuff polarizer:* the iodine is replaced by organic dyes. This type of polarizer is more heat resistant but less efficient.

- *KE polarizer:* PVA film is itself chemically changed instead of being stained with iodine or dye. This type combines both advantages.

- *nanowire grid:* nanoscale wires reflect light polarized parallel to the wires and pass light across the wires.

2.5.7.2 Polarization and Quantum Physics

A common misinterpretation of polarization assumes light passing a linear polarizer to be attenuated according to its polarization angle.

This could explain why 50% of randomly polarized light passes a polarizer filter. It could also explain why there is additional attenuation with two polarizers in sequence, and why the second polarizer being turned entirely orthogonal would no longer allow light to pass.

Challenging this would be the insertion of a third polarizer between the two, turned to an angle of 45°. All of a sudden, 1/8 of the light will now appear behind the third filter.

This is not consistent with the simple interpretation. It can be explained only if the filters actually change the polarization characteristics of the light in some way. More detailed measuring of this reveals that actually one part of the light is leaving the filter polarized according to the filter's orientation, and the remainder is reflected, with a polarization orthogonal to it.

If we consider the electric field vector of the wave as consisting of two orthogonal components, one in filter orientation, a $\cos(\varphi)$ law follows for the amplitudes (Figure 2.23).

Yet, we know that light comes in packets called *quanta*. What would happen to a single quantum, what rules if it passes or gets reflected, and how does this relate to the result for the macroscopic description?

In fact, the correct explanation for the polarizer is entirely quantum theoretical [242], [85]. A photon's polarization vector is *measured* by the filter to be either parallel or orthogonal, with no other possibilities. The probability of being *measured* in one direction over the other depends on the relation of the vector components of the photon's polarization vector to parallel or orthogonal direction.

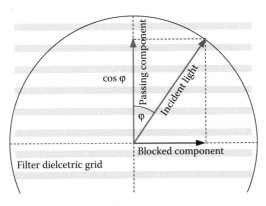

FIGURE 2.23 Polarizer (symbolized by gray bars), and an electric field vector split into two corresponding components (note that this shows amplitudes, not intensities).

After passing the filter, a photon is polarized in filter direction.[*] All photons not passing the filter are reflected instead, and are now polarized orthogonal to that.

The probability of a quantum being at a certain location is the absolute square of the wave amplitude, hence, if we use this accordingly and consider a $\cos(\varphi)$ law for the vector components, the probability of the photon passing is $\cos^2 \varphi$.

Macroscopically, $\cos^2 \varphi$ is the light intensity belonging to the amplitude. So the passing and reflected components together carry the same energy as the original light beam, as required for energy conservation.

Note that $\int \cos^2 \varphi d\varphi$ for $0°$ to $90°$ is 0.5, so an even distribution of polarizations (as before the first filter) also yields 50% of photons passing, just as expected.

For a photon at $45°$, $\cos^2 \varphi$ is 0.5 as well and we also get 50% probabilities for passing or being reflected.

Applying this to the aforementioned experiment, we get 50% attenuation by any of the three filters, or 1/8 of the original light intensity after the third filter, the same as we have measured.

A complete treatment of polarization in optics is done by formula frameworks known as *Jones Calculus and Mueller Calculus* [60,122].

2.5.7.3 Turning Polarization

Certain crystals and fluids can turn polarization continuously. *Liquid crystals* for example consist of lengthy dipole molecules tending to align, forming sort of a "fence" lattice forcing passing light to become polarized. If the orientation of the molecules changes continuously from one end of the volume to the other, the polarization of passing light will also be turned.

One might wonder if these many little polarizers in series would cause losses. But this is not the case: if already polarized light passes a polarizer with a small angle difference φ, there is a small probability it will not pass. The probability to pass is $\cos^2\varphi$. Concurrently it gets a new main polarization direction turned by φ. The total attenuation for n such steps is

$$A = (\cos^2 \varphi)^n \tag{2.34}$$

and the total angle is

$$\alpha = n\varphi \tag{2.35}$$

thus

$$A = (\cos^2(\alpha/n))^n \tag{2.36}$$

With n going to infinity, this leads to $A = 1$, quite obviously due to the fact that $\cos^2 \alpha$ very quickly approaches 1 for small α. Hence, a quasi-continuous polarizer such as a liquid crystal can turn polarization with zero loss.

2.5.8 Circular Polarization

Circular polarized light is composed of two perpendicular polarized plane waves of equal amplitudes and 90° (1/4 wavelength) phase shift.

The electric field vector of circular polarized light that propagates toward an observer would appear to rotate instead of oscillating between + and −. With counterclockwise rotation (when looking at the source), this is called *right-circular polarization*. The opposite is called *left-circular polarization*.

If the two plane wave amplitudes are unequal, we speak of elliptic polarization.

Circular polarization can be used to separate left and right images of stereo displays, in similar fashion to linear polarization: the screen emits two opposite polarized images and the viewers wear polarizer glasses. Circular polarization has the advantage that tilting the head sideways does not cause crosstalk.

Historically, circular polarizers have been difficult to manufacture and were relatively expensive. Recent developments, however, have changed this entirely. Currently, the addition of 3D ability to a TV by means of circular polarization increases overall costs so little, that it has become a very common feature.

2.5.8.1 Producing Circular Polarized Light

Certain materials such as *calcspar*, have different permittivity (ϵ, see Section 3.3.1.2 at page 59) in two perpendicular directions. This is called a *birefringent medium*. Light with different polarization travels in birefringent media at different speeds, causing a phase shift between them. A plate of such material thick enough to cause a 90° delay, is called a *quarter-wave plate*. Such a plate can turn linear-polarized light into circular-polarized light. The light has to enter the crystal at a 45° angle between its fast and slow orientations (Figure 2.24).

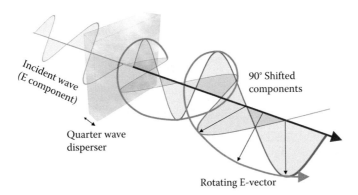

FIGURE 2.24 Principle of circular polarization with a quarter-wave plate. All waves show *E*-vectors. In reality, the plate is many wavelengths thick to achieve the quarter-wave runtime difference between horizontal and vertical polarization.

---

* Note that quantum theoretical sources often prefer to say that just x and y vector amplitudes have changed. This allows keeping all following calculations in the same coordinate system. For our considerations here, it is simpler to use new vectors in filter orientation.

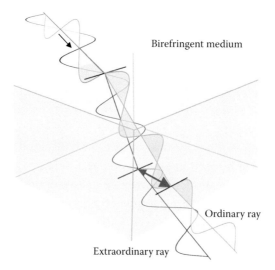

Birefringent medium

Ordinary ray

Extraordinary ray

FIGURE 2.25 Splitting of polarizations in a birefringent medium: different propagation speeds result in different refraction indices.

Otherwise, the beam would pass faster or slower but unaltered. Circular polarizers consist of a linear-polarizer filter plus a quarter-wave plate.

A birefringence medium also causes split refraction (Figure 2.25). Nonpolarized light is refracted into the fast (called the *ordinary*) direction and the slow (called the *extraordinary*) direction. Both components are polarized, travel at different velocities, and their waves become out of phase.

Note that liquid crystals as used in LC displays also show birefringence.

2.6 SUMMARY

We have treated the principles of electromagnetic radiation, light generation and measurement, as well as the physics of light. It becomes evident that all these matters can be understood from a small set of principles: radiation laws, light generation by moving charges, and quantum effects.

Knowing these principles from the outset will ease the understanding of their future applications in the course of the very rapid evolution of display technology. The developments in display technology that we explored in this chapter were, to a great extent, unknown just a few decades, or even years, ago. New techniques of light generation or modulation are found almost every year, and the large selection of other technologies such as semiconductor and thin film devices, allows the application of any of these principles to complete displays quite as quickly.

Learning how to judge all of these new developments requires a broad knowledge of the foundations of the underlying technologies, which are not limited to certain disciplines. Involved here are physics (which we just touched upon), optics, physiology, electronics, even physical chemistry (the latter being an especially wide field that we can treat only as far as naming the ingredients), diffraction optics, photogrammetry and computer science.

We will now proceed with the chapter on optics.

CHAPTER 3

Principles of Optics

3.1 INTRODUCTION

In the previous chapter, we learned a lot about the physical nature of light. We explained how it is generated, how it propagates through space, how it is modulated by matter, and how it can be measured. Visible light is the basis for all displays. But it has to be "shaped" or "formed" by optics to generate useful images.

In this chapter, we will discuss the principles of optical-image generation. Because we know that light is basically electromagnetic radiation, we will recap the fundamentals of wave optics in Section 3.2. For many optical devices and displays it is essential to consider the wave properties of light, such as wavelength, amplitude and phase. Holograms (discussed in Chapter 5) and CGH displays (discussed in Chapter 9), for instance, would not be imaginable without these considerations. We will see that light can interact not only with matter, but can also show certain effects with light itself. Light waves, for example, can interfere constructively or even destructively, depending on their phase relative to each other.

In many cases, it is important to produce "clean" light that interacts in a controlled way. Lasers are very fascinating light sources that produce special light – light that consists of a single wavelength only (called *monochromatic*) and that is in phase (called *coherent*). Normal white light, for instance, is a mixture of many out-of-phase waves of different wavelengths. Such "dirty" light, in many cases, cannot be used when it becomes essential that light waves interact in a controlled way (e.g., for holograms, as we will see later). Because of the importance of lasers, we will explain their principles in Section 3.5 at page 81.

Wave optics, however, is not always crucial to the optical design of instruments or displays. For the generation or detection of macroscopic image points, which are a lot larger than the wavelength of light (e.g., pixels being projected onto a screen or captured by a regular camera), the wave properties of light can often be ignored. In geometric optics (Section 3.3 at page 57), we assume that light always travels the shortest distance between two points in a homogeneous medium. By completely ignoring its wave properties and using a more abstract representation of light rays optical designs can be simplified a great deal. Instead of complex principles of wave propagation, simple vector notations and operations are sufficient for describing the behavior of optical systems.

We will explain the most basic concepts of image point formation (Section 3.4 at page 64) based on laws of geometric optics. Various ordinary optical elements, such as lenses, mirrors, and apertures, as well as their effects in optical devices are discussed. Before we end this chapter, we will also introduce the plenoptic function and its relationship to new imaging, display and lighting systems that are based on entire light fields rather than on focused light rays.

3.2 WAVE OPTICS

In Chapter 2, we learned that light is an electromagnetic wave. As it is the case for all waves, electromagnetic waves share wave properties such as frequency, amplitude, and phase. For many optical elements, such as holograms, it is necessary to consider all of these wave properties in order to explain particular phenomena. This branch of optics is referred to as *wave optics*.

In Chapter 2, we presented examples for physical phenomena of light that relate to its wave nature, such as interference, polarization, and birefringence. Below, we will provide a short general overview of wave optics before we propose yet another abstraction: geometric optics.

Light waves emitted from a point source will propagate in all directions, if not occluded. Points of equal phase form a surface called a *wavefront*. The wavefront is spherical if waves are emitted from a point, and is called a *spherical wavefront*. It consists of infinite planes that are orthogonal to the propagation direction if light waves are emitted from an infinite number of points in a plane. This is called a *planar wavefront*. For light waves emitted from an arbitrary surface, the wavefront forms the same shape near to that surface (Figure 3.1).

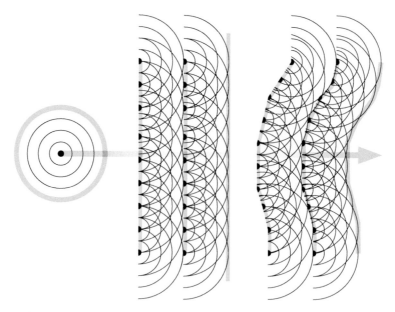

FIGURE 3.1 Spherical wavefront (left), planar wavefront (center) and arbitrary wavefront (right) from multiple point sources.

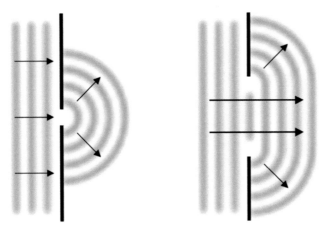

FIGURE 3.2   Diffraction at different slit sizes.

What is important: Any complex wavefront can be formed from a collection of multiple (virtual) point sources and their spherical wavefronts, as shown in Figure 3.1. If a wavefront encounters an obstacle, waves from the virtual point sources next to the obstacle's border can therefore spill light behind the obstacle. This is called *diffraction*. It is often referred as "*bending*" of light, but this is a very misleading interpretation.

Diffraction occurs with all waves (light, sound, water, etc.). If a planar wavefront passes through a slit equal to or smaller than its wavelength, a lot of diffraction occurs, and a more or less cylindrical wavefront results (Figure 3.2(left)). With a slit larger than the wavelength, little diffraction occurs (Figure 3.2(right)).

The amount of diffraction hence depends on the wavelength. The larger the wavelength, the higher the amount of diffraction. Stephen Benton's (a pioneer of rainbow holography) rule of thumb for this is: *red rotates radically*, or RRR.

With slits a few wavelengths wide, fringe patterns are created because different parts of the wave have to travel different distances across the width of the slit, and are phase shifted in this manner. On a screen placed behind such a slit, line patterns of alternating constructive and destructive interference can be observed if the light is sufficiently coherent (quite similar to the double slit experiment in Figure 2.17 on page 38).

Multiple dense slits (or holes) are called a *diffraction grating*. A wavefront passing through a diffraction grating forms a more complex wavefront and interference pattern that depends on the properties of the grating. This is the basis for optical holography, and will be discussed in detail in Chapter 5. If you understand the principles of diffraction and interference, you will understand holography.

So, if you want to explain the color patterns on the surface of soap bubbles, for example, basic knowledge of wave optics is required:

Light approaching a media boundary is reflected. If a wave is reflected from a surface to an optically denser medium (i.e., a material with a higher refraction index), its phase is reversed (180° change of phase, or 1/2 wavelength). If a wave is reflected from a surface to a less dense medium (i.e., a material with a smaller refraction index), its phase is not reversed (Figure 3.3(left)). Since a thin film, such as a soap film, reflects and transmits light

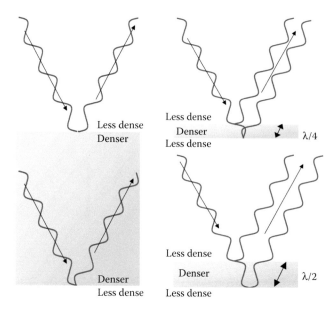

FIGURE 3.3 Light phase after reflection at boundary surface between different media (left) and interference with multiple reflections at thin films (right).

simultaneously, a double reflection on both surface sides occurs (Figure 3.3(right)). This double reflection causes a phase shift which leads to the interference of the two waves. This interference depends on the thickness of the film, and the wavelength of the light. Since the soap film is normally not equally thick everywhere, white light is reflected with different phase shifts and its various spectral components interfere differently. This causes the color effects on soap bubbles. The basic principle behind this is called *thin film interference*. Some optical holograms apply a similar principle, as we will see later.

The examples above clarify, that the phase of light waves plays an important role in wave optics. Most wave optical principles are therefore based on coherent light. If two waves of the same frequency are in phase, they are said to be coherent. Light that consists of one wavelength only is called *monochromatic*. Thus, coherent light must also be monochromatic. Coherent light can be generated with lasers (see Section 3.5). The degree of coherence describes the distribution of phases in a light bundle, and consequently whether two waves interfere constructively or destructively. White light (e.g., sunlight) is a superimposition of many wavelengths at different phase offsets, creating a complex interference pattern. It is therefore neither coherent nor monochromatic, and precise wave optical effects, such as holography, are difficult to achieve with it.

This is called *temporal incoherence* and is illustrated in Figure 3.4. More on this in Section 5.3.9 at page 141. Note that amplitude modulation also causes additional frequencies, hence incoherence, as discussed in Section 2.5.2.4 at page 42.

A second form of coherence is *spatial coherence*. More on this in Section 5.3.10 at page 143.

The amplitudes of several waves at the same place always add up to a single waveform. If we regard two coherent waves of slightly different frequency, this result in a pulsating waveform called a beat (Figure 3.5). What we observe with light waves in this case is the pulsating

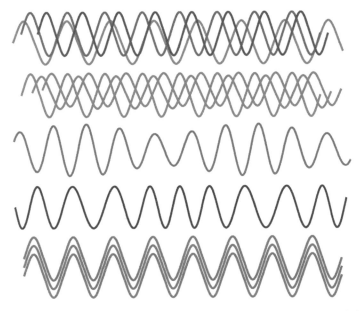

FIGURE 3.4 From top to bottom: multiple color, multiple phase, amplitude modulated, frequency modulated, and coherent light waves.

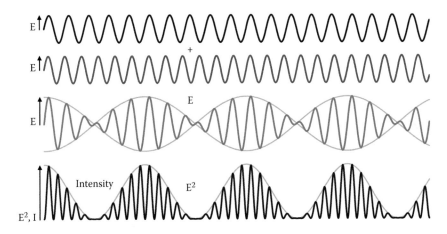

FIGURE 3.5 Two slightly different frequencies adding up to a beat. The lower curve shows the resulting relative intensity, for example, for light waves (amplitude squared). The sinusoidal shape of the intensity hull curve plays an important role in laser interference and in hologram formation.

intensity, which is proportional to the electrical amplitudes squared, and represents a sine wave of its own. We observe likewise sine wave shaped interference patterns also with spatial interferences of wavefronts in two or three dimensions.

3.3 GEOMETRIC OPTICS

It can be difficult to create an accurate mathematical formulation of wave optics that describes compounds of simple optical elements, such as lenses. Therefore, light modulation and optical image formation are often simplified with a geometric representation. Geometric optics considers light as traveling along a straight line, mainly ignoring its wave nature. Although light is more often described as being an electromagnetic wave (and light rays do not even exist from the point of view of quantum physics), rays are simple and straightforward and suited to a geometric analysis. However, to explain more complicated optical effects, such as holograms, a wave representation cannot be avoided. After looking at basic forms of light modulation, we will review geometric optical principles for refractive and reflective optics.

3.3.1 Light Modulation

Depending on material properties, light can be reflected, refracted, scattered, absorbed, and diffracted by matter. We discussed diffraction above. Absorption normally causes the light energy to be converted into heat (unless it is stored, for example, in excited electrons). We will review refraction and scattering below and then we will go on to show that (from a geometric optics point of view) reflection is very similar to refraction.

3.3.1.1 Scattering

When colliding with particles or small surface features, light is scattered (Figure 3.6). Different scattering models exist based on the size the particles. The most relevant are:

- Geometric scattering occurs when the particles are significantly larger than the wavelength of light.

- Mie scattering (after Gustav Mie) happens when the particles are approximately the same size as the wavelength of light.

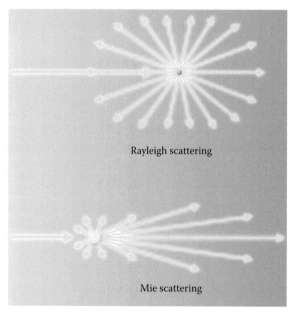

FIGURE 3.6 Rayleigh and Mie scattering.

- Rayleigh scattering (after John Rayleigh) happens when the particles are smaller than the wavelength of light.

Mie and Rayleigh scattering models both occur on small particles or droplets or even on density fluctuations in gases. The effects are wavelength dependent (i.e., there exists a particle-size-to-wavelength relation). However, Mie scattering does not depend on the wavelength to the same degree as Rayleigh scattering does. Rayleigh scattering in a gas volume, for example, is responsible for the blue color of the sky. For geometric scattering, the properties of the particles are widely ignored, and geometric optics can be applied (refraction and reflection). Color aberration with refraction in small droplets, for example, explains the colors of a rainbow. For Mie, Rayleigh, and geometric scattering, the energy (wavelength and frequency) of the light is not changed (except for Doppler effects with fast particles). This is called *elastic-light scattering*. There also are several types of *inelastic light scattering*, such as Brillouin scattering, Raman scattering, inelastic X-ray scattering and Compton scattering. These do cause energy transfer, but they are not significant for light optics because they involve frequencies at least several hundred times higher than those of visible light.

3.3.1.2 Refraction

The speed difference between two media with different optical densities causes a change of direction when light passes their border. This is called *refraction*. The amount of refraction also depends on wavelength, and white light splits into spectral colors. This is best observed with a prism, where two refractions increase the effect (Figure 3.8).

A mathematical description of light refraction was empirically derived from observations by Willebrord Snell, long before the physical fundamentals were known. From today's point of view, this phenomenon is well understood: because light is an electromagnetic wave, its propagation characteristics depend on the material in which it is traveling. The very speed of light depends on the electrical permittivity and magnetic permeability (ε and μ) of the material:

$$c = \frac{1}{\sqrt{\varepsilon\mu}} \tag{3.1}$$

If we consider light in a vacuum

$$\varepsilon_0 \approx 8.8541878176 \cdot 10^{-12} \,[A \cdot s/V \cdot m] \quad \mu_0 = 4\pi \cdot 10^{-7} \,[N/A^2] \tag{3.2}$$

we get the well known propagation speed of light $c \approx 3 \cdot 10^8 \, m/s$ (in vacuum).

In normal glass or water, μ is almost exactly μ_0 but ε varies significantly. The propagation speed c in such a medium is slower (sometimes much slower) than in vacuum.

Regarding a beam of light entering such a medium at an angle φ, we can simply consider the fact that the beam is always perpendicular to the wavefront. The one edge of the wavefront that first enters the medium suffers a certain delay, until the other edge of the wavefront also enters the medium. If we follow the beam backward, the opposite effect would occur. This causes a change of the wavefront's angle, as easily seen in Figure 3.7. The general relation

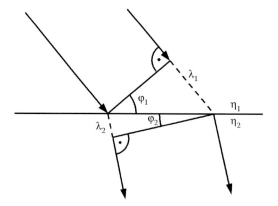

FIGURE 3.7   Snell's law of refraction.

of this is given by

$$\frac{\sin \varphi_1}{\sin \varphi_2} = \frac{\lambda_1}{\lambda_2} = \frac{v_1}{v_2} = \frac{\eta_2}{\eta_1} \approx \frac{\varepsilon_2}{\varepsilon_1} \tag{3.3}$$

where η_1 and η_2 are the refraction indices of the two media, v_1 and v_2 are the light speeds, and λ_1 and λ_2 are the respective wavelengths.

For glass, where μ is negligible, we get:

$$\eta_1 \sin \varphi_1 = \eta_2 \sin \varphi_2 \tag{3.4}$$

So we have derived Snell's law of refraction simply from the change of permittivity.

One fact to be considered here is that the permittivity ε is dependent on the frequency of the wave. In most cases it decreases with wavelength. Hence, short wavelengths usually travel more slowly than longer wavelengths and experience stronger refraction (BRR: *blue rotates radically* – which is reverse to diffraction, as explained in Section 3.2 at page 54). So because the refraction angle is different for different colors, a glass prism, for example, disperses light into its spectral components (Figure 3.8) and is known as color *dispersion*.

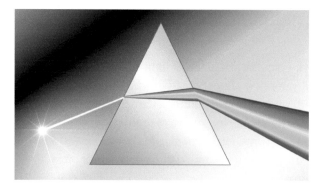

FIGURE 3.8   Color dispersion by refraction in a prism: blue rotates radically, BRR.

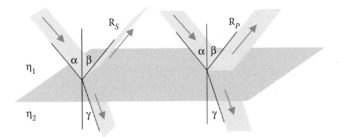

FIGURE 3.9 Partial surface reflection.

Another important fact is that not all of the light that enters the medium is actually refracted. A certain part is always reflected (as anybody ever having seen a window certainly understands) and is polarized perpendicularly to the deflection angle.

Partial light reflection at sharp media-boundaries can be calculated as follows (Figure 3.9):

The reflection angle β trivially equals the incident angle α. The refraction angle γ follows from the refraction index ratio η_1/η_2 (Snell's law of refraction):

$$\sin \gamma = \frac{\eta_1}{\eta_2} \sin \alpha \tag{3.5}$$

The ratio of reflected-light intensity versus the incident-light intensity also depends on polarization. Reflection intensities for polarizations transversal (s) and parallel (p) to the plane spanned by the rays are given by the Fresnel equations:

$$R_s = \left(\frac{\eta_1 \cos \alpha - \eta_2 \cos \gamma}{\eta_1 \cos \alpha + \eta_2 \cos \gamma} \right)^2 \quad R_p = \left(\frac{\eta_2 \cos \alpha - \eta_1 \cos \gamma}{\eta_2 \cos \alpha + \eta_1 \cos \gamma} \right)^2 \tag{3.6}$$

Nonpolarized light accordingly results in different polarization partitions for the reflected beam (Figure 3.10). The total reflection intensity for nonpolarized light is given by:

$$R = \frac{R_s + R_p}{2} \tag{3.7}$$

The remainder gives the intensity of the refracted light, of course. The total reflection intensity for light perpendicular to the surface ($a = 0°$) is:

$$R_0 = \left(\frac{\eta_1 - \eta_2}{\eta_1 + \eta_2} \right)^2 \tag{3.8}$$

At $\alpha + \gamma = 90°$ (called *Brewster's angle*), all reflected light is s-polarized.

3.3.2 Homogeneous vs. Inhomogeneous Media

Light can be interpreted as rays traveling in straight lines only in ordinary media. An *ordinary* medium is one that is *homogeneous* (the same at all points) and *isotropic* (the same

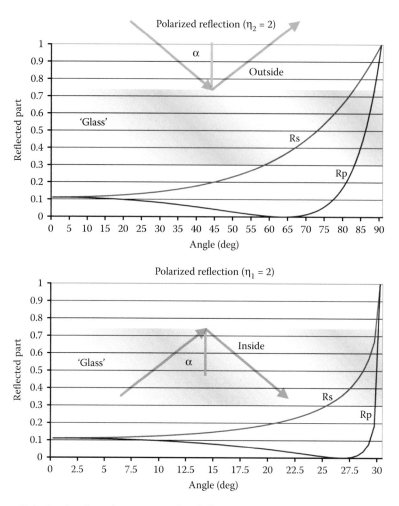

FIGURE 3.10 Polarized reflected intensities for different incident angles into and out of optically denser medium.

for all directions). Geometric optics usually deal with systems of adjacent ordinary media parted by intersection surfaces, as seen above.

Inhomogeneous media, such as atmospheric air with strong temperature differences, will cause light rays to bend, causing phenomena such as *fata morgana*, or heat shimmering over hot street asphalt (Figure 3.11).

For most of the discussions in this book, we consider ordinary media only.

3.3.3 Snell's Law Vectorized

Let's revisit Snell's law from the point of view of vectorization to understand its relation to reflection.

In three dimensions, we can write Snell's law in vector form as follows:

$$\eta_2 r' - \eta_1 r = an \tag{3.9}$$

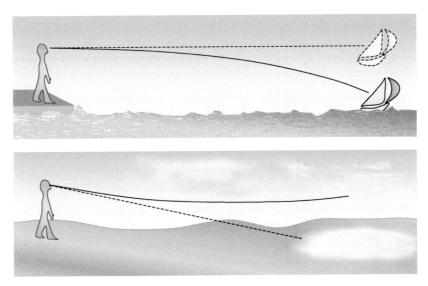

FIGURE 3.11 Atmospheric refraction as an example for inhomogeneous media: cold air near water invoking a "Flying Dutchman" (top) and hot air near ground in a desert, causing the illusion of water (bottom).

A light ray r intersecting a surface point i with normal n at two media with different refraction indices (η_1 and η_2), is refracted into ray r'. With r, r' and n being normalized, and a as an arbitrary real number, we can derive (Figure 3.12(left)):

- Snell's first refraction theorem: the refracted ray r' lies on the plane that is spanned by r and n. This plane is called *plane of incidence*.

$$r' = (\eta_1 r + an)/\eta_2 \tag{3.10}$$

- Snell's second refraction theorem: the cross product of n with the vectorized Snell's law, leads to Snell's law of refraction.

$$\eta_2(n \times r') = \eta_1(n \times r) \tag{3.11}$$

$$\eta_2 \sin(\alpha_t) = \eta_1 \sin(\alpha_i) \tag{3.12}$$

where α_i and α_t are incident angle and refracted angle, respectively.

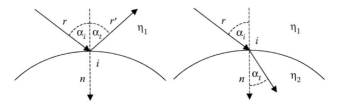

FIGURE 3.12 Snell's refraction theorem (left) and reflection theorem (right).

At a border of a denser and a less dense medium, total internal reflection occurs if a certain incident angle γ, called the *critical angle*, is exceeded:

$$\gamma = \sin^{-1}(\eta_2/\eta_1) \tag{3.13}$$

Light is reflected with an efficiency of 100% instead of being refracted. Therefore, this total internal reflection has great advantages for optical elements and especially for glass fibers, allowing them to conduct light over hundreds of kilometers with only small losses. Note that modern glass fibers have a refraction index that increases toward the edge, and a very thin section –only a few micrometers– of low refraction at the center. This causes light rays to be curved rather than hard reflected, and to concentrate in the thin middle section. Time delays between individual rays are minimized this way, avoiding bandwidth reductions due to interference.

Snell's vectorized law also applies more generally: r and r' can be assumed to be in the same medium with the same refraction index η_1. In this case, r is reflected into r', as shown in Figure 3.12(right):

- First reflection theorem: r' lies on the plane of incidence.

$$r' = r + (a/\eta_1)\, n \tag{3.14}$$

- Second reflection theorem: by the cross product of the vectorized Snell law with n, we can substitute for Snell's law of reflection (this is rather self-evident):

$$n \times r' = n \times r \tag{3.15}$$

$$-\alpha_t = \alpha_i \tag{3.16}$$

for $\alpha_t, \alpha_i = -\pi/2 \ldots + \pi/2$.

Thus, geometrical principles for refraction as well as reflection can be derived directly from Snell's classical law.

3.4 FORMATION OF POINT IMAGES

Optical instruments can form images of a number of point-like sources (called *objects*). The images may be detected, for example, by the human eye or a photographic film.

If all light rays emitted from one object p_o travel through an optical system and converge in the same image point p_i, then p_o and p_i are called a *stigmatic pair* (Figure 3.13). Such an image formation property is called *stigmatism*, and optical systems that support stigmatism between all object-image pairs are called *absolute optical systems*. The basic precondition for stigmatism can be derived from Fermat's principle: the optical path length L of all light rays traveling from p_o to p_i is equal.

If points (objects or images) are formed by a direct intersection of light rays, then these points are called *real*. If light rays do not really intersect within a point (e.g., if they diverge

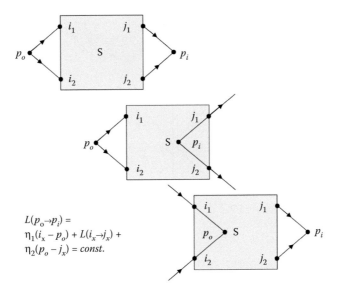

$$L(p_o \rightarrow p_i) =$$
$$\eta_1(i_x - p_o) + L(i_x \rightarrow j_x) +$$
$$\eta_2(p_o - j_x) = const.$$

FIGURE 3.13 Point image formation with an optical system S: real object and image (top), real object and virtual image (center), virtual object and virtual image (bottom). The general equation for optical path length.

after leaving the optical system), they can still form virtual images, because these rays appear to diverge from points inside the optical system. The location of the virtual image is found by extending the light rays in negative direction. As this portion of the optical path is negative, it must be subtracted from the total path length. Objects can also be virtual. In this case, the light rays again have to be extended in order to find the location of the corresponding object. The subpath to a virtual object also has to be subtracted from the total path length.

Producing absolute optical systems is difficult, because the only surfaces that are easy to build and that support stigmatism are planar or spherical surfaces. Most optical instruments just approximate stigmatic image formation. The deviation from the ideal image introduced by this imperfection is called *aberration*.

Recent developments have enabled the manufacturing of aspherical or even asymmetric optical surfaces (free-form optics) [245]. Among the applications especially profiting from this are several types of near-eye displays (NEDs).

Below, we will review how reflective and refraction optical elements form optical images.

3.4.1 Reflective Optics

Consider an optical system exclusively made up of reflecting surfaces (e.g., mirrors). Further conceptualize that the mirrors are surrounded by air or, at least, that the medium the light rays are traveling through is ordinary.

The optical path length can be simplified in this case:

$$\eta_2 = \eta_1 = 1, i_x = j_x \tag{3.17}$$

$$L(p_0 \rightarrow p_i) = (i_x - p_0) + (p_i - j_x) = const \tag{3.18}$$

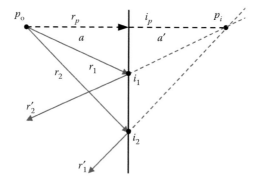

FIGURE 3.14 Planar mirror geometry.

3.4.1.1 Planar Mirrors

With planar mirrors, objects are real and images are virtual (Figure 3.14). The mapping of objects and images is bijective, invertible, and symmetrical for all points; stigmatism exists between all objects and images. Planar mirrors are therefore absolute optical systems.

If the mirror plane is defined by a plane equation, then reflected rays can be computed with Snell's law of reflection (Section 3.3.3 at page 62), and geometric mapping between objects and images can directly be computed as well:

$$f(x, y, z) = ax + by + cz + d = 0 \tag{3.19}$$

$$r' = r - 2n(nr) \tag{3.20}$$

$$p_i = p_0 - 2(np_0 + d)n \tag{3.21}$$

where $n = (a, b, c)$ is the normal of the mirror plane.

3.4.1.2 Spherical Mirrors

Nonplanar mirrors (Figures 3.15) do not provide stigmatism between all objects and images. In fact, only a few surface types generate just one true stigmatic pair for objects in certain positions. For all other objects, the corresponding images have to be approximated. With known radius r of the spherical surface, the focal point f can be easily determined:

$f = -r/2$	$f = r/2$	$f = 0$
convex	concave	planar

The distance between surface and focal point is called *focal distance* or *focal length*.

3.4.1.3 Concave Parabolic Mirrors

Of the types of spherical mirrors, parabolic mirrors can bundle parallel entering light rays into a single point (Figure 3.16).

Concave parabolic mirrors can generate both real and virtual images from real objects. Reflected rays diverge or converge, depending on the location of the object. If the object is located at infinity, a real object is created at focal distance.

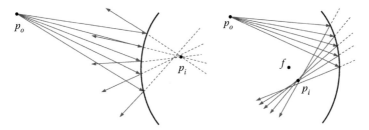

FIGURE 3.15   Convex mirror geometry (left) and concave mirror geometry (right).

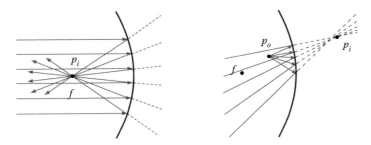

FIGURE 3.16   Concave parabolic mirror geometry.

If the object is located behind the focal point, the reflected light converges and bundles in a real image (also located behind the focal point). Images formed from multiple image points appear as enlarged, flipped, and distorted versions of the reflected object.

If the object is located in front of the focal point, the reflected light diverges and bundles in a virtual image (also located in front the focal point). Images formed from multiple image points appear as enlarged and deformed versions of the reflected object, but the image is not flipped. If the object is located at the focal point, then its image is located at infinity.

3.4.1.4 Convex Parabolic Mirrors

If, with a convex parabolic mirror (Figure 3.17), the object is located at infinity (again, real by definition), its image is virtual and located at focal length. If the object is not located at infinity (real), the virtual image is not located at the focal point. Rays in this case bundle around a virtual image point (with aberration).

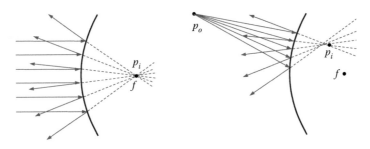

FIGURE 3.17   Convex parabolic mirror geometry.

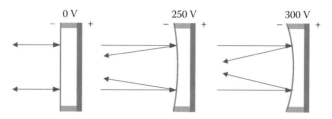

FIGURE 3.18 Varifocal mirror (electrostatic drive).

3.4.1.5 Varifocal Mirrors

A varifocal mirror can, for example, be built with a flexible mirror membrane deformable by air pressure, electrostatic (Figure 3.18), or piezo electric forces. This principle can be used for wavefront corrections in telescopes and microscopes, or for building 3D displays (rapidly generating different real and virtual images appearing at different distances).

3.4.2 Refractive Optics

Refractive optical systems (e.g., lenses) are based on refraction index changes between adjacent media. The optical path equation can be idealized and simplified for a single interfacing surface surrounded by air (the refraction index of air is ≈ 1):

$$\eta_1 \neq \eta_2, \quad i_x \neq j_x$$
$$L(p_0 \longrightarrow p_i) = (i_x - p_0) + \eta_2(p_i - j_x) = \text{const} \tag{3.22}$$

Because the refraction indices of real materials are wavelength dependent, lenses not only have geometric, but also chromatic aberrations. By combining several lenses of different materials and shapes, optical systems can be built that are highly corrected for aberration and other errors, such as geometrical distortions in the image plane. Almost any photographic lens, as well as other optical instruments are compounds of many individual lenses.

Note that current digital cameras with fixed lenses usually abandon full geometric and chromatic aberration compensation. A large part of geometry errors and lateral color aberrations are compensated electronically. This allows for lighter and cheaper lens constructions as well as improved specifications (wider zoom range).

3.4.2.1 Lenses

Lenses have traditionally been produced in spherical shape because the grinding machines used consisted of two concentric half spheres, in between which many glass plates were mounted. Rubbing the spheres together in complex concentric moves, under an addition of a grinding powder slurry, allowed for producing spherically shaped lens surfaces. No other shape could be made this way.

Because of their spherical surfaces, such lenses do not have exact focal points, they have bundling areas instead (in contrast to some mirrors with parabolic surfaces). Therefore, they cannot generate true stigmatic pairs. For practical applications, an optimization toward ideal imaging properties is necessary in almost any case. This is achieved by combining multiple lenses of different curvature and refraction index.

For modern camera lenses, more complex *aspherical* surfaces are produced as well, which allows for more exact correction, compact designs, and higher resolution.

Plastic lenses can nowadays be molded directly to their final shape, with micrometer precision. Early varieties, however, suffered from reflections and poor scratch resistance. Today, advanced coatings deliver both almost-perfect reflection cancellation and very hard surfaces. The plastics materials used have also improved, especially their longevity and resistance to UV light; plastic lenses can now offer optical quality equal to that of glass lenses, and their technical properties remain stable for decades.

A special advantage of plastic lenses is that any shape can be produced inexpensively. One disadvantage is the relatively low refraction index of plastics materials, limiting the freedom of design. In smaller digital cameras, plastic lenses are quite common today; they are even more common in eyeglasses, where their light weight is a distinct advantage. Eyeglasses lenses are manufactured by directly molding their basic shape, convex or concave, but because of the numerous eye conditions there would be too many molding forms to produce. Hence, after the basic shape is molded, one surface is afterward often milled to its final shape, according to the visual system requirements. This is possible because surfaces can nowadays be directly milled to optical quality, using precision diamond tools.

When milling is finished, the glasses get their final treatment, the coating, usually by a sol-gel process (see Section 6.6.3.1 at page 229). Plastic eyeglasses, therefore, are very inexpensive to produce; their pricing is more reflective of market conditions than production costs.

Another parameter of a lens is its spectral transmissivity. Ordinary glass cuts off infrared and ultraviolet light. For ultraviolet (UV), quartz glass can be used. For a large *infrared* (IR) range, Germanium lenses are common (germanium is nontransparent in visible light but like glass for IR). Some plastics materials are transmissive to UV, and some even to very far IR (lens sheets of IR motion detectors actually are plastic Fresnel lenses).

3.4.2.2 Converging Lenses

This is the most ancient type of lens. Objects at infinity create real images in the focal plane (Figures 3.19(left), 3.20, 3.21). Objects at focal points create images at infinity. Images and objects are both real. However, by definition, these two possible focal points of a lens are named differently, depending on the imaging direction:

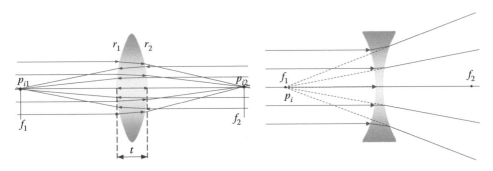

FIGURE 3.19 Converging lens geometry (left) and diverging lens geometry (right).

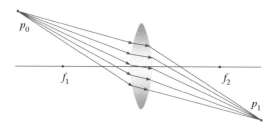

FIGURE 3.20 Converging lens example: real objects behind one focal point create real images behind the other focal point. Images formed by multiple image points in this case appear to be a flipped version of the refracted object.

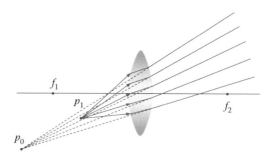

FIGURE 3.21 Converging lens example: real objects in front of one focal point create virtual images in front or behind the same focal point. In this case, images formed by multiple image points appear not flipped.

Parallel rays that enter the lens focus at the *back focal point*. The plane that is perpendicular to the lens' optical axis and on which the back focal point is located is called the *back focal plane*. Reversely, light rays that diverge from the *front focal point* exit the lens as parallel rays. The plane that is perpendicular to the optical axis and on which the front focal point is located is called the *front focal plane*. Thus, parallel rays on one side of the lens are mapped to the focal point on the other side. Nonparallel rays (i.e., belonging to object or image points that are closer than infinity) do not map to the focal point. But light rays that cross these points from the same angle always cross on the opposite focal plane.

The focal length of a spherical lens can be computed as:

$$\frac{1}{f} = (\eta_2 - 1)\left(\frac{1}{r_1} - \frac{1}{r_2}\right) + \frac{(\eta_2 - 1)^2}{\eta_2}\frac{t}{r_1 r_2} \tag{3.23}$$

where r_1 and r_2 are the two radii, and t is the central thickness.

The behavior of converging lenses is similar to the behavior of concave mirrors, but reversed.

3.4.2.3 Diverging Lenses

With diverging lenses, objects at infinity create virtual images at the focal plane (Figure 3.19(right)). Real objects always create virtual images, independent of their location.

The behavior of diverging lenses is similar to the behavior of convex mirrors, but reversed.

3.4.2.4 Plane Parallel and Curved Parallel Lenses

Objects behind a thick glass plate appear slightly enlarged because of refraction, an effect that is increased if the glass is curved toward the observer. This fact is important for the design of cathode ray tubes with their very thick front panels.

3.4.2.5 Varifocal Lenses

Varifocal in this context does not address zoom lenses for photographic equipment, which are built of several complex (rigid) lens groups that are moved forward and backward to change focal length. Instead, varifocal lenses are lenses that can change their surface shape. This is more difficult to achieve than with mirrors, and is usually confined to very small lenses. They are also sometimes referred to as *liquid lenses*.

Varifocal microlenses can, for example, be built by enclosing a conducting aqueous solution (e.g., a salt solution) and a nonconductive oil (e.g., silicon oil) in a small cavity. Surface tension and a hydrophobic wall coating cause the intersection between the fluids to be curved and to work as a lens because of the different refraction indices of the two liquids (Figure 3.22). By applying voltage, electrostatic force changes the intersection curvature [260]. Example figures for products of this type are 2.5 mm opening diameter, 9 ms response time, and 1 mW operating power (Varioptic SA.).

The liquid lens principle can also be used for individual pixels in certain display designs. A similar approach is to use variable prisms for directing beams in autostereoscopic displays (see Section 9.5.6.2 at page 399).

The possible refraction index modulation of liquid crystals can also be used for gradient refractive index (GRIN) lenses and prisms (Figure 3.24 on page 73). Particular uses are variable or switchable lens barrier rasters for autostereoscopic 3D displays.

Another type of varifocal lenses is based on an electroactive polymer. A good overview of this and other technologies, also often referred to as "*artificial muscles*" is found in [198]. These techniques have many applications, possibly also for near-eye-displays (see Section 10.16.5.2 at page 484).

A varifocal lens can be constructed with a polymer lens mounted in a ring of electroactive polymer that pulls the rim of the lens outward when voltage is applied, similar to the focusing principle of a human eye lens. Example figures for products of this type are 10 mm opening diameter, 10 ms response time, and 0–2 W operating power (**Optotune** AG).

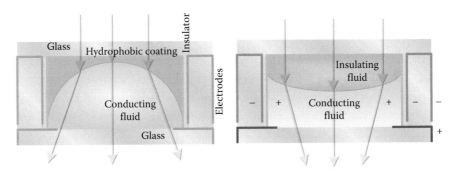

FIGURE 3.22   Example of a varifocal microlens.

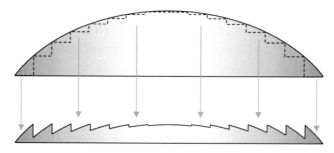

FIGURE 3.23 Fresnel lens construction from normal lens shape.

Flexible or inflatable lenses of several millimeters in size have been used for experiments with focus variations in near-eye displays (see Section 10.11 at page 452). Generally, fluid or flexible varifocal lenses have less optical quality than rigid lenses, which may limit their fields of application.

3.4.2.6 Fresnel Lenses

The refractive behavior of thick lenses can also be approximated by concentric prism rings of varying slopes (Figure 3.23). This is called a *Fresnel lens*. Though this approach allows production of lenses that are both thin and highly refracting, the disadvantages are obvious: the steps between the prism rings produce unwanted glare and blur.

One main application of Fresnel lenses are thin foil lenses of poor quality (e.g., fisheye optics for car rear windows, or "enlargement" lenses for vintage TVs).

Nevertheless, a similar principle is sometimes found in display systems: prism stripe arrays are used in autostereoscopic displays, where they are employed to direct different pictures to each eye (avoiding the drawbacks in quality of a simple Fresnel lens, if properly implemented). We will explain this in a later section.

3.4.2.7 GRIN Lenses

An entirely different kind of refractive lens uses a variation of the refractive index inside the lens. These *Gradient Refractive Index* or GRIN lenses have recently gained some importance as variable liquid crystal lenses in 3D display screens (see Section 9.4.1.3 at page 375).

Figure 3.24 shows a basic example (there are many other shapes and types). Its geometric form is plane parallel, and the refractive index increases from the edge to the center. The different light propagation speeds in the center and edge regions cause a deformation of the wavefront.

The calculation of GRIN lenses works a bit different from that of conventional geometric optics, as the behavior of a light ray propagating along a path of constant refractive index but with an index gradient perpendicular to the path, is difficult to conceive. As light "rays" always are perpendicular to the wavefront, their bending can however be calculated, most conveniently, by regarding the wavefront. To converge toward a focus point, the wavefront should become concentric at the exit side of the lens (then the according rays also converge). An accurate shaping of the wavefront is required for a crisp focus point formation; this depends on properly chosen gradients for the refractive index. The gradient function

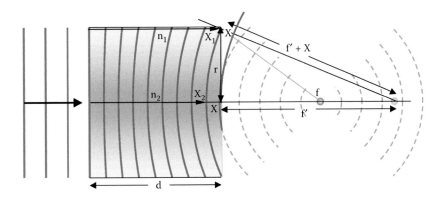

FIGURE 3.24   GRIN lens, wavefront formation.

required depends on many factors (in the case of liquid crystal lenses, e.g., on the electrode shapes, lens thickness, etc.) and in practical cases, also three-dimensional gradient functions may occur. An exact calculation would have to include the entire refractive index gradient and would therefore become quite complicated.

The following approach allows for a simple assessment of the principal capabilities of GRIN lenses. For the calculation of the focus length, here, we suppose a proper index gradient function as given, and only regard the edge and center indexes needed for a certain radius of a concentric exit wavefront.

The focus length can be calculated relating the light path lengths x_1, x_2 to the refraction indices n_2, n_1, and assuming x_1 as the lens thickness d:

$$x = x_1 - x_2 = x_1 - x_1\frac{n_1}{n_2} = d\left(1 - \frac{n_1}{n_2}\right).\ \text{With Pythagoras } (f'^2 + r^2 = (f'+x)^2)\ \text{we get}$$

$$r^2 = 2f'x + x^2,\ \text{hence } f' = \frac{r^2}{2x} - \frac{x}{2}\ \ \text{and}\ \ f' = \frac{r^2}{2d\left(1 - \frac{n_1}{n_2}\right)} - \frac{d\left(1 - \frac{n_1}{n_2}\right)}{2}$$

An additional refraction occurs at the exit surface, leading to a shorter focus length. It can be calculated by Snell's law (see Section 3.3.1.2 at page 59). For small angles and an exterior refraction index of 1, we can approximate $f \approx f'/n_1$ and we get

$$f \approx \frac{r^2}{2n_1 d\left(1 - \frac{n_1}{n_2}\right)} - \frac{d\left(1 - \frac{n_1}{n_2}\right)}{2n_1} \tag{3.24}$$

Calculations show that the right term can be neglected for an approximation.

Another application of the GRIN principle leads to the equivalent of a prism. This can, for example, be used for light-directing elements in autostereoscopic displays. It requires a continuous index slope from one side of the optical element toward the other. Figure 3.25 illustrates a calculation of light bending by index modulation. We assume a propagation

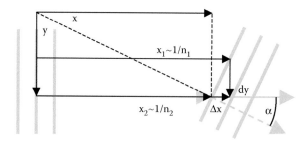

FIGURE 3.25 GRIN lens, calculation of beam deflection.

speed, hence path length x changing in y direction. For small areas, we get the simple relation $\Delta x/dy = y/x$. Assuming a small $dn = n_2 - n_1$, we can conclude from the figure that $\Delta x \approx x\, dn/n$. For a small x, the deflection angle resulting is $\alpha \approx \Delta x/dy$. This leads to $\alpha \approx x\, n\, dn/dy$. Explicitly writing this for small increments, we get

$$d\alpha = dx\, n\frac{dn}{dy} \tag{3.25}$$

This does not behave like the instant deflection at a glass surface; the deflection here obviously increases progressively with distance passed. Using $\Delta x/dy = y/x$ and writing the vertical deflection increment $\Delta x/dy$ as a constant a, we can integrate

$$y = \int a\, x\, dx = \frac{1}{2}\, a\, x^2 \tag{3.26}$$

Hence, for a constant propagation speed gradient across the light path,[*] a light beam behaves as if being *accelerated* in that direction. This similarity to a falling object (where the textbook formula goes $y = \frac{1}{2}gt^2$) is not just incidental: there is a most interesting analogy that we should mention here, between the behavior of light in a medium with varying refractive index and light in a gravitational field, where the propagation speed depends on the gravitational potential (clocks run slower near heavy masses than in free space). Gravitational effects can hence be calculated from the gradient of the gravitational potential and the according gradient of relativistic time dilation. A "gravitational lens" formed by the gravity of a galaxy cluster is indeed a cosmic equivalent of a GRIN lens (but behold that according to relativity theory, the speed changes are accompanied by equivalent length distortions due to space curvature, doubling the refraction effect).

3.4.3 Properties of Optical Systems

Optical systems can be characterized by principal parameters such as focus and aperture. But there are also a variety of effects leading to blurred and distorted images. These are generally called aberrations. We will first discuss different types of aberrations and other parameters, and then address the topic of resolution, which seamlessly leads to basic insights

---

[*] This is not the same as a constant index gradient, as $v \sim 1/n$.

for the subsequent section on lasers. The following considerations apply to lens, mirror, and combined optics as well. We will show them either for lenses or for mirrors, whichever allows for a better demonstration.

3.4.3.1 Apertures

Lenses can be blocked from light by apertures (normally located at their back focal planes, see Section 3.4.2.2 at page 69). The opening of a lens (the size of the aperture) is normally expressed with the f-number (f/N), which is the ratio of its focal length (f) to its open diameter (a):

$$N = f/a \tag{3.27}$$

In general, the f-number describes the light-gathering ability of the lens. If the magnification m from the object to the image is considered, then it is defined as:

$$N_w = (1 - m) \cdot N \tag{3.28}$$

This is also referred to as a *working f-number*. The aperture determines the amount of light reaching the focal plane, as well as the depth of field (of objects in the scene) or the depth of focus (of the image plane). Photographic lenses have variable "iris" apertures, adjustable in steps. Each step cuts light intensity in half; the usual steps (called *f-stops*) are 1, 1.4, 2, 2.8, 4, 5.6, 8, 11, 16, 22....

Smaller and larger values are possible but rare. Lenses with an f-stop of 1 or below are also very expensive, because the difficulty of lens correction increases with the size of the aperture. The iris aperture of a typical lens system is located in the middle of the lens assembly (Figure 3.26), at the plane of maximum defocus (called *aperture plane*, so the aperture itself is not depicted in the image.

Very small apertures are used for large format cameras, for example, in landscape photography. Their large depth of field effect can be adverse, however, because the maximum angular resolution of a lens depends on its size. We will discuss this in Section 3.4.3.6 at page 79.

The image of an aperture that is produced by an optical system which follows it is called the *exit pupil*. Similarly, the image of an aperture as seen through a preceded lens at the front of an optical system is called the *entrance pupil*. Consider a compound camera lens: The image of the aperture that one can see by looking through the lens from the front is the entrance pupil, while the image of it that can be seen from the back is the exit pupil. Only light rays that pass the exit pupil can actually exit the optical system (i.e., the compound lens in this example). In the case of magnifying optical systems, such as a microscope or a telescope for instance, the exit pupil can be very narrow, making it difficult to match with the entrance pupil of a human eye. Therefore, the eyes have to be positioned exactly.

In the case of optical systems for NED, a certain (as large as possible) degree of eye rotation has to be supported. The total exit pupil range in this case is also called the *eyebox*. We will return to this in Chapter 10.

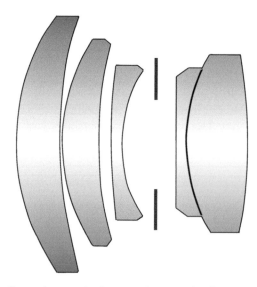

FIGURE 3.26 Example of a modern multielement photographic lens, with the aperture mechanism in the middle (**Zeiss Sonnar**).

If no preceding lens is used in front of the aperture (e.g., in the case of a pinhole system), the physical aperture equals the entrance pupil. Otherwise, the entrance pupil is a virtual image of the physical aperture.

For some optical systems, like microscopes, the *numerical aperture* is more important than the f-number (which is frequently used in photography). For the image side of an optical system, it is defined as:

$$NA = \eta \cdot \sin(\theta), \tag{3.29}$$

where η is the refraction index of the host material of the optical system (i.e., $\eta = 1$ for air), and θ is the half-angle of the cone of light that is generated by the optical system. For air, we can approximately correlate the f-number and numerical aperture as:

$$N \approx \frac{1}{2 \cdot NA} \tag{3.30}$$

or as:

$$N_w = (1 - m) \cdot N \approx \frac{1}{2 \cdot NA} \tag{3.31}$$

if we use the working f-number that considers the magnification m. For the object side, the numerical aperture is correlated to the working f-number as follows:

$$N \cdot \frac{(m - 1)}{m} = \frac{1}{2 \cdot NA} \tag{3.32}$$

If the aperture at the focal plane is sufficiently small, then the lens is called *telecentric*, and the aperture is often called a *telecentric stop*. Mainly parallel light rays are considered in

FIGURE 3.27 Working principle of an image and object-space telecentric lens.

this case. A telecentric stop at the front focal point for instance, causes parallel exit rays (i.e., an exit pupil at infinity). This is called *image-space telecentric* and is useful for image sensors that do not tolerate a wide range of incident ray angles.

Similarly, a telecentric stop at the back focal point causes *parallel* entrance rays (i.e., an entrance pupil at infinity). This is called *object-space telecentric* and causes a *magnification invariance* of objects at different distances or positions. This is very different from a typical photographic lens, where the entrance rays are diverging and distance objects are depicted to be progressively smaller. It also indicates that with an object-space telecentric lens, the front lens has to be at least as large as the depicted object. Therefore, some types have very large front lenses. Figure 3.27 shows an example of a two-sided telecentric lens.

3.4.3.2 Vignetting
Different types of *vignetting* exist that cause a gradual loss of intensity at the borders of an image that is captured with an optical system. Light rays of an object entering an optical system from off-axis directions can be partially blocked. This happens, for example, if multiple internal lens elements are applied as they reduce the effective opening of the lens. This is called *optical vignetting*. External elements, such as filters or secondary lenses, can also block such light rays, and this is called *mechanical vignetting*. Finally, the intensity of unblocked light rays falls off with respect to the cosine fourth ($\cos^4(\alpha)$) of their entrance angle (α). This is called *natural vignetting*. Usually it is used to keep light distribution within optical systems as even as possible, and to minimize vignetting.

3.4.3.3 Aberrations
The aberration of optical systems or elements, such as lenses or mirrors, is a complex topic that we will not discuss here in detail. Of certain interest for displays are the so-called "3rd order aberrations" (also called *primary* or *Seidel* aberrations):

- Spherical aberration: Different focus length for center and edge beams
- Astigmatism: Different focus length for the lateral and vertical axis, caused, for example, by cylindrical surfaces, or when light rays are hitting an optical element at an angle (off-center configuration)
- Coma: Similar to astigmatism, but for wider parallel light bundles
- Chromatic aberration: Different focus length for different colors (wavelengths)

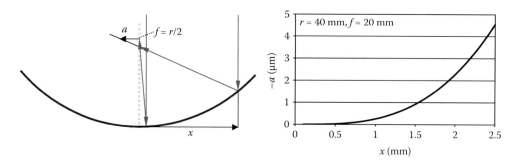

FIGURE 3.28 Spherical aberration by the example of a concave mirror.

Also, often mentioned in context with aberrations are field curvature (the foci for different pixels of an image not lying in a plane) and distortion (lateral distortion of images).

The following examples for spherical aberration and astigmatism have implications for some topics in Chapter 10.

3.4.3.4 Spherical Aberration

Spherical aberration occurs when optical elements are not appropriately shaped to focus beams at their center and edges to the same point. Figure 3.28 illustrates this by the example of a spherical mirror. The focus error and hence the lateral deviation of the reflected beams grows progressively with distance from the center axis. For mirrors with a very large focus length (e.g., astronomical telescopes), spherical aberration is small. For smaller focus lengths (i.e., instruments with larger fields of view), optimized mirror shapes are required.

3.4.3.5 Astigmatism

Mirror optics often have off-axis configurations. Examples are astronomical *Schiefspiegler* (which means slant deflector) telescopes, and NED (see Section 10.7.5 at page 440). For spherical mirrors, this results in a considerable deviation between the focus lengths for the horizontal and vertical beam cross sections (astigmatism, as shown in Figure 3.29).

An elliptic mirror shape can reduce this problem: in an ellipsoid, all rays originating from one focal point are perfectly converging in the other (Figure 3.30). Various combinations of mirrors based on elliptic and parabolic shapes are used in modern high-resolution telescopes. The principle is illustrated in Figure 3.30.

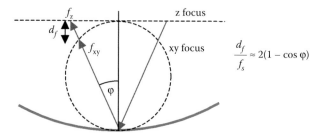

$$\frac{d_f}{f_s} \approx 2(1 - \cos \varphi)$$

FIGURE 3.29 Off-axis astigmatism of a spherical mirror: the focus lengths in the xy (drawing) plane and perpendicular to it deviate progressively.

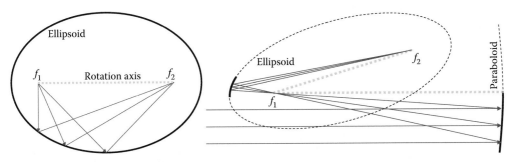

FIGURE 3.30 Left: elliptic mirror principle. Right: example off-axis application using the focus convergence of a paraboloid and an ellipsoid.

3.4.3.6 Resolution

The resolution of a lens or a mirror (also often referred to as its *diffraction limit*) is an important parameter with many implications on our topic. Usually in wave optics, rather complicated derivations are used to approach lens resolution. However, we can approximate in a simpler way for lenses with a larger focal length, as illustrated in Figure 3.31.

We regard a coherent wavefront approaching the lens and two partial wavefronts from the lens edges (they contribute most to resolution) meeting at the focus point.

Remember that for small angles we can assume that $\alpha \approx \tan \alpha$. With this, we get $\frac{a}{2}/f \approx \frac{\lambda}{2}/\frac{d_0}{2}$, and hence $d_0 \approx 2\lambda f/a$. Given the way d_0 refers to the amplitude pattern, the actual focus point diameter d is less than half of d_0, depending on the amplitude value we take as a border for the point. Wavefront portions from inner parts of the lens (i.e., with smaller a, and larger d_0) will, however, spoil the result toward larger focus points.

Hence we could simply define $d = d_0/2$ and the following as an approximation to lens resolution:

$$d = \lambda f/a \qquad (3.33)$$

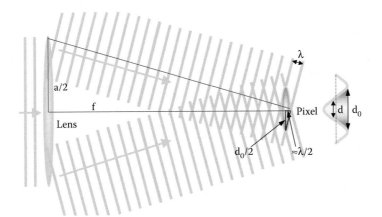

FIGURE 3.31 Approximation to lens resolution.

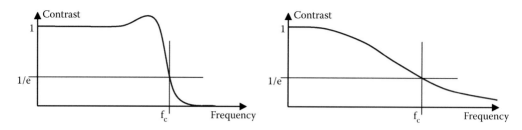

FIGURE 3.32 Examples of different contrast transfer functions with equal resolution figure.

Another look at our approximation on lens resolution reveals that

$$\Phi = d/f = \lambda/a \tag{3.34}$$

which is the angular resolution (still assuming that $\alpha \approx \tan \alpha$ holds) in radians.

A rigorous but more complicated approach would be integrating wavefronts coming from the lens for the entire angular range (leading to the Gaussian solution as shown in Figure 3.37 on page 85). The angular resolution from this approach (formula for $z \to \infty$) is $\Phi = (4/\pi)\,\lambda/a$, just differing by a factor of $4/\pi$ or 1.27. This greatly depends on the contrast value definition used (and also on λ). Moreover, the same resolution figure can result for very different contrast transfer functions (see below, also cf. Figure 3.32).

For the discussion of optical principles in connection with various display applications, we will therefore refer to Equations 3.34 and 3.33, as they are adequate and most easily remembered.

We can use Equation 3.33 for such practical matters as deriving that it would take a lens or mirror almost a mile wide to see the remainders of lunar missions on the moon, or that an HDTV (high definition TV) camera with optics could fit into a 1/8″ (3 mm) cube, or that the human eye can see crispy to one arcmin of angular resolution (more on this in Section 4.2.5 at page 95).

Detailed resolution information for a specific image point is given by the modulation or *contrast transfer function*, describing the ratio of the object contrast reaching the image, for different spatial frequencies.

Contrast transfer functions can show a shallow or steep decline toward higher spatial frequencies, as illustrated in Figure 3.32. Two optical systems with equal numerical resolution (usually the spatial frequency at a contrast of 1/e or 37%) can produce quite different visual impressions, due to different contrast transfer functions. The curve to the left indicates a relatively crisp image impression, while the curve to the right indicates a softer, less crisp appearing image, although it contains more higher frequencies. Contrast transfer functions are therefore necessary for a complete characterization of an optical system. Often, these functions are also given as separate curves for several spectral colors.

3.4.3.7 Depth of Field

The same simple assessment shown for resolution may likewise be used for calculating the depth of field of a lens (Figure 3.33). Note that we talk about *depth of field* if we consider

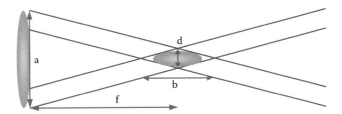

FIGURE 3.33 Depth of field of a lens.

the object space in front of an optical system, but if we consider the image space behind an optical system, it is called *depth of focus*. For the sake of simplicity, we use only the term depth of field in the following explanations.

The depth of field can be approximated with[*]:

$$b \approx 2df/a \approx 2\lambda f^2/a^2 \tag{3.35}$$

In the case of limited pixel resolution of the detector (<lens resolution) we get:

$$b \approx 2\lambda f^2/(a_0 a) \quad \text{for } a_0 < a \tag{3.36}$$

where a_0 is the aperture corresponding to this resolution. In other words: b increases linearly with the sensor pixel size as soon as this becomes larger than the focus spot of the lens.

Interesting to remark is that the depth of field b for an optimal aperture ($a_0 = a$) depends on the focal point size d only:

$$b \approx 2d^2/\lambda \tag{3.37}$$

Hence, the depth of field becomes quadratically lower with shrinking dimensions (which is an issue for microscopes, for example).

We have now covered everything that is necessary to understand lasers and the properties of laser beams, which are related to what we have just learned about lenses and focusing.

3.5 LASERS

It is important for us to discuss lasers because many applications in optics, for instance, optical holography and computer-generated holography would not be possible at all without lasers as sources of monochromatic coherent light. As discussed above, this is a requirement for achieving controlled and precise wave optical effects, such as interference.

Laser is the abbreviated term for *Light Amplification by Stimulated Emission of Radiation*. So let's see what this actually means.

3.5.1 Stimulated Emission

A laser is based on the principle that an excited electron in close proximity to a photon whose excitation energy matches its own energy can emit another photon of exactly the same phase, frequency, polarization, and direction of travel (Figure 3.34). This, of course, implies that the original photon came from another atom or molecule of the same type.

---

[*] Again here, the Gauss/Rayleigh solution (Figure 3.37 on page 85) is just slightly different.

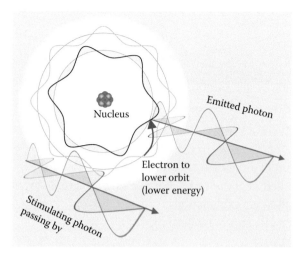

FIGURE 3.34 Principle of stimulated light emission.

This effect is called *stimulated emission* and was predicted by Einstein in 1916. With many atoms with excited electrons enclosed in a necessarily transparent volume, this may result in an avalanche-like multiplication of photons, provided that many electrons are excited beforehand by some kind of stimulus.

This stimulus may be an intense electromagnetic (light, microwaves, etc.) or other radiation source, a gas discharge, or (in the case of a semiconductor laser) an electric current. In a homogeneous material, all excited electrons will experience the same energy level change, and will emit photons of identical wavelength when relaxing. This leads to coherent and monochromatic light.

The light avalanche can be given a certain direction by enclosing its volume with two parallel mirrors, one of them partly transparent (Figure 3.35). Photons propagating toward the mirrors will multiply much better than others, as they are reflected in the same direction multiple times. Between the mirrors, standing waves occur. Due to quantum uncertainties (see Section 2.5.2.4 at page 42), a small selection of narrow-by modes (numbers of waves

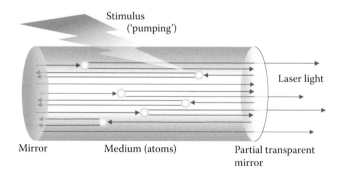

FIGURE 3.35 Principle of a conventional laser: An external stimulus excites atoms in a medium, photons of a certain direction are promoted by a mirror (left) and a partially transparent mirror (right). The beam leaves though the partially transparent mirror.

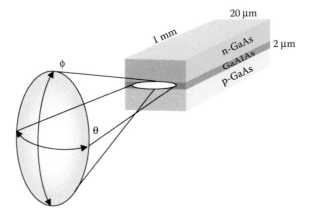

FIGURE 3.36 Principle of a laser diode: electroluminescence causes light emission. The beam leaves the structure by the partially transparent front mirror.

over the mirror distance) are possible, so the laser spectrum will not be a single sharp line but several lines distributed in a Gauss-shaped hull curve.

Only a small portion of the light exits through the partially transparent mirror (between <1% and <50% depending on the actual construction). Hence the field amplitude inside the laser is much stronger than the resulting beam amplitude.

Especially interesting for display applications are semiconductor lasers. These are planar diodes with very thin layers (Figure 3.36). The light generated is propagated along a p-n junction layer and is reflected at a mirror and a half-transparent mirror at its end.

Because the emitting surface is narrow perpendicular to the junction but wide in the across direction, the emitted beam is anisotropic (e.g., 16° by 40° opening angle) and needs anamorphic optics to be formed into a more or less round, narrow beam.

For display purposes, red, green and blue lasers are required. While LEDs are available in numerous colors from infrared to ultraviolet, the application with laser diodes is far more difficult.

Laser wavelengths can be designed only according to the properties of the materials available. Green diode lasers are a problem because until very recently, no materials were available for them. The usual alternative is an infrared laser coupled to a nonlinear optical material working as a frequency doubler. Typical materials used for lasers are BBO (β-barium borate), KDP (potassium dihydrogen phosphate), KTP (potassium titanyl phosphate), and lithium niobate.

Current types of laser diodes with wavelengths useful for displays are (without claim of completeness):

- 405 nm Indium Gallium Nitride (InGaN), used in Blu-Ray and HD DVD drives).

- 445 nm InGaN, blue laser diode (published 2010).

- 520 ... 530 nm InGaN (several publications 2009/2010).

- 635 nm used in laser pointers and for LIDAR (light radar).

- 650 nm used in DVD drives.

- 670 nm used in inexpensive laser pointers and in bar code readers.

- 780 nm used in CD drives and in laser printers.

- 808 nm Pumping of Nd:YAG Lasers and primary source in green laser pointers.

- 980 nm Pumping of Nd:YAG Lasers.

- 1064 nm Pumped Nd:YVO4 crystal used in green laser pointers and fiber optic communications.

Blue, and especially green, laser diodes proved difficult to build, but remarkable progress has been made recently. In December 2010, for example, a 524 nm laser diode with 50 mW continuous light output was demonstrated by Osram. While this is not yet perfect green (that would be 550 nm), a look at the chromaticity diagram reveals that it is already perfectly fit for a combination with blue and red lasers, providing an extremely wide color gamut that includes any existing standard color triangles (e.g., see Figure 6.15 on page 194). Other green laser diodes demonstrated included those from Sumitomo (520 nm), Nichia (510 nm), and Kaai (523 nm).

A blue laser diode demonstrated by **Kaai** Inc. in 2010, features 60 mW of 445 nm single mode output power. It is based on proprietary InGaN semiconductor technology fabricated on GaN substrates.

The 405 nm laser used in Blu-Ray drives would be a better primary color, but eye sensitivity is very low at this wavelength, so a lot of light power is required. With near-eye displays (see Chapter 10), this would be less of a problem, of course.

Current green and blue laser pointers work with frequency multiplication.

A typical green laser pointer for example uses an 808 nm infrared laser diode pumping a Neodymium doped Yttrium Orthvanadate (Nd:YVO4) crystal, emitting light at 1064 nm, then doubling the frequency to 532 nm by a Potassium Titanium Oxide Phosphate (KTiOPO4) crystal. A 20 . . . 30% efficiency could be achieved in theory but in practice, less has to be expected.

A blue laser device can be built using an 808 nm laser diode pumping a Neodymium Yttrium Vanadium Oxide or Nd:YVO4 crystal for a 946 nm output, then frequency doubled to 473 nm by Lanthanum Boron Oxide (LBO). Here the efficiency is only 3 . . . 5%.

Laser diodes have generally become very efficient in terms of light generation, yielding up to 50% in the infrared and up to 30% for some of the visible frequencies.

The laser effect, however, requires a minimum energy; laser diodes won't operate below a certain voltage or current threshold. Impedance and actual output intensity are also very temperature dependent, and the devices are sensitive to overload. Therefore, many laser diodes have integrated light sensitive monitor diodes allowing control of their light output (and driving current) by a dedicated electronic regulator.

Because photons are also waves, the particle metaphor gives an incomplete picture of the laser effect. A laser beam is not as perfectly bordered as is often assumed: a single photon constitutes a wave with a wide opening angle. Only the overlay of a very large number of photons originating from a planar area very much larger than the light wavelength results in a wavefront sufficiently planar to give the impression of a straight beam (more below).

Lasers also generally tend to oscillate in several *modes* concurrently. These are waves with different counts of half-wavelengths fitting between the end mirrors. They tend to form a line spectrum with a Gauss-shaped intensity distribution around a central frequency. The very small frequency differences between the modes cause periodically changing interferences, a phenomenon called a *beat* (Figure 3.5 on page 57). This may cause nasty effects in many applications and should normally be avoided. Intentionally adding many modes can, however, be used to generate more complicated beat shapes, like sequences of well-separated ultrashort pulses. More about the behavior of pulse series and frequency combs will be encountered in Section 6.4.2 at page 203. Note that laser frequency combs are a tool for the ultraprecise measurement of light wavelengths.

3.5.2 Laser Beam Divergence

Laser beams are often simply thought of as ideal rays of light, being arbitrarily thin and long. Real laser beams, however, diverge widely.

An exact description of laser beam divergence is derived from the electromagnetic field equation, which explains the formation of a so-called *Gaussian beam* (Figure 3.37), that either diverges or converges. Convergence can be accomplished up to a minimum waist size that is determined by the convergence angle and the wavelength; conversely, a smaller source size causes a larger divergence. Beam divergence can, however, be derived a lot more easily, using the approach to explain lens resolution given in Section 3.4.3.6 at page 79.

Let's assume the lens in Figure 3.31 on page 79 is bundling coherent, monochromatic light (as the drawing would suggest anyway). The light bundle will diverge after the focus spot, with the same angle at which it entered. With coherent light, the focus spot can be interpreted as the source of a laser beam.

The lens that converges light at the focus spot can be seen as the optical dual to the laser that diverges from its source: geometrically, both are identical (Figure 3.38). A larger

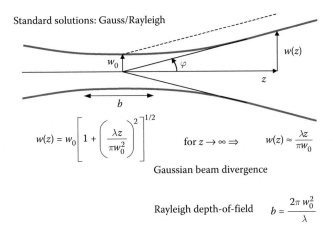

Standard solutions: Gauss/Rayleigh

$$w(z) = w_0 \left[1 + \left(\frac{\lambda z}{\pi w_0^2} \right)^2 \right]^{1/2} \qquad \text{for } z \to \infty \Rightarrow \qquad w(z) \approx \frac{\lambda z}{\pi w_0}$$

Gaussian beam divergence

Rayleigh depth-of-field $\qquad b = \frac{2\pi w_0^2}{\lambda}$

FIGURE 3.37 Gaussian beam standard equations.

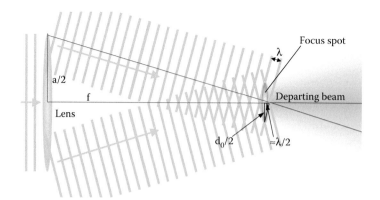

FIGURE 3.38 Laser beam divergence explained with lens focusing.

focus spot, or, beam origin, therefore results in a less diverging beam, and a smaller origin results in a more diverging beam. The beam divergence formula results from the one for lens resolution.

Hence, the beam divergence shown in Figure 3.39 can be computed with:

$$a \approx \lambda f / d \tag{3.38}$$

The beam divergence angle can be approximated (for small angles, $x \approx \tan x$) with:

$$\Phi = 2\varphi \approx \frac{a}{f} \approx \frac{\lambda}{d} \tag{3.39}$$

Hence, a laser beam needs to converge from an original diameter of at least a in order to be able to focus in a spot of diameter d (this is the original lens-resolution derivation again).

The value from the usual Gauss solution in Figure 3.37 is $\Phi = (4/\pi)\lambda/d$. According to our derivation of lens resolution (see Figure 3.31 on page 79), we may again argue that this also greatly depends on the contrast value definition as well as on λ; so, we may use Equation 3.39 as an easily remembered rule of thumb for our further considerations.

Figure 3.40 offers another explanation for laser-beam divergence. It shows many coherent point-light sources that remain at constant distances from each other forming a planar wavefront. With a continuous large surface and arbitrarily narrow light sources, the edge waves can be a sum of any possible phases and can interfere almost perfectly to zero. Nevertheless, a tiny part will deviate in all directions, and the planar part of the wavefront will widen up

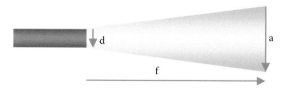

FIGURE 3.39 Laser beam divergence.

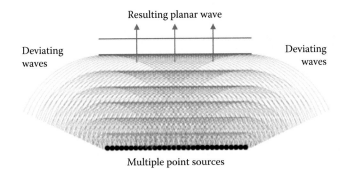

FIGURE 3.40 Laser beam interpreted as interference of waves from multiple point sources.

progressively. Macroscopically, what we get here is a typical laser beam coming from a finite source area.

For any kind of laser application, the following relevant conclusions should be considered:

- A laser beam intended to stay narrow for a long distance can't be arbitrarily narrow at its origin.

- A laser beam intended to be focused to a tiny spot needs a considerable diameter to start from.

- The usual concept that a laser beam is an ideal line is not factual.

These results are important for laser projectors, both for large scale projection and for near-eye projection (retina scanning) as well. One other consequence for laser scanners is that the beam deflection mirror must not be arbitrarily small, because the laser beam cannot be arbitrarily small.

The quality of a laser beam, in terms of spectral and spatial definition, is called its *coherence*. We will address this in more detail in Section 5.3.9 at page 141.

3.6 THE PLENOPTIC FUNCTION

In general, the *plenoptic function* describes the radiance along all light rays that propagate within a 3D space under constant illumination. Each light ray vector can be addressed by three origin coordinates (x, y, z) and two angle directions (θ, ϕ). Thus, the classical plenoptic function is five dimensional: $L(x, y, z, \theta, \phi)$ (Figure 3.41(right)).

Several approaches are made to reduce the dimensions of the plenoptic function to four dimensions by parameterizing it with, for example, two parallel planes (Figure 3.41(right)) or spheres (Figure 3.41(center)). A light ray that passes a sphere or two parallel planes can be addressed with only four intersection points (s, t, u, v) within the 4D parameter space. Thus, the ray-space representation becomes 4D and can be measured with cameras or can be presented with displays. This 4D representation has clear limitations, as it cannot represent all rays within the 3D space. It is limited to rays that are passing through the convex hull

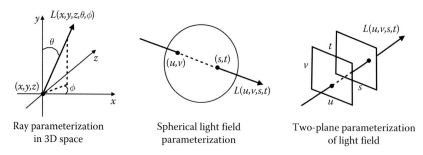

Ray parameterization in 3D space

Spherical light field parameterization

Two-plane parameterization of light field

FIGURE 3.41 Ray parameterization for 5D plenoptic function (left), 4D ray parameterization for light fields: spherical (center) and two-plane (right).

of the scene. Light rays that are inter-reflected by other scene points cannot be represented with this approximation. In electrical engineering, such 4D approximations of the plenoptic function is called *photic field* (1981), while in computer graphics and computer vision it is referred to as *light field* (1996). We will refer to it as light field.

The light rays passing a lens of a camera carry the information of an entire light field. However, when light rays are focused on, and integrated by, the camera sensor the information about the radiance of individual light rays arriving from different angles is lost. We end up with a 2D image, rather than with a 4D light field. This is illustrated in Figure 3.42(left).

Replacing the sensor with a micro lens array and placing the sensor behind it preserves the angular information, as illustrated in Figure 3.42(right). The light rays that have focused on the same sensor point before are now imaged (with a low resolution) on a small area on the new sensor position [210].

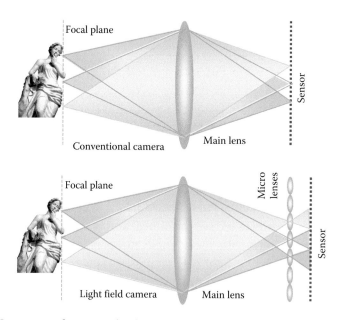

FIGURE 3.42 Conventional camera (top) and possible implementation of a light field camera (bottom).

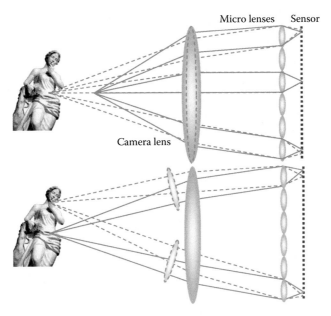

FIGURE 3.43 Principle operation modes of a light field camera: refocusing (upper) and selection of viewing angles (lower).

Figure 3.43 illustrates how different effects can be achieved with this approach, by different selections of sub pixels.

The resolution of the microlens array corresponds to the spatial resolution of the light field, while the resolution of lens-individual sensor regions corresponds to the angular resolution of the light field. Spatial resolution times angular resolution always equals the sensor resolution in this case. The limited resolutions of camera sensors clearly provide one restriction to this approach. Depending on the application, angular and spatial resolutions might have to be carefully balanced, but imaging with a spatial resolution that equals the original sensor resolution is obviously not possible with this approach.

There are certainly several alternatives in addition to the example that was given above, to capture light fields. Using 2D camera arrays or special aperture masks inside cameras are only two of them. Greater focus on light field imaging is clearly beyond the scope of this book. Reproducing a light field with a display is of more pertinent interest. We will explain this in Section 9.5 at page 388.

3.7 SUMMARY

This chapter focused on those principles of optics that are necessary for understanding the remaining topics in this book. It is, by far, not complete and is not meant to replace an optics textbook. Yet, it gives a concise overview of the most important concepts.

We will see that wave optics becomes essential to understanding the principles of holography (Chapter 5) or CGH displays (Chapter 9). Geometric optics plays an important role for describing optical components and their behavior in general display technology. The plenoptic function will probably play a more dominant role for displays in the future than it currently does. We will see this in Section 9.5 at page 388. Dynamic image formation can today be solved only by mainly mechanically moving optical elements. Focusing of a lens is a good example. These mechanical constraints will vanish with optics that capture and generate light fields – yet, at the cost of a much higher and partially redundant amount of information that needs to be processed. But we can expect that memory and processing limits will also be pushed further in future.

However, image-forming optics is only one side of the coin. Efficient display technology almost always considers the final detectors of those images as well. These are human observers. Therefore, human visual perception is as important for displays as advanced optics. Basics of visual perception will be our next topic in Chapter 4.

CHAPTER 4

Basics of Visual Perception

4.1 INTRODUCTION

One might ask: Why are we covering human visual perception in a book about display technology? The answer is simple: Displays are human computer interfaces that transport information through the visual perception system. Not considering this final part of the display pipeline would be critical, and would most likely lead to ineffective display devices.

For the design of displays, limitations of the human visual perception systems should be considered. For example, we don't need screens with resolutions that cannot be resolved by the eyes under common viewing conditions. We don't need to display colors that are outside the visual spectrum. We want to ensure that a display is capable of presenting gray scales in a way that can be differentiated by human observers; if not, it could be fatal when monitors are used for medical diagnostics.

Consideration of the human visual system and its limitations is as important for displays as the understanding of optics; not only is display hardware influenced but also display algorithms.

Nevertheless, describing the limitations of human vision should not leave the impression that the eye is a flawed construction. It is extremely optimized to its purpose, and its integration of optics and signal processing is exemplary for advanced camera concepts. Moreover, display technology still hasn't succeeded in delivering the perfect picture, in spite of all the limitations of human vision.

In this chapter, we will give an overview of the most important aspects of human visual perception insofar as they concern display technology. We will start with an outline of the human visual system in Section 4.2, and its essential sensory properties, including resolution, contrast, dynamic range, and temporal response. Section 4.3 at page 97 will explain the basics of colorimetry, which is the science of color perception, measurement, and representation, and its relationships to various color models being used in displays. One major topic in this book is 3D displays (Chapters 5 and 9); Section 4.4 at page 107 summarizes various depth cues that are more or less relevant for depth perception. Later, we will see that most displays will support only a subset of these depth cues, which of course affects depth perception with regards to 3D displays. Finally in Section 4.5 at page 119 we will explain certain perception pitfalls for motion picture creation and display and common solutions that are implemented in consumer displays.

The appendix at the end of this book provides an additional coverage of several aspects of human perception, in the context of perceptive display calibration.

4.2 THE HUMAN VISUAL SYSTEM

In the following sections, we will briefly review the most important sensory properties of the visual perception system that are relevant to the design of many display systems and we will present their driving algorithms.

4.2.1 The Eye as an Optical System

The human eye is a complex optical system, resembling, in principle, a camera but built rather differently (Figure 4.1). Its diameter is about 25 mm and it is filled with two different fluids (both having a refraction index of ≈ 1.336). The iris regulates the amount of incident light by expanding or shrinking, changing the eye's aperture. The cornea and the elastic biconvex lens (refraction index ≈ 1.4) behind the iris bundle light and focus it on the light sensitive background of the eye, the retina. The lens can adjust its shape to different focal lengths, a deformation and reformation of the lens called *accommodation*. The human eye can accommodate to a focal length between infinity and <100 mm (near accommodation, degrading with age). The image on the retina is, of course, upside down and flipped, as with any biconvex lens.

The retina consists of small conic and cylindrical light-detecting cells called *photoreceptors* (size $\approx 1.5 \ldots 5 \ \mu m$). The photoreceptors are categorized into rods (perceiving intensities, with a sensitivity maximum at about 500 nm) and cones (three different types with different color responses). The area on the retina with the highest resolution is called the *fovea* (it provides the highest density of receptors).

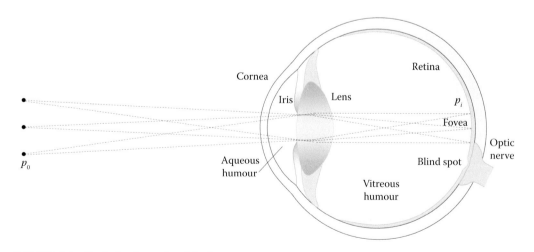

FIGURE 4.1 Optical schematic of the human eye.

The resolution of the eye depends on the density of these cells, among several other factors. Color perception and spectral sensitivity are slightly different for daylight-adapted vision (*photopic/cone vision*) and night-adapted vision (*scotopic/rod vision*).

4.2.2 Saccades

Our vision is sharp at the very center of the retina only. We don't normally notice it, but any time we want to see anything very clearly, we will direct our eyes toward it. Larger scenes are perceived by quick eye movements called *saccades* that flick between certain points of interest, overlooking minor details. In addition to saccades there are *microsaccades*. These are omnipresent little motions not consciously perceived. Most researchers believe that they allow for correcting eye drifts, but their true function is still debated.

4.2.3 Temporal Response

Fast intensity changes are integrated (evened out) perceptually. The response of the human visual system is simply too slow to perceive high frequencies. Below certain frequencies however, changes are perceived as flickering. The frequency at which the signal appears to be steady is called *flicker fusion threshold* or *flicker fusion rate* (Figure 4.2), and it depends on the brightness of the signal (the brighter, the higher) and on the location of the signal on the retina. In the periphery of the visual field, higher flicker frequencies can be perceived. This explains why vintage TVs at a distance don't flicker at 50 Hz, while old computer monitors that are close to our field of vision sometimes do, because they cover a larger field of view.

More than 70 Hz are required for a steady impression with high light intensities at the periphery, while just a few Hz can be sufficient at the foveal area with very low light conditions (obviously, our eyes can do what sensitive cameras also do – integrate light over time). Refresh rates of displays should never fall below the flicker fusion threshold.

Flickering, however, can also be detected well above 70 Hz: in cases of high-speed motion (either object or eye), they may result in *stroboscopic* multiple images, or in dotted multicolor blur. This is called *phantom array effect* (also known as *rainbow effect* with DLP projectors).

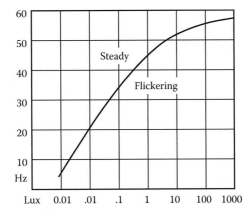

FIGURE 4.2 An average flicker fusion curve for the human eye: frequency (*y*) vs. brightness (*x*).

4.2.4 Contrast and Dynamic Range

The eye can see in a brightness range of about nine orders of magnitude, but not simultaneously (i.e., not over the same scene). This covers a very large range of light intensity. It starts from about 1/1000 lux (starlight) and goes up to approximately 100,000 lux (sunlight). Our eyes adapt to this immense range in several ways. For example, pupil size may vary from about one mm to more than seven mm. This corresponds to a brightness variation of, for example, 1:50 (but for elder people the maximum pupil diameter usually is four or five mm). The sensitivity regulation of the receptors allows for an even wider range.

Another applicable principle is the grouping of receptors by the retina neuronal network (we see less clearly in the dark) and the longer integration times for light received (we don't perceive changes as quickly in the dark).

The retina's structure actually allows for an effective grouping of more than 1000 rods if required. The central part of the retina (the fovea) cannot detect very dim light, because it contains only cones. A well known consequence of this is that we have to look a bit "beneath" stars if we want to see them.

A very powerful mechanism in pitch darkness is the chemical sensitization of the rod and cone receptors, mainly by enrichment of *rhodopsin* (visual purple). The rhodopsin is a pigment of the retina that regulates the formation of photoreceptor cells. It takes approximately 20–30 minutes to fully adapt to complete darkness by producing rhodopsin; at the same time, brightness sensitivity increases at four to six orders of magnitude, and the eye's spectral sensitivity changes as well. The reverse process also takes time, approximately five minutes, during which the rhodopsin is destroyed by light.

Although our visual systems have a wider brightness range than any single electronic camera, it would be false to assume that we can correctly perceive extremely high contrast ranges in a single scene. For example, we are easily blinded by bright lights, while certain camera chips are largely unaffected by them. Our eyes get damaged if we look into the sun, while our video cameras hardly take notice.

The eye's response to brightness levels is essentially logarithmic, similar to the responses of many other human senses. The actual relation can be given by an exponent (*Weber-Fechner law*) or, within certain ranges, as a gamma value. Figure 4.3 shows an empirical relation between subjective brightness perception and brightness. The logarithmic law here holds for about five orders of magnitude. Because perception is always subjective, such relations can never be exact; the results may also show individual variations.

The contrast that can be perceived simultaneously within the same image depends on adaptation, brightness, and spatial-detail frequency in the image. If, for instance, the contrast between two (even large) image features is too low, they might not be differentiable. For persons of approximately 20 years of age, perceived contrast maximizes at a spatial frequency of two to five *cycles per visual degree* (cpd) in the visual field. The contrast range we can resolve also depends on stray light occurring in the eye and may vary from person to person. Figure 4.4 illustrates the threshold contrast with respect to contrast and spatial frequency.

In addition to perceived contrast, the maximum number of intensities that a human can distinguish under given viewing conditions is also important for displays (think about diagnostic monitors that are used in radiology).

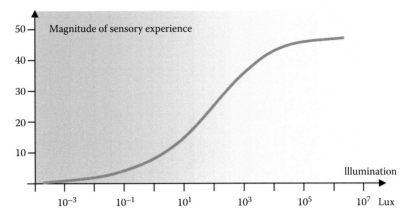

FIGURE 4.3   Magnitude of sensory experience vs. brightness.

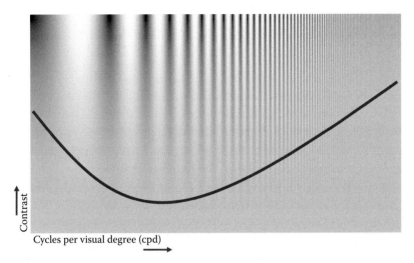

FIGURE 4.4   Contrast sensitivity function: perceived threshold contrast (plotted line) for given contrast (y) and spatial frequency (x). The threshold contrast line might shift to left or right, depending on the viewing distance.

The smallest step of intensity that can be perceived is called *just noticeable difference* (JND) (Figure 4.5). How many JNDs a human can distinguish simultaneously in an image depends mainly on the brightness of the image. Note that the JND values obtained greatly depend on the type of pattern detected [188]. The curve shown was intended for typical display artifacts and reasonably high detection probability.

4.2.5 Resolution

From the lens resolution derived earlier (Equation 3.33 on page 79), we can instantly tell the theoretical resolution of the human eye. We have a system with a lens diameter of between one and nine mm and a focal length of about 20 mm. The larger pupil diameters are quite rare and usually occur only with young people who still have a very flexible iris tissue. Most people have upper lens diameters of 4…6 mm. Under fairly good lighting conditions, we can assume about two mm or less.

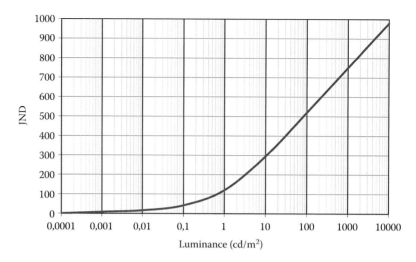

FIGURE 4.5 Mapping function from luminance to JND steps. (Data from Kil Joong Kim, Rafał Mantiuk, and Kyoung Ho Lee. Measurements of achromatic and chromatic contrast sensitivity functions for an extended range of adaptation luminance. In Bernice E. Rogowitz, Thrasyvoulos N. Pappas, and Huib de Ridder, editors, *Human Vision and Electronic Imaging*, page 86511A, 2013.)

For a wavelength of $\lambda = 550$ nm and a pupil diameter of $a = 2$ mm, we get an angular resolution of $\Phi = 1/3600$ in radians or, more commonly written, one arcmin. (This corresponds to 30 cpd), and a focus spot on the retina of about $6\,\mu$m.

This also equals the value physiologists have found for the best resolution a human eye can deliver, and this is also what TV standards consider to be "crisp".

Although this is a theoretical value derived from optical constraints only, it is by no means surprising that the measured crispness values of human eyes are just this good. Evolution tends to optimize physiology according to requirements. At larger pupil diameters, resolution could theoretically be better, but the density and size of retinal receptors sets a limit to this. At low light levels, larger receptors are of advantage because they can receive more photons. Resolution therefore has to be traded off for sensitivity. Unlike the eyes of an eagle or of a cat, human eyes are not specialized for day or night vision. Consequently, the human eye lens does not deliver more resolution with an increasing aperture (iris opening); on the contrary, the resolution drops due to increasing aberration (cf. Section 3.4 at page 64).

Outside the center of view, eye resolution decreases dramatically (Figure 4.6) – a lot more than could be expected from the decreasing receptor density (Figure 4.21 on page 108) [116]. The exact crispness requirements are a complex function of contrast, focus of attention and other factors [295].

The lower receptor density outside the center fovea goes hand in hand with higher light sensitivity, as discussed in Section 4.2.4 at page 94.

It should be noted that for most practical purposes concerning displays, a resolution of 1.5 arcmin is perfect already, as eye resolution also depends on object contrast. A resolution of one arcmin is possible with 100% contrast at best, and two arcmin are at least sufficient. Actual screen projections in cinemas are often worse than this.

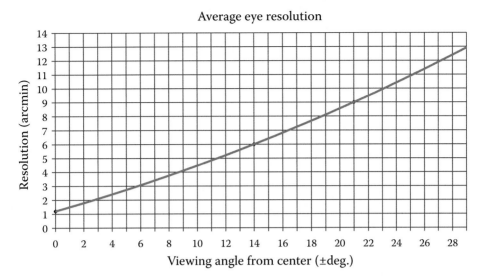

FIGURE 4.6   The average resolution of the human eye (y) with respect to the visual field (x).

The visibility of detail also depends on the structures involved. While parallel lines – the usual pattern for resolution tests – can easily be resolved to below 1.5 arcmin, interleaved point patterns may appear as a gray surface at 2 arcmin already: in Figure 6.4 on page 178, the point pattern in the center equals lines of only 70% width and lower contrast as well, compared to the straight lines to the left.

An important difference exists between monoscopic and stereoscopic pictures. For example, if we look with one eye we see a little less crisp; our brain combines both eye images for higher resolution. Stereoscopic pictures therefore look crisper, and this is not simply because they appear more vivid. In practice, with only one eye the maximum resolution of one arcmin is rarely achieved at all.

For the outer ranges of the visual field, the achievable resolution is further reduced, because the human eye can only rotate up to a certain limit. The rotation limit is approx. ±45° horizontal and vertical. This is important for NED: the periphery of a wide-angle NED will always remain in the periphery of the visual field, and therefore cannot be seen sharp in any case. Figure 4.7 shows the limitations of eye rotation and the resulting decrease of resolution outside the maximum rotation range. At least outside of this range, we may therefore allow for a decreasing display resolution or a degrading optical quality, or both.

4.3 COLORIMETRY

In Sections 2.4.1 and 2.4.2, we discussed radiometry and photometry. This section is about *colorimetry*, which is the science of color perception, measurement, and representation.

Years ago it was assumed that the human eye uses three separate types of color sensors: *red, green and blue* (R,G,B). Experiments with color reception and mixing pointed to that. The trichromatic theory of color vision, also known as the *Young-Helmholtz three-component theory*, was the basis for the development of the three-color (red, green, blue) based system commonly used in color recording and display technology.

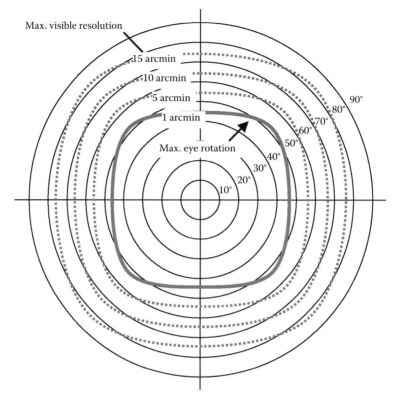

FIGURE 4.7 Range of eye rotation in polar coordinates (may vary for different persons), and maximum possible resolutions outside of it, according to eye peripheral resolution [118].

Today we understand the retina's cone receptors, and we know that they are responsible for seeing color. It has been confirmed that, indeed, one sensor type is assigned for each of red, green, and blue, although their sensitivity curves are far from being purely spectral. We perceive monochrome light as blue at a wavelength of about <450 nm, green at ≈530 nm and red at >650 nm. The sensitivity curves of the eye's receptors are overlapping. For many spectral colors, two or all three cone types react, although with different degrees of sensitivity. Humans can distinguish about 10 million different colors (with a color variation of approximately two nm) and brightness variations of roughly 2%.

Although the principle is quite clear, finding accurate response curves for human receptors proved difficult. This may be attributed to the fact that a lot of image processing takes place in the retina, combining signals from different cones as well as, probably, rods.

When color perception was first assessed with displays in mind, it was not possible to analyze the neuronal signal response of single receptors in the retina. Indirect methods were used to retrieve response curves of hypothetical red, green, and blue receptors. We will first show this approach, because it is the most versatile for practical purposes. Later we will show some physiological results that were discovered decades later.

In a series of experiments done in the late 1920s ([296],[106]), the issue was approached as follows by the International Commission on Illumination (CIE): Subjects were shown a

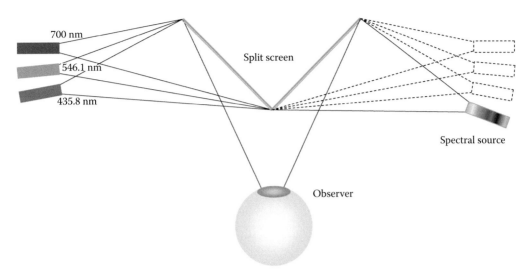

FIGURE 4.8 CIE color-matching test setup.

split screen, one half of it illuminated by a monochromatic light source that could be tuned throughout the entire visible spectrum (Figure 4.8). The other half was illuminated by three arbitrarily chosen monochromatic light sources of red (700 nm), green (546.1 nm), and blue (435.8 nm) color, which could be dimmed individually. With the assumption of three color receptors and linear additive color mixing, the same impression as with any individual spectral color should be possible to synthesize with the three sources – making the screen appear to be evenly lit.

4.3.1 CIE Color-Matching Functions

The experiments described above led to the CIE 1931 color-matching functions [58], which could be attributed to three receptor types, corresponding to their sensitivities. These curves, however, had negative parts, resulting from the fact that some of the monochrome sources sometimes had to be used on the other side of the screen (Figure 4.9).

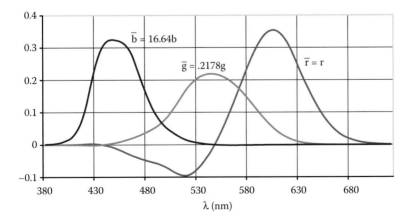

FIGURE 4.9 Original CIE 1931 RGB color-matching functions (normalized).

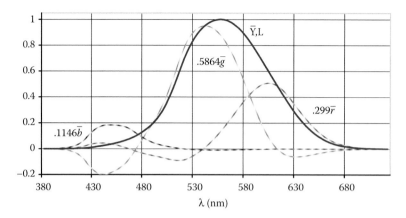

FIGURE 4.10 FCC RGB color matching functions in real ratio (dashed), and resulting luminance (L) curve (black).

Negative receptor responses are certainly not physically possible. Thus, these odd results might have been caused by either the choice of the primary colors or by signal processing in the retina (perhaps cross inhibiting to add color contrast).

As spectral sources were impractical for implementation, the FCC later on defined new functions $\bar{r}$, $\bar{g}$, and $\bar{b}$ based on the colors of available screen phosphors (NTSC, Section 6.3.1 at page 194). These functions are derived by a linear transformation of the CIE 1931 functions. Figure 4.10 shows their real values and that their sum still results in the luminance curve:

$$L = 0.2990\bar{r} + 0.5864\bar{g} + 0.1146\bar{b} \tag{4.1}$$

For practical purposes (camera design), sensitivity curves had to be found that could be attributed to real receptors – showing positive parts only.

A linear transformation had to be found to convert the curves. Because there are infinitely many possible ones, and nobody knew which was "right" because the real receptor curves were still unknown, an additional condition had to be introduced. From the similarity of the luminance curve to the green curve (Figure 4.10), a transformation was chosen that would deliver three color curves where the green one was perfectly proportional to the luminance curve. This would have the advantage that, with color cameras, one could simply take green for the luminance signal in black-and-white TV transmissions, and encode red and blue separately, for color transmission only.

The transformation is as follows:

$$\bar{X} = 0.6070\,\bar{r} + 0.1734\,\bar{g} + 0.2006\,\bar{b}$$
$$\bar{Y} = 0.2990\,\bar{r} + 0.5864\,\bar{g} + 0.1146\,\bar{b} \tag{4.2}$$
$$\bar{Z} = 0.0000\,\bar{r} + 0.0661\,\bar{g} + 1.1175\,\bar{b}$$

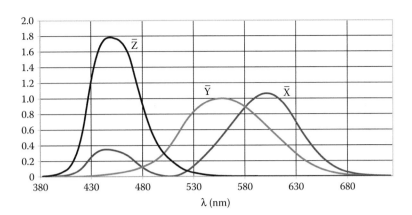

FIGURE 4.11   CIE 1931 standard observer color matching functions.

or in matrix notation:

$$\begin{bmatrix} \bar{X} \\ \bar{Y} \\ \bar{Z} \end{bmatrix} = \begin{bmatrix} 0.6070 & 0.1734 & 0.2006 \\ 0.2990 & 0.5864 & 0.1146 \\ 0 & 0.0661 & 1.1175 \end{bmatrix} \begin{bmatrix} \bar{r} \\ \bar{g} \\ \bar{b} \end{bmatrix} \tag{4.3}$$

where $\bar{X}$, $\bar{Y}$, and $\bar{Z}$ are the new red, green and blue values. It is obvious that $\bar{Y}$ has the same equation already presented (Equation 4.1 on page 100) for luminance, just as intended (Figure 4.11).

The inverse transformation can easily be derived:

$$\begin{bmatrix} \bar{r} \\ \bar{g} \\ \bar{b} \end{bmatrix} = \begin{bmatrix} +1.9097 & -0.5324 & -0.2882 \\ -0.9850 & +1.9998 & -0.0238 \\ +0.0582 & -0.1182 & +0.8966 \end{bmatrix} \begin{bmatrix} \bar{X} \\ \bar{Y} \\ \bar{Z} \end{bmatrix} \tag{4.4}$$

4.3.2 The CIE Chromaticity Diagram

A representation of all colors, independent of brightness can be obtained if we transform the primary color values as follows:

$$x = \frac{\bar{X}}{\bar{X} + \bar{Y} + \bar{Z}} \quad y = \frac{\bar{Y}}{\bar{X} + \bar{Y} + \bar{Z}} \quad z = \frac{\bar{Z}}{\bar{X} + \bar{Y} + \bar{Z}} \tag{4.5}$$

With brightness normalized to 1 ($x + y + z = 1$) we may use just x and y ($z = 1 - x - y$ is redundant in this case). By drawing all possible color values in an $x - y$ coordinate system, we get the CIE chromaticity diagram (Figure 4.12), also sometimes called *horseshoe diagram* for its shape. This diagram illustrates the entire perceivable color space. The elliptical area that is shown here shows all color values that could actually be produced by mixing the primary sources of the 1931 CIE experiment.

The outer edge of the diagram (called the *spectral locus*) represents the pure visible wavelengths. The straight line at the bottom (called *purple colors*) represents all mixtures between

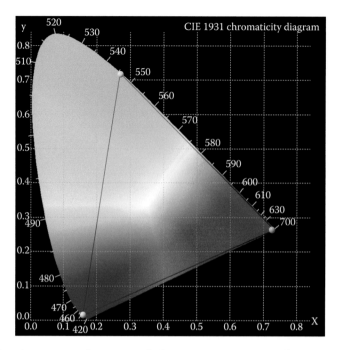

FIGURE 4.12 CIE chromaticity diagram, with the CIE 1931 experiment's spectral sources.

blue and red (they don't have inverse counterparts). The area itself represents all mixtures of pure visible wavelengths. The uncolored spot (called *white point*) in this diagram lies at $x = y = 1/3$.

It is a nice feature of the chromaticity diagram that all reproducible colors simply lie within a triangle or a polygon between the primary color dyes or phosphors used in a display. Hence, this is an easy way to evaluate the perceivable color space a particular display can reproduce (more in Section 6.3.1 at page 194). The plotted triangle in Figure 4.12 is an example for the color space of a display that applies three quite saturated primary colors. Hence, it spans a large color space. The area that a display covers within the chromaticity diagram is called the *display gamut*.

4.3.3 Color Separation of the Eye

The chromaticity diagram can also be used to show the color separation ability of the human eye. In Figure 4.13, ellipses of different sizes, named McAdam ellipses, show the maximum distance for the equal appearance of colors. Note that these ellipses are drawn 10 times larger than they normally are.

In order to get a chromaticity diagram with color distances better representing human capabilities, the CIE 1960 UCS (Uniform Color Space) was defined. It uses two coordinates, u and v, which are related to x and y as follows:

$$u = 4\bar{X}/(\bar{X} + 15\bar{Y} + 3\bar{Z}) = 4x/(-2x + 12y + 3) \tag{4.6}$$

$$v = 6\bar{Y}/(\bar{X} + 15\bar{Y} + 3\bar{Z}) = 6y/(-2x + 12y + 3) \tag{4.7}$$

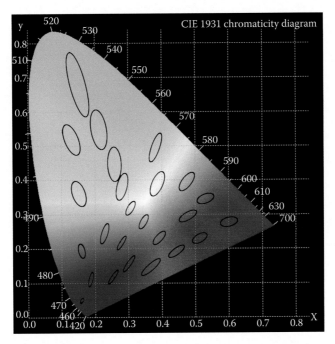

FIGURE 4.13 CIE chromaticity diagram, with Mc Adam ellipses indicating human color separation ability (ellipses enlarged by 10).

$$x = 3u/(2u - 8v + 4) \tag{4.8}$$

$$y = 2v/(2u - 8v + 4) \tag{4.9}$$

Figure 4.14 shows the McAdam ellipses in the CIE 1960 UCS. The color distances here better fit to human separation ability, shown in the ellipses which are much less different in size.

The white spot here lies at:

$$u = 4/19, \quad v = 6/19 \tag{4.10}$$

This colorspace was intended to replace the CIE 1931 version, but until today, both are in use. Of course other (even perceptually more uniform) colorspaces exist, such as CIE Lab. But discussion of these is not within the scope of this book.

4.3.4 Color Recording

Color beam splitters as used in professional 3-chip TV cameras could be designed to match the sensitivity curves of the human eye. Hence, the color signals from cameras of this kind would contain all information that could be visible and would have a color separation similar to that of the eye, making maximum use of the information channel capacity. The three color outputs could then be sent over a matrix circuit that would recalculate them into three standardized R, G, and B color values to match the dyes of standard displays. This could

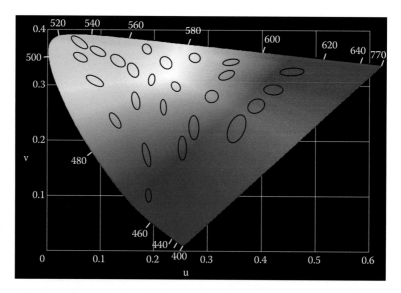

FIGURE 4.14 CIE 1960 UCS diagram with McAdam ellipses (enlarged by 10).

create an additional overlapping and reduce the color space. With smart signal processing it has already been shown that this process is at least partly reversible.

Alas, the design of real color cameras is not this ideal. Figure 4.15 shows, the color sensitivity curves of a typical studio camera. In the ranges *a*, *b*, and *c* no separation of spectral colors is possible at all, because this would require at least two color channels delivering signals for comparison. The same applies for a large range of mixed colors. With cameras, wide overlapping with a maximum variation in sensitivity ratios, rather than extreme spectral separation between channels, is required.

Poor camera designs, as in the example above, are quite common. Considerations about ideal color reproduction such as those we show in the following, however, assume proper implementations.

The color-matching functions found for the human eye are much more discriminating, as we will show using the CIE 1964 color-matching functions (Figure 4.16).

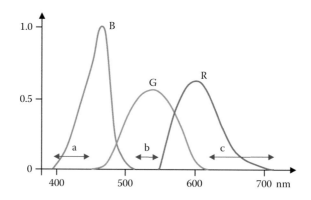

FIGURE 4.15 Spectral response curves of a typical studio camera.

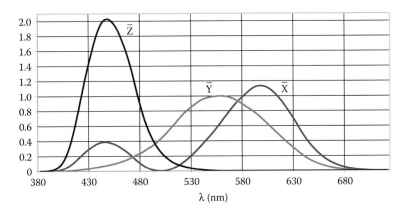

FIGURE 4.16   CIE 1964 (10°) color-matching functions.

These functions were measured for a 10° viewing angle rather than for the 2° angle used for the 1931 functions. There are, therefore, more rod influences.

Figure 4.17 shows the ratios between the three color functions. First we see that there are unambiguous values allowing good discrimination in the green range, quite different from the camera example. Regarding the extreme blue part, we see that the extra part of the red curve in the blue range is necessary to discriminate spectral colors between 380 nm and 420 nm. Actually, the curves in parts (1) and (2) diverge by about 15%, enough for a reasonable amount of discrimination. The red range is discriminated by a similar ratio between about 640 and 680 nm. Over 680 nm there is no difference remaining at all.

No matter how perfectly the CIE curves actually describe the discrimination abilities of the human eye, we see that for good results, the curves being used always have to be reproduced entirely, including any overlapping parts, up to the ends of the spectrum.

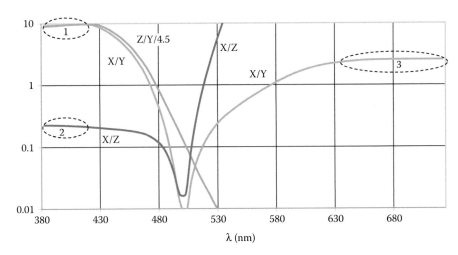

FIGURE 4.17   Color discrimination prerequisites of the human eye, approached by the relations of the CIE 1964 color-matching functions.

4.3.5 Neuro-Physiological Results

Figure 4.18 shows the normalized color absorption of human retina pigments. These look quite different from the CIE response curves, which can partly be explained by influences such as pigment density and light absorption in the eye.

It also appears that rods could contribute to color perception (leading to a four-color model), yet this is not entirely true. Rods and cones are distributed very differently throughout the retina, and most important, the retina does a lot of preprocessing before image data actually gets to the brain. It can be assumed that the processing (not the sensory) model is prevalent and is actually based on an inherent three-color scheme.

Another very important fact is the extreme difference between light sensitivity of rods and cones. It can be as much as a factor of 1000 (Figure 4.19). This seems incredible, but consider that "all cats are gray" at about one lux already while starlight can have one millilux

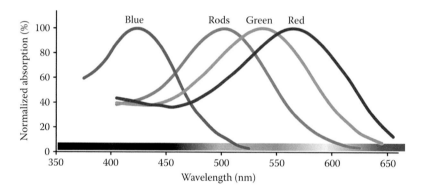

FIGURE 4.18 Measured spectral absorption curves of cone (red, green, and blue) and rod pigments. (Data from Bowmaker, J.K. and Dartnall, H.J., *J. Physiol.*, 298, 501–511, 1980.)

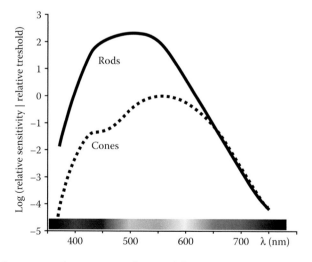

FIGURE 4.19 Absolute spectral sensitivity of cones (photopic) and rods (scotopic). (Data by Wald from H. Davson. *Physiology of the Eye.* Macmillan Academic and Professional Ltd., 5th edition, 1990.)

FIGURE 4.20 The Mach band: although each of the gray bars is entirely uniform, it appears as if their brightness is changing toward the neighboring bar, increasing the contrast at the borders.

and still our cones deliver some (faint) signal. This is also the reason why we cannot see dim stars by directly looking at them; we always (unintentionally) look a little bit beneath, using a retina area with many rods.

4.3.5.1 Retinal Image Processing

Preprocessing in the retina also yields motion vectors. The entire image perceived is accompanied by signals representing directions and speeds of motion for each and every image part. Other preprocessing detects basic geometric shapes. All in all, what passes the visual nerve is not actually a pixel-by-pixel image as is used in technology, but a rather complex compound of preprocessed data of shape and vector elements rather than single pixels. This is even necessary in a way, because the visual nerve hasn't nearly enough "wires" to transport all receptor signals individually.

An indication for lateral inhibition in the retina is the *Mach band*. Adjacent brightness values influence each other in a way that increases visual contrast (Figure 4.20).

The rod and cone density on the retina is depicted in Figure 4.21. Obviously, cones are dense only in an extremely small area at the center. Hence, we can see fine color detail in this small area only. Rods are much denser in most areas. Their number degrades with angular distance from the center, but, by far, not as much as the actual resolution decreases, as measured in experiments (Figure 4.6 on page 97).

Another indication for the importance of preprocessing is the discovery that the off-center resolution of the eye can vary according to the attention to off-center objects. Though it is not certain that this actually happens in the retina, it indicates that the human visual system is a rather complex image processing system (which is not very surprising at all).

4.4 DEPTH PERCEPTION

3D perception of our environment is essential for orientation. Our ways of achieving this have, of course, been optimized during evolution, because they are important for survival. The basic toolbox of mammal nature contains only two eyes. However, not all species have developed them for "stereo" perception. Rabbits, for example, can see 360°, but hardly at all in stereo. Yet they can still navigate in 3D quite well, because there are several other depth or distance cues a visual system can exploit.

Reproducing real 3D impressions optically on a display is a tricky endeavor. Perspectives as seen by a camera or a live observer can be correctly reproduced only if display size and

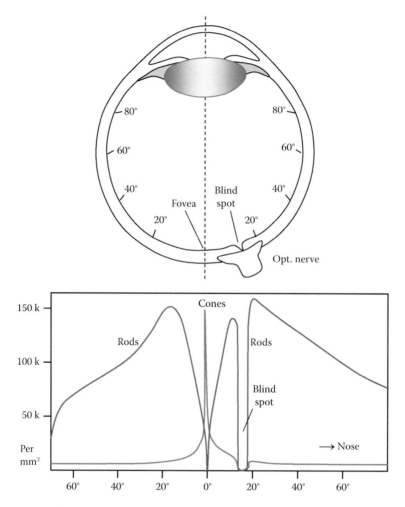

FIGURE 4.21 Distribution of cones and rods in the eye. (Data from Osterberg G. Topography of the layer of rods and cones in the human retina. *Acta Ophthalmol Suppl.*, 6:1–103, 1935.)

distance allow for producing the same picture on the observer's retina, thereby producing the same converging perspective lines as in the original situation.

An image taken with a wide-angle camera lens for example, needs a wide angle display in order to be seen correctly – a screen that is large in relation to its distance, reproducing the original field of view. Conversely, a tele-shot would require a small display to reproduce the original perspective, but this would be counter productive because it would eliminate the enlargement effect. Moreover, we always take notice of the real distance of a display screen because of our stereo vision. The human visual apparatus is quite able to learn and to adapt to these peculiarities, so actors appearing 20 m tall on a cinema screen no longer disturb us.

The situation intensifies with 3D TV. Here the discrepancy between real and displayed perspectives becomes more obvious. Will we get used to this, as we got used to the imperfections of 2D displays? Some doubt may be justified. In any case it will be much better if

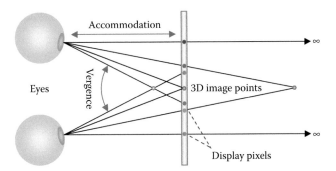

FIGURE 4.22 Stereo image point formation, accommodation, and vergence.

we correct for perspective errors as much as possible by adapting images to the actual position of the viewer. There will be more on this in the 3D displays chapter (Chapter 9). In the current chapter, we will have a look at the basics of the human perception of stereoscopic images.

The perceptual difference between two image projections on two retinas is called *stereopsis*. Due to the horizontal eye separation (interocular distance 6.3 cm on average) the two images are slightly shifted, horizontally. The relative 2D displacement of two image projections of the same object is called *retinal disparity*.

If retinal disparity becomes too large (e.g., for too-close objects) the object appears twice. This is called *diplopia* or *double vision*. The eyes can rotate around their vertical axis. This is called *vergence*, see Figure 4.22 (inward: *convergence*, outward: *divergence*).

4.4.1 The Human Visual Field

The total scope of the environment that can be seen by each eye individually is called the *monocular field*. It covers about 180° horizontally and 130° vertically.

The part of the visual field being shared by both eyes simultaneously is called *binocular field* [108] (Figure 4.23).

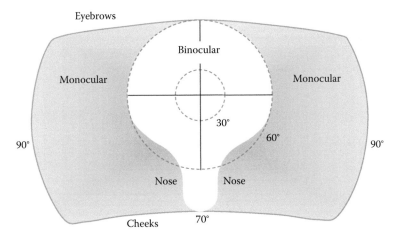

FIGURE 4.23 Monoscopic (monocular) and stereoscopic (binocular) parts of the human visual field.

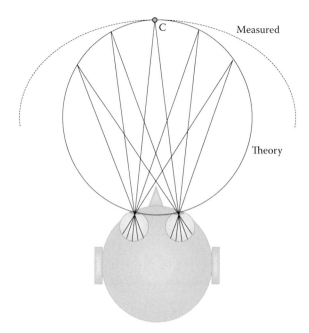

FIGURE 4.24 Horopter: The eyes are focused on point C. The other points form a theoretical horopter. Empirical results, however, more closely resemble the dashed curve.

It covers 120° horizontally and 130° vertically. A smaller portion of the binocular field of view is the area where both eyes can see in focus, called the *foveal field*. It covers only 60° horizontally and vertically.

All points with a fixed position to the eyes are mapped to corresponding positions on the two retinas from a surface that is referred to as *horopter* (Figure 4.24). Points that are located too far from the horopter lead to diplopia. Note that the horopter changes for different eye positions (i.e., when converging to different scene depths).

With these constraints in mind, it is interesting to think about optimal designs of stereoscopic near-eye displays. This will be discussed later, in Chapter 10.

4.4.2 Depth Cues

A short summary of many of the hints and methods available for 3D orientation reads as follows:

- Convergence (both eyes converge, matching their images for one object)
- Retinal disparity (each eye sees a slightly different image)
- Accommodation (change of the eye's lens focus)
- Focus effects (blurring of objects not in the lens focus)
- Haze (softened image parts appear more distant)
- Color (bluish objects appear more distant)

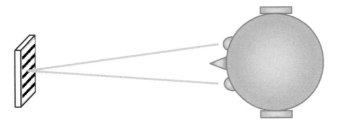

FIGURE 4.25   Convergence (up to 10 m).

- Motion parallax (images change when the head moves)
- Motion dynamics (objects change sizes and positions, in motion)

These will be reviewed below.

4.4.2.1 Convergence

As explained already, convergence is the inward rotation of the eyes when targeting a distant object (Figure 4.25). The state of the eye muscles gives us a hint about depth for up to ten meters. However, we don't get extremely fine angular resolutions at this distance.

4.4.2.2 Retinal Disparity

For longer distances, the difference between the two images projected onto the retinas (called *retinal disparity*) is far more efficient than convergence. Near objects block distant ones at slightly different positions, resulting in different images generated by the left and right eyes (Figure 4.26).

The differences at object edges can be perceived up to the crispness limit of our vision. With a typical eye-to-eye distance (also called *interocular distance*) of about six centimeters and an angular resolution of one arcminute, we get a distance of 200 m where retinal disparity may just be perceivable (Figure 4.27). So we can assume that this kind of stereo vision

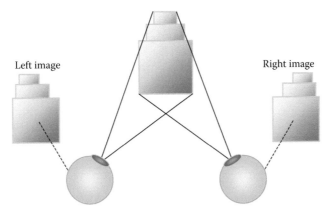

FIGURE 4.26   Binocular (stereo) view and resulting left and right image (stereo pair).

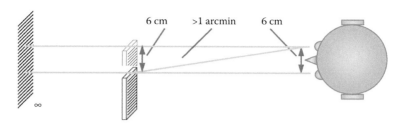

FIGURE 4.27 Retinal disparity (up to 200 m, 6 cm/tan(1/60°)).

may work for up to 200 m in the extreme or, for practical situations and average vision, it will work up to about 100 m.

Our ability to detect differences in distance using stereoscopic cues is called *stereo acuity*. It is given by the smallest difference in the images presented to the two eyes that can be detected reliably.

A closer assessment is shown in Figure 4.28. Here, e is the eye distance (e = 62 mm) and φ is the maximum eye resolution (φ = 1 arcmin = 0.000291). For large distances v, the extensions of the smallest resolvable voxel (x,z) are given by $x = \varphi v$ and $1/z = e/(xv) = e/(\varphi v^2)$.

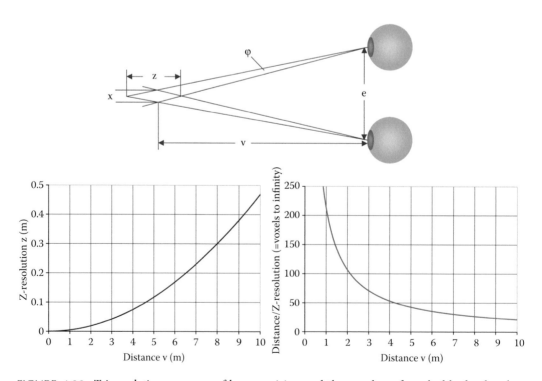

FIGURE 4.28 Triangulation accuracy of human vision and the number of resolvable depth values (stereo acuity) as a function of distance.

We see that in general, *stereo acuity* is inversely proportional to the square of the viewing distance. For the total count of resolvable z-values from v_0 to infinity, n_z, we can calculate

$$n_z = \int_{v_0}^{\infty} \frac{1}{z} = \frac{e}{\varphi} \int_{v_0}^{\infty} \frac{1}{v^2} dv = \frac{e}{\varphi v_0} \tag{4.11}$$

Thus, the range at which disparity is effective depends mainly on the interocular distance, the convergence of the eyes, and the distance of the object. Points that are located close to the horopter (see Section 4.4.1 at page 109) can be fused correctly. The range around the horopter at which this is possible is called *Panum's fusion area*. However, in addition to absolute disparity, other factors affect disparity-based depth perception. For example, the gradients of the disparities (i.e., the depth gradient) influence depth perception and make disparity-based depth perception content dependent. Furthermore, the speed at which disparity is processed and depth is perceived can vary significantly between conflicting cues (e.g., inconsistent convergence and accommodation, see Section 4.4.2.3 at page 113) and nonconflicting cues, and an upper limit to the temporal modulation frequency of disparity exists.

It is important to point out that disparity-based depth perception is a key ingredient for the perception of fast-moving objects. Most often, there is no time to point one's eyes properly, let alone converging them on an object. A lot of everyday orientation is based on the (subconscious) perception of disparity, in the entire field of view. This also applies to fast-action scenes viewed with 3D TV or cinema technology.

A good discussion on disparity-based depth-perception can be found in [127].

4.4.2.3 Accommodation

While convergence and retinal disparity are the main source of depth perception, there are others.

Accommodation (i.e., visual focus) delivers another suitable depth cue. It works mainly for short distances. Distinguishing between closer distances is possible if these are separated by at least the depth of field b (Figure 4.29). According to our lens equations given in Section 3.4.3.7 at page 80), this can be computed as follows :

$$b \approx 2\lambda f^2 / a^2 \tag{4.12}$$

In line with these calculations, a closest distance b_i, for a depth of field from b_i to infinity can be derived as illustrated in Figure 4.30:

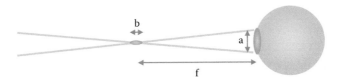

FIGURE 4.29 Accommodation and visual depth of field.

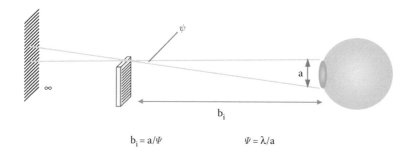

FIGURE 4.30 Depth of field toward infinity.

Assume the eye focuses at distance b_i. Toward infinity, for a sharp vision the rays should not deviate by more than an angle ψ. This angle should equal b_i/a (remember $\sin \alpha = \tan \alpha = \alpha$ for small angles). The maximum resolution of the lens is given by λ/a. As we may also allow the light rays to deviate before the crispness point, a factor of two has to be introduced for the full depth-of-field value. This leads to

$$b_i \approx a^2/2\lambda \tag{4.13}$$

(The same also follows from the depth-of-field calculation shown in Section 3.4.3.7 at page 80, if we just intuitively set $b = f = b_i$).

This formula presumes the receptor behind the lens has at least the same resolution that the lens can deliver. If it has less, the depth-of-field value b_i proportionally increases. Likewise, we could calculate depth of field for the diameter of a lens delivering just this resolution. For the eye, we simply need to take $a = 2$ mm, the pupil size matching the best eye resolution of one arcmin ($1/60°$).

With a pupil of $a = 2$ mm (representing maximum eye resolution) and $\lambda = 0.5\ \mu m$, we get a depth of field from $b_i = 4$ m to infinity. Hence, we cannot count on a contribution of focus to depth perception for distances above 4 m.

For the construction of displays generating virtual focus, or focus cues, it is also useful to know how many distinct distance values can be separated by focus accommodation alone. For the total count of resolvable d-values from a certain focus value f_0 to infinity, n_b, we can integrate $1/b$ from f_0 to infinity using Equation 4.12:

$$n_b = \int_{f_0}^{\infty} \frac{1}{b} = \frac{a^2}{2\lambda} \int_{f_0}^{\infty} \frac{1}{f^2} df = \frac{a^2}{2\lambda f_0} \tag{4.14}$$

Some volumetric displays try to provide a natural depth experience by generating a number of separate images in different distances. Here, we should take into account, that both edges of any depth of field range have a certain blur in addition to the generic lens diffraction. If we just enqueue several such ranges, we get this additional blur at the junctions and hence resolution values recognizably changing with distance. A volumetric display should therefore better provide about $2n_b$ distinct image layers.

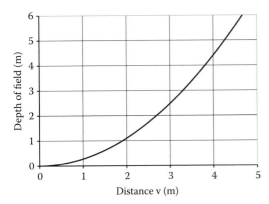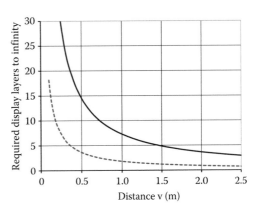

FIGURE 4.31 Eye depth of field (left) and number of volumetric display layers required from certain minimum distances up to infinity (right), for resolutions of $\Phi = 1$ arcmin and $\Phi = 2$ arcmin (dashed line).

For the human eye, the maximum number of distance values results for $a = 2$ mm, as this corresponds to the maximum eye resolution. Larger a are not valid in this case. Figure 4.31 shows the eye depth of field for $a = 2$ mm and the number of separate image layers required for $a = 2$ mm and $a = 1$ mm (corresponding to display resolutions Φ of 1 and 2 arcmin).

Accommodation is not a good absolute distance indicator also because our lens muscles would need to provide a very accurate, absolute feedback for this purpose.

We may conclude from this that focusing is not something we have to care for when dealing with large screens, such as a large-screen TV or a cinema screen. Even at screen distances almost down to 1 m, no major problems should arise [286].

Nevertheless, we have to keep in mind that eye convergence and accommodation are automatically aligned to a certain accuracy, and this becomes important for closer viewing distances or if 3D objects are rendered to appear before a larger screen, nearer to the viewer. With virtual objects displayed at virtual distances above one m, this should not really be a problem [286]. It takes a considerable act of will, however, to see a really close-up picture sharply if both retinas receive images with a disparity indicating large distances. Therefore, the combination of accommodation, disparity, and convergence remains a problem for many stereoscopic displays.

4.4.2.4 Focus Effects

Apart from accommodation, the blurring of distant or very near objects (related to the eye depth of field) is a very effective source of depth information. Shooting a picture that is just crisp all over, may be tempting, especially with HD equipment, but it is not smart in all cases. With 2D, photographers or cameramen always had this in mind and adjusted depth of field by selecting an appropriate aperture. A strong 3D impression can also be invoked by changing the distance setting of the lens from near to far, or vice versa within an otherwise quite static scene (*rack focus effect*). 3D or stereoscopic material, however, has to be recorded crisp all over, because anything else would appear unnatural.

For stereoscopic movies in cinemas, strong out-of-focus effects seem to be problematic. The blurred image portions make the fusion of the stereo pairs very difficult in these venues. Another problem is that, in reality, we can naturally re-adapt focus to out-of-focus objects. This, however, is obviously not possible with certain focus settings used for recording. In particular, if blurred regions are mixed with focused regions that support stronger depth perception, then this situation can also lead to problems for cognitive interpretation of the scene. This seems especially to be the case for defocused foreground objects with focused objects in the background. The viewer may also tend to look about in scene areas not intended as the center of attention, especially with screens covering large fields of view. A blurred background, often used for an impression of depth in 2D, then appears most unnatural.

Currently, directors of stereoscopic movies try to avoid strongly out-of-focus effects for these reasons [276]. But as you can imagine, depth of field and focus are important tools for cinematographic story telling. So there may be a challenge here that might influence the future success of 3D cinemas.

4.4.2.5 Haze

Abundant vapor in the atmosphere, as well as under water, makes distant objects lose contrast and their edges soften (not blur). This is a "soft" depth indicator but, nevertheless, it has to be taken into account for a naturally appearing 3D presentation.

4.4.2.6 Color

From our experience in natural environments, color is a source of depth information as well. Blue objects always appear more distant. This results from the fact that, in nature, the atmosphere has a slightly higher absorption for warm colors, and items at the horizon appear bluish. This is deeply ingrained in our psychology of vision and is therefore also valid for close-up objects that are just simply blue. Combining blue color and blur can give a dramatic 3D effect even on a 2D display.

4.4.2.7 Motion Parallax and Motion Dynamics

Another important depth indicator is the change of perspective when we move our heads. This is called *motion parallax*. Even very small head movements result in a change of tiny image detail at least, and edges of close-up objects blocking or partially blocking even small areas of a distant object cause a depth impression. Therefore, this is almost as powerful as retinal disparity.

Instead of the observer, the scene could be moving. In the case of very small movements, the observer may not even notice what actually is going on. But if a cameraman moves his camera just a little sideways while keeping the object of interest in place (Figure 4.32), the small perspective changes that occur may be perceived as a result of our own motion. Our subconscious makes the images appear three-dimensional. To a certain degree this also happens with a simple pan as the camera usually rotates around an axis apart from the center of the lens. Perspective changes in almost any kind of camera motion will deliver some depth clues (zooming, however, won't). A conscious look at newer film productions reveals that some directors are using these techniques quite often, while older movies usually were filmed

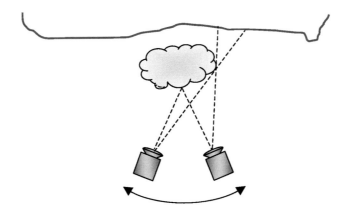

FIGURE 4.32   This camera trick makes any still shot look 3D: Simply shift the camera sideways or upwards a bit while fixing one point. Everything suddenly has depth!

with fixed camera positions or very simple moves, also because of the heavier equipment, of course.

An object moving sideways before a distant background also causes perspective relations identical to stereoscopic viewing.

Observers or objects moving up or down deliver even more information than just stereo viewing, enhancing even 3D movies. Observers moving forward and backward cause more difficult changes of perspective, but even these can be exploited for depth information. In practice, all motion effects mentioned might deliver even more 3D effect than just stereo viewing, especially for distant objects where the stereo basis of our eyes is a bit small in comparison. A movie showing an helicopter ride around distant mountains, for example, appears perfectly three dimensional if we just deliver the appropriate parallax for infinity (i.e., deliver both eyes exactly the same image). Mixing real stereoscopic and monoscopic views in the same movie may even go unnoticed if the monoscopic views deliver depth information by motion.

All motion effects mentioned above can also be exploited for an automatic conversion of 2D into 3D movies, because missing perspectives can, in many cases, be derived from previous and subsequent frames (Figure 4.33). Moreover, subsequent frames may deliver more object pixels than a single one (e.g., if an object is displaced by a half-pixel, information about in-between pixels can be derived from the other frame). Hence, 2D movies may not only be converted to 3D but also upscaled to a higher resolution in the same process [158].

The discussion above leads us to the following conclusions:

- Any movie scene can be made to appear 3D by carefully inserting some motion.

- Conventional movies can be converted to 3D by exploiting motion in scenes, delivering information even about blocked image parts, because these image parts may be revealed shortly before or after (Figure 4.33). Such conversions have already been tried with remarkable success. They do not work well in all cases, but true stereo views and mono views can be mixed quite seamlessly if necessary.

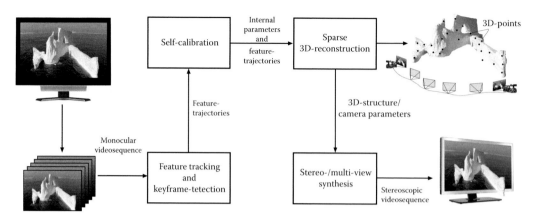

FIGURE 4.33 Image motion can be exploited to make 3D movies from existing 2D films: Perspective changes between subsequent frames are analyzed and different perspectives generated. Image courtesy: Sebastian Knorr [158].

- Stereo displays can be built in two ways or a combination thereof:
  - just delivering retinal disparity
  - delivering different monoscopic perspectives according to the changing position of the observer
  - delivering both stereoscopic images and adapting them to observer's motion (e.g., using head-tracking technology) – making it possible to intentionally look behind objects.

A special type of 3D effect by scene motion will not be neglected when we talk about displays: rotating an object on a simple 2D screen. This is very powerful in visualizing the 3D structure of objects, especially if the rotation can be influenced interactively. This way, our brain is able to analyze very complex objects or transparent 3D structures from just raw 3D image data, displayed by a simple coordinate transforming process, even in cases when the computer would not have a chance to isolate any structures in the same data set. This can be referred to as *motion dynamics*.

4.4.3 Stereo Picture Recording

Apart from the constraints regarding the recording of high-resolution motion pictures (Section 4.5 at page 119), recording pictures for stereo movies (currently dubbed "3D") requires certain additional techniques.

First, a meticulous management of stereo basis and camera convergence is required for achieving a certain credibility of the picture content and avoiding side effects like headaches or motion sickness. Current 3D camera equipment even allows these parameters to change dynamically during zooms and camera moves. We will return to the different stereo effects in conjunction with displays later, in Section 9.2.1 at page 347.

Second, we need to know that depth-of-field effects (blurring of near or far objects) are inadequate for 3D movies, as explained in Section 4.4.2.4 at page 115. This combined with the requirement for crisp motion recording, may prove to be a significant problem: short exposure times, low apertures, and high resolution are contradicting parameters requiring extremely sensitive camera chips or extremely bright recording lights.

A solution may be light field cameras (as mentioned in Section 3.6 at page 87). They may combine large lenses, very large camera chips, and wide apertures with the ability to record crisp near- and far-field pictures simultaneously, by combining various subpicture patterns in real time. Their current limitations, however, are either a low spatial resolution (e.g., when microlenses are used with one camera sensor) or extremely complex setups (e.g., when 2D camera arrays are applied).

4.5 MOTION PICTURES

The principle of motion pictures is common knowledge: Show many slightly different pictures in a fast sequence, and the content of the pictures seems to move.

An impression of smooth motion can be achieved with sequential pictures at a sufficient rate. But what rate is sufficient?

There are several answers. Just animating a person or a cartoon character, for example staying in place with just arms or legs moving, can be done with as little as 8 pictures (frames) per second. Moving the background of a scene, or panning with a camera (moving the entire image) can require very high frame rates. The usual 24 *frames per second* (fps) of cinema film require keeping pans slow. Camcorders and TV film standardly have 50 or 60 fps and allow pans at almost any desirable speed. For arbitrary mixtures of character and scene motion, anything between eight to over 60 fps may be required (cartoonists may move a background each frame but provide a new drawing of a character only every third frame).

4.5.1 Displays and Motion Blur

A common misunderstanding assumes that it would be necessary to hold a single frame until the next frame can be displayed, and that phosphors of cathode ray tube (CRT) screens are laid out to afterglow until the next frame.

In reality, CRT phosphors are designed to glow just a few milliseconds. The reason for this can easily be understood with regard to a typical motion-scene situation.

The most dynamic motion in moving pictures usually occurs when a small object moves against a background. Inevitably, the eye will follow the object. The eye, however, will do this with a more or less continuous motion. If we display the object at a constant position during the entire frame length, the observer's eye will still move during this time. The result is that the object will be motion-blurred (Figure 4.34).

If we show the picture for just a tiny moment instead, it will appear crisp. We might suspect that, in this case, the object may appear to jump or stutter from position to position, like a stroboscopic picture, but actually this will occur only if we choose a very low frame rate. At the usual 24 fps of a movie, moving objects in the scene will appear consistent, at least, if they are not too big and are not moving too fast.

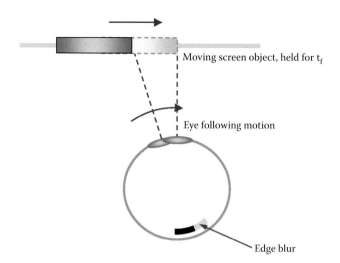

FIGURE 4.34 Motion blur due to frame persistence.

If the entire scene is moving (e.g., camera panning), a severe stuttering effect will occur if the speed becomes too fast.

What causes motion blur on conventional LCD screens is the fact that, for the best utilization of the backlight source, they usually hold a frame for its entire duration. For computer displays this may once have been an advantage, because it reduces flicker at low frame rates (again, refer to the flicker fusion threshold that was discussed in Section 4.2.3 at page 93), and computer screens, at least in offices, show still pictures most of the time. As soon as people started to view TV or play animated games on their PCs, however, the problem became apparent. A better generation of LCDs are flashing their backlights. In this case, an image flashes up for only a tiny fraction of the frame duration, just by switching its light source. Alternatively or in combination with this, the frame rate is increased by computing intermediate frames. More about motion issues with various display types in Chapter 7. An overview of necessary frame rates for displays – depending on display size and resolution – is given in Section 6.2.4 at page 186.

4.5.2 Film Projection

Mechanical film projection is a dying art, but we will mention a few words to be thorough. With the 24 fps of current movies, or even more so the 16...18 fps of historic films, flickering would become unbearable if the shutter would turn off light only while the film moves from one frame to the next. In film projectors, the shutter is closed for two to three extra times per frame duration. This increases the flicker frequency and makes flickering disappear (refer to the flicker fusion threshold that was discussed in Section 4.2.3 at page 93). This, however, does not improve motion effects it only reduces flickering.

4.6 SUMMARY

Considering human visual perception is as important as optics for the design of effective display technologies. This does not apply only to 2D screens, but also to displays that support 3D.

Many of the discussed visual perception properties have been understood for decades, and they have been applied to display design as early as the first television sets that occupied our living rooms. Knowledge about the perception requirements on refresh rate, resolution, and color compression were always relevant for consumer displays, such as TVs and computer monitors.

Interestingly, we can still witness a continuous improvement of display technology based on old findings in visual perception research. Flashing backlights in modern TVs or monitors that enhance temporal perception of slow LCDs is just one example.

As stereoscopic display technology is entering movie theaters and even the home-entertainment market now, methods that enhance depth perception for such displays become more and more relevant. One evidence of this is the recent activity surrounding the development of disparity retargeting methods for stereoscopic movies [166]. Even though stereoscopy has been around for more than 170 years, we have just started to seriously think about how depth perception of stereoscopic content can be improved.

For many stereoscopic displays, inconsistent depth cues lead to issues concerning depth perception. We come back to this topic later in Chapter 9 when we compare different 3D display approaches. In the next chapter, we'll take a glimpse at the ultimate approach to 3D image presentation for which such inconsistencies do not exist: holography.

CHAPTER 5

Holographic Principles

5.1 INTRODUCTION

The basic principles of holography were originally developed by Dennis Gabor (1947), while he was seeking improvements for electron microscopy. Gabor's wavefront reconstruction process led to recorded patterns that he called *holograms* (Greek: holos = whole). After the invention of lasers (1960), Leith and Upatnieks (U.S.) and Denisyuk (Russia) adapted Gabor's technique to produce the first optical holograms.

The unique virtue of holograms is that they record and replay all the characteristics of light waves (i.e., phase, amplitude, and wavelength) going through the recording medium (e.g., a photographic emulsion). Hence, there is ideally no difference between seeing a natural object or scene, and seeing a properly illuminated optical hologram of it. This also implies that the entire original scene can still be seen when the eye moves close to the recording medium. Hence, any tiny piece of a hologram, in principle, contains a complete picture of the original scene (from a single perspective of course). A large hologram can therefore be interpreted as a collection of many single perspective views of the recorded scene. But it is more than that, because even phase information in the original light is restored.

The most fascinating aspect about holograms may be the principal simplicity of recording and reproduction: illuminate a scene with a laser (i.e., coherent, monochrome light exhibiting regular wave fronts), and expose a photographic plate to the light from the scene, as well as a part of the illuminating beam guided directly to the photo plate (the "reference beam"). When the plate has been developed, simply illuminate it by a laser beam equal to the reference beam, and the original scene appears behind the photo plate like magic. Using three colored laser beams, even full-color reproduction is possible. Of course, we will discuss this in much more detail later.

Holograms can reproduce all aspects of a scene with extreme crispness. Unlike simple stereo pictures, they even reproduce proper distance and exhibit no differences between parallactic distance and eye focusing. Because they contain many perspectives at once, they can be used for reliable storage of arbitrary data, or for recording not only separate perspectives but separate distinct images as well.

White-light holograms even serve as their own light filter, being able to select just those wavelengths suitable forming an image from a white light source. Hence, it is not always necessary to use a laser for reproduction.

Because holograms can reproduce natural objects in all visible aspects, they can also form optical elements such as prisms, lenses, or mirrors. *Holographic optical elements* (HOE) are a very important application of holography.

The drawback of optical holograms lies in their complicated production (holographic studios or laboratories are required for advanced display holography) and their mainly static image format, compared with 3D displays that are fully interactive.

Holograms also require immense amounts of image resolution (they rely on fringe patterns in the order of light wavelength, hence, micrometer range), so their application in electronic imaging is utterly difficult. Nevertheless, computer-generated holography holds many promises for the future, as we will see in the following.

Today, many applications for holography exist, including display holograms, biomedical application, interferometry, copy protection, data storage, holographic optical elements, and many more.

The reason why we explain the holographic principle in this book is that it is the key to truly understanding 3D display technology. Once we understand how holograms work as the ultimate 3D image generation, we will also understand the drawbacks of different 3D display technologies that will be discussed in Chapter 9. Most electronic 3D displays don't come even close to what holograms are capable of.

We will start our journey with a summary on holography in Section 5.2, followed by a more detailed discussion of the two fundamental wave-optical ingredients for holography – interference and diffraction– in Section 5.3 at page 127. We will look at holographic optical elements (Section 5.4 at page 144) and classical optical holography for display holograms (Section 5.5 at page 158), before we finish this chapter.

5.2 HOLOGRAPHY: A SUMMARY

Holography is a commonly known principle although its foundations are still an enigma to many. We will try to explain not only the application but the founding principles thoroughly, and in a way that will be comprehensible to all of our readers. We will first give an overview of the principles as a preface to the following detailed analysis.

The first principle reads as follows: If an optical recording medium (e.g., a photographic film plate) is transgressed by two different coherent wavefronts, interference of the wavefronts will cause microscopic fringe patterns to be recorded in the medium. If the developed medium is later transgressed by one wavefront similar to one of the original recording wavefronts (called *reference wavefront*, or *reference beam*), the second wavefront (called *object wavefront*, or *object beam*) is reproduced, by interaction of the light with the fringes in the medium. While the formation of fringe patterns in itself is not strange, the reproduction of wavefronts with it sounds a bit miraculous at first. We will therefore spend a larger part of this chapter proving it. For this first overview, we will just assume it to be true.

The second important principle regards the superposition of holographic fringe patterns: If the object wavefront consists of light emitted from all surface points in a real three-dimensional (3D) scene, the reference wavefront could perhaps also reproduce the entire wavefront of this scene and therefore its holographic 3D image. Yet this object wavefront is utterly complex. We might be able to prove reproducibility of a single, clean wavefront originating from one point, but would the superposition of many such wavefronts still be workable?

A single point on an object in a scene emits only a small amount of the entire light, hence its spherical wavefront exposes very little of the recording medium. Such a faintly modulated hologram would of course turn only a very small fraction of a reference wavefront into an object wavefront at reconstruction, but this is OK because a single object point doesn't need a lot of light in order to be seen.

With many point sources, or object points in a scene, any of them will likewise cause only a very small modulation of the medium. All of these faint patterns finally add up to a 100%-modulated hologram.

At first it would appear that with – for example – one million object points, we would need an amplitude range for the hologram fringes to cover millions of distinct gray levels (or refraction levels); as theoretically, contributions from all these points could be present at any part of the hologram and would have to contribute to the modulation without distortions (nonlinearity, inhomogeneities) by the recording medium.

No recording film could fulfill such requirements. Yet, the highly irregular addition of wavefronts of numerous points from a natural scene results in a behavior similar to that of the addition of random noise signals. For n random noise signals with amplitudes $a_1 \ldots a_n$, the resulting mean amplitude a is given by:

$$a = \sqrt{a_1^2 + a_2^2 + a_3^2 \ldots + a_n^2} \tag{5.1}$$

Hence, $a = 1000$ for $n = 1{,}000{,}000$ and $a_1 \ldots a_n$ all $= 1$. Since the amplitude distribution for a random noise signal is Gaussian, the maximum amplitudes to be expected are indeed very limited. Perfectly adding pattern contributions from many point sources requires a lot fewer separate gray levels than the theoretical maximum, 1000 times less for the one million points, for example.

A medium still falling short of this or not being entirely linear will still deliver a complete image, because the fringe patterns for any point are distributed over a large hologram area. If pattern crosstalk and distortions lead to some incorrect wavefronts being formed, they will only cause a faint blur or haze in the image, because the theoretical image resolution of an optical hologram is extremely high.

5.2.1 Holographic Object Recognition

This is a special topic and it has little relation to displays, but it is very useful for a more thorough understanding of the principles of holography, before we even go further into detail.

The general principle of a reference wavefront invoking the object wavefront, and vice versa, when illuminating a hologram, implies that if we would apply the original wavefronts from a recorded scene to the hologram of that scene, we would reproduce the reference beam with great strength. Any other combination of wavefronts (from a different scene) would not do this.

The scene could be any object or set of objects or even a simple flat photograph. The hologram could be used to recognize a particular object or photograph. The more closely the object resembles the original one, the stronger the reproduction of the reference beam. This works best for photos, because we can properly position them much more easily than we can 3D objects.

By measuring the strength of the reference beam reproduction, the method could measure similarities among different photos, and recognize persons, for example, a technique that has been widely explored in the past but has lost its importance in lieu of the rapid progress in digital computing.

Finally, we should state that the reproduction principle applies to any combination of the original wavefronts. The wavefront of a single original scene point would reproduce all other wavefronts, hence a scene image and the reference wavefront as well (though very faintly).

5.2.2 A Basic Hologram Setup

Consider that any picture or scene we can see consists of a single point. A single point emits a spherical wavefront. A natural scene can be thought of as many such sources, one spherical wavefront for each point in it.

We will regard a very simple hologram photography assembly (Figure 5.1): a single laser delivers a reference beam to the recording film and also illuminates an object. This guarantees identical frequencies and stable phase relations for both branches.

The reference beam (reference wavefront) in hologram recording does not have to be planar. But in practice, it would almost always be a planar wavefront that is formed from an original divergent beam using a *collimator* (i.e., a lens or curved mirror).

Choosing an illumination angle from the side has the advantage that unwanted modes, such as ghost images (details on this later), are also shifted to angles outside the viewing range.

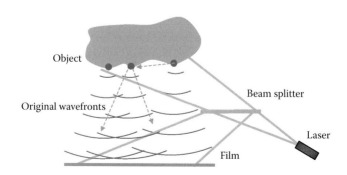

FIGURE 5.1 Simple hologram recording setup.

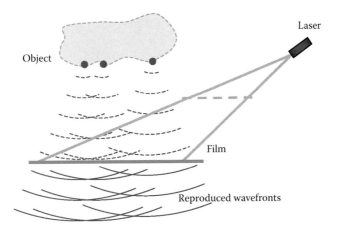

FIGURE 5.2 Simple hologram playback setup.

Wavefronts from three points on the object are shown as an example in Figure 5.1. These wavefronts interfere with the reference beam and form fringe patterns on the film.

Note that scene points will be illuminated not only by the laser sources directly, but also by light reflected from other points. This is an unwanted effect of optical hologram recording, because with the used coherent light it causes various interferences, noticed as speckle.

If at some later point, another laser (normally of the same, but possibly of a different wavelength and position) reproduces the reference beam and illuminates the patterns on the developed film (Figure 5.2), each and any of the recorded patterns results in light wavefronts as though emitted by the individual points of the original scene. The fusion of these wavefronts reproduces the entire original scene.

So we have recorded and reproduced all pixels simultaneously, together with their proper distances, in other words, the entirety of light waves from the original scene.

The holographic fringes on the film may be flat gray value patterns. However, they may also be developed into reflecting patterns, or into patterns of different refraction index. The latter also allows for 3D structures in the film, called *volume holograms* (to be discussed later). Actually, most optical holograms you may encounter are volume holograms.

In the following, we will consider the construction, properties, and use of those various types of fringe structures. In the course of our discussion, we will also explain in detail how and why the miraculous wavefront reconstruction works.

5.3 INTERFERENCE AND DIFFRACTION

Holography works with interference patterns. These occur when coherent waves (e.g., laser light) from different origins add or annihilate (i.e., interfere) according to their phase and propagation direction.

In order to illustrate the point formation of a hologram, we regard the very simplest of all holographic setups (Figures 5.3 and 5.4). Consider a point source of (coherent) light. This could also be just one point P of a scene illuminated by a laser. In addition, we consider a totally planar wavefront R derived from the same laser source (i.e., entirely synchronous).

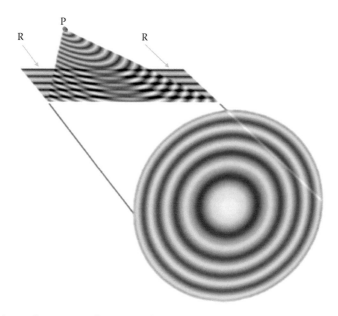

FIGURE 5.3   Holographic pattern formation for a single point.

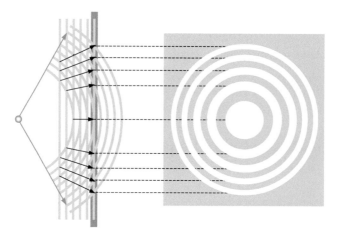

FIGURE 5.4   Zone-plate construction.

On a receptor (e.g., a photographic plate) in front of this, we get an interference pattern of concentric circles. This is called a *zone plate*. These circles are not equidistant; their diameters are a function of the distance between the scene point and the receptor. For a first demonstration of principles, we will consider the photographic plate to be very thin, although in most practical cases the photographic emulsion is thick (relative to the recording wavelength).

It should also be noted that we are not recording just a snapshot of the pattern. The amplitude pattern shows the two interfering waves to be moving in propagation direction, and the recording medium receives a temporal average of them for nearly all practical recording assemblies. Details of this process will be discussed later, with volume holograms.

Next we take the developed photographic plate and illuminate it from behind, with a planar wavefront as in the recording assembly. The transparent rings of the recorded zone plate will act as wave origins, and they are tiny enough that a single cylindrical wave emerges from each of them.

What is fascinating about this is that because of the varying distances between the rings, all these wavefronts will add up to form a single spherical wavefront, and this wavefront will be identical to the wavefront that came from our point source at recording.

Such a basic pattern of concentric rings (i.e., a zone plate) works like a lens. Photographers sometimes like to use them for artistic effects, but such simple zone plates are not entirely ideal as lenses. We will see this in the following.

5.3.1 The Grating Equation

We will now have a closer look at the workings of a diffraction pattern. Any small part of a zone plate for example, can be regarded as a pattern of parallel, equidistant lines. Just imagine a planar wavefront approaching a surface with very narrow reflecting lines. This is an example that is based on reflection. But the same would happen on a transmission basis for a grating with very narrow slits. Any of these lines will become a source of a cylinder wave, and all these cylinder waves have different phases according to the angle of the incident light and the pattern line position. They will combine into another planar wave of a certain angle, very different from the reflection angle of a simple mirror surface. This actually describes the behavior of any pattern detail of any hologram, and it should be interesting enough to be examined in more detail (Figure 5.5):

With a reflective hologram as depicted in Figure 5.5, we can easily see that *constructive interference* of waves from the different wave origins (the bright parts of the pattern) occurs when $\underline{CD} - \underline{AB} = n\lambda$ (a multiple n of the wavelength λ), but also when $\underline{CD} + \underline{AB} = n\lambda$ (the underlinings denote distances). So actually two conjugated departing wavefronts X and Y are generated. Hence, the *grating equation* is derived by

$$n\lambda = \underline{CD} \pm \underline{AB} = d \sin\alpha \pm d \sin\beta \tag{5.2}$$

with

$$\beta = \pm \arcsin(n\lambda/d - \sin\alpha) \tag{5.3}$$

where $n = 0, 1, 2, 3, \ldots$ (only $n = 1$ usually is of interest).

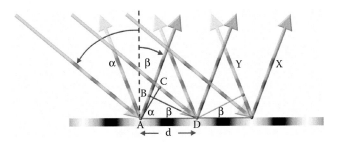

FIGURE 5.5 Construction of the grating equation.

Due to symmetry, there are $2n - 1$ conjugate constructive interference angles per line, for $n = 0, 1, 2, 3 \ldots$ multiples of the wavelength. Sometimes, n is given in positive and negative integers $(\ldots, -2, -1, 0, 1, 2, \ldots)$ to indicate the symmetry. These directions are called *diffraction orders* or *diffraction modes*. The direction at $n = 0$ is called *zero mode* (with first order/mode: $n = 1/-1$, second mode: $n = 2/-2$, etc.). The interference pattern intensity reduces with higher diffraction modes. As we see from the grating equation, the diffraction angles depend also on the wavelength (different colors are diffracted into different angles).

Note, that higher modes would be suppressed for a grating with a sine wave such as a gray value pattern (i.e., only $n = 0, 1$ exist). Strong higher-order modes are created with binary Fraunhofer holograms.

5.3.2 Holographic Point Formation in Detail

From the grating equation, we see that incident angles around zero deliver several reflected beams also at unwanted angles or modes (Figure 5.6).

As explained above, these exit angles can also be positive or negative. A "plain vanilla" zone plate therefore shows ghost images and is both a collecting and diverting lens (Figure 5.7). Using this kind of pattern in a hologram will also produce a conjugated real image in front of the plane (right side in the figure), and even more real and virtual images for higher modes. Moreover, there is a hotspot (at $n = 0$).

This is the reason why the example hologram recording assembly shown in Figure 5.1 on page 126 used slanted beams. If so desired, a hologram appearing in front of the plane could still be generated, and used as the main picture. There are several more tricks that can be applied with optical hologram recording, which can be found in specialized literature [251].

Let's take a more detailed look at the workings of a zone plate, since it represents the most fundamental of all holographic fringe patterns – that of a point source. Illustrating this with

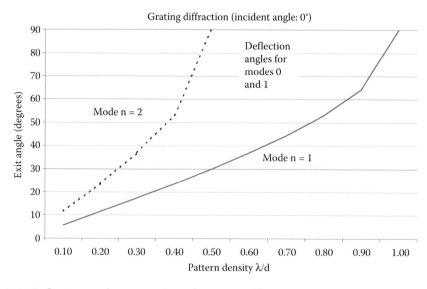

FIGURE 5.6   Reflection modes zero and one for a vertical beam.

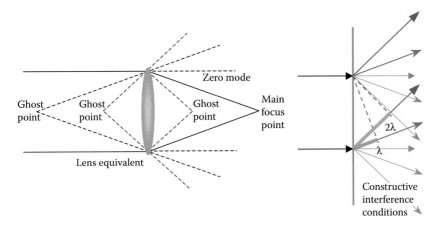

FIGURE 5.7   Zone-plate lens equivalent with different modes.

the entire wavefront is difficult, because the effect only becomes obvious with many zone rings involved.

In Figure 5.8 we have sectioned the wavefront into several parts in 10° steps, so for each of them the phase relations can still be seen. Slanted incident recording beams create patterns of parallel lines with different width, according to the grating equation (refer to Section 5.3.1 at

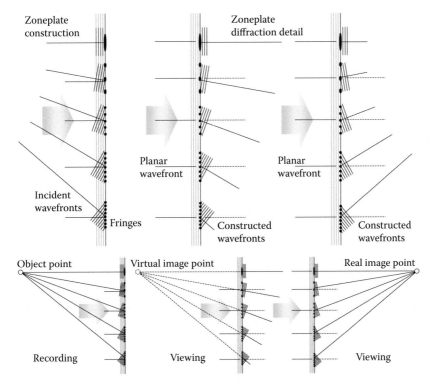

FIGURE 5.8   Top: principle of a zone plate, with single ray interference line pattern construction (left) and ray reconstruction (right). Bottom: different modes, real and virtual focus points resulting.

page 129). Later, the fringes turn the illuminating beam into point sources releasing spherical waves. Slanted beams result for angles where these sources are in phase: the reconstructed beams (upper center), but also the zero mode (dashed lines) and the mirrored angle (upper right). The modes cause real as well as virtual images of the focus point (bottom).

Conversely, if we illuminate the pattern with a concentric wavefront as emerging from our point, a planar wavefront will result. One beam from the recording assembly can generate the other, by use of the recorded pattern.

5.3.3 Phase Holograms

A classical type of a hologram is called an *amplitude hologram*. It records fringes as varying gray-tone patterns that modulate the amplitude of the reference beam.

Simple amplitude holograms will inevitably absorb at least 50% of the light, just by their gray levels. Moreover, light is distributed among several exit beams (modes), even in cases where these may just go unnoticed because of their extreme angles. We also have to consider that light power is amplitude squared, so regarding power effectiveness, the result is intensified.

Yet couldn't we find a way of making better use of a reference beam's light power?

The solution is to record holograms as variations in phase shift, and not in density (i.e., absorption property). Revisiting the grating as shown in Figure 5.5 on page 129, we could conceive a hologram where the dark areas also reflect light, but with a phase delay of $\lambda/2$. These waves would then also increase the total amplitude.

This can actually be achieved with a hologram of a certain thickness and a varying refraction index. Higher refraction index means nothing but a decrease in light speed (see Equation 3.1 on page 59). So if light has to pass through such a layer, parts of it are delayed against others. Varying this phase shift continuously and periodically between fringe lines, we can achieve a 100% output contribution from any location in the hologram (Figure 5.9). These types of holograms are called *phase holograms*.

Specially developed photographic emulsions and certain plastic films can record light as variations of refraction index. Using photo emulsions is the most common way to record holograms. The light-absorbing silver halide in photo emulsions can easily be converted into silver bromide in a process called *bleaching*. Silver bromide has a high refraction index. Very detailed information about this can be found in [251].

Properly developed (and laminated onto a mirror surface if we want a reflection hologram), this will simply replace dark by a phase shift of $\lambda/2$.

FIGURE 5.9 Phase modulating mirror (index type).

In-phase
reflections

Runtime by
distance changes

FIGURE 5.10 Phase modulating mirror (relief type).

As the phase shift achieved depends on the path length in the medium, and therefore the angle of the light beams, properly designed phase holograms cannot only suppress higher-order modes, but also the zero-order mode, to a great extent.

5.3.4 Embossed Holograms

Phase shifts may also be achieved using a mirror surface with engraved patterns that cause different light-path lengths. For example, a photoresist lacquer on a substrate can be exposed with a hologram fringe pattern and then developed, leaving a landscape of higher and lower lines (Figure 5.10). The engraved pattern can either be galvanized with a mirror surface, or replicated by appropriate techniques. Even a metal stamp can be made this way, which allows the imprint of a pattern into plastic surfaces. Metallizing such a surface afterward yields a special type of a reflection hologram, which is referred to as an *embossed hologram*.

These holograms are widely used for authenticity seals on products, credit cards etc., because they are cheaply replicated but difficult to forge.

Again, unwanted diffraction modes can be widely suppressed by appropriate fringe structures.

5.3.5 Color Dispersion

From the grating equation $\beta = \pm \arcsin(n\lambda/d - \sin\alpha)$ it is obvious that the exit angle β varies with the wavelength λ. Hence, light of different colors is diffracted at different angles. This effect can be used to separate white light into its spectrum, as with a classical prism. Applications are certain types of artistic holograms as well as scientific instruments and certain display types.

A prominent application of color dispersion is the Grating Light Valve display (see Section 7.3.7 at page 256). It is a reflective light modulator whose single pixels consist of evenly spaced gratings with an up- and down-moving ribbon for every second grating line, making the grating appear or disappear (i.e., even out). Red, green, and blue pixels have different grating widths, so they reflect their desired color only within the desired exit beam range (Figure 7.20 on page 256).

5.3.6 Volume Gratings

Amplitude holograms are very inefficient (only a few percent yield), there is a much better way: As we have seen already, the photographic film can be developed to perform refraction index modulation instead of amplitude modulation. And this is not all.

Most photographic holograms are thick compared with the wavelength. Thick holograms are generally called *volume holograms*. Volume holograms consist of 3D patterns, called *volume gratings* or *Bragg gratings*.

Bragg gratings can yield a light effectiveness of nearly 100%. They can also be almost entirely transparent to ordinary light and show their special behavior for light of a certain wavelength only, coming in at a certain angle only.

Let us explore this in some detail. To avoid unnecessary complications, in the following considerations we will ignore light refraction by the substrate material. The real angles of light and the diffraction patterns within the material will therefore be a bit different from the drawings, but this will not affect the general principle.

5.3.6.1 Volume Grating Construction

A volume hologram contains the interference pattern of light waves, translated into regions of different levels of gray, or (in almost any case) the refraction index. The formation of these patterns is shown in Figure 5.11. With volume gratings, beams coming from the same side will form a transmission hologram, while beams coming from opposite sides will form a reflection hologram.

Here it is very important to recognize that wavefronts are not standing waves. The amplitude patterns of the two interfering waves are moving in a direction that is just the vector average of the wavefront directions (white arrows). A still picture is not really adequate to show this; please refer to the book's website for an animated version (www.displaysbook.info).

We also have to emphasize that black and white in this picture mean negative and positive maxima of the sine waves, and these are both interfering while the film is exposed. So the actual interference pattern arises in a fairly complex way: spots of plus and minus amplitude travel through the emulsion, exposing it along certain lines, while between these lines, only zero crossings occur, and those do not expose the film.

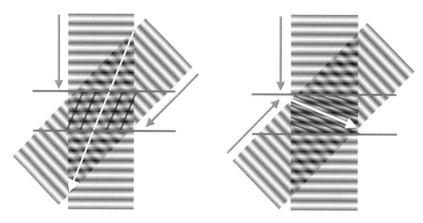

FIGURE 5.11 Holographic volume grating construction. Transmission hologram (left) and reflection hologram (right).

So this is not just about "freezing" the interference patterns in the film. Such a simplification can be used only for very thin emulsion layers, with certain restrictions. The actual interference pattern needs even a (very) short time in order to be properly recorded.

What we should also add at this point is that the intensity patterns caused by the interfering wavefronts always have sinusoidal intensity shapes, which becomes obvious from Figure 3.5 on page 57. With a linear photographic emulsion, this also results in sinusoidal density or refraction index gradients, which are ideal for the holographic point formation and wavefront reconstruction.

5.3.6.2 Volume Grating Reconstruction

The really fascinating part of this is that even with volume holograms, and despite the quite indirect pattern formation (compared to amplitude holograms), the resulting 3D diffraction grating causes light to be refracted or reflected in the same angular proportions as with the constructing beams (Figure 5.12). So the basic principle for holograms, the mutual reconstruction of wavefronts, still applies here.

Reflection or deflection of the wavefront is never accomplished by just one fringe layer; these are the effects of multiple layers in combination (as in Figure 5.15 on page 138).

This is based on the fact that light gets reflected (or refracted, in the case of volume transmission holograms) at any surface where the refraction index changes (Figure 3.9 on page 61), even if it hits the surface perpendicularly. Although only a small part gets reflected from each individual layer, reflections from the multiple layers within a hologram can add up to almost 100%. As an example, simply think of even planes parallel to the film surface,

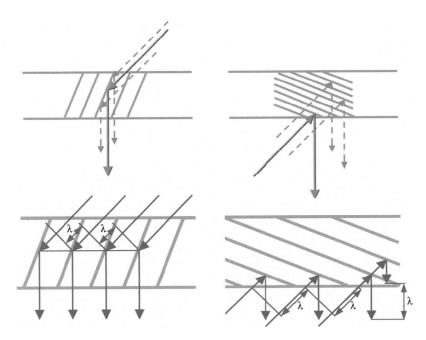

FIGURE 5.12 Holographic volume grating reconstruction. Same as in Figure 5.11. Transmission hologram (left) and reflection hologram (right).

with λ/2 spacing. Any reflected wave returns with a delay of $n\lambda$, or with the same phase, and they will all add up.

Such a mirror, also called a *distributed Bragg reflector*, is as good as a silver mirror, for the particular wavelength(s) it works with. Distributed Bragg reflectors have applications of their own, for example, as reflecting surfaces in wave guides (optical fibers), or as reflectors in lasers and laser diodes.

The image of one point source in a hologram can be illustrated much more easily with a volume hologram than with the flat zone plate (Figure 5.13).

We always have to consider that light reflected several times, from different layers or even back and forth between layers (the single reflections shown in some of our illustrations are just a simplification) may cause some spatial and temporal dispersion, but the effect is so tiny, it can hardly be perceived.

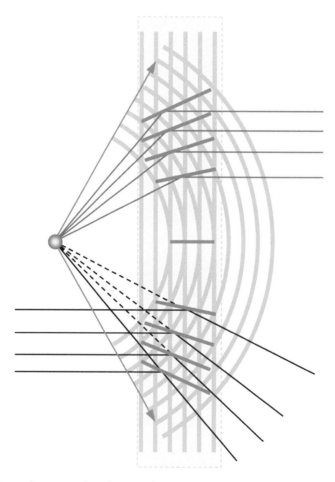

FIGURE 5.13 Zone-plate equivalent (image of a point source) for a transmission volume hologram. A reference beam creates a real image of the recorded object point from one side (upper part), or a virtual image of the point from the other side (lower part). This, of course, is reciprocal.

As stated, with sufficient thickness of the film, the constructive interference effect is very wavelength and direction selective. The operation (spectral) range depends on the thickness of the medium.

We should note, however, that the same holographic mirror reflecting light at λ could also work with 2λ or 3λ, as it finds some surfaces of the right distance.

Because the human visual range covers only about 400...700 nm, a wavelength ratio of less than 1:2 is usually not a big problem. Nevertheless, dealing with color (especially when combining volume holograms for full-color reproduction) is not a trivial task.

Combining three layers of volume holograms for red, green, and blue basic colors has successfully been demonstrated. In order to minimize interferences between colors, however, it proved best to use three-color reference beams from different angles, as widely separated (horizontally and vertically) as possible. More on color holograms in Section 5.5.5 at page 165.

5.3.6.3 Resolution Requirements

The resolutions necessary for a volume hologram can be calculated from the relative beam angles and the incident angle toward the emulsion (the beams in Figure 5.14 are depicted perpendicularly for simplicity only, it has no implication on the universality of the formulas obviously derived from it). The usual notation is θ for half the degree of angle between the beams, and φ for the angle of the interference planes against the substrate.

5.3.6.4 Bragg's Law

The resolution figures above also yield the size of the fringe patterns and can be inverted in order to derive the beam angles (beams generate patterns, patterns generate beams, the principle of holography again). Simply setting $n\lambda$ instead of λ, we get all reflected (diffracted) beam modes:

$$d = \frac{n\lambda}{2 \sin \Theta} \tag{5.4}$$

$$n\lambda = 2d \sin \Theta \tag{5.5}$$

This is Bragg's law, originally developed to derive the lattice width of a crystal in x-ray crystallography (distances between atoms are in the order of <1 nm, so with radiation of

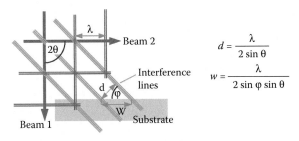

FIGURE 5.14 Holographic volume grating resolution.

about one MeV (i.e., x-rays) these crystal lattices show grating properties – exit-beam patterns can therefore be used to analyze crystal structure). The angle of an exit beam can be derived from this by just extracting Θ and adding φ, straightforwardly.

5.3.6.5 Color Dependency

One important fact to consider is that volume gratings show reflection maxima for different wavelengths at different angles (Figure 5.15). This doesn't affect applications where only monochrome light occurs. Otherwise, Bragg gratings might exhibit some unwanted effects, limited to narrow light bands but possibly disturbing nevertheless.

For the perpendicular ray, Figure 5.15(left) also shows the phase-inverted reflections at the dense/less dense borders, which are always present with volume gratings. If the wavelength for a perpendicular ray is λ_0, then the wavelength for a ray at the angle α is $\lambda_x = \lambda_0 \cos \alpha$ (only 0° reflections are shown in the drawing). This may look counterintuitive at first glance, as the Bragg lines look wider for a slanted beam; hence one could expect them to work for larger λ. But the reflected light also needs to be in phase for all lines, which then is not the case. Consider the incident and reflected beam constructing the hologram, as in Figure 5.11 on page 134: steep beams provide a close line pattern, while shallow beams provide a wider one. Hence, for the shallow beams to provide a narrow line pattern as well, their frequency indeed needs to be higher. As explained before, applying one of the constructing beams to a hologram will reproduce the other – the reflected beam, in this case.

Finally, we should note that with thick holograms, there is no color dispersion. Exit angles are defined by beam and grating angles, just as with a classical mirror.

With true color holograms (explained in Section 5.5.5 on page 165), secondary images may be created that have to be kept at angles where they do not disturb. This is achieved by a properly chosen recording and playback geometry. This is usually possible because, in this case, only three monochromatic light sources are present, and the unwanted modes are very limited because the maximum wavelength difference is considerably less than 2:1. Here, it is of advantage that the visible spectrum is only one octave wide, so unwanted modes tend to occur outside of it.

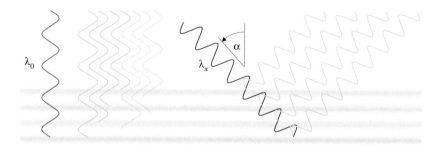

FIGURE 5.15 Volume grating behavior for different angles and wavelengths. On the left is also shown the reflection at dense/less dense borders.

5.3.6.6 Point Formation in a White-Light Hologram

What we have learned so far enables us to understand the principle of a white-light hologram, even a color hologram: an exposure with r, g, and b lasers results in overlaid Bragg structures for the three colors (Figure 5.16). These structures reflect only three narrow bands r, g, and b from the light source. They act like a convex mirror delivering a small image of the light source, which actually is what we see as one point in the holographic image. Hence, the size of the light source limits the resolution.

The illustration also shows that the Bragg layers becoming thicker with shallower incident/outgoing light angles, to correspond to the same wavelength. Further, the spectral selectivity of the Bragg structures rises with their total thickness (this is quite similar to a Fourier transform of the spatial Bragg structure to the frequency domain). Thin Bragg structures (down to a single faint refraction index boundary surface, that would just behave like an ordinary mirror) reflect a wider spectral range, but still at defined angles forming image points. The hologram, viewed with a halogen lamp, then looks white or only little colored, even if it has been recorded with a single laser wavelength. Nevertheless, we cannot record a white-light hologram with white light, as this is not temporally coherent and therefore cannot form stable fringe patterns. We need one or several coherent, hence monochromatic sources. Three sources of red, green, and blue (r, g, b) colors can provide the illusion of white light to our eyes, they can serve as primaries for a white or colored hologram. If the r, g,

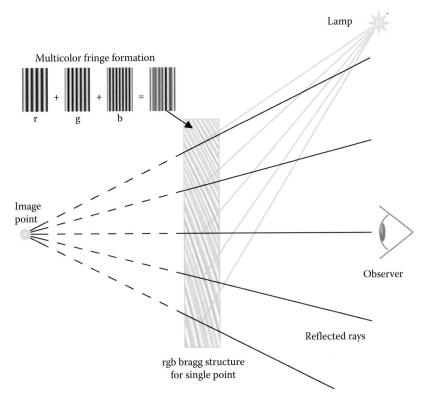

FIGURE 5.16 Formation of a single point in a white-light hologram.

and b parts of the Bragg structure have different strengths, the image point becomes colored. This reproduces the colors of the recorded image. The white-light hologram then becomes a color hologram. Real holographic film materials, however, often are sensitive to one color only. Therefore, three separate holograms for r, g, and b, stacked upon each other, are often used instead of a single, combined one. The light source must be at the same positions as the reference sources at recording. Otherwise, color shifts and geometry distortions in the holographic image will result, because wrong parts of the Bragg structures will then reflect light to the viewer, and will select different color bands from the light source.

A perfect color hologram in one layer can better be produced using three laser sources from different directions (e.g., top, left, and right), as in this case the Bragg structures cross over at considerable angles and do not influence each other too much even if the hologram film does not have perfect properties.

5.3.7 Hologram Efficiency

As explained above, amplitude holograms waste most of the light and exhibit a bad effectiveness, while phase holograms can yield up to 100% effectiveness. This is not entirely true for thin phase holograms, since these allow for several exit modes, stealing power from the main mode. The possible effectiveness for several types of holograms is shown in Table 5.1.

5.3.8 Holograms and Displays – Basic Considerations

Interference patterns such as those on a photographic film may also be simulated with computers and reproduced with a display. With optical hologram recording, we can't exclude the above-mentioned self-interference. With synthetic holograms, this and other adverse effects can easily be avoided by proper pattern generation. Synthetic holograms can also be derived from practically feasible recording assemblies, such as camera arrays delivering spatial information, while optical hologram recording is practically impossible in most situations, because it would require laser illumination and very large film areas. Synthetic holograms are therefore an interesting technology for displays as well as for signal processing.

The resolution necessary for a hologram depends on the angle of the incident light: The larger the viewing angle we want to reproduce, the higher the resolution required (Figure 5.17). Let us assume that fringe patterns (e.g., gray values of an amplitude hologram) constitute sine waves or superpositions of them (wavelength $= \lambda$). Let's also assume that we want to display the fringe pattern on a *spatial light modulator* (SLM) that consists of discretized pixels. According to the sampling theorem [261], the fringe patterns can be reproduced with at least two pixels per wave. Thus, we need pixel sizes of about $d/2$, or less, because we need to reproduce the exact position of the interference patterns. Waves

TABLE 5.1   Maximum Diffraction Efficiency of Various Hologram Types

Thickness	Thin			Thick		
Modus		Transmission			Reflection	
Type	Amplitude	Phase	Amplitude	Phase	Amplitude	Phase
Effectiveness	6.25%	33.9%	3.7%	100%	7.2%	100%

Source: Data from Udo Reinert. *Holographie - Medium der Zukunft*. Holtronic GmbH, 1986.

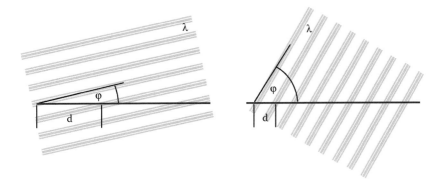

FIGURE 5.17   Incident angle and resolution.

reproduced by a digital signal processing system, that just satisfy the sampling theorem, however, do not guarantee a proper phase at the edge of the frequency range. In any case, it is absolutely important to reproduce exact gray values for the hologram fringes.

If the SLM is illuminated almost perpendicularly, φ is the angle between illumination (reference) wave and resulting (object) wave. Thus, the pattern resolution just depends on the degree of deflection, or the viewing angle, required. Because wavelengths of visible light can be as low as 0.4 μm (blue light), we will need pixel sizes between about 0.2 and 20 μm, depending on the illumination and deflection angles desired.

For big screens, this would normally not require megapixels of resolution –as it would for classical displays– but terapixels (trillions of pixels). It would seem that any attempt to implement holograms with current technology, therefore, would be forfeited (and we did not consider computational and memory requirements here). With very small displays, however, terapixels are not needed and the procedure is not as difficult. There are already first applications of such a technology.

5.3.9 Temporal Coherence

Sometimes the question arises: How good does our light source have to be, in terms of "cleanliness" (i.e., coherence). Consider a small light source with a bandwidth delta λ (we use wavelength instead of frequency, as usual with light). After a certain distance, two signals at the band edges will erase each other. Going further, the entire signal gets irregular and loses its phase information.

We can define the coherence length l_c (as in Figure 5.18), up to where the signal is sufficiently in phase. A usual, haphazard assumption is a phase difference of 360°/π (i.e., 2rad or 114.59°). Anything using constructive interference will work only within approximately the coherence length:[*]

$$\Delta\lambda \approx \lambda^2/\pi l_c \qquad (5.6)$$

---

[*] $\Delta\lambda$ is the bandwidth of the signal, or the difference between the longest and shortest wavelengths contributing and interfering. Usually it would be expressed in terms of frequency (ν), but for this consideration wavelength (λ) fits much better.

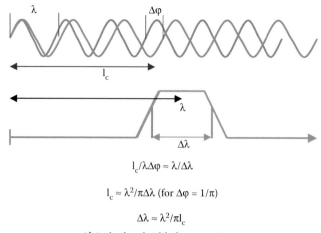

$$l_c/\lambda\Delta\varphi \approx \lambda/\Delta\lambda$$

$$l_c \approx \lambda^2/\pi\Delta\lambda \ (\text{for } \Delta\varphi = 1/\pi)$$

$$\Delta\lambda \approx \lambda^2/\pi l_c$$

$\Delta\lambda$ is the *bandwidth,* for convenience
(some optics texts use this for *half bandwidth*)

FIGURE 5.18 Coherence length.

For optical holography, the coherence length limits the useful operation distance range. Therefore, huge coherence lengths are desirable (e.g., as are possible with laser light). For hologram reconstruction, we need a coherence length long enough only for allowing constructive interference from the contributing fringes. To calculate this, we need the size of the fringe pattern forming a point, and the distance of the point from the pattern.

We use our former simplification for the pattern size, setting it equal to eye aperture (Figure 5.19). The viewer's eye has a lens that delays the inner part of the beam, there we have no interference effects. The interesting phase differences occur at the source point. Hence, we take $f = f_p$, and get:

$$l_c \approx a^2/4f_p \tag{5.7}$$

With $f_p = 200$ mm and $a = 2$ mm, we get $l_c \approx 5$ μm. With $\lambda = 0.5$μm, $\Delta\lambda$ is 16 nm.

Since any display hologram must represent any 3D point only within a fringe pattern size as big as the viewer's eye aperture, a light source with, for example,16 nm bandwidth should

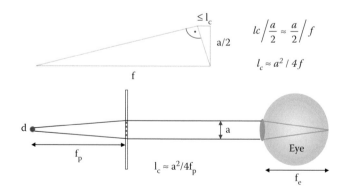

FIGURE 5.19 Coherence requirements.

be sufficiently coherent in many cases. This is not something difficult to achieve: any color light source should have a bandwidth of <100 nm, or it would not be clean enough for any purpose.

5.3.10 Spatial Coherence

Another kind of cleanliness for a light source is its spatial coherence. A clean laser beam can be focused down to a spot about that is limited by the laser beam divergence, as discussed in Section 3.5.2 at page 85 (Figure 5.20). This works because a laser source delivers waves in phase for its entire surface. It defines a fully coherent wavefront as is required for good holography.

A light source that cannot be focused this narrow is spatially less coherent. We could use a pinhole to enforce coherence, but we may lose a lot of light this way. If we want to use a source other than a laser, such as an LED, we have to consider that any part of its surface emits its own light phase. To get a measure for the achievable quality in this case, we need to define a measure for spatial coherence and to calculate how spatially coherent a light source has to be for certain applications.

Consider a light source of diameter d illuminating a fringe pattern of diameter a from distance f (Figure 5.21). Beams from the edges of the light sources travel the same distance to the center of the fringes but different distances to their edges. This difference $\Delta\lambda$ should be smaller than one wavelength, otherwise we get destructive interference. Note that in the

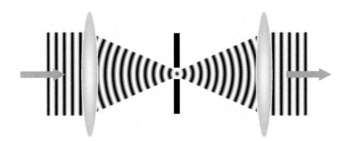

FIGURE 5.20 Beam collimation.

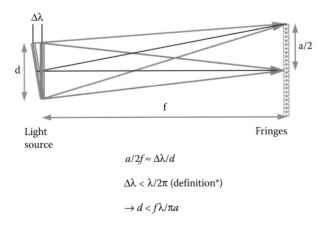

$$a/2f \approx \Delta\lambda/d$$

$$\Delta\lambda < \lambda/2\pi \text{ (definition*)}$$

$$\rightarrow d < f\lambda/\pi a$$

FIGURE 5.21 Spatial coherence.

diagram, we consider $\Delta\lambda$ to be at the source side and the source to be tilted accordingly, since it greatly simplifies the derivation of the formula, which should be obvious this way.

According to general custom, we can define $\Delta\lambda < \lambda/2\pi$ or $\approx 60°,$[*] which over the full pattern width a results in $\approx 120°$ or a maximum amplitude loss of ≈ 0.5.

Thus, we get:

$$d < f\lambda/\pi a \tag{5.8}$$

As an example, we calculate the maximum diameter of a light source for an auto holographic display (more about this in the chapter on 3D displays, Chapter 9):

$$a = 2\,\text{mm}, \quad f = 200\,\text{mm}, \quad \lambda = 500\,\text{nm} \rightarrow d < 16\,\mu\text{m}$$

This would be very small for an LED chip, so even with the high efficiency of LEDs (much better than with laser diodes), we see that squeezing an LED's output for better coherence will have its limits.

5.3.11 Laser Speckle

A well-known issue with lasers is the appearance of randomly flashing speckle patterns when a laser beam hits a rough surface. This occurs because of the fact that laser light is very coherent: parts of the beam are reflected in different directions by the surface grains. The reflected parts interfere at different phase offsets. As neither the beam's coherence length is infinite, nor is the entire assembly free of vibrations, this causes random flickering effects whose mean frequencies are lower the better coherence and stability are. Speckle is constant if observer and assembly are perfectly static.

With incoherent white light, such effects are still present but at extremely high frequencies, hence invisible.[†] Speckle noise is best avoided by making the beam less coherent.

Spatial coherence can be lowered by a diffuser. Laser beams usually are concentrated and squeezed through pinhole blinds for collimation, and this is the best place for a diffuser. It increases the spot size and allows for a defined spatial coherence setting without destroying the final beam.

Temporal coherence can be lowered by modulating the laser light, either by an electro-optical modulator or by varying the driving current of a laser diode. This causes side spectra left and right of the laser frequency to occur (compare amplitude modulation in Section 2.5.2.4 at page 42). By a Fourier transform, modulations for any kind of desired side spectra can be calculated.

5.4 HOLOGRAPHIC OPTICAL ELEMENTS (HOE)

Holographic patterns cannot only represent images, but also optical elements such as lenses and mirrors. We have already seen this with the simple zone plate in Section 5.3 at page 127. Volume holograms, used as optical elements, exhibit even more interesting properties. They

---

[*] Some sources allow only half as much, but we try to stay consistent with temporal coherence.
[†] The frequency differences between any contributing partial wavefronts tend to be very large; remember that light has about 10^{15} Hz.

can emulate lenses, mirrors, prisms, and also entire assemblies consisting of several conventional optical elements, as well as new kinds that, for example, divert one beam into many, with total control over angles and intensities. These are called *holographic optical elements* (HOEs).

HOEs, however, are not identical in behavior compared with their classical counterparts: they are dependent on wavelength, typically specialized on monochrome light, they have different geometric behavior (e.g., optical path lengths with a holographic lens are different from those with a real one), and they build resultant light fields by interference and diffraction rather than by refraction, causing a multitude of subtle differences. So their applications are specialized, nevertheless, very interesting for many aspects of display technology.

5.4.1 Head-Up Displays

One interesting application of HOE is *head-up displays* (HUD). These have been used in fighter jets for more than 20 years. Their purpose is to mirror information from instruments and to aim devices directly into a pilot's field of view (Figure 5.22).

The principal optical layout consists of a display and a half-transparent parabolic mirror, delivering the display picture at a virtually infinite focal distance (Figure 5.23). Ideally, this converts pixel positions on the display into angles, so for the pilot, the image appears at

FIGURE 5.22 Left: Head-up display (top mounted) in a WC-130J Hercules. Right: The pilot's view of sunset through the head-up display after flying into Hurricane Ike. Image courtesy: U.S. Air Force, 403rd Wing, Photos by Major Chad E. Gibson.

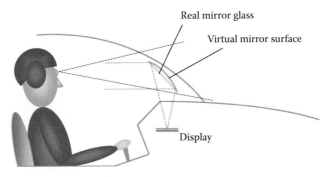

FIGURE 5.23 Head-up display (HUD) in an airplane (principle).

a fixed position on the horizon, and no additional alignment mechanism is necessary for adjusting the picture to distant targets.

Such displays are also known as *collimated displays*, because they deliver parallel (in other words, collimated) light bundles from points at virtual infinity (more in Section 7.10.13 at page 298).

The mirror has to meet certain requirements. Foremost, it should not deliver unwanted reflections from bright objects around it, and it should absorb as little light as possible. HOEs, as stated, are very color and direction sensitive, so they can be designed to reflect light from the display only. Therefore, HUD mirrors were produced as HOEs even as long as decades ago, despite the difficulties and cost of their production. Very recently, HOEs have been introduced into civil aviation.

If the display used is not monochromatic but has a wider spectral emission range (like a CRT phosphor or an LCD dye), light hitting the holographic mirror at different angles will be selected for different narrow color bands from the emission spectrum (Figure 5.15 on page 138). The exit angles, however, will always only be determined by the incident angles and the orientation of the holographic fringe layers. This makes the holographic mirror work quite similar to a conventional one, reflecting at a considerable range of angles, but there will be angle-dependent color changes and the efficiency of the reflection will be considerably affected because only parts of the display spectrum are reflected.

5.4.2 Construction of a HOE

How a hologram can act as a HOE is obvious from our prior considerations: record the picture of a single point with a planar reference wavefront, and this point will be the focal point of the resulting HOE (in the case of a single lens or mirror element). There are more uses for HOEs, but let us first consider the basic applications in some detail.

Regard the construction of a mirror element for the HUD (Figure 5.24). Because we want to make a mirror, the constructing beams have to come from opposite sides of the photographic film plate. One beam arrives at parallel from behind, representing the image of a

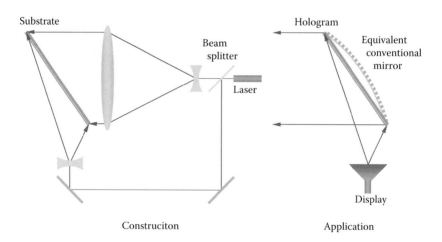

FIGURE 5.24 HOE construction (left) and application (right).

point at infinity. The other beam comes from a single point below, representing the same point on the display, also, in this case, the focal point of the mirror element produced. As with any hologram, one beam will later reproduce the other. The pattern is developed into a reflection volume index hologram that will convert parallel into concentric beams and vice versa, just like a parabolic mirror. Hence, any point on the display will produce a beam from infinity, as intended.

The direction sensitivity of a hologram is not perfect. It depends on the thickness of the hologram film, and we may not even want it to be too large, as we want our mirror to work for all points on the display, not just for a single one, and we may also not want a too big wavelength selectivity if we use noncoherent light. Therefore, we will use a hologram film whose thickness is optimized for the selectivity as well as the operating range we require. We may also overlay several hologram structures within one film, in order to provide mirror functionality for a wider range of angles (similar to the method shown in Figure 5.30 on page 153).

5.4.2.1 A Detailed Construction Setup

The possible angular variation range also allows us to simplify the construction setup a little (Figure 5.25).

A huge lens to imitate infinity is unpractical, so we use the lens equation to form an equivalent holographic mirror from finite focal points:

$$1/F = 1/f_1 + 1/f_2 \tag{5.9}$$

Real laser beams are thick, so we use crossover concentrating lenses to form point-like sources, and some blinds with tiny holes of some micrometers in diameter, to clear incoherent parts from the laser beams (the collimation technique used with practically any hologram recording).

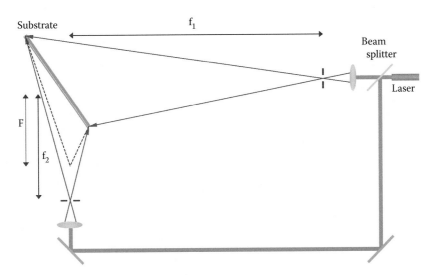

FIGURE 5.25 Detailed construction of a HOE.

5.4.3 HOE Angular and Frequency Response

Calculating HOE characteristics in detail is a very complicated task involving wave optics. We will try to give a simple approach leading to approximate results for the angular and frequency selectivity of HOEs. Obviously, these figures are dependent on the thickness, or number of layers of different refraction indexes, of the hologram. The more layers that are involved, the more selective the hologram will be.

Figure 5.26 illustrates our approach for describing angular response. A number of $n\lambda/2$ layers has a thickness of $2\pi n$ and causes a phase shift $\Delta\varphi$ at a beam angle of $\alpha/2$.

Thus, we get

$$\Delta\varphi = 2\pi n \left(1 - \cos\left(\alpha/2\right)\right) \tag{5.10}$$

or, for small a α:

$$\Delta\varphi = \pi n\alpha^2/4 \tag{5.11}$$

This indicates a relatively wide α range for only ten layers that we assume here: With $\Delta\varphi = 2$ and $n = 10$ we get alpha = 30°.

HOEs, like any hologram, may in certain cases exhibit diffraction modes, but this applies for thin holograms and becomes progressively weaker with a growing number of layers (i.e., with volume holograms). In practical applications, selectivity should not be driven too high of course, because a certain effective range of operation is required.

The spectral response of a HOE or volume hologram can be approximated accordingly. Figure 5.27 indicates a relatively high frequency selectivity, which explains why optical color holograms working with white light can be made: They select almost monochromatic base

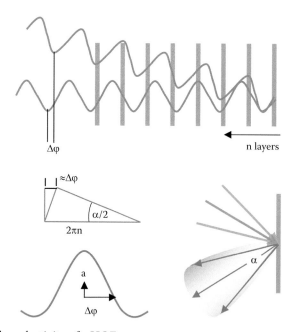

FIGURE 5.26 Angular selectivity of a HOE.

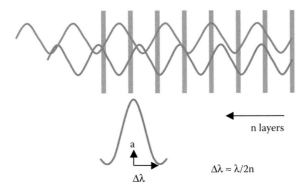

FIGURE 5.27   Frequency selectivity of a HOE.

colors from the white spectrum.[*]

$$\Delta\lambda \approx \lambda/2n \qquad\qquad (5.12)$$

Higher orders (effects at n times the base wavelength) are not likely to occur, because the difference relation between blue and red wavelengths used for displays is only about 1:1.5. It would take a considerable angular deviation in addition to get to a wavelength ratio of, for example, 1:2 (400...700 nm).

5.4.4   HOEs vs. Conventional Optics

In Figure 5.28 we see the basic functions of conventional lenses replicated by HOEs using transmission-volume holograms. Although HOEs are mostly used in off-axis configurations (slanted beams only) in order to cancel out unwanted modes, volume holograms exhibit a mode selectivity sufficient to regard them for examples at least, directly comparing their properties with those of conventional lenses.

Figure 5.28(top) shows a HOE working like a diverging lens. The configuration producing such a HOE is obvious: one parallel and one diverging beam from the same side (although combining them in the same axis may be difficult).

Producing the equivalent of a converging lens (Figure 5.28(bottom)) is more difficult, because we would need converging rays hitting the hologram plate from a wide angular range.

Here a simple maneuver helps: by simply flipping the diverging lens HOE, we get a converging lens HOE. Unlike glass lenses, the HOE is direction dependent. The line patterns shown inside the HOE cross sections represent the volume gratings. A perfectly flat (non-volume) hologram, to the contrary, would be a converging and diverging lens in one, from both sides, as explained earlier.

---

[*] The bandwidth of the signal is $\Delta\lambda$, or the difference between the longest and shortest wavelength contributing and hence interfering. Usually it would be expressed in terms of frequency (ν), but, for this consideration, wavelength (λ) fits much better.

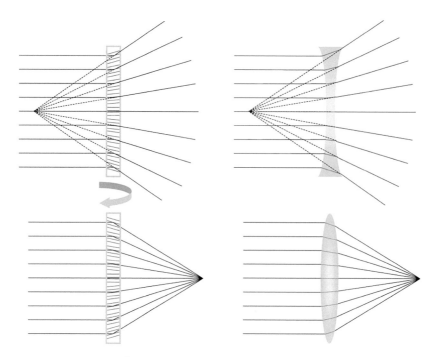

FIGURE 5.28 HOEs compared to conventional lenses. Diverging lens (top) and converging lens (bottom).

The same principle applies to reflection volume holograms (Figure 5.29). Here we can use the recording configuration shown in Figure 5.29(bottom left), producing the hologram easily. From one side, this hologram will be like a conventional convex mirror, from the other side it will be a concave mirror.

Looking back at the HUD example, in producing it we have already used the same trick (i.e., flipping the hologram, using it from the other side).

5.4.5 Camera Lenses with HOEs

Holographic mirrors have been tried for camera objectives. An issue to be considered here is wavelength dependency. A holographic mirror constructed with monochrome light will select angle-dependent frequencies from normal (more or less white) light, which may work for black-and-white photos but at very inferior performance. Using methods as illustrated in Figure 5.16 on page 139, however, a more efficient mirror can be conceived. Nevertheless, HOEs never prevailed as products in photography.

5.4.6 Virtual HOEs

Another kind of HOE can be found in some display holograms, when optical components have been holographed together with a scene (e.g., when you holograph a magnifying glass, for instance). This is not a typical kind of HOE, however, since it acts only on objects inside the picture, not on external light.

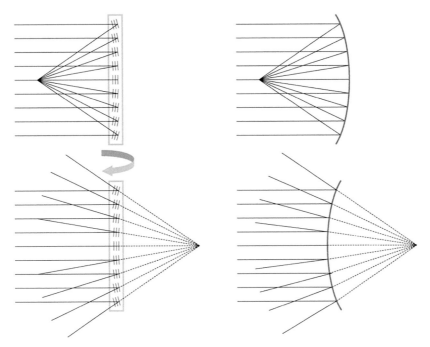

FIGURE 5.29 HOEs compared with classical mirrors. Concave mirror (top) and convex mirror (bottom).

5.4.7 Spatial Light Modulators

Displays with extremely small pixel sizes, usually working in reflective-phase-modulation mode are a special kind of HOE. Certain LCD displays work this way, modulating phase instead of polarization (or amplitude when they are combined with polarization filters). Computer-generated patterns on such displays are used to dynamically shape the beam of a laser in certain measurement applications, for example. These LCD displays are available as conventional polarizing displays, but also as phase-modulating displays, offering much greater efficiency.

As phase can also be modulated by surface engravings in a mirror, beam-shaping microdisplays have also been made from silicon chips, carrying a dense grid of micro mirrors that can be moved downward from their rest position by electrostatic force, thereby forming a phase-modulating array.

5.4.8 Beam Splitters and Diverters

HOEs can do many things that classical lenses or optical elements cannot do. For example, we may want to split a laser beam into three equally bright beams with different angles. Then, we simply have to record the hologram of one bright reference beam (representing the original beam) and three weaker object beams at certain angles (i.e., those that we want to be produced). Any of the three beams will form a different hologram (corresponding fringe patterns) with the reference, and these three holograms will overlay each other. At reconstruction, any of these hologram layers will simply "steal" one-third of the incoming laser light, just as any single point recorded in a typical hologram will always result in a partial pattern stealing part of the illuminating beam at reconstruction. Constructing complex beam splitters for many angles, as well as other beam-shaping elements of any kind, is therefore possible with HOEs.

5.4.8.1 Switched HOEs
With liquid crystal technology, Bragg holograms can be created which can be switched to "clear glass" behavior by applying voltage (e.g., Digilens, see Section 7.3.13 at page 260).

5.4.9 Holographic Projection Screens
Screens with transparent structures forming HOEs can provide complex but well-controlled behavior, such as bundling light into a specific angle and vice versa, or dispersing light from a specific angle into many directions. This is possible because optical holograms can be superpositions of many different structures, each with a different behavior. This way, a light beam passing such an element can be split into many directions with perfectly controllable distribution. A *holographic projection screen* (HOPS) should divert rays from a certain singular location (a projector lens) into a range of angles pointing toward all desired viewer positions.

The projector itself is a normal image projector. It would work best with three narrow-banded colors of laser light, but it may also use white light, because the HOPS extracts the colors it can use, by itself. The HOPS surface is illuminated with the projected image, just as the surface of a canvas screen is illuminated with a normal projector.

Holographic optics offers a wide variety of possible designs. The screen, for example, can itself be an image of a mirror, a beam splitter, or a canvas screen, lying behind the physical screen area.

Just imagine a display hologram of a white surface: illuminated by a simple light source, the surface appears uniform, but if the light source's intensity is angle dependent, the surface has location-dependent intensities, forming an image on it. So the image of the white surface in the hologram behaves in the same manner as the original that it was recorded from.

The manufacturing of a screen-sized hologram providing a well-defined behavior is fairly complicated, requires several steps, and also has to involve several different wavelengths, otherwise the screen would not allow color projection.

One method of HOPS making uses a spherical wavefront from the desired projector location, interfering with a multitude of beams for any desired viewing angle (Figure 5.30). The interference patterns for all locations combine with holographic beam-splitter elements and later divert the projector beams to all viewing angles. With a sufficient number of beams from various angles, a continuous light distribution over the entire viewing area is obtained, because of the fact that finite Bragg patterns (either by finite screen thickness or by splitting the screen area into discretized pixels) have a nonzero angular range. For a color screen, the entire process has to be repeated for all primary colors (usually red, green, and blue).

A commercially available screen for back projection is shown in Figure 5.31.

Let us consider HOPS in a little more detail. One important fact of this application is that volume gratings show reflection maxima for different wavelengths at different angles (see Section 5.3.6.5 on page 138).

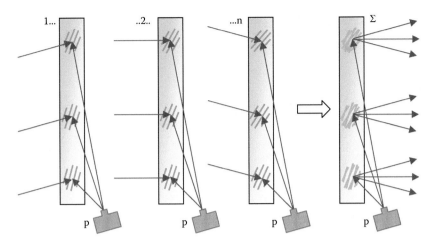

FIGURE 5.30 Holographic screen making with a multitude of beams for any desired viewing angles (1... n, only a few are shown here).

FIGURE 5.31 Holographic screen projection setup (back projection), with touch screen function. Image courtesy: **Sax3d** GmbH.

Figure 5.32 shows details of the reflection behavior of a HOPS, considering parasitic color diffraction. Two partial Bragg diffraction fringes (f_m, f_n) are shown, for $-15°$ and $+15°$ exit angles with red light from projector p.

A black back enclosure inhibits stray light from behind. We see that only light from below (e) in the extreme red range finds modes reflecting it partially to the audience. This could further be reduced, for example, by a black floor mat (m) or a (macroscopic) blind structure (j).

The figure also indicates that we only have to consider short wavelengths (here, 450 nm). For the green and blue active fringes, these effects are negligible anyway, with unwanted modes in the infrared range.

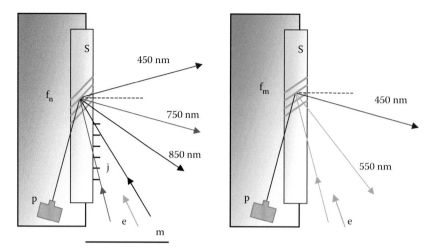

FIGURE 5.32 Holographic back projection screen (s): two partial Bragg diffraction fringes are shown, reflecting projector (p) beams to + or −15°. Several modes of external light (e) reflection are also shown.

The abilities of HOPS by far exceed those of any other kind of projection screen. Of course, a good antireflection coating on the screen front is also necessary for best results. Because holographic screens work best with very slanted projection angles, they allow the creation of very flat projection assemblies.

Front projection screens have more modes, that could possibly cause glare, but they are confined to narrow bands of color (e.g., 3 x <10 nm) for any specific angle, so only 10% of any ambient light can be reflected toward the viewer, even in the worst case (Figure 5.33).

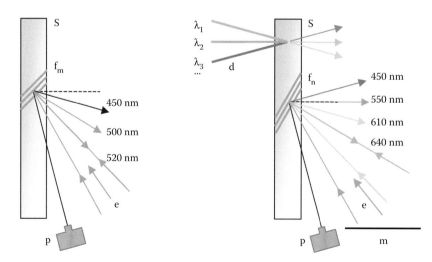

FIGURE 5.33 Holographic front projection screen (s): two partial Bragg diffraction fringes are shown, reflecting projector (p) beams to + or −15°. Several modes of external light (e) reflection are also shown. The screen is almost transparent from both sides (only some narrow-banded modes (d) are faintly reflected).

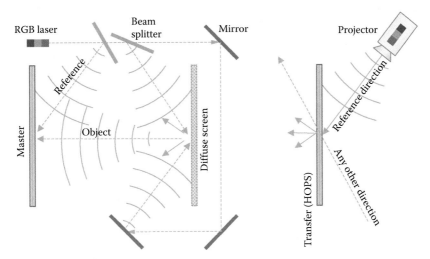

FIGURE 5.34 An example of holographic projection screen (HOPS) manufacturing with virtual canvas. Recording (left) and application after an additional transfer step (right). Note that light of the same wavelength as the recording wavelength will be reflected by the HOPS. Only other wavelengths will pass it.

Conversely, 90% of the light from the backside may pass the screen. The effect is that of a glass window suddenly showing bright images, when the projector is started. If this is not intended, a black plate has to be added behind the screen.

Figure 5.33 shows details for a front projection screen (s): two partial Bragg diffraction fringes (f_m, f_n) are shown, again for $-15°$ and $+15°$ exit angles with red light from projector (p). We see that yellow-to-green rays from below (e) will find modes reflecting them partially to the audience. This is true for one narrow-banded color of any single direction only, so the entire glare is quite small. A black floor (m) can further reduce it. The screen is transparent from both sides for most colors/directions with only some modes being reflected.

There are several other options for the manufacturing of HOPS. One of them involves making an optical hologram of a real sheet of canvas (Figure 5.34).

Again there are numerous manufacturing options for HOPS. In the actual example, numerous exposures with illuminations from different angles are combined, for maximum control over the angular response of the HOPS. The canvas image is placed behind the actual screen, with a distance defined by the position of the real canvas during recording. For applications in cars, even a virtual distance of 10 ft. was conceived. Note that the virtual canvas shows only up where lit by the projector, so it would not block normal sight.

5.4.10 Visual Perception of Holograms

Let's take a short look at the perception limitations of holograms.

For a single viewer, a 3D image point can be represented only by a certain screen area, actually a tiny zone plate. This is because of the limitations of the optical path that any light ray moving toward the eye can take (Figure 5.35). In case of a point at infinity, this zone plate

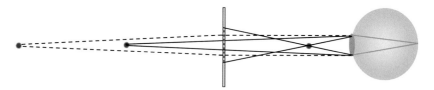

FIGURE 5.35 Effective pattern sizes of zone plate.

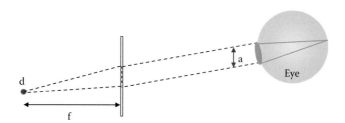

FIGURE 5.36 Hologram image resolution.

cannot be bigger than the pupil. For a nearer point, it becomes smaller, and for image points in front of the hologram plane, it can also get bigger than the pupil.

For general consideration we can simply assume a zone plate just as big as the pupil (Figure 5.36) (again, keep in mind that with flat holograms we always have to use slanted arrangements in practical implementations, closing out unwanted diffraction modes). Instead of analyzing various configurations with different reference beams, we can simplify the situation by assuming the zone plate to be focusing light to a point with diameter d at distance f. This is even accurate, when the distance between the eye and the hologram gets very small.

This simplifying step allows us to apply the formula for lens resolution to the zone plate and to calculate a diameter for the scene point, hence the resolution that the hologram can exhibit to an observer.

As we have seen in Section 3.4.3.6 at page 79, the resolution a lens (and therefore also a zone plate) can deliver, follows very simply from the actual point size that wavefronts from different parts of the lens are able to form:

$$d = \lambda f / a \tag{5.13}$$

Typical results for this point diameter are between 0.3 and 0.5 mm. Hence, the theoretical resolution possible with light (in the micrometer range) is not achieved for practical viewing situations. In order to do this (i.e., to exploit the full theoretical resolution of the hologram) we would have to use a lens/zone plate diameter as big as the hologram itself (of course leading to some other disadvantages, such as a very small depth of field).

Figures 5.35 and 5.36 also show what will happen if we depict a point at infinity. Obviously our planar reference beam would also approach the eye as a planar wavefront. What would happen? Again, light from a pupil-sized patch on the hologram would enter the eye, it would form a single point on the retina, and we would just see a point at infinity, from the direction of the wavefront approaching. If we move sideways, this point would also appear to move sideways, like a distant star, as all objects at infinity do. Depicting a point at a different position would mean it would have to appear at a different angle, and this would require a planar wavefront from a different angle. At infinity, position means angle.

5.4.11 Keyhole Holograms

Within the hologram of a complex scene, the same fringe pattern has to deliver the information for many viewing angles at once (Figure 5.37), even for the entire image, because it can be regarded from any angle within the eye's aperture range. This imposes high demands on image quality, especially dynamic range, resolution, and graininess (noise).

It also tells us that this tiny pattern holds the information for the entire scene, because we could imagine moving our eye toward the pattern and looking through it like through a keyhole, seeing anything from just one single point of view (behold the eye close to the screen in Figure 5.37). We want to refer to such a little hologram patch as *keyhole hologram*. It has no real 3D information any more but still has some distance information replicating the proper focus distance. Here again, pixel position translates into angle. Note that the term keyhole hologram is sometimes also used for special display holograms that record physical apertures or keyholes [251].

What we learn from this: if we break up a hologram plate into parts, any of these parts still has some information about the entire scene. Holograms carry a tremendous amount of redundancy!

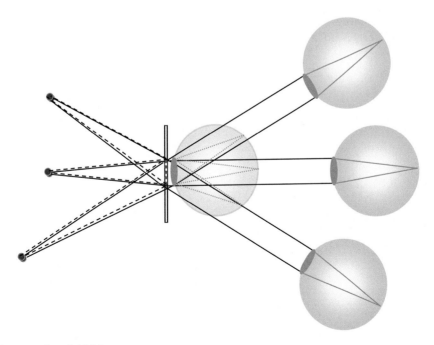

FIGURE 5.37 Overlaid fringe patterns.

5.5 OPTICAL HOLOGRAPHY

This section refers to methods developed in the field of optical holography and their implications on display technology. With optical holography, we understand capturing holograms on photographic film, and replaying them from film.

Optical holograms represent the most traditional form of holography, and are mainly applied as display holograms in museums. "Display" in this case refers to the initial meaning of the word before computer screens were invented: the exposition of objects. Having been around for decades now, optical holography has developed into a veritable art of its own, and many tricks and techniques discovered in this field will also be useful for information-display technology.

An *optical hologram* is a photometric emulsion that records interference patterns of light waves. The basics of interference and diffraction have been discussed in Section 5.3 at page 127. There will be some repetition here in the context of optical holography.

To recap what we have discussed above: for recording (Figure 5.38(left) and Figure 5.1 on page 126), a coherent light source (i.e., a laser beam) is split into two planar (usually collimated) wavefronts – one directed toward the emulsion (called a *reference beam*) and the other directed toward the object to be recorded. The object reflects the light to the emulsion, and by doing so it causes local phase shifts and interference effects, creating a distorted wavefront (called an *object beam*). The plane wave of the reference beam and the distorted wave of the object beam interfere and expose the emulsion to locally different amplitudes, causing a distinct interference pattern (called a *fringe pattern*). This interference pattern forms a diffraction grating which is not regular as it is for two interfering plane waves (see Section 5.3 at page 127) .

After processing and developing the emulsion (basically, a high-resolution photographic film), the recorded fringe pattern causes the incident light to be diffracted uniquely. If the reference beam is diffracted at the fringe pattern, local diffraction together with interference effects form exactly the same complex wavefront (called *image beam*) as the one that was reflected by the object initially (Figure 5.38(right) and Figure 5.1 on page 126). Note that the image beam and the object beam should ideally be identical. In optical holography, however, we do want to differentiate between both to indicate the case of recording (object beam) and

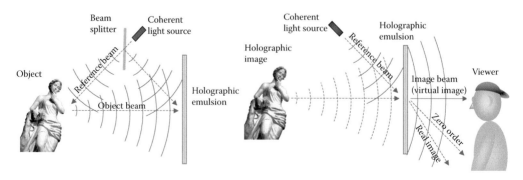

FIGURE 5.38 Recording (left) and replaying (right) a transmission hologram. Conceptual illustration.

replay (image beam). A certain amount of light is not diffracted and passes straight through the emulsion (zero order or zero mode).

Consequently, there is –in theory– no difference between perceiving the light wave that is reflected by a real object and the wavefront that is replayed by its holographic recording. In contrast to simple photographs, which can record only amplitude and wavelength information, holograms can record and reconstruct complete optical wavefronts. This is what makes holograms so unique and fascinating. The replayed holographic image appears 3D and (in contrast to many other 3D displays) it supports all depth cues .

Replaying a hologram as shown in Figure 5.38(right) creates two optical images of the same recorded object. A virtual image and a dim real image are formed simultaneously in front of the emulsion when replaying the hologram from the direction of the reference beam.

A brighter real image can be formed when replaying the hologram from the opposite direction of the zero order (called a *conjugate beam*). Alternatively, the emulsion can simply be flipped. As explained in Section 3.4 at page 64, light rays physically intersect in real images, thus they can be projected onto screens. This principle is used in some approaches that apply real optical holographic images for 3D shape measurement. Ultrafast holographic cameras (25 µs), for instance, have been modified to allow capturing 3D objects, such as faces [43] or bodies [90]. A fast-pulsed laser with short exposure time is used in these cases for holographic recording free of motion artifacts. The depth information is then reconstructed by replaying the hologram. Topometric information is retrieved by digitizing the real holographic image being projected onto a diffuse plate. Moving the plate in the depth direction (away from the holographic plate) results in several 2D slices through the holographic image. These slices are finally combined to form the corresponding 3D surface. Note that the virtual image is orthoscopic while the real image replayed with the conjugate beam appears pseudoscopic (i.e., with reversed depth). A new approach [51] uses a high-resolution *complementary-metal-oxide-semiconductor* (CMOS) camera to record the holographic wavefront and allow a direct calculation of the surface shapes. On the processor of a high-end graphics card, this takes only seconds.

5.5.1 Optical Distortion

If the reference beams used for recording and replaying do not share exactly the same properties, such as wavelength or direction, the holographic images appear geometrically distorted. The warping of the image under these circumstances is view dependent. Thus, the recorded object does not only appear distorted, but also moves and changes its geometric appearance depending on the viewing position. This geometric imaging behavior is mathematically well understood and is explained in [54]. If we assume the holographic image is being viewed from infinity, the view-dependent properties can be neutralized, and only the parameters of recording and replaying reference waves will influence the image formation. This is explained below and is illustrated in Figure 5.39(left).

With respect to Figure 5.39(left), the following geometric laws for image formation can be defined:

With known distances of a recorded object point o (R_o), of the recording r (R_r) and of the replaying c (R_c) reference beams to the center of the emulsion, as well as the wavelengths of

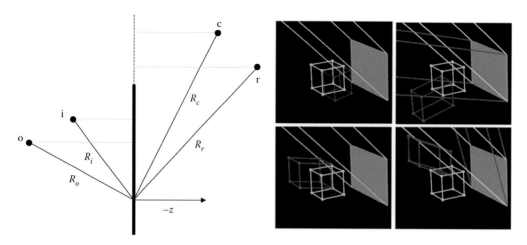

FIGURE 5.39 Geometric formation of holographic image points (left) if recording and replay reference beams differ (viewed from infinity). Simulation of image formation (right): Object recorded with 45° and 550 nm (green) reference beam, replayed from 45° with 550 nm, 400 nm (blue) and 700 nm (red), and with 400 nm from 15° and 75° [14].

recording (λ_r) and replaying (λ_c) beams,

$$\frac{1}{R_i} = \frac{1}{R_c} + \frac{\lambda_c}{\lambda_r}\left(\frac{1}{R_o} - \frac{1}{R_r}\right) \tag{5.14}$$

is the distance of the image i (R_i) from center of emulsion,

$$\frac{x_i}{R_i} = \frac{x_c}{R_c} + \frac{\lambda_c}{\lambda_r}\left(\frac{x_o}{R_o} - \frac{x_r}{R_r}\right) \tag{5.15}$$

is angle of i subtended in x direction, and

$$\frac{y_i}{R_i} = \frac{y_c}{R_c} + \frac{\lambda_c}{\lambda_r}\left(\frac{y_o}{R_o} - \frac{y_r}{R_r}\right) \tag{5.16}$$

is angle of i subtended in y direction.

It is easy to see that if recording and replaying reference beams are equal (geometrically and in wavelength), the replayed image i will appear exactly at the position of its original object o. If this is not the case, the holographic image appears geometrically distorted.

Based on this model, a numerical method has been derived that estimates the image position of recorded objects for cases in which the recording reference beam does not match the replay reference beam, and a known perspective viewing situation is assumed [14]. These principles have since been applied for reconstructing the depth of a holographic image that is replayed under different lighting conditions [34].

Note, that a hologram (i.e., the holographic emulsion) does not necessarily have to be planar. It can be (almost) arbitrarily shaped as long as it is replayed in the same way as it was recorded in order to avoid artifacts. Most popular nonplanar shapes are cylindrical or conical holograms. Furthermore, a hologram does not have be recorded on an optical film; the fringe patterns can also be embossed onto a plastic film backed with reflective aluminum foil, as is the case for the *embossed holograms* (see Section 5.3.4 at page 133) that are mass produced (e.g., for credit cards). Many different classes and types of holograms exist that vary in the way they are recoded and replayed. We have briefly mentioned them in earlier discussions on the basics of holography, and we will discuss them in a bit more detail in the context of optical holography below. For even more details on practical holography the interested reader is referred to [251].

5.5.2 Transmission Holograms

The type of hologram illustrated in Figure 5.38 on page 158 is called a *transmission hologram* because the holographic image is formed by diffraction of transmitted light. More precisely, this would be called a *laser transmission hologram* since transmission holograms that can be replayed with white light will be treated specially (will be discussed in Section 5.5.4 at page 163).

Transmission holograms are recorded with reference and object beams coming from the same side of the emulsion, and they are replayed with the reference beam and the viewer located on opposite sides. Note that if a mirror is placed behind the holographic emulsion, a transmission hologram can also be replayed from the side of the viewer. When processing the emulsion of a recorded transmission hologram, the fringes shape a diffraction grating of visible opaque and transparent areas (in nanometer scale) on the film. They cause the light of the replay beam to be diffracted during replay.

If the laser beam is explicitly divided by a beam splitter to form the reference beam and the beam that illuminates the object, this type of hologram is referred to as a *two-beam hologram*. Yet, configurations are possible where splitting the laser beam is not necessary, and the same beam can be directed toward the emulsion as well as toward the object (where it is then reflected toward the emulsion). Such holograms are called *single-beam holograms*. Note that two-beam holograms are more common since they force fewer restrictions during recording or replaying and viewing. Single-beam transmission holograms are mainly a theoretical construct and are not common in practice. Single-beam reflection holograms, however, do have a practical relevance, as we will learn in the next chapter.

5.5.3 Reflection Holograms

Reflection holograms are another class of optical holograms that differ from transmission holograms in the way they are recorded and replayed. As illustrated in Figure 5.40, reflection holograms are recoded with a reference beam and an object beam intersecting the holographic emulsion from different sides. During replay, the reference beam and the viewer are located on the same side of the emulsion.

If the emulsion is thick, the recorded fringe patterns are stored in layers. As we already know, thick holograms are referred to as *volume holograms* (see Section 5.3.6 at page 133). In case the object beam and the reference beam intersect a thick emulsion from the same side (as would be the case for transmission holograms) the fringe layers are approximately

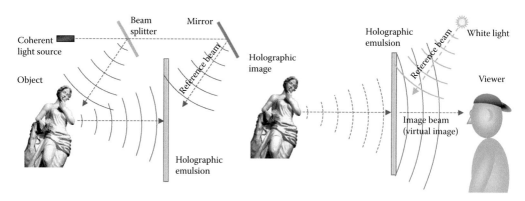

FIGURE 5.40 Recording (left) and replaying (right) a reflection hologram. Conceptual illustration.

perpendicular to the surface of the emulsion (Figure 5.12(left) on page 135). If, however, object beam and reference beam intersect the emulsion from different sides (as for reflection holograms) they form an interference pattern that creates different layers of fringe patterns that are approximately parallel to the plane of the emulsion (Figure 5.12(right) on page 135). Note that if the incident angles of object and reference beams relative to the emulsion plane are equal, the fringe patterns will be perfectly parallel or perpendicular to the emulsion plane, as indicated in Figure 5.15 on page 138. If this is not the case, they will be slightly tilted, relative to the difference between both angles. In both cases, the spacing of the fringe patterns also depends on the incident angles of reference and object beams (as well as on their wavelengths).

Thus, when replaying such a reflection hologram, Bragg diffraction (see Section 5.3 at page 127) becomes the dominating factor for image formation. While images are produced by transmission in the former case, they are created by reflection in the latter case. However, since the recorded dark fringe patterns absorb most of the light, the efficiency of such a reflection hologram is rather low. It can be increased through bleaching as part of the developing process, which turns the dark fringe patterns into silver bromide, showing a high refraction index, higher than the emulsion's gelatin. This leads to alternating layers of plain gelatin (with lower refraction index) and gelatin with silver bromide fringes (with higher refraction index). During replay, the layers act as weak mirrors. The result is called a *phase hologram* or *phase grating* and it modulates the optical distance within the recording material. In contrast to this, *amplitude holograms* or *amplitude gratings* modulate the absorption of the material.

In the case of reflection holograms, the Bragg condition (see Section 5.3 at page 127) becomes so powerful that they can be replayed with white light point sources. Using white light instead of monochromatic laser light, reflection holograms select only a narrow band of wavelengths, leading to a mainly monochrome image (Figure 5.41).

The color of the image is mainly dependent on the wavelength of the recording beam, but can be influenced later by modifying the emulsion's thickness through shrinking or swelling it after recording (see Section 5.5.5 at page 165). Such a hologram is referred to as a *white-light reflection hologram*.

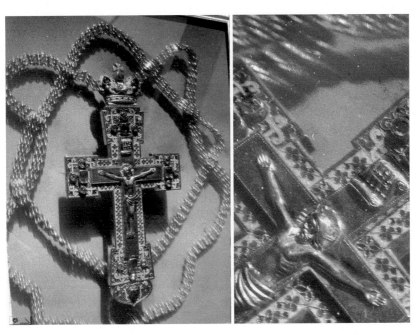

FIGURE 5.41   Photograph and close-up of a white-light reflection hologram.

Single-beam and two-beam configurations exist for reflection holograms. In a single-beam configuration, the undistorted laser beam is directed to the emulsion from one side (this is the reference beam), and is transmitted by the emulsion toward an object located on the other side, where it is reflected back to the emulsion (this forms the object beam). These types of holograms are called *Denisyuk holograms*. The real image and the zero-order beam are mainly suppressed by such holograms. Yet, for the same reasons as those for transmission holograms, two-beam configurations are more common.

5.5.4 Rainbow Holograms

Replaying laser transmission holograms with white light leads to blurred images. As explained in Section 5.5.1 at page 159, the geometric appearance of a holographic image depends on several factors, such as the angle and the wavelength of the reference beam. The latter is responsible for the blur when laser transmission holograms are replayed with white light. The reason for this is that the spectral components of the white light are diffracted at different angles at a grating.

This is illustrated in Figure 5.42. In opposition to dispersion, diffraction bends lower-frequency light waves (e.g., red) more than higher-frequency waves (e.g., blue). Remember Stephen Benton's popular rule of thumb (see Section 3.2 at page 54): RRR=red rotates radically. Since the different spectral components are diffracted at different angles, the multiple holographic images overlap in an unregistered way, which this causes the blur.

One possible way to overcome this is to replay the holographic image only from a very small portion of the holographic emulsion. As explained earlier, each portion of the holographic film replays a full image of the recorded scene.

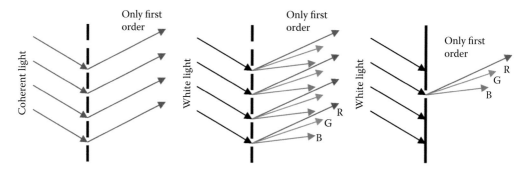

FIGURE 5.42 Larger wavelengths (e.g., red) of white light diffract more than shorter wavelengths (e.g., blue). At the grating of a laser transmission hologram, this causes the replay of multiple, unregistered images that in total lead to a blurred image.

Masking the film physically with a very narrow horizontal slit aperture, as shown in Figure 5.42(right), would prevent replaying overlapping images, and consequently prevent blur. Yet, the holographic image still consists of differently diffracted spectral components of the white light. The slit masks only prevent the creation of multiple such images at different grating slits that would overlap in the end and cause blur (Figure 5.42(center)). In fact, the smaller the slit, the sharper the replayed image. This image will not appear monochromatic, but contains all spectral components from red (top) to blue (bottom) light. Because of this property, such holograms are called *rainbow holograms*.

Rainbow holograms have three distinct characteristics: First, they are (normally) transmission holograms that can be viewed under white light. Second, they replay the holographic image focused and rainbow colored. Third, they do not replay a full parallax image, as is the case for the other hologram types. This is because the horizontal mask slit prevents replaying multiple overlapping images in a vertical direction. Consequently, the vertical parallax portion of the recorded scene cannot be replayed. The horizontal slit replays the horizontal parallax only, and therefore it belongs to the group of *horizontal parallax only* (HPO) holograms. HPOs prevent depth perception if viewed with both eyes aligned on the vertical emulsion direction. Viewing holograms with both eyes aligned in a horizontal direction relative to the film is most common. Thus, HPOs are still applicable.

To record a rainbow hologram in a single step, the recorded scene can be physically masked. In practice however, most rainbow holograms are recorded in a different way. Instead of recording a laser transmission hologram and masking it with a physical horizontal slit, the slit mask is holographed in a two-step process (Figure 5.43). In the first step, a conventional laser transmission hologram is recorded as explained in Section 5.5.2 at page 161 (Figure 5.43(right)). This is called the *master hologram* or H1. The H1 is flipped by 180° and is replayed with its conjugate beam to produce a pseudoscopic real image as explained in Section 5.5 at page 158. By doing so, the flipped H1 is physically covered by the slit mask (Figure 5.43(center)) to suppress the vertical parallax. The replayed real holographic image is then recorded in the second step into what is called the *transfer hologram*, or H2. Replaying a real image instead of a virtual image has the advantage that the H2 can be positioned either before, behind or in between it. This allows the final image to appear either in front

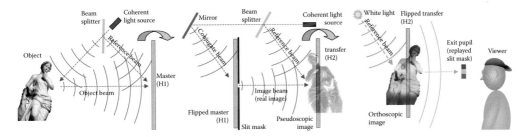

FIGURE 5.43 Two-step process of recording a rainbow hologram: record a laser transmission (master) hologram (left), flip and mask it, replay it with its conjugate beam and record the appearing pseudoscopic real image with another (transfer) hologram (center), flip the transfer hologram to produce an orthoscopic image with white light (right).

of or behind the emulsion, or even half-and-half. Finally, the H2 must be flipped again by 180° to replay an orthoscopic and focused rainbow image when illuminated with white light. Note that similar master-transfer processes exist also for reflection holograms.

When replaying the H2 of a rainbow hologram, the image of the slit mask that covered H1 will also be replayed. It appears as an exit pupil in front of the holographic plane (Figure 5.43(right)). If the viewer is located too far in front of or behind it when observing the hologram, the holographic image might partially be clipped (Figure 5.44(left)).

Illuminating a rainbow hologram with multiple, vertically aligned white light sources again creates multiple overlapping images. This can be explained with the laws of holographic image formation described in Equations 5.14–5.16. This time the angle of the replaying reference beams differ (all in a vertical direction) and cause the formation of multiple overlapping images. If positions of the light sources are carefully selected, all rainbow images overlap in such a way that geometrically corresponding wavelengths add up to white light and the final image appears slightly blurred but achromatic. This is shown in Figure 5.44(right).

5.5.5 Color Holograms

The hologram types explained so far are either monochromatic or achromatic. Of color holograms, two basically different categories exist: *true-color holograms* and *pseudo-color holograms.*

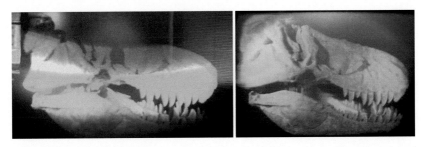

FIGURE 5.44 Rainbow hologram replayed with a single white light source (left) and with multiple, vertically aligned light sources (right).

Single exposure true-color holograms are true-color holograms that require the holographic emulsion to be sensitive to multiple wavelengths (i.e., all wavelengths that must be recorded). In this case, the laser beam that is used for recording is a composition of multiple wavelengths (e.g., red, green, blue) produced by individual monochromatic laser sources which are optically aligned (usually with beam combiners, such as half-silvered mirrors). The individual wavelengths are reflected differently from the object's surfaces, depending on its local reflectance. This is recorded by emulsion (usually a thick volume hologram to avoid cross-talk effects). Figure 5.45 illustrates such a single exposure true-color reflection hologram recorded on an 8 nm (grain size) emulsion called *ultimate film*.

Recording true-color with a single exposure requires a special emulsion that is sensitive to all recording wavelengths. Alternatively, several holograms can be recorded for individual wavelengths and combined after recording. These are called *multiexposure true-color holograms*, and they have the advantage that emulsions which are sensitive to only one wavelength can be applied. Thus, for example, the red fraction of an object is recorded with a red laser on an emulsion that is sensitive to red light (and so on for green, blue, and possibly other wavelengths). This requires multiple exposure steps and precise geometric registrations of the emulsions after recording (which are glued together). Another possible way to create a multiexposure true-color hologram is to record multiple single color (e.g., RGB) master holograms as before, and transfer them sequentially into a *rainbow transfer hologram* as explained in Section 5.5.4 at page 163. Thereby, each master contains only the image of those surface portions that reflect the corresponding wavelength. When recording the transfer hologram, the master holograms have to be aligned precisely in such a way that when being replayed as rainbow holograms, the color spectrum of each master is shifted depending on the wavelength-dependent diffraction angle (Figure 5.46). This shift causes the individual color components of each master's spatially overlapping replay wavefronts to always add up to white light (if all spectral components are present) or to an arbitrary other color, depending on the reflection from the object's surface.

Pseudocolor holograms can be produced without the need for emulsions that are sensitive to different wavelengths, but will normally not replay the true reflected colors of the recorded objects. As explained in Section 5.5.3 at page 161, the color of an image that is replayed from

FIGURE 5.45 Singleexposure true-color reflection hologram (left) with close-up (right).

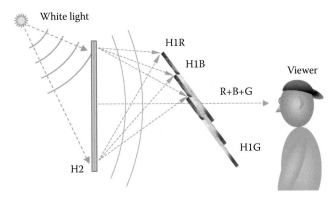

FIGURE 5.46 Multiexposure true-color rainbow hologram: The recorded masters are transferred in such a way that the spatially overlapping replay wavefronts are shifted to allow the reconstruction of all colors.

a white-light reflection hologram is dependent on the emulsion's thickness and can be modified after recording through shrinking or swelling the holographic film. This is exactly what is being done for pseudocolor holograms: Multiple master holograms of the same object are recorded on different emulsions. They are then transferred sequentially to the same film whose thickness is varied before each transfer step (i.e., by swelling the film). The thickness of film in each step determines the different color.

This produces a color hologram that in most cases has nothing to do with the true colors actually being reflected from the recorded scene. The advantage is, such holograms can be produced with conventional types of emulsions, but require a great deal of manual labor. Figure 5.47 depicts an example of a pseudocolor reflection hologram.

5.5.6 Multichannel Holograms

Multiple exposures during recording are not only useful for creating color holograms, as explained in Section 5.5.5 at page 165, they can also be used to record special effects and animations into a single hologram. As mentioned earlier, recording multiple objects sequentially into the same hologram by exposing the emulsion several times is possible. The hologram will finally replay a composition of all recorded objects simultaneously. A *multichannel hologram* is an optical hologram that has been exposed to multiple 3D objects sequentially. There are different ways of recording special effects and even animations into a single multichannel hologram, which are in general very similar (illustrated in Figure 5.48). Let's assume, as an example, that three master holograms are recorded, of three different scenes (e.g., a red point, a green point, and a blue point, as shown in Figure 5.48). Cutting the three masters into equal thirds, pasting (edge to edge) the pieces (R, G, and B) together, transferring the result into a transfer hologram and replaying it would lead to the fact that the red point would be visible when viewing the hologram from the left, the green point would be visible when viewing it from the center and the blue point would become visible when moving toward the right. The different points are visible in the exit pupils formed by the real images of the three master holograms. Since their positions can freely be chosen

FIGURE 5.47 Pseudocolor hologram.

during the transfer step, the exit pupils do not necessarily have to be located on the holographic plane (as indicated in Figure 5.5.6), but also in front of it. Seeing through the exit pupils is similar to seeing through adjacent windows (whereby a completely different scene can appear behind each window). If the viewer is located too far away from the exit pupils, multiple windows (and the different scenes behind them) might be visible simultaneously. This also happens during transitions from one exit pupil to another. Consequently, it is a good idea to (optically) offset the exit pupils and bring them closer to the viewer. A two-step transfer recording process makes this possible, as explained in Section 5.5.4 at page 163. The effect that would be visible in our example (Figure 5.48) is that the point changes color from red, to green, to blue when looking at the hologram and moving from left to right. Of course, the individual channels (i.e., the recorded masters) can contain different types of content, ranging from completely different objects and scenes to animation effects with the same object or scene, such as shown in Figure 5.48. Each channel is an individual hologram and consequently replays a full 3D image.

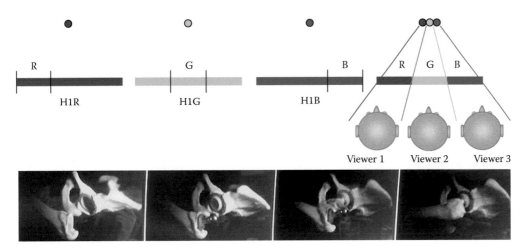

FIGURE 5.48 Multichannel hologram: principle (top) and example for three channels showing an animation of the installation of a hip joint endoprosthesis (bottom).

Another possibility for recording multichannel holograms is to –instead of cutting multiple masters apart– cover a single master with an aperture mask and shift this mask step-by-step through multiple exposures. Thus, different contents are recorded directly on different portions of a single master hologram. Finally, the master is transferred into a transfer hologram, as with the first method. Note that both techniques do not require the transfer hologram to be planar. In fact, many cylindrical multichannel holograms exist that allow the viewer to walk around them. Yet, the more channels that are recorded and replayed with a multichannel hologram in horizontal direction, the more of the horizontal parallax will be suppressed in each view. The masters can also be masked vertically (i.e., with horizontal strip masks) to create a multichannel hologram. In this case, the horizontal parallax is fully preserved, but the animation effects appear through the vertical shift of the observer.

5.5.7 Holographic Stereograms

As well as of recording an optical hologram of a 3D object as outlined above, holograms of 2D pictures can be captured in exactly the same way. Replaying a hologram of a picture would, of course, lead to a visible 2D image of it (or a 3D image of its image plane, if the picture is not located on the holographic plane). Recording a two-channel hologram of a stereo pair of photographs would replay one photograph on one side, and the other photograph on the other side of the transfer hologram. A viewer looking straight at the replayed images –having one eye located on the left side and the other one located on the other side– would perceive both images simultaneously, but separately for each eye. Since the two recorded photographs are a stereo pair, the viewer would perceive the depth of the photographed scene based purely on a stereopsis effect (see Section 4.4 at page 107). As for all such stereoscopic viewing techniques, this leads to a good depth perception mainly because of retinal disparities and convergence of the eyes, but accommodation (i.e., focus) is only possible for

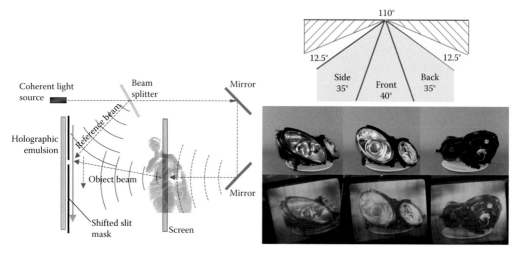

FIGURE 5.49 Holographic stereogram: Basic recording principle (left), and example (right) – 360 perspectives photographs compressed into three individual viewing zones with a total of 110°.

the 2D image planes of the recorded photographs. It is easy (at least theoretically, not so much in practice) to go one step further, from a two-channel hologram of two photographs to a multichannel hologram of multiple photographs. The recording process is exactly as explained in Section 5.5.6 at page 167. The main difference, however, is that only 2D images are replayed, yet they can be perspective images supporting stereoscopic depth perception (single viewer for two channels, and multiviewer for multiple channels). In the case that 2D images, such as photographs, are multiplexed, these holograms are referred to as *holographic stereograms* [17]. Since digital images are recorded (photographs or computer generated), they are also called *digital holograms*.

Holographic stereograms can be recorded as illustrated in Figure 5.49(left). The 2D images are displayed on a screen. This can, for example, be a transparent LCD panel without backlight that transmits laser light, a diffuse screen onto which the image is projected using laser light, or a DMD panel reflecting the image formed by laser light. Of course, the holographic recording process still requires the object beam and reference beam to be coherent.

Each time a new image is displayed on the screen, it is recorded through a slit mask that is shifted by the slit's width for every individual exposure. If the images are perspective images, the slit is aligned vertically (and moved horizontally), and many channels are recorded, this will create a fully autostereoscopic multiview horizontal parallax only (HPO) stereogram [72]. If the aperture mask forms a rectangular opening that is shifted in both directions rather than a slit that is moved in only one direction, this will allow recording a *full parallax (FP) stereogram* [157]. In this case, the displayed images must also provide vertical perspectives with respect to their corresponding exposure area on the holographic film. The result is an autostereoscopic image that does not suppress the vertical parallax as in the HPO case.

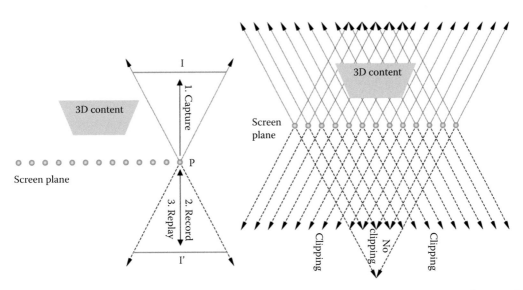

FIGURE 5.50 The holographic stereogram principle taken to its limit: capturing, recording, and replaying all possible light rays – for one point (left) and for all points (right) on the emulsion.

While HPO stereograms are similar to autostereoscopic parallax displays, FP stereograms can be related to autostereoscopic integral images (Section 9.4 at page 373). Instead of applying an aperture mask for recording different channels, a lens optics can be used for focusing the image that is displayed on the screen onto a particular region of the film during exposure. In many cases the film itself is moved instead of the optics for recording. Because of a similarity to print technology, these recording devices are sometimes referred to as *holographic printers*.

Figure 5.50 takes this principle to its limit: placing a camera at position P and capturing a photograph in step one would record all light rays that are reflected or emitted by the scene and would focus them in the optical center of the camera. The recorded image I can be flipped (I') and can be recorded to the area of the holographic emulsion at P in step two. When replaying this fraction in step three, exactly the same light rays that have been recorded will be reproduced. This is illustrated in Figure 5.50(left). Figure 5.50(right) shows what happens if this is repeated for all (infinitely small) points on the holographic plane: all light rays that are reflected or emitted by the scene and intersect the holographic emulsion will be captured and reproduced. Due to a clipping at the boundaries of the emulsion, not all ray possibilities can be generated for these areas. However, the triangular area in the center will replay the full scene description. In computer graphics, this light ray representation is sometimes called *light field* [174] (see Section 3.6 at page 87).

The advantage of holographic stereograms in contrast to conventional optical holograms is that an arbitrary content can be recorded into a hologram. Everything that can be displayed in an image is possible, while traditional holography is limited to physical objects that can be set up in a holographic studio. In contrast to this, holographic stereograms can contain video footage (recorded indoors or outdoors), photographs, and even completely synthetic computer graphics, potentially showing physically impossible content. Besides perspective images, arbitrary animations can also be recorded in holographic stereograms.

Figure 5.49(right) shows an example of a holographic stereogram of a car's headlight. It was generated by taking 360 perspective photographs from different angles (in 0.5 degree steps to cover a 110° total viewing zone plus two 35° clipping areas, head-light was rotated on a turntable). The perspective photographs were multiplexed into different subzones (40° = 80 images for the front view +2 x 35° = 140 images for the side and rear views +2 x 12.5° = 50 images to fill the partially visible clipping area outside the 110° total viewing zone +2 x 22.5° = 90 images to fill the invisible clipping area outside the 110° total viewing zone). Consequently, three different partial views (front, rear, and side) can be observed by moving within the total viewing zone of 110°.

Recent developments in *photorefractive polymeric materials* have enabled the creation of self-developing and rewritable holographic films. Recorded diffraction gratings decay fast in such materials, especially under illumination or when being rewritten with a new grating (this erases the previously recorded grating). Using recording beams that are spatially multiplexed with a microlens array, for instance, it is now possible to update the holographic images every two seconds [37]. For color holograms, three different sub-holograms are recorded at different reference angles. They are then simultaneously replayed from these reference angles with differently colored LEDs (red, green, blue for full color). Since relatively fast rewriting and replaying can occur simultaneously from the film side that is opposite from the viewer, photorefractive polymers and adequate scanners are a true alternative to classical computer-generated holographic display systems, as discussed in Section 9.6 at page 399. If we consider that a set of perspective 2D images are transmitted or broadcasted each video frame, and are scanned quickly onto the film for displaying a holographic 3D image video frame, we also see the potential of this technology for future 3DTV systems.

5.5.8 Digital Volumetric Holograms

Digital volumetric holograms [121] (not to be confused with volume holograms) are a special form of multichannel holograms. Similarly to holographic stereograms, image content can be recorded and replayed by multiplexing the exposure process. However, instead of recording multiple images into individual portions of the emulsion –either horizontal/vertical slits for HPO or rectangular areas for FP– the whole emulsion is exposed multiple times to different full images.

For doing this, the holographic emulsion is not covered by an aperture mask during recording. Instead the screen is moved away from the emulsion for each exposure step. During each step, one single image is displayed in the screen, which is recorded on the holographic film (compare Figure 5.51(left)). As for multiple exposures when recording real objects (e.g., see Sections 5.5.5 or 5.5.6), all recordings will be visible simultaneously when replaying the final result. In the case of digital volumetric holograms, a series of stacked 2D images will appear. If the recorded images are the corresponding slice images of a volumetric dataset (e.g., from *computer tomography* (CT) or *magnetic resonance imaging* (MRI) techniques), such a dataset can be stored on and displayed with a holographic film (see Figure 5.51(left)).

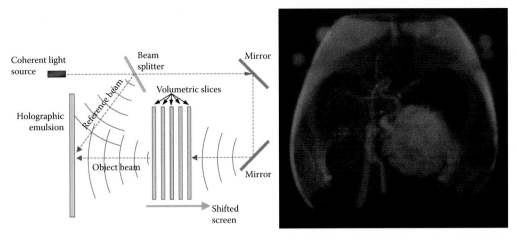

FIGURE 5.51 Digital volumetric holograms: basic recording principle (left) and example (right).

5.6 SUMMARY

We have seen that holographic techniques are not limited to static (museum) display applications but also offer a lot of possibilities for optics and electronic display technology.

The reason why we have discussed holography to this extent is that optical holograms represent a good reference on the search for the ultimate 3D display technology of the future. An optimal 3D display should produce an optical image of an object or a scene that cannot be distinguished from the optical image that the object or the scene produces by reflecting light. It should also support an infinite number of viewers, perspectives, and viewing distances simultaneously and without any delay. All of this has been possible with optical holograms for almost 40 years! One essential additional requirement, however, is still missing. That is the capability of displaying 3D images interactively with holograms. Therefore, we have been seeking alternatives for almost the same period of time. Many of these alternatives (most of them are explained in Chapter 9) support interactive and real-time presentations of 3D images, but none of them reaches the complexity and the completeness of optical holograms even closely.

We will see in upcoming chapters that the holographic principles do not only play a role for image-forming elements of all kinds, being applied for spatial-screen displays and near-eye displays, but that it also becomes more and more important for image processing and encoding.

So while the hype about the possibilities of optical holography may have faded during the last 40 years, the potential of holographic principles is still far from being fully explored.

CHAPTER 6

Display Basics

6.1 INTRODUCTION

In the previous three chapters we explained the physics, optics, and physiology basic to the functioning of displays. However, there is more that needs to be considered in order to get a full picture. In addition to optics, for example, electronics plays an important role in display technology. The display electronics is mainly responsible for digital signal processing and for driving optical elements. But the assembly of optical, electronic, and possibly mechanical parts is also important, and can be as challenging as optical design. Assembly has to be designed well to give displays small form factors and to deal with other less obvious challenges, such as electromagnetic and thermal constraints. Many different components are tightly packed into display housings and some of them are not even used directly for image generation, as is the case for touch-screen technology. Finally, what are the criteria that can be used for objectively describing the capabilities (and with that, the quality and the application fields) of individual displays?

In this chapter we will explain the remaining fundamentals and general principles of display technology beyond the physics, optics, and physiology, which can be widely applied in the context of the large pallet of display approaches that will be presented in the following chapters.

Section 6.2 first treats fundamental display measures such as resolution, speed, brightness, contrast, and dynamic range or angular range. Then we will explain in Section 6.3 at page 193 how colors and intensities are produced in general, and how this information can be represented in typical image and video formats. Basic signal and image processing related to displays will be our next topic, in Section 6.4 at page 202. Here, we will learn more about signal transmission and sampling, and various image processing operations (like antialiasing, resizing, or deinterlacing). Section 6.5 at page 215 briefly reviews fundamental display electronics, such as semiconductors, multiplexing, and passive and active matrix systems. Finally, in Section 6.6 at page 224, we will describe how different display components, such as lighting, filters and coatings, driving and image processing electronics, and touch-screen technology, can play together when they are assembled in one housing.

6.2 FUNDAMENTAL MEASURES

In the following sections, we will explain several fundamental measures that are features of different displays. They relate directly to the properties of human visual perception, as discussed in Chapter 4.

6.2.1 Resolution

Most display types are *raster-scanning displays*, reproducing pictures as a matrix of picture elements (pixels) arranged in rectangular coordinates. These pixels are set to different colors and brightnesses, thereby forming the image. In most practical cases, these values are written sequentially line by line, or "scanned" (Figure 6.1), as with laser scanners (raster type) or cathode ray tubes (CRT). In principle, however, the image may first be written into a storage layer within the display panel, providing continuous signals to the single pixels for a frame duration, as, for example, in LC displays. Though the usual application of raster scanning is line by line, it may be done in any other order, including random writing of single pixels (random stroke display).

The number and size of the pixels determine the amount of information that can be shown, and also the maximum size for a display to be perceived with a crisp, smooth appearance (Figure 6.2).

Vector displays are a less frequently used type of display. These draw images with contour lines (Figure 6.3). The most common vector displays are vector laser scanners and certain applications of CRTs. The images generated have no solid areas (unless filled by many

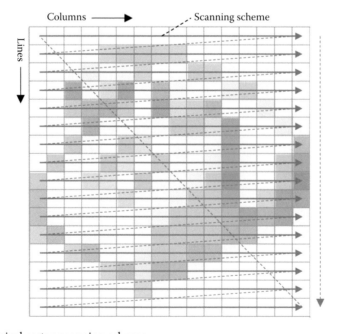

FIGURE 6.1 Typical raster-scanning scheme.

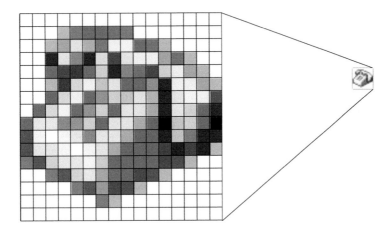

FIGURE 6.2   Raster displays: pixels merging into an image at sufficient distance.

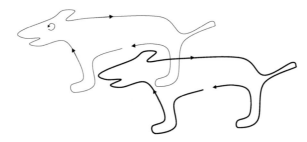

FIGURE 6.3   Vector displays draw images by contour lines.

parallel lines as with a raster image). Common applications include light show displays, oscilloscopes, and radar screens (including the vector display of numerical digits).

Radar screens use afterglowing phosphors, so they store the image for some time.

Older radar screens, for example, use beam deflections starting from the screen center with each radar pulse emitted, at an angle synchronized with the rotation of the radar antenna. This way, the outward deflection is proportional to the running time of the radar pulse. The beam intensity is modulated by the returning echoes. Thus, any echo creates a bright spot on the screen corresponding to its geographical position. With an afterglowing phosphor, a complete and steady picture emerges.

A newer application of the vector display principle can be found in certain near-eye displays with laser scanners (virtual retina displays). These are addressed in Chapter 10.

The resolution of any display can be expressed as

- lines or columns (absolute resolution),

- pixel size or density (dots per inch, as used in printing applications),

- angular resolution (the viewing angle a single pixel occupies, usually measured in arc minutes, equaling $1/60°$).

Angular resolution is of special importance for near-eye displays, because their screen size is virtual and display crispness can best be evaluated by comparing the display's angular resolution to that of the eye (approximately 1 *arcmin* at best). One arcmin implies that the smallest item resolved by the eye can measure about 1/3000 of the viewing distance.

The resolution of a vector display is given in terms of line thickness (similar to the pixel size of a raster display).

The resolution of a raster display is usually expressed in pixels per lateral length. With lenses and with analog photography or film, line pairs per mm (*lp/mm*) are commonly used. Line pairs are the maximum number of adjacent black and white line pairs still visible. In the case of raster displays, this equals half the number of lines, or pixels (50 lp/mm = 100 pixels/mm). This difference has to be considered when comparing analog and digital photography standards.

Matrix displays do not only have resolution values for the horizontal and vertical direction, but also for the diagonal. If we understand resolution to be the maximum number of separable black and white lines, the diagonal may be $\sqrt{2}$ times better than in the h/v directions but at a lower contrast, as in Figure 6.4 (middle), or it may be $\sqrt{2}$ times worse but at high contrast, as in Figure 6.4 (right). Obviously this is not a trivial issue and has been treated in many papers concerning advanced spatial filtering.

Display screens are characterized by their pixel count in horizontal and vertical direction, their size (usually the diagonal extension), and their aspect ratio, giving the relation between horizontal and vertical extension. To simplify matters, usually most parameters conform to certain standard formats (VGA, PAL, etc.) and only the display's diagonal size is further needed for a full characterization.

Anamorphic is the term to describe pictures whose vertical and horizontal pixel sizes are different. The first anamorphic pictures were wide-screen movies recorded on standard format film, the horizontal compressed with cylindrical lenses. Another example is 16:9 encoding of TV pictures in the same 720×576 pixel format formerly used for 4:3 (which also had been a bit anamorphic, as 4:3 normally would translate to 768×576). Indeed, many usual formats have nonsquare pixels.

Projected displays often allow for a large range of projected image sizes, so the horizontal and vertical pixel counts are the extent of what is usually understood as resolution.

Another important feature of displays is their refresh rate (or temporal resolution), in other words, how many times per second a new image is drawn on the screen. With CRT displays, a low frequency may cause a flickering image. Frequencies below approximately

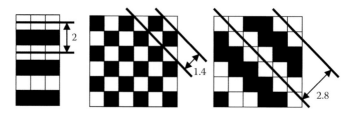

FIGURE 6.4 Raster displays: orthogonal vs. diagonal resolution.

TABLE 6.1   A Selection of Current
Computer-Display Formats

Name	Resolution (H × V)	Aspect Ratio
VGA	640 × 480	4:3
SVGA	800 × 600	4:3
XGA	1024 × 768	4:3
WXGA	1365 × 768	16:9
SXGA	1280 × 1024	5:4
WSXGA	1680 × 1050	16:10
UXGA	1600 × 1200	4:3
WUXGA	1920 × 1200	16:10
QXGA	2048 × 1536	4:3

50 Hz for TV or 75 Hz for computer displays (which cover a larger peripheral field of view) are perceived as flickering (see Section 4.2.3 at page 93). LCDs, which are currently most often used in flat panels, usually have no dark phase between pictures, so flickering is not refresh-rate dependent. For a fluent display of motion pictures however, the refresh rate is very important (Section 4.5 at page 119).

While computer displays may, in principle, have any format and especially any refresh rate (see Table 6.1 for an overview of common formats), TV recording requires more conformity. This has been inevitable because of the fact that before digital technology, format conversions were extremely difficult. This applied not only to frame-rate conversions – still intricate even with digital technology, but also to size conversions. Apart from this, almost any image resizing involves interpolations between neighboring pixels, hence loss of crispness, and frame rate conversions are often accompanied by a certain amount of stuttering or speed errors even today.

6.2.1.1 Digital vs. Film

Analog pictures usually are haunted by graininess. The more sensitive the film, the coarser the grain. Grain in analog pictures looks very similar to signal or pixel noise in digital pictures. Good digital cameras today surpass analog equipment in terms of light sensitivity and reduced noise.

In comparing movie film with TV, resolution as well as grain have to be considered. The maximum resolution of an analog camera, usually only achievable with very insensitive film, remains theory under almost any practical circumstances. The crispest color film (Kodachrome, discontinued) has about 50 lp/mm. Practical averages with most film types are only half as much. This indicates that 16 mm film (image format 10.25 × 7.5 mm), has to be used for TV reports. 35 mm film (image format 22 × 16 mm) usually is worse than HDTV, especially as the digital picture mercilessly reproduces film grain. Analog motion pictures are nowadays often treated with *temporal noise filtering*, a method exploiting similarities between subsequent pictures, to achieve a clean picture that does not show grain noise on high-resolution displays.

6.2.2 Interlacing

In the early days of TV technology, bandwidth was precious, because all transmission signals had to share the same "ether". Until today's computer technology had been invented, reducing bandwidth by compression was not possible. Image information had to be transmitted sequentially line by line and reproduced on a screen exactly in the same timely manner as it had been recorded. One simple measure, however, reduced bandwidth by half, without major disadvantages: transmitting the even lines in one image (*half-image* or *frame*), and the odd lines in the next (Figure 6.5). At a frame rate of 50 or 60 Hz, the image flickering is inconsequential enough to not be perceived, at least at a normal TV viewing distance. The lines are tiny enough that their alternating occurrence is also not perceived at that distance. This technique, called *Interlacing*, therefore enables high-resolution pictures while allowing high frame rates. Non-interlaced pictures (with sequential lines in a single frame) are called *progressive*.

Interlaced formats may disappear sooner or later, since they offer no advantage with digital image transmission: the compression formats used (see Section 6.4.8 at page 210) exploit similarities between subsequent frames, which increase with frame rate, thus only a little more bandwidth is needed for twice the frame rate.

Nevertheless, a large part of any archival material available is interlaced and will be used for a long time to come. Moreover, even the current European *High-definition TV* (HDTV) standard is interlaced, with 1920 pixels by 1080 lines, 50 half-frames per second. Therefore, interlacing will remain an important issue in display technology for many years.

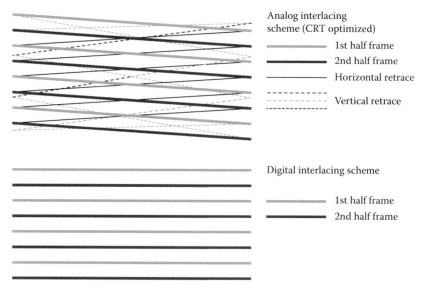

FIGURE 6.5 Typical interlacing schemes. The retrace lines in the analog scheme (top) are referring to beam retracing in a CRT. Note that the beam does not do an instant vertical retracing. This happens while several horizontal lines are written, which are set to below black level to hide them. The digital scheme (bottom) needs no retrace lines.

Note that digital interlaced encoding (Figure 6.5) can be done with the *top field first* (TFF), or the *bottom field first* (BFF). Most formats (MPEG2 with DVDs, see Section 6.4.8 at page 210) use TFF, but the *Digital Video* (DV) format used in the first digital camcorders uses BFF.

With flat-panel displays and their rigid pixel raster, new picture-size standards, and the frequently arising necessity to resize images, interlaced formats became a major problem. Even though fast LCD displays having exactly the required 1920 × 1080 resolution (*full HD* resolution) are cheaply available now and could, in principle, also display interlaced pictures, this is not done except for rare ALiS displays (see Section 7.6.3.1 at page 272). But even then, the question remains, how to handle resolutions not native to the display, such as any low-definition material.

Resizing an interlaced image can be done by resizing each half-frame separately and retrieving the lines for a resized interlaced picture from those frames. This avoids any problems that could occur from deinterlacing. Yet, as stated, this doesn't help with most of today's flat-panel displays, because they are not designed for an interlaced format.

Interlaced pictures can, however, be converted to progressive pictures, by image processing. We get back to this in Section 6.4.9 at page 212.

6.2.3 TV Standards

Most digital formats are related to or derived from those used for TV, so they may be referred to simply as "*TV standards*" (although there are others, digital cinema, for example).

We will give an overview of the most important standards, because they are directly related to display design.

Important early television standards are PAL (*Phase Alternating Line*), SECAM (*Séquentiel couleur à mémoire*) and NTSC (*National Television Systems Committee*). PAL and SECAM use the same raster size and scan frequencies but different color transmission methods. NTSC is different in both respects. Usually today, "PAL" (or "European standard") is the term for 625 lines 50 Hz (25 full frames/sec) interlaced, and "NTSC" (or "US standard") is the term for 525 lines 60 Hz (exactly, 29.97 full frames/sec interlaced; see Section 6.2.2 at page 180).

The (half-frame) image frequency was chosen to be the same as the power-line frequency; with early tube-based electronics it would have been very expensive to filter the power-supply voltage sufficiently from the signal path in order to avoid any flickering. There were other standards such as the British 405 or French 819 lines, but those have long been abandoned.

PAL and NTSC have rather similar line frequencies (15625 Hz vs. 15750 Hz). Line frequencies could not be chosen arbitrarily high, because problems with circuitry, inductances and so forth would multiply. This became another reason to use interlacing.

Common to all these early standards is a relation between line and image frequency being a multiple of small prime numbers. This is due to the fact that mother frequency generators had to be realized with several frequency dividers of simple design (analog synchronized oscillators). Examples are $625 = 5*5*5*5$, $525 = 5*7*3*5$.

In analog standards, many of the lines, as well as the beginning and the end of each line, had to be reserved for the *retrace time* (the electron beam in a CRT returning for the next line or frame). Synchronization for proper picture reproduction was done by transmitting levels below "black" within these retrace times (see the oscillogram in Figure 1.3).

18 lines of the 625 were set aside for vertical retrace with PAL, for example. The large tolerances of CRTs also required a considerable bleed for the image borders. Only about 580 lines reliably remained in the image area with PAL. 576 lines were finally standardized for the digital version. For NTSC, 480 lines became standard.

The first implementations of digital TV used square pixels, resulting in 768 horizontal pixels for PAL and 640 for NTSC, given the 4:3 aspect ratio (horizontal:vertical size) of the images. The first computer display standard (*VGA*, 640 × 480) was directly derived from NTSC, as ordinary TVs were often used for computer displays at the time.

Meanwhile, today, practically all digital formats encode PAL as well as NTSC with 720 horizontal pixels. This includes DV, MJPEG, MPEG (DVD or digital satellite), AVC (*Advanced Video Coding*). The pixels in these cases are not exactly square of course.

Other digital formats used in the interim had 704 or 480 horizontal pixels. The latter value reflected the fact that analog material in almost any case had less horizontal than vertical resolution, due to bandwidth compromises. This format appeared in SVCD (*Super Video Compact Disc*) as well as (sometimes until today) in satellite transmission.

Images with 16:9 aspect ratio have widely replaced the older 4:3 formats. They are either encoded using the full area (*anamorphic encoding*), or with black areas at the top and bottom of the frame.

Current HDTV formats have square pixels as they were defined for 16:9 aspect ratio from the beginning. Usual cinema film formats are *widescreen* (1.85:1) or *Cinemascope* (2.35:1). These are often encoded in TV formats both anamorphic and with black areas at the same time. 16:9 in comparison equals about 1.78:1.

Completing the chaos, many TV sets from the transition age between low- and high-definition TV had arbitrary native resolutions, (e.g., 1320 × 768 or 1280 × 768), with the odd result that even the US HD standard of 1280 × 720 could be displayed only with scaling, hence interpolating pixels and reducing crispness (leaving black borders might be better in this case).

Table 6.2 on page 182 gives an overview of currently used TV formats. Figure 6.6 shows a size comparison (for equal pixel resolution) of these formats. These give an impression of the respective display sizes required for equal resolution.

TABLE 6.2   Current TV Standards

Name	Resolution (H × V)	Refresh Rate	Aspect Ratio
PAL (625/50)	720 × 576	50 i	4:3 or 16:9
NTSC (525/60)	720 × 480	60 i	4:3 or 16:9
720 line HDTV	1280 × 720	30, 50 or 60 p	16:9
Full HD	1920 × 1080	50 i or p, 60 i or p	16:9
UHD	3840 × 2160	50 p, 60 p, . . .?	16:9
		i = interlaced; p = progressive	

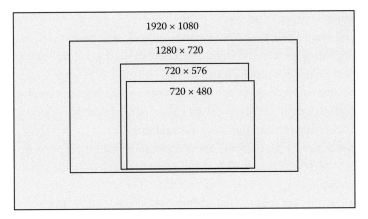

FIGURE 6.6   Size comparison of current TV standards.

For cinema applications, common resolutions also are 4 K (4096 × 2160) or 5 K (5120 × 2880). Progressive frame rates of 50 Hz or more are also gaining grounds in film production.

6.2.3.1   The Kell Factor

Early TV standards had analog signal processing line by line, but in effect, the line raster itself – the vertical, that is – was a fixed raster, just as in digital TV. The analog signal can transport image detail at any positions (no raster), so there are no aliasing effects and detail can always be transported up to the limit given by the bandwidth. In the vertical, image detail fitting to the line raster is transported well, while otherwise it suffers, possibly up to complete annihilation. The effective vertical resolution is therefore lower than the vertical, and without means of prefiltering (as it was in the analog age), nothing can be done about it.

Having different effective horizontal and vertical resolutions, though, makes little sense. The resolution difference was determined by tests with human viewers. In 1934, Raymond D. Kell and his associates determined a value of 0.64. Later measurements led to slightly higher values. Consequently, the bandwidth of a 625 line/50 Hz TV signal, for example, was chosen to be 5 MHz, instead of about 7 MHz as would have been appropriate without the Kell factor. This is also one reason for choosing only 720 pixels horizontal resolution instead of 768 pixels for the digital version of the same signal (actually still too much).

While the Kell factor for analog systems is history, its underlying principles still reappear in many aspects of signal processing even in the digital age. Owing to the fixed pixel raster, a similar factor – of about 0.8 . . . 0.9 – can be found for digital systems as well. Here, it is not a ratio between horizontal and vertical resolution, but a ratio between the maximum resolution possible and the real resolution achievable without disturbing aliasing and Moiré effects. With digital systems, advanced filtering techniques allow to extend the resolution limits close to the maximum (also see Section 6.4.5 on page 208). Using a higher-resolution system for the image recording than for the final film allows for an even more efficient postprocessing. The improvements in the final image are significant.

6.2.3.2 Eye Resolution and Displays

Raster displays will show their best performance only if their resolution, respective of their size and the distance they are viewed from, are tuned so their pixels are just melting together (i.e., have a size just below eye resolution).

With a distance too small or a screen too big, single pixels become visible, destroying the impression of a natural image. In the opposite case, not all detail provided by the display can be seen and the image appears smaller and less realistic.

The eye's maximum resolution of one arcmin equals a resolution of about 570 pixels on a screen at distance d and height $d/6$. This is the resolution used for classic TV standards (to be precise: 576 or 480 lines).

At 2.5 m distance, the TV screen would then have to be about 40 cm high, or 67 cm in diagonal with a 4:3 image aspect ratio. 67 cm was about the maximum size of TV tubes for decades, and with the usual viewing distance of about 3 m for home TV, we see that there was little demand for a better resolution.

A HDTV display, with typically 1080 lines, needs to have a diagonal of more than 1 m ($\approx 40''$) to show its full resolution at a normal viewing distance. This requires projection or flat-panel technology, as a CRT of this size is unacceptably heavy. Projectors, however, never became widely marketable because of their limitations in brightness and usability. So HDTV had to wait for plasma and LCD screens.

In Japan, where viewing distances usually are much smaller, HDTV made sense even with TV tubes. This is one major reason why HDTV transmissions started in Japan more than a decade before they emerged in Europe or the US.

In order to see individual scan lines or pixels on a screen separately, we would need to see the "black" between them.[*] This would require seeing twice as sharp as the line raster. Therefore, even though for utter crispness the TV would have to be at a distance to make one line equal 1 arcmin, we would have to get twice as near to see the scan lines separately.

With interlacing, however, line artifacts may occur as soon as we get below the *1 arcmin* distance. This occurs for several reasons:

- Even very small vertical eye movements may cause the lines of the half frames to merge now and then, because they are displayed at different times.

- With picture tubes, the two line rasters of the two half-frames are not always exactly aligned. Even a small mismatch causes them to merge more or less, and a raster with only half the line count appears.

With an interlaced display, we therefore have to keep a proper distance to avoid these effects. But what about computer screens?

A typical vertical computer screen resolution currently is 1080 lines, a typical viewing distance may be 70 cm, and a proper screen height for this would be 34 cm (27″ screen). With a good display, images look utterly crisp in this configuration. A short calculation

---

[*] Note that due to the soft shape of an electron beam spot, real black will not appear, but usually in a good picture tube the beam is focused well enough to make line separation visible.

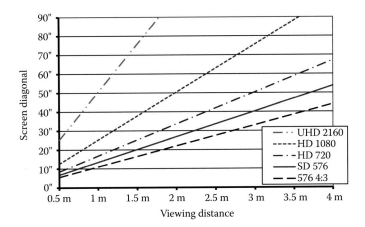

FIGURE 6.7   Best display sizes for different resolution standards and viewing distances.

however reveals that one pixel in this example equals only about 1.5 arcmin. Nevertheless, there are no interlacing artifacts, no line structure (on a good-quality screen), no flicker, and usually a perfectly crisp and antialiased image generation.

For a perfectly built display, resolution requirements may therefore be smaller than anticipated. More decisive are the quality of signal generation and presentation. We also have to take into account that the ideal maximum eye resolution is only achieved at brightness levels that are uncommonly high for home or office applications (see Section 4.2.4 on page 94).

Figure 6.7 shows the proper display sizes vs. distance for 1 arcmin resolution. The ideal display size for a certain application may differ from these values, for several reasons.

As we have argued before, the visibility of detail below 1.5 arcmin or even just below 2 arcmin depends on brightness and structure types (see Section 4.2.5 on page 95). A Kell equivalent factor of about 0.9 or less (cf. Section 6.2.3.1 on page 183) may also have to be considered. This might indicate to use bigger screen sizes. For desktop computing applications where we want to see even the smallest detail, this is a reasonable choice.

With TV applications, however, we have to consider that a large part of all media available will be of lower resolution for a long time ahead, and these look unfavorable or even awful on a screen that is too big. Even newer HD material often falls short of its full resolution, and a current display will mercilessly reveal this. A typical TV should therefore be chosen a bit smaller than the full HD resolution (1920 × 1080) figures would indicate.

The diagram shows that screen sizes grow extremely large for formats above HD. A UHD screen for a common viewing distance of 3 m would be about 150″ diagonal, or 1.9 m high and 3.4 m wide. For desktop computing with a typical distance of 70 cm and a typical requirement of 1.5 arcmin resolution, we get about 53″ (0.7 × 1.2 m), just a bit more acceptable.

Crisp and smooth motion reproduction can be more valuable than very high resolution (see Section 6.2.4 on page 186). A 1280 × 720 p (p for *progressive*) recording at 50 fps will almost always look better than a progressive "full HD" (1920 × 1080 p) recording at only 30 fps as produced by cheap cameras.

Consequently, 1280×720 p/50 is used by many European TV stations. Viewers hardly notice this at all, to a great part due to the fact that full HD equipment is commonly used for the production. Owing to the many signal conversions involved with cutting and video effects in a professional production, even digital signals lose quality. But with a smaller end format, this is not a problem anymore. The lower resolution may therefore look just as good as the original one with the quality loss. For the same reason, more recent SD material – usually produced with HD equipment already – most often looks a lot better than old material produced all in SD. Consequently, UHD – although a bit over the top for typical TV transmission and display – will at least significantly improve the production quality of normal HD video.

6.2.4 Display Resolution and Motion

Most of today's flat-panel displays have real problems not with static resolution but with motion, because they show each frame for its full duration (see Section 4.5.1 on page 119). This is an entirely display-specific effect. Other effects adding to motion blur are long frame-exposure times during recording (which entirely depends on the personal preferences of the director), and effects caused by exaggerated signal compression.

The bigger the screen gets, the easier it is to see motion blur. This may have annoying consequences: a resolution suddenly dropping to a fraction of the value for still pictures, even at the slightest motion, may destroy any illusion of realism and is catastrophic in terms of image quality.

Starting out from the above explanation of motion blur due to frame persistence (see Section 4.5.1 on page 119), we will try a quantitative assessment of the impact of motion as a function of frame frequency (if frames are flashed, the reciprocal of the flash pulse duration applies instead of frame frequency). The parameters are

- Pan time t_p (duration for a full frame width sweep, also equivalent to the time for a moving object to pass the entire screen width)

- Horizontal screen resolution a (full HD = 1920 pixels)

- Frame frequency f (if we consider flashing backlights, we can take $1/pulse\ duration$, or $1/t$, instead)

The pan itself allows for a maximum resolution b of *frame frequency**pan time ($f * t_p$). The effective resolution r results from b and the static resolution a. For the evaluation of required frame frequencies, however, the static resolution plays a lesser role. We have to consider that for fast motion, the eye needs a certain time to catch up to the moving objects, physically. This indicates that a crisp display of moving objects is only required up to speeds of $4 \ldots 2$ seconds/frame width. Moreover, imprecisions in the tracking render crisp viewing quite difficult, so a drop to half the static resolution will hardly be noticed. Figure 6.8 shows the motion resolution curves for different resolution standards, assuming half of the static resolution to be required, and a range of speeds perceived as quality levels "acceptable" through "excellent." We see that a 1280×720 display at 100 Hz is OK, while at 50 Hz,

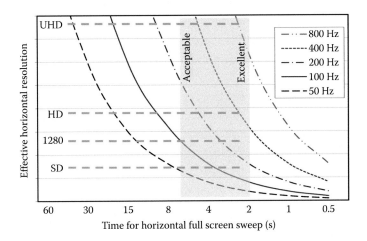

FIGURE 6.8 Display resolution: effects of motion and display speed.

it would not be acceptable anymore. Full HD or UHD will profit considerably from frame rates up to 800 Hz. Note that here we assume a proper viewing distance, matching the display resolution. Viewers sitting closer to the display may appreciate somewhat higher frame rates.

Current TV sets have claimed image frequencies up to 1600 Hz; this is by no means the real frame rate, but is a combined value of real frame rate and the effective impression caused by a flashing or scanning backlight modulation. The combined effect is expressed as the frequency of an equivalent real frame rate. Several manufacturers have invented their own names for this parameter. Some of these are (in alphabetical order and without claim of completeness): **Grundig**: Picture Perfection Rate (PPR), **LG**: Motion Clarity Index (MCI), **Philips**: Perfect Motion Rate (PMR), **Samsung**: Clear Motion Rate (CMR), **Sony**: Motionflow XR, **Thomson**: Clear Motion Index (CMI), **Toshiba**: Active Motion Rate (AMR).

"1600 Hz" will actually indicate a backlight pulse duration of 1/1600 seconds (with a usually much lower real frame rate). Frame synthesis has its limits due to processing speed. Nevertheless, it has to be accomplished up to 100 Hz at least, in order to avoid flickering with a flashing backlight.

Even the most sophisticated motion processing can however not mend all shortcomings of the media sources involved. In film production, motion is routinely blurred by intentional use of long exposure times, in order to avoid stuttering and stroboscopic effects in cinema projection. These habits are changing but slowly, since the introduction of digital cinema and 50 fps production equipment.

6.2.5 Brightness

In addition to spatial and temporal resolution, brightness is an essential display parameter.

The total visible light output of a lamp or a projector is measured in lumen, as discussed in Chapter 2. The same applies for the total emission from a projection screen or a display panel.

The perceived brightness of a projected image or a panel display depends on the total energy emitted, the emission spectrum, the size of the image, and the angular emission characteristics of the projection or display image. It is best characterized in cd/m^2 (see Section 2.4.2 at page 32).

For a good image presentation, the display should produce brightness levels at least as high as those of its surroundings. Otherwise, the image will partly or entirely disappear as the viewer's eyes adapt to these surroundings, and also as reflections of surrounding light appear on the screen, brighter than the image produced. Necessary brightness levels for displays could therefore range from below 100 cd/m^2 for projection in a dark room, to many thousand cd/m^2 for displays used in a room with bright lighting or even in daylight.

6.2.6 Contrast and Dynamic Range

Natural scenes may contain brightness levels between less than 1/1000 lux (starlight) up to 100,000 lux (sunlight), a range of more than eight orders of magnitude. With a little extra margin for high brightness, the human eye can cover almost nine orders of magnitude, though not within the same scene, as discussed in Section 4.2.4 at page 94.

In practical situations, most displays produce brightness values varying in a range of about 200:1 at best, for various reasons. First, a display surface will usually reflect more or less of the environment light, limiting the contrast achievable. An effective anti-reflective coating is required for high contrast. Even near-eye displays have similar problems, because of light reflected from the eye.

Projectors are limited in contrast, because their own light is reflected from the screen into the room and back onto the screen, lighting up any dark areas in the picture. A measure against this is the use of direction- and/or color-selective screens, such as holographic screens (see Section 5.4.9 at page 152). Furthermore, light may also be dispersed or reflected within the projector, resulting in higher black levels. Holographic screens cannot reduce this.

Also important is the proper color of the screen material itself. CRT phosphors, for example, always tended to have natural colors of light green to light gray (inactive). A dark front glass is a usual measure here to increase contrast.

Another contrast-limiting factor is signal processing. Less expensive TV electronics may use only 8-bit signal encoding (reportedly even less bits per color in some cases), allowing for a contrast of no more than 1:256 (assuming the display is linear). The number of grayscale levels that can be displayed is called *tonal resolution*. It is 256 for an 8-bit display.

An insufficient tonal resolution leads to visible brightness or color steps (fringes) in otherwise smooth, gradient areas. Sometimes, the tonal resolution has technical limits, for example, if a display panel can only process a certain number of bits per pixel. In such circumstances, *dithering* is commonly used to regain a smooth impression. This means generating a dense pattern of pixels with alternating brightness or color levels. As argued in Section 4.2.5 on page 95, dot patterns are less visible than equally wide line patterns. The visibility of fine detail also degrades with contrast. Hence, if the differences between the neighboring pixels are low, fine alternating patterns go unnoticed. Missing tonal values can therefore be generated by patterns of pixels with alternating values below and above the desired value. To avoid possible Moiré effects, random patterns can be used. Dithering is also common in other applications, such as image printing. More details about dithering are discussed in the Appendix, Section A.4 on page 520.

With LCD panels, the remaining transmissivity of pixels even in their "off" position may also limit the achievable contrast, although this feature has greatly improved with recent products.

With HDR (*high-dynamic range*) displays (see Section 7.8 at page 278), better values can be achieved. The main reason for HDR is brighter highlights, making the picture appear more brilliant. A high brightness range of the entire panel can also be useful, since it allows adaptation to very different surroundings, from rooms filled with daylight to dark theater or living rooms.

6.2.7 Gamma

Many parts of the signal chain from camera to display have (perceptually) nonlinear brightness-to-signal relations, also named contrast transfer functions. These may be applied either for brightness in general or as different functions for different primary colors.

Gamma correction is the most common compensation method for contrast nonlinearity. The most usual type of such a correction (the gamma function) is expressed as follows:

$$V_{out} = V_{in}^{\gamma} \tag{6.1}$$

where γ can be <1 (gamma compression) or >1 (gamma expansion), with $V_{in} = 0 \ldots 1$, typically.

Gamma can be interpreted as the slope of a straight line representing the output/input relation in log-log space (see Figure 6.9):

$$\gamma = \frac{\log (V_{out})}{\log (V_{in})} \tag{6.2}$$

The gamma function therefore most naturally takes into account the logarithmic brightness response of the human eye. It provides for an adaptation to different dynamic ranges by a contrast compression perceived as linear, hence, natural.

A typical example for an application of gamma correction is the nonlinearity of a CRT, typically corresponding to a gamma value of 2.2, which is precorrected by a gamma of 1/2.2 in TV standards (Figure 6.9).

Incorrect gamma is quite a common problem with many recording devices. Classical photography had many issues with it; these were addressed by special emulsions, developing procedures, or even by applying especially produced soft negatives (contrast masks). Today, many digital cameras and amateur camcorders in particular record pictures too hard (low gamma), probably because this makes pictures appear a little more "brilliant" or "sunny", but this is mere "eye candy" (Figure 6.10). Correcting this with software is quite easy but needs some attention: gamma compression of a picture always results in a lower average contrast, which is intended, but also implies lower color saturation, which is usually not intended. Correcting gamma therefore may require a color contrast adjustment as well.

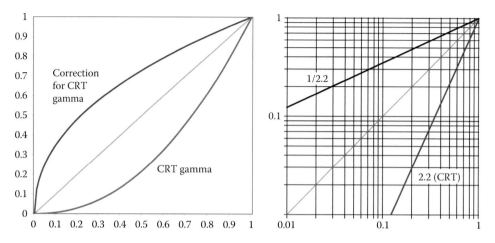

FIGURE 6.9 CRT gamma correction (TV standards), in linear (left) and logarithmic scales.

FIGURE 6.10 Typical gamma error of an amateur camcorder (left), appropriate correction (middle) and overcorrection (right).

More details about gamma correction for displays are discussed in the Appendix, Section A.1.1 on page 508.

6.2.8 Geometry

A proper reconstruction of the original image geometry is not always granted. As a matter of fact, flat-panel displays are about the only ones that are inherently linear and do not require any geometry compensation.

Optics always cause more or less geometric distortion, hence cameras are affected by this, as well as projection displays. Cathode ray tubes (CRT) are inherently nonlinear and require diverse measures, like applying static as well as dynamic magnetic fields, to get an acceptable image.

With digital image processing, distortions can also be compensated by remapping the pixel raster. This is now common in almost any electronic camera. Beneath geometry, color

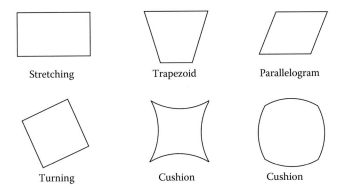

Stretching   Trapezoid   Parallelogram

Turning   Cushion   Cushion

FIGURE 6.11 Basic types of geometric image distortion.

aberrations are also compensated this way. This allows to acquire high-quality images with cheaper and more compact lenses.

Figure 6.11 shows the basic types of geometry distortions. Three-dimensional displays know additional forms of distortions (see Section 9.2.3 on page 353). With near-eye displays, another issue is field curvature (see Chapter 10).

6.2.9 Angular Range

Most displays are surface emitters, whereby the radiation density seen is a function of the angle under which the surface is observed (see Lambert emitter, Section 2.4.1.2 at page 30).

With certain 3D display types, light originates from an entire (transparent) volume; these are volumetric emitters (see Section 2.4.1.2 at page 30).

6.2.9.1 Viewing Cone

Displays can usually be seen from many different directions. It is important here that neither brightness, nor contrast, nor color are significantly changed for different viewing angles. Even with only a single observer, the angle of view is always different for different parts of the display area, as long as the viewer is not at an infinite distance (Figure 6.12).

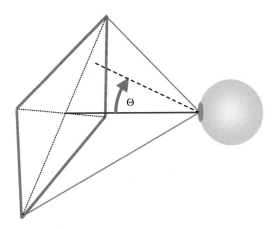

FIGURE 6.12 Viewing distance and resulting viewing angle deviations.

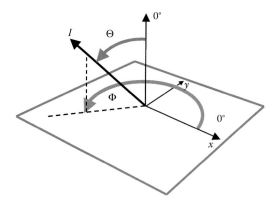

FIGURE 6.13   Coordinates for the viewing angle.

The angular response of a display is assessed by measuring brightness, contrast, and color deviation for a given point on the screen, with a point-like sensor, from various angles in space.

The angles are defined from the surface normal (Θ), and either by a second angle Φ (in polar coordinates) or by x and y values on the screen plane, determining the direction from the screen center (Figure 6.13). A range of viewing directions in this case is cone shaped, hence it is called a *viewing cone* (ISO 13406-2:2001). The data measured is distributed over a half-sphere, which can be mapped into a flat diagram by delineating Θ values in equal distances from the center and Φ (respectively x, y values) accordingly.

The brightness values themselves are visualized by different colors. Ideally, the entire area should be of just one color if the display is a perfect Lambert emitter, so we have to apply the inverse cosine when drawing the intensities (Figure 6.14). Real displays have diagrams showing the maximum intensity present within a certain angular range only. The larger this

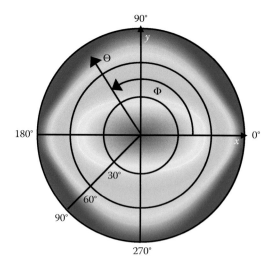

FIGURE 6.14   Example of angular response diagram of a display.

range, the better. The viewing cone diagram allows comparison of different displays at a single glance.

Experiments [271] indicate that with growing Θ, a decrease of luminance is more acceptable than a decrease in contrast.

Note that the technical data given for consumer displays usually always contain viewing angle specifications of either 170 × 160° or 178 × 178°. The higher value indicates the display has PVA, IPS, or other wide viewing range technology. Apart from that, these values obviously are not to be taken seriously.

6.2.10 Speed

A display's ability to switch between different gray or color values as fast as possible is important, and this is true not only for motion pictures. As explained above and in Section 4.2.3 at page 93, this ability is strongly related to the temporal response of the human visual perception system.

The switching ability is usually expressed by the switching time. This is the time it takes for the output parameter of a system to change between 10% and 90% if the input parameter is switched between 0 and 100%. This is also accompanied by a switching delay that may or may not have to be considered.

At 50 fps, a typical TV rate, one frame is just 20 ms long. Switching between frames hence requires a switching time of a few milliseconds.

A short preview of the display technologies treated in later chapters should give an impression about the implications of this requirement:

Phosphors react almost instantly to excitation, but light is remitted over some time, at an exponentially falling rate. After a half-life time, emission is half of the initial value, after twice the time it is 1/4, and so on. Half-life times can range from a millisecond (TV picture tube) to seconds (analog radar picture tube) to many hours (photoluminescent gadgets "glowing" in the dark).

LCD cells may have switching times in the 100 ms range, but current products are a lot better already. Advertised times of 2.6 ms promise very good motion performance, but they are usually measured for switching from full black to white and back, with overshooting driving voltages. Switching between gray levels may take a lot longer, so the advertised times have to be regarded with caution; especially with 3D TV applications showing left and right images alternately, LCD switching times are problematic even today.

Ferroelectric LCOS (*liquid crystal on silicon*) displays are very fast, but are usually available only in small sizes, for projector applications.

Plasma display cells are very fast due to their pulsed operation.

Probably the fastest display technologies are LED and OLED; these have switching times below a microsecond, beyond anything one could wish for.

6.3 COLOR AND INTENSITY PRODUCTION

Next, we will review basics of the color- and intensity-production capabilities of displays. Again, there is a strong relationship to the color and brightness perception capabilities of the human visual system, as discussed in Chapter 4.

6.3.1 Color Gamut

The color space a display can reproduce may be derived very easily, by marking the locations of the display color dyes or phosphors in a chromaticity diagram (see Section 4.3.2 at page 101) and drawing lines between these three (or more) points. This is called the *color gamut* of the display. Figure 6.15 shows the color gamut that typical TVs can reproduce by their *red*, *green* and *blue* (R,G,B) phosphors according to the first standard as defined by NTSC, and the later standard adapted to high-performance phosphors by the EBU (*European Broadcasting Union*). The NTSC triangle which had been developed for phosphors that were available in 1953, has become obsolete. A new color triangle for HDTV (Rec.709) is very similar to EBU triangle. Obviously there is a large deficit in reproducible colors, especially in the range of blue-green (cyan) and also blue-magenta ("purple").

Given the deficiencies of color and also of contrast reproduction, tuning the signal processing for an optimum visual impression has become an important and highly developed art, known as display calibration. Visual calibration methods – working without measuring instruments – are discussed in the Appendix.

6.3.2 Wide-Color-Gamut Displays

With screen colors closer to the edge of the chromaticity diagram (hence, more narrow-banded or spectral colors), a wider range of colors can be displayed. Such displays are called *wide-color-gamut* displays. Typical implementations are laser displays, LED displays, or LCD displays with LED backlight. In the case of LCDs, usually there is an LCD screen with traditional pixel-wise dye filters, but an illumination with three almost pure colors can select narrow parts from the filter curves, resulting in much more clearly defined colors. Hence, even with dye filters this can result in very high transmission and color separation.

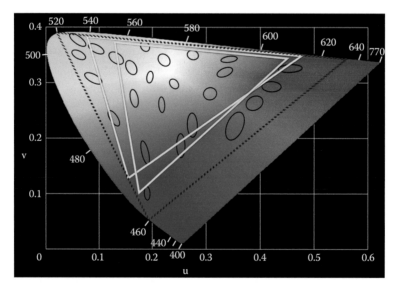

FIGURE 6.15 CIE 1960 UCS diagram with NTSC colors (yellow), EBU colors (cyan) and hypothetical wide color gamut primaries (dashed).

Nevertheless, a simple triangle in the chromaticity diagram could never contain all visible colors. The reason is obvious: the strong overlapping of the eye's sensitivity curves (see Section 4.3 at page 97) causes almost any single spectral color to be received by two or three of the receptor types. Especially for green this causes a severe degradation of color definition.

So even if a good TV camera could record exactly what the eye's separate receptor types can perceive, bringing this information into the eye requires the reproduction of the original color spectrum outside of the eye, and as accurately as possible. This could in theory result in a perfectly accurate color reproduction, but as we have seen in Section 4.3.4 at page 103, cameras usually don't reproduce eye characteristics properly, there even are gaps in their color discrimination ability.

The considerations about ideal color reproduction examined in the following section assume proper implementations of the principles, especially considering camera characteristics. Otherwise, the real effectiveness of wide-color-gamut or multicolor displays will be compromised.

The dashed triangle in Figure 6.15 shows a viable compromise with three spectral primary colors, where the standard color range is contained and the red and blue wavelengths are in an area of relatively high eye sensitivity. Even though we could still choose a shorter wavelength for blue, we would sacrifice some colors from the standard range and some in the cyan area in this case. So this is the approximate best result with only three colors.

6.3.3 Multicolor Displays

By adding more colors, we can produce a larger gamut, because we can simulate the spectrum of the original color more effectively. Especially with the green and cyan, a large improvement can be achieved, yielding a more natural reproduction, particularly of landscapes (plants, sky, sea). Printing media already use six or more colors, but primarily to compensate for idiosyncrasies of dyes and print-specific color mixing.

Genoa developed a five-color system that was intended to be marketed in a high-end projection TV, together with Philips (gray line in Figure 6.16). Eizo has a computer display using an additional cyan color (dotted white line in Figure 6.16). Multicolor displays have not been successful with TV so far, but are sometimes used in professional graphics applications.

Wide-color-gamut displays, however, could enter the mass market almost effortlessly, because LED illumination provides almost pure spectral colors without additional cost. An issue is that to extreme red and blue, the eye is very insensitive. This is a reason for the only multi-color TV technology being marketed so far. Such TVs add a yellow color, however, all producible colors still fit entirely into the range of the EBU color triangle, so the addition of the yellow is not really intended to achieve an extended color range, but to increase the brightness of yellow (which otherwise has to be mixed with green and red, being limited by the low eye sensitivity for red).

We have seen that any older video can be reproduced with a color quality dependent on the playback equipment, provided the recording cameras use filters conforming to eye response. Yet, this is not really the case with most cameras. Using wide-gamut or multicolor display for video reproduction nevertheless makes sense for older materials, because there are heuristic (guessing) methods which may provide a fairly good reconstruction

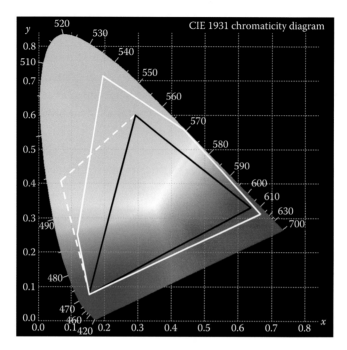

FIGURE 6.16 CIE chromaticity diagram with a typical LCD color range (black), five-color display example (Genoa, gray) and four-color-example (Eizo, dashed gray).

of the original impression. Genoa, for example, developed a proprietary method for this, improving the usability of their five-color display.

6.3.4 Additive and Subtractive Color Mixing

Luminescent displays usually provide color by a fine raster of alternating red, green and blue pixels. Since the eye's resolution for color is only 1/4 of that for brightness, the total raster density does not have to be higher than with a black-and-white display. This color mixing from adjacent pixels is called *additive*, because the brightness values of the pixels add up to any colors within the color gamut (on a discrete basis, of course), including white.

6.3.4.1 Subtractive Color Mixing

Using an additive RGB scheme for displays not being self-luminescent (such as for reflective or light-valve displays) results in a significant brightness loss: Only 1/3 of the display area can be active for each of the primary colors, so at least 2/3 of the total light is lost. Instead, three stacked films of yellow, cyan, and magenta can be arranged for mixing all visible colors by subtracting parts of the spectrum from white light (Figure 6.17). The definition of these *subtractive* base colors is:

$$yellow = red + green$$

$$cyan = blue + green$$

$$magenta = blue + red$$

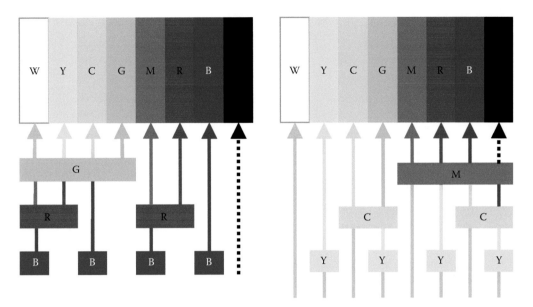

FIGURE 6.17 Standard TV test pattern and its mixing from base colors: additive mixing (left) vs. subtractive mixing (right).

These are not all spectral colors, but nevertheless all colors can be mixed from them. Color films use subtractive mixing, and so do color printers.

Subtractive color mixing has not been very popular with display devices, because it requires stacked layers with transparent pixels and, for working effectively, circuits, but its application has been revived with certain types of electronic paper that have recently been made available for real implementations (see Section 7.3.10 at page 258).

6.3.5 YUV-Formats

Native color-image data would require three times the bandwidth or storage space of black-and-white image data. The human eye however has significantly less – approximately a quarter – of the resolution for color than for intensity.

This fact can be exploited by calculating separate brightness and color signals from the RGB signals of the TV standard. We need three resulting signals to carry the entire information. The most common transformation used is RGB-to-YUV, with Y defined as the luminance signal,

$$Y = 0.299R + 0, 587G + 0, 114B \qquad (6.3)$$

and U and V as the chrominance or color difference signals:

$$U = 0, 493(B - Y) \quad V = 0, 877(R - Y) \qquad (6.4)$$

All factors in the above formulas are exact by definition. Note that this is not identical to the y, u, v parameters that we have learned in the general color considerations in Section 4.3.3 at page 102. Classic TV standards separate brightness and color for backward compatibility to b/w systems, and also for bandwidth savings: the chroma components are modulated on a separate carrier signal in the luminance signal, whose frequency is high enough to show no disturbance on a b/w screen. In order to avoid moving Moiré effects that could be very disturbing, the carrier frequency is locked to the line frequency and the signal is inverted from line to line, resulting in a static dot pattern that is hardly visible from a distance.

NTSC and PAL use, respectively, 3.58 and 4.43 MHz carriers. Color bandwidth is modulated with approximately 1/4 the intensity bandwidth. *U* and *V* are encoded on the same frequency but with a 45° phase shift between suppressed carriers. This is called *quadrature amplitude modulation* (QAM). As one carrier has its zero transition when the other has its maximum (sine and cosine functions), they can be separated if their phase is exactly known. For demodulation, the carrier including its proper phase is reconstructed from a so-called *burst signal*, a short sample carrier transmitted in the line retrace time. Phase shifts may however occur, in signal processing or transmission, hence NTSC suffered from color changes which had to be adjusted manually (hence the nickname Never The Same Color). PAL overcame this by reverting phases from line to line, so shifts would also alternate and could be compensated for.

The SECAM system was also designed to improve color fidelity. It uses a frequency modulated carrier and transmits *U* and *V* alternately from line to line.

Both PAL and SECAM use a one-line memory (ultrasound delay line) to reassemble full-color information for each line. PAL can also do without ("simple-PAL") but this causes saturation losses in the case of larger phase errors.

Analog video recorders use systems derived from these principles, usually encoding *U* and *V* alternately from line to line, because the lower resolution of our eyes for color can of course be exploited in the vertical aspect. This results in a two-line (because of the interlacing) color displacement downward, that visibly accumulates with subsequent copying.

Separating and multiplexing brightness and chroma components is less trivial than depicted above, because it involves low-pass filtering of the chroma signal, which results in a time delay as well. Hence, recombining the RGB picture requires a time delay of the luminance signal or there will be colored edges.

With digital signal processing, these complications are not present. Digital formats also exploit lower chroma resolution, by encoding chroma with 1/2 or 1/4 the pixel count in horizontal or in both horizontal and vertical direction. There are packed formats (storing Y, U and V in pixel groups) and planar formats (storing separate Y, U and V images.

Dozens of different YUV varieties exist whose detailed description would by far exceed the scope of this book. The most important ones for example are:

- YUY2, reducing U and V resolution by two in the horizontal only. Very frequently used as an intermediate storage format in digital video.

- YV12, reducing U and V by two in both horizontal and vertical. It is the common format used in MPEG and AVC codecs, hence for almost any TV application.

- YVU9, reducing U and V by four in both horizontal and vertical. This format was introduced by **INTEL**.

6.3.6 Dyes and Filters

Many display constructions rely on pixel-wise color filters of red, green and blue color primaries to allow for the formation of arbitrary mixing colors. Available filter technologies, in principle, are organic or inorganic dyes, and *dichroic filters*. While the latter can be designed to any specification at high accuracy, manufacturing raster displays with them would be complicated and expensive.

Complying with color standards, on the other hand, requires a wide selection of possible materials to choose from. Organic dyes usually are the best option here. Finding suitable substances is not a simple task and requires huge efforts in testing and experimenting. It took quite a while until satisfactory results had been achieved for all three colors, as dyes in LCD panels for example.

Still, the transmission curves of any natural dyes are never ideal. They may overlap, may absorb some light even in their transmission bands, or may have any kind of odd transmission curves, although visually they appear as more or less pure colors. Moreover, fluorescent backlights, still most commonly used for LCDs, tend to have jagged spectra with dominant emission lines, which may interfere with natural colors in most unpredictable ways. Dye colors and illumination therefore have to be viewed and designed together.

6.3.7 Light Sources

LED backlights can be used to improve the spectral and temporal characteristics of LCDs. The disadvantages of dye colors may be surmounted by intentionally illuminating the panel with only three narrow-banded light sources ("RGB LED", see Figure 6.18). Varieties with "white LED" backlight are quite similar to the fluorescent light in Figure 6.18, because they use the same principle of generating "white", with a phosphor mixture (usually showing some predominant spectral lines). RGB LED Backlight causes narrow-banded, better defined primary colors and delivers a more accurate color rendition than even CRT (Figure 6.19) or plasma displays.

Quantum dots (cf. Section 2.5.6 on page 47) are increasingly used to convert the emission of LEDs into narrow-banded spectral emissions: either as single color layers for separate red, green, and blue LEDs, or as compound layers delivering white light consisting of three narrow r, g, and b spectral lines, from an originally blue or near-UV LED.

6.3.8 Luminescent vs. Light Valve Displays

Contrast/brightness and viewing angles of the existing technologies are extremely diverse.

Luminescent displays (or emissive displays) most often are Lambert emitters, showing a very large viewing angle (LED, OLED, CRT).

Light valve displays such as LCD or DMD suffer from limited viewing angle and false colors/gamma at large angles.

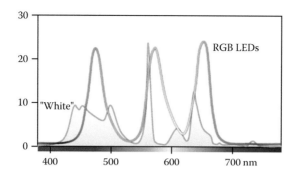

FIGURE 6.18 Typical spectra of three-color LED backlight for an LCD display vs. "white" fluorescent backlight.

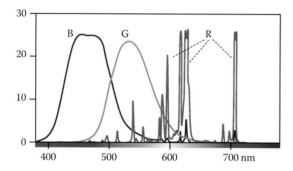

FIGURE 6.19 Some typical spectra of color CRT phosphors).

The brightness of LCDs can compete with the brightness of luminescent displays, while projection displays typically have disadvantages. Projectors can, however, provide the largest images.

Reflective displays such as electronic paper, can operate in bright sunlight, giving them a very large advantage for outdoor applications.

Generally, all technologies have specific advantages for specific purposes. There is no generalized grading scale to suggest one is better than the other. We will discuss all of these different technologies in detail in the next chapter.

6.3.9 Test Pictures

Displays as well as image transmission chains are often tested with certain basic image contents (Figure 6.20), suited to reveal basic errors in gray value or color reproduction, geometry (important for CRTs, projectors, and scanners), and resolution. The resolution triangle consists of converging lines and contains line densities up to (theoretically) infinity. Resolution can be read directly from where the lines melt to gray (at about "5" or "6" in the example shown in Figure 6.20).

The geometry pattern contains straight lines (the eye is sensitive to bended lines) and circles (the eye is also very sensitive to their distortions). Gray steps easily reveal if a display

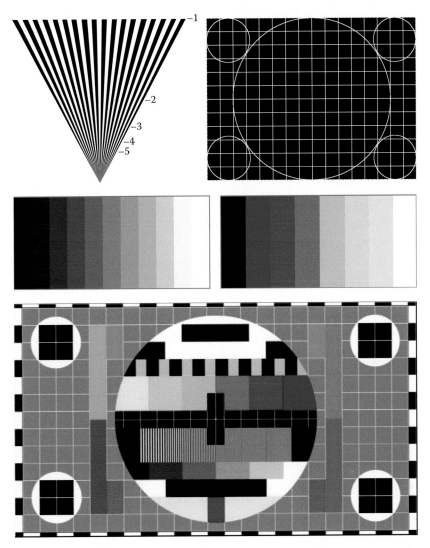

FIGURE 6.20 Display test pictures: resolution triangle (top, left), geometry grid (top, right), gray steps (center, left), color bars (center, right), and a typical TV test picture, with deficiencies caused by signal processing and transmission (bottom). Note that the color bars will also appear as gray steps when viewed on a black-and-white screen.

has a satisfactory brightness and contrast adjustment. The color bar is a rather coarse instrument, but it can at least show if colors are pure. Other test "patterns" are uniform color areas (for testing evenness of intensity and color), and also natural images, necessary to test the fine tuning of colors (e.g., with skin tones) and color contrast. Practical test images are often combined from many of the elements mentioned, allowing several basic errors to be seen at a glance.

The TV test picture shown in Figure 6.20 (bottom) is a recording from digital satellite. Despite the digital transmission, its crispness is not very good and obviously there are some problems with the vertical resolution (visible line steps at the circles). This is a quite common result given the current chaos of TV standards, often leading to numerous format conversions throughout the transmission chain.

6.4 SIGNAL AND IMAGE PROCESSING

In the following sections, we will discuss general signal and image processing techniques that are implemented in the electronics of most consumer displays.

6.4.1 Signal Transmission

Displays should replicate the appearance of natural objects with locally distinct brightness and color. This should be possible for still images as well as for videos or interactive content.

Contrary to physiological systems like the human eye, technical systems cannot transfer a large number of signals in parallel at acceptable complexity and cost. The individual pixel signals are therefore serialized, taking advantage of the simplicity of high-frequency handling with technical transmission channels.

Spatial changes in brightness therefore translate into temporal changes, spatial resolution into bandwidth. Analog transmission channels have a bandwidth that is limited by system design, and their frequency response is crucial for the image resolution and quality.

In analog systems, analog filters are used for signal treatment. Filters may be used to sharpen or smooth out pictures, or to separate color and brightness signals from a TV transmission. Filters may have a response to signal steps that may include edge overshooting, ringing, or edge asymmetries (Figure 6.21). Obviously, these response characteristics affect image quality, hence, care has to be taken with video signal filtering, especially concerning the proper reproduction of edges. The choices of useful analog filters are limited: mainly Bessel filters (characterized by certain relations of their filter coefficients) are used, since they cause low ringing and have a useful phase-shifting behavior.

If signals are transmitted over filters of different bandwidths (color and brightness, for example, approximately 1.2 MHz vs. 5 MHz for PAL TV), the high-bandwidth signal has to be delayed to avoid misalignments. The small delay times necessary ($< 1\,\mu s$) can be achieved by special coils with defined parasitic capacitance, or coaxial cables of low impedance. Such devices behave like a medium with high dielectricity ϵ_r or also permittivity μ_r, causing

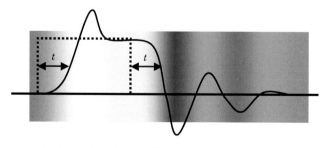

FIGURE 6.21 A rectangular input signal (dotted) and a filtered signal with overshooting and ringing. Also shown is the delay time t and the resulting brightness impression (background).

electromagnetic waves to run significantly slower than in vacuum (see Section 3.3.1.2 at page 59).

Such short-time delay lines should not be confused with those used to recombine phase-inverted lines in PAL TV. The delay time of, for example, 64 μs that is necessary here requires other solutions, usually an ultrasound signal propagating in a crystal. A digital signal could of course be delayed much more easily, with a simple storage device, requiring the availability of inexpensive converters and memory. Today, this is no longer a problem.

Digital filters offer several more options than analog filters do. They can either mimic analog designs by stepwise integration, or use different approaches, such as finite-response filters whose coefficients directly encode a desired output step response.

6.4.2 The Sampling Theorem

Today, the greater part of all signal processing components in displays has become digital. Digital means that we convert the analog signal curves into binary numbers. In order to do so, we must measure them in short time intervals, taking *samples* of the signal. This is commonly known as *analog-to-digital* (A/D) conversion. We will not go into the many methods of A/D conversion here. Rather than that, we will provide some fundamentals of signal theory, just enough for understanding signal processing in displays.

An important point is the sampling theorem, also known as the *Nyquist/Shannon theorem*, which states that in order to properly digitize an analog signal with maximum frequency f_s, we need to take samples with a frequency $F > 2f_s$.

We could simply think of a sine wave at f_s for which we take samples at each of its maxima and minima. These would represent the most important aspects of the function. But what if we take samples at its zero crossings? This would yield no information about the function at all, yet, in practice we have to consider that with $F > f_s$, this phase condition can't last for long.

A beat[*] between sampling and signal frequency could result from phase changes, but we have to consider that near f_s, no signal modulation can be allowed, since this would cause side bands (Equation 2.27), and parts of these would exceed f_s. So we have to keep a certain distance to $F/2$, or our signal sampling won't give very accurate results.

Note that the phase of the sampling pulses doesn't count, because there is no absolute phase relation between sampling sequence and sampled signal. We should also note that it may make sense to use signal averages between sampling times instead of point-wise samples, but this doesn't make much difference as we will see. The sampling theorem is not just a condition, but also dictates that we have to apply a very good low-pass filter before sampling.

A mathematical derivation of the sampling theorem can be rather abstract, so we will try to show this in a different way. We need to sidetrack briefly to *Dirac pulses*.

6.4.2.1 Dirac Pulse Series

A Dirac pulse δ is a mathematically ideal, single pulse, defined as having an amplitude of infinity at $x = 0$ (x could be time t) and an amplitude 0 otherwise. Its integral is

---

[*] Wave with periodically rising and fading amplitude (Figure 3.5 on page 57).

defined to be 1.

$$\delta(x) = \begin{cases} +\infty & x = 0 \\ 0 & x \neq 0 \end{cases} \tag{6.5}$$

$$\int_{-\infty}^{\infty} \delta(x)\, dx = 1 \tag{6.6}$$

This is a theoretical concept since real pulses never are this narrow. It essentially serves as a description of one of the sampling pulses that we used above.

Mathematically, the entirety of the sampling pulses in the above example can be described as a Dirac pulse series:

$$\triangle_T(t) = \sum_{n=-\infty}^{\infty} \delta(t - nT) \tag{6.7}$$

Where T is the pulse interval. The Fourier transform of this is (we will prove this later in a more intuitive way):

$$\mathcal{F}\{\triangle_T\}(f) = \frac{1}{T} \sum_{k=-\infty}^{\infty} \delta\left(f - \frac{k}{T}\right) \equiv \frac{1}{T} \triangle_{\frac{1}{T}}(f) \tag{6.8}$$

The right side of the equation already contains an important finding:

The infinite pulse series with interval T transforms into a spectrum with infinitely many lines with intervals $F = 1/T$. Remarkably the original and the transformed in this case are identical functions. Mathematicians speak of a *fixed point* of the Fourier transform; another fixed point of the transform is the Gauss curve, which we encountered in Section 2.5.2.4 at page 42.

6.4.2.2 Pulses and Sampling

Now recall the sampling procedure as shown in Figure 6.22. In principle, it is nothing but a multiplication of the analog signal with a series of pulses.

The clue is that this multiplication can also be done in the frequency domain. We take a signal with spectrum $0 \ldots f_s$ and multiply it with a series of sine waves with frequencies $0, F, 2F, \ldots$. This is an amplitude modulation as treated in Equation 2.27 on page 43, because

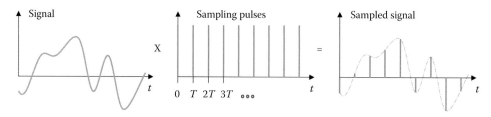

FIGURE 6.22 Digital sampling of an analog signal.

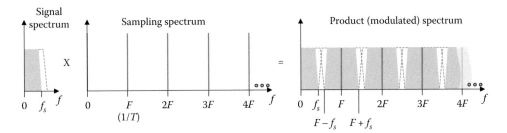

FIGURE 6.23 Modulation (multiplication) of the spectrum of a Dirac pulse series with a signal spectrum from $0 \dots f_s$. If the modulating spectrum is extended too far (dashed lines) interferences will occur, making a later retrieval of the original modulating spectrum impossible.

any of these frequencies can be interpreted as carrier frequencies. What we get from the modulation (or multiplication), are side spectra (also called *side bands*) left and right of these carriers, each resembling the modulating signal spectrum (remember that $a \sum b_i = \sum ab_i$).

Note again that the phase of the carrier frequencies doesn't count, because a phase relation to the sampled signal is not defined in any practical applications.

If these carriers correspond to the spectrum of the above treated Dirac pulse series, we also get a base spectrum $0 \dots f_s$ from the $f = 0$ component. This makes sense since we can conclude from Figure 6.22 that a simple low pass filter over the sample amplitudes would also yield an analog signal that is similar to the original analog signal.

If we extend the modulating spectrum as indicated by the dashed lines in Figure 6.23, then the side spectra of all neighboring carriers interfere with each other and cannot properly be demodulated later. In other words, if we try to reconstruct the analog signal from the samples in this case, we get a signal that also contains unwanted difference frequencies from these interferences in the modulation spectrum.

Therefore, as stated above, we need $F > 2f_s$.

Thus, if we want to digitize a signal we always have to ensure that it contains only frequencies below $F/2$. This is done by applying a low-pass filter, also in this case often called an *"anti-aliasing filter"*. We also speak of aliasing effects when analog image contents are mapped to a fixed pixel raster (see Section 6.4.4 at page 207). This is indeed similar to sampling. There however, the term aliasing is more used for effects such as step effects with slanted lines. Effects caused by interference of image frequencies and pixel raster are more often referred to as *Moiré* (see Section 6.4.5 at page 208).

6.4.2.3 Fourier Transform of the Dirac Series

We now give an intuitive explanation for the Fourier transform of the Dirac series.

Suppose we add infinitely many sine waves of different frequencies. We chose their phases so that all have a maximum at $t = 0$ (i.e., we have cosine functions), Hence, all wave amplitudes will add at $t = 0$, forming a peak. If our cosine waves all have non-correlated frequencies, amplitudes at other points (on the time scale) will have an even distribution of values between $+1$ and -1. The contribution of these values, compared to the peak at zero, will practically vanish. The result is a Dirac pulse, a perfect "needle". We may conclude that

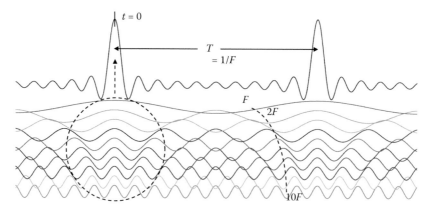

FIGURE 6.24 Formation of a pulse series: example with ten cosine waves with harmonic frequencies.

a Dirac pulse must have an infinite, evenly distributed spectrum, because the waves we used for creating it create exactly this.

Now consider that we use not arbitrary cosine waves, but such with harmonic frequencies (i.e., $F, 2F \ldots nF$; F being a certain base frequency; we can omit $n = 0$ because it doesn't change the waveform). In this case, all frequencies will have common (periodic) maxima when the wave with the base frequency F also has its maximum, hence after time $T = 1/F$ (see Figure 6.24).

Thus, with n approaching infinity, we get a series of infinitely high and narrow pulses, with period length T. The ripple frequency in between goes to infinity, hence evens out in practice.

What we get is a perfect look-alike of the Dirac pulse series. The spectrum of a Dirac pulse series hence equals a sum of infinitely many cosine[*] functions ("carriers") of frequencies being a multiple of F.

This is exactly what we intended to show.

6.4.2.4 Back to Analog

Digital signals have to be converted back to "natural" analog signals at some point. This is called *digital-to-analog* or *D/A conversion*. In principle, this process is simple: Set an analog storage element (e.g., a capacitor) to the sample amplitude, let it hold this amplitude and set it to the value of the next sample after duration T. This results in a stepwise signal that has to be smoothed by low-pass filtering afterward. What we have to consider is that very steep low-pass filters tend to cause *ringing* (oscillations after signal changes). In addition, fast amplitude changes of signals close to the sampling limit will be evened out. This has to happen, since it merely reflects the fact that (side band) frequencies $>f_s$ aren't allowed. There are several advanced D/A conversion methods (all limited by the sampling theorem, of course), but their discussion is beyond the scope of this book.

---

[*] Sine waves with max. at $t = 0$.

6.4.3 Tonal Resolution, Signal Noise, and Transfer Function

Converting analog signals to digital needs to take into account the required dynamic range:

1. the brightness and color distinction abilities of the eye;

2. reserves for internal calculations and transformations (rounding errors, boundaries).

Even if 8 bits would reflect the achievable tonal resolution of many displays, this will easily lead to visible artifacts, such as intensity or color steps (called *banding*) for example, especially when signal processing is also done with no higher resolution. At least 10, 12, or 16 bits per color channel are therefore used for calculations in many of today's image processing chips.

Tonal resolution also relates to noise figures. The least significant bit always tends to be random. Hence, a signal encoding with 8 bits causes a noise level of approximately −48 decibels (dB).[*]

In analog systems, noise is also omnipresent. Thermal noise of a resistor (any signal source can be treated as an equivalent to a resistor) increases with the square root of the bandwidth. So a 5 MHz channel has a tendency to produce a greater noise than, for example, a sound channel that needs only 20 kHz.

Fortunately, the eye is not very sensitive to small local brightness changes (see Section 4.2.4 at page 94). While an acoustic system may well require 80 dB or more of signal-to-noise ratio (10000:1), a video image appears clear with 40 dB. Again, the many conversion steps in a video transmission chain may lead to an accumulation of noise and require a much better noise figure for any of the single devices involved.

Linearity of the brightness-to-voltage relation (called *transfer function*) is a major issue, especially with analog processing.

Nonlinear transfer functions are used in most consumer cameras and displays to match nonlinearities of the human visual system (see Chapter 4). The most common transfer function is the gamma curve (see Section 6.2.7 at page 189).

6.4.4 Antialiasing

Processing image data (or generating it artificially) may result in slanted lines or edges encoded in hard steps according to the pixel raster. Such pixel-sized steps destroy the impression of a natural image and may even be visible from a distance.

Generally this is solved by inserting some pixels of intermediate gray levels to smooth the impression, at least for distant viewing (Figure 6.25). The process is called *antialiasing*.

This problem should not occur when recording natural images with a camera (hard edges automatically cause partial exposure of raster pixels along the edges). A proper antialiasing algorithm should therefore guess the real edge location in a finer raster and should simulate the exposure process. Brightness levels of the coarse raster points have to be calculated to reproduce the local averages of a blurred picture of the finer raster.

---

[*] dB is a logarithmic measure for signal ratios. 20 dB equal a ratio of 1:10.

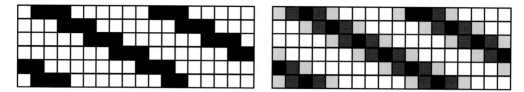

FIGURE 6.25 Rough display of slanted lines with visible steps, and de-aliased version with steps less visible from a distance.

Aliasing was not a common problem in the analog era, especially not with CRTs, because these cause a certain blurring already and the electron beam would write lines that overlap a bit.

With raster displays, even more so if the fill factor (i.e., sum pixel area vs. total display area) is not 100%, antialiasing has to be used quite often. It is also very important with resizing (sub- and super-sampling) operations.

6.4.5 Moiré

Rasterizing images has a certain disadvantage if object patterns are present that show similar spatial frequencies to the image raster. In this case, lines on the object may in some locations be in phase with the display raster, and in other locations not. A black-and-white structure on the object, having a frequency causing one pixel to be black and the neighboring to be white can be reproduced with high contrast if in phase, but shifted by just 1/2 pixel it would result in nothing but gray.

This is also usually referred to as "aliasing effects."

When patterns are tilted or distorted against each other, or have different frequencies, interference structures (beat frequencies) will appear on the screen (Figure 6.26).

This effect is called *Moiré*, and it is present in any raster image processing, be it with print media or with electronic displays. An appropriate measure against it is low-pass filtering, removing disturbing patterns before they can interfere, and avoiding Moiré effects that result from image frequencies above the raster frequency. The effects occurring here are the same as discussed in Section 6.4.2 at page 203.

If this occurs at the camera's side – object patterns interfering with the camera pixel raster – little could be done about it except for optical integration by a softening filter directly at the chip (which causes a certain amount of blurring), or some (less effective) filtering of the resulting signal. This is the reason why jackets with houndstooth patterns and shirts or ties

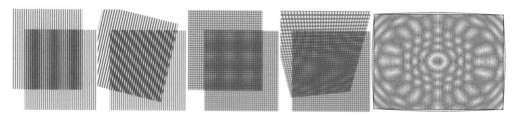

FIGURE 6.26 Example of Moiré patterns for line (left) and distorted raster overlays (center). Right: interference of straight and and cushion distorted dot patterns (e.g., color CRT mask).

with narrow stripes were often banned from TV studios; stripes especially can cause strong low-frequency patterns (beats, see Figure 3.5 on page 57), running through the picture at the slightest movements of the objects.

In the analog age, little more was available than one-dimensional filtering – in the time domain. Aliasing problems with the TV lines could hardly be corrected at all.

An approach often found in TV applications is *comb filtering*. It removes one frequency and its harmonics but preserves frequencies in between for improved crispness. This was of particular interest for line sequential signals as used in analog TV standards. Comb filters can, for example, be constructed by adding a signal with a delayed copy of itself.

With digital imaging, filters in most cases are two-dimensional, applied to the image plane. There are at least as many approaches to this as there are for one-dimensional filters.

Object patterns close to the pixel raster size can result in very disturbing dynamic effects, such as flickering and fast-moving beat frequencies. Three-dimensional filtering algorithms (combining subsequent frames) can be used to exclude this, while retaining a resolution close to the theoretical maximum.

Quite often the necessity arises to remove smaller Moiré patterns remaining after improper prefiltering, or to smooth out image rasters before resizing. The following convolution filter is an example from practice that proved to be a good general approach (of course it has to be adapted to the actual pattern sizes occurring). Note that this is not simply a low-pass filter, but a filter with a horizontal/diagonal anisotropy, which combines a good Moiré suppression with little blurring:

$$\begin{bmatrix} 0 & {}^1\!/_5 & 0 \\ {}^1\!/_5 & {}^1\!/_5 & {}^1\!/_5 \\ 0 & {}^1\!/_5 & 0 \end{bmatrix} \tag{6.9}$$

Such a convolution filter matrix is used like this: each pixel at location x, y of the output image is a weighed sum of a 3×3 pixel block around location x,y from the input image, according to the factors in the matrix.

A very effective measure against moving Moiré patterns are temporal filters, which integrate subsequent frames.

6.4.6 Resizing

When, for example, a PAL signal of 720×576 pixels is displayed on a medium HD screen of, for instance, 1320×768 pixels it is not possible to map any pixel in the original image to just one or two particular pixels on the screen. This could result in severe edge stepping and running line effects with motion images. Hence, any pixel has to be mapped to more pixels on the screen, with varying factors. Also, object edges have to be de-aliased again. All of this results in significant image blurring. Hence, the crispness on the higher-resolution screen is actually lower than on a screen with the original image resolution. The effect is less significant if the screen has a much higher resolution.

More advanced resizing approaches than linear scaling or stretching are available today (not all of them commercially, yet). Video retargeting approaches such as those described by [55,160,282,283], for example, apply a nonlinear rescaling of input footage to fit it into other format ratios. Video upsampling techniques described by [88,125], as another example, increase the spatial resolution of video footage by either registering and blending video frames within a consistent coordinate system or by learning the correspondence between low- and high-resolution image patches from a database.

6.4.7 Noise Reduction

Using a simple low-pass filter for noise reduction has the disadvantage of sacrificing image resolution. Resolution can be improved when bandwidth is dynamically changed with signal amplitude, so the filter only kicks in for flat areas and leaves edges intact (an analogy to dynamic de-noising in audio).

A more powerful de-noising is achieved by exploiting the timely similarities between motion picture frames. Any noise bits will be random from frame to frame, while the image content will be quite similar. This way, a very efficient noise reduction is achieved without loss of crispness. Such methods are often referred to as *three-dimensional filtering*. A disadvantage of this approach is a tendency toward motion blur. Adding dynamic behavior, such as disabling the filter in areas with strong motion, can improve the results significantly. A good "temporal" noise filter such as this delivers astonishing improvements in quality. The technology is frequently used for TV transmissions of old movies.

6.4.8 Image Compression

Very few images today are transmitted without some type of signal compression. Digital image processing allows the exploitation of the spatial and also the temporal similarities between adjacent image pixels or frames. Additional efficiency is achieved by exploiting the eye's low sensitivity to small brightness changes in small areas or around edges.

Practically all current image compression standards are based on an operation called *discrete cosine transform* (DCT).

Another method extensively researched is wavelet transform. It has not found its way into major motion picture standards, so far, but it is often used in still-image compression (JPEG 2000).

DCT is quite similar to a Fourier transform, wherein absolutely any shape of a wave can be constructed from sine waves of integer multiples of base frequencies, with appropriate amplitudes and phases. The DCT, however, is based on *real* cosine waves only (no phase values).

If we regard a number of adjacent pixels and see their brightness values as a wave, we could split this wave into Fourier coefficients and use these coefficients to describe it, instead of the original signal encoding. For images, the very similar DCT is better suited. Actually, for an idealized image source, the Kharhunen-Loève transform [76] theoretically proved to be best. Its basis functions are computed via *principle component analysis* (PCA) of sample images.

A good pragmatic choice for the DCT basis functions is a "wave" just 8 pixels wide. The DCT method is then expanded into two dimensions with 8×8 pixel patches in the image. Any image is therefore partitioned into separate 8×8 fields that are separately encoded.

A typical DCT is written as follows:

$$X_k = \sum_{n=0}^{N-1} x_n \cos\left[\frac{\pi}{N}\left(n + \frac{1}{2}\right)k\right] \quad k = 0, \ldots, N-1 \tag{6.10}$$

In two dimensions, the formula becomes:

$$X_{k_1,k_2} = \sum_{n_1=0}^{N_1-1}\sum_{n_2=0}^{N_2-1} x_{n_1,n_2} \cos\left[\frac{\pi}{N_1}\left(n_1 + \frac{1}{2}\right)k_1\right]\cos\left[\frac{\pi}{N_2}\left(n_2 + \frac{1}{2}\right)k_2\right] \tag{6.11}$$

All possible base DCTs for an 8×8 pixel array are shown in Figure 6.27 ($N_1 = N_2 = 8$). Any 8×8 pixel image patch can be 100% encoded by a weighed linear sum of all these 64 DCT bases. Hence, the original 8×8 pixel matrix is replaced by an 8×8 weight factor matrix for the 64 DCTs.

Subsequently, the smallest coefficients can be set to zero, vastly reducing the space required for them in the signal encoding and hence saving bandwidth. This results in some changes in the fine structure of the image of course, but these are barely visible to the human eye. A further improvement can be achieved by reoptimizing the matrix with the zero coefficients in place. Also, the coefficients can be encoded with different thresholds and bit resolutions according to their importance. This weighing matrix can be optimized according to the type of image material; movies or cartoons may have optimal results with very different matrix factors.

FIGURE 6.27 All possible 8×8 DCT bases.

The basic compression method described above is the main ingredient of the JPEG (*Joint Picture Experts Group*) compression standard for still images. It can be expanded for motion pictures by exploiting temporal similarities. Such techniques identify motion by comparing subsequent frames, calculating motion vectors, and if areas in the current frame still resemble those in the previous frame but just a bit shifted, a reference to the previous frame area together with the motion vector is encoded, saving a lot of bandwidth.

These methods are known as *MPEG* (*Motion Picture Experts Group*), DivX, AVC (*Advanced Video Coding*) or H.264 (the usual format for HD), and the latest approach, HEVC (*High Efficiency Video Coding*) or H.265, the proposed format for UHD. Compared to raw video, a compression factor of 50:1 or more is commonly achieved without any visible loss of quality.

The newer formats are more optimized toward exploiting the physiological properties of the human visual system for further signal compression. For example, low-contrast background detail may be softened before the encoding. Such effects are visible if a still picture is inspected and directly compared to the original, but they are hardly perceivable in a motion picture sequence.

Another advanced feature concerns psychological aspects. Faces, for example, always attract attention, even if hardly visible due to small size or low contrast. Saving encoding bandwidth here will result in very visible defects. An advanced encoder will recognize such features and assign them higher priority.

6.4.9 Deinterlacing

Interlaced pictures can be converted to progressive pictures (i.e., pictures with all lines) by image processing (Figure 6.28). Simple approaches use one or more of the following methods:

1. Add half-frames into full frames as they are (a method dubbed "BOB"). This retains resolution for still pictures but results in considerable jagged edges with motion.

2. Blend the half-frames by crossover addition into one full frame (called "*BLEND*"). This avoids jagged edges but retains neither full motion nor vertical resolution and is certainly the worst of all approaches, especially because it produces heavy motion blur.

3. Motion resolution is retained if only one field (half frame) is taken and just doubled to replace the other (called "*FIELD*"). This approach, however, sacrifices half the vertical resolution.

A simple combination of FIELD and BOB is often used as a more intelligent approach (*adaptive* deinterlacing). Methods can be switched for separate parts of an image, by detecting the differences between half-frames: for small differences, BOB is used, and for large differences possibly indicating motion, the FIELD method is used. As the loss of resolution is less apparent with fast motion, this may be more effective than the simple approaches. The decision when to switch is more complex than it first appears, and there is a large probability for visible artifacts if the decision algorithm fails too frequently.

FIGURE 6.28 De-Interlacing methods: Interlaced picture with sideways motion (upper left), BLEND: field blending (upper right), FIELD: field doubling (lower left), and smart deinterlacing by correct combination of motion shift compensated half frame parts (lower right).

With qualified estimates about the motion of picture parts, called *motion vectors*, an improved deinterlacing can be obtained; in this case, missing pixels can very likely be replaced from the other half-frame or even half-frames of subsequent pictures. With such a motion estimation, very few pixels really have to be "guessed" by interpolation. The generation of motion vectors is a very well-researched field; it is essential for satisfactory interframe compression such as MPEG or AVC, the main standards for TV signal compressing. The vectors are even readily available when decoding such signals.

It is obvious that any deinterlacing can deliver progressive frames (full pictures) either at half-frame or full-frame frequency (e.g., from 50i* either to 50p or 25p). It's also obvious that

---

* A frequent notation for interlacing modes uses the frame or half frame rate and a letter p for progressive or i for interlaced. 60i for example, means 60 half frames interlaced. 50p is 50 full frames progressive.

motion resolution is retained only if the original half-frame rate becomes the new full-frame rate (e.g., converting 50i to 50p).

Nevertheless, most TV appliances currently use very simple deinterlacing and almost always to the full-frame rate (e.g., from 50i to 25p). Even 100 fps are insufficient for crisp motion display if the frames are shown for their full duration (Section 4.5.1 at page 119).

A major difficulty with deinterlacing arises from the frequent presence of strong noise in analog pictures. Our eyes are very insensitive to picture noise, or grain if we're talking about film. 40 dB (1:100) are perceived as perfect already. Even 20 dB (1:10) are often accepted as film grain, in dark scenes for example.

A deinterlacing algorithm, however, will experience difficulty with this kind of signal, because it is very difficult to distinguish picture detail from noise at the pixel level. Therefore, images that look good on a classic TV may look awful on a modern flat panel, especially if inexpensive deinterlacing chips are employed.

A special problem arises with old film scanners that are still often used in TV studios. These may not be synchronized with the actual frame changing of the film transport. Then the half-frames are shattered between adjacent full frames and there is "interlacing" where there should not be any. A deinterlacer should be able to detect this. Reassembling the half-frames in this case is simple.

Another frequent TV problem arises with 24 or 25 fps movies usually being converted to the approximately 30 fps of the NTSC TV format by inserting half-frames (a process named *pulldown*) in order to retain a minimum of smooth motion (adding ten half-frames per second looks smoother than five full frames). Flat-panel sets trying to convert this to 30p will produce considerable motion stuttering at least, and if such TV tapes are converted a second time (as often seen when NTSC tapes are transmitted by stations in PAL (25i) countries), any kind of unpredicted results may arise. Even sawtooth-like forward/backward motion can often be observed with current TV sets in these cases.

Smart flat-panel TVs should in principle be able to recognize converted cinema material, reassemble the half-frame to the original 24 fps (*inverse pulldown*) and then perhaps also apply a frame doubling algorithm for smooth motion.

If the video source is not TV transmission but DVD, one should know that DVDs are recorded only at 25 fps (movie accelerated by 4%) for PAL countries and 24 fps for NTSC countries, where the DVD player then performs the pulldown operation to get 30 (exactly: 29.97) fps, interlaced. The latter is an unnecessary step and can be bridged with flat-panel displays. Many displays, and also projectors, offer this "24p" playback option.

As we have seen, even the latest advances in digital image processing are no guarantee against inappropriate designs, ignoring existing TV standards, and the basic knowledge any engineer dealing with TV should normally have.

The challenge is increased by the existence of various different old standards and the creation of many new ones requiring frequent size and frame-rate conversions, often four or five of them in a single transmission chain. This and the fundamental flaws in motion reproduction of many current display types often result in dramatic loss in quality, substandard even to the performance of a tube TV.

6.5 ELECTRONICS

Although electronics is a wide field already, display technology expands it even further, in directions as exotic as transparent semiconductors. We will not try to cover electronics in general here, but will focus on special, display-related issues.

6.5.1 Semiconductors

Before proceeding to display driving circuits, we will give a (very short) overview of semiconductor types for display purposes.

Certain materials, especially four-valent elements like germanium, silicon, or carbon, or combinations of three- and five-valent or two- and six-valent elements, conduct poorly in their genuine state but may be altered in their behavior by changing their mixture balance or by inserting small amounts of other elements such as indium or antimony (a process called *doping*). This causes a surplus of electrons (n-type material) or a lack of electrons (p-type).

Both electrons and locations of missing electrons (called *holes*) can wander through the material, letting electric current flow (Figure 6.29). Holes are considerably slower (they wander by being filled with an electron that causes another hole to open nearby). Materials showing these effects are called *semiconductors*.

From a quantum physics perspective, in a semiconductor there can be only certain energy levels of electrons (called *bands*), just as in an atom. If we join an n-type material directly to a p-type one, current between them can flow only in one direction and only if a certain threshold (depending on the voltage gap between the energy bands in them) is surpassed. In the other direction, the junction does not conduct (at least not until a certain voltage is reached). What we have then is a typical semiconductor diode, used for rectifiers, etc.

Diodes are (almost) nonconducting in reverse direction until a certain voltage (breakdown voltage) is reached. This voltage can be tailored for values between a few volts to over 1000 volts. Such diodes (Zener diodes) are widely used for voltage stabilization and references (Figure 6.30).

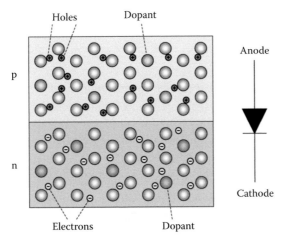

FIGURE 6.29 Electron-hole model of a semiconductor compound and corresponding diode symbol.

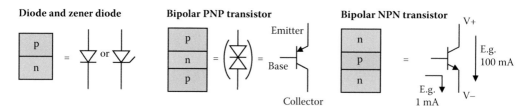

FIGURE 6.30 Planar diode and bipolar transistor principles.

TABLE 6.3　Band Gaps and Typical Applications of Selected Semiconductors

Material	Band Gap	Applications
Cadmium arsenide	0.14 V	Infrared detectors
Indium antimonide	0.17 V	Thermal cameras
Indium arsenide	0.35 V	FIR detectors, Terahertz emitters
Germanium	0.67 V	Early transistors (also IR lenses)
Silicon	1.12 V	IC technology, light sensors
Gallium arsenide	1.43 V	RF circuits, IR LEDs
Selenium	1.74 V	Rectifiers, Transparent circuits
Cadmium selenide	1.74 V	Quantum dots
Gallium phosphide	2.26 V	LEDs
Silicon carbide types	2.4…3.2 V	LEDs
Zinc tin oxide	3.3…3.9 V	Transparent circuits
Gallium nitride	3.44 V	High efficiency blue LEDs
Carbon (diamond)	5.47 V	High temperature sensors

Some typical band gaps and application fields for a few of the numerous known semiconductor materials are shown in Table 6.3.

Some of the materials (not silicon, germanium, or diamond) can emit photons when electrons change between energy levels. The wavelength of the photons corresponds to the band-gap voltage (i.e., the electron energy in electron volts).

Though not able to emit photons, silicon diodes can absorb electrons, and generate current flow. Large diodes from thin layers of p- and n-type materials are, for instance, used in solar cells.

Two diodes face-to-face would normally not conduct. Closely integrated, however, current flow in one diode induces charge carriers in the other and makes the entire assembly conductive. Depending on the asymmetry of the device, the resulting total current may be 10 to 1000 times stronger than the steering current. This device is a bipolar transistor (Figure 6.30). We distinguish PNP and NPN types.

In the beginning, all transistors were of bipolar type. Planar transistors and diodes can be arranged in large numbers on a single silicon wafer, structured by multiple steps of photo masking, etching, vapor diffusion or ion implanting.

Oxidizing silicon yields a very good insulator (silicon dioxide, which is quartz), and connections can be arranged by depositing aluminum structures. This enabled the first integrated circuits.

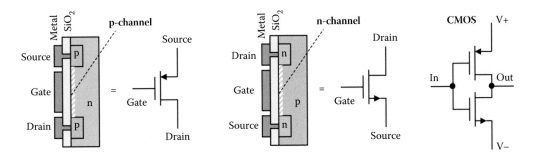

FIGURE 6.31 MOSFET transistor and CMOS principles.

A transistor type more important today and for our topic as well, is the *Metal-Oxide Semiconductor Field Effect Transistor* (MOSFET). It uses two strongly doped patches in the silicon surface (called *source* and *drain*), with a poorly or non-doped patch in between (called the *channel*). The entire structure is covered with an insulator (SiO_2) and then with a metal electrode. Voltage applied to the electrode (called *gate*) can influence the band gaps and cause current to flow through the channel.

The device is more or less symmetric, and the gate voltage may lie outside the drain- and source-voltage range. Hence, the device can in some cases even be used to switch alternating current.

Other than with bipolar transistors, the D-S path behaves like a variable resistor. Also, there is no driving current; only the gate capacity has to be charged. There are *p-channel* and *n-channel* MOSFETs in several variations. The polarity is usually indicated in the circuit diagram by an arrow at the source or gate (Figure 6.31). Their main difference is inverted gate polarity.

Combining two complementary MOS transistors for pulling current toward plus- and minus-supply, results in a basic CMOS (*Complementary MOS*) gate (Figure 6.31). It draws current only when changing states. The advantage of their infinite DC current gain as well as their simplicity, made CMOS gates the elements of choice for highly integrated circuits, including all kinds of current microprocessors.

Large numbers of parallel MOS transistors on a single silicon chip are used to make power MOSFETs. Their "on" resistance can be as low as 10 mΩ, with no threshold voltage. Being very fast as well, these elements are ideal for switching power supplies as well as many other applications.

For displays, one often needs transparent electrodes or even transparent semiconductors and transistors. Indium tin oxide (ITO) is the material of choice for most transparent electrodes. Very thin evaporated layers of metal may also be used, but conductivity is low in this case, so this is a choice only for full area electrodes.

Several new materials have been tried for transparent semiconductors. Materials, for example, based on zinc, selenium, or their oxides show promising results (selenium is not entirely new in electronics, most power rectifiers in the electron tube age were made of it and were known for their sensibility and their bad smell when blown up).

Another important new semiconductor class is polymer based. Some that are able to emit photons are of particular interest to display technology. These are used in organic light emitting diodes (see Section 7.6.6 at page 273).

Carbon nanotube based materials also are really new. More on this in Section 6.6.6.3 at page 236.

6.5.2 Passive Matrix Displays

LED (not OLED) displays can usually also work with short, high-power pulses instead of lower continuous current, so separate capacitors maintaining pixel voltage are not required.

Simple numeric LED displays, for example, can be driven by a matrix, consisting of PNP and NPN transistors with the segments as rows and the digits as columns (Figure 6.32).

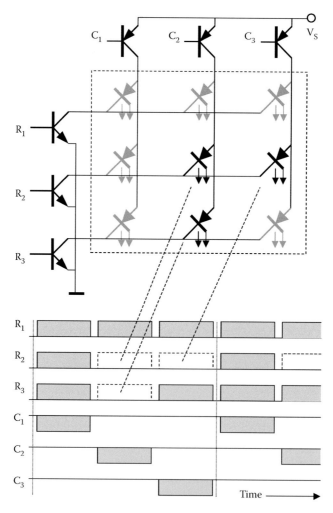

FIGURE 6.32 Basic multiplexed matrix display with nine LEDs, here with bipolar driver transistors, and corresponding driving voltage sequences (three LEDs in this example are dark).

If the LED drivers deliver high peak currents, even large numbers of LEDs can be driven at high refresh rates. The single LEDs flash shortly in this case, but for motion pictures, this is an advantage.

6.5.3 Multiplexing and Connection

Matrix displays obviously need a special circuit addressing the pixels, one at a time or line by line, analog to the electron beam in a CRT, or in any other suitable manner, in order to form an image. Basic video signals arrive by a single wire, time sequentially. A driver circuit has to demultiplex this timely signal in order to address the pixels.

Usually single lines are addressed time sequentially. No matter what type of line address-ing signal we have, we won't want to do this outside the display panel, because it would require a substantial amount of wiring connected to the display. Therefore, these demul-tiplexing circuits usually are mounted directly onto the rim of the display panel as chips with bonding connections or *Surface-Mount-Technology* (SMT) soldering, or the circuits are created right in place from polysilicon, amorphous silicon, or other materials.

If we keep the analogy to CRT for the moment, pixel-wise driving signals for the lines have to be provided as well, and usually with a great variety of possible voltages supporting analog brightness levels. This part of the circuitry therefore is a bit more complex. We won't dive into the numerous possibilities for analog, digital, or hybrid solutions here, but will show the principle of a generic matrix display.

In the example shown in Figure 6.33, four chips perform the line addressing. Each has a little address decoder *d*, responding to only one of the four combinations possible for bits 1 and 2. Bits 3 and 4 are decoded to four individual address lines in each chip, but only if bits 1 and 2 select the chip. In other types, another chip may be used for decoding bits 1 and 2, but the example shown here allows for a quite compact layout.

For line-pixel driving, we have assumed that here we will use an analog circuit, a *Charge-Coupled Device*. The CCD (which may also consist of several smaller CCDs in series) has a *shift clock line* commanding the progression of the signal pattern by one pixel. By another steering line *t*, a separate circuit stage (a sample-and-hold stage) takes over the entire pixel pattern when shifting is complete, so the display gets a steady driving signal for the line duration.

With inorganic LED displays, this is simply all, because for these displays – with their high pulse/continuous power ratio – it is sufficient to flash line after line (even better for most video-related purposes). With LCDs, a separate matrix of thin film transistors in the display array would take the line signals by the *t* steering pulse and charge a capacitor with them, keeping the pixel voltage constant for the entire frame duration. The same may apply for organic LEDs (OLED), because they allow for less peak current than LEDs.

Connecting ultra-thin films on glass with other electronics requires specific techniques (simple soldering is not an option here). The usual solution for passive matrix LCD is a "worm" consisting of alternating slices of conductive and nonconductive rubber, which is simply pressed between the connections on the panel and on the circuit board (Figure 6.34). The usually fully metalized front panel can be connected to the back panel wiring at one point inside the display.

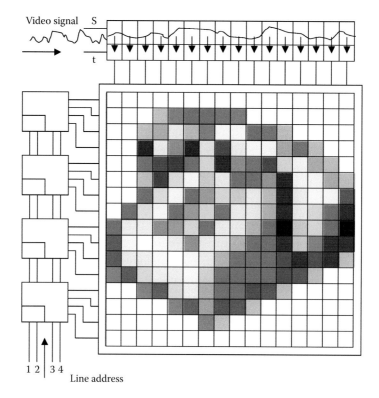

FIGURE 6.33 Basic schematic for an analog matrix display with digital line addressing and CCD pixel addressing.

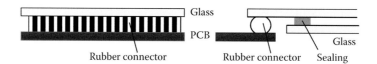

FIGURE 6.34 Typical LCD display connector (side views).

With appropriate mechanical support and connection technology, one may also connect thin mylar *printed circuit board* (PCB) foils directly to the panel (as in Figure 6.35). The connection itself may be performed with conductive glue. Parts of the wiring foils also have to be glued to the panel surface for sufficient mechanical support. The ends of the flexible PCB foil are thickened and carry an additional metal layer (e.g., gold) for inserting them directly into plug sockets.

6.5.4 Active Matrix Displays

Light modulating displays such as liquid crystal (LC) or electronic paper, cannot be operated like some self-luminating displays, which activate single lines or one pixel time sequentially at high intensity, letting the eye do the averaging.

In a matrix configuration (necessary to keep the number of driving lines low even with high pixel numbers), image content has to be stored so the pixels can keep their state for an

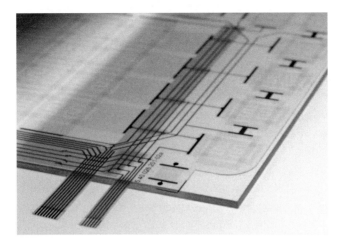

FIGURE 6.35 Example: foil PCB wiring connected directly to a panel (in this case, a glass touch panel). Image courtesy: **RAFI** GmbH.

entire image duration. Even in flashing backlight displays, the entire image has to be present at a certain time. In any case, this requires a storage capability at any single pixel.

Therefore, larger matrix LCDs have one CMOS transistor or diode (*thin film transistor*, TFT, or *thin film diode*, TFD) and one capacitor per cell (Figure 6.36). As rows are driven sequentially, the (small) capacitor serves to hold cell voltage for the image duration. The capacitor can also be the cell capacitance itself. The transistors or diodes are manufactured as thin film devices of amorphous or polycrystalline silicon, or, in latest developments, as transparent semiconductors from certain inorganic materials or organic polymers, directly on the panel, in between or – in case of transparent materials – even above the pixel areas.

Amorphous silicon currently is the technology of choice for direct display panel deposition because it can be deployed in a vacuum process at relatively low temperature (380°C), allowing the use of normal glass or even plastic films. Its disadvantage however is low electron mobility, hence poor conductivity and speed. Polycrystalline silicon is much better but needs higher temperatures to deploy (650°C): it requires quartz glass carriers and is therefore mainly used for small displays like LC or LCOS, for projection applications. Workarounds for the problem are being explored and may find their way into production. Amorphous

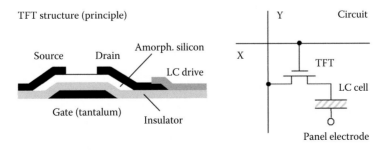

FIGURE 6.36 Structure of an amorphous silicon TFT.

silicon layers can, for instance, be caused to crystallize by applying energy, such as with a short laser pulse, thus avoiding excessive heat on the carrier.

Other materials based on zinc, tin or selenium, are quite new in this field but have great prospects for creating conductors, semiconductors, and transparent circuits. Another alternative are organic compounds, especially polymer enriched with carbon nanotubes, which can serve as conductors or semiconductors depending on composition. Because only small additions of carbon nanotubes are required, transparency can be obtained (see Section 6.6.6.3 at page 236).

An alternative driving technology for LC that should be mentioned is *plasma activated LC* (PALC). It uses a gas-filled plasma discharge layer behind a layer of LC cells. Voltage at the (passive) electrode matrix causes local discharges making the gas conductive (ionizing it) and forming "virtual" electrodes for a certain time; this approach has not yet become marketable, however.

An important fact is often neglected in the description of LCD driving techniques: Applying DC voltage to a cell will change transmissivity in a more or less proportional way, and will result in a simple driving circuit. DC applied to a fluid, however, will also cause electrolytic effects. This "polarization" will quickly destroy the display cells. Changing the polarity of the driving voltage as often as possible will avoid this, and is a necessary requirement for any LCD driving circuits.

The CMOS transistors used in TFT displays can also be inverted (with the gate voltage outside the drain and source voltage range). This symmetric behavior of the CMOS transistors allows the exchange of drain and source voltages, hence AC driving can in principle be provided by inverting the entire supply.

TFD displays (Figure 6.37) are a compromise between performance and complexity. The threshold voltage of the diodes enables the selection of particular rows. Again, one capacitor per cell holds the driving voltage until the next refresh cycle. The "diodes" used are bidirectional Zener diodes, their only purpose being to provide threshold voltages suppressing crosstalk (only a sufficiently high difference between line and row voltage will allow current to go to a pixel). So TFD can work with both polarities as well. Simply changing polarity from frame to frame would result in a certain amount of flicker, since the circuits usually are not perfectly symmetric. The usual procedure therefore, is to drive consecutive lines with opposing voltages and to change these polarities from frame to frame. Usually the local brightness levels are evened out by visual blur, and the eye is also less sensitive to flicker with

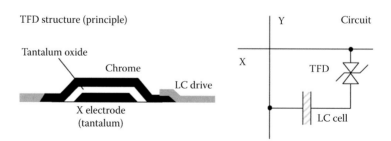

FIGURE 6.37 Structure of a metal insulated TFD.

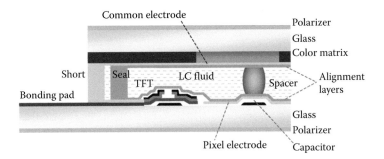

FIGURE 6.38 LCD panel structure with chip structure, spacers, and metalization layers.

small detail. Since the flicker amplitude is also small, the effect disappears entirely. Even with the polarity-changing mechanism, circuit layout has to provide additional measures to avoid any unwanted long-term current imbalance.

Driving voltages typically are in the 20 ... 30 volts range, while current requirements are low (mainly a capacitance is driven). Simple passive matrix displays, such as of clocks, require microamperes or even a lot less. Current requirements increase with refresh frequency and cell size, hence video LC displays (with a large total cell size) have the highest driving power requirements. Nevertheless, this is minute compared to the power drain of the backlighting. Figure 6.38 shows a cross section of a complete TFT display structure.

6.5.5 Smart Displays

Active display panel driving circuits can, in principle, incorporate much smaller structures than the display matrix itself, and be up to orders of magnitude more complex. This especially applies for inorganic CMOS structures, but can also be expected to apply for future organic materials.

Such circuit structures can be used for a wide variety of processing tasks. This could, for example, include parts of the video signal decompression, image postprocessing like deinterlacing, crispening, temporal noise reduction, or super-resolution algorithms. The entire topic is very new, with only a few publications so far. A first application that has been demonstrated is light field generation with dedicated processors integrated into the display (see Section 9.5.6 at page 398).

Intelligent circuitry can, for example, be used to improve motion response, or to provide multiresolution inlays, a feature most useful for near-eye displays and that we will discuss in detail in Section 10.10 on page 450.

For large panel displays, providing intermediate frames for fast motion right in the display itself could be an advantage. The key to this is a technology known as charge coupled device (CCD). In a CCD, charges stored in adjacent circuit cells are moved to the neighboring cells by means of a circuitry between the cells. An entire charge pattern can be moved along a cell line, step by step, controlled by trigger pulses. CCD camera chips have used this principle since decades, for a sequential read-out of image data, pixel by pixel. Only for displays, this is still a new approach. With CCD hardware integrated into the display panel, the

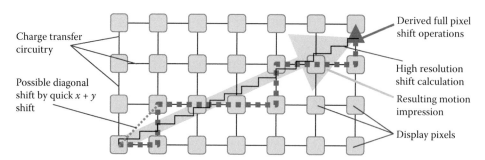

FIGURE 6.39   Image shifting scheme for a planar micro display [117].

entire frame or parts of it could be shifted, instead of supplying new frames at high speed (see Figure 6.39).

What should be shifted and how fast can be determined quite easily. Any video compression standard today relies on motion vectors, which are contained in the compressed signal. These could be used to supply two signals x and y, in addition to the r, g, and b signals, to dedicated processors located at any pixel. With these signals, a CCD circuitry could execute a pixel shifting in x and y direction at any nth or mth pulse of a common, high-speed clock signal. This would provide an effective frame rate of several kilohertz, without requiring a flashing backlight. See Section 10.10.1 on page 450 for further considerations about this technology.

A critical factor for the circuits is electron mobility, determining the processing speed possible. This has been very low for early organic semiconductors, but significant progress has been made, in particular with the introduction of carbon nanotube-enhanced plastics [172].

6.6   ASSEMBLY

Manufacturing technology, including assembling and connection technologies, housing, and functional design, are prerequisites for the success of any mass-market products, such as displays. Without good solutions for any of these, no display technology can be more than a laboratory gadget.

6.6.1   Panel Construction

Most flat-panel displays require some kind of transparent enclosure for functional reasons or for protection. Glass is a preferred material here, not only because of its rigidity and scratch resistance, but also because it has a low vapor diffusion. Plastic materials are light and can be coated against scratching, but their rigidity may in some cases be too low (LCD needs a dense array of spacers to maintain cell thickness), and plastic also has a certain transmissivity to vapor, so humidity can get inside, or fluid or gaseous display components can diffuse outside and be lost.

Vapor diffusion is a major concern with any electronic components in terms of durability. Integrated circuits, for example, can get defective quite early in a humid climate because diffused humidity causes corrosion. Military-grade equipment is therefore usually required to have metal or ceramic encapsulated semiconductors.

With LCD panels, enclosure is especially important. Even if glass plates are used, the edge sealing may be prone to diffusion. For extreme requirements, a low-temperature glass solder may be used as the ultimate ratio here. Most commercially available panels rely on organic materials to hold the plates together and seal the edges.

6.6.2 Backlighting

LCDs (and other possible light valve displays) require an evenly distributed, bright and color-neutral backlighting. The latest variety uses a matrix of red, green and blue LED which

- improves color gamut by delivering three narrow band colors,
- can be flashed to improve motion resolution,
- can deliver different brightness values for different display areas, improving contrast and reducing power drain (*high dynamic range display* (HDR), see Section 7.8 at page 278).

Nevertheless, most current displays don't have all these features. HDR backlighting is particularly delicate because it requires equally bright LED or an adjustment to guarantee equal light distribution.

RGB LEDs are not common in spite of their theoretical advantages; the vast majority of currently available displays are using white LED (blue or UV LED with white emitting phosphor). A reason for this is the difficulty to compensate for different brightnesses of individual LEDs, as well as the different aging of red, green, and blue LEDs. It is easier to tune the phosphors of white LED for spectra with narrow-banded red, green, and blue maxima. Especially efficient here are quantum dot-enhanced phosphors. These can deliver spectra even surpassing anything possible with an RGB LED assembly.

LCD displays with LED backlight have misguidingly been introduced as "LED displays," and this name has become common for them. For *true* LED displays, the correct term "OLED displays" (as all actual products use organic LED) has prevailed.

Edge backlighting is commonly used for smaller displays (handheld devices, notebooks) and if a flat design is required. A slim fluorescent lamp or a row of LEDs is placed at the bottom of the panel (with large screens, also at top and bottom, or at all four sides) and a *light guide* (essentially a glass plate wherein the light is kept by total reflection) distributes the light over the area. Substantial effort is taken for even intensity and angular distribution. The basic methods for this are (Figure 6.40)

- Light guides with little, unevenly spaced rims (diffuse surface extraction).
- Glass wedges, also with rims but more evenly distributed.
- Either variety combined with *tuning films* intended to make the extracted light perpendicular to the surface (pyramid-shaped structures on the glass surface have a tendency to do this).
- Diffractive or Bragg structures respectively light guides, similar to those described in Section 10.14 on page 464. These can be perfectly transparent, allowing for special applications (see Section 7.5 on page 264).

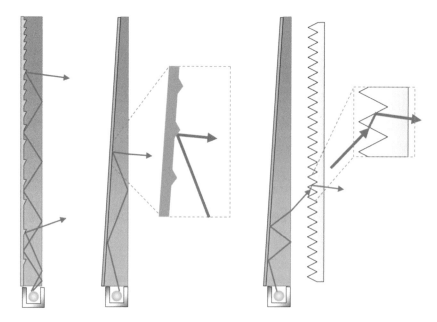

FIGURE 6.40 LCD back panel light extraction: planar light guide (left), wedge (center), tuning film (right).

Fluorescent tubes used for edge backlights are extremely thin (e.g., 2 mm) and are cold cathode types driven by a high voltage supply typically located in the display frame. The light produced is only partly effective, as the very narrow tube casing cannot guide light from the back side of the tube into the display panel. LED stripes are simpler to use, and also more efficient because they emit to only one side anyway.

With four-sided LED edge lighting, a selective dimming can provide for a limited improvement of black level for large areas, but it is by far not as effective as a modulated area backlighting.

Large panel TVs often use direct backlighting through the rear of the panel, consisting of a grid of parallel fluorescent tubes (Figure 6.41). This greatly contributes to the thickness of

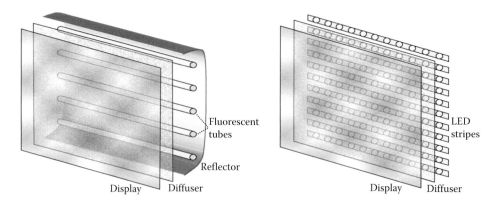

FIGURE 6.41 Fluorescent area backlight (left) and LED stripe area becklight (right).

older LCD TVs. Modern displays most often have edge LED or full area LED backlighting with LED stripes or LED arrays, also allowing for selective dimming or HDR features for high-end displays (see Section 7.8 on page 278).

LED stripes can also be used for backlight flashing (scanning backlight, cf. Section 6.2.4 on page 186).

Another interesting option for a display backlight we should mention here are full area OLED foils.

6.6.3 Antireflective Coatings

Antireflective coatings should be able to absorb incident light without affecting outbound light. There is only one really sufficiently working technology for this: thin layers of different refraction indexes are coated on the surface; multiple gradual reflections from the different layers work together to eliminate reflected light by interference.

A simple $\lambda/4$ layer (Figure 6.42) may be sufficient in many cases. This works perfect only for one wavelength of course, but a coating absorbing mainly green will leave only weak violet reflexes, due to the eye's sensitivity curve.

For equal strength of both partial reflections, required for total extinction, the coating should have a lower refraction coefficient than the glass (see Section 3.2 at page 54).

In order to work for the entire color range, several coatings thinner or even much thinner than a light wavelength may be combined (Figure 6.43). The entire process is identical to the manufacturing of dichroic filters (Section 10.6.1 at page 428). Multi-layer coatings are typical for high-performance camera lenses.

High-grade antireflex coating has in fact been around with computer displays for many years, for example, the CRT display of the **DEC** (Digital Equipment Corporation) PC at

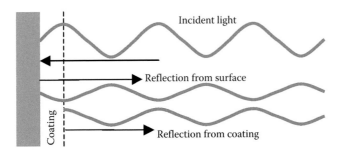

FIGURE 6.42   Antireflective effect by interference.

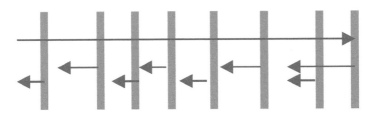

FIGURE 6.43   Fine-tuned vacuum-deployed layers of different refraction indices, each reflecting part of the light.

about 1985. Especially useful with CRTs is a coating that is also conductive, because when grounded, it eliminates the electrostatic charge that has always been a nuisance with CRT computer displays (with home TVs, it may be seen as a virtue because it is an efficient fine-dust absorber).

Another type of antireflective coating is a matte surface, simply dispersing the light and thus avoiding direct reflexes. This causes some contrast loss because all of the display surface then reflects some of the light into the observer's direction, and it may also cause a slight blurring of the display image. Nevertheless, such matte surfaces together with tinted panels have been developed to highly efficient solutions.

With *nano structures* etched into the surface, an even stronger effect, similar to continuous refraction index reduction can be achieved [255]. This can be attributed to the fact that the structures themselves are smaller than the light wavelength and their effective material density, and hence the resulting refraction index, decreases toward the edge. A simple example of a continuous index changing structure is shown in Figure 6.44 (this reminds at a lotus effect surface, indicating that such surfaces could even be dirt repellent). Similar structures are also found in biological optical surfaces. TVs with advanced coating technology of this class ("moth eye") have been presented, for example, by **Sharp** and **Phillips**.

It cannot be pointed out adequately enough that without an efficient antireflective coating, any claim of high-contrast figures for a display is baseless. In spite of the availability of several efficient and affordable antireflective coating technologies, most current displays, especially TV panels, are greatly lacking this feature. A common problem are screens with a surface of black-tinted glass and poor coating, sharply mirroring any lights and brighter items in a room. This may yield high contrast if there are no bright items in the line of direct reflection, but nevertheless it causes a poor viewing experience in most practical situations. Matte screens as used in LCD computer monitors and earlier TVs already perform a lot better in normal use.

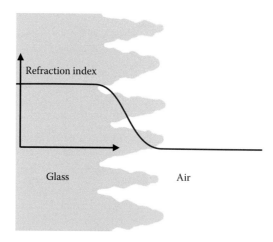

FIGURE 6.44 Continuous refraction index change by nano-etched surface structutres.

6.6.3.1 Sol-Gel Coating

Antireflective coatings can be produced either by vacuum deployment of metal or metal oxide vapor, or by the *sol-gel* process. Vacuum coating is indispensable for high-precision coatings (narrow-band filters, for example) since it is very easily controlled. Electric fields are used for directing the vapor deployment. This in principle also works with plastic glass, because there are materials with which the deployment can be done at temperatures low enough to not damage the material surface.

Sol-gel is another coating technique, working with nano dispersions of metal oxides or metal fluorides. Traditionally, metal oxides are dispersed in water and a thin liquid film is deployed on the glass by spin coating (deploying a droplet and having it diverted into a thin film by quickly rotating the target), or by applying it on a panel surface with a wiper (a fast and inexpensive method for large panels). The liquid quickly evaporates, leaving a thin film of metal oxide that is not only transparent and serving as an antireflective coating if the thickness is correct, but is also very scratch resistant. Plastic spectacles today are coated this way, giving them a durability almost comparable to real glass.

Fluorides lately have been shown to be easily deployable as well, by a sol based on alcohol [297]. Their advantage is their low refraction index, resulting in a better antireflective effect on plastic glass. MgF_2 for example has a refraction index of 1.38 whereas TiO_2 has 2.5...2.9, depending on the deployment process.

Sol-gel coatings are less dense than a solid material, because the molecules tend to arrange with atomic scale gaps left by the evaporating carrier fluid; which is an advantage because it reduces refraction even further. Sol-gel coatings with an overall uniformity of about 3% have been demonstrated, which is good enough for antireflection applications but not for narrow-band filters. Nevertheless, multilayer coatings (e.g., with alternating MgF_2 and TiO_2 layers), have been demonstrated as well. Advances in manufacturing technology could therefore possibly lead to sol-gel processes allowing dichroic filter or mirror applications.

6.6.4 Touch Screens

Directly pointing at certain objects on a screen is an efficient type of interaction for graphical user interfaces.

Essential for this is the recognition of fingertip positions. One variety of such actions – gesture recognition by cameras – we will not address here because it is not actually display technology.

Detecting direct touch calls for a very close integration of the technology into display panels. In the following we will explain the most important and promising technologies.

6.6.4.1 Force Sensors

Placing pressure sensors at the corners of a display front panel allows for the detection of the location of any direct touch, because the force applied will be distributed between the sensors according to the leverage law (Figure 6.45). Appropriate force sensors can easily be implemented using piezoelectric elements. This principle (also a bit misleadingly referred to as *strain gauge*) allows for thick and rugged panels and is therefore ideal in public places, touch screens in automatic teller machines, for example. Obviously, static force from the

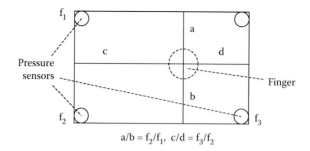

FIGURE 6.45 Position detection by force balance (leverage law).

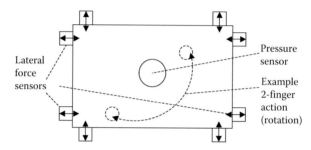

FIGURE 6.46 Detection of sideways action on a surface.

weight of the panel itself has to be compensated for, either by a calibration step or by some more or less intense high-pass filtering. If the detectors are used to detect short pulses only, the method is referred to as *acoustic pulse recognition*.

A disadvantage here is the lack of multitouch detection (several fingers at once). A recent patent application by Nokia (US 0090256807), however, promises to allow multitouch detection on a force-operated screen as well. The principle is to detect lateral forces caused by the friction of fingers moving on the screen. This is combined with pressure force detection for a wide variety of possible actions (Figure 6.46).

6.6.4.2 Surface Wave Detection

Dispersive Signal Technology (DST, cf. Figure 6.47) is based on the progression of bending waves along a glass panel. Piezoelectric sensors at the glass edges detect these waves, caused by touching the panel, and calculate the location from the different arrival times of the mechanical bending waves. Static forces are ignored, the device only "sees" pressure changes and is specialized for applications with single-touch operations (e.g., depressing displayed keys).

6.6.4.3 Light Grid and Optical Imaging

By placing multiple light sources and detectors around the edges of a display, a grid of light beams traveling closely above the display plane can be produced and detected. Placing a fingertip on the display will interrupt certain beams, hence position can be detected. With simple LEDs, photo diode detectors and tiny plastic lenses, this principle can be

FIGURE 6.47 DST touch panel controller. Image courtesy: **3M Touch Systems**.

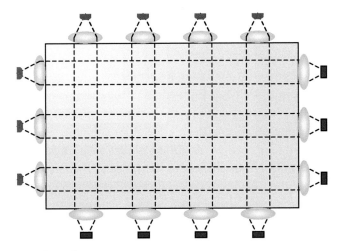

FIGURE 6.48 Light-grid touch screen.

implemented quite inexpensively. It allows for some multitouch operations and it is also quite rugged.

The individual light detectors in Figure 6.48 may be replaced by one-dimensional camera sensors. This way, only stripe-shaped light sources at two edges and, for example, two cameras in the display corners are required, resulting in a much simpler assembly.

6.6.4.4 Bidirectional Display Touch Detection

With light-sensitive pixels integrated into a display, "touch" actions can also be detected by reflection of light from fingertips, or by shadowing of environment light. Such an assembly can achieve a very high resolution. In certain cases a separate illumination may be necessary, for example, by infrared-emitting pixels also integrated in the display panel.

6.6.4.5 Resistive Panels

Two foils with transparent electrodes can be put together in a way that resistance between them changes when pressure is applied. With electrode layers made of resistive material

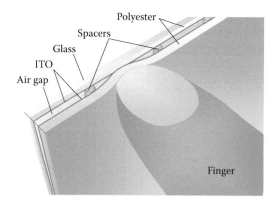

FIGURE 6.49 Resistive touch screen.

and a grid of spacers keeping the foils apart by default, pressing the foils together will cause smaller or larger parts of the surfaces to get into contact, and electrical resistance between the electrodes will change accordingly (Figure 6.49). A common electrode material for this technology is indium-tin-oxide (ITO) [225].

Location aware resistive panels may uses two resistive foils, one with electrodes at the top and bottom and one at the left and right edges of the display (*four-wire* system, Figure 6.50, left). Touch position is determined by the resistance relationships measured. A simpler assembly uses only one resistive foil while the other is highly conductive. The resistive foil has connections at all four corners. Again, resistance relationships (this time from the conductive foils to each of the four corners of the resistive one) are used for determining the position. This is usually called a *five-wire* system due to its connections (Figure 6.50, right). The measurement in this case is performed by first applying the same voltages to both upper and both lower connections and then in a second step to both left and both right connections. Diagonal measurements may optionally follow.

More sophisticated resistive panels work with a structured electrode matrix. In this procedure, positions of multiple touches can be detected, as well as force (as the area pressed together determines the total resistance). This allows for multitouch applications, even with high resolution (up to 4k × 4k pixels reported).

The major disadvantages of resistive touch panels are the mechanical vulnerability of the sensor foils, usually plastic material, and their interaction with passing light, possibly resulting in multiple reflections or a certain amount of blurring.

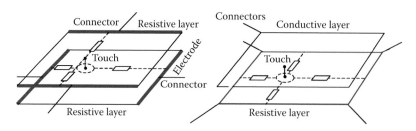

FIGURE 6.50 Principle of "four-wire" and "five-wire" resistive panels.

6.6.4.6 Percolation

A more proportional response to touch pressure can be achieved with metal or carbon particles embedded in composites. Some of the particles will always be in contact, creating a certain resistive behavior. If pressure is applied, more particles come into contact, opening more conduction paths and causing a decrease in resistance. This mechanism is named *percolation*.

6.6.4.7 Quantum Tunneling Composite (QTC)

The latest development in resistive pressure detection uses the tunneling effect (see Section 2.5.5 at page 46). In this technology (**Peratech** Inc.), metal particles are enclosed in silicone rubber, not touching each other. The particles in this case, however, have spiked surfaces, with microscopic needles concentrating electric charges to high field intensities, causing electron transport between spikes of adjacent particles by the tunneling effect. Hence, an electric current can flow between the particles without them actually touching. The current flow is also a function of particle distance, continuously changing with the pressure applied.

6.6.4.8 Surface Capacitance

Applying an electric signal to a single (transparent) conductive layer above the display, a "parasitic" capacitance is formed by a finger approaching the area, drawing energy from the field. Basically, this gives an indication of finger distance. If the layer is also structured or resistive, different effects measured from different sides of the display area may allow for a rough detection of finger positions as well.

6.6.4.9 Projected Capacitance (PCT)

Placing an addressable matrix of neighboring, transparent electrode pads behind a thin glass plate (Figure 6.51(left)) enables the detection of an approaching fingertip by capacity changes between the electrodes (Figure 6.51(right)).

A major advantage with this type of detection: The panel can be rugged (although not too thick) glass, fingers can be detected without actual contact, and by sequential addressing of individual row and column electrodes, precise and fast multitouch detection is possible.

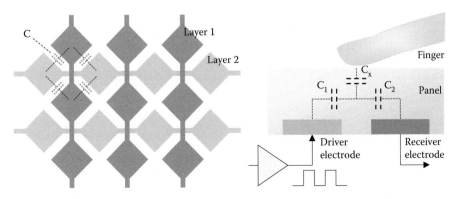

FIGURE 6.51 PCT capacitive touch panel. Left: electrode matrix. Right: working principle.

Especially with big screens, the principle can provide a "gesture recognition" appeal, because fingers can be detected at some (short) distance.

PCT panels are the technology of choice for most current touch screens, whether mobile phones or large PC monitors, in a wide variety of applications [225].

6.6.4.10 Inductive Touch Panels

This variety works in similar fashion to a graphics tablet. It requires a pen with an inductive coil (no direct finger operation possible). Because the effect works over some (small) distance, the tablet structure can be positioned behind the display panel.

6.6.4.11 Touch Panels with Tactile Feedback

One drawback of the smooth touch panel surfaces from an interaction point of view is that they do not provide the tactile sensation that one is used to from classical input devices, such as keyboards. Novel touch panel technology, however, is able to produce tactile feedback with respect to the touch position. This can be realized in different ways. Generating mechanical vibrations is one classical option but it has the disadvantage that the whole device will vibrate.

Electrovibration to control electrostatic friction between a touch surface and the user's finger is a new approach that proves to be a better alternative that does not require any moving parts [13]. By applying a periodic electrical signal to a transparent electrode sheet on top of the panel, a tactile sensation is generated directly at the fingertip. By chaining the amplitude and frequency of the signal, different surface textures (e.g., rough or sticky surfaces) can be felt.

6.6.5 Flexible Electronics

Flexible, rollable, or stretchable displays will allow for many new applications, for example as compact rollout displays for electronic devices, as flexible display areas integrated into clothing, or as "display wallpaper" that could perhaps be manufactured inexpensively from polymer material by roll-to-roll printing and simply be glued to walls, forming active display screens of arbitrary size.

The term "flexible" is often used with different meanings:

- Flexible in terms of bendable. This requires little elasticity and can be a property even of tin, for example.

- Flexible in terms of stretchable. This requires highly elastic material, like certain polymers or silicone.

We will therefore use bendable or stretchable in the following text for clarity. A very simple type of stretchable electronics consists of separate chips molded into flexible polymer or silicone foils (MID, *Molded Interconnect Device*). Stretchable wiring is obtained using tortuous horseshoe-shaped metallic wiring, embedded in a matrix of, for example, PDMS (poly-dimethyl siloxane) [45].

This wouldn't provide a reasonable flexible display assembly however, apart from wiring some separate LED points.

Examples for bendable displays are assemblies of flexible foils with printed wiring and polymer devices such as polymer OLEDs. Metallic wiring may also be bendable if it is thin enough.

With conductive plastics wiring, devices can even be stretchable. Conventional conductive plastics, however, have poor conductivity, sufficient only for certain display types like "electronic paper". Carbon nanotube enriched plastics offer entirely new possibilities, even for fully transparent active drivers (TFT) (see Section 6.6.6.3 at page 236).

A technology already used for solar cell production deploys amorphous silicon on polymer foil (**PowerFilm** Inc.). The silicon layer is thin enough to be fully flexible. Several silicon layers can be applied in a continuous roll-to-roll process. The process provides a layer structure but hardly any spatial structure (except for solar cell wiring that can be integrated already). Circuit structures as are necessary for displays would have to be created by lithographic processes resembling classical semiconductor manufacturing. This technology is still in development. Advantages are said to be better conductivity and speed than with current organic semiconductors.

6.6.6 Transparent Electronics

Many display types use conductive layers, in front of the display cells, for applying electric fields or current. A sufficiently thin metal layer may be used as a nearly transparent conducting surface. Indium tin oxide (ITO) is well suited to this purpose and is very frequently used in current display constructions. A competing transparent conducting material is aluminum zinc oxide (AZO).

Certain display solutions will profit from integrating an active, transparent driving circuitry into the panel. Apart from possibly higher efficiency due to an increase in the active pixel area, these techniques still have limited use for normal displays. For special types of light valves however, such as transparent OLED or masking displays for augmented reality glasses, they may become of major importance. Several technologies have been demonstrated for this.

6.6.6.1 Transparent Semiconductors

Transparent semiconducting materials allow for complete active matrix driving circuits layered on top of the display cells. These materials are relatively new and are still being explored. Since 2003, several of them have been demonstrated with transparent electronics.

Examples are:

- indium gallium zinc oxide (or a-IGZO) [214]

- zinc oxide (ZnO) [89]

- tin oxide (SnO_2) with silicon dioxide (SiO_2) insulation [305]

- zinc tin oxide (ZTO) and indium doped zinc tin oxide (IZTO), showing higher electron mobility than Zno or SnO alone [56], [80]

6.6.6.2 Organic Transparent Semiconductors

Most polymer materials still suffer from low electron mobility and are therefore very slow. A promising variety so far is polymer materials enriched with carbon nanotubes. These materials may also be transparent, depending on the polymer material used as a basis, and they have already been demonstrated for display driver circuits.

6.6.6.3 Carbon Nanotubes

In 1991, Sumio Iijiama discovered tube-like carbon structures of some ten nanometers diameter as a collateral product when trying to produce fullerenes. It turned out that these structures consisted of hexagonal grids of carbon atoms forming hollow cylinders (Figure 6.52). Depending on the orientation and offset (thread slope) of the wrapping, these tubes behave like conductors or like semiconductors. As conductors, they show *ballistic conduction*, almost like a superconductor, and can endure a current density more than 1000 times higher than with copper. As a semiconductor, the tubes show band gaps starting from 0.1 V, depending on their diameter. Practical diameters are between 0.4 and 100 nm, and also tubes of multiple concentric layers can be produced.

Even a single carbon nanotube between two metal electrodes can already form a practically useful field-effect transistor (Figure 6.53). Theoretically it should be possible to design ultrahigh speed, ultralow power circuits with structure sizes of one or two nanometers. Even three-dimensional structures would be realistic because of the high thermal conductivity, hence, power dissipation capability of the material.

Interest in carbon nanotubes is very high also because their tensile strength is about 20 times higher than with steel, and their thermal conductivity and heat resistance are comparable or even better than a diamond. Carbon nanotube powder can meanwhile be produced at a high level of purity, in a *chemical vapor deposition* (CVD) process. Producing longer tubes is under intense investigation; meanwhile, carbon nanotubes can also be grown on a silicon crystal, almost like hair (**Infineon**, [161], see Figure 6.54).

The tubes are grown from the ground of tiny holes by a CVD process and can be used as layer interconnections for wiring. The method also gives rise to hope for power transistors with ultra-low voltage loss and ultra-high current density.

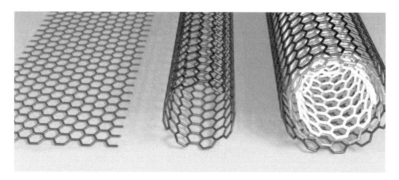

FIGURE 6.52 Carbon nanogrid and carbon nanotubes, grid structure. Image courtesy: Franz Kreupl, **Infineon**.

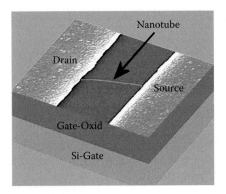

FIGURE 6.53 Single nanotube transistor. Image courtesy: Franz Kreupl, **Infineon**.

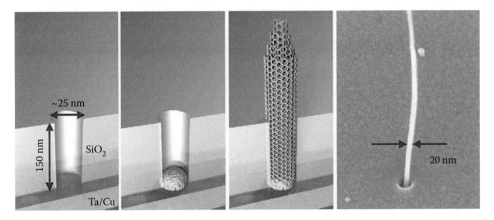

FIGURE 6.54 Growing carbon nanotubes on silicon. Image courtesy: Franz Kreupl, **Infineon**.

Mixing conducting or semiconducting nanotubes into plastics makes the plastic itself a good conductor or semiconductor. A low density of nanotubes is sufficient because of the extreme conductivity of the single tubes. Hence, transparent plastics material remains almost 100% transparent. The tubes do not even need to be directionally orientated, and they are not expensive because simple "nanotube dust" is sufficient for the purpose. Complete circuits of this kind have successfully been demonstrated for TFT displays ([247], Figures 6.55 and 6.56).

6.6.7 Printed Displays

Classical manufacturing methods for panel displays are derived from semiconductor technology and involve lacquering, exposure, and etching processes that are relatively slow and expensive. Novel technologies based on polymers for light emission and also electronic conductors and circuits allow for a direct, structured deposition of various materials on a substrate. As these materials often behave like lacquer or ink, well-established printing methods can be used for deployment.

Materials being developed for printed circuits include carbon nanotube enriched plastic, but also more "classical" semiconducting materials, such as zinc tin oxide (ZTO) have

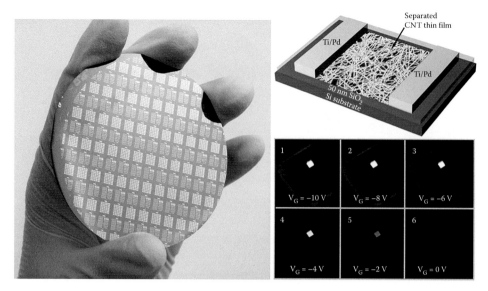

FIGURE 6.55 CMOS transistor wafer from nanotube filled polymer [247]. Image courtesy: Chongwu Zhou, University of Southern California.

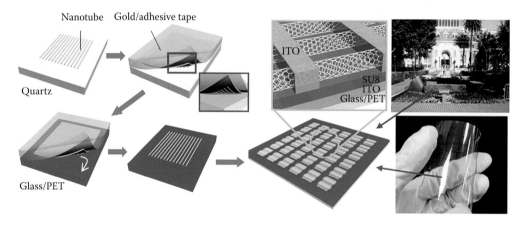

FIGURE 6.56 Transparent and flexible circuit assembly based on carbon nanotubes [135]. Image courtesy: Chongwu Zhou, University of Southern California.

been used with inkjet printing instead of the more usual vapor deposition [149]. Various electronic components, even batteries (see Section 7.3.8 at page 257), can be produced by printing.

An often-used method for electronic circuit printing is *silk-screen printing*. A fine mesh of fibers is covered with wax or other material, making it tight against color in certain areas while remaining open in others. Placing the mesh over a substrate and applying color to it lets color diffuse through the open areas and create a pattern on the substrate. This is a slow and delicate process but it has nevertheless been used for a long time, in the production of electronic components such as thin or thick film modules.

The other most common printing technology, *offset*, is much faster; it uses a metal roller with microscopic engravings according to the intended printing pattern. Color is brought

FIGURE 6.57 Left: printed polymer electronics on roll. Right: endless printed logic circuits for RFID tags. Image courtesy: **PolyIC**.

onto the metal roller with a wiper that prevents excessive deposition, then a rubber roller with defined roughness picks up the color and deposits it on a long roll of paper or other material. This *reel-to-reel* or *offset* printing is the least expensive and fastest method and is currently the foundation of almost any mass printing.

More easily controllable than offset printing is inkjet printing, which uses microscopic cavities filled with fluid (ink) by capillary forces. Either by piezo actors, or by tiny heating wires evaporating part of the fluid, tiny droplets are shot from the cavities toward a target. The perfect controllability of the material amount deposited, and the ease of creating well-defined structures, make inkjet a very interesting technology for high-quality display manufacturing.

The technology is being used for this purpose already. While not as fast or inexpensive as offset, it is still very competitive and can produce almost any size display without the need for expensive masking, handling, and etching installations, as is needed in the classical processes derived from semiconductor manufacturing.

Semiconductor structures based on polymers have gained importance in recent years. The electron mobility in polymers, however, is extremely low, so the first circuits could only work at a few Hertz. Recent development has brought faster materials and complementary transistors allowing for organic CMOS circuits (e.g., [150]). Speed has been improved to about 200 Hz, allowing for applications like intelligent display tags (e.g., variable price tags), RFID tags and more [36]. Even roll-to-roll printing is already used for polymer integrated circuits (Figure 6.57), [196,308].

Flexible electronics with carbon nanotube-enhanced materials, offering high electron mobility and fast signal processing, have made significant advances during the last years (e.g., [172]). We may expect this to gain importance for display technology in the future, perhaps together with polymer (OLED) displays.

6.7 POWER CONSUMPTION

The power consumption of a display greatly depends on its size. With modern flat-panel displays, mere light generation is the determining factor. Classical tube displays had a significant overhead for heating, high voltage generation, etc., which led to power requirements from 300 W for early all-tube devices to below 100 W for later devices greatly based on semiconductor technology.

Flat-panel displays, due to larger screen sizes, may also draw up to several 100 W. This, however, is very dependent on the brightness setting. A typical 40″ LED–LCD TV may draw between 30 and 120 W (the latter at its default brightness!). The data sheet of the very same device may list 160 W. Moreover, measurements on a similar device but with fluorescent backlight may deliver almost identical values. Screen size should make a difference, but sometimes different sized devices share similar light units.

This said, general conclusions about power consumption are impossible, except for the fact that data sheet values are usually wrong, all depends on brightness, and most devices in use – when operated at default settings – are drawing way more power than necessary.

Even technology differences hardly matter in comparison: plasma devices – less efficient – tend to be operated at lower brightness, and OLED – most efficient – tend to be set to eye-hurting brightness values for sales.

We therefore recommend always to *measure* power consumption with a power factor compensated power meter and brightness set to reasonable values.

6.8 SUMMARY

In this chapter we have learned a lot about the basics of display technology and many related topics such as TV standards, signal processing, and general requirements for proper display construction.

One conclusion that we can draw is that many display principles closely follow basic principles of visual perception, as explained in Chapter 4. This is a wise concept because displays are nothing other than human-computer interfaces to the human visual system (HVS). By reviewing what has been explained in Chapter 4, for example, we can directly correlate display resolution with eye resolution, display refresh rate with flicker fusion rate, color-space coverage with color perception, display contrast and tonal resolution with contrast sensitivity and just noticeable differences.

Another conclusion that we can draw at this point is that most existing displays are far from ideal, in particular when considering consumer displays where the cost factor is relevant. It is not easy to reach with electronics and optics what evolution has achieved in millions of years. This is reason enough to dig a bit deeper.

In the following chapter, we will cover spatial light modulation technologies that are essential for the implementation of current screens and projection displays. And we will learn more about alternatives and possibilities for improvement of today's displays.

CHAPTER 7

Spatial Light Modulation

7.1 INTRODUCTION

Light is modulated by matter, as was seen in Chapters 2 and 3. But displays and other optical instruments require a controlled way of modulating light temporally and spatially. Optical components supporting this are referred to as *spatial light modulators* (SLM). They will be discussed in this chapter.

A large variety of SLMs exist that are based on the transmission (Section 7.2), the reflection (Section 7.3 at page 247), a combination thereof called *transflection* (Section 7.4 at page 262), or the emission (Section 7.6 at page 264) of light.

In general, SLMs modify the intensity and possibly the color of light at different spatial positions. Classic examples are LCDs that filter light by polarizing and transmitting it through polarization filters, or digital micro-mirror devices (DMD, also known as *DLP*) used in digital light projectors which apply pulse-width modulation when reflecting light from an array of microscopical, moving mirrors.

Bi-stable SLM, such as e-ink or electronic paper are often used in ebook readers. Their advantage is their low power consumption since they can hold their display state without constantly applying power. A wide variety of less common SLM have been developed, such as dyed guest host displays or *electrowetting* displays. These and other forms of SLM will also be discussed in this chapter.

Using multiple SLM in a series enables advanced displays, such as high dynamic range (HDR) screens that can present high-contrast images. Stacking two 8-bit LCD panels with a contrast of 400:1 each, for instance, theoretically leads to a 16-bit SLM with a contrast of 160,000:1. This principle is called *double modulation*. The same can be achieved with other combinations of SLM, such as LED and LCD. In Section 7.8 at page 278 we will explain the basic principles of HDR displays and rendering based on double modulation.

Light-sensitive elements can be integrated into SLM. Displays with SLM of this type can generate and record images simultaneously. They are called *bi-directional displays* and are briefly discussed in Section 7.9 at page 281.

Projection displays have the advantage over other displays in that they can generate images which are larger then the actual display device itself. They also apply SLM of various types, but require additional optics imaging them onto screens. We will treat the basic components and functioning of projection displays in Section 7.10 at page 281.

7.2 TRANSMISSIVE DISPLAYS

In general, transmissive displays employ spatial light modulators to filter light. Normally they contain continuously operating light sources and generate intensities and colors by applying some sort of transmissive filtering.

The term has also been used as a specific name for displays emitting to one side while being transparent from the other (**Toshiba**, 2013). A useful application could be NED (see Section 10.8 at page 441).

7.2.1 LCD

Liquid crystal displays (LCDs) use nematic liquid crystals between two glass plates with polarizer filters. Liquid crystals were discovered as long ago as 1888, by Friedrich Reinitzer. There are *nematic*, *smectic*, and *cholesteric* liquid crystals, with increasing levels of order in their molecular structure. Most displays today use nematic liquid crystals. In 1973, the first nematic liquid crystals that worked at room temperature and were suitable for display technology were discovered by George W. Gray. Since then, LCDs have made rapid progress and are now the dominant technology for display screens.

The liquid crystal (LC) consists of lengthy dipole molecules tending to align in parallel, forming a structure that polarizes passing light.

A polyamide film on the inside glass surfaces, with parallel carvings only a few nanometers wide, aligns the LC molecules parallel to the carvings. The coatings on the upper and lower surfaces are arranged in an angle of, for example, 90° relative to each other, and the molecules tend to align to their neighbors as parallel as possible, resulting in a continuously changing orientation, twisting the polarization of passing light by 90° (Figure 7.1).

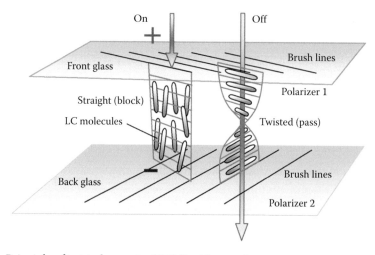

FIGURE 7.1   Principle of twisted nematic (TN) liquid crystals.

Two polarizers are added to the glass plates. They can be oriented in a 90° angle, then light passes in the off state because the LC fluid also twists polarization by 90°. They can also be oriented in parallel, which causes light to be blocked in the off state.

With an electric field applied between the plates, all LC molecules are forced into one direction (toward the electrodes), and the polarization turn is zero. With the polarizer filters added on the glass plates, the LC assembly either switches from black to transparent or vice versa, depending on their orientation. Even in the transparent state, however, the polarization filters usually absorb half of the incident light. This can be avoided by only using already polarized light.

This basic principle is called *twisted nematic* (TN) and is used in many current displays. Figure 7.2 shows the complete layer structure of a typical color display. Another early technology is *super twisted nematic* (STN), which uses an addition of cholesteric LC, has a twisting angle of over 90° and, most important, a very steep voltage response. STN is useful for simple passive matrix displays, because it reduces cell crosstalk, but it has no application in modern (active matrix) display screens.

A critical issue, especially for color displays, is the viewing angle. Simple displays show severe angular anisotropies and even a negative picture at large angles. Often the orientation foils and polarizers are not arranged in horizontal/vertical direction but diagonally, which creates the largest viewing angle ranges for the display.

An improvement of angular behavior is achieved with a design in which the LC molecules are vertically arranged in the *off* state and turned into more or less slanted directions in the *on* state. The *multi-domain vertical alignment* (MVA) design was developed by Fujitsu in 1996. It uses interleaved electrodes on the top and bottom plates to turn the LC molecules in alternately slanted angles (Figure 7.3(left)). Further improvements can be made with a zig-zag layout of the electrodes, making the overall behavior of the display less angle dependent.

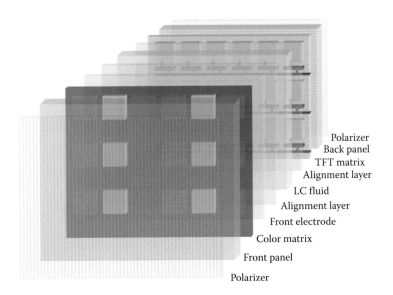

Polarizer
Back panel
TFT matrix
Alignment layer
LC fluid
Alignment layer
Front electrode
Color matrix
Front panel
Polarizer

FIGURE 7.2 Layer structure of an LCD display.

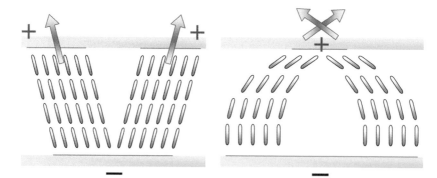

FIGURE 7.3 Principle of MVA or PVA (left) and ASV (right) electrode assemblies for improved angular range. The electrodes may also be pre-tilted perpendicular to the molecule orientations by a corresponding panel surface profile [152].

The *patterned vertical alignment* (PVA) design by **Samsung** works quite similarly to MVA but uses four different slant angles per pixel, provided by four sub-pixel electrodes. A further development of this is *super-PVA* (S-PVA), which works with eight subpixels; this is still the common technology for high-end computer monitors.

A remaining effect at large viewing angles with these display types is a certain decrease of contrast.

Another solution, currently used in many LC TV displays, is *advanced super view* (ASV). ASV uses point-like electrodes on one side and large ones at the other. This arranges molecules in a multitude of angles and in a star-like pattern around the pixel electrodes and yields specified viewing angles up to 170°.

A very different technology improving angular behavior is *in-plane switching* (IPS), as shown in Figure 7.4. There the LC molecules are aligned in one planar direction (without a twist) in the off state, and are turned by 90°, still parallel to the glass plates. This requires a comb-like electrode structure and sacrifices a lot of display area, hence light efficiency, for the electrodes. The angular range of these displays is comparable to PVA, with even less change in gamma characteristics with angle.

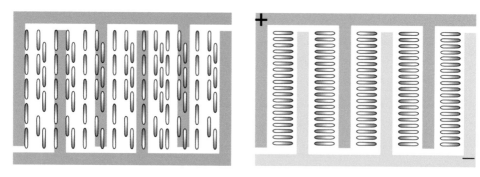

FIGURE 7.4 IPS LC principle, seen from above: off state (left) and on state (right). Both electrodes are on one side of the panel, and the molecules are floating above them.

The black level typically increases substantially at large angles. More expensive IPS panels compensate this to a certain degree by a regionally dimmable backlight (HDR display principle).

IPS is used for some high-end handheld devices, computer monitors, and recently also commonly in TVs. The latest version is dubbed *super-IPS* (S-IPS).

7.2.1.1 Driving LC Displays

The application of modulating voltage is done in various ways, depending on the intended application. For simple displays of the type used in clocks, very thin, transparent metal coatings (usually ITO) are sufficient. These allow only simple matrix structures, and speed may be limited because of electrical resistance and capacities emerging with larger structures of this kind.

For complex displays like TV screens, active driver structures are required. These are implemented as thin film transistors, either vapor deployed or, in case of organic (polymer) semiconductors, possibly silk screen-, inkjet- or offset-printed.

Switching times of LCDs have always been a major difficulty. Modern designs deliver switching times of a few milliseconds, also achieved by forced driving technologies.

With a *predictive* driving voltage generation and an overshooting voltage during the LC transition time, LC response can be accelerated (Figure 7.5). The fast switching times listed in current LC data sheets describe full black-to-white transition by default; switching from one gray level to another may take a lot longer. This is especially problematic for time-multiplexed 3D applications, where left and right pictures are displayed in an alternating way. Switching times can still lead to crosstalk in this application.

A type of LCD especially important for motion pictures are flashing backlight displays; in these the picture flashes up for only a tiny fraction of the frame duration, just by switching its light source. Switching time effects are reduced because the transitions can be hidden in the black phase.

Suitable backlights for these screens are high-powered LEDs. Flashing the usual fluorescent tubes has also been tried, but in this operation mode it is very difficult to maintain an acceptable life expectancy of the tubes, and scanning backlight would require many tubes, making LED the better alternative in any case.

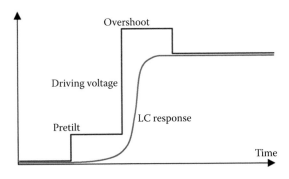

FIGURE 7.5 Forced driving pulses for an LC display, decreasing switching times.

Because LCD screen pixels are addressed sequentially and their switching delays are not negligible, an even more effective variety are scanning backlights, which illuminate any part of the screen just in the middle of its addressing time. Such a display delivers a light pattern over time, very much resembling that of a CRT screen.

A more difficult approach to improving the motion performance of LCD involves using active image processing to calculate – or rather estimate – intermediate motion frames, thus doubling or multiplying the frame rate. From about 200 Hz on, a flashing backlight is no longer necessary; the image is maintained for the entire duration of the frame, without major disadvantages.

7.2.2 FLC

Ferroelectric LC (FLC) displays are LCDs with *chiral smectic C phases*, exhibiting ferroelectric properties. They are more difficult to produce than normal LCDs, but offer very short switching times ($< 10 \mu s$, rather than $< 10 ms$ as with normal LCDs).

7.2.3 TMOS

Time multiplexed optical shutter (TMOS, [258]) displays are based on polymer films with numerous little pockets, close to a glass plate, which can be electrostatically moved toward the glass, disrupting total reflection at the surface. The "off" distance of the film pockets from the glass is only about 1 μm, and switching times are as short as 2 μs, enabling color display by sequentially switched illumination. Potentially inexpensive to produce and allowing for a high power efficiency, this display type is still in development.

7.2.4 Dyed Guest Host Displays

A dyed guest host (DGH) display is usually made of dichroic, rod-shaped dye particles diluted in liquid crystal fluid (Figure 7.6). The dye particles align parallel to the LC molecules, changing their orientation with them when voltage is applied.

Voltage between the display glass plates orients the dyes parallel to the path of the light, where they hardly influence it.

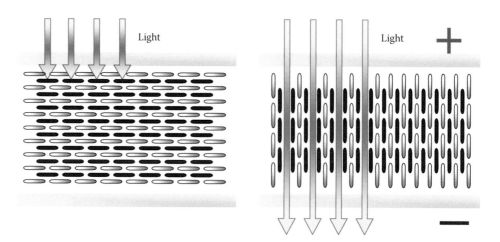

FIGURE 7.6 Dyed guest host display principle.

Without voltage, the LC molecules align with the glass plates, and are forced toward a certain direction by a brushed foil at the inside of the glass, as with common LC displays. Due to the rod shape of the dye particles, light polarized perpendicular to their orientation may still pass the display. In order to achieve strong attenuation, a polarizer is added (Hellmeyer type [124]), which incurs a base attenuation, however.

Better results are achieved with two display layers of orthogonal polarizations (double-layer DGH display).

Another type of DGH displays are *phase change* (PCGH) or White-Taylor GH [291]. Here the dye is embedded in cholesteric LC, and oriented in all directions due the spiral LC arrangement. In the off state, only a narrow color spectrum remains. In the on state, only a small absorption is present.

Contrast values reported for dyed guest host displays are up to 10:1 [275]. Response times are relatively slow due to the viscosity increase induced by the dye.

7.2.5 Other

Numerous other physical effects causing visible changes could be used for display technology.

A few more possibilities for transmissive displays will be addressed in the near-eye displays chapter, in conjunction with mask displays (Section 10.17.3 at page 487).

7.3 REFLECTIVE DISPLAYS

In contrast to transmissive displays, reflective displays apply SLMs that modulate intensities (sometimes also colors) on a reflective basis. In this section, we will discuss the most common reflective displays.

7.3.1 LCoS

Liquid Crystal on Silicon (LCoS) are LCD displays using a silicon wafer as a driving backplane. They work reflectively and allow for smaller pixel footprints (and thinner LC layers).

A liquid crystal material is coated over the surface of a silicon CMOS chip (not between polarized glass, as in normal LCD). The CMOS chip is given a reflective surface. Polarizers are located in the light path before and after the light is reflected (Figure 7.7). LCoS can

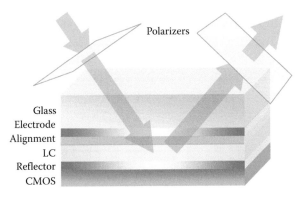

FIGURE 7.7   Reflective LCoS display principle.

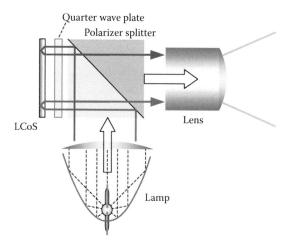

FIGURE 7.8 Projector optics for reflective LCoS.

be used as reflective micro displays, but their main application is for projectors. A working optical assembly for an LCoS projector is shown in Figure 7.8.

Compared to normal LCDs, LCoS

- are easier to manufacture

- allow for higher resolution (denser electronic circuits are in the chip)

- can be smaller

7.3.1.1 F-LCoS

Ferroelectric LCoS (F-LCoS) displays combine LCoS and FLC (ferroelectric liquid crystal) technologies; they may be produced with very small pixel sizes (currently 8 μm, but 4 μm or less are said to be possible) and currently are the technology of choice for high-resolution virtual reality goggles as well as synthetic holography. These displays are very fast. HD LCoS displays with 1920 × 1200 pixels may have a pixel size of 8 μm for example (Figure 7.9). Color is typically produced by sequential illumination, switching the light source rather than working with color filters in the display itself, a particular advantage with reflective displays.

The actual implementations of LCoS may vary for many reasons. An important consideration is the chemistry and materials used. While most LCoS varieties tend to degrade over time because of changes in their organic components due to heat and light stress, LCoS with an inorganic (SiO$_x$) alignment layer are also available (*Digital Direct Drive Image Light Amplifier* or D-ILA). These have a very long life expectancy, claimed to be similar to that of DMDs.

7.3.1.2 Phase Shifting LCD

LC fluids can not only turn polarization but also change their effective refraction indexes with voltage. This property is commonly used in laser beam shaping. Layer thickness also plays a role here since it is necessary for obtaining a sufficient phase shift.

FIGURE 7.9 Example of F-LCoS displays with 1920 × 1080 resolution. Image courtesy: **HOLOEYE Photonics** AG.

An innovative projector using LC fluids for holographic light-field synthesis (Fourier holograms) is already available, using a phase shifting LCoS display. Light field shaping together with laser sources could also be an interesting technology for near-eye displays. Also refer to Section 7.3.13 at page 260.

7.3.2 Bi-Stable LC Displays

Cholesteric[*] liquid crystal fluid (also known as *chiral nematic liquid crystal*) between two adjacent plates tends to align molecules parallel to the plates (*planar* state); the molecules further arrange themselves in spirals with axes perpendicular to the plates[†] (Figure 7.10).

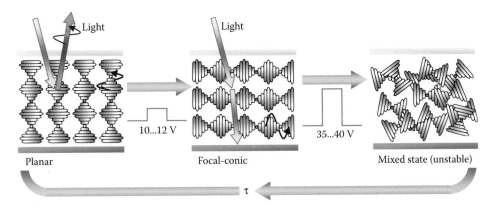

FIGURE 7.10 Principle of Cholesteric LCD.

---

[*] This phase was first observed by Friedrich Reinitzer in 1888 in derivatives of cholesterol.
[†] Spirals have a certain winding orientation, therefore *chiral*, which means asymmetric.

When voltage is applied (10 . . . 12 V typically), the molecules can also be aligned mainly vertical to the plates, but keeping their spiral local structure (*focal-conic*, Figure 7.10). This state is then maintained when voltage is removed.

Short, higher voltage pulses (35...40 V e.g.) can put the molecules into a *mixed* state that then rapidly settles to the planar state again.

Hence, it is possible to switch these LCs between two states (planar and focal-conic), and they will remain stable indefinitely even after all voltage has been removed.

In the planar mode, the molecules reflect light. The reflection is mainly a Bragg reflection (see Section 5.3.6.2 at page 135), combining up partial reflections from single molecules if the distance between them keeps all refections in phase. Hence, a certain light color is mainly reflected (typically a bandwidth of about 100 nm) [299].

Because the spiral arrangement of the molecules, the circular polarized component of the light that has the same twist as the molecule spiral is reflected, but not the other. In the focal-conic state, light can pass almost unaffected. No polarizers are required to form an image, and the plates do not need to be brushed. Simple, transparent electrode structures made from ITO, with about 25 nm of polyimide cover, are all that is needed, and cell thickness (5 μm typically) is not critical.

Normally these cells are used in reflective mode, with a black area behind. In this case they switch between black (cell transparent) to a monochrome tone (about 40% reflectance).

This kind of display is often referred to as *electronic paper* (though there are many other technologies for this purpose as well). They are a good application for ebooks, with a contrast of 25:1 even in bright sunlight, and no power consumption as long as the page is not changed. Moreover, they can also be manufactured with thin plastic foils instead of glass plates which makes them very flexible. Even coating them on textiles is possible (Figure 7.11(left)). With switching times of about 5 ms at room temperature, ebook page refreshes can still be done with passive matrix driving, line by line.

Special driving techniques can also put the LC into persistent mixed states, allowing for 16 gray levels at least. With such techniques and three colored LC screen layers for subtractive color mixing, full-color displays have been demonstrated (e.g., Kent Technologies).

FIGURE 7.11 Left: Flexible cholesteric color display on clothing. Right: Cholesteric LCD full display, 1/4 VGA resolution, supporting motion, color. Image courtesy: **Kent Displays**, Inc.

With active matrix drivers, this technology could even provide for a TV display, with the major advantage that it is brilliant in full sunlight (Figure 7.11(right)).

7.3.3 DMD

Digital Micromirror Devices (DMD), also known as *Digital Light Prcessing* (DLP), are arrays of tiny, micromechanical mirrors able to switch between two tilt positions, directing light either to the projection optics or away from it into a light trap. Due to their binary mode of operation, gray levels with DMDs are produced by pulse-width modulation (also known as *pulse-length modulation*). Switching times of typical DMD micromirrors are about 5 μs, enabling a wide range and high resolution of gray levels, even for motion picture applications.

DMD technology was developed by **Texas Instruments** more than a decade ago. From a single silicon wafer, all of the mechanical and driver structures are etched or diffused in up to 43 processing steps. A sophisticated technology, but it became affordable with progress in semiconductor technology.

Recently, the demand for mobile phone microprojectors has given DMDs a strong impulse, because their high light efficiency and the better cost effectiveness of smaller, lower-resolution types makes them competitive with the main alternative, laser projectors. While laser projectors are said to deliver crispness independent of distance, this is also true of DMDs when they are combined with laser sources (see projection displays, Section 7.10 at page 281), and with DMDs it is much easier to build high-resolution projectors, whereas laser scanners have difficulties because of the high deflection frequencies needed.

Figure 7.12 shows typical DMD elements. The mirrors are suspended on two tiny spring hinges. Even smaller spring tips serve as dampers, for a smooth settling at the end positions. The mirrors shown are 13 μm wide and are coated with aluminum for better reflectivity. Mirrors of pico displays for mobile phones are less than 8 μm wide (Figure 7.13).

Moreover, the mirrors of pico DMD are arranged diagonally and flip in the direction of the display axes rather than diagonal as with conventional DMD. This keeps the optical path entirely level and allows for a more compact projector design (see Figure 7.59 on page 292).

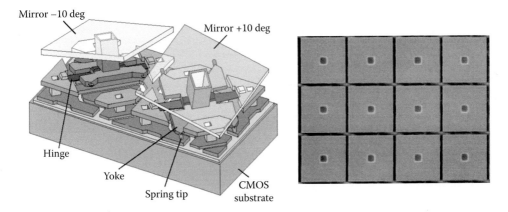

FIGURE 7.12 Left: Two DMD mirrors. Right: DMD mirror array (Courtesy: **Texas Instruments**).

FIGURE 7.13 Example of a complete pico DLP light engine, including LED, DLP and optics (**Young Optics**).

Because the spring hinges are etched from monocrystalline, pure, semiconductor-grade silicon, tilting the mirror does not impose any wear on them. Simply, each and every atom stays in place, contrary to many macroscopic springs made from inhomogeneous, amorphous, or polycrystalline materials. So these springs are losing no energy (an effect named hyperelasticity), and their life expectancy is almost unlimited. Another advantage of DMDs is their temperature resistance and very low thermal drift. Together with their excellent linearity and perfectly even brightness distribution, this makes them a prime choice for all kinds of high quality projection, including measurement applications.

7.3.3.1 Driving DMDs

DMDs are typically used at a minimum "on" pulse duration or clock of 22 μs. For 256 gray levels, pulse width hence has to go from 22 μs to about 5.5 ms, resulting in a maximum frame rate (for gray scales only) of about 180 per second (Figure 7.14). Since DMDs do not modulate color on their own, there are two ways for color projection:

Either three DMDs are combined with a dichroic beam combiner (see Section 7.10.8 at page 293), or three base colors are projected sequentially (see Section 7.10.6 at page 291).

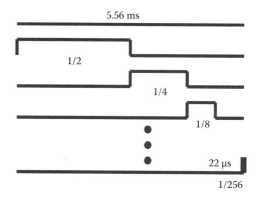

FIGURE 7.14 Example for gray level production with PWM: Gray level 42% = 100%*(1/4 + 1/8 + 1/32 + 1/64). Exactly: 42,1875%.

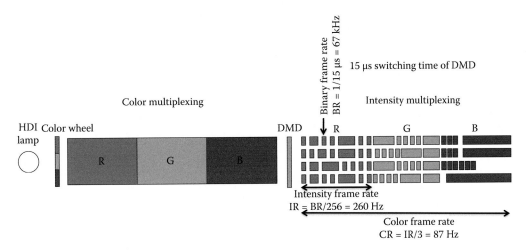

FIGURE 7.15   Example for gray level and color production with DLP projector.

The first variety is used in high-end professional cinema projectors, typically also employing ultra-resolution DMD's. Such devices are a prime choice for replacing traditional large film formats.

This solution, however, is expensive (DMD chips are expensive), so the standard solution for commercial projectors involves a color wheel, switching between base colors 150 or 180 times per second, enabling 50 or 60 Hz progressive color display. This works quite well, but there are major disadvantages:

A lot of light is wasted (only 1/3 can pass at a time), and there are color fringes visible at object edges in the picture as the viewer moves his eyes (*rainbow effect*, see Section 4.2.3 at page 93).

Objects moving inside the picture will also have rainbow edges, as they are usually followed by the eye, while the three color frames are identical (object in same position) but produced sequentially.

The latter effect can be precompensated by intelligent object shifting (involving substantial image processing), the first effect, however, is unavoidable (unless one could predict erratic eye movements and there was only one viewer).

Figure 7.15 illustrates an example for the image generation principle of a DLP projector. If we consider a shortest DMD "on" time of 15 μs (slightly faster than what has been discussed above), 256 gray scales per color channel, and 3 primary colors, then the frame rate to display a binary image (BR) is 67 kHz, the frame rate to display one gray scale image (IR) is 260 Hz, and therefore the frame rate to display one color image is 87 Hz.

7.3.4 Advanced Driving Techniques

Faster image sequences could reduce color fringes, but this alternative needs special measures:

If we use LED lighting for example, and modulate these LEDs to light with full, 1/2, 1/4, 1/8 intensity until 1/128, for 15 μs each, we could use the DMD to switch to "on" for

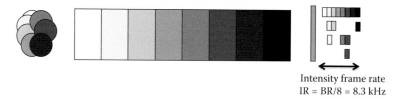

Intensity frame rate
IR = BR/8 = 8.3 kHz

FIGURE 7.16 Example for gray level and color production with potential high-speed DLP projector.

an arbitrary selection of these intensity pulses, forming a binary word of intensities, adding up to any of 256 gray levels desired.

Figure 7.16 illustrates this example. Assuming the same DMD switching speed of 15 μs (hence the same *binary rate* (BR) of 67 kHz), as in the example above, we can now achieve an *intensity rate* (IR) of BR/8 = 8.3 kHz, and a *color rate* (CR) of IR/3 = 2.8 kHz (assuming three primary colors again). Note, that the color modulation is not visualized in Figure 7.16. Color must be realized with multicolor LEDs, as the color wheel faces mechanical constraints at these high speeds.

This, however, is a purely theoretical example that considers DLP technology only. The other problem that has to be solved is the data-transfer of the images to the projector at this speed. Assuming a simple XVGA (1024 × 768 pixels) resolution, would require 6.6 GB/s upload rate at 2.8 kHz, if the images are totally uncompressed. Even a fraction of the theoretically achievable, 200 color fps for example, would nevertheless be a big improvement for motion picture projection, and could definitely be handled by current technology.

The analog amplitude modulation could spoil the perfect linearity of the DLP projector (also the color definition if the LEDs for red, green and blue have different characteristics). It would therefore be better to modulate the LED sources digitally, generating intensity by pulse-width modulation again.

This may, for example, require LED "on" times of 22 μs/128 or approximately 172 ns (Figure 7.17), hence, transition times well below this. Such parameters are achievable with many of today's devices.

This driving technique could of course be used for other switching displays (e.g., F-LCoS) as well.

Note that compared to the normal driving technique as explained in Section 7.3.3.1 at page 252, the gained acceleration comes at the price of a lower overall brightness.

7.3.5 PISTON-Type Micromirror Displays

Micro electro mechanical systems (MEMS) displays with parallel up-and-down moving mirrors are still being researched topic. Their main purpose is phase modulating holograms, for laser beam shaping or deflection, or for image projection using Fourier hologram techniques (see Section 9.6.3 at page 402).

In principle, their construction resembles that of DMDs, although the mirror suspensions used are quite different and usually they allow for a continuous motion rather than just two switching positions (Figure 7.18). This is a very important feature for holographic applications, because exact phase values are absolutely crucial for a clean and efficient hologram

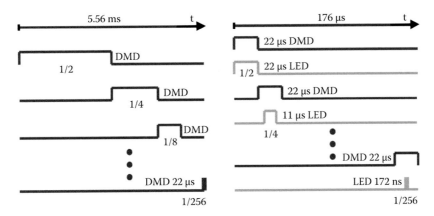

FIGURE 7.17 Driving DMD for up to 2000 color pictures per second with digital precision, with pulsed LED light (right) compared with the classical DMD driving scheme (left).

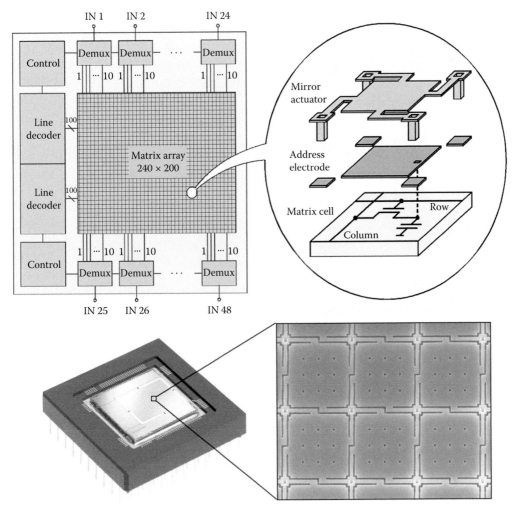

FIGURE 7.18 A 240 × 200 piston micromirror array. Image courtesy: **FhG-IPMS**.

(see Section 10.13.1 at page 461). As usual in these size ranges, the mirrors are moved by electrostatic force.

7.3.6 MLM

Moving Liquid Mirror (MLM) displays carry a liquid film on a CMOS substrate with an electrode array, undulating the film by electric forces [294]. Still a subject of research, this technology could be used for beam shaping by phase modulating (reflection or refraction). Reaction times reported are substantially longer than with micromechanical displays so far (ms vs. μs).

7.3.7 GLV

Grating Light Valve (GLV) displays are linear (1D) arrays of microscopic aluminum coated ribbons each about 100 μm long, 100 nm thick and about 3 μm wide, suspended closely above the substrate. Being switched down by elecrtrostatic force, they can either form a virtually continuous mirror or an interference grid (Figure 7.19). Because the structure is only one-dimensional, it is typically used for laser beam shaping in one axis, while the other projection axis is implemented by mechanical scanning. Color pixels are provided by different grating pitches (Figure 7.20).

GLVs switch in about 20 nanoseconds, fast enough for picture scanning with a one-dimensional GLV array and also for producing gray levels and color by pulse-length modulation. Because of their high light efficiency (reportedly up to 95%), GLVs have mainly been employed for large scale projectors (Figure 7.21).

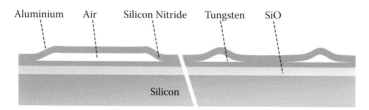

FIGURE 7.19 GLV display working principle: The left ribbon is in "off" position, the right ribbon is in "on" position, attracted to the substrate by electrostatic force.

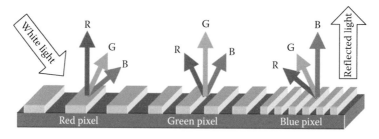

FIGURE 7.20 GLV display color generation: Arranging ribbons in different spaces makes them work like a diffraction grating, reflecting colors in different directions. Typical GLV pixels consist of six ribbons (three of them moving). Only one color per pixel is sent into the projector's light path.

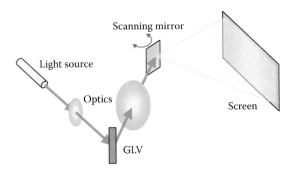

FIGURE 7.21 GLV projector example: The GLV line generates one vertical display line at a time, the image is generated by horizontal scanning.

7.3.8 Polymer Displays

This term is used (appropriately) for any kind of organic displays, such as polymer based OLEDs, for example. Formerly, only reflective varieties (*electronic paper*) were summarized under this term. We chose to list the different varieties of polymer technology (from OLED to electronic paper) under their specific names later.

7.3.8.1 Electrochromic Polymers

Electrochromic polymer displays switch between a transparent state and selective color band absorption.

Several colors are available, but current products use them one at a time. The NanoChromics technology by **NTERA** for example, uses electrochromic, cabon-based viologen molecules between two plastic sheets with transparent electrodes and a white TNO layer (which gives the display a white background for e-paper applications). The rear electrode is made up of antimon-doped ZnO and gives the display a bi-stable behavior (image remains when power is switched off). **NTERA** very recently demonstrated a prototype containing not only a printed display of said type, but also a printed battery ("Disbattery") manufactured in the same run (Figure 7.22), allowing the display to run on its own, like, for example, an intelligent tag [199].

FIGURE 7.22 First printed display with integrated battery printed in same process. Image courtesy: **NTERA**.

7.3.9 E-Ink

E-Ink (*electronic ink*) is a proprietary technology already found in mass applications, such as ebook readers for example. It consists of myriads of microcapsules less than 1/10 mm small. Each microcapsule contains positively charged white particles and negatively charged black particles suspended in a clear fluid. With an electric field applied, the white particles move to the top of the microcapsule where they make the surface appear bright to the viewer. By inverting the field, the black particles appear at the top of the capsule, now making the surface appear dark.

With dense electrode arrays, single e-ink capsules could also be excited partly or at an angle, resulting in the appearance of a gray dot. Yet in any practical implementation the electrodes are a lot bigger than the capsules (Figure 7.23). Combining areas of capsules with color dyes, color displays can be achieved. The maximum reflectivity for white however, is very limited in this case.

For production, the microcapsules are suspended in a liquid medium allowing them to be printed onto virtually any surface, also allowing for flexible displays (Figure 7.24) or applications in *intelligent clothing*.

7.3.10 Electrowetting Displays

Electrowetting displays (EWD) are based on a layered structure consisting of a water-repellent electrode array, covered by a thin oil film and a thin water film above. Applying a voltage between the water and the electrodes causes this stable state to change, with the water moving toward the electrode and pushing the oil on that pixel aside. The pixel color thus changes between the color of the oil and the color (or reflectance) of the electrode. High reflectance and contrast can be achieved this way, the display requires little power and the technology is fast enough for video.

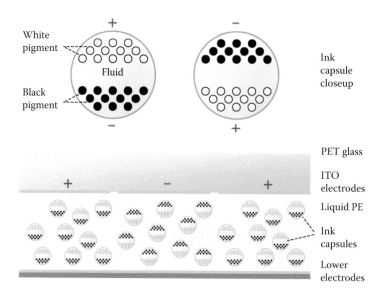

FIGURE 7.23 Working principle of **e-ink**: single capsules with voltage applied (top), display assembly (bottom).

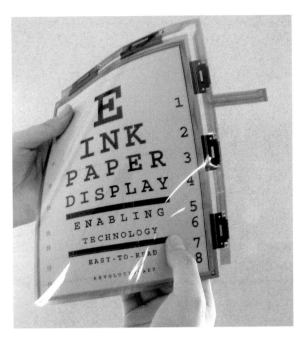

FIGURE 7.24   Example of flexible **e-ink** display. Image courtesy: **LG Philips LCD**.

With transparent electrodes, several pixels with different transparent-colored oils can be stacked, allowing for a subtractive color composition with high brightness and contrast. A working color ebook reader with a 6″ electrowetting display was presented in 2010 and is supposed to become commercially available in 2011 (**Liquavista**, a **Philips** spin-off).

7.3.11 Electrofluidic Displays

Electrofluidic displays [123] have small reservoirs of an aqueous color dispersion for each pixel (approximately 10% of the area). Electrical force is used to press the liquid into the main pixel area, while capillary force serves to retract it. The active pixel area here is larger than that of electrowetting displays.

7.3.12 iMOD Displays

This technology, called *interferometric modulator display* (**iMOD**), works with thin transparent membranes approximately 1 μm above a silicon chip. Light rays reflected from the chip and the membrane interfere, resulting in brightness change and colorizing (the same effect that creates colors on butterfly wings). Applying voltage draws the membrane to the silicon by electrostatic force, changing reflection characteristics. The display elements are bi-stable.

The distance between membrane and chip in rest position defines the pixel color, while brightness is modulated by pulse width, exploiting the fast switching speed of $\approx$50 μs. An example is the **Mirasol** display by **Qualcomm** (2010), a 5.7″ XGA display capable of playing video at full frame rate. Reflectivity for the specific color band in **iMOD** displays can be similar to that of a (dichroic) mirror, hence quite optimal. A problem may be the directional sensitivity of the spectral response (the gap defining the interference gets relatively bigger with 1/cosine of the incident angle).

Because the color of a pixel is fixed, separate pixels are necessary for the base colors, which limits brightness for white to less than 1/3. Hence, while this technology can be used for reflective color displays, the image will appear darker than an average printed photo (in which subtractive color mixing is used).

Analog versions of this principle could be conceived; in this case, the spectral color of each pixel could be freely selected, and brightness could be modulated by pulse width due to the fast reaction time of the pixel elements. Several colors could be combined, sequentially, in a single pixel; yet, the total maximum reflectivity of the display would not increase this way.

7.3.13 Refractive Index Modulation

Certain chemicals change their refraction index when voltage is applied.

For example, liquid crystals can be used in modes exploiting their refraction changes only. With LCoS displays, a common application is laser beam shaping by modulated fringe patterns. Figure 7.25 shows an LCoS display modulated with a zone plate pattern.

Polymer Dispersed Liquid Crystal (PDLC) consists of droplets of LCs inside a polymer [84], [202]. Inside these droplets, ranging from 0.3 to 3 μm in size, the LC molecules arrange in random directions (Figure 7.26(left)). In this state, light experiences a refraction index change upon entering a droplet. Hence, light is scattered at any of the droplets, with characteristics dependent on droplet size (Rayleigh- or Mie scattering, see Section 3.3.1.1 at page 58). From the incident side, the material looks brighter, from the other side it gets darker, perhaps very dark if the material has a certain basic attenuation, increasing its effect when the light has to travel further.

If voltage is applied, all LC molecules align perpendicular to the enclosing glass plates and so approximately parallel to light rays passing the display (Figure 7.26(right)). In this arrangement, the molecules have almost no influence. If the LC fluid is matched to the enclosing polymer, the entire volume appears homogeneous and light passes unaffected.

FIGURE 7.25 High-resolution LCoS micro display showing zone plate fringe patterns (left). Enlargement of a single pattern, made visible by polarized light (right). (Image courtesy: **HOLOEYE Photonics** AG.)

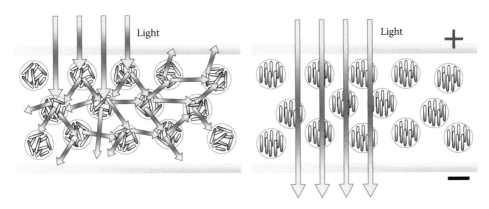

FIGURE 7.26   Light switching by refraction index modulation.

A special application of refraction index modulation is the **DigiLens** by **SBG Labs**, Inc. This is a Bragg hologram (see Section 5.3.6 at page 133) recorded in a nanocomposite material called a *Reactive Monomer Liquid Crystal Mix* (RMLCM). The hologram is recorded as usual, by interfering laser light. In the material this creates regions with numerous liquid crystal microdroplets, parted by regions of clear photopolymer. Applying a voltage via electrodes reorientates the LC droplets, reducing the refractive index modulation. The diffraction efficiency then changes from very high to nearly zero, in less than a millisecond. The technology can be used for switching optical elements, but also for potentially forming display pixels with very special behavior.

7.3.14 Electronic Paper

The term *electronic paper* relates to reflective displays that can be read under strong ambient light, like real paper, preferably holding images also when driving voltage is removed, operate at very low power and hence can be used in light-weight, large-screen devices serving to replace classic print media.

This should not be confused with "digital paper", which relates to a technology that allows the user to virtually write on a touchscreen with a pen. In many cases, electronic paper displays are also flexible, although current ebook readers don't make use of this feature. Several technologies exist for e-paper, as mentioned above.

The earliest varieties were bi-stable cholesteric LCDs, which allowed several distinct properties such as flexibility. Their contrast, however, was a weak point. Meanwhile, the reflectivity of some varieties has become competitive and color displays with video compatible response times are also possible (Kent Technologies).

The most popular e-paper technology currently is electronic ink (**e-ink**), used in the **Kindle** ebook reader for example.

iMOD displays are generically colored due to their pixel forming by interference and could perhaps even be used for subtractive color mixing.

Electrowetting displays are close to market entry and can provide for very bright color e-paper. The same applies for electrofluidic displays but these are not as close to practical application.

Considering possible reflective 3D displays, these could be built with microlenses (autostereoscopic or light field) or possibly using DigiLens elements which could provide for spatial or even color modulation, perhaps also combined with conventional display technology. This would greatly surpass the simple mimicking of real paper (moving pictures of course are doing so as well). Hence, electronic paper will not just remain flat and static, it will give rise to entirely new media types and experiences.

7.4 TRANSFLECTIVE DISPLAYS

Transmissive displays rely on some kind of rear illumination. This works well indoors, but outdoors ambient light may get so bright that no kind of illumination could provide enough contrast; the display image would simply become invisible. The same applies for self-luminous displays (i.e., emissive displays, as explained in Section 7.6 at page 264).

Reflective displays use the environment light itself and become more effective the brighter it is. Indoors, however, they may deliver poor results, and without ambient light they show nothing. LC technology allows to combine transmissive and reflective behavior in one *transflective displays.*

Several methods are possible for implementing transflective LC displays:

- A partial reflector behind the LC allows light to pass from an additional light source behind it.

- The backlighting may be implemented as a light emitting foil that itself has a white surface color.

- The light guiding panel of an LC display's back illumination may be equipped with a white backside.

- The backside polarizer of an LC panel may be a film that reflects light of one polarization but gives pass to the other (**Vukuti** film by **3 M**).

A transflective mode is efficient only for displays capable of a reflective mode already. Transmissive color LCDs commonly used for TV and computer screens will not work, because only a very small amount of light passes to the back panel, and the display will look almost black with no additional backlighting.

Displays suitable for electronic paper are transparent enough for a reflective mode as well as for a transmissive mode, although not all types may be ideal for this purpose.

Transflective displays have been in use for many years, but their largest market segment was simple black-and-white applications, in mobile phones, pocket calculators, PDAs or GPS devices.

For a high-quality color display, there must be a smooth transition from back illuminated to reflective mode. In reflective mode light passes the display twice, so contrast in this case is much higher than in the "shine-through" case.

FIGURE 7.27 Comparison in full sunlight, of a normal notebook display and a **PixelQi** display, delivering an additional black-and white reflective mode. Image courtesy: **Pixel Qi** Corp.

An approach to increase reflective contrast (by PixelQi, see Figure 7.27), combines a transmissive color mode with a reflective black-and-white mode (and a third mode with reduced color). Of course, a black-and-white image is still better than none. The b/w mode also has a higher resolution; it uses each single pixel in the color triplets separately.

One method to overcome the color-contrast problem is to use separate pixels for each mode. This reduces reflective light by half, so it is not recommended for a high performance display.

Sensing the external light and adapting the display backlight concurrently with the contrast of the displayed image is a quite successful approach. This way, a smooth transition between modes can be achieved (e.g., Figure 7.28).

For fast-changing light conditions, a color temperature adaptation of the backlight or the display image may also be considered.

FIGURE 7.28 Naval transflective display, night through daylight adaptive. Image courtesy: **WRSYSTEMS**.

If a sufficient *reflective* display technology is available, an alternative to the transflective display could an additional illumination of the reflective display, from the front side. The main advantage to this approach is that it is not necessary to adjust contrast. Usually this requires some space above the display, but a light-guiding panel in front of the display could also be used. For example, a glass plate filled with light from the sides and equipped with numerous microscopic (practically invisible) tilted mirror elements within the front plane, reflecting parts of the light toward the display, could be a useful solution.

With the growing number of portable computing devices also demanding high-quality color displays, the demand for transflective displays or reflective displays with illumination will be greater than ever. Emerging technologies in the *electronic paper* field may deliver an overall performance not only making displays competitive with print media but also adding the feature of built-in illumination.

7.5 TRANSPARENT BACKLIGHT DISPLAYS

Edge backlights with light guides using diffractive or Bragg structures can be entirely transparent, and allow to build translucent light valve displays (e.g., LCD). According products have been presented (**Samsung, LG**). The **Smart Window** by **Samsung,** for example, can be used instead of a real window. It uses daylight or a transparent backlight unit with a diffractive light guide, and it incorporates a transparent touch screen as well. As the display is occlusive, it can also be used as a window blind. A specific advantage, apart from some practical usability aspects, is the low power consumption when the backlight is not needed.

OLEDs are another option for a transparent backlight. For OLED layers, typically less than $1\,\mu m$ thin, transparency is common, and display-sized light foils are achievable. A complication is the generation of white light.

7.6 EMISSIVE DISPLAYS

Emissive displays are characterized by their self-luminous screen. They are different from transmissive or transflective displays, which may have a quite similar appearance but rely on separate light sources.

7.6.1 CRT

CRTs (*Cathode Ray Tubes*) work with electron beams emitted from an (usually heated) electrode and traveling to a phosphor-coated screen from which the electrons cause visible light to be emitted. The entire assembly is inside a vacuum tube (allowing the electrons to travel freely).

The electron source has a negative charge and is called the *cathode*, while the glass tube has a positive charged electrode called the *anode*, causing the electrons to accelerate toward the screen.

Heated materials emit electrons that can be drawn away from the material by application of an electric field. The first cathodes simply were heated metal threads. Soon they were replaced by a combination of a heated thread and an oxide layer with an orders of magnitude higher electron emission. In modern CRTs, highly optimized emission materials are used;

the heating up of the cathode causes a power-on delay, which has been minimized to a few seconds with modern tubes by applying a short, well-defined current surge.

The phosphorous screen coating of the CRT emits light because the accelerated beam electrons push other electrons in the screen's atoms to higher energy levels. When they fall back to their rest level after a random time, these electrons release energy by emitting photons. By appropriate mixing of chemicals, "phosphors" emitting various colors can be created.

CRTs were first marketed in about 1922. These first tubes had rather round screens (easier to manufacture and sturdy enough to withstand the pressure of air against the vacuum inside) and a screen emitting more or less white light.

Poor beam definition and light spreading behind the curved screen and inside the phosphor gave these CRT a rather "soft" picture and poor contrast. Modern CRTs have special coatings and black grids between the phosphors, minimizing these effects.

Geometrical errors of early CRTs were large, and the analog signal processing by electron tube circuits caused all sorts of nonlinearities and drifts, requiring frequent manual image adjustment. In 1953, color TV was first introduced in the US. The simple CRT concept used was three electron sources emitting three almost parallel beams, being deflected by the same magnetic field. These three beams maintain a certain convergence/divergence even when approaching the screen (Figure 7.29).

A *shadow mask* behind the screen, essentially a metal plate with holes, causes images of the three electrodes to appear on the screen, just like little pinhole cameras. Each appropriately positioned phosphor dot of a primary color hence receives electrons from just one of the cathodes (Figure 7.30(center)). One hole in the shadow mask is fitted to any phosphor triplet. This simple principle requires little precision other than appropriate positioning of the mask holes relative to the phosphor pattern. The electron beams approach their proper color dots only by means of their incident angle and the shadow mask. Typically, each beam always

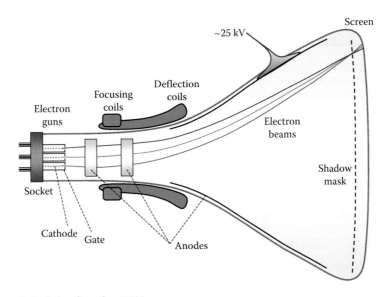

FIGURE 7.29 Principle of a color CRT.

 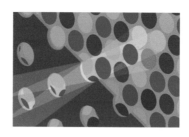 

FIGURE 7.30 Left: deflection unit of a modern color CRT with optimized copper coils. Center: principle of the shadow mask. Right: **Trinitron** (top) and stripe mask (bottom).

lights several dots (of the same color) at a time. The approach wastes a lot of beam power, however, since most of the electrons are absorbed in the shadow mask.

More elaborate constructions have been devised during the about 50 years since CRTs were the only color image displays available. The mask has been reduced to a stripe mask, or a wire comb in the extreme (**Trinitron** tube), with the cathodes lying in a straight row. Wire combs require extreme tension in order not to vibrate, adding a heavy frame to the construction, and even then the wires have to be stabilized by thin cross wires of tungsten.

The *stripe mask* essentially is a comb with numerous bridges between the wires (Figure 7.30), and it became popular with most manufacturers. All these developments increased the transmissivity of the original color mask from about 15% to about 20%.

All shadow mask CRTs have intrinsic problems with the convergence of the electron beams. The larger the tube's deflection angle, the more the three beams tend to misalign, especially in the screen corners, which results in colored fringes around objects. Elaborate circuits were devised for compensation, because due to manufacturing tolerances, early color TVs had dozens of convergence adjustment screws, making adjustment a veritable art. Later color CRTs required very little adjustment although they had larger deflection angles, because of computer-optimized construction and minimized production tolerances of tube and deflection coils (Figure 7.30(left)).

One attempt to get away from the poor mask transmissivity was the Chromatron, with a wire mask allowing the application of high voltages between adjacent wires, deflecting and concentrating the (one) beam electrostatically after the mask, addressing each of three color phosphor stripes per wire pair sequentially. This works with just one electron gun and hence avoids convergence problems. However this system never became reliable enough for market entry.

Another variety, *index CRTs*, need no mask. They work with UV-emitting *index* stripes between color stripes, providing the driver circuit with timing references for correct addressing of the phosphors. This type has mainly been used for very small color CRTs. It has never been in wide use, because color purity depends on beam focusing, and the electronics required were quite expensive at times when electron tubes were most popular.

CRT screens have become more and more flat and square, imposing huge difficulties on tube stability. Large "flat" CRTs require an immense glass thickness, making them prohibitively heavy and limiting screen sizes, which is one reason why large LCDs quickly gained large market shares once they became affordable.

The contrast of a CRT largely depends on the material color of the phosphors. These are usually bright colors; without special measures the screen would reflect too much ambient light for good contrast. A gray-dyed front glass reduces this effect, since ambient light has to pass it twice, but the screen light only once. Implementing the gray screen with lead glass also serves to reduce X-ray emissions from the screen efficiently.

Soft X-rays are emitted from all larger CRTs because of the abrupt deceleration of the electrons at the screen. Their energy is given by the anode voltage: with 25 kV for example, typical for a color CRT, X-rays of 25 keV are emitted. This is at the very low end of X-ray spectra used for medical diagnostics. Nevertheless, these rays obviously have a damaging effect on cells and need to be shielded.

Other forms of emissions from CRTs are electrical fields. The electrostatic charge of the front screen is a nuisance. It causes CRT TV's to attract lots of fine dust from the surroundings, so frequent cleaning is required.

Magnetic fields from the deflection are suspected to cause health hazards, but this is still a rather controversial topic. In summary, possible health hazards are one argument for replacing CRTs with other technologies.

An advantage of CRTs is that they are not rastered. The deflection of a CRT can continuously be adapted to arbitrary image frequencies and line numbers. Hence, image signals can be displayed at their native resolution, with no requirement for scaling. Nevertheless, fine image structures can still cause Moiré effects with the shadow mask. This can be an issue with computer monitors, which therefore often have special electronic provisions against it.

CRTs are the only displays so far reproducing interlaced TV signals correctly, except for certain kinds of plasma screens, where it is possible to use interlacing, but only in their native HD resolution (**AliS**, see Section 7.6.3 at page 269). Although LCD with appropriate line numbers could also do this, all products known so far use deinterlacing and scaling. We focused on interlacing and deinterlacting in Section 6.2.2 at page 180.

Disadvantages of CRT mainly are geometrical distortions, color aberrations and lower sharpness – but all in moderate dimensions with advanced CRTs.

7.6.1.1 Deflection

The electron beam is deflected by a magnetic field in order to write an image onto the screen, line by line. As the deflection coils basically are inductors, they are driven by a constant voltage (causing constantly increasing current) to draw a line. To retract the beam, voltage is turned off, causing the current to break down at maximum speed (and a high back-firing voltage to occur at the coil, usually also exploited to generate the anode voltage).

The beam is modulated with the image content while the line is written and clamped to black level at retrace. Since retrace time cannot be zero, a certain reserved time had to be written into TV standards, also because capturing an image was relying on tubes as well.

While writing line by line, the beam also has to be deflected vertically, at a much lower frequency, usually also by magnetic coils integrated in the deflection unit.

7.6.2 FED and SED

The principle of the CRT also works for single pixels. From a large number of tiny single-pixel tubes, a flat panel display can be constructed. The main obstacle is finding a cathode that works without heating and at as low a voltage as possible.

Pin emitters are one approach. At the tip of a pin, electric fields concentrate in an extreme way, making electron emission a lot easier. From about 10^7 V/cm on, the tunneling effect starts to enable electron emission.

For CRTs, this has not been implemented, because the current flow would have burned away the pin. The same problem on a smaller scale occurs in single pixel assemblies. The first *field emission displays* (FED) suffered from poor durability.

An alternative approach was tried, using highly effective area cathodes (e.g., palladium oxide). The principle of such a *Surface-conduction Electron-emitter Display* (SED) cell is shown in Figure 7.31; it proved difficult to bring into mass production.

A breakthrough with FEDs was accomplished with cathodes made of microstructured carbon pins (Figure 7.32). While there may be several ways to do this, the best approach is using many parallel carbon nanotubes. Nanotubes are extremely thin, making up ideal pins, and they are also extremely rugged and durable.

Growing carbon nanotubes almost hair-like on a silicon wafer has been demonstrated (see Section 6.6.6.3 at page 236).

Displays built from micro CRT cells have been demonstrated as large flatscreen TVs already. Their advantages are a wide viewing angle, fast switching times, and large color gamut. Important for success are manufacturing costs of course. HDTVs were announced for 2007 (**Toshiba**), but we are still waiting and it seems the massive price drop with LCD had its impact here.

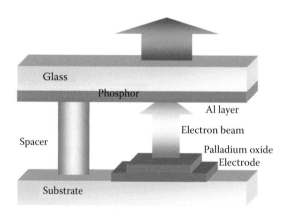

FIGURE 7.31 Surface-conduction Electron-emitter Displays (SED) cell principle.

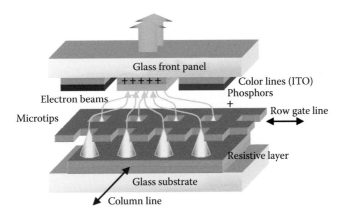

FIGURE 7.32 Pixel scheme of a FED. The gap between the glass plates is approximately 2.5 mm.

7.6.3 Plasma Displays

Plasma displays have a small fluorescent gas discharge cell for each individual pixel. The cells have a low-pressure gas filling of neon or xenon. Horizontal row electrodes and vertical column electrodes generate high-voltage pulses (passive matrix driving). Any voltage change causes a discharge current pulse that causes an ionization of the gas atoms and the release of UV photons (Figure 7.33). The intensity of the light flash generated depends on the electric energy of the discharge. The color phosphor layer coated onto the inside walls of the cells is stimulated by UV light to emit visible light. Other designs simply using two opposite electrodes (dubbed *DC*) have been tried, but failed for poor performance.

Figure 7.34 shows three plasma cells and the top electrodes coated on a glass panel, with ITO as transparent layers and additional narrow metal bus wires, which are necessary because of the relatively high resistance of the ITO. A very important ingredient is the about-500-nm-thin MgO layer. It protects the dielectric from sputtering and provides a secondary electron emission under ion impact. MgO so far is the only material able to provide

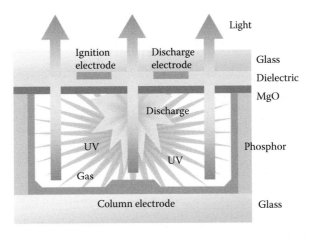

FIGURE 7.33 Working principle of a plasma display cell (the ignition and discharge electrodes have been drawn to 90°. Turned for better visualization; actually they would go from left to right).

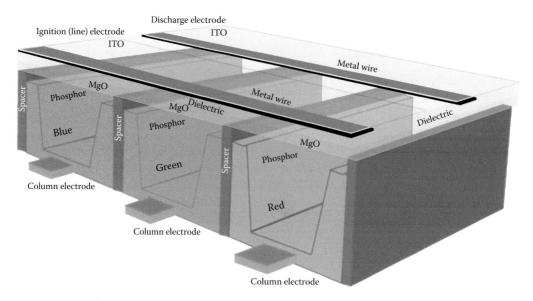

FIGURE 7.34   Three cells of a plasma display (principle).

high efficiency as well as endurance. Without the discovery of MgO as an electrode material, there would have been no plasma displays.

The most common driving scheme is *AC-powered side discharge*. It uses a high-voltage pulse to ionize the gas and thereafter a smaller AC voltage for the discharge. Charge carriers are seeded to a cell if voltage is applied between the ignition (line) and the column electrode (raster scan), causing a UV-emitting discharge to occur when afterward the (AC) discharge voltage is applied to the ignition and discharge electrodes of the entire panel. Figure 7.35 shows an example that is easily explained and should be helpful to introduce the general principle. Note that several detail variations exist in actual circuits and driving schemes of plasma panels. More advanced schemes also allow for an interleaving of scan and sustain phases [144]. A detailed treatment of many aspects of plasma display technology can be found in [41].

What we have described so far, could only provide two brightness levels per pixel: on or off. Gray levels have to be assembled by sequences of images of different duration (and hence different brightness contribution), called *subfields*. This is a similar approach as with DMD, shown in Figure 7.14 on page 252. It sometimes leads to an effect called *false contour* with fast-moving objects, as different brightness layers of the object are drawn at different times. More expensive plasma displays may contain signal processing for a pre-compensation of this effect by motion-sensitive pixel shifting.

False contour is not a predominant effect, however, as only the larger gray-level steps (bits) may become visible as double edges. Hence, even cheap plasma panels compete with 100…200 Hz LCD for motion resolution. Figure 7.36 shows a comparison of plasma pulse series at two different brightness levels (widest pulse on or off) with analog pulse shapes approximating a temporal average of the digital pulse sequence.

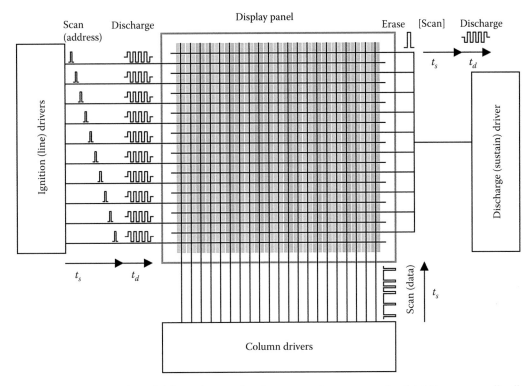

FIGURE 7.35 Exemplary driving scheme of a plasma panel: an erase pulse (right) prepares all cells for writing, then scan address and data pulses seed charges to individual cells (t_s), and then an AC discharge voltage is applied for t_d. t_d is different for each subfield.

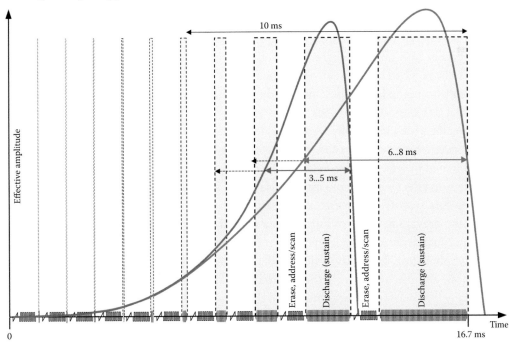

FIGURE 7.36 Approximation of effective perceived pulse duration.

The minimum pixel size of a standard plasma display is about 0.3 mm; so, this technology is specialized for large displays, viewed from a distance of 1 m or more.

7.6.3.1 ALiS

A technology especially suited for high resolution was developed by **Fujitsu** in 1999. The **ALiS** (*Alternate Lighting of Surfaces*) structure [20] has no closed cells but two large panels with electrodes and spacers. The discharge occurs between adjacent line electrodes, alternately for even and odd lines. The electrodes alternately take the roles of ignition and discharge electrodes, and the discharge occurs in ionized patches between them. This requires only half as many electrodes, and the electrodes cover less front panel area, so more light can be emitted.

The alternating display of even and odd lines works like interlacing, and can be used to display interlaced sources.

Originally this was developed for high-resolution computer displays since it allows for much smaller cells than the conventional approach. Interlacing, however, does not work well for such monitors because they are always viewed from a close distance and small structures (characters, etc.) are affected by line flickering.

A dedicated application for this technology was high-resolution TV. There, a genuine interlaced operation can be an advantage, especially for the 1920×1080 format. False contour effects may still occur, however, so this does not work quite as ideal as a CRT.

Plasma displays were often criticized for high energy consumption. Power drain is specified for an entirely white picture, so with a self-luminescent display, the actual power consumption is highly dependent on picture content. Typical LCD displays, on the other hand, draw continuous power and most of it is wasted (absorbed) in the display panel.

Plasma screens made considerable progress regarding power consumption. A recent plasma screen in typical applications (TV) now competes with an earlier LCD screen. Recent LCD, especially with LED backlight, however, restored the distance to plasma again.

Plasma displays had a better color rendition than early LCD, their useful viewing angle is wider than with many LCD types, and partly also their contrast range, given the problems of some LCDs to provide deep black.

One specific problem initially were burn-in effects, occurring when static pictures were displayed over a long time, but this is not likely in typical TV applications and has greatly been eliminated by a factory pre-aging of the panels.

The burn-in effect with plasma displays is not the same as known from early TV or computer monitors with CRT screens, which occurred due to bad phosphors.[*] With plasma displays, the prevailing cause of burn-in is a degradation of the MgO layer by sputtering, causing an MgO deposition on the phosphor (which actually is not phosphor degradation). A genuine phosphor degradation due to the aggressive plasma has also been supposed. But anyhow, the life expectancy the plasma displays has meanwhile been improved so substantially that plasma has become one of the most durable technologies [243].

---

[*] Note that phosphor aging and burn-in, contrary to many sources, has *not* been a relevant issue with color CRT since decades now; these tubes would age by cathode degradation, especially of the "red" cathode (which has to deliver the largest current).

As prices for plasma displays had dropped with time, even below the level of LCDs, they became a viable alternative if price was regarded more important than power consumption or maximum brightness. Nevertheless, plasma displays have meanwhile been discontinued (and the same applies to fluorescent backlight LCD displays).

7.6.4 Electroluminescence Displays

Although electroluminenscence (EL, see Section 2.3.9 at page 28) is present in numerous display types such as LED or OLED, the term EL display usually refers to devices where an inorganic material (a "phosphor") is caused to luminate by means of high AC voltage and resulting (capacitive) current flow (see Figure 7.37). Because of the high driving voltages, these displays are not very popular any longer.

7.6.5 LED

LED (see Section 2.3.9 at page 28) displays are mainly useful for giant screens built from a large number of matrix modules containing many individual LEDs. Small inorganic LED displays are impractical because of the difficulty of integrating GaAs LED chips on a silicon driving chip, although a few *LED on silicon* products were developed before they were all replaced by OLED on silicon. Plain LED displays are seeing a revival as backlights for large LCD screens, where little resolution is needed. LEDs, with their narrow color bandwidth, improve the color definition and energy efficiency of LCDs and can also increase contrast by forming a low-resolution dynamic backlight screen (see Section 7.8 at page 278). Moreover they can easily produce a *flashing backlight*, improving motion definition. In current products advertised as LED TVs, actually an LCD panel works with an LED backlight panel.

7.6.6 OLED

OLED (*organic light emitting diodes*) are based on organic materials emitting light when being transgressed by electric current.

The two major types are *polymer OLEDs* based on large molecules (Figure 7.38), and *small-molecule OLEDs* (Figure 7.39).

OLED displays have already found many commercial applications, from miniature color displays to lamps for room lighting. Their efficiency has approached that of anorganic LEDs.

Similar to other technologies, OLEDs are also divided into passive driven displays or lamps (POLED) and active matrix driven displays (AMOLED).

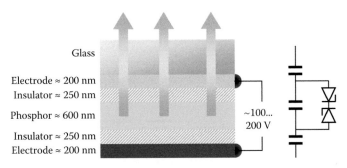

FIGURE 7.37 Electroluminescent (EL) display principle.

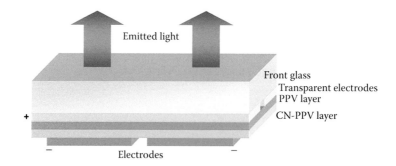

FIGURE 7.38 Principle of polymer OLED pixels.

Current active matrix OLED displays mostly work with inorganic TFT structures.

The use of organic semiconductor structures by inkjet printing (mainly for polymer materials) has been demonstrated in several ways already (see Section 6.6.7 at page 237) and may make these displays very affordable in the future, if problems with electron mobilty (speed) can be resolved.

With microdisplays, classical manufacturing processes (wafer technology, vacuum deployment with small molecule materials) are not so expensive and are the option of choice (OLED on CMOS, for example).

OLED displays can provide good motion rendition because of fast switching times, high contrast and color fidelity, and a wide viewing angle. A specific advantage is their low power consumption because of the self-luminating principle. Their life expectancy will also become very high.

Figure 7.39 shows a sectional cut through an OLED chip, Figure 7.40 a pixel driver circuit, including a pixel storage capacitor. There are two principal layer sequences for the OLED stack, either emitting the light through a transparent anode and the (in this case: glass) substrate, or through a transparent cathode (Figure 7.41).

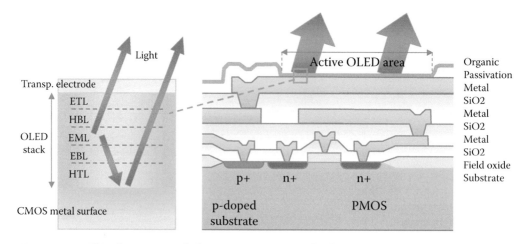

FIGURE 7.39 Chip design example for OLED-on-CMOS display pixels.

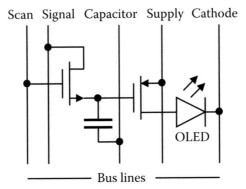

FIGURE 7.40 Typical circuit of an OLED-on-CMOS display pixel.

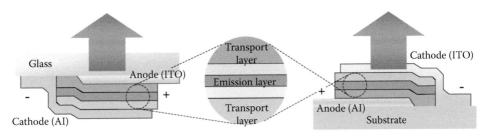

FIGURE 7.41 OLED display pixels as bottom emitter (left) and top emitter (right).

A problem with early OLED displays was their peak current tolerance. To increase the size of single pixels and reduce current density, special color subpixel schemes, the so-called **PenTile** schemes, have been invented. An exemplary variety consists of red, green, blue, and white subpixels (Figure 7.42). The white pixels allow for higher brightness for less saturated colors. The main advantage is that the scheme allows writing non colored image detail only two sub pixels wide, without risking color Moiré effects. With the classic RGB pixel scheme, three sub-pixels are required.

Newer OLED displays tend to have normal pixel patterns, such as r,g,b or r,b,g,b. Currently there are two different implementations: **Samsung** uses red, green, and blue OLED pixels, while **LG** uses white pixels with red, green, and blue color dye filters, which are reportedly simpler to produce.

Consumer OLED TVs went into mass production about 2013. The price level however dropped very slowly, due to production yield problems. Also considering the improvements achieved with LED–LCD panels, such as better color range by quantum dot-enhanced phosphors, a replacement of these panels by OLED products may take its time. Nevertheless, OLED displays involve less components and should therefore, on the long run, even become cheaper than other technologies.

7.6.6.1 Transparent OLED

Transparent OLED (TOLED) are transparent like a glass plate when inactive; pixels "glow" when addressed but the display remains transparent even when active. If combined with a

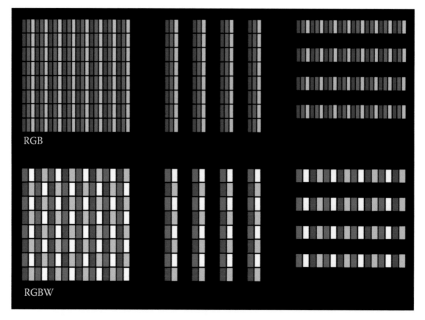

FIGURE 7.42 A **PenTile** subpixel scheme used for OLED displays (bottom) compared to usual RGB subpixel scheme of LCD or CRT (top). Formation of monochrome lines (right).

black back panel, TOLEDs reflect very little light when inactive and hence allow for high contrast even in bright environments. There are passive and active driven TOLEDs (the former mainly for illumination purposes). Typically an active TOLED display consists of a TFT driver matrix of zinc-tin-oxide (ZTO) that is over 90% transparent, and transparent organic OLED layers. Currently the largest active TOLED panel, a prototype of a 14 inch TOLED notebook display, was presented by **Samsung** at the **CES 2010**, reportedly with a transparency of 40%. Novaled presented a panel with 60-70% transparency at the Finetech 2010 in Japan.

The TOLED principle can also be used to build *stacked OLED* (SOLED), consisting of three layers of primary-color-transparent OLED and driver structures. An SOLED based on "small-molecule" OLEDs, built using vacuum deposition, was presented by **Universal Display Corporation** in 1999. The advantage of the SOLED that any pixel can provide all colors, but the technology is complicated.

7.6.6.2 OLED on CMOS

OLEDs on CMOS work with vacuum-deployed layers of organic LED material on CMOS semiconductor chips. An additional (transparent) metal layer is added on top of the OLED as a counter electrode. With the CMOS base, sophisticated chip assemblies are possible. The chip may contain complex driver circuits and, a special advantage, light-sensitive structures allowing the integration of a camera right into a display structure, as a retina tracker, for example (see Section 10.16.3 at page 480).

FIGURE 7.43 Example of a vacuum-fluorescent VCR display (color effect added by dye filters).

7.6.7 Vacuum Fluorescence Displays

This has been a very popular display type used in VCRs (example in Figure 7.43), clocks and car dashboards. It works with heated tungsten wires coated with alkaline earth-metal oxides as cathodes, grids of fine wires as gates, and phosphor-coated anode plates forming symbol elements to be displayed. With the gates, the display works like multiple triode tubes. Cathodes and gates can be steered as a matrix display, greatly reducing the number of wires needed and allowing for fairly large and complex display panels. A big advantage for applications in car dashboards is their ability to work at very low temperatures, conditions which cause great difficulties for LCDs.

7.6.8 Cold Cathode Tubes

Cold cathode or *nixie* tubes have been very popular for numeric displays and many other applications but have become outdated. They contain multiple cathode wires shaped like symbols and a grid-like (see-through) anode. A neon gas filling with mercury and/or argon causes an orange glowing discharge around an activated cathode. Although no heated cathode is used, life expectancy of these devices can't compete with modern LED or matrix displays.

7.7 TILED DISPLAYS

Large public installations and events require displays that are several meters wide. Apart from projection-based approaches, a typical solution is using many display boxes or tiles arranged in a matrix. Early variants often employed CRT screens, with the disadvantage of large gaps between the individual boxes. Another possibility were boxes with a matte front screen and a built-in projector—offering small edges but also suffering from low brightness.

Flat panel displays offer a new solution: many TV sets as well as industrial monitors have a built-in capability to select a specific section of a video signal for display. This allows to arrange many displays (usually up to 5 × 5) as a giant screen, with no extra hardware required. Some display types have extremely slim edges, which are hardly visible from a distance. As these displays are relatively cheap, mass-produced products, this is also a very economic solution.

Extremely large public displays are often built of modules using arrays of individual LEDs or lamps. This allows for a very high brightness, sometimes even enabling operation under full sunlight. Current installations can include up to several million LEDs and complex custom-built signal processing and driving assemblies.

A new approach aimed at large public installations, is the **TriLite** display. It uses individual MEMS laser scanners as display pixels, allowing to produce a detailed light field for 3D viewing. If affordable, this could eliminate the necessity for glasses with 3D cinema.

7.8 HIGH DYNAMIC RANGE DISPLAYS

The human visual system can adapt to a large range of contrast (see Section 4.2.4 at page 94). Usual recording techniques as well as displays are limited in their contrast by several orders of magnitude (Figure 7.44).

Common *hight dynamic range* (HDR) imaging techniques combine multiple *low dynamic range* (LDR) exposures of the same scene. An alternative to combining multiple LDR images is to improve the total contrast range itself. Consumer digital camera chips can deal with extreme contrast ranges if their signal processing is implemented accordingly, but professional HDR cameras already exist that apply various techniques and technologies to capture full HDR images directly. To discuss HDR imaging in detail is not within the scope of this book. We refer the interested reader to [241][240]. Our focus is on displays instead.

The reflectance of the display screen is very decisive for image contrast. This applies even with no external light sources: even in a dark room, light from the display itself will illuminate the room and cause reflections from the screen. This especially limits the contrast range of projection displays. Their screens usually are quite reflective in order to get a bright projection image, and so are more prone to ambient light reflections. Special varieties like holographic screens may perform much better.

Classical CRTs had little provisions against stray electrons and even against screen light being reflected inside the tube. This was greatly improved with modern color tubes.

LCDs used to have a problem with their maximum absorption, but this has been mended for some types. Nearly all panels in production show very bad reflection suppression; TV displays usually have a blank, glassy surface and the only measure helping to keep reflections low is a low refraction index of the front glass. Computer monitors usually come with a matte surface that inevitably scatters ambient light.

FIGURE 7.44 Photographs of typical natural motif with under- (left) and over-exposed (right) parts. The naked eye sees this scene entirely differently, with a still perfectly bright foreground.

Another limiting factor is image signal processing. With analog technology, nonlinearities and black-level drifts are eminent. With digital processing, less expensive solutions are limited by the number of bits used, normally 8 per color, yielding a tonal resolution of maximum 256 values.

Panel reflections can effectively be reduced by optical coatings as explained in Section 6.6.3 at page 227. For HDR displays this is mandatory.

With LCDs, active backlights consisting of a LED matrix may be used to extend the dynamic range (Figure 7.45). This technology exploits the fact that the eye also has a certain lateral crosstalk that prevents contrast reductions directly beneath bright lights from being seen.

Hence, a LED matrix with much lower resolution than the LCD display may be used, being fed with a coarser variety of the image. A diffuser screen renders a very blurry image from this, supporting the contrast yield of the display image for large areas.

Problems with this approach are efficiency and linearity deviations between individual LEDs, and aging effects that may be different for each LED. This results in an uneven brightness and color distribution on the screen. As a measure against this problem, a dense array of photo receptors (ideally one for each LED) can be integrated into the panel and the individual LED currents can be actively controlled. As silicon photo diodes - for example - do not age and are linear, a perfectly even illumination can be achieved.

At edges, the LCD image has to be modulated to compensate for the blurring caused by the LED matrix. If the properties of this matrix and its diffuser are known well enough, the LCD can achieve this quite perfectly (Figure 7.46).

This principle is called *double modulation* (or *dual modulation*), since the backlight is premodulated by the LEDs, and then modulated again by the LCD. Because only a fraction of the backlight area is active in most cases, much brighter highlights can be realized for LCDs with the active backlight matrix, which normally would require the entire backlight

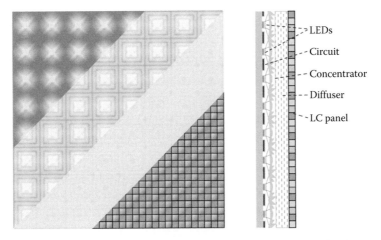

FIGURE 7.45 Backlighting and principle of panel construction of an HDR display. Hexagonal LED grids are found in products.

FIGURE 7.46 Backlight (left) and combined display (right). Image courtesy: Wolfgang Heidrich, University of British Columbia.

to be running at this high intensity all the time, consuming large amounts of power and generating heat.

The double modulation principle can be realized in several other ways (e.g., two sandwiched LCD panels or a back projector and an LCD panel). HDR LCD displays have been built which are capable of displaying a luminance range of 10000 cd/m^2 to 0.1 cd/m^2 (again, such extremes are rather theoretical as they neglect ambient light reflections). As explained above, these displays normally combine a high resolution transmissive LCD and low resolution, monochrome backlight raster composed of bright LEDs (which sacrifices color rendition improvements possible with LEDs at least if the LEDs are not built with triple RGB chips). If both the LCD and the LEDs have 8-bit luminance resolution, their driving signals can be combined to form a 16-bit HDR image.

We will discuss approaches of HDR projectors that apply double modulation to increase tonal resolution and contrast, in Section 8.6.3 at page 337. Furthermore, SLMs (such as e-paper displays) have also been used as screens to lead to high-contrast, high-tonal-resolution images for projection system, benefitting from double modulation of projector and screen.

7.8.1 Rendering for HDR LCD Displays

If two modulators with a contrast of 1 : a and 1 : b and x and y-bit tonal resolution are combined, the result is a display with a contrast of 1 : $(a * b)$ and a tonal resolution of $x + y$ bits (which is only theoretically true).

One possibility for computing the two components for LCD and LED matrices (see Figure 7.46) can be summarized with the following example [256] (Figure 7.47):

The square root of the original HDR image with intensity I is taken. The target intensities I^L are the derived for every LED by first downsampling to the LED matrix resolution. Nonlinearities in the LED response are corrected by applying the inverse of the LED response function r_1.

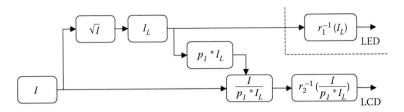

FIGURE 7.47   Rendering chain for LED and LCD parts of an HDR display, after [256].

The LCD image is computed in such a way that it basically compensates for differences between the displayed LED image and target image I. Since the LED intensities will actually spatially overlap, their point-spread function p_1 has to be known and considered. The interaction between neighboring LEDs is approximated by Gauss-Seidel iterations in [256]. The low-resolution version of the LED intensities IL is convoluted with the LED point-spread function and is then upsampled to full resolution of the LCD to simulate the image presented by the LED display. The original HDR image I is divided by the resulting LED simulation $p_1 * I_L$ to compute the complementary LCD part. Finally, the inverse of LCD response function r_2^{-1} has to be applied to obtain the displayed LCD image.

7.9 BIDIRECTIONAL DISPLAYS

A bidirectional display has additional light-sensitive pixels, distributed over the screen area. It is a display and a camera sensor in one.

While this could theoretically work with almost any type of display, concrete examples known are restricted LCD screens (large displays) and OLED on CMOS (microdisplays). The latter variety we will address in the near-eye displays chapter (see Figure 10.74 on page 481).

Light-sensitive pixels in a large screen may be used in various ways.

One is the formation of a sort of a large camera. This only works if each pixel has a tiny lens and the entire assembly forms the equivalent of a fly's eye. The advantages of this approach over an additional compact camera are questionable.

Another application is touch screens, as either the shadow of fingers or reflected light from the display's own pixels may be sensed and located (see Section 6.6.4 at page 229).

Also interesting is an application recently presented by **LG**: the sensor pixels are used to scan documents placed on the screen. The display here works as illumination. While the resolution of such a scanner won't match that of a classical desktop scanner, this will surely be useful for all kinds of portable computers, including pad computers.

7.10 PROJECTION DISPLAYS

Projectors can generate large images with small devices, while for screen displays, the devices are always larger than the images they generate. This makes projectors advantageous in many respects.

When the first movie projectors were invented, no technology had been available for screen displays at all. Screen displays are very complicated in comparison and the only reason for their invention originally had been the development of television.

Nevertheless, screen displays usually have a certain advantage over projectors: their screens can be relatively dark when inactive, not reflecting much ambient light, while projection screens usually have to be very reflective. Typical projectors therefore can be used only in dark rooms, while screen displays (including CRTs) can be used in normal room lighting without disadvantages.

Another problem with large-scale projection is the thermal radiation of the projection lamps, which may damage the display (or film) if no appropriate countermeasures are taken. Cinema film projectors may even instantly catch fire if the film transport stops and a single frame stays in the projection beam for too long.

With emerging new technologies, projectors have come to be used for many new applications.

High-power, high-resolution projectors with digital displays can reproduce digital content on giant movie theater screens, with excellent quality.

Tiny microprojectors can be integrated into mobile phones, allowing the projection of moderately large images (almost) anywhere. Projectors are scalable in resolution and image size, and more versatile to use than screen displays.

Multiple projectors may be combined for large displays or surround displays, without borders between the single images.

Projectors together with cameras can be used to actively measure the 3D shape of objects, or to project images on any surface regardless of shape or color, compensating for these parameters and generating an image as if projected on an even, uniform screen. We will discuss such projector-camera approaches in Chapter 8.

Typical projector applications today are:

- presentations and entertainment (home, cinema, theme parks, etc.)
- visualization, simulation, virtual reality (especially in the context of large immersive displays)
- mobile devices (image larger than device)
- spatially and temporally coded illumination (e.g., in microscopy, 3D measurement)

Projection images can be generated in many different ways. With respect to the spatial light modulation (SLM) technologies discussed, the basic principles are:

- emissive raster displays (e.g., CRT, OLED, laser raster)
- transmissive raster displays (e.g., LCD)
- reflective raster displays (e.g., LCoS, DLP)
- vector image generation (e.g., laser scanners)
- diffraction based (e.g., GLV, Fourier holograms)

Light valve projectors filter white light by their SLMs (either by transmission, reflection, or diffraction). For example, LCD, LCoS, DLP, and GLV can be included in this category. For emissive projectors, their SLMs are self-luminous and therefore don't filter white light. For instance, CRT, laser, OLED belong to this group. In general, images can be generated by vector scanning (as done with laser projectors), or by rasterization (as done by most projectors).

The following sections give a brief overview over different basic aspects of projection displays. For more details on projector fundamentals, the interested reader is referred to [44]. Various specialized high-speed, high-resolution, large depth-of-field and HDR projector solutions are explained in Chapter 8.

7.10.1 Projector Optics Overview

Figure 7.48 illustrates a simplified model of a slide projector. Modern digital projectors are conceptually not different.

Most projector lamps are volume emitters, so the first measure for light collection is a spherical concave mirror, reflecting the rear rays back into the emitting volume. With arc or halogen lamps this results in many of these rays going right through the emitting volume and coming out again in front. A correct alignment between lamp and mirror is important for achieving highest light output.

Next, a large lens, the condenser, collects rays from a large solid angle Ω. The condenser focuses the lamp's light cone right into the center of the projection lens. A light valve (i.e., a transmissive SLM, such as a slide or an LCD panel) may be placed right after the condenser. This is the place where light rays get spatially modulated with a projected image. The projection lens of course has its focus on the projection screen. The condenser throws an image of the light source into the projection lens. A condenser collecting light from a large solid angle has a short focal length toward the source as opposed to a long focal length toward the projection lens, hence a greatly enlarged image of the source appears in the projection lens. To avoid light losses, the projection lens requires an opening of at least this size, which may result in a small depth of field both toward the projection display and toward the screen. Smaller light sources allow for smaller projection lens apertures, resulting in a larger depth of field.

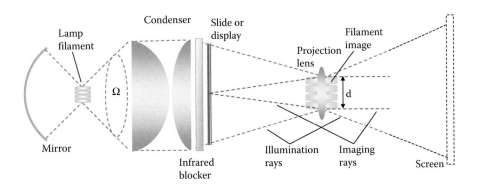

FIGURE 7.48 Optical path of a typical slide projector.

With most emitters, a certain loss of light is inevitable. The beam of a laser source, in contrary (also emitting at one side only), can be focused into a small spot and then come out of it almost like an ideal point source, with a sharply limited opening angle. In this way, virtually all of the light can be collected and directed through an extremely small opening in the projection lens, causing a huge depth of field (no matter how big the lens aperture really is).

The light rays generating a real image of the lamp (its filament or arc) in the projection lens are said to belong to the illumination (or lighting) path. They are called *illumination rays* or *lighting rays*.

The light rays generating a real image of the image plane (i.e, the SLM) on the screen plane are said to belong to the imaging path. They are called *imaging rays*.

The condenser often consists of plane-convex lenses. It has to be designed for an even light distribution in the SLM plane.

In most cases, an infrared-absorbing glass panel is placed behind the condenser to protect the display (or film) from overheating.

Figure 7.48 illustrates how the lamp filament is depicted in the projection lens, determining the beam diameter and hence the effective aperture. Hence, the depth of field of a projector depends on the size, or the spatial coherence, of the light source, whether it is a slide projector, a laser scanner or a DLP projector. There is no generic advantage in depth of field of a laser scanner over a projector. All that counts is the light source.

So far we have shown the principles of a basic light-source assembly. More complicated optical paths are possible and may be necessary, such as with reflective displays, or with combinations of three separate displays for primary colors.

An elliptic mirror may be used, instead of the spherical mirror/lens assembly for light collection. In an ellipsoid, any rays coming from one of the focus points ($f1$, Figure 7.49) is deflected toward the other ($f2$). Despite the apparent symmetry of the optical path, the resulting beam diameter still depends on the solid angle from which light is collected, due to nonlinearity of the imaging.

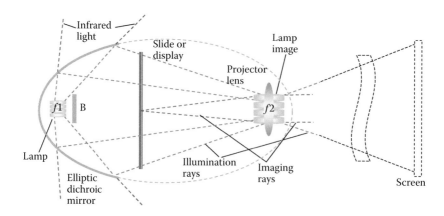

FIGURE 7.49 Projector with cold light mirror.

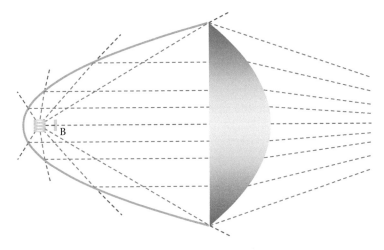

FIGURE 7.50 Light source with parabolic mirror.

A parabolic mirror in conjunction with a lens serves the same purpose, the light is first parallelized by the mirror and then focused by the lens (Figure 7.50).

Many current projector lamps come with an integrated elliptic, parabolic, or spherical mirror that is transmissive for thermal radiation (hence the name *cold light mirror*) and can be mass manufactured in a fairly inexpensive process. Because focus is critical with such a mirror, integrating it with the lamp makes sense. As infrared is not reflected, an additional heat-blocking filter can often be omitted.

Halogen as well as arc and high-performance lamps are available in conjunction with cold-light mirrors. The mirror can collect light from a very large solid angle, but light from the front of the lamp normally cannot be guided using another lens (except with a spherical mirror), since this results in two entirely different light beams, hence poor coherence.

A blocking item (B) may be added, blocking light or at least filtering infrared from the lamp front. It may also be shaped for recycling light back into the mirror.

Lambert emitters can also be combined with parabolic or elliptic mirrors (Figure 7.51). In this case, nearly 100% of the emitted light can effectively be collected. Another often-used assembly contains a forward mounted Lambert emitter in a concave mirror with a large lens in front. The mirror in this case collects only the light outside the solid angle covered by the lens. This assembly collects light efficiently but has a poor beam coherence.

A problem more difficult to assess than just light collecting is the evenness of light distribution at the SLM. Measures ensuring this largely depend on the particular application.

For more complicated projector optics, such as three-panel color projectors, the light has to span longer distances toward the optics and is often reflected and redirected several times. In these cases, a reflecting tunnel (called *integrator rod*) may be placed in the focus of the light-source optics (Figure 7.52). Multiple reflections inside the tunnel mix light beams to form a fairly homogeneous light bundle with a narrow opening angle, which can be shaped by additional lenses as desired. This incurs a certain light loss as well.

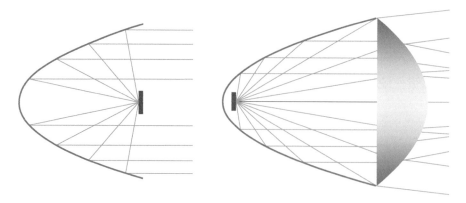

FIGURE 7.51 Light collectors for Lambert emitters (LED): parabolic reflector (left) and lens with peripheral mirror (right).

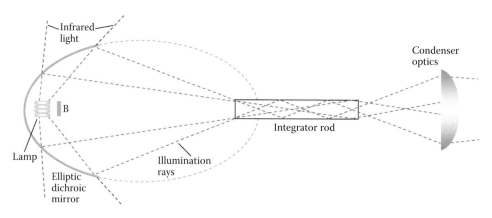

FIGURE 7.52 Projector with integrator rod.

7.10.2 Projection Lenses

Projection lenses may have fixed focal length or may be zoom lenses, allowing for image size changes without repositioning the projector. Important characteristics of a projection lens are:

- throw ratio = distance to screen/image width

- aspect ratio = image width/image height

7.10.2.1 Offset Projection

Very often a projector cannot be placed centered in front of the screen, or it is not desired to do so (e.g., if we want to mount a projector to the ceiling). Normally this would result in a distorted picture on the screen, and perhaps render a correct focusing of all image parts impossible. Tilting the SLM (called *Scheimpflug correction*) can solve the focus problem, but the image will still be distorted.

The problem is solved by using a lateral displacement (*lens shift*) of the projection lens (or the display panel). How this works is easily imagined by thinking of a wider projection angle

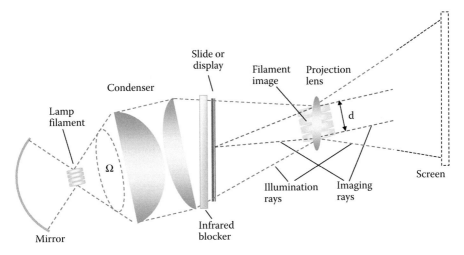

FIGURE 7.53 Projection with lens shift for perspective correction. Also shown is an illumination path offset for efficient and even illumination.

and then eliminating most of the display area except one part at the lower edge (Figure 7.53). Simply doing so however sacrifices most of the light in a projector not generically designed for it.

A lateral tilting of the illumination path (called *illumination path offset*) solves for this, as it turns the center of illumination toward the display center again. It also keeps the light bundled toward the lens center, so a smaller lens can still be used, compared to the case of lens shift alone.

7.10.3 Projector Lamps

Most projector systems today use *high-intensity discharge* (HID) lamps (Figure 7.54(left)). These are glass-confined arc lamps filled with material that is a vapor at operating

FIGURE 7.54 Discharge lamp of a regular projector (left), LED chip of a pocket projector (right).

temperature. At room temperature this material can be a gas (e.g., xenon), a liquid (mercury) or a solid (metal-halide salt), or a combination thereof.

Xenon arc lamps have a very continuous spectrum, while the spectrum of the more efficient metal-halide arc lamps shows considerable predominant lines (Figure 7.55).

For high-performance applications, *ultrahigh performance* (UHP) lamps have been developed. Their mercury filling has to be evaporated by a high-voltage (5 kV), high-energy pulse, while the operation voltage is about 65 V. Due to an arc concentrated to about 1 mm and operating at about 200 atmospheres pressure and very high temperatures, their efficiency is more than two times better even than metal-halide lamps (a 100 W lamp can emit almost 6000 lumen), and their spectrum is more continuous. A special glass is required to withstand the extreme temperature and pressure (e.g., quartz glass, having a melting point above 1500°C). UHP lamps are expensive and require special precautions. They have to be safely encapsulated to prevent damage in case they should explode, and evaporating mercury in such a (quite rare) case is an incident one would not really like to have occur in one's home. Another consideration is ozone generation due to UV parts in the spectrum (a typical color temperature for UHP lamps is 7600 K).

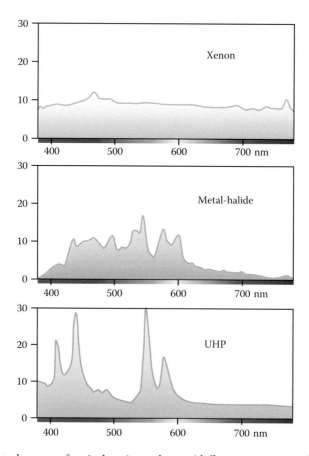

FIGURE 7.55 Spectral curves of typical projector lamps (different intensity scales).

While UHP lamps can last very long (up to 10000 hours), most projector discharge lamps last between 2000 and 4000 hours, and so they would become a considerable cost factor if projectors were to be used for everyday home TV.

A few low-end and portable projectors still use tungsten halogen lamps. These lamps are more affordable and easier to operate but their efficiency is only a fraction of that of arc lamps, and color rendition suffers from the poor blue partition of their spectrum.

With the recent advent of high-power LEDs (Figure 7.54(right)), portable projectors have become light weight, inexpensive to operate and highly efficient. Small varieties even fit into mobile phones. These aren't yet very bright, however (100 lumen).

Laser diodes can also be built with high continuous-power output today, and they are very efficient for projectors since almost 100% of the output beam can be utilized for the projection image. A problem with them has always been the green color, as discussed in Section 3.5.1 at page 81.

Recently a projector has been introduced by Casio, that combines LED, Laser, and – for the green color – a green luminous phosphor dot excited by laser light. The total light output is reported to be 1600 lumen!

7.10.4 CRT and OLED Projectors

Screen phosphors of CRT tubes (see Section 7.6.1 at page 264) can deliver an extreme brightness. The limiting factor, however, is always the cathode that burns out when current gets too high. This implies that small CRTs with strong cathodes and high driving voltage can concentrate an electron beam power as large as that of a big tube on a small screen, producing images as bright as a slide in a projector. Hence, it is possible to project bright images from these tubes with moderately large optics.

With the rapidly increasing performance of OLED displays, these are possible candidates for direct projection as well. The technical implications for the projection optics are quite similar.

CRT projectors normally use three CRTs with different phosphors for red, green and blue. These are either projected by three lenses (their beams converging on the screen, Figure 7.56)

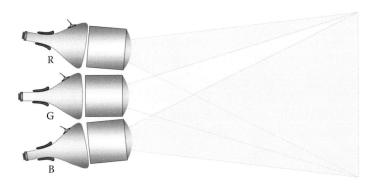

FIGURE 7.56 Principle of a CRT projector with three tubes and three lenses. The lenses are partially tilted to correct for alignment.

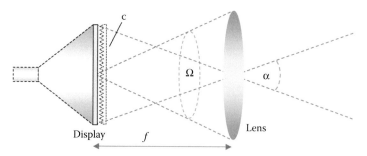

FIGURE 7.57 Projector principle with emissive SLM display.

or with a dichroic combiner prism and a single lens. While the principle works quite well, the projection nevertheless is not very bright (generally 300–500 lumen).

Other than with a point-light source, no condenser concentrates light into the projection optic. Hence, the light amount collected depends on the solid angle covered by the aperture of the projection lens (Figure 7.57). A very large projection lens has to be used to collect at least a fraction of the light produced by the CRT tube. The same applies to any self-luminous projection display, hence also for OLEDs.

The situation intensifies if we want a longer focal length, but special lens constructions[*] can partially avoid this. A concentrator foil (c) similar to what we have seen with LCD back panels may concentrate more light toward the optics. The foil of course has to be very close to the SLM pixels or it would blur the picture. With CRTs, it would definitely have to be placed inside the front panel.

Crispness is a problem because the large aperture causes a small depth of field. With CRTs, focusing the electron beam and avoiding stray light within the CRT is also not simple.

Advantages of CRT projectors are the absence of the pixel raster effects, and fast update rates (>120 Hz). A professional adjustment for convergence and balance of the three color images is required. Today, CRT projectors have widely been replaced by modern technologies such as DLP.

7.10.5 LCD Projectors

LCD (see Section 7.2.1 at page 242) projectors are quite common because their displays are relatively affordable. Being active-matrix light valves, their switching devices may become visible as dark spots between pixels (or within the actual pixel footprint) when magnified by the projection lens.

In reflective active matrix-light valves (e.g., based on LCoS, see Section 7.3.1 at page 247) electronics is integrated in the silicon chip, resulting in less pixel visibility and better area effectiveness. LCoS pixels may actually yield a 100% area coverage due to edge effects around the closely adjacent electrode areas.

---

[*] Think of modern camera lenses where the distance between lens and film can be very different from the effective focal length.

Color images can be combined from raster pixels or from separate panels:

- Single panel: RGB subpixels in the panel reduce efficiency as well as resolution (not severely, since the eye has less color resolution anyway).

- Three panel: each color channel has the full panel resolution, color filtering is done by dichroic combiners (Figure 7.61 on page 293), light efficiency is boosted by lossless splitting with one source, or by using three monochrome sources.

7.10.6 DLP and GLV Projectors

The general functioning of projectors using DMDs based on digital light processing (DLP) has been explained in Section 7.3.3 at page 251.

They offer high efficiency; the micromirror devices have negligible light absorption and a large active pixel area. The devices acquire less heat and are also very heat resistant, making them a prime choice for high-power projectors. Moreover, they behave like a plane mirror, so the coherence advantage of laser sources can be fully retained.

Professional DLP projectors use three chips, an assembly quite similar to LCoS. The more common single-chip variety has a rotating color wheel time-multiplexing color (Figure 7.58). The chip is operated at triple frame rate and the wheel brings alternating red, green and blue sectors into the light path. Light efficiency is three times lower this way.

Another possibility is to electronically switch three colored LED or lasers, a more energy-efficient method.

Compact pico DLP projectors, for example (see Figure 7.13 on page 252), use three LEDs, as shown in Figure 7.59 on page 292.

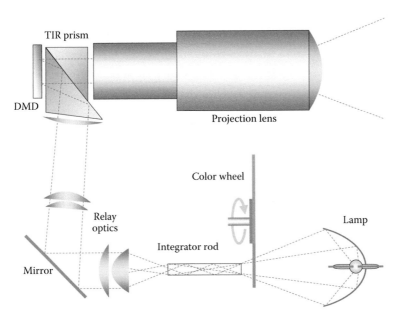

FIGURE 7.58 Example for single-chip DLP optics.

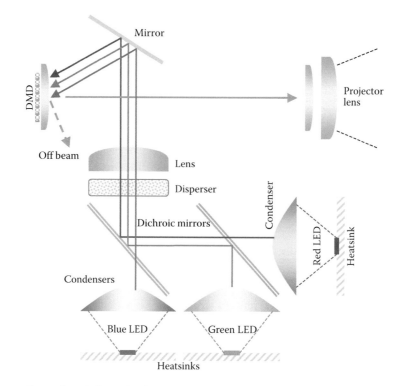

FIGURE 7.59 Exemplary light path of a pico DLP projector.

Any time-sequential color mixing will, however, cause colored fringes around objects when the viewer moves his eyes. This *rainbow effect* is the biggest disadvantage of inexpensive DLP projectors (see Section 4.2.3 at page 93).

The principle of the GLV (grating light valve) technology has been explained in Section 7.3.7 at page 256. They are also reflective SLMs, just like DMDs. Color, however, is provided by different grating pitches, while intensities are still created via pulse-width modulation. Projectors based on GLV have been demonstrated for professional applications.

7.10.7 Eidophor Projector

For video projection on very large screens, the **Eidophor** system (Figure 7.60) was the only choice for many decades, before DLP took over. The principle is as follows: A high-power lamp is placed in the focus of a concentric mirror, via a grid of mirror bars. The mirror bars are shaped to reflect all light back to the lamp as long as the mirror works normally.

A thin oil film on the mirror is distorted by an electron beam, causing little deviations in beam angles, making the light beams pass through the gaps in the mirror bar grid. Vacuum is necessary of course, to support an electron beam. If the electron beam writes a TV image onto the mirror, a very bright and crisp image can be derived behind the grid and projected onto a screen by a lens.

Color systems use three parallel projectors. The system is suited for cinema-sized screens, but it also needs a lot of maintenance. Every 100 hours, the oil film and the cathode have to be replaced, and during operation a vacuum pump has to run, removing traces of oil vapor.

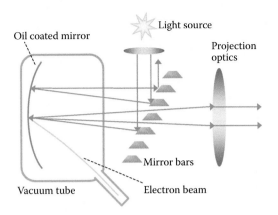

FIGURE 7.60 **Eidophor** projector principle.

So this technology was confined to very professional applications. Eidophor projectors were invented in the 1930s. Their production ended in 1997.

7.10.8 Dichroic Combiners

Projection displays are often constructed using three monochrome (gray level) SLM chips or panels, one for each of the three basic colors (RGB). Color extracts of the projection light have to be distributed to the SLMs accordingly and afterward recombined without major energy loss.

This is best achieved by a prism assembly with several dichroic mirrors. As dichroic mirrors reflect certain colors and give pass to the remainder, they are useful as beam splitters and combiners as well, and are virtually lossless.

Figure 7.61 shows such an assembly with three LCoS panels as SLM displays. As LCoS use light polarization, additional polarizer splitters are included for better efficiency. These basically work by the principle of polarization splitting with partial surface reflection, but use special techniques such as birefringent materials to achieve a 100% effect at 45°.

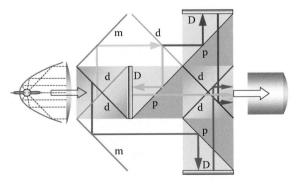

FIGURE 7.61 Assembly of an LCoS projector, consisting of three displays (D), three polarizer/splitters (p), two mirrors (m) and five dichroic color mirror/filters (d).

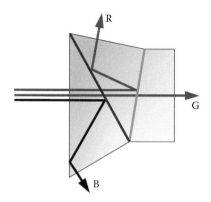

FIGURE 7.62 Dichroic color splitter of a Philips 3-CCD camera.

Figure 7.62 shows an assembly as is used in video cameras (3-chip cameras) or in self-luminous display or DLP projectors. With no necessity to care for polarization, the optical construction here can be kept very simple.

7.10.9 Fourier Holographic Projector

Figure 7.63 shows the principle of a holography-based projection display, generating 2D pictures on a projection screen. In contrast to other laser projectors, the image does not have to be scanned, but shares the advantages of laser projection (i.e., vivid color reproduction, image is always in focus).

A 2D Fourier transform renders an angle/intensity interference pattern that forms the projected image on the screen. The principles of this are explained in detail in Section 9.6.3 at page 402. With the small angles involved, an LCoS display of 13 μm pixel size (**CRLO Displays**, Ltd.) is adequate here.

Holographic laser projectors like this work with a special processor chip able to generate the interference patterns in real time. The algorithms are certainly the most important innovation in this technology. Practical implementations include 3 display chips for full-color reproduction.

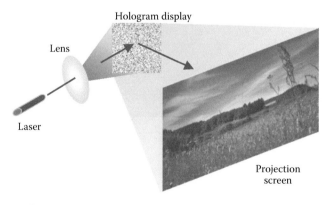

FIGURE 7.63 Fourier holographic 2D projector. Image courtesy: **Light Blue Optics**.

This technique can so far be expected to work for a deflection angle of about 10° total, enough for a projector with some dedicated optics. F-LCoS pixels could be made even smaller, enabling larger angles as well. The structural size of the driver patterns itself is not the limit, as silicon structures can be manufactured way below 0.1 μm.

7.10.10 Projection Screens

The sole purpose of a projection screen is to receive light from the projector and distribute it evenly to the audience.

Ideally, the screen would react only to light coming exactly from the projector direction and would confine its reflection exactly to the angular range where observers are located. This can be approached with holographic techniques, but usually these screens are considerably less perfect. Typical reflection characteristics of normal screens are shown in Figure 7.64.

Diffuse reflection is the simplest case and applies for canvas or white walls. Such screens reflect lots of ambient light, and therefore require a dark projection room in order to provide sufficient contrast. They also do not preserve polarization, hence are inappropriate for certain stereo techniques.

Retro-reflective materials have microstructures reflecting light into its incident direction. For projection applications this should not be too selective. A good compromise is tiny glass balls applied on a screen. This trick is also used for super-reflective traffic signs and number plates. Disadvantages are the imperfectly defined reflection area, and crispness losses due to lateral light dispersion between the glass balls. Retro-reflective screens like this have long been the standard solution for slide projection. For professional applications, more elaborate microstructures such as microlens stripes or arrays may be used. Retro-reflective screens are also used to realize projector-based autostsreoscopic displays, as explained in Chapter 9.

Screens with small metallic particles (*silver screens*) are highly retro-reflective and preserve polarization, making them useful for 3D projection with polarized light. They also appear darker (less ambient light influence) and are often used for projection in (moderate) room light.

Screens with transparent structures forming holographic optical elements (see Section 5.4.9 at page 152) can provide very complex but well controlled behavior, such as bundling light into a specific angle and conversely dispersing light from a specific angle into many directions. The resulting screens can be reflective (appearing almost perfectly transparent, or black if mounted on a black background) or transmissive (for rear projection, appearing black if mounted in front of a black box).

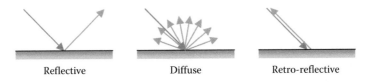

FIGURE 7.64 Different basic screen types: reflective (left), diffuse (center), and retro-reflective (right).

A particular variety of projection screens are made of *Polymer Dispersed Liquid Crystal* (PDLC), which can be switched from transparent to dispersive reflecting. Such screens are used for interactive projection displays that require a camera to capture images through the screen when it is in its transparent state, while images are projected onto it in the diffuse state. More on this in Chapter 9.

7.10.11 Rear Projection

Rear projection was the main technology for large screen TVs before large LC screens became possible. First models used CRT projection, later ones LCD and DLP projection. Main objectives in development were screens appearing dark to environment light while transporting as much projected light as possible, and an optical construction making the devices as flat as possible.

While a remarkable flatness and miniaturization of the projection unit could be achieved (see, e.g., Figure 7.65), the screens remain a weak point. Always a main problem to solve is the *hotspot* of the projector: if light is not sufficiently dispersed by the screen, the center area carries some almost direct projection light, making it way too bright. On the other hand, a very dispersive screen may appear bright, but also direct much of the light to the backside, where it is lost.

More sophisticated constructions than just matte screens have been developed, using lenslets, light guides, and so forth, but proved too difficult or expensive. The ultimate solution, holographic screens, was developed too late to play a major role in rear projection TVs before they were replaced by flat panel displays.

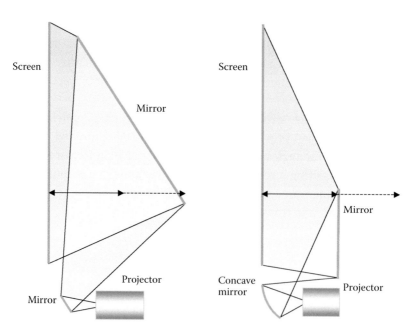

FIGURE 7.65 Simple rear projection optics (left), advanced optics of a device almost half as deep (right).

7.10.12 Wedge Displays

This rear projection display type has been developed by Cambridge Flat Projection Display, Ltd. (**CamFPD**).

The principle is quite simple: Beams entering a flat glass wedge from the side or from below will be total reflected inside until their angles get steep enough to leave the glass (Figure 7.66). The entry angle determines the number of reflections necessary, hence the exit position. A projection lens converts positions on the projection display into angles, the wedge converts them into positions on the screen.

As the exit angle of the light rays from the screen is not suitable for viewing, a deflection and a diffuser foil are needed in front of the panel. The projector emission can be expanded in the horizontal, by sending it through a glass slab where it is multiply reflected between the faces. This way the construction can be kept flat.

By folding the glass slab on itself and behind the screen, the total depth of the assembly can be kept at a few cm (the wedge itself needs only to be three millimeters thick).

Obviously there are constraints on vertical resolution, because of the flat beam angles involved. Beam divergence or spatial coherence of the projection assembly plays a role here. The wedge also requires a perfectly kept thickness gradient (bending the entire wedge is not so critical). Moreover, reflection does not sharply end at a certain angle, so the beam will be reflected inside the wedge several more times, each time losing part of its intensity. This will also cause a certain amount of vertical blurring that must be kept at bay by using a very thin wedge. The principle of the wedge display can also be inverted, using the screen as an area camera.

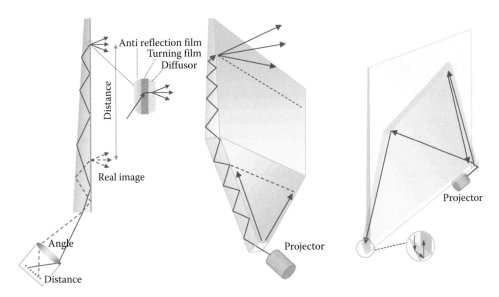

FIGURE 7.66 Wedge display principle. Multiple reflections and beam exit when total reflection angle is passed (left). Expanding the projector beam selectively in horizontal direction, incurring multiple zig-zag reflections in a folded glass slab (middle). Folding the slab, keeping the entire construction extremely flat (right).

Using diffraction gratings instead of the total reflection principle, can deliver a better-defined image. This inherently different approach, the *Quantum Display*, is currently used for NED only. It is described in Section 10.14.2 at page 467.

7.10.13 Collimated Displays

Collimated display technology uses optics, usually a concave mirror, to create an image appearing at infinity. Typically, a conventional display screen (self-luminous, projection, rear projection, etc.) provides the image, and the concave mirror converts positions in the display into angles, in other words, rays from any particular display pixel are turned into wide, parallel light bundles appearing to come from infinity. Parallels merge at infinity, so this is equivalent to light from one point at infinite distance. Such rays entering the eye pupil of an observer will be focused to a single point. As parallel light is also dubbed collimated light, such displays are called *collimated displays*. What is important, is that the image will appear in the same direction for all observers within the aperture of the light bundles. In a flight simulator for example, this perfectly simulates a real outside view (Figure 7.67). Not only will all crew members see the scenery in the same position, the distant objects depicted will also stay in place relative to the cockpit if one crew member moves his head. Moreover, eye adaptation is at infinity just as in the real plane.

A less intricate version of this is the head-up display we have already encountered in Section 5.4.1 at page 145).

Collimated display layouts may also be used with near-eye displays, where they greatly simplify the alignment of displayed images with the direct view (see Section 10.7.1 at page 434).

A remarkable working principle for a collimated NED display is the **Quantum Display** by **BAE Systems**. It is explained in Section 10.14.2 at page 467.

7.10.14 Laser Projectors

While lasers can generally be used as a light source for many types of displays or projectors, their most typical projection application is vector scanners.

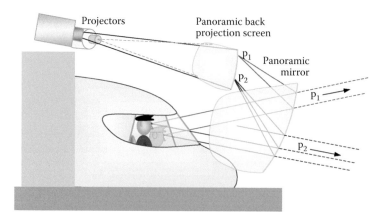

FIGURE 7.67 Display of a professional flight simulator: the virtual image appears at infinity, so any crew member sees it at the same position relative to the airplane.

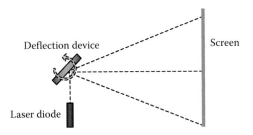

FIGURE 7.68 Basic laser projection assembly.

Laser scanners are based on the narrow light beams of lasers or laser diodes, modulated for brightness changes and deflected in horizontal and vertical directions (Figure 7.68), writing an entire image onto a screen or directly into the eye (we will discuss retinal displays in Chapter 10).

Their advantages are the relative simplicity of the light source, the ability to generate pictures with large brightness (almost 100% of the light produced can be brought to the screen), wide color gamut (if multiple primary sources are used) and a little easier focusing than with most of the classical projectors (because of their larger depth of field).

The following considerations are based on the basic principles discussed in Section 3.5.2 at page 85.

A problem resulting from very coherent light sources is the appearance of speckles. This can be avoided by using appropriate projection screens and controlling the coherence level of the beam (see Section 5.3.10 at page 143).

A major problem with laser scanners has always been beam deflection, because very high speeds are necessary for high resolution images. Moreover, any deflecting mirrors must be of a minimum size.

Laser beams are always diverging or converging (Section 3.5.2 at page 85). Maybe the most important characteristic for our purpose here is spatial coherence (Section 5.3.10 at page 143). It corresponds to the smallest focus point we can achieve when trying to concentrate the beam. In a scanner, the diameter of the scanning mirror is crucial for this property.

With a near-field scanner, as a virtual retina display, the intended focus spot size can retroactively be interpreted as a light source imposing a certain beam divergence toward the scanner mirror. Hence, this mirror needs to have a minimum diameter, growing with the image resolution desired.

Laser scanners can be near-field (e.g., as used for retinal displays or some pocket projectors) or far-field (as used in planetariums).

Far-field scanners can be designed in a way that the resulting beam divergence causes the beam to enlarge along with the image size growing over distance. The mirror can be interpreted as the light source itself, causing a certain beam divergence angle, getting larger the smaller the source is. Hence, with growing image resolution, it also requires a larger scanning mirror. The relation is given by Equation 3.39 on page 86. We regard a total divergence angle $\Phi(= 2\varphi)$ and a mirror diameter d:

$$d \approx \frac{\lambda}{\Phi} \qquad (7.1)$$

For near-field scanners, the beam has to be focused on the projection screen. The smaller the focus point desired, the larger the scanning mirror has to be. We invert the beam divergence formula (Equation 3.38 on page 86) and for a focus point size a at distance f we get a mirror diameter d:

$$d = \lambda f / a \qquad (7.2)$$

This value d is also the necessary size for a lens in a conventional projector if the light source is perfectly collimated (e.g., a laser). Particular laser colors are often generated by frequency doubling or tripling from other colors. The efficiency of such conversions varies. Some examples are listed in Section 3.5.1 at page 81.

7.10.14.1 Far-Field Laser Projectors

Far-field vector laser scanners are mainly used for professional applications, such as light shows and planetariums. The beam may be deflected mechanically by mirrors with electrostatic or electromagnetic drive, or by special optical crystals reacting to mechanical pressure (acusto-optical deflection).

Far-field laser scanners with the sole objective of providing a raster display are usually built with polygonal mirror wheels, at least for the fast (line or horizontal) scanning axis. Such a mirror wheel can spin extremely fast, requiring very little driving power. The requirements for its accuracy, however, are very high. As subsequent mirror segments write adjacent image lines, even the slightest angular errors would result in jagged image edges. If used for vertical deflection, inaccuracies would result in a jittering image. Hence for this direction, an oscillating mirror or a simple, rotating double-sided flat mirror is an alternative.

7.10.14.2 MEMS Scanners

For vector scanners, only freely tilting (respectively oscillating mirrors) can be used. *Micro-electro-mechanical systems* (MEMS) are often used for multi-way scanning mirrors. This scanning technology basically requires a single mirror which can be produced as a microdevice together with its hinges and even driving circuitry, but in a much simpler manufacturing process than, for example, for DMDs. Hyperelasticity and small sizes can create a super fast and reliable MEMS element from silicon or other materials by etching, laser cutting, or other methods.

This is also the method of choice for micro raster scanners as can be used for pocket projectors or near-eye displays.

In order to achieve large deflection angles, both axes have to be decoupled by an intermediate frame and independent hinges (h) for horizontal and vertical guidance (Figure 7.69).

Electrostatic forces get stronger with smaller dimensions, so they are usually the method of choice for the mirror deflection in MEMS. Magnetic drive is an alternative for larger devices.

Unwanted resonances and parametric effects have to be addressed by a proper driver design and damping. Heating of the mirror, caused by the projection light, may cause geometrical errors that are difficult to address.

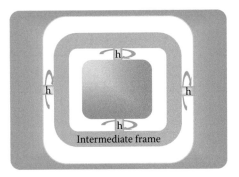

FIGURE 7.69   Principle of a two-way scanning mirror.

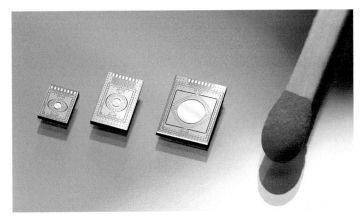

FIGURE 7.70   Various MEMS scanning mirrors. Image courtesy: **FhG-IPMS**

Resolutions of up to 800×600 have been achieved with a single MEMS mirror (**Microvision, FhG-IPMS**). In [112], a combination of up to three coaxially arranged mirrors of different sizes is suggested, able to create an image with inlays of increasing resolution. This is a solution only for personal near-eye displays however, because the inlays have to follow eye movements in order to be effective.

Various MEMS scanning mirros are shown in Figure 7.70. Figure 7.71 graphs voltage vs. deflection for a MEMS mirror. Current devices reach up to $23kHz$ for a $1.2mm$ mirror, at $\pm9,5°$ deflection and $150V$, $300\mu W$ driving power (**FhG-IPMS**, 2011).

7.10.15 Beam Deflection Modes

Raster laser scanners draw pictures line by line, like a classic TV picture tube. In a TV, a sawtooth-like voltage is used to deflect the electron beam from side to side with nearly constant velocity, then bring it back much faster, to draw the next line in sequence (Figure 7.72(1) on page 302 [116]). Moving a mirror this way would incur very violent accelerations.

The smoothest way of moving a mass forth and back is in a sine wave-like motion. But this results in an uneven line and brightness distribution (Figure 7.72(2)). Brightness could be compensated for, but we see line patterns at the image edges that would only disappear

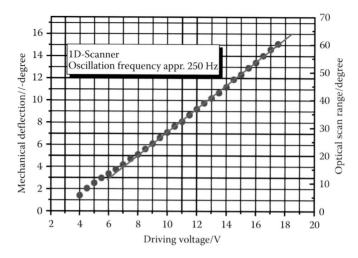

FIGURE 7.71 MEMS mirror: voltage vs. deflection. Image courtesy: **FhG-IPMS**

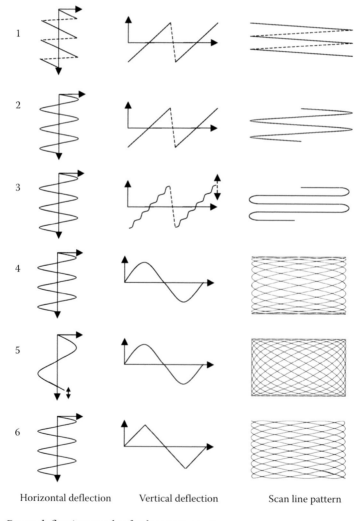

FIGURE 7.72 Beam deflection modes for laser scanners.

at very high resolutions. One method to address this problem would be modulating the deflection mirror with a small high-frequency sine wave also in the vertical, that would keep the lines about horizontal over most of the display area (Figure 7.72(3)).

The edges could then simply be dimmed out and we would get a fairly even line pattern with smoothly moving mirrors.

Current laser scanners most often use the Lissajous mode, deflecting both directions by a sine wave. Figure 7.72(5) shows an example with two sine waves of similar frequency, drawing a tumbling ellipse inside a square area. Obviously the lines get denser at the edges. This also applies for sine waves of very different frequencies (Figure 7.72(4)). The useful area in this mode is about 80% of the deflection angle, and even then we have to compensate for nonlinearities and, more important, for different brightness and resolution.

A versatile solution could be Figure 7.72(6): A triangle for the low and a sine for the high frequency axis deliver an almost even line density while reducing accelerations to a minimum [112].

7.10.15.1 Scanning Fiber Projection

Optical glass fibers are very thin and flexible. The so-called monomode fibers have a very thin core in which light can be transported over many kilometers, at very small loss.

Scanning fiber projectors move the loose end of a fiber in a spiral pattern, scanning a complete circular area. The fiber end produces a light spot about 3 μm wide, according to the core diameter of the optical fiber. If the fiber end is in resonance, very fast excitations are possible requiring little energy. Practical implementations with a piezo actuator can be driven at resonance frequencies of up to about 30 kHz and with excitations of about ±0.5 mm. A dedicated lens assembly projects the resulting light pattern onto a target.

These scanners can be very small, 1 mm in diameter for example. One of the applications are surgical micro-endoscopes, where the light pattern is used to sequentially illuminate a small area, and additional fibers pick up the reflected light to be assembled as an image [314].

In another application, the light is modulated with an image content, and the device directly works as an image projector (cf. [313]). With certain types of near-eye displays,

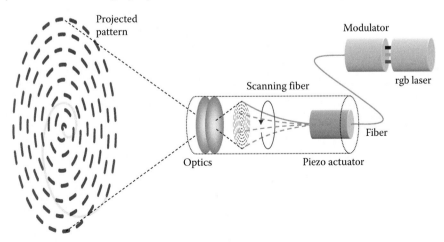

FIGURE 7.73 Scanning fiber projector, working principle.

the output of such a micro-projector is fed into an optical waveguide (see Section 10.14.2 at page 468 for more detail).

Figure 7.73 shows the working principle of the projector. A 3 μm spot size allows for about VGA resolution if the scan field is up to 2 mm wide, with frame rates of about 30 or at best 60 Hz. In [315], the use of a multi-core fiber, producing seven pixels at once, for example, is suggested to improve resolution.

As with all analog deflection devices, the image geometry may be subject to distortions and drift. Another concern may be durability. Test devices have been continuously operated for many months however, with no problems reported so far.

7.11 SUMMARY

With the information presented in this chapter, we have given an overview of currently available spatial light modulation technology used for displays. Table 7.1 benchmarks the most common types used for TV sets.

Betting on the future, it turns out that only OLED seems to enable displays that are good in all aspects. Remarkable is the still-acceptable performance of CRT and the often-bashed plasma screens. CRT is unbeaten for motion since it is the technology available in real products that allows interlacing, beneath the rare **ALiS** displays (see Section 7.6.3 at page 269). LCDs are a compromise in many aspects, except for devices with flashing RGB LED backlight, which are still rare.

Given the billion-dollar investments currently going into large panel OLED fabrication sites, skepticism about the success of these displays seems to be outdated.

Our comparison in Table 7.1 on page 304 considers only realistic approaches for TV applications. Large reflective displays, such as electronic paper, that could fit in here are still in the lab stage and their achievable contrast ratio would be a bit limited anyway (like that of printed paper). Front- and back-projection displays are limited to certain applications and most of them require special viewing setups (movie theater) and/or are suffering from contrast issues.

In conclusion, TV display technology is currently in an intermediate state where none of the many new approaches have reached perfection. The future will hopefully bring a lot of improvements.

TABLE 7.1   Performance of Large Scale Display Technologies

Display	Brightn.	Contrast	Color	Motion	Angle	Flat	Power
OLED	+	+	++	+	+	+	+
Plasma	+	+	+	+	+	+	-
CRT	+	+	+	++	+	-	o
LED - LCD	+	o+/+[1]	-/++[2]	-/+[3]	o -	+	o
LCD	+	o+	-	-	o -	+	o
DLP - projection	+	o	o +	o -	o	-	-
LCD - backproj.	-	-	-	-	o	o -	- -
LCD - projection	-	-	-	-	o	-	- -

[1] + if HDR; [2] with RGB LED, or quantum dots, else -; [3] + with flashing backlight.

CHAPTER **8**

Projector-Camera Systems

8.1 INTRODUCTION

Their increasing capabilities and declining cost make video projectors widespread and established presentation tools. Being able to generate images that are larger than the actual display device, virtually anywhere is an interesting feature for many applications that cannot be provided by desktop screens. Several research groups discovered this potential by employing projectors in unconventional ways to develop new and innovative information displays that surpass simple screen presentations.

Today's projectors are able to modulate displayed images spatially and temporally. Synchronized camera feedback is analyzed to support a real-time image correction that enables projections on complex and ordinary surfaces that are not bound to projector-optimized canvases or dedicated screen configurations.

This chapter reviews current projector-camera-based image correction techniques. Section 8.2 at page 306 begins with a discussion on the problems and challenges that arise when projecting images onto nonoptimized screen surfaces. Geometric warping techniques for surfaces with different topology and reflectance are described in Section 8.3 at page 308. Section 8.4 at page 314 outlines radiometric compensation techniques that allow the projection of static and dynamic scenes and configurations onto colored and textured surfaces. Also explained are state-of-the-art techniques that consider the limitations of human visual perception to overcome technical limitations of projector-camera systems. In both Sections (8.3 and 8.4), conventional structured light-range scanning as well as imperceptible coding schemes are outlined that support projector-camera calibration (geometry and radiometry). While the previously mentioned sections focus on rather simple light-modulation effects, such as diffuse reflectance, the compensation of complex light modulations, such as specular reflection, interreflection, refraction, and so forth, are explained in Section 8.5 at page 325. This section also shows how the inverse light transport can be used for compensating all measurable light-modulation effects. Section 8.6 at page 331 is dedicated to a discussion on how novel (at present, mainly experimental) approaches to high-speed, high-dynamic

FIGURE 8.1   Application example of a multiprojector system with real-time, per-pixel geometry correction and radiometric compensation: Projecting onto the stage settings during live performance of the Karl May festival in Elspe, Germany. Image courtesy: **VIOSO** GmbH.

range, large depth-of-field and super-resolution projection may, in the future, overcome the technical limitations of today's projector-camera systems.

Image-correction techniques for projector-camera systems have proved to be useful tools for scientific experiments, but also for real-world applications. An example is illustrated in Figure 8.1. Current applications include on-site architectural visualization, augmentations of museum artifacts, video installations in cultural heritage sites, outdoor advertisement displays, projections onto stage settings during live performances, and ad-hoc stereoscopic VR/AR visualizations in everyday environments. Besides these rather individual application areas, real-time image correction techniques will potentially address future mass markets with applications such as pocket projectors for flexible business presentations, miniature projectors integrated into mobile devices such as cellphones, and game-console driven projectors for the home-entertainment sector.

Note that this chapter does not discuss general single- or multi-projector calibration for simple screen surfaces, such as planar and curved white diffuse canvases. The interested reader is referred to [185] for details on such standard techniques.

8.2 CHALLENGES OF NONOPTIMIZED SURFACES

For conventional applications, screen surfaces are optimized for projection. Their reflectance is usually uniform and Lambertian across the surface, and their geometrical topologies range from planar and multiplanar to simple parametric (e.g., cylindrical or spherical) surfaces. In many situations, however, such perfect screens cannot be applied. Some examples are mentioned in Section 8.1 at page 305. The modulation of the projected light on these surfaces can easily exceed simple diffuse reflections. In addition, blending with different surface pigments and complex geometric distortions can degrade the image quality significantly. This is shown in Figure 8.2.

The light of the projected images is modulated on the surface together with possible environment light. This leads to a color, intensity, and geometry distorted appearance (Figure 8.2(left)). The intricacy of the modulation depends on the complexity of the surface. It can contain interreflections, diffuse and specular reflections, regional defocus effects, refractions, and more. To neutralize these modulations in realtime, and consequently to reduce the perceived image distortions is the aim of many projector-camera approaches.

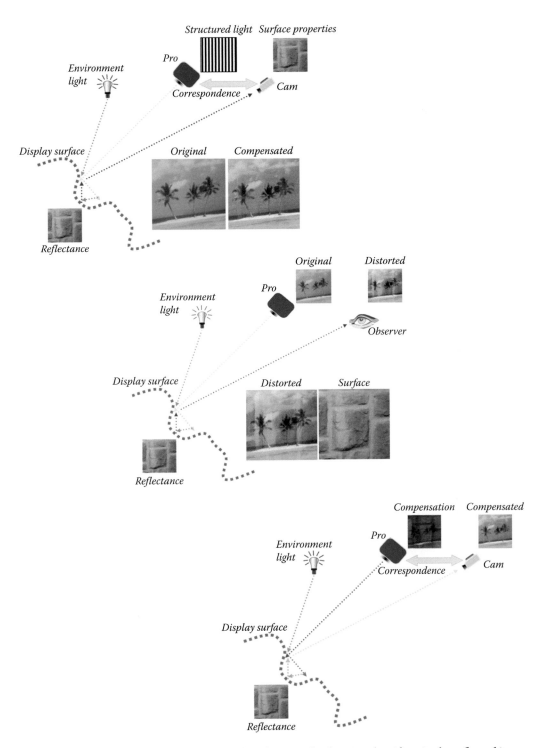

FIGURE 8.2 Projecting onto nonoptimized surfaces can lead to visual artifacts in the reflected image (top). Projector-camera systems can automatically scan surface and environment properties (center) to compute compensation images during run-time that neutralize the measured light modulations on the surface (bottom).

In general, two challenges have to be mastered to reach this goal: first, the modulation effects on the surface have to be measured and evaluated with computer vision techniques, and second, they have to be compensated in realtime with computer graphics approaches. Structured light projection and synchronized camera feedback enable the required parameters to be determined and allow a geometric relation between camera, projector, and surface to be established (Figure 8.2(center)). After such a system is calibrated, the scanned surface and environment parameters can be used to compute compensation images for each frame that needs to be projected during runtime. If the compensation images are projected, they are modulated by the surface together with the environment light in such a way that the final reflected images approximate the original desired images from the perspective of the calibration camera/observer (Figure 8.2(right)).

The forthcoming sections will review techniques that compensate individual modulation effects.

8.3 GEOMETRIC REGISTRATION

The amount of geometric distortion of projected images depends on the complexity of the projection surface. Different techniques are applied for individual surface topologies. While simple homographies are suited for registering projectors with planar surfaces, projective transforms can be used for nonplanar surfaces of known geometry. For geometrically complex and textured surfaces of unknown geometry, image warping based on lookup operations has frequently been used to achieve a pixel-precise mapping. Most of these techniques require structured light projection to enable a fully automatic calibration. Some modern approaches integrate the structured code information directly into the projected image content in such a way that an imperceptible calibration can be performed during runtime.

Such geometric projector-camera registration techniques will be reviewed in this section.

8.3.1 Uniformly Colored Surfaces of Known Geometry

For surfaces whose reflectance is optimized for projection (e.g., surfaces with a homogenous white reflectance), a geometric correction of the projected images is sufficient to provide an undistorted presentation to an observer with known perspective. Slight misregistrations of the images on the surface in the order of several pixels lead to geometric artifacts that – in most cases– can be tolerated. This section gives a brief overview of general geometry correction techniques that support single and multiple projectors.

If multiple projectors (*pro*) have to be registered with a planar surface via camera (*cam*) feedback (Figure 8.3(left)), collineations with the plane surface can be expressed as 3x3 camera-to-projector homography matrix H:

$$H_{3x3} = \begin{bmatrix} h_{11} & h_{12} & h_{13} \\ h_{21} & h_{22} & h_{23} \\ h_{31} & h_{32} & h_{33} \end{bmatrix} \tag{8.1}$$

A homography matrix can be automatically determined numerically by correlating a projection pattern to its corresponding camera image. Knowing the homography matrix

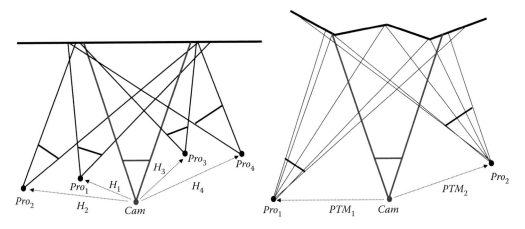

FIGURE 8.3 Camera-based projector registration for untextured planar (left) and nonplanar (right) surfaces of known geometry.

H_i for projector pro_i and the calibration camera cam, allows the mapping from camera pixel coordinates $cam(x, y)$ to the corresponding projector pixel coordinates $pro_i(x, y)$ with $pro_i(x, y, 1) = H_i \cdot cam(x, y, 1)$. The homographies are usually extended to homogenous 4x4 matrices to make them compatible with conventional transformation pipelines and to consequently benefit from single pass rendering [231]:

$$A_{4x4} = \begin{bmatrix} h_{11} & h_{12} & 0 & h_{13} \\ h_{21} & h_{22} & 0 & h_{23} \\ 0 & 0 & 1 & 0 \\ h_{31} & h_{32} & 0 & h_{33} \end{bmatrix} \tag{8.2}$$

Multiplied after the projection transformation, they map normalized camera coordinates into normalized projector coordinates. An observer located at the position of the (possibly off-axis aligned) calibration camera perceives a correct image in this case. Such a camera-based approach is frequently used for calibrating tiled screen projection displays. A sparse set of point correspondences is determined automatically, using structured light projection and camera feedback [250]. The correspondences are then used to solve for the matrix parameters of H_i for each projector i. In addition to a geometric projector registration, a camera-based calibration can be used for photometric (luminance and chrominance) matching among multiple projectors. A detailed discussion on the calibration of tiled projection screens is not within the scope of this chapter; multiprojector techniques that are suitable for conventional screen surfaces are not covered. The interested reader is referred to [46] or [185] for an overview of state-of-the-art techniques. Other approaches apply mobile projector-camera systems and homographies for displaying geometrically corrected images on planar surfaces (e.g., [233]).

Once the geometry of the projection surface is nonplanar but known (Figure 8.3(right)), a two-pass rendering technique can be applied for projecting the images in an undistorted way [232,236]: In the first pass, the image that has to be displayed is rendered off-screen from a target perspective (e.g., the perspective of the camera or an observer). In the second step, the geometry model of the display surface is texture-mapped with the previously rendered image while being rendered from the perspective of each projector *pro*. For computing the correct texture coordinates to ensure an undistorted view from the target perspective, *projective texture mapping* is applied. This hardware-accelerated technique dynamically computes a texture matrix that maps the 3D vertices of the surface model from the perspectives of the projectors onto the texture space of the target perspective.

A camera-based registration is possible in this case as well. For example, instead of a visible (or an invisible – as will be discussed in Section 8.3.3 at page 312) structured light projection, features of the captured distorted image that is projected onto the surface can be analyzed directly. A first example was presented in [301] that evaluates the deformation of the image content when projected onto the surface to reconstruct the surface geometry and refine it iteratively. This approach assumes a calibrated camera-projector system and an initial rough estimate of the projection surface. If the surface geometry has been approximated, the two-pass method outlined above can be applied for warping the image geometry in such a way that it appears undistorted. In [139] a similar method is described that supports a movable projector and requires a stationary and calibrated camera, as well as the known surface geometry. The projector's intrinsic parameters and all camera parameters have to be known in both cases. While the method in [301] results in the estimated surface geometry, the approach of [139] leads to the projector's extrinsic parameters. The possibility of establishing the correspondence between projector and camera pixels in these cases depends always on the quality of the detected image features and consequently on the image content itself. To improve their robustness, such techniques apply a predictive feature matching rather than a direct matching for features in projector and camera space.

However, projective texture mapping in general assumes a simple pinhole camera/projector model and does not take the lens distortion of projectors into account. Together with flaws in feature matching or numerical minimization errors, this can cause misregistrations of the projected images in the range of several pixels – even if other intrinsic and extrinsic parameters have been determined precisely. These slight geometric errors are normally tolerable on uniformly colored surfaces. Projecting corrected images onto textured surfaces with misregistrations in this order causes immediate visual intensity and color artifacts that are well visible, even when applying a radiometric compensation (see Section 8.4 at page 314). Consequently, more precise registration techniques are required for textured surfaces.

8.3.2 Textured Surfaces and Surfaces of Unknown Geometry

Mapping projected pixels precisely onto different colored pigments of textured surfaces is essential for an effective radiometric compensation (described in Section 8.4 at page 314). To achieve a precision on a pixel basis is not practical with the registration techniques outlined in Section 8.3.1 at page 308. These techniques are also unappreciable if the surface geometry is unknown. Instead of registering projectors by structured light-sampling followed by numerical optimizations that allow the computation of projector-camera correspondences via homographies or projective transformations, they can be measured pixel-by-pixel and

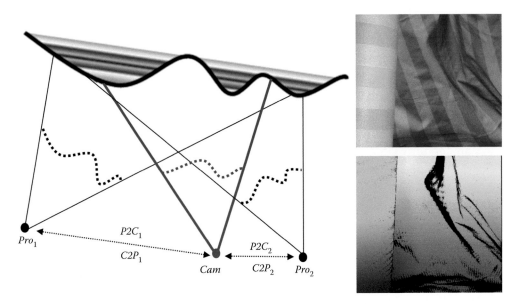

FIGURE 8.4 Camera-based projector registration for textured surfaces and surfaces of unknown geometry (left). The camera perspective on a scene (top-right) and the scanned lookup table that maps camera pixels to projector pixels. Holes are not yet removed in this example (bottom-right).

queried through lookup operations during runtime. Well-known structured light techniques [250] (e.g., Gray code scanning) can be used as well for scanning the one-to-n mapping of camera pixels to projector pixels. This mapping is stored in a 2D lookup texture having a resolution of the camera, which in the following is referred to as *C2P map* (Figure 8.4). A corresponding texture that maps every projector pixel to one or many camera pixels can be computed by reversing the *C2P* map. This texture is called *P2C map*. It has the resolution of the projector.

The one-to-n relations (note that n can also become 0 during the reversion process) are finally removed from both maps through averaging and interpolation (e.g., via a Delaunay triangulation of the transformed samples in the *P2C* map, and a linear interpolation of the pixel colors that store the displacement values within the computed triangles). Figure 8.4(right) illustrates the perspective of a camera on a scene and the scanned and color-coded (red = x, green = y) *C2P* texture that maps camera pixels to their corresponding projector pixel coordinates. Note that all textures contain floating point numbers.

These lookup textures contain only the 2D displacement values of corresponding projector and camera pixels that map onto the same surface point. Thus, neither the 3D surface geometry, nor the intrinsic or extrinsic parameters of projectors and camera are known.

During runtime, a fragment shader maps all pixels from the projector perspective into the camera perspective (via texture lookups in the *P2C* map) to ensure a geometric consistency for the camera view. We want to refer to this as *pixel displacement mapping*. If multiple projectors are involved, a *P2C* map has to be determined for each projector. Projector-individual fragment shaders will then perform a customized pixel-displacement mapping during multiple rendering steps, as described in [27].

In [33] and in [310], pixel-displacement mapping has been extended to support moving target perspectives (e.g., of the camera and/or the observer). In [33] an image-based warping between multiple $P2C$ maps that have been pre-scanned for known camera perspectives is applied. The result is an estimated $P2C$ map for a new target perspective during runtime. While in this case, the target perspective must be measured (e.g., using a tracking device), [310] analyzes image features of the projected content to approximate a new $P2C$ as soon as the position of the calibration camera has changed. If this is not possible because the detected features are too unreliable, a structured light projection is triggered to scan a correct $P2C$ map for the new perspective.

8.3.3 Embedded Structured Light

Section 8.3.1 at page 308 has covered registration techniques (i.e., [139,301]) that do not require the projection of structured calibration patterns, such as Gray codes. Instead, they analyze the distorted image content, and thus depend on matchable image features in the projected content. Structured light techniques, however, are more robust because they generate such features synthetically. Consequently, they do not depend on the image content.

Besides a spatial modulation, a temporal modulation of projected images allows integrating coded patterns that are not perceivable due to limitations of the human visual system (see discussion on temporal response in Section 4.2.3 at page 93). Synchronized cameras, however, are able to detect and extract these codes. This principle has been described by Raskar et al. [236], and has been enhanced by Cotting et al. [61]. It is referred to as *embedded imperceptible pattern projection*. Extracted code patterns, for instance, allow the simultaneous acquisition of the scene's depth and texture for 3D video applications [284],[279]. These techniques can be applied to integrate the calibration code directly into the projected content to enable an invisible online calibration. Thus, the result could be, for instance, a $P2C$ map scanned by a binary Gray code or an intensity phase pattern that is integrated directly into the projected content.

The first applicable imperceptible pattern projection technique was presented in [61], where a specific time slot (called *binary image exposure period* (BIEP)) of a DLP projection sequence is occupied exclusively for displaying a binary pattern within a single color channel (multiple color channels are used in [62] to differentiate between multiple projection units). Figure 8.5 illustrates an example.

The BIEP is used for displaying a binary pattern. A camera that is synchronized to exactly this BIEP will capture the code. As it can be seen in the selected BIEP in Figure 8.5, the mirror-flip sequences are not evenly distributed over all possible intensities. Thus, the intensity of each projected original pixel might have to be modified to ensure that the mirror state that encodes the desired binary value at this pixel is active. This, however, can result in a nonuniform intensity fragmentation and a substantial reduction of the tonal values. Artifacts are diffused using a dithering technique. A coding technique that benefits from reconfigurable mirror-flip sequences using the DMD discovery board is described in Section 8.6.4 at page 341.

Another possibility for integrating imperceptible code patterns is to modulate the projected image I with a code image that results in the image I_{cod}, and to compute a

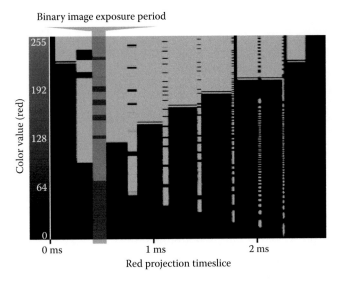

FIGURE 8.5 Mirror-flip (on/off) sequences for all intensity values of the red color channel and the chosen binary image exposure period (BIEP) [61]. Image courtesy: Computer Graphics Laboratory, ETH Zurich.

compensation image I_{com} in such a way that $(I_{cod} + I_{com})/2 = I$. If both images are projected with a high speed, human observers will perceive I due to temporal integration. This is referred to as *temporal coding* and was shown in [236]. The problem with this simple technique is that the code remains visible during eye movements or code transitions. Neither can be avoided for the calibration of projector-camera systems using structured light techniques. In [104] properties of human perception (threshold contrast and flicker fusion threshold) are taken into account for adapting the coding parameters depending on local characteristics such as spatial frequencies and local luminance values of image and code. This makes a truly imperceptible temporal coding of binary information possible. For binary codes, I is regionally decreased ($I_{cod} = I - \Delta$ to encode a binary 0) or increased ($I_{cod} = I + \Delta$ to encode a binary 1) in intensity, while the compensation image is computed with $I_{com} = 2I - I_{cod}$. The code can then be reconstructed from the two corresponding images (C_{cod} and C_{com}) captured by the camera with C_{cod}-$C_{com} <=> 0$. In [218] another technique for adaptively embedding complementary patterns into projected images is presented. In this work the embedded code intensity is regionally adapted depending on the spatial variation of neighboring pixels and their color distribution in the YIQ color space. The final code contrast of Δ is then calculated depending on the estimated local spatial variations and color distributions. In [309], the binary temporal coding technique was extended to encoding intensity values as well. For this, the code image is computed with $I_{cod} = I\Delta$ and the compensation image with $I_{com} = I(2 - \Delta)$. The code can be extracted from the camera images with $\Delta = 2C_{cod}/(C_{cod} + C_{com})$. Using binary and intensity coding, an imperceptible multistep calibration technique is presented in [309] which is visualized in Figure 8.6, and is outline below.

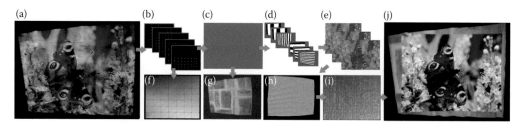

FIGURE 8.6 Imperceptible multistep calibration for radiometric compensation [309].

A recalibration is triggered automatically if misregistrations between projector and camera are detected (i.e., due to motion of camera, projector, or surface). This is achieved by continuously comparing the correspondences of embedded point samples. If necessary, a first rough registration is carried out by sampling binary point patterns (Figure 8.6(b)) that leads to a mainly interpolated *P2C* map (Figure 8.6(f)). This step is followed by an embedded measurement of the surface reflectance (Figures 8.6(c,g)), which is explained in Section 8.4.2 at page 319. Both steps lead to quick but imprecise results. Then a more advanced three-step phase shifting technique (Figure 8.6(e)) is triggered that results in a pixel-precise *P2C* registration (Figure 8.6(i)). For this, intensity coding is required (Figure 8.6(h)). An optional Gray code might be necessary for surfaces with discontinuities (Figure 8.6(d)). All steps are invisible to the human observer and are executed while dynamic content can be projected with a speed of 20 Hz.

In general, temporal coding is not limited to the projection of two images only. Multiple code and compensation images can be projected if the display framerate is high enough. This requires fast projectors and cameras, and will be discussed in Section 8.6.4 at page 341.

An alternative to embedding imperceptible codes in the visible light range would be to apply infrared light as shown in [262] for augmenting real environments with invisible information. But it is not used for projector-camera calibration.

8.4 RADIOMETRIC COMPENSATION

For projection screens with spatially varying reflectance, color and intensity compensation techniques are required in addition to a pixel-precise geometric correction. This is known as *radiometric compensation*, and is used in general to minimize the artifacts caused by the local light modulation between projection and surface. Besides the geometric mapping between projector and camera, the surface's reflectance parameters need to be measured on a per-pixel basis before using them for real-time image corrections during runtime. In most cases, a one-time calibration process applies visible structured light projections and camera feedback to establish the correspondence between camera and projector pixels (see Section 8.3.2 at page 310) and to measure the surface pigment's radiometric behavior of the surface pigments.

A pixel-precise mapping is essential for radiometric compensation since slight misregistrations (in the order of only a few pixels) can lead to significant blending artifacts – even if the geometric artifacts, are marginal. Humans are extremely sensitive to even small (less than 2%) intensity variations (see Chapter 4). This section reviews different types of radiometric compensation techniques. Starting with methods that are suited for static scenes and projector-camera configurations, it will then discuss more flexible techniques that support dynamic situations (i.e., moving projector-camera systems and surfaces). Finally, most recent approaches are outlined that dynamically adapt the image content before applying a compensation based on pure radiometric measurements to overcome technical and physical limitations of projector-camera systems. Such techniques take properties of human visual perception into account.

8.4.1 Static Techniques

In its most basic configuration (Figure 8.7), an image is displayed by a single projector (*pro*) in such a way that it appears correct (color and geometry) for a single camera view (*cam*). Thereby, the display surfaces must be Lambertian, but can have an arbitrary color, texture, and shape. The first step is to determine the geometric relations of camera pixels and projector pixels over the display surface. As explained in Section 8.3 at page 308, the resulting $C2P$ and $P2C$ lookup textures support a pixel-precise mapping from camera space to projector space and vice versa.

Once the geometric relations are known, the radiometric parameters are measured. One of the simplest radiometric compensation approaches is described in [27]: With respect to Figure 8.7(left), it can be assumed that a light ray with intensity I is projected onto a surface pigment with reflectance M. The fraction of light that arrives at the pigment depends on the geometric relation between the light source (i.e., the projector) and the surface. A simple representation of the form factor can be used for approximating this fraction: $F = f * \cos(\alpha)/r^2$, where α is the angular correlation between the light ray and the surface normal and r is the distance (considering square distance attenuation) between the light source and the surface. The factor f allows scaling the intensity to avoid clipping (i.e., intensity values that exceed the luminance capabilities of the projector) and to consider the

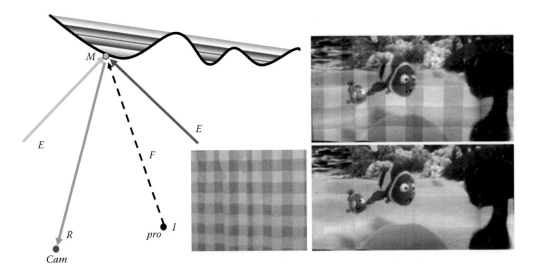

FIGURE 8.7 Radiometric compensation with a single projector (left) and sample images projected without and with compensation onto window curtains (right) [27].

simultaneous contributions of multiple projectors. Together with the environment light E, the projected fraction of I is blended with the pigment's reflectance $M : R = EM + IFM$. Thereby, R is the diffuse radiance that can be captured by the camera. If R, F, M, and E are known, a compensation image I can be computed with:

$$I = (R - EM)/FM \tag{8.3}$$

In a single-projector configuration, E, F, and M cannot be determined independently. Instead, we capture an image while projecting a white flood image ($I = 1$) first. This image contains $C1 = FM + EM$. Repeating this under a black flood projection ($I = 0$), the captured image contains only $C2 = EM$. While EM is simply equivalent to $C2$, FM corresponds to $C1 - C2$. Note that EM also contains the black level of the projector. Since this holds for every discrete camera pixel, R, E, FM and EM are entire textures and Equation 8.3 can be computed together with pixel displacement mappingin realtime by a fragment shader. Thus, every rasterized projector pixel that passes through the fragment shader is displaced and color compensated through texture lookups. The projection of the resulting image I onto the surface leads to a geometry and color corrected image that approximates the desired original image $R = O$ for the target perspective of the camera.

One disadvantage of this simple technique is that the optical limitations of color filters used in cameras and projectors are not considered. These filters can transmit a quite large spectral band of white light rather than only a small monochromatic one. In fact, projecting a pure red color, for instance, usually leads to nonzero responses in the blue and green color channels of the captured images. This is known as the *color mixing* between projector and camera, which is not taken into account by Equation 8.3.

Color mixing can be considered for radiometric compensation: Nayar et al. [208], for instance, express the color transform between each camera and projector pixel as pixel-individual 3x3 color mixing matrices:

$$V = \begin{bmatrix} v_{RR} & v_{RG} & v_{RB} \\ v_{GR} & v_{GG} & v_{GB} \\ v_{BR} & v_{BG} & v_{BB} \end{bmatrix} \tag{8.4}$$

Thereby, v_{RG} represents the green color component in the red color channel, for example. This matrix can be estimated from measured camera responses of multiple projected sample images. It can be continuously refined over a closed feedback loop (e.g., [92]) and is used to correct each pixel during runtime. In the case that the camera response is known while the projector response can remain unknown, it can be assumed that $v_{ii} = 1$. This corresponds to an unknown scaling factor, and V is said to be normalized. The off-diagonal values can then be computed with $v_{ij} = \Delta C_j/\Delta P_i$, where ΔP_i is the difference between two projected intensities ($P_{1i} - P_{2i}$) of primary color i, and ΔC_j is the difference of the corresponding captured images ($C_{1j} - C_{2j}$) in color channel j. Thus, six images have to be captured (two per projected color channel) to determine all v_{ij}. The captured image R under projection of I can now be expressed with: $R = VI$. Consequently, the compensation image can be computed with the inverse color mixing matrix:

$$I = V^{-1}R \tag{8.5}$$

Note that V is different for each camera pixel and contains the surface reflectance, but not the environment light. Another way of determining V is to numerically solve Equation 8.5 for V^{-1} if enough correspondences between I and R are known. In this case, V is unnormalized and v_{ii} is proportional to $[FM_R, FM_G, FM_B]$. Consequently, the off-diagonal values of V are 0 if no color mixing is considered. Yoshida et al. [303] use an unnormalized 3x4 color mixing matrix. In this case, the fourth column represents the constant environment light contribution. A refined version of Nayar's technique was used for controlling the appearance of 2D and 3D objects, such as posters, boxes and spheres [101]. Sections 8.4.2 and 8.4.3 also discuss variations of this method for dynamic situations and image adaptations. Note that a color mixing matrix was also introduced in the context of shape measurement based on a color coded-pattern projection [53].

All of these techniques support image compensation in realtime, but suffer from the same problem: if the compensation image I contains values above the maximal brightness or below the black level of the projector, clipping artifacts will occur. These artifacts allow the underlying surface structure to become visible. The intensity range for which radiometric compensation without clipping is possible depends on the surface reflectance, on the brightness and black level of the projector, on the required reflected intensity (i.e., the desired original image), and on the environment light contribution.

Figure 8.8 illustrates an example that visualizes the reflection properties for a sample surface. By analyzing the responses in both datasets (FM and EM), the range of intensities for a conservative compensation can be computed. Thus, only input pixels of the desired original image $R = O$ within this global range (bound by the two green planes: from the maximum value EM_{max} to the minimum value FM_{min}) can be compensated correctly for each point on the surface without causing clipping artifacts. All other intensities can potentially lead to

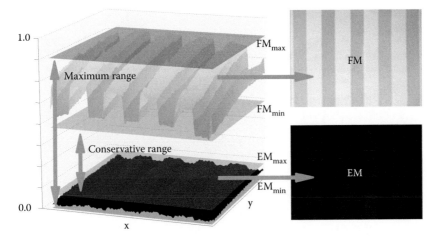

FIGURE 8.8   Intensity range reflected by a striped wall paper [105].

clipping and incorrect results. This conservative intensity range for radiometric compensation is smaller than the maximum intensity range achieved when projecting onto optimized (i.e, diffuse and white) surfaces.

Different possibilities exist to reduce these clipping problems. While applying an amplifying transparent film material is one option that is mainly limited to geometrically simple surfaces, such as paintings [25], the utilization of multiple projectors is another option.

The simultaneous contribution of multiple projectors increases the total light intensity that reaches the surface. This can overcome the limitations of Equation 8.3 on page 316 for extreme situations (e.g., small FM values or large EM values) and can consequently avoid an early clipping of I. Therefore, [27] presents a multiprojector approach for radiometric compensation: If N projectors are applied (Figure 8.9(left)), the measured radiance captured by the camera can be approximated with: $R = EM + \sum_i^N (I_i \cdot FM_i)$. One strategy is to balance the projected intensities equally among all projectors i, which leads to:

$$I_i = (R - EM)/ \sum_j^N (I_j \cdot FM_j) \tag{8.6}$$

Conceptually, this is equivalent to the assumption that a single high-capacity projector (pro_v) produces the total intensity arriving on the surface virtually (Figure 8.9(right)). This equation can also be solved in realtime by projector-individual fragment shaders (based on individual parameter textures FM_i, $C2P_i$ and $P2C_i$ – but striving for the same final result R). Note that EM also contains the accumulated black level of all projectors. If all projectors provide linear transfer functions (e.g., after a linearization) and identical brightness, a scaling of $f_i = 1/N$ used in the form factor balances the load among them equally. However, f_i might be decreased further to avoid clipping and to adapt for differently aged bulbs. Note however,

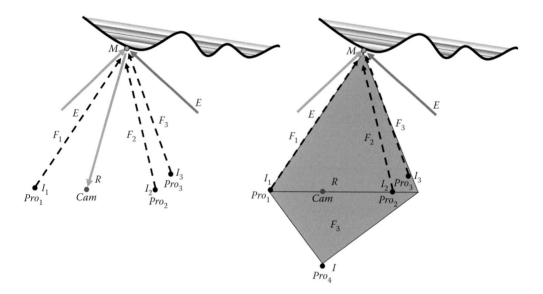

FIGURE 8.9 Radiometric compensation with multiple projectors.

that the total black level increases together with the total brightness of a multiple-projector configuration. Thus, an increase in contrast cannot be achieved. Possibilities for dynamic range improvements are discussed in Section 8.6.3 at page 337.

Since the required operations are simple, a pixel-precise radiometric compensation (including geometric warping through pixel-displacement mapping) can be achieved in real-time with fragment shaders of modern graphics cards. The actual speed depends mainly on the number of pixels that have to be processed in the fragment shader. For example, framerates of >100 Hz can be measured for radiometric compensations using Equation 8.3 on page 316 for PAL-resolution videos projected in XGA resolution.

8.4.2 Dynamic Surfaces and Configurations

The techniques explained in Section 8.4.1 at page 315 are suitable for purely static scenes and fixed projector-camera configurations. They require a one-time calibration before runtime. For many applications, however, a frequent recalibration is necessary because the alignment of camera and projectors with the surfaces changes over time (e.g., because of mechanical expansion through heating, accidental offset, intended readjustment, mobile projector-camera systems, or dynamic scenes). In these cases, it is not desired to disrupt a presentation with visible calibration patterns. While Section 8.3 at page 308 discusses several online calibration methods for geometric correction, this section reviews online radiometric compensation techniques.

Fujii et al. have described a dynamically adapted radiometric compensation technique that supports changing projection surfaces and moving projector-camera configurations [92]. Their system requires a fixed coaxial alignment of projector and camera (Figure 8.10(left)). An optical registration of both devices makes a frequent geometric calibration unnecessary. Thus, the fixed mapping between projector and camera pixels does not have to be recalibrated if either surface or configuration changes. At an initial point in time zero the surface reflectance is determined under environment light $(E_0 M_0)$. To consider color mixing as explained in Section 8.4.1 at page 315, this can be done by projecting and capturing corresponding images I_0 and C_0. The reflected environment light E_0 at a pigment with reflectance M_0 can then be approximated by $E_0 M_0 = C_0 - V_0 I_0$, where V_0 is the unnormalized color mixing matrix at time zero, which is constant. After initialization, the radiance R_t at time t captured by the camera under projection of I_t can be approximated with: $R_t = M_t / M_0 (E_t M_0 + V_0 I_t)$. Solving for I_t results in:

$$I_t = V_0^{-1} (R_t M_0 / M_{t-1} - E_{t-1} M_0) \tag{8.7}$$

Thereby, $R_t = O_t$ is the desired original image and I_t the corresponding compensation image at time t. The environment light contribution cannot be measured during runtime. It is approximated to be constant. Thus, $E_{t-1} M_0 = E_0 M_0$. The ratio M_0 / M_{t-1} is then equivalent to the ratio C_0 / C_{t-1}. In this closed feedback loop, the compensation image I_t at time t depends on the captured parameters (C_{t-1}) at time $t - 1$. This one-frame delay can lead to visible artifacts. Furthermore, the surface reflectance M_{t-1} is continuously estimated based on the projected image I_{t-1}. Thus, the quality of the measured surface reflectance depends

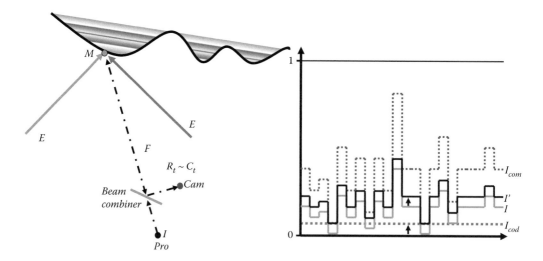

FIGURE 8.10 Coaxial projector-camera alignment (left) and reflectance measurements through temporal coding (right).

on the content of the desired image R_{t-1}. If R_{t-1} has extremely low or high values in one or multiple color channels, M_{t-1} might not be valid in all samples. Other limitations of such an approach might be, first, the strict optical alignment of projector and camera that could be too inflexible for many large-scale applications; and second, that it does not support multiprojector configurations.

Another possibility for supporting dynamic surfaces and projector-camera configurations that do not require a strict optical alignment of both devices was described in [309]. As outlined in Section 8.3.3 at page 312, imperceptible codes can be embedded into a projected image through a temporal coding to support an online geometric projector-camera registration. The same approach can be used for embedding a uniform gray image I_{cod} into a projected image I. Thereby, I_{cod} is used to illuminate the surface with a uniform floodlight image to measure the combination of surface reflectance and projector form factor FM, as explained in Section 8.4.1 at page 315. To ensure that I_{cod} can be embedded correctly, the smallest value in I must be greater than or equal I_{cod}. If this is not the case, I is transformed to I' to ensure this condition (Figure 8.10(right)). A (temporal) compensation image can then be computed with $I_{com} = 2I' - I_{cod}$. Projecting I_{cod} and I_{com} with a high speed, one perceives $(I_{cod} + I_{com})/2 = I'$. Synchronizing a camera with the projection allows I_{cod} and therefore also FM to be captured. In practice, I_{cod} is approximately 3–5% of the total intensity range, depending on the projector brightness and the camera sensitivity of the utilized devices. One other advantage of this method is that, in contrast to [92], the measurements of the surface reflectance do not depend on the projected image content. Furthermore, Equations 8.3 or 8.6 can be used to support radiometric compensation with single or multiple projectors. However, projected (radiometric) compensation images I have to be slightly increased in intensity, which leads to a smaller (equal only if $FM = 1$ and $EM = 0$) global intensity increase of $R = O$. However, since I_{cod} is small, this is tolerable. One main limitation of this method in contrast to the techniques explained in [92], is that it does not react to changes quickly. Usually a few seconds (approximately 5–8 s) are required for an imperceptible geometric and radiometric recalibration. In [92] a geometric recalibration is not necessary. As explained in [104], a temporal coding requires a sequential blending of multiple code images over time, since an abrupt transition between two code images can lead to visible flickering. This is another reason for longer calibration times.

In summary we can say that fixed coaxial projector-camera alignments as in [92] support real-time corrections of dynamic surfaces for a single mobile projector-camera system. The reflectance measurements' quality depends on the content in O. A temporal coding as in [309] allows unconstrained projector-camera alignments and supports flexible single- or multiprojector configurations, but no real-time calibration. The quality of reflectance measurements is independent of O in the latter case. Both approaches ensure a fully invisible calibration during runtime, and enable the presentation of dynamic content (such as movies) at interactive rates ($\geq$20 Hz).

8.4.3 Dynamic Image Adaptation

The main technical limitations for radiometric compensation are the resolution, framerate, brightness, and dynamic range of projectors and cameras. Some of these issues will be addressed in Section 8.6 at page 331. This section presents alternative techniques that adapt the original images O based on the human perception and the projection surface properties before carrying out a radiometric compensation to reduce the effects caused by brightness limitations, such as clipping.

All compensation methods described so far take only the reflectance properties of the projection surface into account. Particular information about the input image, however, does not influence the compensation directly. Calibration is carried out once or continuously, and a static color transformation is applied as long as neither surface nor projector-camera configuration changes, regardless of the individual desired image O. Yet, not all projected colors and intensities can be reproduced, as explained in Section 8.4.1 at page 315 and shown in Figure 8.8 on page 317.

Content-dependent radiometric and photometric compensation methods extend the traditional algorithms by applying additional image manipulations that depend on the current image content to minimize clipping artifacts, while preserving a maximum of brightness and contrast in order to generate an optimized compensation image.

Such a content dependent radiometric compensation method was presented by Wang et al. [281]. In this method, the overall intensity of the input image is scaled until clipping errors that result from radiometric compensation are below a perceivable threshold. The threshold is derived by using a perceptually-based physical error metric that was proposed in [230], which considers the image luminance, spatial frequencies, and visual masking. This early technique, however, can be applied only to static monochrome images and surfaces. The numerical minimization that is carried out in [281] requires a series of iterations that make real-time rates impossible.

Park et al. [217] describe a technique for increasing the contrast in a compensation image by applying a histogram equalization to the colored input image. While the visual quality can be enhanced in terms of contrast, this method does not preserve the contrast ratio of the original image. Consequently, the image content is modified significantly, and occurring clipping errors are not considered.

A complex framework for computing an optimized photometric compensation for colored images is presented by Ashdown et al. [7]. In this method the device-independent CIE L*u*v color space is used, which has the advantage that color distances are based on human visual perception. Therefore, an applied HDR camera has to be color calibrated in advance. The input images are adapted depending on a series of global and local parameters to generate an optimized compensated projection: the captured surface reflectance as well as the content of the input image are transformed into the CIE L*u*v color space. The chrominance values of all input images' pixels are fitted into the gamut of the corresponding projector pixels. In the next step, a luminance fitting is applied by using a relaxation method based on differential equations. Finally, the compensated adapted input image is transformed back into the RGB color space for projection.

This method achieves optimal compensation results for surfaces with varying reflectance properties. Furthermore, a compensation can be achieved for highly saturated surfaces due to the fact that besides a luminance adjustment, a chrominance adaptation is applied as well. Its numerical complexity, however, allows the compensation of still images only. Figure 8.11 shows a sample result: An uncompensated projection of the input image projected onto a colored surface (top, left) results in color artifacts (top, right). Projecting the adapted compensation image (bottom, left) onto the surface leads to significant improvements (bottom, right).

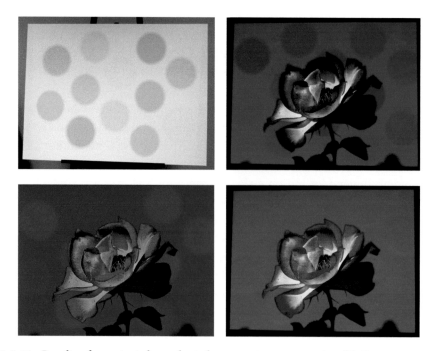

FIGURE 8.11   Results of a content-dependent photometric compensation [7]. Image courtesy: Mark Ashdown.

Ashdown et al. proposed another fitting method in [8] that uses the chrominance threshold model of human vision together with the luminance threshold to avoid visible artifacts.

Content-dependent adaptations enhance the visual quality of a radiometric compensated projection compared to static methods that do not adapt to the input images. Animated content such as movies or TV broadcasts, however, cannot be compensated in realtime with the methods reviewed above. While movies could be precorrected frame-by-frame in advance, real-time content such as interactive applications cannot be presented.

In [105], a real-time solution for adaptive radiometric compensation was introduced that is implemented entirely on the GPU. The method adapts each input image in two steps: first it is analyzed for its average luminance that leads to an approximate global scaling factor that depends on the surface reflectance. This factor is used to scale the input image's intensity between the conservative and the maximum intensity range (Figure 8.8 on page 317). Afterward, a compensation image is calculated according to Equation 8.3 on page 316. Instead of projecting this compensation image directly, it is further analyzed for potential clipping errors. Errors are extracted and blurred, also. In a final step, the input image is scaled globally again depending on its average luminance and on the calculated maximum clipping error. In addition, it is scaled locally based on the regional error values. The threshold map explained in [230] is used to constrain the local image manipulation based on the contrast and the luminance sensitivity of human observers. Radiometric compensation (Equation 8.3 on page 316) is applied again to the adapted image, and the result is finally projected. Global, but also local scaling parameters are adapted over time to reduce abrupt intensity changes in the projection which would lead to a perceived and irritating flickering.

This approach does not apply numerical optimizations and consequently enables a practical solution for displaying adapted dynamic content in realtime and with increased quality (compared to traditional radiometric compensation). Yet, small clipping errors might still occur. However, especially for content with varying contrast and brightness, this adaptive technique enhances the perceived quality significantly. An example is shown in Figure 8.12: Two frames of a movie (b,e) are projected with a static compensation technique [27] (c,f) and with the adaptive real-time solution [105] (d,g) onto a natural stone wall (a). While clipping occurs in case (c), case (f) appears too dark. The adaptive method reduces the clipping errors for bright images (d) while maintaining details in the darker image (g).

8.4.4 Enhancing Contrast

In contrast to the radiometric and photometric compensation techniques that are explained above, similar methods boost the contrast of existing surfaces rather than fitting arbitrary image content into their limited contrast range [5,30]. Such structured illumination techniques can be used if a low-contrast reflection or transmission under ordinary uniform illumination is problematic, since they enhance existing surface features.

This basic principle of *double modulation* is visualized in Figure 8.13. Instead of using uniform (low-frequent) light for illumination, a high-frequent (projected) light is applied. This allows a controlled spatial and temporal modulation with reflective or transmissive matter. Since the modulation behavior of the matter is measured initially or on the fly, a carefully

FIGURE 8.12 Two frames of a movie (b,e) projected onto a natural stone wall (a) with static (c,f) and real-time adaptive radiometric compensation (d,g) for bright and dark input images [105].

computed illumination image can be projected, which is contrast modulated by the matter itself. The formed image can then exceed the contrast that is possible with a uniform illumination alone by several orders of magnitude. Besides reflective surfaces, such as radiological paper prints, e-paper displays, and other real-world surfaces, this technique potentially finds

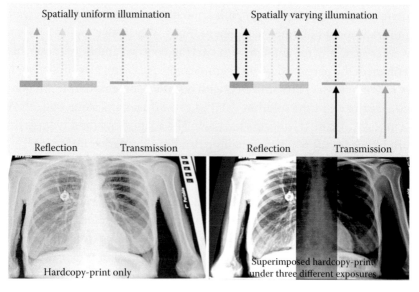

FIGURE 8.13 Top: Basic principle of double modulation with transmissive or reflective matter: the illumination is premodulated by the projector, and is modulated a second time by being reflected, transmitted or absorbed by real matter. Bottom: Example of contrast enhancing a radiological paper print from less than 100:1 to over 60.000:1. [30].

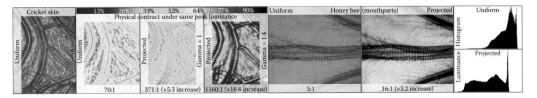

FIGURE 8.14 Double modulation of transmitted illumination while observing a honey bee under a microscope. Compared to a simple uniform illumination, a projected illumination enhances contrast [23].

applications in microscopy, endoscopy, or restoration – basically in areas that demand a contrast-enhancing light source. Figure 8.14 shows an example for the application of this concept in microscopy [23].

8.5 CORRECTING COMPLEX LIGHT MODULATIONS

All image-correction techniques that have been discussed thus far assume a simple geometric relation between camera and projector pixels that can be automatically derived using homography matrices, structured light projections, or coaxial projector-camera alignments.

When projecting onto complex everyday surfaces, however, the emitted radiance of illuminated display elements is often subject to complex lighting phenomena. Because of diffuse or specular interreflections, refractions, and other global illumination effects, multiple camera pixels at spatially distant regions on the camera image plane may be affected by a single projector pixel.

A variety of projector-camera based compensation methods for specific global illumination effects have been proposed. These techniques, as well as a generalized approach to compensating light modulations using the inverse light transport will be discussed in the following subsections.

8.5.1 Interreflections

Eliminating diffuse interreflections, or scattering, for projection displays has recently gained a lot of interest in the computer graphics and vision community. Cancellation of interreflections has been proven to be useful for improving the image quality of immersive virtual and augmented reality displays [29]. Furthermore, such techniques can be employed to remove indirect illumination from photographs [257]. For compensating global illumination effects, these need to be acquired, stored, and processed, which will be discussed for each application.

Seitz et al. [257], for instance, measured an impulse scatter function (ISF) matrix B with a camera and a laser pointer on a movable gantry. The camera captured diffuse objects illuminated at discrete locations. Each of the sample's centroid represents one row/column in the matrix as depicted in Figure 8.15.

The ISF matrix can be employed to remove interreflections from photographs. Therefore, an interreflection cancellation operator $C^1 = B^1 B^{-1}$ is defined that, when multiplied to a captured camera image R, extracts its direct illumination. B^{-1} is the ISF matrix's inverse and B^1 contains only direct illumination. For a diffuse scene, this can easily be extracted from B

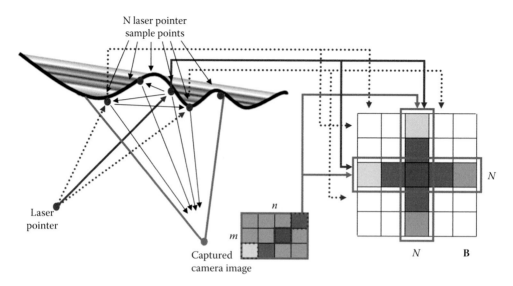

FIGURE 8.15 A symmetric ISF matrix is acquired by illuminating a diffuse surface at various points, sampling their locations in the camera image, and inserting captured color values into the matrix.

by setting its off-diagonal elements to zero. A related technique that quickly separates direct and indirect illumination for diffuse and non-Lambertian surfaces was introduced by Nayar et al. [207].

Experimental results in [257] were obtained by sampling the scene under laser illumination at approximately 35 locations in the camera image. Since B is in this case a very small and square matrix it is trivial to be inverted for computing B^{-1}. However, inverting a general light-transport matrix in a larger scale is a challenging problem and will be discussed in Section 8.5.3 at page 328.

Compensating indirect diffuse scattering for immersive projection screens was proposed in [29]. Assuming a known screen geometry, the scattering was simulated and corrected with a customized reverse radiosity scheme. Bimber et al. [24] and Mukaigawa et al. [200] showed that a compensation of diffuse light interaction can be performed in realtime by reformulating the radiosity equation as $I = (1 - \rho F)O$. Here O is the desired original image, I the projected compensation image, 1 the identity matrix and ρF the precomputed form-factor matrix. This is equivalent to applying the interreflection cancellation operator, introduced in [257], to an image O that does not contain interreflections. The quality of projected images for a two-sided projection screen can be greatly enhanced as depicted in Figure 8.16. All computations are performed with a relatively coarse patch resolution of about 128×128 as seen in Figure 8.16(c).

While the form factor matrix in [24,200] was precomputed, Habe et al. [107] presented an algorithm that automatically acquires all photometric relations within the scene using a projector-camera system. They state also that this theoretically allows specular interreflections to be compensated for a fixed viewpoint. However, such a compensation has not been validated in the presented experiments. For the correction, a form-factor matrix inverse is required, which again is trivial to be calculated for a low-patch resolution.

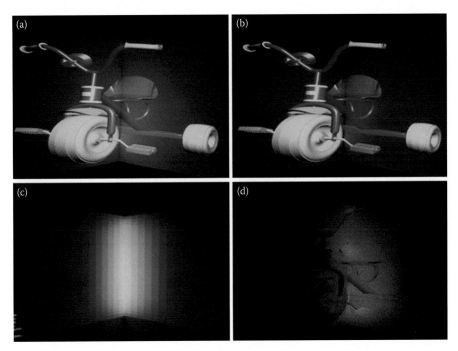

FIGURE 8.16 Compensating diffuse scattering: An uncompensated (a) and a compensated (b) stereoscopic projection onto a two-sided screen. Scattering and color bleeding can be eliminated (d) if the form factors (c) of the projection surface are known [29].

8.5.2 Specular Reflections

When projecting onto non-Lambertian screens, not only diffuse and specular interreflections affect the quality of projected imagery, but specular highlights may also distract a viewer. Park et al. [219] presented a compensation approach that attempts to minimize specular reflections using multiple overlapping projectors. The highlights are not due to global illumination effects, but to the incident illumination that is reflected directly toward the viewer on a shiny surface. Usually, only one of the projectors creates a specular highlight at a point on the surface. Thus, its contribution can be blocked while display elements from other projectors that illuminate the same surface area from a different angle are boosted.

For a view-dependent compensation of specular reflections, the screen's geometry needs to be known and registered with all projectors. Displayed images are predistorted to create a geometrically seamless projection as described in Section 8.3 at page 308. The amount of specularity for a projector i at a surface point s with a given normal n is proportional to the angle θ_i between n and the sum of the vector from s to the projector's position p_i and the vector from s to the viewer u:

$$\theta_i = \cos^{-1}\left(\frac{-n \cdot (p_i + u)}{|p_i + u|}\right) \tag{8.8}$$

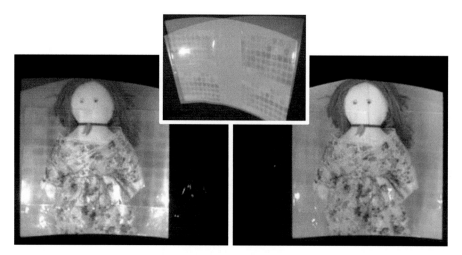

FIGURE 8.17 Radiometric compensation in combination with specular reflection elimination [220]. Image courtesy: Hanhoon Park, **NHK** Science and Technology Research Laboratories, Tokyo.

Assuming that k projectors illuminate the same surface, a weight w_i is multiplied to each of the incident light rays for a photometric compensation:

$$w_i = \frac{\sin(\theta_i)}{\sum_{j=1}^{k} \sin(\theta_j)} \tag{8.9}$$

Park et al. [220] extended this model by an additional radiometric compensation to account for the color modulation of the underlying projection surface (Figure 8.17). Therefore, Nayar's model [208] was implemented. The required one-to-one correspondences between projector and camera pixels were acquired with projected binary Gray codes [250].

Specular highlights were also suppressed for coaxial projector-camera systems used in microscopes to enhance viewing conditions when observing wet tissue [23].

8.5.3 Radiometric Compensation through Inverse Light Transport

Although the previously discussed methods are successful in compensating particular aspects of the light transport between projectors and cameras, they lead to a fragmented understanding of the subject. A unified approach that accounts for many of the problems that were individually addressed in previous works was described in [290]. The full light-transport between a projector and a camera was employed to compensate direct and indirect illumination effects, such as interreflections, refractions, and defocus, with a single technique in realtime. Furthermore, this also implies a pixel-precise geometric correction. In the following subsection we refer to the approach as performing radiometric compensation. However, geometric warping is always implicitly included.

In order to compensate direct and global illumination as well as geometrical distortions in a generalized manner, the full light-transport has to be taken into account. Within a projector-camera system, this is a matrix T_λ that can be acquired in a preprocessing step,

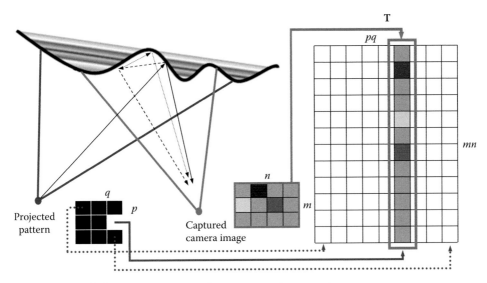

FIGURE 8.18 The light-transport matrix between a projector and a camera.

for instance as described by Sen et al. [259]. Therefore, a set of illumination patterns is projected onto the scene and is recorded using HDR imaging techniques (e.g., [71]). Individual matrix entries can then be reconstructed from the captured camera images. As depicted in Figure 8.18, a camera image with a single lit projector pixel represents one column in the light-transport matrix. Usually, the matrix is acquired in a hierarchical manner by simultaneously projecting multiple pixels.

For a single projector-camera configuration the forward light-transport is described by a simple linear equation as

$$\begin{bmatrix} r_R - e_R \\ r_G - e_G \\ r_B - e_B \end{bmatrix} = \begin{bmatrix} T_R^R & T_R^G & T_R^B \\ T_G^R & T_G^G & T_G^B \\ T_B^R & T_B^G & T_B^B \end{bmatrix} \begin{bmatrix} i_R \\ i_G \\ i_B \end{bmatrix}, \tag{8.10}$$

where each r_λ is a single color channel λ of a camera image with resolution $m \times n$, i_λ is the projection pattern with a resolution of $p \times q$, and e_λ are direct and global illumination effects caused by the environment light and the projector's black level captured from the camera. Each light transport matrix $T_{\lambda_c}^{\lambda_p}$ (size: $mn \times pq$) describes the contribution of a single projector color channel λ_p to an individual camera channel λ_c. The model can easily be extended for k projectors and l cameras:

$$\begin{bmatrix} _1 r_R - _1 e_R \\ _1 r_G - _1 e_G \\ \vdots \\ _l r_B - _l e_B \end{bmatrix} = \begin{bmatrix} _1^1 T_R^R & _1^1 T_R^G & \cdots & _1^k T_R^B \\ _1^1 T_G^R & _1^1 T_G^G & \cdots & _1^k T_G^B \\ \vdots & \vdots & \ddots & \vdots \\ _l^1 T_B^R & _l^1 T_B^G & \cdots & _l^k T_B^B \end{bmatrix} \begin{bmatrix} ^1 i_R \\ ^1 i_G \\ \vdots \\ ^k i_B \end{bmatrix} \tag{8.11}$$

For a generalized radiometric compensation, the camera image r_λ is replaced by a desired image o_λ of camera resolution and the system can be solved for the projection pattern i_λ that needs to be projected. This accounts for color modulations and geometric distortions of projected imagery. Because of the matrix's enormous size, sparse matrix representations and operations can help to save storage and increase performance.

A customized clustering scheme that allows the light-transport matrix's pseudo-inverse to be approximated is described in [290]. Inverse impulse scatter functions or form-factor matrices had already been used in previous algorithms [24,107,200,257], but in a much smaller scale, which makes an inversion trivial. Using the light-transport matrix's approximated pseudo-inverse, radiometric compensation reduces to a matrix-vector multiplication:

$$i_\lambda = T_\lambda^+ (o_\lambda - e_\lambda),\qquad(8.12)$$

In [290], this was implemented on the GPU and yielded real-time framerates.

Figure 8.19 shows a compensated projection onto highly refractive material (f), which is impossible with conventional approaches (e), because a direct correspondence between projector and camera pixels is not given. The light-transport matrix (Figure 8.19(b)) and its approximated pseudo-inverse (visualized in (c)) contain local and global illumination effects within the scene (global illumination effects in the matrix are partially magnified in (b)).

It was shown in [290] that all measurable light modulations, such as diffuse and specular reflections, complex interreflections, diffuse scattering, refraction, caustics, defocus, and the like can be compensated with the multiplication of the inverse light-transport matrix and the desired original image. Furthermore, a pixel-precise geometric image correction is implicitly included and becomes feasible, even for surfaces that are unsuited for a conventional structured light scanning. However, due to the extremely long acquisition time of the light-transport matrix (up to several hours), this approach will not be practical before accelerated scanning techniques have been developed.

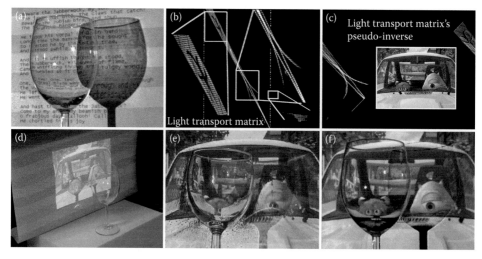

FIGURE 8.19 Real-time radiometric compensation (f) of global illumination effects (a) with the light-transport matrix's (b) approximated pseudo-inverse (c).

8.6 OVERCOMING TECHNICAL LIMITATIONS

Most of the image-correction techniques that are described in this chapter are constrained by technical limitations of projector and camera hardware. A too low resolution or dynamic range of both devices leads to a significant loss of image quality. A too short focal depth results in regionally defocused image areas when projected onto surfaces with an essential depth variance. Too slow projection frame rates will cause the perception of temporally embedded codes. This section is dedicated to giving an overview of novel (at present mainly experimental) approaches that might lead to future improvements in projector-camera systems in terms of focal depth, high resolution, dynamic range, and high speed.

8.6.1 Increasing Depth of Field

Projections onto geometrically complex surfaces with a high depth variance generally do not allow the displayed content to be in focus everywhere. Common DLP or LCD projectors usually maximize their brightness with large apertures. Thus, they suffer from narrow depths of field and can only generate focused imagery on a single frontoparallel screen. Laser projectors, which are commonly used in planetaria, are an exception. These emit almost parallel light beams, which make very large depths of field possible. However, the cost of a single professional laser projector can exceed the cost of several hundred conventional projectors. In order to increase the depth of field of conventional projectors, several approaches for deblurring unfocused projections with a single or with multiple projectors have been proposed.

Zhang and Nayar [304] presented an iterative, spatially-varying filtering algorithm that compensates for projector defocus. They employed a coaxial projector-camera system to measure the projection's spatially-varying defocus. Therefore, dot patterns as depicted in Figure 8.20(a) are projected onto the screen and captured by the camera (b). The defocus kernels for each projector pixel can be recovered from the captured images and encoded in the rows of a matrix B. Given the environment light EM including the projector's black level and a desired input image O, the compensation image I can be computed by minimizing the sum-of-squared pixel difference between O and the expected projection $BI + EM$ as

$$\arg\min_{I, 0 \leq I \leq 255} \|BI + EM - O\|^2, \qquad (8.13)$$

which can be solved with a constrained, iterative steepest-gradient solver as described in [304].

An alternative approach to defocus compensation for a single projector setup was presented by Brown et al. [47]. Projector defocus is modeled as a convolution of a projected original image O and Gaussian *point spread functions* (PSFs) as $R(x, y) = O(x, y) \otimes H(x, y)$, where the blurred image that can be captured by a camera is R. The PSFs are estimated by projecting features on the canvas and capturing them with a camera. Assuming a spatially-invariant PSF, a compensation image I can be synthesized by applying a Wiener filter to the

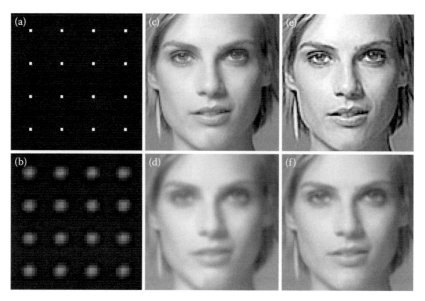

FIGURE 8.20 Defocus compensation with a single projector: An input image (c) and its defocused projection onto a planar canvas (d). Solving Equation 8.13 results in a compensation image (e) that leads to a sharper projection (f). For this compensation, the spatially-varying defocus kernels are acquired by projecting dot patterns (a) and capturing them with a camera (b) [304]. Image courtesy: Shree Nayar, Columbia University.

original image:

$$I\left(x,y\right) = \mathcal{F}^{-1} \left\{ \frac{\tilde{H}^* \left(u, v\right) \tilde{O} \left(u, v\right)}{\left|\tilde{H}\left(u, v\right)\right|^2 + 1/SNR} \right\}. \tag{8.14}$$

The signal-to-noise ratio (SNR) is estimated a priori, $\tilde{O}$ and $\tilde{H}$ are the Fourier transforms of O and H, respectively, and $\tilde{H}^*$ is $\tilde{H}$'s complex conjugate. $\mathcal{F}^{-1}$ denotes the inverse Fourier transform. Since the defocus kernel H is generally not spatially-invariant (this would only be the case for a frontoparallel plane) Wiener filtering cannot be applied directly. Therefore, basis compensation images are calculated for each of the uniformly sampled feature points, using Equation 8.14. The final compensation image is then generated by interpolating the four closest basis responses for each projector pixel.

Oyamada and Saito [215] presented a similar approach to single-projector defocus compensation. Here, circular PSFs are used for the convolution and are estimated by comparing the original image to various captured compensation images that were generated with different PSFs.

The main drawback of single-projector defocus compensation approaches is that the quality is highly dependent on the projected content. All of the discussed methods result in a pre-sharpened compensation image that is visually closer to the original image after being optically blurred by the defocused projection. While soft contours can be compensated, this is generally not the case for sharp features, which result in ringing artifacts. These are mainly because of the aforementioned divisions by zeros introduced by circular projector apertures.

The resulting PSFs act as low-pass filters on projected light by irreversibly canceling out high spatial frequencies. Decreasing the size of the aperture opening reduces the number of low Fourier magnitudes, thus it effectively enhances the depth of field of a projection system. Using narrower aperture openings (down to pinhole size), however, will naturally decrease the light throughput significantly, which is unacceptable for most projection-based displays.

Coding a projector's aperture plane with adaptive patterns, together with inverse filtering allows the depth of field of projected imagery to be increased. Such coded apertures can be broadband masks [102], or adaptive masks [103] that filter an image-specific frequency band. Thus, they are better suited for projector defocus compensation based on inverse filtering than low-pass apertures. In contrast to narrow apertures, they preserve a high light throughput. In [103], two prototypes (Figure 8.21) and corresponding algorithms for static and programmable apertures are presented. It is explained how these patterns can be computed at interactive rates, by taking into account the image content and the limitations of the human visual system. Applications such as projector defocus compensation, high-quality

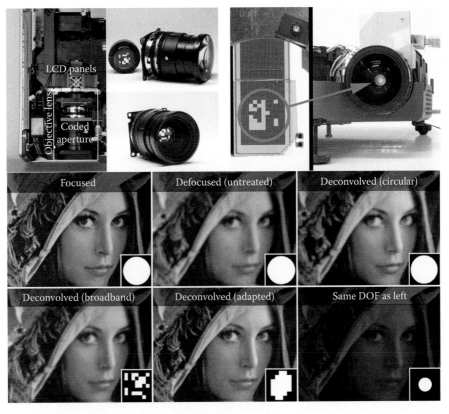

FIGURE 8.21 Two prototypes with a static broadband mask and an image-adaptive coded aperture realized with a programmable liquid crystal array (top). Focused and defocused image before and after deconvolution with different apertures (low-pass circular, broadband, adapted), and comparison of light loss when achieving the same depth of field with a circular aperture as with an adaptive coded aperture (bottom) [103].

projector de-pixelation, and increased temporal contrast of projected video sequences can be supported. Coded apertures are a step toward next-generation auto-iris projector lenses.

An alternative approach that is less dependent on the actual frequencies in the input image was introduced in [26]. Multiple overlapping projectors with varying focal depths illuminate arbitrary surfaces with complex geometry and reflectance properties. Pixel-precise focus values $\Phi_{i,x,y}$ are automatically estimated at each camera pixel (x, y) for every projector. Therefore, a uniform grid of circular patterns is displayed by each projector and recorded by a camera. In order to capture the same picture (geometrically and color-wise) for each projection, these are pre-distorted and radiometrically compensated as described in Sections 8.3 and 8.4.

Once the relative focus values are known, an image from multiple projector contributions with minimal defocus can be composed in realtime. A weighted image composition represents a trade-off between intensity enhancement and focus refinement as:

$$I_i = \frac{w_i (R - EM)}{\sum_j^N w_j FM_j}, \quad w_{i,x,y} = \frac{\Phi_{i,x,y}}{\sum_j^N \Phi_{j,x,y}}, \tag{8.15}$$

where I_i is the compensation image for projector i if N projectors are applied simultaneously. Display contributions with high focus values are upweighted while contributions of projectors with low focus values are downweighted proportionally. A major advantage of this method, compared to single-projector approaches, is that the depth of field of the entire projection scales with the number of projectors. An example for two projectors can be seen in Figure 8.22.

8.6.2 Super-Resolution

Super-resolution techniques can improve the accuracy of geometric warping (see Section 8.3 at page 308) and consequently have the potential to enhance radiometric compensation (see Section 8.4 at page 314) due to a more precise mapping of projector pixels onto surface pigments. Over the past years, several researchers have proposed super-resolution camera

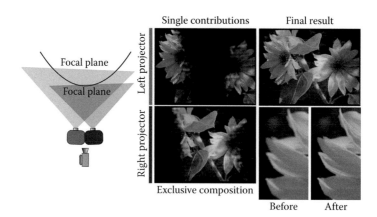

FIGURE 8.22 Defocus compensation with two overlapping projectors that have differently adjusted focal planes [26].

techniques to overcome the inherent limitation of low-resolution imaging systems by using signal processing to obtain super-resolution images (or image sequences) with multiple low-resolution devices [221]. Using a single camera to obtain multiple frames of the same scene is most popular. Multicamera approaches have also been proposed [293].

On the other hand, super-resolution projection systems are just beginning to be researched. This section introduces recent work on such techniques that can generally be categorized into two different groups. The first group proposes super-resolution rendering with a single projector [4], [203]. Other approaches achieve this with multiple overlapping projectors [66,67,138].

In single-projector approaches, so-called *wobulation* techniques are applied: Multiple subframes are generated from an original image. An optical image shift displaces the projected image of each subframe by a fraction of a pixel [4]. Each subframe is projected onto the screen at slightly different positions using an optomechanical image shifter. This light modulator must be switched fast enough so that all subframes are projected in one frame. Consequently, observers perceive this rapid sequence as a continuous and flicker-free image while the resolution is spatially enhanced. Such techniques have been already realized with a DLP system (**SmoothPicture, Texas Instruments**).

In [203], this idea was extended by masking a DMD with a static aperture grating to reduce the pixel footprints on the screen down to 1/25th of their original sizes. Shifting the image in 25 steps per frame leads to a final resolution of 25 times the original resolution without overlap, as in classical wobulation. This, however, also requires projectors that support a 25-fold frame rate.

The goal of multiprojector super-resolution methods is to generate a high-resolution image with the superimposition of multiple low-resolution subframes produced by different projection units. Thereby, the resolutions of each subframe differ and the display surfaces are assumed to be Lambertian. Super-resolution pixels are defined by the overlapping subframes that are shifted on a subpixel basis as shown in Figure 8.23. Generally, the final image is estimated as the sum of the subframes. If N subframes $I_{i=1...N}$ are displayed, this is modeled as:

$$R = \sum_{i}^{N} A_i V_i I_i + EM \tag{8.16}$$

Note that in this case the parameters R, I_i, and EM are images, and that A_i and V_i are the geometric warping matrix and the color mixing matrix that transform the whole image, as opposed to these parameters representing transformations of individual pixels (Sections 8.3 and 8.4).

Figure 8.23(bottom, right) shows a close-up of overlapping pixels to illustrate the problem that has to be solved: while $I_1[1...4]$ and $I_2[1...4]$ are the physical pixels of two projectors, $k[1...4]$ represent the desired "super-resolution" pixel structure. The goal is to find the intensities and colors of corresponding projector pixels in I_1 and I_2 that approximate k as closely as possible by assuming that the perceived result is $I_1 + I_2$. This is obviously a global optimization problem, since k and I have different resolutions. Thus, if O is the desired original image and R is the captured result, the estimation of subframe I_i for projector i is in

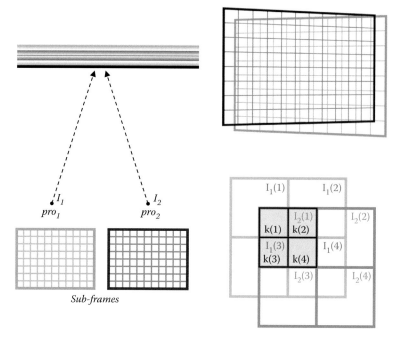

FIGURE 8.23 Super-resolution projection with a multiprojector setup (left), overlapping images on the projection screen (top, right) and close-up of overlapped pixels (bottom, right).

general achieved by minimizing $||O - R||^2$:

$$I_i = \arg\min_{I_i} ||O - R||^2 \tag{8.17}$$

Jaynes et al. first demonstrated resolution enhancement with multiple superimposed projections [138]. Homographies are used for initial geometric registration of multiple subframes onto a planar surface. However, homographic transforms lead to uniform 2D shifts and sampling rates with respect to the camera image rather than to nonuniform shifts of general projective transforms.

To reduce this effect, a warped subframe is divided into smaller regions that are shifted to achieve subpixel accuracy. Initially, each such frame is estimated in the frequency domain by phase shifting the frequencies of the original image. Then, a greedy heuristic process is used to recursively update pixels with the largest global error with respect to Equation 8.17. The proposed model does not consider V_i and EM in Equation 8.16, and a camera is used only for geometric correction. The iterations of the optimization process are terminated manually in [138].

Damera-Venkata et al. proposed a real-time rendering algorithm for computing subframes that are projected by superimposed lower-resolution projectors [67]. In contrast to the previous method, they use a camera to estimate the geometric and photometric properties of each projector during a calibration step. Image registration is achieved on a subpixel

FIGURE 8.24 Experimental result for four superimposed projections: single subframe image (left) and image produced by four superimposed projections with super-resolution enabled (right) [67]. Image courtesy: Nelson Chang, **Hewlett-Packard** Laboratories.

basis using Gray code projection and coarse-to-fine multiscale corner analysis and interpolation. In the proposed model, A_i encapsulates the effects of geometric distortion, pixel reconstruction, point-spread function, and resample-filtering operations.

Furthermore, V_i and EM are obtained during calibration by analyzing the camera response for projected black, red, green, and blue flood images of each projector. In principle, this model could be applied to a projection surface with arbitrary color, texture, and shape. However, this has not been shown in [67]. Once the parameters are estimated, Equation 8.17 can be solved numerically using an iterative gradient descent algorithm. This generates optimal results but does not achieve real-time rendering rates.

For real-time subframe rendering, it was shown in [67] that near-optimal results can be produced with a noniterative approximation. This is accomplished by introducing a linear filter bank that consists of impulse responses of the linearly approximated results which are precomputed with the nonlinear iterative algorithm mentioned above. The filter bank is applied to the original image for estimating the subframes.

In an experimental setting, this filtering process is implemented with fragment shaders and real-time rendering is achieved. Figure 8.24 illustrates a close-up of a single projected subframe (left) and four overlapping projections with super-resolution rendering enabled (right). In this experiment, the original image has a higher resolution than any of the subframes.

8.6.3 High Dynamic Range

To overcome the contrast limitations that are related to radiometric compensation (see Figure 8.8 on page 317), HDR projector-camera systems are imaginable. Although there has been much research and development on HDR camera and capturing systems, little work has been done so far on HDR projectors.

In this section, we will focus on state-of-the-art HDR projector technologies rather than on HDR cameras and capturing techniques. A detailed discussion on HDR capturing/imaging technology and techniques, such as recovering camera response functions and tone mapping/reproduction is not within the scope of this book. The interested reader is referred to [241]. HDR displays in general have been explained in Section 7.8 at page 278.

Note that for the following we want to use the notation of dynamic range (unit decibel, dB) for cameras, and the notation of contrast ratio (unit-less) for projectors.

The dynamic range of common CCD or CMOS chips is around 60 dB while recent logarithmic CMOS image sensors for HDR cameras cover a dynamic range of 170 dB (**HDRC**, **Omron** Automotive Electronics GmbH). Besides special HDR sensors, low-dynamic range (LDR) cameras can be applied for capturing HDR images.

The most popular approach to HDR image acquisition involves taking multiple images of the same scene with the same camera using different exposures, and then merging them into a single HDR image.

There are many ways for making multiple exposure measurements with a single camera [71] or with multiple coaxially aligned cameras [2]. The interested reader is referred to [205] for more information. As an alternative to merging multiple LDR images, the exposure of individual sensor pixels in one image can be controlled with additional light modulators, such as an LCD panel [205] or a DMD chip [206] in front of the sensor or elsewhere within the optical path. In these cases, HDR images are acquired directly.

The contrast ratio of DMD chips and LCoS panels (without additional optics) is about 2,000:1 [75] and 5,000:1 (**SXRD, Sony** Corporation) respectively. Currently, a contrast ratio of around 15,000:1 is achieved for high-end projectors with auto-iris techniques that dynamically adjust the amount of the emitting light according to the image content. Auto-iris techniques, however, cannot expand the dynamic range within a single frame. On the other hand, a laser projection system achieved the contrast ratio of 100,000:1 in [22] because of the absence of light in dark regions.

Multiprojector systems can enhance spatial resolution (see Section 8.6.2 at page 334) and increase the intensity range of projections (see Section 8.4.1 at page 315). However, merging multiple LDR projections does not result in an HDR image. Majumder et al., for example, have rendered HDR images with three overlapped projectors to demonstrate that a larger intensity range and resolution will result in higher quality images [184]. Although the maximum intensity level is increased with each additional projector unit, the minimum intensity level (i.e., the black level) is also increased. The dynamic range of overlapping regions is never greater than the largest one of each individual projector.

Theoretically, if the maximum and the minimum intensities of the ith projector are I_i^{max} and I_i^{min}, its contrast ratio is I_i^{max}/I_i^{min} : 1. If N projectors are overlapped, the contrast ratio of the final image is $\sum_i^N I_i^{max} / \sum_i^N I_i^{min}$: 1. For example, if two projectors are used whose intensities are $I_1^{min} = 10, I_1^{max} = 100$ and $I_2^{min} = 100, I_2^{max} = 1000$ (thus both contrast ratios are $10 : 1$), the contrast ratio of the image overlap is still $10 : 1$ $(10 = (I_1^{max} + I_2^{max})/(I_1^{min} + I_2^{min}))$.

Recently, HDR display systems have been proposed that combine projectors and external light modulators. Seetzen et al. proposed an HDR display that applies a projector as a backlight of an LCD panel instead of a fluorescent tube assembly [256]. As in Figure 8.25(top), the projector is directed to the rear of a transmissive LCD panel. The light that corresponds to each pixel on the HDR display is effectively modulated twice (*double modulation*): first by the projector and then by the LCD panel. Theoretically, the final contrast ratio is the product of the individual contrast ratio of the two modulators. If a projector with a contrast ratio of

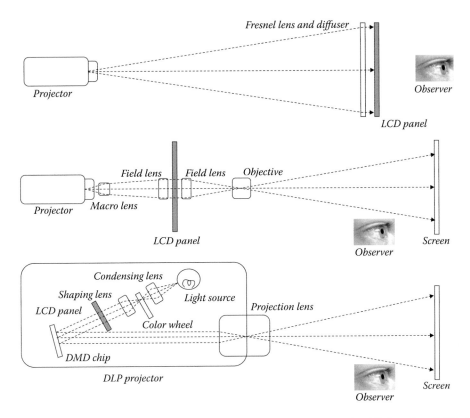

FIGURE 8.25 Different HDR projection setups: using a projector as backlight of an LCD (top), modulating the image path (center), and modulating the illumination path (bottom).

$c_1 : 1$ and an LCD panel with a contrast ratio of $c_2 : 1$ are used in this example, the contrast of the combined images is $(c_1 \cdot c_2) : 1$. In an experimental setup, this approach achieved a contrast ratio of $54,000 : 1$ using an LCD panel and a DMD projector with a contrast ratio of $300 : 1$ and $800 : 1$ respectively. The reduction of contrast is due to noise and imperfections in the optical path.

The example described above does not really present a projection system since the image is generated behind an LCD panel, rather than on a projection surface. True HDR projection approaches are discussed in [65,70]. The basic idea of realizing an HDR projector is to combine a normal projector and an additional low-resolution light modulating device. Double modulation decreases the black level of the projected image, and increases the dynamic range as well as the number of addressable intensity levels. Thereby, LCD panels, LCoS panels, and DMD chips can serve as light modulators.

HDR projectors can be categorized into systems that modulate the image path (Figure 8.25(center)), and into systems that modulate the illumination path (Figure 8.25 (bottom)). In the first case, an image is generated with a high-resolution light modulator first, and then modulated again with an additional low-resolution light modulator. In the latter case, the projection light is modulated in advance with a low-resolution light modulator before the image is generated with a high-resolution modulator.

In each approach, a compensation for the optical blur caused by the low-resolution modulator is required. The degree of blur can be measured and can be described with a PSF for each low-resolution pixel in relation to corresponding pixels on the higher-resolution modulator. A division of the desired output image by the estimated blurred image that is simulated by the PSF will result in the necessary compensation mask which will be displayed on the high-resolution modulator.

Pavlovych et al. proposed a system that falls into the first category [223]. This system uses an external attachment (an LCD panel) in combination with a regular DLP projector (Figure 8.25(center)). The projected image is resized and focused first on the LCD panel through a set of lenses. Then it is modulated by the LCD panel and projected through another lens system onto a larger screen.

Kusakabe et al. proposed an HDR projector that applies LCoS panels that falls into the second category [164]. In this system, three low-resolution (RGB) modulators are used first for chrominance modulation of the projection light. Finally, the light is modulated again with a high-resolution luminance modulator that forms the image.

The resolution of the panel that is applied for chrominance modulation can be much lower than the one for luminance modulation because the human visual system is sensitive only to a relatively low chrominance contrast. An experimental result is shown in Figure 8.26. The proposed projector has a contrast ratio of 1,100,000:1.

FIGURE 8.26 Photographs of a part of an HDR projected image: image modulated with low-resolution chrominance modulators (top, left), image modulated with a high-resolution luminance modulator (top, right), output image (bottom) [164]. Image courtesy: Yuichi Kusakabe, **NHK** Science and Technical Research Laboratories.

8.6.4 High Speed

High-speed projector-camera systems hold the enormous potential to significantly improve high-frequency temporal coded projections (see Sections 8.3.3 and 8.4.2). It enables, for instance, projecting and capturing imperceptible spatial patterns that can be efficiently used for real-time geometric registration, fast shape measurement, and real-time adaptive radiometric compensation while a flicker-free content is perceived by the observer at the same time. The faster the projection and the capturing process can be carried out, the more information per unit of time can be encoded. Since high-speed capturing systems are well established, this section focuses mainly on state-of-the-art of high-speed projection systems. Both together, however, could be merged into future high-speed projector-camera systems. For this reason, we first want to give only a brief overview of high-speed capturing systems.

Commercially available single-chip high-speed cameras exist that can record 512x512 color pixels at up to 16,000 fps (**FASTCAM SA1**, **Photron** Ltd.). However, these systems are typically limited to storing just a few seconds of data directly on the camera because of the huge bandwidth that is necessary to transfer the images. Other CMOS devices are on the market that enable a 500 fps (**A504k**, **Basler** AG) capturing and transfer rates.

Besides such single-camera systems, a high capturing speed can also be achieved with multicamera arrays. Wilburn et al., for example, proposed a high-speed video system for capturing 1,560 fps videos using a dense array of 30 fps CMOS image sensors [292]. Their system captures and compresses images from 52 cameras in parallel. Even at extremely high framerates, such a camera array architecture supports continuous streaming to disk from all of the cameras for minutes.

In contrast to this, however, the framerate of commercially available DLP projectors is normally less than or equal to 120 fps (**DepthQ**, **InFocus** Corporation). Although faster projectors that can be used in the context of projector-camera systems are currently not available as mass-products, we want to outline several projection approaches that achieve higher framerates, but do not necessarily allow the projection of high-quality images.

Raskar et al., for instance, developed a high-speed optical motion capture system with an LED-based code projector [234]. The system consists of a set of 1-bit Gray code infrared LED beamers. Such a beamer array effectively emits 10000 binary Gray-coded patterns per second, and is applied for object tracking. Each object to be tracked is tagged with a photosensor that detects and decodes the temporally projected codes. The 3D location of the tags can be computed at a speed of 500 Hz when at least three such beamer arrays are applied.

In contrast to this approach which does not intend to project pictorial content in addition to the code patterns, Nii et al. proposed a *visible light communication* (VLC) technique that does display simple images [212]. They developed an LED-based high-speed projection system (with a resolution of 4x5 points produced with an equally large LED matrix) that is able to project alphabetic characters while applying an additional pulse modulation for coding information that is detected by photosensors. This system is able to transmit two data streams with 1 kHz and 2 kHz respectively, at different locations while simultaneously projecting simple pictorial content. Although LEDs can be switched with a high speed (e.g., the LEDs in [212] are temporally modulated at 10.7 MHz), such simple LED-based projection systems offer a too low spatial resolution at the moment.

In principle, binary framerates of up to 16,300 fps can currently be achieved with DMDs for a resolution of 1024x768. The DMD discovery board enables developers to implement their own mirror timings for special purpose application [75]. Consequently, due to this high binary framerate some researchers utilized the Discovery boards for realizing high-speed projection techniques. McDowall et al., for example, demonstrated the possibility of projecting 24 binary code and compensation images at a speed of 60 Hz [193]. Viewers used time-encoded shutter glasses to make individual images visible.

Kitamura et al. also developed a high-speed projector based on the DMD discovery board [153]. With their approach, photosensors can be used to detect temporal code patterns that are embedded into the mirror-flip sequence. In contrast to the approach by Cotting et al. [61] that was described in Section 8.3.3 at page 312, the mirror-flip sequence can be freely reconfigured.

The results of an initial basic experiment with this system are shown in Figure 8.27: the projected image is divided into ten regions. Different on/off mirror-flip frequencies are used in each region (from 100 Hz to 1000 Hz at 100 Hz intervals), while a uniformly bright image

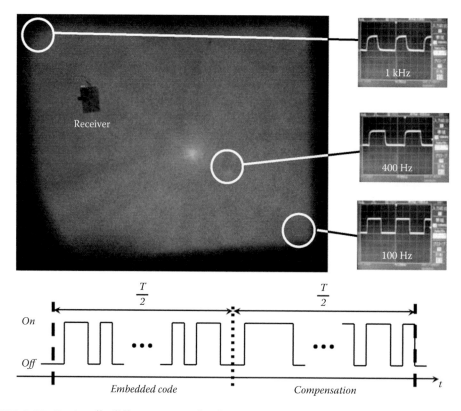

FIGURE 8.27 Regionally different mirror-flip frequencies and corresponding signal waves received by photosensors at different image areas. The overall image appears mostly uniform in intensity (top). Binary codes can be embedded into the first half of the exposure sequence while the second half can compensate the desired intensity (bottom) [153]. Image courtesy: Masahiko Kitamura, NTT Network Innovation Labs.

with a 50% intensity appears in all regions – regardless of the locally applied frequencies. The intensity falloff in the projection is mainly due to imperfections in applied optics. The signal waves are received by photosensors that are placed within the regions, which can detect the individual frequency.

Instead of using a constant on-off flip frequency for each region, binary codes can be embedded into a projected frame. This is illustrated in Figure 8.27(bottom): For a certain time slot of T, the first half of the exposure sequence contains a temporal code pattern (modulated with different mirror flip states) that is compensated with the second half of the exposure sequence to modulate a desired intensity. Yet, contrast is lost in this case due to the modulated intensity level created by the code pattern. Here, the number of on-states always equals the number of off-states in the code period. This leads to a constant minimum intensity level of 25%. Since also 25% of the off states are used during this period, intensity values between 25% and 75% can only be displayed.

All systems that have been outlined above apply photosensors rather than cameras. Thus, they cannot be considered as suitable projector-camera systems in our application context. Yet, McDowall et al. combined their high-speed projector with a high-speed camera to realize fast range scanning [192]. Takei et al. proposed a 3,000 fps shape measurement system (shape reconstruction is performed off-line in this case) [269].

In an image-based rendering context, Jones et al. proposed to simulate spatially varying lighting on a live performance based on a fast shape measurement using a high-speed projector-camera system [140]. However, all of these approaches do not project pictorial image content but rather represent encouraging examples of fast projector-camera techniques.

The mirrors on a conventional DMD chip can be switched much faster than alternative technologies, such as ordinary LCD or LCoS panels whose refresh rate can be up to 2.5 ms (=400 Hz) at the moment.

LEDs are generally better suited for high-speed projectors than a conventional UHP lamp (we do not want to consider brightness issues for the moment), because three or more different LEDs that correspond to each color component can be switched at a high speed (even faster than a DMD) for modulating colors and intensities. Therefore, a combination of DMD and LED technologies seems to be optimal for future projection units.

Let's assume that the mirrors of a regular DLP projector can be switched at $15\mu s$ (=67,000 binary frame rates). For projecting 256 different intensity levels (i.e., an 8-bit encoded gray-scale image), the gray-scale frame rate is around 260 Hz (=67,000 binary frames per second/256 intensity levels). Consequently, the frame rate for full-color images is around 85 Hz (=260 gray-scale frames per second/3 color channels) if the color wheel consists of three filter segments.

Now, let's consider DLP projectors that apply LEDs instead of UHP lamps and a color wheel. If, for example, the intensities of three (RGB) color LEDs can be switched between eight different levels (1,2,4,8,16,32,64,128,256) at a high speed, a full-color image can theoretically be projected at around 2,800 Hz (=67,000 binary frames per second/8 (8-bit encoded) intensity levels/3 color channels). This is an example that we have discussed in more detail in Section 7.3.4 at page 253.

To overcome the bandwidth limitation for transferring the huge amount of image data in high speed, the MULE projector adopts a custom programmed *field-programmable gate array* (FPGA)-based circuitry [141]. The FPGA decodes a standard *digital visual interface* (DVI) signal from the graphics card. Instead of rendering a color image, the FPGA takes each 24-bit color frame of video and displays each of the bits sequentially as separate frames. Thus, if the incoming digital video signal is 60 Hz, the projector displays $60 \times 24 = 1,440$ fps. To achieve even faster rates, the refresh rate of a video card is set at 180–240 Hz. At 200 Hz, for instance, the projector can display 4,800 binary fps.

8.7 SUMMARY

This chapter reviewed the state-of-the-art of projector-camera systems with a focus on real-time image correction techniques that enable projections onto nonoptimized surfaces. Projector-camera related areas, such as camera supported photometric calibration of conventional projection displays (e.g., [46], [143], [21]), real-time shadow removal techniques (e.g., [268], [137], [136]), or projector-camera based interaction approaches (e.g., [227], [77], [87]) were not discussed.

Future projectors will become more compact in size and will require little power and cooling. Reflective technology (such as DLP or LCoS) will increasingly replace transmissive technology (e.g., LCD), which will lead to an increased brightness and extremely high update rates. They will integrate GPUs for real-time graphics and vision processing. While resolution and contrast will keep increasing, production costs and market prizes will continue to fall. Conventional UHP lamps will be replaced by powerful LEDs or multichannel lasers. This will make them suitable for mobile applications.

Imagining projector-camera technology to be integrated into, or coupled with, mobile devices, such as cellphones or laptops, will support truly flexible presentations. There is no doubt that this technology is on its way. Yet, one question needs to be addressed when thinking about mobile projectors: What to project onto, without carrying around screen canvases? It is clear that the answer to this question can only be: onto available everyday surfaces. With this in mind, the future importance of projector-camera systems in combination with appropriate image-correction techniques becomes clear.

CHAPTER 9

Three-Dimensional Displays

9.1 INTRODUCTION

The most interesting varieties of displays have always been those delivering some kind of 3D impression, making things appear more real, just as if one could actually touch them. At first glance this may seem quite simple, as if delivering two pictures instead of one could be sufficient. In practice however, this turns out to be among the most complicated tasks to achieve.

The problem is as simply described as it is omnipresent: pictures produced by a display are generally viewed in a multitude of sizes and positions, not just as they have been recorded. Almost any picture we see does not appear in correct dimension or perspective, but our eyes and brains are quite tolerant of this, as long as only flat pictures are concerned.

With stereoscopic pictures (matching left- and right-eye pictures are called a *stereo pair*), false perspectives, sizes, accommodation, and so on are a lot more problematic. Since refurbishing stereo pictures for different viewing setups (i.e., screen types) is anything but trivial (it usually requires comprehensive 3D image processing), only simpler varieties of 3D media have been in use. Typically, just two pictures shot at about eye distance, projected the same way, are displayed to an auditorium filled with sitting people upright and at a proper distance. This may more or less work in a cinema, but for general use it is quite inappropriate, and so 3D has remained a niche technology.

As displays are concerned, a lot more options would be available, as we will see in the following pages, but we should also keep in mind that widespread use of them requires the availability of sufficient programming material; the selection of 3D movies, to name just one sector is just now growing. Very promising techniques are being developed, and 3D information from existing films is being derived, a task that is proving to be a lot easier than colorizing black-and-white images.

Some decades ago, when holography was invented, it was thought that this would revolutionize filmmaking, and it would be possible to open a virtual window to a scene, with all the characteristics of a real one, eliminating many of the position, size, and perspective problems of other approaches. However, the technology has several drawbacks: true holograms need laser light to shoot, and film or displays with micrometer resolution to reproduce; they cannot be scaled or zoomed, adding color is difficult and may produce artifacts, and so on.

Holographic filming would require a studio with laser lighting and film formats several feet wide, with reels as big as monster truck tires. Effects like self-interference severely limit the quality of naturally recorded holograms. For shooting outdoors, holographic stereograms (see Section 5.5.7 at page 169) represent realistic –but still analog– alternatives.

So for now, dynamic (even interactive) holographic content is confined to synthetic holograms generated by computers (so called *computer-generated holograms*, CGI), either from synthetic scenes or from natural ones. In the latter case, a multitude of cameras and sophisticated image processing would be necessary to record the 3D image data required. So, the displays we use for presenting these 3D scenes will most probably not be truly holographic, since similar viewing experiences may also be accomplished with much simpler technology.

Newest developments are promising pseudo holographic displays, able to deliver a much denser raster of viewing angles (0.8° for example) [9]. Most of them are lenticular or similar working displays in principle. Image generation is still very demanding because so many parallel pictures have to be delivered. More likely to be successful are types delivering just a few separate pictures to a few individual viewers.

This is all very new, and final results cannot yet be drawn, but as developments continue it appears quite possible that good and affordable 3D display screens will soon be leaving the realm of science fiction [15].

Again, the most fascinating approach will most likely not be the ultimate one: pure holographic displays would require a pixel size smaller than 1 μm, as we learned in Section 5.3.6.3 at page 137. This means not millions, but trillions of pixels, in the case of big screens, which simply destroys the feasibility of any approach with current technology. With very substantial efforts, dynamic holograms in postcard size have been demonstrated, with still many compromises (horizontal perspective only), and that's as far as that technology has progressed for now [180].

Nevertheless, special varieties of holography may play a role in future display concepts, not only in the form of holographic optical elements (see Section 5.4 at page 144), but also as relatively coarse-grained interference patterns generated with high-resolution displays, forming and directing light in very innovative ways. We will see more of this later.

Many of today's 3D displays do not even come close to matching the ability of true holograms. Instead of generating a holographic image, they display several perspectives of a 3D scene and rely on the optical separation of these pictures by each of the observer's eyes, as well as on stereoscopic disparity and vergence (see Section 4.4.2 at page 110) as main cues for depth perception.

Separating perspectives for each eye can be done with shutter or polarized glasses and also by integrating the display itself right into the glasses. This approach can make things a lot simpler, but it also has drawbacks. For near-eye displays, the most prevalent problem is the proper fit of the glasses unit on the user's head. Simple optical glasses slide down the nose quite a bit, are tilted and turned, all contributing to an optical misalignment that may impair the proper function of the entire assembly. For general use, strapping glasses to the head, as is often seen in research or industrial applications, is not an option.

Intelligently designed optics and adaptive systems will be important for these types of displays to succeed [109,267]. This and other technological questions warrant a full chapter and will be discussed in Chapter 10.

Our discussion on 3D displays is focused on spatial displays (i.e., screens of some sort). We will cover simple (and not so simple) spatial stereoscopic displays, the whole variety of autostereoscopic screens and computer-generated holographic displays. The chapter begins with a discussion on basic considerations for 3D displays, such as perspective constraints and a comparison between 3D TV and 3D cinema in Section 9.2. We will then review single- and multiviewer stereoscopic displays that require observers to wear some sort of glasses for stereo-channel separation (Section 9.3 at page 358). This is followed by an explanation of the varying types of classical autostereoscopic displays (Section 9.4 at page 373) that fall into the categories of parallax displays and volumetric displays. More advanced 3D display concepts, such as light field displays (Section 9.5 at page 388) and computer-generated holographic displays (Section 9.6 at page 399) are presented next. We'll close this chapter with a discussion on 3D media encoding for light fields and holograms (Section 9.7 at page 410).

9.2 THREE-DIMENSIONAL DISPLAYS: BASIC CONSIDERATIONS

Stereoscopic displays seem to become more and more popular in the context of 3D cinema and 3D TV. Let's start our journey with several basic considerations on stereoscopic content production and presentation. Later on, we will take a close look at appropriate display technology.

9.2.1 Orientation

Classical stereoscopic displays, as we know them from IMAX theaters for example, are characterized by delivering separate pictures to each eye.

These stereoscopic pictures are, for example, taken by two cameras of approximately the distance between human left and right eyes and these pictures are then reproduced without any modulation. Yet, they can also be fully computer generated, using two virtual cameras instead, filming a virtual scene.

One problem with stereoscopic techniques is that in order to see the picture correctly, the viewer must literally have his head fixed in a screw mount. Figure 9.1 shows a classical assembly with stereo cameras, a CRT display with a light shutter in front, and the viewer

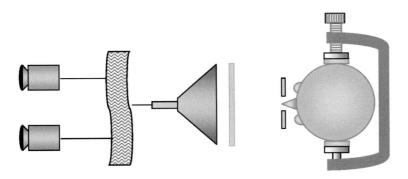

FIGURE 9.1 Simple stereo displays require an almost fixed head position.

wearing shutter glasses. For a correct reproduction, display size and distance cannot be varied, zooming is almost impossible without very disturbing false perspectives, etc. Everything is defined by the recording equipment, once and for all.

Any deviation from the correct position and distance causes errors, and, what is most often neglected, sideways tilting of the head forces one eye to move up and the other down, a very unnatural situation. Watching stereo TV while lying on a couch is therefore impossible. While moderate sideways tilting can be compensated by eye movement, this always causes dipvergence (i.e., misalignment in the vertical direction). Dipvergence causes double images in the vertical direction that the observer's brain cannot compensate for. Dizziness and headaches can be the result [146]. Watching stereo TV while lying on a couch is impossible, as one would have to move one eye up and one down, a truly acrobatic feat.

9.2.2 Distance and Depth

Tele- and wide-angle shots have very dissimilar viewing angles. Reproducing such divergent situations correctly would require different viewing environments with different screens, and zooming would not be possible. In order to reproduce the original perspective, the viewer would have to be precisely at the position of the recording cameras.

If viewer distance and original camera distance diverge too much, as illustrated in Figure 9.2, images and objects appear very unreal – making the entire effort to produce 3D quite useless – and very often this results in loss of stereo vision, or diplopia. If we try to retain the original perspective at least, large parts of the real display area may remain unused (as in Figure 9.2(bottom right)), or the image might not entirely fit on the screen.

With the processing power to generate different perspectives synthetically, one could retain use of the full display and also construct a physiologically correct perspective. The only useful strategy for shooting 3D zoom and teleshots without such capabilities would be to enlarge the stereo basis and to increase the focal length. This would deliver the same

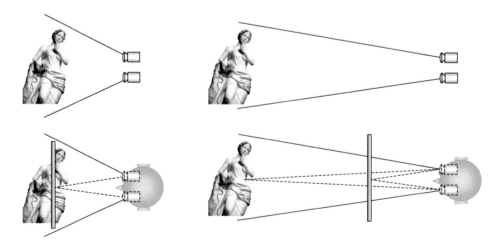

FIGURE 9.2 Tele and wide angle shots have very different viewing angles. Trying to reproduce the original perspective with an arbitrary screen distance might cause an inefficient usage of the screen area and a misfit between vergence and accomodation (bottom right).

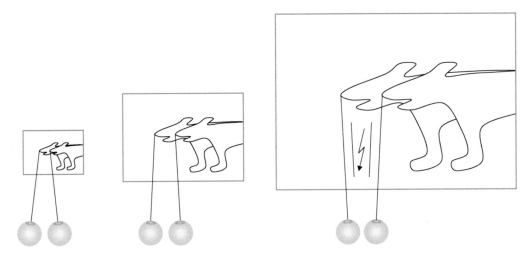

FIGURE 9.3   Stereo disparity for different screen sizes.

distance separation in a teleshot as in a normal shot and would render a natural-looking reproduction much more easily.

Experiences with cinema productions however have shown that there is much viewer tolerance for enlarged depiction, especially on a large screen. The opposite, downscaled scenes on a small screen, is perceived as much less real (puppet theater effect).

Stereoscopic images are in principle bound to a proper reconstruction of the original recording geometry. Stereo disparity will be proportional to screen size if no special precautions are taken. Figure 9.3 shows that an image with proper stereo effect (middle) may turn into puppet theater with a small screen (left) or be entirely unacceptable because of impossible eye divergence on a big screen (right). The problem can be addressed in part by adding a lateral pre-shift to the images, at least for removing the exaggerated disparity for large screens. Nevertheless the entire depth range will remain distorted.

With a simple stereo screen, the perceived distance of an object depends on its stereo disparity d on the screen (Figure 9.4). With eye distance e and screen distance v we can calculate the perceived distance z as:

$$\frac{d}{z-v} = \frac{e}{z} \quad \longrightarrow \quad z = \frac{ev}{e-d} \tag{9.1}$$

A negative disparity results in an object appearing before the screen. This is an impressive effect; overdoing it may, however, result in clipped objects (this and other clipping effects are known as the *framing problem*). The clipping could be rendered more naturally with a virtual 3D frame box displayed, but this may be more distracting than the clipping itself. So the only safe measure is to use this effect with caution, and only for objects in the middle of the screen.

Note, that depth perception in this case is based purely on retinal disparity and convergence. We learned in Chapter 4 that depth perception with stereoscopic displays has its own issues: inconsistent accommodation and convergence, to name one. It turns out that if stereo disparity becomes too large (in particular for negative disparity), stereo pairs become hard

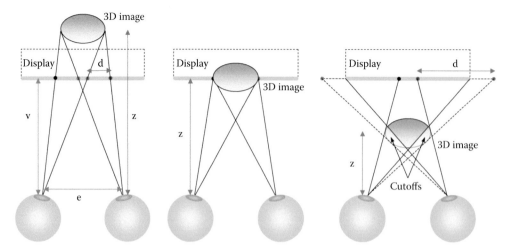

FIGURE 9.4 Stereo disparity and resulting depth impression (right: clipping due to exaggerated foreground effect).

to fuse and diplopia will frequently occur. In fact, stereo fusion (and with that, depth perception) is much easier for 3D content behind the screen plane than for content in front. Recently developed algorithms apply disparity constraints to 3D content to render depth perception for stereoscopic displays more naturally (e.g., nonlinear disparity mapping for stereoscopic 3D [166]).

The basic configuration for stereo recording is two cameras straightly parallel, in eye distance (e.g., 6.5 cm). This yields a natural perspective if camera opening angle and display angular size are equal. 3D production equipment allows for other configurations and even moves between configurations, for certain effects (Figure 9.5). If an object is intended to appear in the display plane regardless of display size, the cameras are pointed to converge on it. Simply tilting the cameras, however, results in misaligned geometry as both frames have

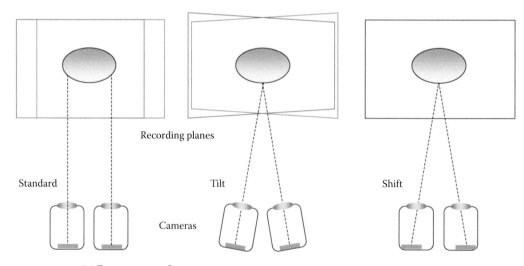

FIGURE 9.5 Different types of camera convergence.

opposite trapezoid distortions. This can lead to dipvergence and can be avoided either by an electronic geometry correction, or by using a shift-capable camera (Figure 9.5(right)).

To ensure a proper reproduction of 3D material, disparity has to fit to the display size, and this over the full depth range. Adapting the disparity range for smaller screen sizes by simply shifting the images results in a certain object flattening , making persons look like cardboard panels. Methods for disparity range adaptation are known as *disparity mapping*. Considerable effort currently goes into developing better algorithms [166].

With enough information recorded and enough computing power, this can be done at playback. At the current state of technology, the parallel production of cinema and TV versions, with different recoding camera geometries, may be the least problematic approach.

To illustrate the methods for this, we regard a common scene type: actor's portraits close-up, filling most of the screen. In reality, we would only see faces this "large" if we were close to them. Trying to simulate this short distance with a cinema screen, however, would lead to strange results: large stereo offset, focus/convergence disparity, vignetting etc. Most astonishingly, there is hardly any problem if the faces are shown with a stereo disparity near zero, hence perceived at screen distance, even though this turns the actors into giants (maybe because we are already used to this experience from many 2D movies). The according object distance can be achieved with the shift camera assembly as in Figure 9.5(right).

If the home TV screen would deliver the same viewing angle as in the theater, a proper stereo offset restoring infinity (approximately 6.5 cm disparity for the background) could simulate the depth range of the theater, for example, the faces at 10 m virtual distance. This would appear strange however and would also suffer from strong distortions when viewed off-axis. Moreover, typical TVs, even large flat screens, cover a smaller field-of-view than the typical cinema screen, be it alone for space limitations in the living room. Hence, showing the faces at a virtual distance equal to screen distance would be the best way. Concurrently, the background image should be the same, otherwise the film's composition would come out differently.

Several parameters are important here: eye distance (e), distance (z) of an object intended to be at screen distance, intended screen distance (v), and camera stereo basis (b). Figure 9.6 gives the schematic for this calculation. It requires that the field of view (or opening angle) at playback equals the camera opening angle at recording. The result in this case is that we only need to get the cameras to the right object distance, where it appears at the intended size, shift the camera sensors (or afterward, the images) to have the object at zero disparity and, this is the only parameter fixing everything, set an according camera stereo basis.

We get:

$$\frac{b}{z} = \frac{e}{v} \quad \longrightarrow \quad b = \frac{ez}{v} \tag{9.2}$$

(with e approximately 6.5 cm)

Which for example implies: We approach an actor to 1 m, assume a screen distance in the cinema of 10 m, so we have to set a stereo basis of 0.65 cm. Then the actor appears screen-filling with zero disparity, and the background landscape with 6.5 cm disparity, equaling infinity. For a TV screen being at approximately 3 m distance, we need a camera stereo basis

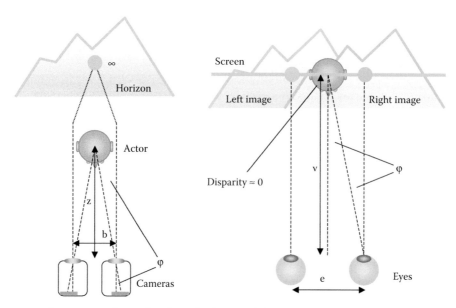

FIGURE 9.6 Geometric scheme for the calculation of the camera stereo basis required to map an object distance z to the screen distance.

of ≈ 2 cm. For a natural reproduction (all proper size and distance) we would have $z = v$ and $s = 6.5$ cm.

If we leave our above simplification and allow for the playback screen to have arbitrary sizes (resulting in different fields-of-view and angular detail sizes), we need to adapt s even further. For example, if our TV is half as big, we need a twice as large disparity at infinity. Assuming we want our object as above still to be at screen distance, its disparity remains zero anyway and all we have to do is to choose a two times larger stereo basis. This automatically doubles the disparity for the distant background. We can instantly expand our above formula by a scale factor s ($s = 1/2$ meaning a display half as big as necessary for reproducing the original viewing angle).

We get:

$$b = \frac{ez}{vs} \tag{9.3}$$

Now we may, for instance, have stereo bases of 0.65, 2, and 4 cm concurrently, for cinema and two different sizes of home TV. Please note that these small stereo bases are just results for a special scene type. Others may require much larger bases. It shows the general principle however: all that it takes for a universally exploitable 3D film production obviously is to provide several, not only two camera perspectives. The three mentioned stereo bases could already be recorded with only four (not six) cameras, as a camera can be the right channel for one basis as well as the left channel for another one. For the small stereo bases involved here, multiple cameras are although not necessary. Just two cameras with a larger stereo basis will in most cases deliver any information from partially occluded image parts required for the smaller bases, so computing these additional views is not a problem.

The adaptation to different display sizes can be done at production, but it can also be done at playback. Current technology would allow to implement this in a TV set. Hence, all that it needs is a simple stereo setup with two parallel cameras, and information about the stereo basis, lens opening angle, and intended on-screen distance. Smaller stereo bases can be computed, and shifting for convergence adaptation can be done electronically. This also allows for more sophisticated, distance or detail-dependent handling of stereo disparity, like the non-linear disparity mapping treated in [166]. The transmission of more than two channels, although possible and even defined in standards already, is therefore not necessary for a mere stereoscopic reproduction. Future developments nevertheless may involve light field recording, with several more separated perspectives.

In spite of all these possibilities, generating proper viewer perspectives is essentially an art, like movie-making in general. In current stereoscopic film productions, variable camera base distances and converging angles are controlled by specialized personnel, doing nothing but trying to achieve an acceptable stereo impression, at least for the most common viewing geometries. These roles will soon be as common and indispensable as the traditional jobs of sound mixing and camera direction. This will not become obsolete, even with light field recording and other advanced technologies emerging, as dramaturgical effects and technical restrictions will always require intelligent and aesthetically acceptable adaptations.

As there is no technology currently available for multiperspective productions in practice, various efforts are made to achieve the most natural 3D impression possible. For example, the aforementioned close-up of an actor's face could be improved by recording it with camera perspectives converging at the face, because in the natural situation, the observer's eyes would also converge there. The special kind of left and right perspective-related distortions resulting from this are delivered to the left and right eyes, even if the object is reproduced on a screen in a very different size. Although neither accommodation nor vergence is compliant with this, the viewer can easily experience the reproduction as a close-up perspective, with a little acclimatization at least. This kind of recording would however result in a huge background disparity when played back greatly enlarged on a cinema screen. Therefore, this is usually done by recording the actor alone, with a special (usually green) uniform background (Figure 9.7). Afterward, a separately recorded background is inserted into the green areas. This method, called *greenscreening*, is most common in 2D cinema and TV productions as well.

For a maximum flexibility regarding various recoding tricks, the cameras need to have flexible adjustments for stereo basis and convergence. As cinema cameras are relatively large, placing the lenses arbitrarily narrow is impossible. Therefore, two cameras are combined using a half-transparent mirror. Figure 9.8 shows the principle. Actual implementations are also featuring servo motors and controllers allowing for programmable dynamic action.

9.2.3 Perspective

Typically, no viewer sits exactly within the center line of the screen. So a displayed 3D scene will appear tilted toward the viewer (Figure 9.9) and objects will be distorted and will appear very unreal as the entire scene seems to tilt toward the viewer and follow any of his movements.

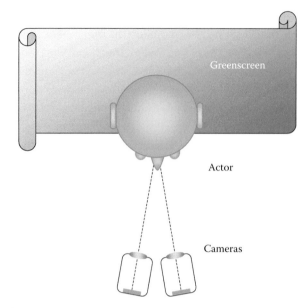

FIGURE 9.7 Natural closeup recording, separate of background.

Proper images for large lateral viewing angles are difficult to calculate even with enough computing power and truly 3D data, because the cameras recording the original scene always have a limited field of view (Figure 9.10). This results in a funnel-like impression behind the display plane. The image tilting inevitably has to be accepted, with simple stereo recordings at least. Dynamic perspective corrections could still be implemented for small head movements. A correction for distance distortions would be another possible improvement.

With camera array recordings (recording a light field, see Section 3.6 at page 87), a large camera opening angle would retain a 3D impression for a sufficient range of viewer displacement (Figure 9.10(right)). The extra angular range however will incur additional complications in production (e.g., unwanted scene objects have to be kept outside).

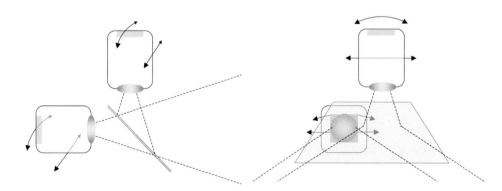

FIGURE 9.8 Principle of a 3D movie camera assembly.

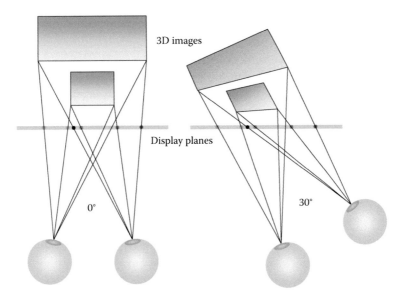

FIGURE 9.9 Spatial distortion for different viewer positions with a simple stereo display.

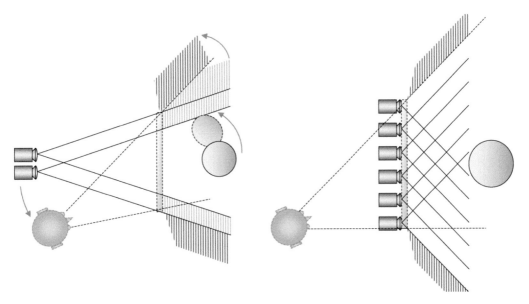

FIGURE 9.10 Camera and lateral displaced viewer fields of view: two cameras recording stereo pairs (left), and camera array recording a light field (right).

9.2.4 3D: Screen Size Matters

We have seen that quite a large number of parameters can cause serious problems for stereoscopic video production and display. In cinemas, the viewing conditions are quite predictable. So it is possible to adjust all parameters at production for best possible cinematic effects.

With home TV, all kinds of display sizes and viewing positions have to be allowed, which turns the advantages of 3D into disadvantages in many cases.

Technology will deliver basic stereo picture capability at marginal cost. Backward compatible encoding formats exist, allowing one channel for both 2D and 3D receivers. The cost here is at distribution, requiring additional bandwidth.

Time-sequential stereo has been supported for a long time by fast CRT computer monitors (recently also with plasma and with fast LCD screens), requiring only shutter glasses and an appropriate software or graphics board driver.

Time-sequential 3D playback can cause very distracting motion effects, growing with screen size (we will show this in Section 9.3.1.2 on page 361), so together with the expensive glasses necessary, it is not a viable choice for cinema. With computer screens, however, it works well and one may wonder why it has been used so little, and only for special applications like 3D design or a few games.

It may just be that 3D is not considered necessary enough by most users, and it's certainly so that the problems with static 3D displays (false perspective, false size, false focus) are just annoying, and for good 3D TV, computer screens are too small, resulting in puppet theater effect and strong disparity between eye convergence and accommodation. For the latter problem, glasses with corrective lenses could be used to generate a longer focus distance (more on this in Chapter 10).

Even though this has long been done by amateurs as well, almost since film was invented, 3D cinema has had a niche existence until quite recently, when increasing competition with TV brought forth monster and surround cinemas and any possible enhancement of the viewing experience was strongly demanded.

A key factor here again is digital technology. Classic film projection relied either on two separate projectors or on a split image recorded on one film and combined with special optics to separate and stretch the pictures. The former approach has often been used but has severe problems: film sometimes rips and has to be repaired, but with 3D both reels have to be cut to retain synchronicity. Eve a one- or two-frame offset has been shown to cause discomfort, sometimes even severe discomfort, in viewers. Moreover, mechanical tolerances let projected film images wiggle a little, which normally nobody notices, but with stereo, a disparity of approximately 6.5 cm (minute compared to the screen size) for scenes at infinity has to be retained accurately. Hence, even very small position changes of the two images make the perceived object distance pump quite heavily, making viewers seasick. These problems may have greatly affected 3D acceptance.

For cinema, techniques using polarized glasses are common, and such glasses are inexpensive. The provider is required to have two projectors and a screen that preserves polarization. Such a screen, in cinema size, can be very expensive. A development simplifying the introduction of 3D in cinemas is the wavelength multiplexing technology (Figure 9.16 on page 364). With this, cinemas just need a second projector, but no new screen as when using polarizers.

Nowadays, many big movie projects are also produced in a 3D version. Nevertheless, most of the successful 3D productions so far are computer generated films, delivering 3D with relatively little effort (just rendering for two virtual camera positions instead of one).

One factor delaying the introduction of a new technology is the scarce availability of programming material. Producing this is only rewarding if enough viewers can be reached. With little material available, customers may adopt the new technology only if it comes at little extra cost. This has been the case with HD and also with color, although movies with these properties were already available. Movies, however, are just small part of TV programming. Color was not really affordable in the beginning but it is very attractive and the difference is huge on any display. HD has no advantage in may cases, so its advance was delayed until the cost difference became very slight.

Unlike color or HD, there isn't even yet a considerable selection of 3D movies to start with.

Converting old movies to 3D is not only difficult in terms of image processing, but it will not work well because 3D needs an entirely different script. Assembling action scenes by quick cuts does not work anymore, defocus and rack-focus effects look unnatural, some closeup and tele shots may work or may not, and in general the sequence of scenes has to be much slower and involve fewer cuts. Directors working in 3D admit they had and still have to re-develop many techniques.

Viewing habits pose another problem, specifically for TV. Although anybody with a large TV set can participate in certain 3D events, he/she must be willing to sit upright and at proper distance and position, and these requirements alone may already confine 3D TV to niche applications.

While affordable costs could help 3D TV to become a regular option quite seamlessly, a large part of all programming and viewing will remain monoscopic for the reasons given above, at least until fully active, viewer-specific 3D rendering and display becomes possible. Next we will address technologies that may deliver these possibilities.

9.2.5 Toward Light Field Displays

Applying any kind of viewer-position dependent perspective correction will work best if we can cause the impression of looking through a window, onto a real scene. This is largely equivalent to having a hologram or a light field display. We discussed the plenoptic function and the concept of light fields in Section 3.6 at page 87. A light field display would be able to generate all exit beams from any point on the display in any direction. In contrast to a hologram, however, no phase information is required by a light field display for this. We will discuss the technical details for light field displays later in this chapter.

We regard comprehensive light field data taken by a camera array A, with a lens opening angle φ (Figure 9.11).

Virtual screen windows of appropriate size at different distances (a, b, c) can give the viewers an entirely correct viewing experience, if the display windows are individually adapted for them.

The usable horizontal viewing range will depend on the screen size here, other than with a "flat" 2D display. As we have seen in earlier sections, the window paradigm can only be fulfilled as far as the viewing angle of the recording cameras allows it (i.e., delivers image data for extreme side views).

The array cameras have to deliver crisp pictures from (almost) zero to infinity, if we intend to record the light field correctly. Depth-of-field blur will occur at reproduction only. Thus, a properly recorded light field should be entirely crisp anywhere.

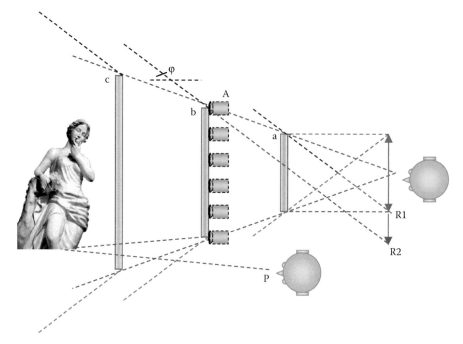

FIGURE 9.11 Characteristics of light field 3D display.

What a screen display does not deliver (at least if it is not truly holographic) is proper focusing. We have seen that this is not of major concern for large displays with at least 3...4 m viewing distance (see Chapter 4), at least if none of the objects displayed are intended to appear before the screen. Simulating proper focus is very difficult to realize with screen displays (we will see some approaches later on).

With near-eye-displays (i.e., head-attached stereo glasses) this is more easily achieved by dynamically changing the system's focal length according to the user's viewing direction and eye convergence (more in Chapter 10).

9.3 SPATIAL STEREOSCOPIC DISPLAYS

As explained above, spatial stereoscopic displays show two or more perspectives on a spatial screen, such as a monitor or a projection screen. These images contain projections of the presented 3D content as seen from the slightly different positions of the observer's left and right eye (either recorded or computer generated). We want to focus on computer-generated content rather than on recorded content, as stereo recordings face challenges of their own.

In the most general case, only two images are rendered for the two eyes of a single viewer. By knowing the viewer's position and orientation relative to the image plane (or surface) of the display, the positions of the two eyes can be approximated. Having a description of the presented 3D scene (also relative to the screen surface) allows computation of individual perspective projections for each eye position. This is illustrated in Figure 9.12.

Note that this is fairly different from stereoscopic recording (i.e., with real stereo cameras), as the scene geometry is known and the stereo pairs can be computed dynamically, depending on the viewer position.

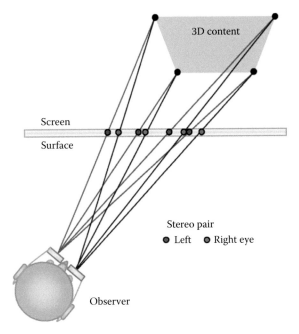

FIGURE 9.12 Stereo pair for one observer and defined 3D content projected onto known screen surface.

This concept can easily be extended to support multiple observers by displaying multiple stereo pairs, as will be explained in Section 9.3.3 at page 368. The essential question for single-viewer or multiviewer stereoscopic displays is how to ensure that each eye of each viewer perceives only the perspective that was rendered for its corresponding position. This is usually referred to as *stereo-channel separation*. Different techniques exist with their individual advantages and disadvantages. They are summarized in Section 9.3.1 at page 359.

9.3.1 Stereo-Channel Separation

For stereoscopic near-eye displays, the stereo-channel separation is realized by providing an individual screen to each eye (see Chapter 10). Both perspective images are displayed simultaneously and separated optically.

The main difference of stereoscopic spatial displays with respect to near-eye displays is that the same screen surface is used for displaying the stereo pair(s). Various techniques for stereo-channel separation have been developed for spatial displays. They can be categorized into active stereo-channel separation and passive stereo-channel separation techniques.

9.3.1.1 Active Stereo-Channel Separation

Active stereo techniques cover the eyes alternately, in synchronization with the display rate to ensure that each eye will see only the correct perspective image. This can be done optically (with LC shutters) or mechanically.

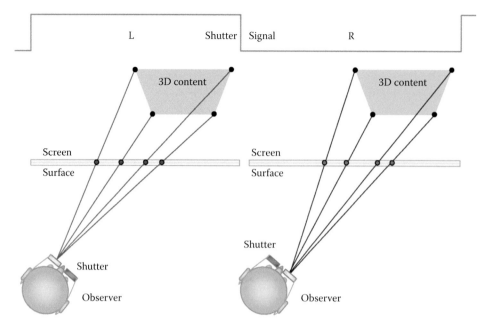

FIGURE 9.13   Active stereo technique through time-sequential shuttering.

Thus, the right eye is stopped down when the image for the left eye is displayed and vice versa, as illustrated in Figure 9.13. If this is done fast enough (at a display rate of 100 Hz–120 Hz, giving an update rate of 50...60 Hz per eye, which ensures it to be above the flicker-fusion threshold, as explained in Section 4.2.3 at page 93), no flickering will be perceived. The perceived brightness is reduced by more than a factor of two (because of the fact that each eye is shut down half of the time, and a transmission factor of the LC shutters is lower than one).

Active stereo-channel separation has the advantage of being invariant to the lateral tilt of the observer's head, in contrast to various passive techniques. Note that this is only the case if the stereo pairs are computer generated. If they are captured, then a stereoscopic presentation will not be orientation invariant, because the base line between the stereo camera pair is normally fixed relative to each other, and the camera orientation does not follow the head rotation of the viewer (see Section 9.2.1 at page 347).

Furthermore, active stereo-channel separation can only be applied in combination with display technology able to provide a display rate high enough to avoid visible flickering. CRT monitors and projectors have historically been used for professional and semiprofessional active stereo displays. Phosphor types used in CRT displays for stereoscopic applications need to have a persistence below the display rate. Otherwise parts (image portions or individual color channels) of one perspective image might still be visible for the other eye. This leads to an effect that is referred to as *ghosting* or *crosstalk*, which reduces or even eliminates the depth perception.

Crosstalk between stereo channels may occur with passive separation techniques as well. A variety of different cross-talk reduction techniques for passive [156] and active [159,175] stereo exist. They mainly estimate the appearing ghosting in one stereo channel and subtract it from the other one. This way, physical crosstalk can be compensated if the content in the stereo images is brighter than the perceived crosstalk itself.

9.3.1.2 Time-Sequential 3D Displays and Motion

If moving objects are displayed time sequentially, their perceived relative position on the screen – or the viewer's retina – depends on the time at which they are displayed. For 3D material recorded in the same – time-sequential – manner, this is of little concern (historic time-sequential 3D systems worked this way [266]). But for material where both images are recorded simultaneously (which is the case for about any current 3D cameras), this can result in a significant displacement between left and right images, causing fast and dramatic changes of disparity and hence, perceived distance.

A quantitative assessment is shown in Figure 9.14. Consider a screen of (horizontal) extension h, observed at a distance v. An object moves horizontally with speed s_h, causing a motion-related displacement d_m. We get

$$e/d_m = (v - \Delta z)/\Delta z; \text{ hence, } \Delta z = v/(e/d_m + 1). \text{ If } f \text{ is the frame rate,}$$

$$\text{then } d_m = s_h/f \text{ and } \Delta z = v/(ef/s_h + 1).$$

If T is the time for the object to pass the entire horizontal screen width, then $s_h = h/T$ and we can also write

$$\Delta z/v = 1/(efT/h + 1) \tag{9.4}$$

Hence, the relative distance error $\Delta z/v$ is approximately proportional to screen size h already, so the effect increases more than proportionally with screen size.

Some numbers (assume $e = 6$ cm): for a screen 1 m wide seen from 3 m distance, an object moving across the entire screen width in 1 s at $f = 120$ Hz$(2 * 60$ Hz$)$, the distance error Δz is approximately 37 cm. This is not extremely disturbing but also not negligible. For a cinema-sized screen, 10 m wide seen from 10 m distance, with the same speed parameters as above, we get a Δz of 5.8 m. An object starting at the screen edge and accelerating to

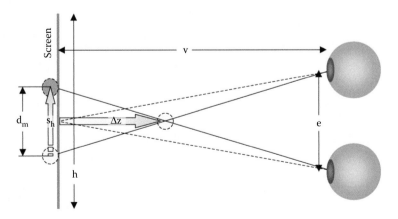

FIGURE 9.14 Motion induced parallax.

a speed of 1 screen width/s would therefore appear to fly halfway toward the viewer. If it moves in the opposite direction (negative s_h), it flys away, until it appears to be 36 m behind the screen. Quite obviously, shutter technology is not viable for cinemas. Historic concepts for shutter techniques assumed films with also sequentially recorded left and right frames; hence, timing errors could only occur with changes in motion speed. This is a small effect, in comparison, but already considered too big for cinema applications in [266].

We also have to consider faster-moving objects. These are difficult to follow with full accommodation, but evidently full accommodation is not a necessity for our brain to compute a 3D impression: in any natural scene, the eyes can converge to one object but we see others consistent and at proper distance, simultaneously. Otherwise, we would have real problems to orientate in 3D in real time. Hence, the larger distance errors resulting in fast action scenes will play a role and will result in an unreal impression consisting of dissected image fragments. Viewing experience backs this analysis.

So far, we have discussed horizontal motion only. The effect will, however, also cause a similar displacement with vertical motion (also mentioned in [266]). Human eyes are not prepared for vertical parallax. We already pointed this out as a problem occurring when a viewer tilts his head laterally (head roll). A recent study confirms that viewer tolerance to this is indeed small, and it is causing significant discomfort [146]. We should note that head roll effects depend on initial displacement and on screen distance (they are rather small in a cinema). With shuttered 3D displays, however, vertical parallax problems can be expected with any kind of vertical motion and at any distance.

9.3.1.3 Passive Stereo-Channel Separation

Passive stereo-channel separation techniques are not based on time multiplexing of the stereo images, but display all images simultaneously. A separation is then achieved through filtering. As for active stereo, special glasses have to be worn by the users. But instead of shutters, different optical (color or polarizing) filters stop down the individual images. In these cases, crosstalk results from imperfections of the filters in blocking light.

9.3.1.4 Anaglyph and Wavelength Multiplexing Separation

Anaglyph stereo-channel separation techniques apply color filters transmitting only a small spectral band, such as red and green or red and cyan for the left and right eyes, respectively. The color channels of the stereo images are modified accordingly before being displayed on the screen. Different methods apply different weights for modifying the color channels, as illustrated in Figure 9.15. The corresponding color mixing matrices are provided below. Here, r_l, g_l, b_l and r_r, g_r, b_r are the red, green and blue color components of the original left and right stereo images, and r_a, g_a, b_a are the R,G,B channels of the final anaglyph. Again, crosstalk can be present due to imperfections of the filters.

The true anaglyphs (Figure 9.15(top left)) produced with Equation 9.5 cause almost no crosstalk, but appear relatively dark and in false colors.

$$\begin{bmatrix} r_a \\ g_a \\ b_a \end{bmatrix} = \begin{bmatrix} 0.299 & 0.587 & 0.114 \\ 0 & 0 & 0 \\ 0 & 0 & 0 \end{bmatrix} \begin{bmatrix} r_l \\ g_l \\ b_l \end{bmatrix} + \begin{bmatrix} 0 & 0 & 0 \\ 0 & 0 & 0 \\ 0.299 & 0.587 & 0.114 \end{bmatrix} \begin{bmatrix} r_r \\ g_r \\ b_r \end{bmatrix} \quad (9.5)$$

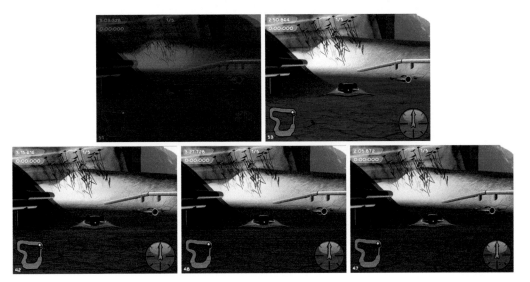

FIGURE 9.15 Anaglyph examples (top left to bottom right): true anaglyphs, gray anaglyphs, color anaglyphs, half-color anaglyphs, optimized anaglyphs.

The gray anaglyphs (Figure 9.15(top right)) produced with Equation 9.6 cause more crosstalk than with Equation 9.5, but appear in gray scales.

$$
\begin{bmatrix} r_a \\ g_a \\ b_a \end{bmatrix} = \begin{bmatrix} 0.299 & 0.587 & 0.114 \\ 0 & 0 & 0 \\ 0 & 0 & 0 \end{bmatrix} \begin{bmatrix} r_l \\ g_l \\ b_l \end{bmatrix} + \begin{bmatrix} 0 & 0 & 0 \\ 0.299 & 0.587 & 0.114 \\ 0.299 & 0.587 & 0.114 \end{bmatrix} \begin{bmatrix} r_r \\ g_r \\ b_r \end{bmatrix} \tag{9.6}
$$

The color anaglyphs (Figure 9.15(bottom left)) produced with Equation 9.7 appear in color, but might enforce retinal rivalry due to brightness variations of colored objects that lead to misinterpretations during disparity-based depth perception.

$$
\begin{bmatrix} r_a \\ g_a \\ b_a \end{bmatrix} = \begin{bmatrix} 1 & 0 & 0 \\ 0 & 0 & 0 \\ 0 & 0 & 0 \end{bmatrix} \begin{bmatrix} r_l \\ g_l \\ b_l \end{bmatrix} + \begin{bmatrix} 0 & 0 & 0 \\ 0 & 1 & 0 \\ 0 & 0 & 1 \end{bmatrix} \begin{bmatrix} r_r \\ g_r \\ b_r \end{bmatrix} \tag{9.7}
$$

The half-color anaglyphs (Figure 9.15(bottom center)) produced with Equation 9.8 appear less saturated, but also with less retinal rivalry than color anaglyphs.

$$
\begin{bmatrix} r_a \\ g_a \\ b_a \end{bmatrix} = \begin{bmatrix} 0.299 & 0.587 & 0.114 \\ 0 & 0 & 0 \\ 0 & 0 & 0 \end{bmatrix} \begin{bmatrix} r_l \\ g_l \\ b_l \end{bmatrix} + \begin{bmatrix} 0 & 0 & 0 \\ 0 & 1 & 0 \\ 0 & 0 & 1 \end{bmatrix} \begin{bmatrix} r_r \\ g_r \\ b_r \end{bmatrix} \tag{9.8}
$$

The optimized anaglyphs (Figure 9.15(bottom right)) produced with Equation 9.9 appear less saturated (except red colors), with almost no retinal rivalry.

$$\begin{bmatrix} r_a \\ g_a \\ b_a \end{bmatrix} = \begin{bmatrix} 0 & 0.7 & 0.3 \\ 0 & 0 & 0 \\ 0 & 0 & 0 \end{bmatrix} \begin{bmatrix} r_l \\ g_l \\ b_l \end{bmatrix} + \begin{bmatrix} 0 & 0 & 0 \\ 0 & 1 & 0 \\ 0 & 0 & 1 \end{bmatrix} \begin{bmatrix} r_r \\ g_r \\ b_r \end{bmatrix} \qquad (9.9)$$

In general we can say that the main disadvantage of anaglyph stereo is that it does not preserve the original color of the displayed content – although individual color mixing techniques have their own advantages and disadvantages. However, anaglyph stereo glasses are relatively affordable compared with shutter-glasses and work quite well if adjusted correctly on all different types of color displays and even print media.

Wavelength multiplexing is yet another passive stereo separation technique that applies interference filters transmitting three primary colors in slightly different wavelength subbands for each eye. For example, the filter for the left eye transmits red colors within a small spectral band around 629 nm, green color around 532 nm, and blue around 446 nm. The right eye transmits these primary colors with a slight offset (red: 615 nm, green: 518 nm, and blue: 432 nm). As long as the spectral bands of the corresponding primaries don't overlap (Figure 9.16), crosstalk can be eliminated. To produce the bandpass filtered images initially, two projectors are applied with different filters attached in front of their lenses. Thus each projector displays only one stereo image and bandpass-filters it according to the wavelength filter used for the corresponding eye. Both projectors have to be calibrated (geometrically and photometrically). Wavelength multiplexing overcomes many problems of anaglyph stereo in terms of color reproduction, crosstalk, and retinal rivalry. However, it

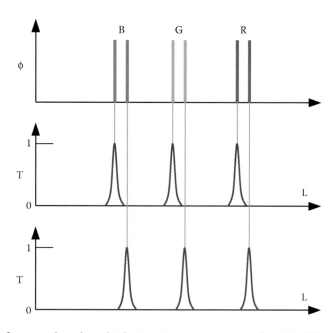

FIGURE 9.16 **Infitec** wavelength multiplexing. Image courtesy: **Infitec** GmbH.

does not reach the quality of active shuttering techniques since bandpass filtering further reduces the color gamut of the projectors. A major advantage over the polarization-based methods is that there is no need for a polarization-preserving projection screen.

9.3.1.5 Polarization-Based Separation

One of the most common passive separations of stereoscopic images is achieved through polarization (see Section 2.5.7 at page 48 for details on polarization). Instead of color filters, polarizers are integrated in glasses and on the display side (e.g., in front of a screen or projector lenses). Linear polarizers can be used for polarizing displayed stereo images in a particular orientation that is transmitted only by corresponding eyeglass filters with the same orientation. Left and right stereo images can thus be polarized with an orientational difference of 90° for minimized crosstalk. If projection displays are equipped with such a polarization technology, the projection screens have to preserve the polarization. Organic screen materials will depolarize the reflected light, so specially coated (e.g., metallized) screens have to be used.

Micropolarizers can also be applied to alternating pixel columns or scanlines of LCD panels for supporting passive stereo-channel separation. This however reduces the effective resolution per stereo-channel.

Alternatively, a second LC layer (without the additional polarization filters that are usual with LCDs) can be aligned in front of a regular LCD. While the first panel displays the two stereo images simultaneously and in full resolution, the second panel serves for rotating the polarization on a per-pixel basis (not RGB triplets but separately for each R, G and B pixel). Thereby it addresses the distribution of pixel intensities reaching each eye through the stereo glasses. The advantage of this is a full resolution per stereo channel. Since the intensity of each pixel is distributed between each eye, the effective brightness of the display is reduced. This applies for almost any stereo technique.

A combination of time multiplexing and polarization uses a second LC panel in front of a normal LCD display. The second panel only turns polarization for the entire area, either + or −45°. The main display shows left and right images sequentially and the turning display delivers them to the appropriate eye, requiring simple polarized glasses.

Although linear polarization is very common, it has the drawback that a lateral head tilt causes crosstalk between the left and right images because the polarizers are no more aligned. Circular polarizers, meanwhile affordable enough for common use, solve this problem. Figure 9.17 shows the principle of a switched (circular) polarization display.

9.3.1.6 Interlaced Polarizer-Based Separation

As of 2012, advances in production methods have led to the introduction of line-wise alternating circular polarizers in mainstream TV displays (**LG, Philips**). Alternating polarization for even and odd display lines enables a viewing with simple polarizer glasses (Figure 9.18). While this divides the vertical resolution per frame in half, practical tests revealed that the two frames are seamlessly merging together as long as a proper viewing distance is kept. Neither the combined stereo picture appears less crisp, nor are there apparent line raster effects.

FIGURE 9.17   Stereo separation by switched (here: circular) polarization.

The technique is so cheap to produce that meanwhile a large number of even moderately priced TVs come with built-in 3D capabilities based on it, and the necessary circular polarizer glasses are also hardly more expansive than simple, linear ones.

The most important advantage here is the simultaneous delivery of both frames, avoiding the motion effects arising with shuttered displays. A closer examination reveals but one disadvantage: viewing the display vertically off axis may cause crosstalk, because of the distance between the display cell plane and the line polarizer foil, resulting in a parallax. This effect was apparent on the first products (having their polarizer as a foil on the screen front) but has been greatly reduced with next-generation models.

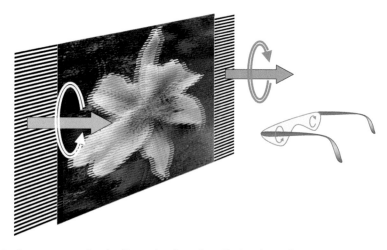

FIGURE 9.18   Stereo separation by line-wise (interlaced) circular polarization.

9.3.1.7 Other Stereo Separation Techniques

Other, less common stereo-channel separation techniques exist. The *Pulfrich effect*, for instance, is more an optical illusion based on the fact that less intense visual stimuli require more time to be processed by our brain than intense (i.e., bright) ones. If an observer wears an intensity filter only on one eye (say the right one) and watches a movie showing a scene with a horizontal camera move (from left to right), then both eyes will process different movie frames at the same time. Although only one frame is displayed at a time, it is perceptually delayed for the darkened eye. The brain fuses this delayed right-eye image with a new left-eye image. If the camera motion is horizontal, a horizontal parallax between both images leads to depth perception. The perceived depth is proportional to the speed of the camera motion, and is consequently only relative. This is not a stereo technique for professional stereoscopic displays requiring absolute depth perception and a less strict relation to the camera motion. However, since video frames do not have to be modified in color and can be watched without loss in quality with an intensity filter, this technique is often applied in broadcasting for ordinary television sets.

9.3.2 Projection Screens

Different screen types for projectors have been discussed in Section 7.10.10 at page 295. We will review them here in the context of 3D displays.

Stereoscopic projection technology is frequently used in cinema theaters, as for example IMAX theaters. Both passive and active separation techniques are common. As we have seen above, passive stereoscopic projection requires a nonorganic screen material to preserve the polarization of the displayed images. Besides such metallic screen materials and simple diffuse canvases, other specialized screen materials exist. Holographic projection screens, for instance, have been described in Section 5.4.9 at page 152. Their advantage over conventional diffuse screens is that they forward light from one particular direction (i.e., the direction of the projector), thus omitting most of the environmental stray light. This results in brilliant images even in daylight situations where normal diffuse screens fail.

Other specialized diffuse screens (sometimes called *diffuse and bright* (DAB) screens) reflect light in a smaller but directed spatial angular range, rather than in a full hemispheric range. This leads to brighter images within a smaller viewing range. Retroreflective screens selectively reflect light back toward the incident direction. Such material is used for traffic signs and for several projector-based head-attached displays [128,133,222]. Projecting individual stereo images from eye-aligned projectors onto a retroreflective screen also supports stereochannel separation, since each image is only reflected back toward the direction of the corresponding eye.

Polymer dispersed liquid crystal (PDLC) screens can be switched to a diffuse and to a transparent state electronically and at a high speed. Such screens can be used in synchronization with projectors and cameras and, for instance, enable tele-immersive experiences [100] (Figure 9.19(left)). Active stereo images are projected during the diffuse state of the screen while video images of the observer can be captured through the screen in its transparent state. If this process is carried out fast enough and is synchronized correctly with the shutter

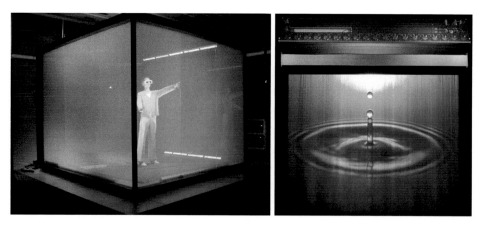

FIGURE 9.19 CAVE-like surround screen projection display using PDLC screens (left), and walk-through screen using falling dry fog (right). Image courtesy: Computer Graphics Laboratory, ETH Zurich (left) and **FogScreen** Inc.

glasses, the observer will see the projected images only on the diffuse screen while video cameras will capture the observer only through the transparent screen.

Walk-through displays project images onto streamed surfaces of dry fog [229] (Figure 9.19(right)) that diffuse light quite well (see Mie scattering in Section 3.3.1.1 at page 58). Since fog is not solid, users can walk or reach through the displayed content. Dynamic image distortions produced by turbulence in the fog flow (especially at some distance away from the nozzles) are one of the main challenges to high-quality visualizations. Such displays are usually found in entertainment, special effects, and advertisement.

Further options for projection screens, such as applying integrated optics for stereo channel separation directly on the screen side or on ordinary everyday surfaces will be discussed in detail in Section 9.4 at page 373 or Chapter 8, respectively.

9.3.3 Screen Configurations and Rendering

Having discussed different screen types and stereo-channel separation techniques, in this section we would like to summarize the most common screen configurations and corresponding rendering techniques for spatial displays. We will assume that if projectors are applied, they are already calibrated (geometrically, radiometrically, and photometrically) with respect to the projection surfaces. Details on such calibration techniques are explained in Chapter 8.

Figure 9.20 illustrates the required parameters for an off-axis projection leading to perspectively correct images of a rendered 3D scene content for observer position c and known screen width w and height h. Note that observer, scene content, and screen plane are defined within the same (right-handed, in our example) coordinate system.

$$near_z = c_z - \max_z -1, far_z = c_z - \min_z +1 \qquad (9.10)$$

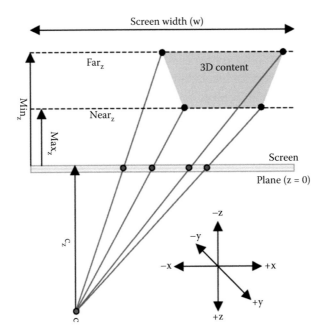

FIGURE 9.20 Off-axis projection for perspective rendering onto single screen plane.

$$near_w = (w * near_z)/(2c_z), near_h = (h * near_z)/(2c_z) \qquad (9.11)$$

$$shift_x = (c_x * near_z)/c_z, shift_y = (c_y * near_z)/c_z \qquad (9.12)$$

Computing the projection parameters with Equations 9.10 - 9.12 configures the transformation pipelines of common rendering libraries. For OpenGL, as an example, they would be used as follows:

Listing 9.1 Off-axis projection in OpenGL.

```
1  ...
2  glMatrixMode(GL\_PROJECTION);
3  glLoadIdentity();
4  glFrustum(-near\_w-shift\_x,near\_w-shift\_x,-near\_h-shift\_y,near\_h-shift\
       _y,near\_z,far\_z);
5  glMatrixMode(GL\_MODELVIEW);
6  glLoadIdentity();
7  gluLookAt(c\_x,c\_y,c\_z,c\_x,c\_y,0,0,1,0);
8  myRenderScene();
9  ...
```

The code fragment above creates the projection and transformation matrices that together compute the correct 2D projections of the defined 3D scene vertices (rendered within *myRenderScene*();) on the screen plane. For stereoscopic applications, this has to be executed twice, for the perspectives of the left and the right eye. This leads to the two stereo images which have to be displayed and separated with one of the techniques described in Section 9.3.1 at page 359.

Usually head-tracking technology is applied in combination with such displays to continuously estimate the viewing perspectives. In other cases –especially if multiple observers are supported and large screens are used, such as in IMAX theaters– a fixed "sweet-spot perspective" is assumed. Viewers located far off this sweetspot will experience perspective distortions, which are tolerable in most cases, if not too extreme.

An off-axis projection can be applied for all planar screen configurations. It is repeated not only for multiple perspectives, but also for multiple screens, as long as they are planar. Screen configurations assembled from multiple planar screen sections are usually referred to as *multiplane screen configurations* or as multisided screen configurations. Examples are multisided surround screen and semi-immersive displays, such as *Cave Automatic Virtual Environments* (CAVEs) [63] or two-sided workbenches [162].

This basically implies that the off-axis projection (as a particular example: the code fragment above) is consecutively applied for each viewer perspective (i.e., observer's eye positions for stereoscopic applications) in combination with each screen plane, but with different screen and perspective parameters. For a three-sided CAVE display and a single-viewer stereoscopic application, for instance, six (three times two) off-axis projections are computed, leading three stereo pairs (one for each screen plane). This is illustrated in Figure 9.21.

Rendering multiple stereo pairs on one graphics card might be an overkill for the applied hardware and can lead to too slow frame rates. Many rendering frameworks capable of driving such displays allow the distribution of the rendering tasks to multiple nodes (graphics processors on single or multiple machines). A three-sided CAVE, for instance, could be driven by three PCs with dual-channel graphics cards (driving two projectors each for passive stereo). It is essential that all the stereo images for the same perspective appear in exactly the same moment and for exactly the same duration on all screens.

To ensure this, it is not sufficient to simply synchronize the distributed software components running on multiple machines (which is sometimes referred to as *frame locking*); the

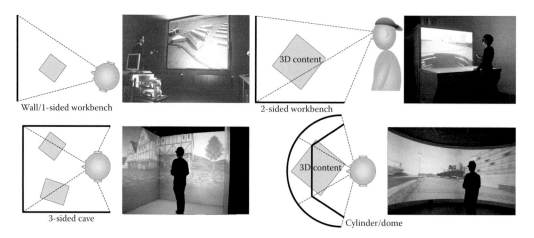

FIGURE 9.21 Off-axis projections for multiscreen configurations, and as discrete approximation to curved screens. Image courtesy: Johannes Kepler University Linz, Leibniz-Rechenzentrum, Technical University Munich.

output signal of all graphics cards also have to be synchronized. This is called *genlocking*, and is supported by professional graphics cards, offering a separate synchronization channel that can be shared by all graphic cards (in the same or in different machines).

In particular for curved screens, an approximation to multiple planar sections becomes quickly inefficient. A per-pixel parametric image warping is much more precise in these cases. This can be implemented on modern graphics cards to support real-time rates. Several approaches have been presented so far. One example is the quadric image transfer function that is used in [235].

9.3.4 Stereoscopic Multiviewer Techniques

The stereo channel separation techniques explained in Section 9.3.1 at page 359 separate two images – one for the left and one for the right eye of one observer. The question is, how such systems can support more than one viewer. There are two general possibilities for extending stereo channel separation to multiviewer scenarios.

In the first, time-sequential shuttering is simply repeated for more viewers (Figure 9.22), as in [3]. This however has clear limitations, since for N viewers, each eye will be exposed to only a fraction $(1/(2N))$ of the frame-display time and is shut for the remaining time $(1 - 1/(2N)$ of the frame display time). This leads to a brightness reduction of $1/(2N)$, compared with the brightness of an image that is being displayed constantly. The loss of brightness with this approach is currently not tolerable for more than two viewers. More viewers can be supported if active shuttering is combined with polarization filtering, as in [35]. Here, a viewer separation is carried out actively. For each instant in time, the shutters of both eyes of one viewer are opened, while the shutters of all other viewers are closed. The two stereo images for the active viewer are then separated through polarization filters attached in front of the projector lenses and to the shutter glasses. Therefore, to support N viewers $2N$ projectors are required because of the passive separation of the stereo pairs. As before,

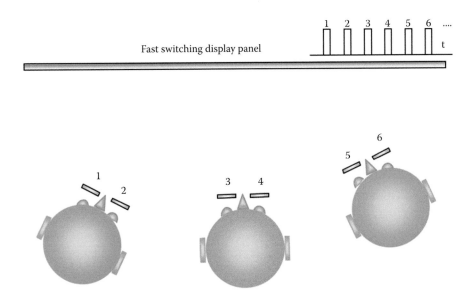

FIGURE 9.22 Time-sequential shuttering for a stereoscopic multiviewer display.

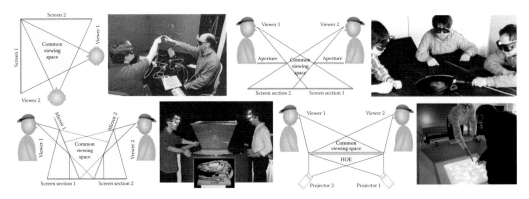

FIGURE 9.23 Spatial viewer separation: private screens (top, left), shared screen space with aperture (top, right), with mirrors (bottom, left) and with holographic projection screen (bottom, right). Image courtesy: Fred Brooks, NIH NCRR GRIP Molecular Graphics National Research Resource, Univ. of N.C. at Chapel Hill, Yoshifumi Kitamura, Tohoku University, Stefan Seipel, Uppsala University.

the brightness of the perceived images is decreased with an increasing numbers of viewers, mainly because of the active cycling around all viewers, but also due to polarization filtering being used in addition to the LC shutters. This technique will become inefficient for more than three viewers.

The second possibility is to separate the images for each viewer on spatially different screen portions through a special optical element, and to separate the individual stereo channels at these screen portions through either one of the standard techniques (i.e., passively or actively). Four approaches have been described that are based on this idea. They differ from each other in the optical elements being used (Figure 9.23). First, each viewer can be assigned to a private screen. If the screens are aligned in such a way that a shared interaction space is formed, such as the corner-shaped configuration in [6], multiple viewers can observe the same spatial scene. The screens have to be aligned in such a way that each viewer can see only his own screen while still looking at a common viewing space. No more than two viewers have been supported by this technique because of these constrains. Other approaches apply mirrors [28] or aperture holes [154] for sharing a common screen space while observing individual sections. Such techniques support four and more viewers. Their disadvantage is that, with an increased number of viewers, they either require a large screen space, or, they can display only small images. A better solution is the application of special holographic projection screens that make images appear only when viewed from particular directions, if these images are projected onto the screen from predefined angles. The system described in [145] supports four viewers with this technique.

Obviously, the separation of stereo images becomes inefficient for stereoscopic displays if supported viewers exceeds a certain number. Another disadvantage is that the separation of each viewer's stereo channels still requires eyeglasses. These two limitations can be addressed with many autostereoscopic displays which are described in detail in Section 9.4 at page 373. They clearly represent the future of multiviewer 3D displays.

9.4 AUTOSTEREOSCOPIC DISPLAYS

Compared to stereoscopic displays as explained in Section 9.3 at page 358, autostereoscopic displays do not require viewers to wear goggles for supporting stereo-channel separation. Yet, basic forms of autostereoscopic displays do display different perspective images. The challenge is to project these images toward individual viewing directions and to ensure that they are only visible when observed from these directions.

Thus for supporting stereo-channel separation without glasses, a special optics is required, projecting perspective images into different zones called *viewing zones*, which are smaller than the eye distance. This will ensure that each eye is always located within a different viewing zone, observing a different perspective.

Consequently, stereo-channel separation is carried out directly on the display rather than with the observer. In general, the term autostereoscopic displays refers to those displays which do allow 3D viewing without stereoscopic glasses, but the principles of 3D image generation are largely different. Most common types of autostereoscopic displays render a set of perspective images into different viewing zones. These are comparable to holographic stereograms, as explained in Section 5.5.7 at page 169. Others produce real 3D image points in space. The following sections will discuss the different forms of autostereoscopic displays.

9.4.1 Parallax Displays

We can say that parallax displays are the digital complement of holographic stereograms (see Section 5.5.7 at page 169). They project perspective images into different viewing zones which are small enough that only one eye can be located in each one. Two different types of micro optics are used in front of a raster display (usually a LCD panel, due to the requirement of an exact alignment) that produce the correct viewing zones: barrier displays and lenticular displays.

9.4.1.1 Barrier Displays

Parallax barrier displays apply an aperture mask (called a *barrier*) in front of a raster display, to mask out individual screen sections that should not be visible from one particular viewing zone. This is illustrated in Figure 9.24. Since the barrier is located at a well-chosen distance pb in front of the display plane, a parallax dependent masking effect is enforced. If a vertical slit mask is applied, then the horizontally aligned eyes of the observer will perceive different vertical screen columns. Every other screen column is masked out, and is only visible by the other eye and vice versa. Thus if two stereoscopic images are divided into vertical stripes being displayed at the correct screen columns, alternating left and right portions, then a viewer located at the correct distance will perceive only the right columns with the right eye and the left columns with the left eye. This corresponds to a horizontal parallax only (HPO) display, meaning that the eyes have to be aligned horizontally and only a horizontal parallax effect is produced.

It is critically important to choose the parameters of the barrier mask appropriately, depending on the viewing requirements. When designing a barrier display, usually the screen distance (p_e) and the pixel pitch (distance between two pixel centers) (p) are known.

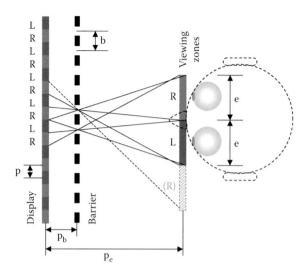

FIGURE 9.24 Principle of a parallax barrier display.

With $p/e = p_b/(p_e - p_b)$, we get the appropriate barrier pitch (b)

$$p_b = (pp_e)/(e + p) \qquad (9.13)$$

and with $2e/b = p_e/p_b$, we get the mask distance (p_b)

$$b = 2p((p_e - p_b)/p_e) \qquad (9.14)$$

The viewing zones (L, R) repeat horizontally in each direction.

With a static barrier, it is possible that the left eye is located in the right viewing zone and the right eye is located in the left viewing zone, which leads to a pseudoscopic impression of the rendered scene. The barrier mask does not necessarily have to be static. It can be dynamically adjusted depending on the viewer's position, with a transparent LCD panel rendering the mask slits dynamically. Adjusting the slits for the locations of the viewer's eyes ensures that each eye is always located inside the correct viewing zone. One important drawback of classical barriers is that the horizontal resolution per eye is half of the horizontal resolution of the underlying display. The same applies to the image intensity, since the barriers block 50% of the light. The resolution limitation can be overcome by applying two stacked SLMs [224]. The back panel (for instance, a fast DLP projection) displays the vertically interleaved stereo image, and the front panel (e.g., a high-speed F-LCD) displays a binary barrier mask. Shifting the barrier mask horizontally at a high speed and updating the stereo image accordingly uses the full horizontal resolution. This is explained in more detail later in this section.

Instead of using slit apertures, any other pattern could be applied. An aperture mask that consists of a dense random-hole pattern enables a view of the display from arbitrary angles (and supports multiple users), if the observer(s) are head-tracked [204].

Refractive elements can be applied in a very similar way as aperture masks, yielding similar effects but at a higher light throughput.

Looking at Figure 9.24, we see that the slits essentially act as pinhole cameras. Hence, replacing each slit with a lens of focus length p_b yields a similar behavior but without the losses. These displays are usually referred to as *lenticular displays* (cf. Section 9.4.1.5 on page 377).

9.4.1.2 Advanced Barrier Patterns

An important disadvantage of barrier displays is the loss of light due to the blocking nature of the aperture mask.

However, classes of alternative stripe or array patterns exist that act almost identical to slit or pinhole patterns, but allow for a much better light transmission, staying at up to 50% even for a pattern equivalent to an array of very small pinholes [98]. An introduction into this topic and applications for displays is found in [169].

These discoveries have led to new classes of displays, using stacked SLM (usually LCD) panels, where one or more displays act as content and/or viewer adaptive barriers. Applications are discussed in Section 9.4.1.4 on page 375, Section 9.5.3 on page 392, Section 10.12 on page 457, and Section 10.12.1 on page 458.

9.4.1.3 Multiperspective Displays

While stereoscopic displays produce only two different sets of viewing zones, adding more display stripes per slit produces a multiplicity of different viewing zones, able to deliver different perspectives at a fine pitch. Figure 9.25 illustrates the principle. Several viewing zones deliver identical sets of perspectives and can be used by multiple viewers. With a sufficient number of separate perspectives, a viewer can move his head sideways inside a viewing zone and experience a seamless perspective change, allowing a – limited – "looking behind" objects. With only a small number of perspectives, this will however lead to an obvious "switching" effect. A particular advantage of this display type is the ratio of perspectives provided and viewers served vs. necessary physical display resolution. This holds if viewing zones and positions of actual viewers can be aligned. A viewer in a wrong position, between two viewing zones, will see a pseudoscopic view, like with stereoscopic displays.

Equations 9.13 and 9.14 still apply in this case, yielding appropriate slit pitch and barrier distance to the display. Changing these parameters changes the size of the viewing zones for a given viewer distance. In principle, this can be used to adapt the viewing zones to the positions of a limited number of viewers. Another adaptation with similar effects can be obtained by changing the registration of perspectives to particular display stripes. Displays with according capabilities have been marketed. They work with lenticular barriers instead of slits (see Section 9.4.1.5 on page 377). Parallax barrier displays can also be made dynamically adaptive and viewer aware, with a barrier realized by an SLM, for example, an LCD screen.

9.4.1.4 Multilayer Barrier Displays

Using multiple barrier layers, complex direction-dependent light modulation can be achieved, up to a complexity approximating the appearance of a full-fledged light field. An

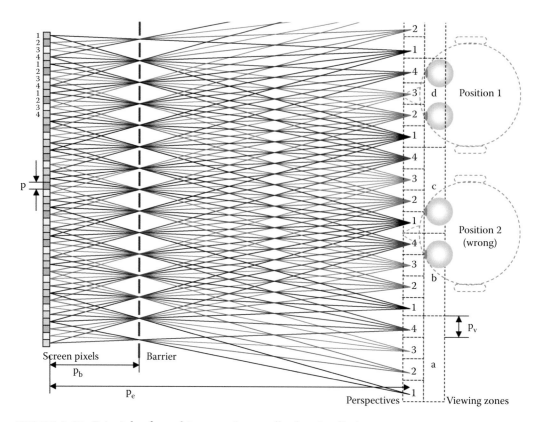

FIGURE 9.25   Principle of a multiperspective parallax barrier display.

experimental implementation using multiple LCD layers is described in [170]. An obvious difficulty arises from the low number of LCD layers and their limited resolution. Figure 9.26 illustrates this. The attenuation patterns required by adjacent display pixels to generate their respective light fields result in conflicting values for any single barrier layer pixel. In the example, attenuation values a_i, b_i, c_i can be chosen to deliver the intensities I_i for the light beams. With four beams and nine LCD cells involved as in the example, the equations have many correct solutions. In reality, there are numerous light beams to provide, and finding a proper set of values for the best achievable light field approximation requires solving large equation systems to an acceptable least mean square approximation. Nevertheless, this can be done in real time using current graphics card hardware [288]. The limitations of layer and resolution figures can partly be overcome using higher frame rates and generating more complex light fields by the temporal merging of fast sequential frames (requiring yet more computing power). The approach is also known as *compressive displays*. Figure 9.27 shows a prototype implementation.

Multilayer barrier displays can also be used in near-eye display designs (see Section 10.12 on page 457). There, the main target is focus synthesis, to a degree where even the oculars normally used for the display enlargement are replaced by appropriate light field rendering.

A difficulty arising is the high attenuation of the multiple barrier layers. With LCD displays, a large improvement is possible by omitting the polarizers of the inner layers. Each

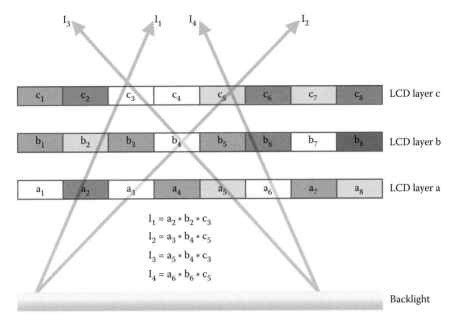

FIGURE 9.26 Principle of an active multilayer parallax barrier display.

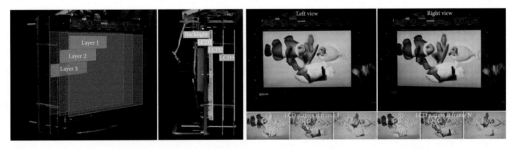

FIGURE 9.27 Compressive light-field prototype with three stacked layers of liquid crystal displays (left). Time-multiplexed patterns for the LCD layers (bottom right). Resulting left and right images (right). Image courtesy: Gordon Wetzstein, Stanford University.

LCD layer then only modulates the polarization turning, causing no attenuation, and only one back and front polarizer is translating the total result from the polarization turns in the different layers into brightness (polarization field display, [168]).

A directional modulation of the backlighting adds another degree of freedom to the creation of a full-fledged light field (tensor display, [289]).

These display types are currently in an experimental state, with several refinements due until a commercial implementation. Theoretically, with arbitrary high resolution and number of display layers, they could come close to a holographic display.

9.4.1.5 Lenticular Displays
Figure 9.28 compares the behavior of slit vs. lens rasters. A focused lens raster can provide fairly separated zones for individual perspectives. Widening slits in a slit mask very soon leads to a crosstalk of perspectives (bottom figure). This may be convenient if a smooth

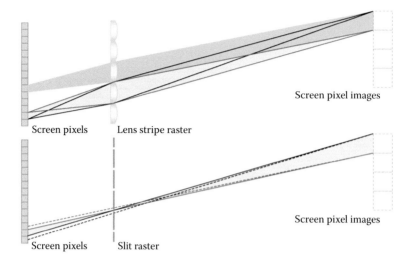

FIGURE 9.28 Comparison of slit mask vs. lens raster.

transition is intended, but even then the slits have to remain very narrow. A similar transition behavior can also be obtained for lenticular displays, by a slight defocus.

Although the multiperspective principle requires a relatively small number of vertical display stripes per actual image pixel, this is still very demanding to current technology. Current implementations usually work with displays of a higher resolution, delivering more pixels in the horizontal and the vertical. In order to exploit both, slanted lens stripes can be used (Figure 9.29). If the lens stripes are slanted by $1/n$ pixels, the usable horizontal resolution and number of perspectives multiplies by n, while the effective vertical resolution is diminished by n. In principle, even single color subpixels can be used to provide separate perspectives. This requires a complex dithering to maintain the correct colors at least for an area average;

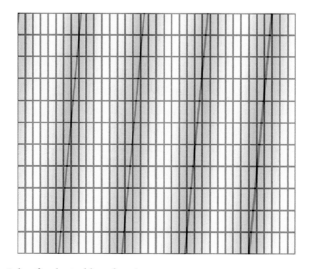

FIGURE 9.29 Principle of a slanted lens barrier raster.

given the fact that the eye resolves fine color detail four times worse than black-and-white detail, this is workable.

A practical implementation of the above-mentioned principles (**Toshiba** 55ZL2G, of 2012), uses a QFHD (3840 × 2160) display for an effective 3D resolution of 1280 × 720. With a lens raster consisting of liquid crystal switchable index modulation (L-GRIN) lenses (cf. Section 3.4.2.7 on page 72), the display can be used both as a 2D QFHD display or a 3D 1280 × 720 display. This device also offers an adaptation to several (static) viewer positions.

Using Equation 3.24 on page 73, we may try a tentative calculation of an L-GRIN screen: A 55″ display with 1280 lenses horizontal has a pixel pitch of about 1 mm. Assuming $r = 0.5$ mm, $n_1 = 1.45$, $n_2 = 1.5$, and $d = 0.5$ mm, we get $f \approx 5$ mm, a reasonable result if compared to Figure 9.25 on page 376.

9.4.1.6 Properties of Lenticular Displays

Lenticular displays use small lenslets with multiple tiny display pixels or stripes positioned behind them. The lenslets themselves are spherical or cylindrical according to their function. While cylindrical lenslets allow a horizontal parallax only, spherical lenslets support full parallax.

This works, in principle, like a micro projector. The display pixel grid behind the lens is projected enlarged onto a distant screen. If the projector has a sufficient depth of field, the pixel grid keeps separated throughout the screens and throughout a large distance range.

Hence, we could think of the projector as emitting separate light beams for each display pixel. Ideally, the position of each pixel is converted into a beam angle. By selecting pixels, individual sectors of space can be addressed, and individual light intensities can be delivered to viewers or single eyes at different positions. These are the viewing zones that are mentioned above.

The simplest version of lenticular displays is made of cylindrical lens stripes and just two display stripes per lens, delivering separate light beams each into different directions (see Figure 9.30). Properly aligned, one viewer can be delivered two stereo perspectives at a time. A simple example of this type are stereo postcards (although these may use rather simple prisms instead of cylindrical lenslets).

The viewer has to keep within a certain distance range to see the picture properly, otherwise incorrect combinations of viewing zones will cause false perspectives.

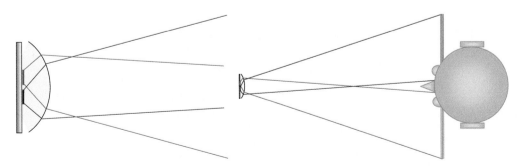

FIGURE 9.30 Two-stripe lenticular display: near field (left) and far field (right).

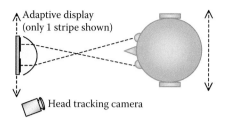

FIGURE 9.31 Principle of adaptive lenticular display.

Optically, one has to ensure that display and lens stripes are properly aligned, and that the lenslets are manufactured accurately enough to ensure their proper function.

As for barrier displays, the following simple equation can be applied for computing the optical parameters of the simplest type of a lenticular display (f = focal length, l = lens pitch):

$$f = pe/(e/p + 1) \tag{9.15}$$

$$l = 2 * p((pe - f)/pe) \tag{9.16}$$

This type of display has very limited abilities (only one viewer can be supported). By moving the display stripes sideways behind the lens, we can adapt the optimal viewing areas to different head positions (Figure 9.31), so each eye will always gets its proper picture, and no overlapping or image switching will occur.

A single lenslet or lens stripe may also support many exit beam angles at once, enabling the delivery of multiple pictures (Figure 9.32). As derived in Section 3.4.3.6 at page 79, the angular resolution of a lens depends on its diameter (a) and is roughly

$$\Phi \approx \lambda/a \tag{9.17}$$

A lens stripe just 1 mm wide, for example, could theoretically support over 1000 separate exit beams ($\lambda \approx 0.5\,\mu m$), producing such a multitude of viewer-position-dependent perspectives that their differences are tiny enough for a seamless transition between them. This allows for either a sophisticated multi viewer stereoscopic setup, or for a light field display. We will take it to light fields later.

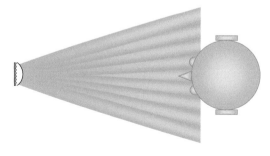

FIGURE 9.32 Multistripe lenticular display with overlapping exit beams.

Finally, we should mention an important aspect of lenticular displays: as lenslets reflect light from any direction, the surface of such a display may look very irritating. An efficient anti reflection coating (as is common with photographic lenses or eyeglasses) is mandatory. Very efficient coatings are available even for plastic glasses.

Screens with gradient refractive index (GRIN) lenses (cf. Section 3.4.2.7 on page 72), for example, a switched or index modulated liquid crystal screen, are not affected by this as their surface is flat.

With displays delivering more exit beams, multiple viewers can be addressed. We could further generate dynamic perspectives according to changing viewer positions, that allow looking behind objects. This would require head tracking again. The exit beams should overlap to a certain amount in order to avoid dark patches in between positions (a controlled defocusing will serve for this).

Head tracking (or, in more sophisticated setups, also eyes tracking) can be done in several ways. Early experimental setups often used commercial electro-magnetic head trackers, but the best way here is with cameras, locating the user by image recognition.

Simple lenslets have chromatic aberration, causing light from different color pixels to be projected toward different directions. To reduce these artifacts, the lenslets may be slightly rotated on the display plane. This *slanted-sheet technique* is therefore applied in most of the current lenticular displays, independent of its also possible effect to increase the number of addressable perspectives (as explained in Section 9.4.1.5 on page 377). Compared to a regular nonslanted situation, this also requires addressing the subpixels differently during rendering.

A vertical displacement of viewers also causes a change in the effective focal length with cylindrical lenses, an effect less grave with simple two-view displays but important with multi view approaches.

9.4.1.7 Time-Multiplexed Displays

One essential disadvantage of most parallax displays is that the resolution of the image visible in each viewing zone is only a fraction of the display resolution. To be more precise, the view resolution is $1/n$ of the display resolution for n different views. If –for an HPO display– only two different views for left and right eye images are generated, as explained above, then the horizontal view resolution is half of the horizontal display resolution, while the vertical view resolution is the full vertical display resolution. If multiple views are generated as explained in Section 9.4.1.8 at page 382, then the view resolution is reduced even further. To overcome this, several autostereoscopic display approaches direct the full display resolution into each viewing zone sequentially through time multiplexing.

Figure 9.33 illustrates the conceptual idea: A high-speed illumination bar turns on one light source at a time. A lens forms a real image of it on the opposite side of the display. While doing this, the light is modulated through a transparent raster display, which could be on LCD basis. While iterating along the bar from light source to light source, the image on the display panel is changed and will appear only within the corresponding (focused) viewing zone. If this can be done fast enough, then many different viewing zones can be created without noticing the sequential multiplexing nature. While the switching speed of

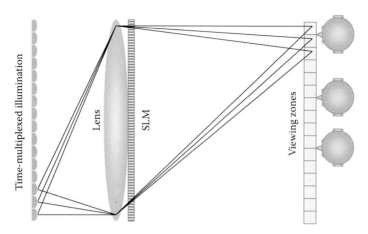

FIGURE 9.33   Concept of a time-multiplexed autostereoscopic display.

light sources, for instance LEDs, is sufficiently high, the switching speed of most LCDs is not. Thus LCDs do not represent an applicable technology for high-speed light modulation.

Therefore these displays are usually built slightly differently, although the basic concept remains the same: instead of the light bar, a CRT screen displays the perspective images at a high speed. Since CRTs cannot modulate light on a transmissive basis, a high-speed shutter bar is used between the CRT and a front lens. In synchronization with the perspective images displayed on the CRT, the shutter bar iterates through the different aperture openings. The front lens will then generate a different viewing zone for each aperture opening. Both shutter bars and CRTs are fast enough for generating multiple, flicker-free viewing zones. As mentioned earlier, the advantage of this approach is that each viewing zone displays the full image resolution of the display (LCD or CRT). The drawback however is the requirement of fast switching speed and the reduction of light with an increasing number of views, as is the case of active multiviewer stereoscopic displays explained in Section 9.3.4 at page 371. The display rate per view must be above the flicker-fusion threshold (see Section 4.2.3 at page 93). It depends on the display brightness, but we can assume this to be 60 Hz. Thus, the overall speed of the display then depends on the number of views (n) to be generated (i.e., $n \cdot 60$ Hz).

As explained in Section 9.4.1.1 at page 373, the same principle was implemented with a DLP projection for the back image and an F-LCD for the front mask. In principle, any SLM combination can be used, as long as they are fast enough.

9.4.1.8 Multi-Viewer Techniques

In an autostereoscopic recording assembly, two or more cameras may pick up the scene from different positions. In the simplest case, the cameras are arranged only in a horizontal row (Figure 9.34). By arranging separate display stripes for each camera picture behind lens stripes, each eye of a viewer should get just the image of a certain camera from a certain viewing angle. In practice, there are areas in between where the two images overlap.

Figure 9.35 visualizes how the screen with its display and lens stripes reproduces the content recorded by the camera array. This is basically a light field display, with a very limited

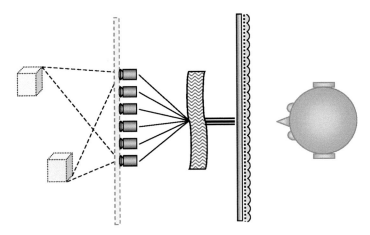

FIGURE 9.34 Recording for multiperspective multistripe lenticular display.

angular resolution. We have shown two viewer positions and a few selected sight lines to virtual objects in the image.

With freely moving observers, many perspectives will consist of an overlay of two images.

Regard the lower viewer and the lower edge of the upper cube. The sight lines go between two camera positions each, so the viewer can't get fitting camera images for this image detail. What his eyes see must be an overlay of two images from the cameras next to the ideal position. We see that autostereoscopy, in spite of the advantage of not requiring glasses, has the disadvantage of producing artifacts because intermediate angles are simply achieved by overlaying two images.

What becomes difficult as well is the realization of large displays, with correspondingly large viewing distances from the display. In order to give every eye its own picture, very small angular deviations have to be resolved, which in turn reduces the "good" viewing area, requiring more viewing zones and more display stripes. The optical separation of display

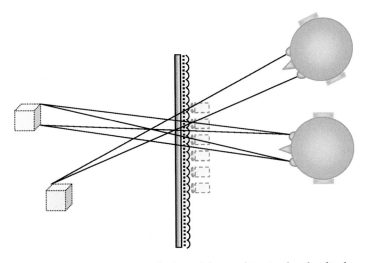

FIGURE 9.35 Multi-viewer perspective rendering with a multistripe lenslet display.

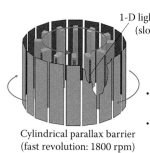

1-D light source array (LED array)
(slow revolution: 100 rpm)

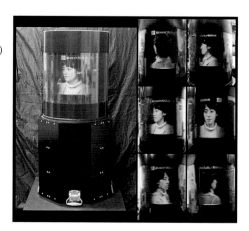

• Directions of the rays are scanned by revolution

• Intensity of each light is modulated in synchronization with revolution

Cylindrical parallax barrier
(fast revolution: 1800 rpm)

Resolution: 1254(H) × 256(V)

FIGURE 9.36 Cylindrical parallax barrier display that supports multiple users [78,302]. Image courtesy: Tomohiro Yendo, Nagoya University.

beams is not a problem, but their exact delivery to a certain viewer is more difficult. This can again be resolved by head tracking, where cameras can also be used to calibrate the display for spatial accuracy (more about this in the section on light field displays).

An example for multi-viewer parallax barrier displays is to use rotating cylindrical parallax barriers and LED arrays for covering a 360° HPO viewing area (Figure 9.36) [78]. Here the barrier interval, the aperture width, the width of the LEDs, and the distance between LEDs and barriers are the essential parameters for defining the produced viewing zones. A very similar –yet single user– barrier display is described in [163]. In this case, the observer is located inside the cylinder, while the barrier mask is inside and LED arrays are outside (pointing toward the cylinder center). Both LED arrays and the barrier mask are fixed aligned with respect to each other, and rotated together.

9.4.1.9 Basic Categories

By applying one of the technological approaches discussed above, autostereoscopic parallax displays can be grouped into three main categories:

1. *Static two-view displays* generate static viewing zones for two perspectives. Multiple observers can use these displays, but will all see the same perspective. During movements, the eye can be located in the wrong viewing zones, projecting the wrong perspectives to the eyes. This leads to a pseudoscopic (inside-out) depth perception.

2. *Tracked two-view displays* avoid pseudoscopic images by head tracking the observer and by realigning the viewing zones toward the actual eye positions (e.g., by mechanically moving the lenslets or barrier mask). These displays support only one user at a time, but also allow the scene to be rendered consistently for the actual perspective of the user.

3. *Multiview displays* generate static viewing zones for multiple perspectives. Head tracking is not necessary (if enough viewing zones can be generated) and multiple users are

supported who can observe the scene from correct perspectives. The drawbacks of these displays are that the more viewing zones that are displayed at the same time (to ensure smooth zone transitions), the slower is the rendering rate of the display. Furthermore, for common approaches the spatial resolution of the display decreases with an increasing number of viewing zones, since multiple pixels will be projected into different zones by a single lenslet or barrier segment. Thus for instance, ten screen pixels will be located under each lenslet / barrier segment or generating ten viewing zones, reducing the spatial resolution of each viewing zone to a 10th of the actual display resolution.

4. *Tracked Multiview displays* can avoid many of these disadvantages; more on this in Section 9.5.6 at page 395.

The spatial resolution of the viewing zones of two-view displays is always half the screen resolution. Only for time-multiplexed displays (explained above), the full spatial screen resolution can be projected into each viewing zone. These displays however reduce the temporal resolution (display frequency) with each additional viewing zone. The same applies to rotating cylindrical parallax displays. The higher the angular or spatial resolution, the higher is the demand on a fast revolving speed. Furthermore, the LEDs have to be narrowly focused for generating smaller viewing zones.

Directing separate images to several observers without using glasses may, however, also be done using holographic fringe patterns for light beam forming. We will turn to this after the prerequisite chapter on computer-generated holographic displays (Section 9.6 at page 399).

9.4.2 Volumetric Displays

Volumetric displays generate 3D voxels in space, rather than 2D pixels on screens. Supporting a natural depth perception (including a consistent accommodation and vergence/stereopsis) of visualized volumetric datasets for an arbitrary number of users is their main advantage over most other stereoscopic and autostereoscopic displays. However, they suffer from other limitations, such as the relatively small form factors and display volumes, and the inability to render surfaces models with correct occlusion or view-dependent shading effects, such as specular surface reflections. The reason for the latter is that all displayed voxels emit light in all directions.

Different possibilities exist for filling a volume with light emitting points. We can categorize them into two main groups: swept volume displays and static volume displays. Their basic principles are described as follows.

9.4.2.1 Swept Volume Displays

Swept volume displays are the most common volumetric displays. They move (sweep, switch, rotate, or translate optically) a passive diffusor (i.e., a screen), an optical element (e.g., a mirror), or an active light emitter (e.g., a LED array or matrix, an LCD panel, or an OLED panel) through a volume at a high speed. This can happen optically, mechanically, or electronically. The voxel elements are created by either projecting points from outside the volume onto moving passive screens, by switching moving active emitters, or by forming optical images through oscillating mirrors. In all cases, the image source and the moving element are synchronized. While the motion itself is too fast to be perceived by the human visual system, the persistence of glowing points displayed along the direction of movement leads to a consistent volumetric image that can be observed as a whole.

Max Hirsch introduced one of the first swept volume displays in 1958 (US patent 2,967,905). A fixed projector was used to illuminate a rotating screen. Several mirrors helped to minimize regional defocus while the screen rotated through the projection volume. In 1960, Richard Ketchpel applied an electron gun to illuminate a rotating phosphor screen [148]. Today's versions of such passive swept volume displays are mechanically, optically, and electronically much more sophisticated, but still follow similar principles. Figure 9.37 illustrates several commercial and noncommercial examples.

The Felix3D display that is shown in Figure 9.37 uses the Helix3D method that was patented by its inventor Rüdiger Hartwig in 1976. With this method, laser beams are projected onto a quickly rotating helix (screw, spiral) in a transparent tube, which generates light spots that as a whole produce a 3D image. In his patent specifications, Hartwig cited, among other things, air traffic control as a possible area for application where the 3D representation would be able to indicate the height and distance of the aircraft.

The fretting of mechanical parts is one limitation of most swept volume displays. The DepthCube display shown in Figure 9.37 avoids this by projecting a sequence of images

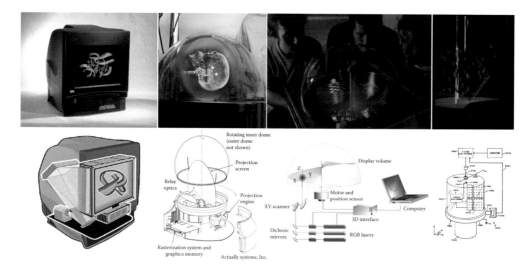

FIGURE 9.37 From left to right: LightSpaceTechnologies' DepthCube applying high-frequency switchable diffusers, Actuality Systems' PerspectaSpatial 3-D Display applying DLP-based micro display chips and relay optics to project RGB images onto a rotating screen from the side [83], Felix3D Volumetric Display [167] from High School Stade applying a helix shaped screen to support a projection from below, and Edwin Berlin's display (bottom-right) that generates volumetric imagery by illuminating LEDs mounted on a rotating panel ([18], US patent 4,160,973), and a photograph of the Solomon HoloDeck Volumetric Imager (top-right). Image courtesy (from left to right): **LightSpace Technologies**, Inc., Gregg Favalora, Knut Langhans, Gymnasium Staade, Edwin P. Berlin, LightSail Energy (bottom-right), and Dennis J. Solomon, **Holoverse**, Inc. (top-right).

(displaying slices of a volumetric model) onto a set of multi-planar switchable diffusers. These are optical elements that can be switched between a transparent and a diffuse mode. The projection is synchronized to the switching process that loops through the diffusers from front to back, diffusing only one plane at a time.

Another possibility for generating a volumetric image is to apply optics to create real and virtual optical image points in space. Alan Traub describes one of the first varifocal displays in 1966 that applies oscillating mirrors to relay image points optically (US patent 3,493,290,[272]). The mirror reflects a fast screen (e.g., a CRT monitor) while vibrating in synchronization to the display rate of the screen. Thereby, the different curvatures of the mirror surface (concave, convex, and planar) create real and virtual reflected images of the screen within a volume surrounding the mirror surface. Several variations (also large-scale systems [194]) exist today. In some systems the mirror optics is set in vibration by a rear-assembled loudspeaker [91], while other approaches utilize a vacuum source [194].

More information on swept volume displays, including a more detailed classification, can be found in [39] and [38].

9.4.2.2 Static Volume Displays

Displays that create 3D volumetric images in space without moving supporting parts through the volume can be classified as static volume displays. Most static volume displays quickly scan a 3D volume filled with a special translucent host substrate (e.g., crystals, fluoride glass, various gases and liquids) with external energy beams, such as those created with high-power infrared lasers located outside the substrate. Optically active ions are excited inside the substrate which then emit visible photons at the intersections of the beams. Elizabeth Downing, for instance, presented such a display in 1994 that applied rare earth doped heavy metal fluoride glass and pairs of infrared lasers [74] (Figure 9.38(left)).

The display developed by **Burton** Inc., **AIST**, Keio University uses a high-power laser beam that is focused at an arbitrary position within a 3D volume of air at a high speed [249] (Figure 9.38(right)). A gas, such as air, ionizes to plasma when a high power laser is focused in it. This process is referred to as *laser induced breakdown*. The breakdown of air results in bluish white emission at the laser-focused position.

Static volume displays are rare, and have not found practical applications thus far; their image quality is not yet sufficient for most applications.

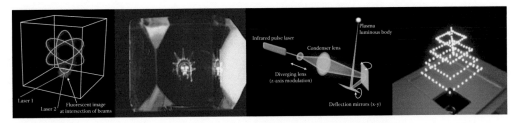

FIGURE 9.38 Rare earth doped heavy metal fluoride glass scanned with pairs of infrared lasers (left) [74], and laser-plasma scanning 3D display (right) [249]. Image courtesy: Elizabeth Downing, **3DTL** Inc. and **Burton** Inc.

9.5 LIGHT FIELD DISPLAYS

An ideal display could look like a window, showing real scenes as if there was no camera, no transmission line, and no display at all. For this purpose, we would usually think of holograms.

Yet there is another way. It begins with light rays passing through a window. If we could catch the direction, intensity, and color of any light ray passing a recording window and reproduce it on a display, it should look like the original scene. We learned in Section 3.6 at page 87 that this is nothing other than a light field. For an image representation consisting of rays going through a plane, the term light field was first introduced in an article by A. Gershun, in 1936 [96].

In order to achieve this, we could segment the window into many small sub windows, each as tiny as a little pinhole, and record the incident light rays for any of these little segments. If these are small enough, they will appear as a solid area from a distance. In principle, this turns out to be quite simple: Any cameras with a sufficiently small aperture will just record angles and intensities of incident light rays and map them onto the pixels of its image sensors (Figure 9.39). Hence small cameras of, for example, 1 mm in size and a sufficient number of (in this case very tiny) pixels can deliver the light field data for just one window segment, which we will call a pixel of the window.

Any camera can in general be seen as an angle-to-position converter. This conversion is relatively robust against geometric errors.

Reproducing the light field on a display is straightforward (at least in theory): we could use identical optical assemblies, this time illuminated micropixel arrays behind pinhole lenses, working as tiny projectors (Figure 9.40).

Each camera/projector pair basically acts like a camera obscura, hence a small hole, and many small holes simply form a window.

What in theory works quite well, will nevertheless cause several problems in practical implementation, as you can imagine. The foremost of these is the sheer number of pixels: If a normal display has n^2 pixels for a nxn resolution, the light field has about n^4 (n^2 pinhole cameras/projectors with n^2 pixels each, to reproduce a light field as dense as the basic

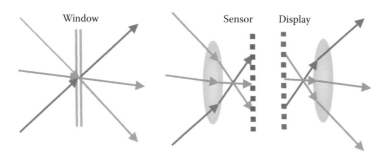

FIGURE 9.39 Light field recording and reconstruction principle: light rays just passing a window (left), light rays converted into pixel values on a tiny image sensor of a pinhole camera (center), light rays reproduced by a tiny projector being just an inverted pinhole camera (right).

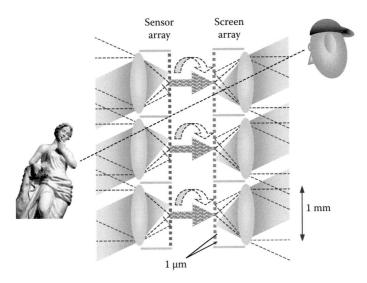

FIGURE 9.40 Principle of a light field display.

image resolution). Without further measures, this would require a prohibitively large transmission bandwidth (same order as a raw hologram) and the technology building such a large and dense assembly is not yet available. Another problem are the tiny camera/projector pixel sizes themselves, down to 1 μm in the extreme, leading to problems with light sensitivity/brightness and noise.

For a practical implementation of light field recording technology, one way is to use a smaller number of cameras, in a less dense array, and calculate the missing window pixels by some kind of interpolation. For this to work properly, it is necessary to retrieve information about the 3D structure of the original scene producing the light field, as edge coverage from distant objects has to be interpolated properly, and this is not possible in any way by just mediating pixel values. A treatise on 3D scene recording with multiple cameras can be found in[57].

Light field displays do not have to be self-luminous. A lens array can also be placed over a reflective high resolution display. With a sufficiently even illumination, outside light will also be well distributed over the micropixels behind any lens element. This renders any 3D image content just as with an active display. That this works is obvious from stereo postcards already. Meanwhile, omnidirectional light field prints are available, using hexagonal plastic lens arrays. Due to the difficulty of aligning lens array and print sheet, only simple patterns are usually chosen as items displayed, but the effect is quite stunning.

9.5.1 Parameterization

An important issue is how to represent and store light field data. We briefly discussed ray parameterizations in Section 3.6 at page 87, and focus now on the common two-plane variation.

Rays can be parameterized in polar or Cartesian coordinates, for example (Figure 9.41). The intuitive approach would be to use intensity and either two tilt angles or a tilt direction

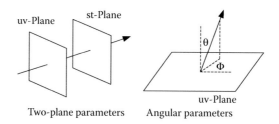

FIGURE 9.41 Light field parameterization: two planes vs. polar ray coordinates.

with an angle. This is very inconvenient for computer calculations however; more common is the two-plane parameterization, which uses a plane before the image plane. The intersection of light rays with this plane encode light ray directions. While the coordinates of the pixel in the image plane are denoted as s, t those in the other plane are denote as u and v.

Because this delivers four values per ray, it is also called a *"four-dimensional"* approach (a bit misleading since delivering four parameters for each point in a 2D field is not really four dimensional).

In some cases we might also have data about a light ray's origin (i.e., its distance to the s, t plane). If so, it requires hardly any effort to store this along with the other four parameters. This would then resemble the full five-dimensional plenoptic function (see Section 3.6 at page 87). If light fields are recorded with camera arrays, however, determining the fifth parameter is not easy, because the distance has to be calculated by matching correspondences.

9.5.2 Light Fields vs. Holograms

While our brains can easily match stereo pictures, computer algorithms have substantial difficulties determining correct pixel correspondences with reflective, transparent, or simply featureless surfaces (which our eyes can circumvent in most cases by regarding an entire scene).

In [306], this approach was used to convert light fields into holograms and vice versa (Figure 9.42). Although still not a safe algorithm, it yields satisfactory results.

Holograms cannot be compressed like conventional pictures; as high-frequency components with this approach are important and have to be reproduced with proper phase and detail, something typical image-compression algorithms like JPEG simply neglect since the human eye is not as picky in this aspect. Algorithms reducing fringe complexity by sacrificing image resolution, as in [180], are also not appropriate for large wavelengths. A proper method could be nonlinear quantization [263].

If the hologram is simply used for image encoding rather than display, the most efficient data reduction is to use larger wavelengths. Since holograms are prone to speckle noise, it may be interesting to mention that [306] introduce an approach to encode n parallel sub-holograms each with a subset (every n^{th} pixel) of the scene. With an additional filtering step, this eliminates speckles efficiently even if $n = 2$. We would diverge too far our topic to talk about all aspects of this approach, but it shows promising methods of combining and transforming light fields and holograms.

Synthetic light fields

Light field   Computed depth field   Hologram rendering

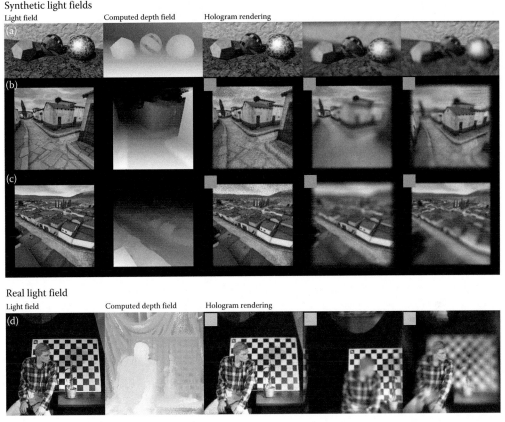

Real light field

Light field   Computed depth field   Hologram rendering

FIGURE 9.42 Turning light fields into holograms and back [306]. Image courtesy: Computer Graphics Laboratory, ETH Zurich.

The simple image-based approach of light fields may always have its limitations. However, we could add depth sensors to classical light field cameras to solve this problem. One possible candidate for this is time-of-flight analysis with a ramp shuttered camera and a short laser pulse for illumination that directly delivers distance encoded into gray levels. Other candidates are projected optical patterns whose appearance on the scene can be analyzed geometrically. In both cases, infrared light can be used since most cameras are sensitive to this.

In case of computer-generated (artificial) scenes, depth data is already available, actually being the basis of it all. So the most natural conclusion is to store "5D" data in any case, which results in a substantial simplification when turning light fields into holograms (yet, only if the distance is stored with high precision, good enough for deriving light phases).

If we do not have distance data, a certain simplification is possible by converting the light ray bundles for any pixel of the light ray image into separate patches of holographic fringe patterns, generating pattern after pattern until all light rays have been taken care of. This method would not attempt to calculate any scenery topology, it would simply try to reproduce light rays as such (see Fourier holograms, Section 9.6.3 on page 402); yet, such an approach has not been practically implemented.

There is a general equivalence between light fields and holograms. A typical viewer may not notice any difference when viewing images produced by a light field display as opposed to a computer-generated hologram. Only in special situations would the difference be noticeable, because holograms form the resulting light field by interference. Such differences may become evident, for example, if coherence responsive optics like holographic optical elements (HOEs) are involved.

For the purpose of displaying 3D images, a light field display offers some advantages. A straightforward implementation can be done similar to classical autostereoscopic displays. This can reduce the complexity of rendering and save a lot of computation. More on this in Section 9.5.6 on page 395.

9.5.3 Light Field Focus Synthesis

In theory, a perfect light field display reproduces focus (virtual pixel distance) correctly. The most obvious implementation would be using a lenslet array. The lenslets should be small enough not to be seen separately, ideally smaller than about 1 arcmin of the field of view, or so near to the eye that they cannot be focused upon. This is a simple requirement, entirely similar to a 2D display.

A screen area consisting of several lenslets can provide a virtual pixel (crossing light rays) closer to the eye, similar to Figure 5.35 on page 156, or also farther away.

A large screen producing virtual images closer to the eye (light beams crossing in front of the viewer) may be useful for a better vergence/accommodation fit with 3D display, or for compensating short-sightedness of the viewer. For mobile phones, it may produce an image at greater distance for long-sighted users.

Figure 9.43 shows an assessment of the resolutions possible for far- and near-sighted focus synthesis. We assume a light field display with an array of lenslets of raster size d (the actual display pixels are not drawn). The "rays" emitted by the lenses have a divergence $\Phi \approx \lambda/d$, caused by the diffraction limit (cf. Equation 3.34 on page 80). This causes a focus spread and hence a blur in the eye, and the angular resolution limit for the eye caused by this is simply equal to Φ. The physical pixel raster of a display at distance D is seen with an angular

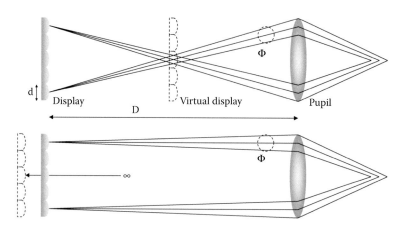

FIGURE 9.43 Light field focus correction for short-sighted (top) and long-sighted viewers.

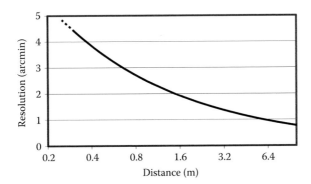

FIGURE 9.44 Focus synthesis resolution for lenslet displays at different distances.

resolution $\Phi_2 \approx d/D$. Combining both equations with the assumption $\Phi = \Phi_2$, we get an approximation of the resolution possible, and it only depends on D:

$$\Phi \approx \sqrt{\lambda/D} \qquad (9.18)$$

Figure 9.44 shows the results with $\lambda = 500$ nm. The angular resolution will be best for distant, hence, large displays. We should point out that these resolution figures are not exact for very close displays. The case of near-eye displays is discussed in Section 10.12 on page 457. They also refer to a virtual display appearing at a focus distance different from the display distance. If the viewer would or could focus his eyes on the real display area, the resolution only depends on the diffraction limit of his eyes and the size of the physical lenslet raster.

Holograms do not have the same focus resolution limitations, as they can be interpreted as if consisting of many individual beam-forming structures – one per image pixel – that are widely overlapping. These structures are therefore sufficiently large not to be affected by the diffraction limit.

An example would be the mirror array shown in Figure 10.47 on page 459. This array, by the way, closely reminds of an array of magnifying boxes (similar to Figure 10.1 on page 418 and Figure 10.9 on page 426), which could be seen as replacing the "good old" approach of a magnifying glass used by elderly people for reading, with an array of smaller lenses. This would not always require a complete light field implementation.

Parallax barriers can be used instead of lenslets. A static demonstration of the principle for a mobile phone, using a fixed parallax barrier, has been presented in [131]. It had a barrier raster of 0.375 mm. Using the much higher resolution of a high-end mobile phone screen, 5×5 pixels were available per field (barrier pinhole). A workable version would use a dedicated barrier display, producing advanced barrier patterns as mentioned in Section 9.4.1.2 on page 375. This, probably in combination with a multilayer configuration, could as well be envisioned for focus synthesis with large displays. Accordingly multilayer approaches however resulted in a crisp image but with an extreme loss of contrast (cf., e.g., [130]).

Another possibility is a pre-filtering of image content, together with a denser lens raster ([131], see Figure 9.45). This, however, also incurs a – moderate – reduction of image contrast.

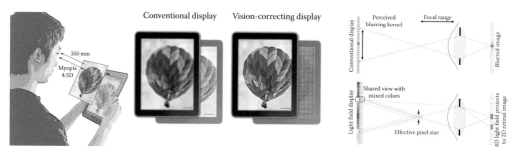

FIGURE 9.45 Focus synthesis with pre-filtering and a denser lens raster. Source: [131]; Image courtesy: Gordon Wetzstein, Stanford University.

A perfect light field display would provide virtual image points at any distance, to achieve a virtually holographic 3D scene reproduction. This is – point by point – identical to focus synthesis, and the same methods as well as the same difficulties apply. A more detailed treatment of this topic with lenslet displays can be found in [190], also discussing approaches to increase resolution.

Finally, we should note that with an HPO (horizontal perspective only) stripe or barrier display, an attempt to reproduce focus would result in a vertical blur, as there would be no proper light ray divergence in the vertical direction. In this direction, the image position would still be perceived at screen distance. This is a result inevitably obtained with the previously discussed rotating HOE display [141] as well.

9.5.4 Depth of Field and Light Field Recording

Cameras recording light fields should deliver as much depth of field as possible, because the ideal light field has to be crisp for any distance, just like a hologram. Lowering pixel noise by using larger lens apertures will therefore not work. It would be interesting to determine the optimum microcamera design and number of cameras to be used for light field capturing. With this information we will get some idea about the design of a microprojector array, as this is dual to the camera array. This is a fairly complex problem, but let's try a simple approach for a first guess.

We can use the already given formulas derived for the depth of field toward infinity (see Equation 4.13 on page 114) – which apply to cameras, projectors, and the human eye.

One solution would be a lens size of a=1 mm, operated at its maximal angular resolution of two arcmin, giving a depth field of of ≈ 1 m to infinity, probably good enough for a typical hologram recording, and yielding ≈ 2000 pixels at 60° horizontal field of view.

The cameras could even be relatively low resolution cameras: utilizing the pixel displacements of these cameras regarding the same object points recorded by many of them, a super resolution algorithm may be applied to upscale the camera pictures to HDTV or more [116].

9.5.5 Light Field Display Implementations

A light field display approach has been demonstrated in a practical experiment. It uses a rotating HOE to produce multiple ray directions sequentially [141]. A projector casts its light from the top onto the 45° tilted HOE (Figure 9.46). The HOE diffuses light in the vertical

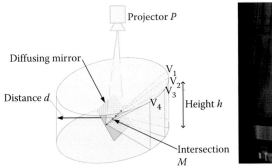

FIGURE 9.46 A 360° light field display: projection optics (left) and rendered 3D graphics example (right). Image courtesy: Paul Debevec, University of Southern California.

direction while it reflects light the horizontal direction. Hence, for horizontal perspective this is like a mirror and in the vertical it acts like canvas.

By rotating the HOE, light from certain pixel columns of the projector is reflected into certain radial directions at certain times. By appropriately addressing these display columns, a viewer cab sequentially receive vertical display lines matching his proper perspective, in all directions that can be served by the mirror (360° horizontally, in this example). This supports a horizontal parallax only, but for a single head-tracked viewer a matching vertical perspective can be displayed. The angular resolution of this rotating light field display is about 1.5°, and it needs thousands of separate images per second to cover all possible perspectives. This is achieved by several ingenious hardware functions that squeeze an acceptable size and resolution out of normal PC graphics hardware.

The disadvantage here is that many pictures are generated although there are actually just a few viewers. Frames generated between those viewed are essentially superfluous. To a larger or smaller extent, this is also the case for other autostereoscopic displays. The mechanical approach makes it impractical for this demonstrator to be mass produced.

In contrast to the similar swept volume displays that apply rotating projection screens (which were discussed in Section 9.4.2.1 at page 385), this display does support consistent occlusion.

There are other light field display approaches that should be mentioned: Other HOEs can be used to direct light from separate screen elements or from multiple projectors in separate directions, forming a light field. This is the more traditional approach and was demonstrated earlier. Another variety, called *diffraction-based holography*, uses dynamically calculated hologram elements to generate a hologram that is actually reduced to light field complexity. We will return to this in Section 9.6 at page 399.

9.5.6 An Adaptive Approach to Light Field Displays

It is not necessary to compute and to display all light rays of a light field display at once. Usually there are a limited number of observers, only so it would be unnecessarily expensive to compute and display a greater number of light rays than those that will be seen. The following discussion is more theoretical in nature, since adaptive light field displays do not yet exist.

Usually it is sufficient to compute horizontal rays only, as in the 360° display explained above. Thus, for a planar light field display we could use an array of cylindrical lenses in combination with display stripes behind them (Figure 9.47). This is indeed an identical optical setup as used for lenticular parallax displays, as described in Section 9.4.1 at page 373. Displaying only those light rays that reach the eyes of each observer (determined with head-tracking technology) is the equivalent of displaying the corresponding viewing zones. Other light rays (or viewing zones) don't have to be computed, which can save a lot of performance, memory, and bandwidth for computer-rendered interactive content.

This approximation will support an individually and dynamically adapted perspective on the same content for each viewer. Even entirely different content for each observer would be possible (e.g., multiprogram TV).

A problem with this approach may arise if adaptive perspectives for one viewer interfere with others, but this will happen only if viewers occupy the same horizontal position (e.g., if people of different sizes are standing behind each other or if some observers are sitting and others standing).

The usual problem with HPO displays (i.e., left and right perspectives falling apart when the observer just slightly tilts his head), can be avoided by dynamically shifting both perspectives accordingly. With large tilting angles, however, as is the case for the stereotypical couch-reclining TV viewer, the stereo effect may have to be abandoned.

Head tracking as we need it here is relatively simple, because it does not matter if tracking cameras fall victim to false impressions (wrongly detected faces, for example). This would just cause some superfluous projection angles. The only requirements are that viewers can continue to observe when looking sideways (it would be disturbing if the picture were to intermediately vanish, even in the periphery), and that the system would also work

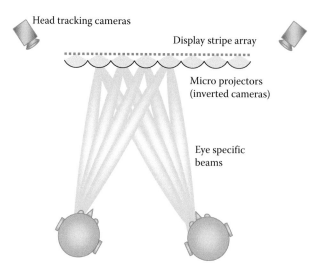

FIGURE 9.47 Adaptive light field display approach [114],[115].

in the dark (it should use an infrared illumination). These problems can be regarded as solved [267].

An adaptive display mode [114],[115] has further advantages over a non-adaptive one. A brute force reproduction of a discretized light field would result in transition effects when the user's eye passes from one beam to the next. In the worst case, little black blotches would separate beams. This problem can be solved either by an optimized optical design or by dynamic brightness adjustment of adjacent beams during a viewer transition between them (which in turn requires eye or head tracking). The adaptive display concept presented has also been addressed extensively in [10].

Adaptive autostereoscopic displays usually change beam directions to follow a viewer's eyes. This can be done by shifting a parallax barrier or lens array positioned in front of the display plane.

With the adaptive light field as described here, however, the beams do not follow the viewer. The viewer walks from beam to beam, while the image perspective rendered is individually fine tuned for him, millimeter by millimeter (Figure 9.48). Hence, he gets a totally smooth perspective transition, as if the objects displayed were real (with a static light field, this could be achieved only with a very large number of very narrow beams).

All beams hitting a particular eye of a particular viewer from any stripe in the display show just this fine-tuned perspective of the displayed objects, and two adjacent beams are simultaneously showing it if the eye is positioned between them. There is no fixed relation between beam angle and perspective rendered, as would be the case with a nonadaptive light field display.

The display panel itself is not depicted in Figure 9.48. We should note that the lens stripes producing the light beams have to be small enough to not be perceived individually on the display panel, equally small indeed as the pixel raster of a conventional display.

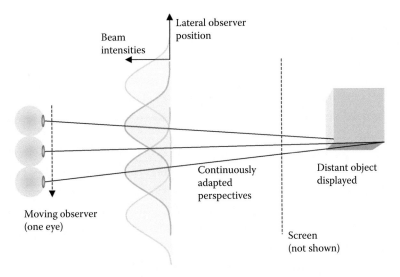

FIGURE 9.48 Adaptive light field display detail: while an observer moves laterally, he passes from beam to beam and simultaneously the displayed image is rendered for corresponding perspectives.

The adaptive display needs less than 100 possible and only a few active ray angles (two for each viewer) compared with at least as many as a hundred for a full quality nonadaptive light field display.

It should be emphasized that this is not a time-multiplexed approach (although it could be operated as such if desired). A small selection of display stripes is illuminated, simultaneously, and their light is projected in a very selective way. With a self-luminous display technology, like OLED, this may save a lot of energy.

The precision demands on the lenslet stripes may seem to be high at a first glance (as, for example, the authors of [267] state for a loosely related approach). But this would be the case only if we wanted to produce beams with exactly defined angles. The essential insight to the functionality of the adaptive light field display regarded here is that any lenslet is a projector, hence an inverted camera, able to produce a multitude of cleanly ordered beams at good resolution without requiring exceedingly high manufacturing precision (any inexpensive camera with a pinhole-sized lens does the same, and some even claim to deliver HD resolution). The main reason for this is that small geometric errors of the lenses will only cause linearity errors when converting stripe positions to beam angles, but the relation will still be monotonic (beams will remain in sequence and not cross over).

Thus, producing such displays at very high precision may not be necessary. Instead, cameras could be used to measure the individual beam angles and brightness profiles and calibrate such a display to dynamically adapt for optimum results in spite of any mechanical or optical tolerances, even for chromatic aberration of the lenses. This has been done in a similar way for random hole autostereoscopic displays [204].

The fine structures necessary for an autostereoscopic light field display will lead to problems with wiring, concerning resistance and frequency response. A measure against this would be using a dedicated processor for each pixel array belonging to one lenslet (or a part of a lens stripe). This technology has recently been demonstrated by **Ostendo Technologies**.

The principle of lenticular stripes with many exit beams has also led to a variation using lenticular mirrors (and a projector) instead of lenticular lenses (Figure 9.49. This probably won't work in practice. However, a discussion is a good exercise for applying what we learned about the diffraction limit in Section 3.4.3.6 at page 79. The approach requires the projector to address different lines on curved mirror ribs in order to send beams to individual eyes of different viewers.

Consider ribs that are 1 mm wide (a normal pixel size for a display 2 m in size), a viewing and projection distance of 3 m and a viewing range that is 3 m wide. Addressing single eyes would require up to 100 separate beams per mirror rib, hence we would need the projector to focus a pixel at d=10 µm. This requires a projection lens of a $= 150$ mm (f $= 3$ m, $d = 10$ µm, $\lambda = 0.5$ µm), when applying the equation for lens resolution that has been discussed in Section 3.4.3.6 at page 79. This applies no matter if we use incoherent or laser light. Not only the projected beams have to be aligned by 10 µm (the resolution of an SLR lens, but this screen is 100 times larger), also the depth-of field would only be about 400 µm (see Section 3.4.3.7 at page 80). A hell of an alignment job, really.

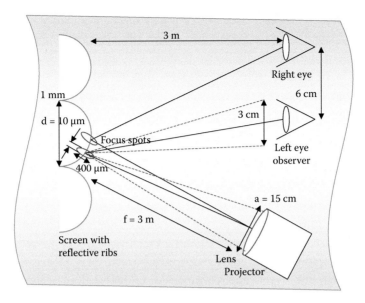

FIGURE 9.49 A proposed lenticular mirror projection display assembly (US pat.7843449B2), analyzed.

9.5.6.1 Diffractive Beam Forming

An approach presented by **Leia**, based on a research project by **Hewlett Packard**, uses an LCD SLM and a backlight with an array of diffraction gratings, concentrating the light for each pixel to a certain angular range. 64 distinct angles (subpixels per 3D pixel) are realized in the prototype. The approach is aimed at mobile phone displays (where the angular resolution requirements are comparably moderate).

9.5.6.2 Electrowetting Prisms and Other Approaches

Other approaches to adaptive light field displays are conceivable. For example, time multiplexed varieties wherein rays for different viewers are produced sequentially, perhaps also with an optical deflection unit directing the light of display elements directly toward the eyes.

Micromechanical mirrors can provide such a deflection, such as with the **TriLite** display (cf. Section 7.7 on page 277).

Another option is variable prisms of liquid crystals with electrically controllable refraction index [267]. We should be aware that liquid microprisms will not work like perfectly planar surfaces and will therefore cause fairly dispersed light beams, probably not addressing the eye specifically enough, except for close-up viewing.

9.6 COMPUTER-GENERATED HOLOGRAMS

We have discussed how holograms or even hologram movies can be recorded optically on photographic film in Section 5.5 at page 158. This is very similar to the recording of traditional pictures or motion pictures. Optical holograms clearly have been insufficient for interactivity. Therefore, the idea of building an interactive display for 3D pictures that is based on holographic principles has acquired a new momentum since computer and display technology opened up new possibilities. Directly recording a motion hologram in natural environments however, will always remain a dream because of the constraints of coherent light. Classical holographic stereograms that are optically recorded from digital content, such as regular images or movies (see Section 5.5.7 at page 169) enable (indirectly) the recording of natural environments (even outdoor environments). However, they are, as autostereoscopic postcard pictures, limited to short, noninteractive animation sequences.

Holographic stereographic displays based on self-developing photorefractive polymeric materials can be quickly re-recorded, as explained in Section 5.5.7 at page 169. If their update rates can be increased further, they represent a potential alternative to previous computer-generated holography (CGH) approaches. What could be realistic for 3DTV technology in the future is the recording of 3D or 2D data with several cameras (or the synthetic generation and rendering of 3D scenes via computer-graphics techniques) and the utilization of holographic techniques (among others) for their encoding and display. Hence, the "encoding" of CGHs has become an important research topic. An understanding of this issue is vital for the design of many future displays as well.

9.6.1 Displaying Computed Fringe Patterns

As we learned in Chapter 5, holographic fringe patterns usually have to be very dense, with a resolution between 0.2 μm and about 10 μm depending on the range of viewing angles to be supported. Photographic film supports this resolution easily.

For experimental setups of CGHs, DMDs or F-LCDs have been used to display computed fringe patterns, with pixel sizes of about 10 μm. SLMs (see Chapter 7) like DMDs and F-LCDs are available only in small sizes, because they are produced for other purposes. Progress in silicon technology however, already allows for structures much smaller than light wavelength, so really versatile holographic displays could be manufactured. Micromechanical piston-type SLMs (see Section 7.3.5 at page 254), producing embossed holograms, are promising alternatives. The total size of such SLMs is of course limited to the size of available silicon wafers ($8''$ ... $12''$ diagonal), and the mere possibility of displaying terapixel resolutions does not yet tell us how to deliver the data necessary to drive them.

9.6.2 Computing a Hologram

Let us first consider what a "brute force approach" to hologram synthesis from conventional 3D data would involve.

Assume we have a scene consisting of surface points. The further away scene objects are located from the holographic screen, the less resolution we need on the holographic screen to cover them. We illustrate this with a volume raster that expands in depth with an angle that corresponds to the viewing angle (e.g., that of a recording camera system or of a computer graphics camera). This is illustrated in Figure 9.50.

Now we have to compute the interference of all scene points (P) at every single screen pixel (q). The illustration in Figure 9.50 shows the virtual wavefront propagating from one scene point to one screen pixel. For determining the correct interference at q, however, we have to sum the interference valves that result from all non-occluded scene points P. Doing

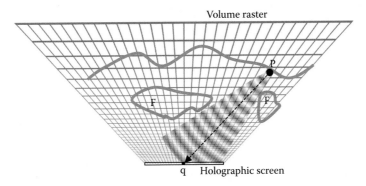

FIGURE 9.50 Holographic rendering with a volumetric raster expanding with distance.

this for all screen pixels results in a holographic diffraction (fringe) pattern that replays the scene holographically. It is obvious that this process is very complex. If we assume that the screen resolution N roughly matches the scene resolution (as above), then N^2 interference computations are required.

For $N = 1$ million screen pixels (very roughly four times the count of a low-resolution TV image), we would have to sum about 1 mio. x 1 mio. individual gray values. These gray values correspond to the amplitudes of the wavefronts from all P that are phase shifted differently when they arrive at q. It is necessary to find algorithms that reduce theses calculations by several orders. We may partly apply Fourier holograms (see Section 9.6.3 at page 402). We may also greatly parallelize the process. But let's develop this a little further:

Getting the wave amplitude that a scene point will cause at a given screen pixel involves calculating the proper distance between both, and then calculating the amplitude from this distance. The amplitude calculation at q can in principle be reduced to a simple lookup in a table that stores a sine wave function (assuming that the distance values are rounded to integers). Calculating the actual distances is not much more difficult, and is even supported by graphics hardware.

If we have the amplitudes of all scene points P at a screen pixel q we have only to compare their phases with the local phase of a virtual reference beam. This gives us information about constructive or destructive interference at q. Keep in mind that these are still about 1 mio. x 1 mio. operations in our example!

With current chips easily reaching billions of clock cycles per second, this is nothing exotic. Current high-end CPUs or graphics processor chips have up to one billion switching elements, this would result in 1000 per screen pixel. Actually, we may hardly need more than this.

High definition holograms would of course need about an order of magnitude more processing power, but even this is not too far fetched, and the brute force approach considered here is still far from optimal.

But there is still one more difficulty: Not all P/q combinations would contribute to the result, since certain background points are occluded by foreground objects F in certain areas of the holographic screen.

This masking of distant points is not simple, and actually represent the core challenge of algorithms for computer-generated holography. Computing mutual occlusion fast is very hard. Recent developments in graphics cards have bred graphics engines about as complex as a high-end CPU and a lot more powerful for specific jobs. These engines also contain circuitry dealing with occlusion, and they have already been successfully employed for hologram synthesis [307].

At least, our simple approach will not suffer from the self-interference (light scattered back from object surfaces) that haunts natural holograms and spoils them with noise (i.e., speckle). The digitally produced fringe patterns can also be further optimized to deliver less diffraction effects than natural ones.

While this section provided a brute force introductory example only, it has to be noted that there are many sophisticated CGH algorithms today that optimize quality and performance of diffraction pattern computations.

9.6.3 Fourier Hologram Synthesis

9.6.3.1 Diffraction Specific Holography

We will now consider an approach in between light fields and holography. This leads to a much simpler way of calculating holograms, and has also been exploited for the very first moving-picture holographic displays by Mark Lucente [180].

Consider a laser beam hitting a display pane. If we produce patterns of equidistant lines on the display, the light beam gets diffracted according to the already discussed grating equation (see Section 5.3.1 at page 129).

By overlaying many patterns of different pitch and amplitude, we can divert the beam into many exit beams of different angles and amplitudes (Figure 9.51). It is of course possible this way to vary the amount of light that a certain viewer's eye, at a certain position, gets from any point on the display. This is not the same as calculating a hologram by simulation of interference. Instead, this is more similar to generating a light field.

In [180], a short holographic area element of this kind is called a *hogel* (holographic element), and the sum of overlaid line patterns in it is called a *fringelet*.

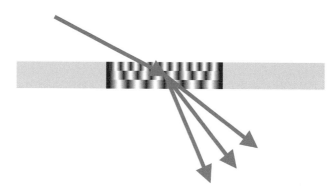

FIGURE 9.51 Several line patterns of different frequencies overlaid, causing several diffracted exit beams at different angles.

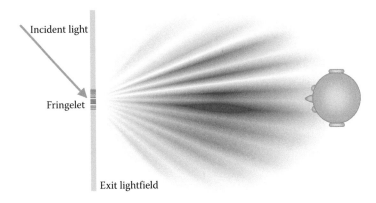

FIGURE 9.52 A hogel with a fringelet resulting in a complex exit light field.

As the pitch (or frequency) of any of the single line patterns constituting a fringelet translates into a certain exit beam angle, the frequency spectrum of the fringelet translates into an intensity curve over the exit angle (Figure 9.52). This is nothing but a Fourier transform (the intensity curve being the spectrum of the fringelet). We therefore refer to a holographic display made up of such fringelets as a *Fourier hologram*.

A complete light field display is made up of many small hogels covering the entire display plane, each of them working like a lenslet of a "conventional" light field display.

While Lucente used 1D hogels constituting a display similar to the lenticular stripe light field approach, the principle works in 2D as well. The computing effort for such a display is much less that for a "full" hologram, particularly as the Fast Fourier Transform algorithm (FFT) can be used here.

The size of the hogels must be small enough not to be recognized individually for a given viewing distance from the display. A sufficient angular resolution for the exit beams may however be achieved by much smaller fringelets in many cases. This can be exploited by computing fringelets of the required size and filling the hogel with several repetitions of them (Figure 9.53).

The fringelets themselves can further be optimized if necessary, for example in order to remove redundancies and to enable the application of compression algorithms. Figure 9.54 shows an approach used, which is based on a Gerchberg–Saxton iterative optimization algorithm [95]).

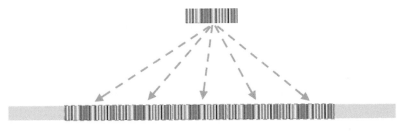

FIGURE 9.53 One fringelet is replicated multiple times to fill the entire hogel area.

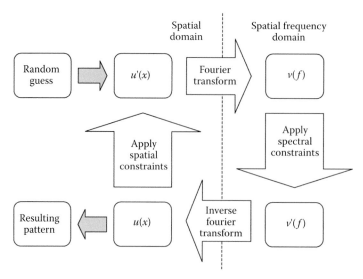

FIGURE 9.54 Iterative fringelet optimization algorithm according to [180].

So this may be a realistic approach to holographic encoding for 3D video recording, especially so as for most scenes, the light field portions emitted from adjacent picture elements (hogels) will have a certain amount of similarity.

The only practical display application of Fourier holograms today, however, is with projection displays (see Section 7.10.9 at page 294).

9.6.4 Adaptive Holographic Displays

Another type of CGH displays was presented in [109,238] (Figure 9.55). The available information leaves some details to the imagination, but the main idea is as follows:

Manny small zone plates (see Section 5.3 at page 127) are displayed on a high-density LC display. These zone plates act as lenslets and form virtual image points at their focus points.

In Section 5.4.10 at page 155, we have seen that the parts of a hologram actually seen by any single observer's eyes are comparably tiny – hardly bigger than an eye pupil. Everything

FIGURE 9.55   20″ adaptive holographic displays. Image courtesy: **SeeReal** Technologies GmbH.

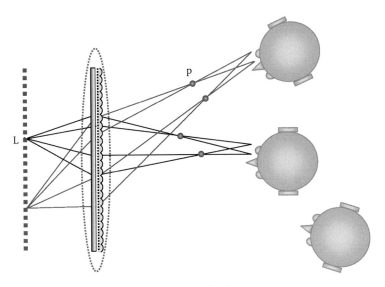

FIGURE 9.56   Principle of an adaptive holographic display.

else is superfluous. By calculating only those patches of a hologram seen by the eyes of a particular observer greatly reduces the complexity of CGH.

It should be pointed out that the actual implementation in Figure 9.55 supports a horizontal parallax only. The claim that this approach also produces proper focus is therefore only half true.

In the following, we will try to analyze the necessary requirements for such a display, as well as the achievable performance figures. Our analysis does not necessarily apply to any particular product. It is mainly intended as a guideline on how such approaches can be assessed.

Figure 9.56 shows the working scheme of an adaptive holographic display. A moving, coherent light source L (or an array of switched light sources) is located behind a transmissive LC screen with a full area Fresnel lens (symbolized by the dotted oval).

In the ideal case, the Fresnel lens roughly concentrates the light of one of the sources to just one eye of one of the users. The LC display here causes parts of the beam to converge at (and also diverge from) different distances, forming optical point (p) in space.

In the following, we assume an LC SLM with cells whose refraction index can be changed. Thus, the transition time t through the display can be varied. Such SLMs exist based on LCoS, but although possible, there is no large scale product availability up to now. The real implementation from Figure 9.55 therefore uses an amplitude modulating SLM. But we will omit this complication, as it is not principally necessary for our considerations.

With the SLM, holographic lenses can be formed, causing the beam to converge or diverge. In Figure 9.57, it converges and forms an optical point that for a distant observer appears in front of the screen. If the beam is shaped to diverge, points behind the screen can be generated.

Note that the actual display, in contrary to this schematic drawing, has a thickness of many wavelengths, allowing minor refraction index changes to sufficiently modulate the beam's

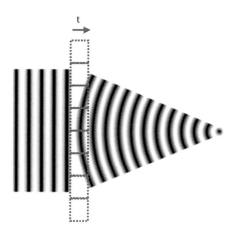

FIGURE 9.57 Beam concentration by refraction index variation.

phase. It is not sufficient, however, to do this for any "lens" size and thickness just by letting the refraction index rise or fall continuously from center to edge. Instead, a zone-plate-like holographic fringe pattern is generated. Hence, the display forms a phase hologram.

Figure 9.58 shows the image-point rendering with an adaptive holographic display. Here we see how tiny virtual lenses (*s*) form image points by beam shaping. One obstacle toward the realization of this principle is the SLM's pixel size. While for minor angular modulations, a pixel size much larger than wavelength should suffice to form a hologram, we see that if large viewing angles are required, part of the display area seen will always be hit by the wave fronts at an angle that normally would require hologram patterns nearly as fine as the wavelength (see Section 5.3.8 at page 140).

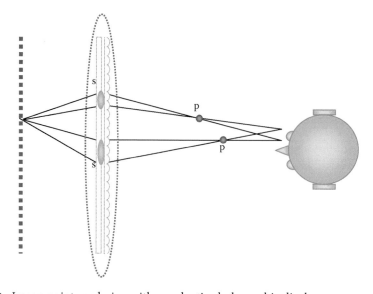

FIGURE 9.58 Image-point rendering with an adaptive holographic display.

FIGURE 9.59   Principle fringe density variation.

Figure 9.59 shows the light path from one light source through the display's large Fresnel lens (here symbolized by an actual lens shape) toward the user's eye. The very different pattern sizes from center to edge, caused by the wave hitting the display area, are obvious.

Two questions arise:

- Can we accomplish a holographic effect, even if one display pixel is much larger than these patterns?

- Can parts of a coherent wavefront passing through "large" adjacent pixels even inter-fere at all? So far, we have argued that any point in the hologram acts as a single point light source emitting a spherical wave. Pixels much larger than wavelength are not point-like.

Here we should remember what we have learned about beam divergence in Section 3.5.2 at page 85. Light from a small source (e.g., a display pixel) cannot form a "straight" beam, instead there will be some divergence depending on the source size.

In Figure 9.60 we have illustrated what happens to light passing through three adjacent pixels of, in this example, 20 μm in size. At one meter distance, the light passing through them has already deviated to 3 cm. Thus the light from these pixels interferes in a fairly wide (three centimeters) area – much larger than a human pupil. This area is of course dependent on distance. If we get closer to the display, we may have an area of just six millimeters at a viewing distance of 20 cm. This is still sufficiently large to cover a human pupil. If we get further away, we may arrive at six centimeters, at a viewing distance of two meters. Because we don't want the light destined for one pupil to also reach the other eye, we can't allow for a lot more. This somewhat limits the possible observer distance. It also shows that a somewhat large pixel size in this application is actually necessary, because it determines the useful observer distance range: smaller pixels cause more beam divergence, hence work, for smaller viewing distances only.

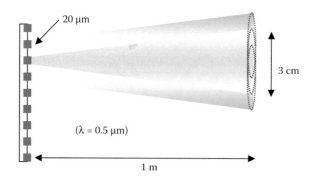

FIGURE 9.60 Pixel beam divergence and merging.

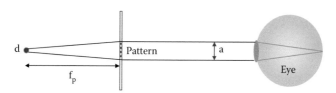

FIGURE 9.61 Effective pattern area.

The area on the display screen forming an image point depends on the point's position and on the eye's pupil diameter (Figure 9.61). For a distant point behind the screen, the pupil diameter a is the limiting factor, since all rays in this case have to arrive at the eye in parallel order to focus on the retina.

For a point appearing between infinite behind the screen and half the observer distance in front of the screen, for example, this effective area diameter is even lower than the pupil diameter (Section 5.4.10 at page 155). In order to get consistent interference over this area, the phase shift should vary as little as possible. The maximum phase shift will occur with those screen pixels located at the edge of the contributing area, since here the deviation from perpendicularity is largest.

In Figure 9.62 we have assumed a pupil diameter of two millimeters (typical at medium bright light) and a relatively close screen distance of 20 cm (which is about the worst condition for this parameter). We can easily see that the phase deviation over an edge pixel would be 0.1 µm, or $^1/_4$ wavelength of blue light. Not really ideal, but sufficient to allow for an unambiguous interference of wavefronts from all screen pixels involved.

In case of multiple observers, secondary diffraction modes from one observer's picture elements may reach the eye of another observer. In this case it would help to change the light-source location for the first observer a little bit, and compensate this displacement by adapting the holographic pattern. The secondary modes will then have a different distribution, which may solve the problem. This is the reason why the light source in the display is movable or switchable.

In the case of too many observers, this may become difficult. Nevertheless each observer needs additional time slots, so their number is somewhat limited.

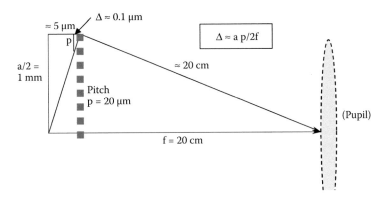

FIGURE 9.62 Intra pixel phase deviation.

But will the large screen pixels still work as intended at the screen edges, where wavefronts are highly slanted, approaching the pixel with different phases at different parts? Figure 9.63 shows two pixels, for the rectangular and the slanted case. The upper pixel has a higher refraction index. A light bundle will pass almost unaltered a pixel that is much larger than the wavelength; only a certain general phase shift will occur, according to the voltage applied. Relative phase shifting between adjacent pixels will work similarly to the perpendicular case, only the phase shift will be somewhat different, according to path length and so forth.

Again, it is necessary to have pixels that are larger than the wavelength for this to work. The same applies when adapting to observer movements by switching light sources, and correcting the angular stepping error by hologram modulation: we have to care only about phase deviations actually contributing to the light bundle entering the eye.

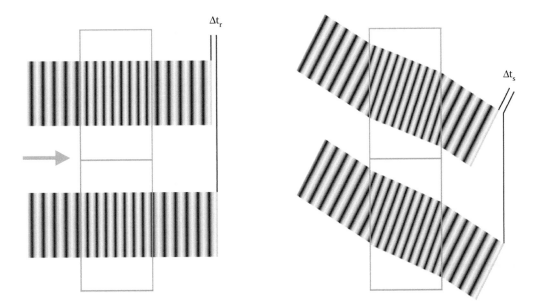

FIGURE 9.63 Interpixel phase stepping for perpendicular (left) and slanted beams (right).

A switched array of red, green and blue LEDs could work for the illumination, better in some aspects than truly coherent light. The LEDs, however, have to be very small, about 20 μm maybe, which in practice will make this difficult (see Section 5.3.10 at page 143). Yet as only one of these LEDs would be active at a time, a simple wire matrix could be used to address them. Another type of illumination would use the spot of a typical lightshow laser beamer, directed to a reflecting screen behind the display. This way, sufficiently fast and bright coherent light could be generated economically. Since a large part of the source light is concentrated just to the observer's eyes, the effectiveness of the display is better than that of a classical panel.

9.6.4.1 Discussion

A display that changes refraction index will only need an additional brightness modulation, as all of the light is either used to form the desired image, or the rest of it has to be deflected somewhere, causing a lot of stray light. This indicates an advantage for amplitude-modulated displays, although we also know that the effectiveness of an amplitude hologram is very poor.

The complexity in the case of an adaptive holographic display is reduced by roughly a factor of 10,000 compared to the brute force CGH technique described above (if we consider the image generation for one eye of one observer only), and even more so with HPO cases. Compared with conventional displays, however, the necessary pixel count is still about 100 times higher, and with any additional observer, this number increases.

For example, with 7500x10000 pixels (20″ diagonal and 40 μm pixel size and six sequential color images per eye pair, we already get a raw data rate of 100 gigabits per viewer. Currently, such approaches still need lots of hardware consuming unacceptable amounts of electrical power.

9.7 3D MEDIA ENCODING

We will now consider another important aspect of 3D displays: Using holographic or similar representations for the actual encoding or compression of 3D image data for signal transport. This topic is most naturally connected to light fields and light field encoding, being just another (but maybe easier) approach to principally the same thing.

One brute force option for 3D media encoding is to reconstruct the entire scene geometry and light-modulation properties. This might be an option for scenes that are entirely computer generated, and where this information is actually defined.

For recorded natural scenes at least, the easiest way might be to encode the actual visible light from the objects, their light field in essence, just to an accuracy that a human observer could see.

9.7.1 Light Field Encoding

Light field data can also be compressed and used as an efficient way of 3D image encoding. For this purpose, simple similarities between the light bundles of adjacent pixels can be exploited, encoding only difference values for the missing ones. Knowledge about the original scene is not necessary for such a compression. In [174] a first approach of this type has been shown (together with a second, entropic compression step).

Light field encoding is an alternative to holographic encoding (described later). Where holographic encoding can reduce data by use of larger wavelengths and fringe pattern compression, light field encoding can use neighborhood similarities.

Light fields can, in principle, also be converted into holograms and back (see Section 9.5.2 on page 390), but we have to take into account their different properties. If we have light field data, for example, we cannot directly calculate holographic fringe patterns for scenery points because the light field rays do not tell us anything about the distance to the scene point they originated from. Hence, we would have to search through the light ray data to find rays originating from the same scene points, and reconstruct the entire scene (see Section 9.6.2 on page 400). A Fourier hologram as described in Section 9.6.3 on page 402 could be obtained much simpler, by generating separate patches of hologram patterns for any pixel of the light field image.

9.7.2 Camera Array (Multiview) Encoding

If we abandon any attempt at object or scene geometry reconstruction from multiple camera images, and only try to encode several camera channels in an efficient way, there is a far simpler approach.

Pictures from neighboring cameras show similarities identical to those in a time sequence from a single camera move. Classical motion encoding (MPEG) can therefore encode such a sequence with ease, as illustrated in Figure 9.64.

In this simplified example, similarities over the X axis of the array are exploited first (i.e., in each row individually). Then the X-compounds are compressed in Y direction, with the sole complication being that some meta data has to be treated as well. Finally, the entire compound including all meta data, is further encoded by exploiting similarities over the time axis (T).

A method like this is not intelligent image processing (i.e., one that identifies objects in the scene), and it will also not deliver any hint about depth. Its only purpose is to encode all camera pictures for later retrieval. Intermediate perspectives would have to be interpolated at playback time. But this can be simplified by the similarity information derived for the available encoding.

A compression method quite similar to this principle has been standardized already (H.264 MVC, multiview coding). It uses interleaved horizontal and time encoding (the principle shown in Figure 9.65). As H.264 uses forward and backward prediction (similarity) vectors, I-frames (full images), P-frames (partial image content) and B-Frames (difference only) are calculated forward and backward in two dimensions. Real implementations normally use many more B-frames, at least in the time axis. Fundamentals are presented in [265] and [195]. The MVC standard (whose details are not crucial for our topic) is engineered for backward compatibility with 2D H.264 (HD and BluRay encoding). Partly because of this, a stereo picture stream is still about 1.5 times larger than a 2D stream.

The scheme shown is for lateral multiview only but could be extended with a vertical dimension.

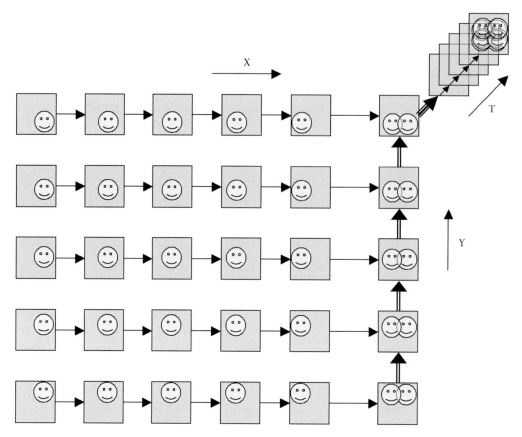

FIGURE 9.64   A basic encoding scheme for camera array recordings.

Because H.264 encoding (very similar to MPEG but more efficient) relies on finding motion vectors between adjacent frames, it already delivers prerequisites for deriving intermediate perspectives.

9.7.3 Holographic Millimeter-Wave Encoding

The diffraction patterns of a hologram contain a great deal of redundancy. In turn, they are able to deliver a resolution limited only by the wavelength of light. A large screen image with 1/1000 mm resolution, however, doesn't make much sense.

With a very small screen, like a keyhole hologram (Section 5.4.11 at page 157), the entire fringe pattern can be reduced to a complexity not much larger than a corresponding 2D picture. This is, however, confined to applications where we can view the hologram through a magnifier, such as near-eye displays, for example (Chapter 10).

But we could benefit from this kind of compression for large holograms, if we could just use a larger wavelength. This won't deliver an optical hologram that could be directly viewed, but it could be a method of 3D scene encoding.

A real millimeter-wave hologram could theoretically be taken by a large array of micro antennas and wouldn't even need a reference beam because these antennas could work directly with an electrical reference frequency, and a complete hologram could be read out

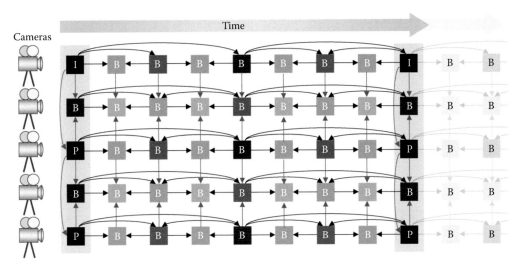

FIGURE 9.65 Principle of multiview encoding adapted to current compression standards.

from the array, as with a giant camera chip. Such waves go through many things that are impenetrable for light (such as clothing, for example).

One way to derive a proper millimeter-wave hologram could be by taking a regular (light) hologram and then enlarging the fringe patterns synthetically (i.e., as if they were recorded with longer waves, $^1/_2$ millimeter perhaps instead of $^1/_2$ micrometer waves).

As optical holograms are rarely at hand, this approach may remain just theory however. The only way of scene recording may again be to use camera arrays and intelligent image processing, and to deliver a 3D model of the scene as a basis for hologram computation.

Such a hologram would essentially carry all superficial and spatial information, yet with less detail resolution, in the order of $^1/_2$ mm, only as much as we need for a large, apparently sharp, natural holographic image. The reduction factor that we achieve in this case is about one million.

Let us regard the properties of this encoding method a bit further. As explained in Section 5.4.10 at page 155, a certain image point (d) can be represented only by a specific area of fringes (actually a tiny zone plate, as shown in Figure 9.61 on page 408).

In Section 3.4.3.6 at page 79 we have already explained that the resolution a lens (and therefore a zone plate) can deliver is $d \approx \lambda f / a$.

In case of a millimeter-wave encoding scheme, the decoding algorithm would have to analyze a much larger area of the hologram, somehow equaling a virtual lens nearly as large as the screen (Figure 9.66). This is necessary to retrieve image points at a sufficient resolution (if $f = a$, then $d \approx \lambda$).

This cannot be carried out all the way, because a very large virtual lens would render perspectives and geometries different from those seen from one single point (in the extreme case, a small near object could be seen from all sides at once). Corrections would have to be applied to get back to a natural result. Another difficulty would be remote objects that can only be seen through gaps between more proximate objects, as these could be properly

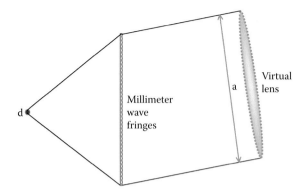

FIGURE 9.66 Effective pattern size with virtual millimeter-wave hologram.

represented only with a higher resolution. It may be necessary to correct for this, for example, by partially inserting layers with smaller wavelengths.

Adding color will in principle increase the complexity of holographic encoding by less than $^1/_4$, because we can just add two color difference channels of half or even quarter resolution, as with classical video (here, half the wavelength).

Holographic millimeter-wave encoding is a relatively new topic, but apart from being published as an idea [111], it has also been explored and verified experimentally [307].

9.8 SUMMARY

We have taken a quite comprehensive look at 3D display varieties. All of them exhibit problems of some sort, and none of them provide what we would consider a life-like 3D experience.

Some of them require the observer to occupy a certain viewing position or sweet-spot area, and even to hold his/her head straight. Even worse, others types will cause headaches because of false convergence and accommodation conditions.

A huge obstacle for the general applicability of 3D display technology is the inflexibility with respect to size and perspective. Modern media should work on a mobile phone display as well as on a wall-sized screen.

The solution to the above mentioned problems will be computerized image processing. Computers have already overcome any format restrictions in conventional productions. In getting rid of formats, a generic description of recorded 3D scenes is called for, that later on produces a device-independent performance, and synthesizes in realtime whatever the desired display arrangement requires.

The acceptance of 3D for large screen-displays will most probably become a lot more acceptable if any viewer is provided his own custom-tailored perspective. We have seen that there is a possibility for an affordable implementation, as a multi-user adaptive light field display.

Tracking of viewers avoids unnecessary rendering and can thus be seen as an advantage, since all computational and display resources can be assigned to the present observers.

TABLE 9.1   Computational Complexity of Spatial 3D Displays

Perspectives	2	2	p	p	n	n
Parallax	H	H+V	H	H+V	H	H+V
Stereoscopic displays	$2n^2$	$2n^2$	pn^2	pn^2	–	–
Parallax displays	$2n^2$	$2n^2$	pn^2	pn^2	–	–
Volumetric displays	n^3	n^3	n^3	n^3	n^3	n^3
Light field displays	$2n^2$	$2n^2$	pn^2	pn^2	n^3	n^4
Holographic displays	$2n^4$	$2n^4$	pn^4	pn^4	n^5	n^6

n = number of display elements (pixels, voxels) in 1 dimension.

Currently, stereo capable TVs are in fashion mainly because adding a time sequential stereo capability has become extremely economical, at least if the display is fast. Many of these displays will run in 2D mode most or all of the time due to the lack of 3D content, but the mere presence of 3D capabilities may induce a creeping change here.

Table 9.1 provides an estimate on the increasing complexity of the various spatial 3D display technologies that have been discussed in this chapter.

Note that for stereoscopic displays, for adaptive light field displays, and for adaptive holographic displays, p is always a multiple of two, while for parallax displays multiple eyes can share the same viewing zone. Our estimate on computational complexity is proportional to scene rendering (if we assume that ray tracing is used) and required display speed (which also depends on number of perspectives and resolution per perspective). Table 9.1 assumes interactive displays that process 3D content in realtime. Interactive light field displays and holographic displays are most complex.

As the number of separate angles served per pixel should be in the order of the pixel count itself for a smooth light field, we get order n^3 for a horizontal (H) or n^4 for a full (H + V) parallax light field. Note that we approximate computational complexity by the (sub-) pixel count here, as any subpixel exactly corresponds to one outgoing light ray.

Estimates for interactive holograms are about n to n^2 times larger than for interactive light fields, since we would need prohibitive amounts of performance to compute a fringe pattern. The simplest way known so far is patch-wise construction from hogels (Section 9.5.2 at page 390). The hologram patches (fringelets) correspond to the macro pixels of a (e.g., lenticular) light field display. We would need a weighed sum of n^2 hogels for each fringelet, resulting in a whopping n^6 sub pixel operations for the whole display. For large holograms, creating the fringelets by a FFT of a corresponding light field display pixel may be a better choice: the 1D FFT has a complexity of $O(n \log_2(n))$, a 2D FFT has $O(n^2 \log_2(n))$. Depending on the actual meaning of O, we may get away with approximately n^3 for the 2D fringelet and n^5 for the entire display, hence about one order of magnitude less. Even with the best approaches known so far, interactive holographic displays are therefore not likely candidates for real displays, especially as a light field can deliver the same optical impression.

However, if we consider pre-rendered or pre-recorded content and omit interactivity, light field displays and CGHs become more efficient since content does not have to be computed in realtime. In case of adaptive or full-resolution light field displays, 4D lookup operations and interpolations are the most complex tasks for rendering and display that have to be carried out, if the light field itself is present. Yet, full 4D light field tables (possibly compressed) would have to be transmitted always for each frame. For holographic displays, only the pre-computed 2D fringe patterns (possibly compressed) have to be transmitted per frame. An adaptation would not be required in this case, since all perspectives would be supported without additional overhead. Only time for decompression has to be considered for light field and holographic content transmission. Yet, this is proportional to their resolutions. Thus, for light fields, 4D tables have to be transmitted while for CHGs 2D fringe patterns are sufficient. The apparent lower complexity of CGHs, however, is misleading if the practical resolution of the data is not taken into account. As we learned earlier, the SLM elements that are required for CGHs are approximately three orders of magnitude smaller than those of ordinary SLMs used for the other display approaches. This means that the 2D fringe patterns at this high resolution would require about as much memory and transmission bandwidth as 4D light fields.

If the content can be stored and transmitted more efficiently (e.g., using 3D datasets) and the rendering on the display side is fast enough (e.g., light field rendering or fringe computations from 3D data), then interactive displays might be most efficient even for static content. As explained above, light field displays will most likely be more efficient for this than holographic displays.

Table 9.2 summarizes different capabilities for 3D content presentation of the various 3D displays. Some are capable of providing an immersive surround presentation, while others enable a walk-around/look-inside experience. Near-eye displays can provide both, simulating surroundings as well as objects, and they support mobile applications, including mobile augmented reality. Theoretically, other display types also support mobile applications, such as recent parallax displays in mobile phones, but they are rather exotic.

Note that a missing tick in Table 9.2 does not necessarily mean that a particular presentation form is not theoretically possible. It rather indicates that it is not likely to be efficient.

In the long run, it might become possible that all kinds of 3D display are seamlessly integrated into an augmented environment. Augmented reality is a paradigm that takes human-computer interfaces beyond spatial screens. Near-eye displays might become the dominant display technology for augmented reality in the future. It supports all presentation forms, as can be seen in Table 9.2. Today, hand-held mobile devices, such as phones, are favored by many because this technology is mature and available to everyone. However, small screens on portable devices will not be a replacement for any spatial screen technology. We will discuss near-eye displays in the next chapter.

TABLE 9.2   Presentation Forms of Spatial 3D Displays vs. Near-Eye Displays

Presentation	Window	Look-inside	Surround	Mobile
Stereoscopic displays	✓		✓	
Parallax displays	✓		✓	
Volumetric displays		✓		
Light field displays	✓	✓	✓	
Holographic displays	✓	✓	✓	
Near-eye displays	✓	✓	✓	✓

CHAPTER 10

Near-Eye Displays (NED)

10.1 INTRODUCTION

Recent mobile phones seem able to replace a PC, a video camera, an ebook reader, a navigator, anything. But how to use all their features in a convenient and efficient way? This technology is facing substantial challenges that increase with the complexity of its applications. The usability of small displays is very limited and large displays are inconvenient for mobile applications.

Technology may soon be improving and changing. Spatial screens could be eliminated in favor of near-eye displays, glasses with a tiny addition that could weigh less than 20 g, and could allow for a multitude of new applications.

Displays of this kind may at some point replace most of today's user interface hardware, screens, keypads (eye steering can turn them into ideal input devices as well), entire installations, and they will do a lot more.

Virtual objects and virtual devices, essentially images that are dynamically generated by powerful but tiny displays sitting right near the eye, could be seamlessly integrated into the real environment, registering with real objects, creating entirely new applications and usage habits.

Desktops mapped to a computer screen could be replaced by operating system surfaces mapped to the real world, linking real objects with information, readily available anywhere and anytime.

The most common term for these kind of applications is augmented reality (AR). Research in this specific field has been ongoing for almost two decades now, but only recently are light and versatile display glasses becoming feasible.

Figure 10.1 shows the principle of a basic near-eye display. Figure 10.2 shows an early but yet very advanced near-eye-display as used in a high-end military deep-flight simulator. It includes most of the desired features that will be discussed later on. Although this was used in a simulator only, fighter-jet pilots today always use some form of AR display, to accompany the head-up display (HUD) on the plane.

For successful consumer applications, however, a light, versatile, and robust display is needed that supports several essential technical features, as we will see in the following sections.

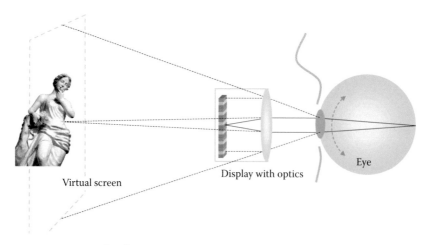

FIGURE 10.1 Basic principle of a near-eye display: a miniature display and optics project directly into the eye, creating a virtual screen. Actual implementations use a large variety of different configurations and technologies, displaying multiple screens or objects, and merging them with the observer's view at the real world.

FIGURE 10.2 1993: HMD for out-of-cockpit view, **Tornado** Simulator; quad LCD projectors coupled by fiber optics, head and eye tracking, high resolution inlays (equivalent resolution 4096 × 4096), field of view 82° × 66° per eye, 33° overlapping [40]. Image courtesy: **CAE** Elektronik GmbH.

Perfect designs should deliver good images regardless of eye movements, incorrect fit, focus, and aperture effects. Moreover, they should not impair direct sight, and they should have very high resolution and support a large *field of view* (FOV). The FOV is an important parameter for NED. It is either specified in degrees horizontal and vertical, or in degrees diagonal.

A near-eye display for everyday applications will have to work without any fixtures to the head exceeding that of simple eyeglasses.

A special requirement in many applications will be a mask display, making virtual objects appear nontransparent by selectively covering the direct view.

For AR applications, fit adaptation and dynamic focus setting, as well as dynamic perspective and registered image generation, can be directed by eye trackers integrated into the display glasses. These could also serve new eye-steered applications.

Another requirement for AR glasses is position sensing. GPS allows this globally, while cameras mounted to the display assembly support this locally and with a high precision.

The **Microsoft Hololens** has most of the orientation features (see Figure 10.3). Behind the front shield are several cameras used for orientation. The device also has inertia sensors, sound, and a number of other features. The FOV is limited, however, and although it is light, it is not yet as easily wearable as some normal eyeglasses. For a closer look at the display itself, see Figure 10.54 at page 466.

Most of the above equally applies to VR applications, where, contrary to AR, the natural view is excluded and the user immerses completely into a virtual scenery. VR has recently gained new momentum in gaming applications. More applications will be possible with the development of convenient and affordable displays. As VR displays can be seen as AR displays without the see-through feature, we will not treat them entirely separate but come back to them wherever appropriate with individual display technology topics.

This chapter will discuss the most relevant aspects of near-eye displays. To a great part it is based on [116], where a comprehensive treatment of AR and additional detail on related technology can be found.

In Sections 10.2 and 10.3 we first compare eye physiology with brightness and power consumption in relation to near-eye displays. We review SLM technologies that can be used

FIGURE 10.3 2015: **Microsoft Hololens** see-through HMD. Features advanced orientation hardware, sound, and diffractive optics. FOV 30 × 17.5°. (Used with permission from **Microsoft** [https://news.microsoft.com/microsoft-hololens-press-materials/]).

for such devices in Section 10.4 at page 423 before we provide various examples for currently applied display principles in Section 10.5 at page 425. Section 10.7 at page 431 outlines today's optical designs and identifies additional requirements for efficient near-eye display development. Laser-based near-eye displays are explained in Section 10.9 at page 445, and differences to spatial displays with respect to consistent focus and accommodation are presented in Section 10.11 at page 452. Holographic image generation principles for near-eye displays are presented in Section 10.13 at page 461 and classical and advanced optical combiners for such systems are reviewed in Section 10.6 at page 428. Section 10.15 at page 470 explains limitations of future contact lens displays. Finally, Sections 10.16 and 10.17 discuss adaptive display solutions and advanced image integration techniques.

Note that many points that are treated in this chapter are theoretical, because this technology is still in development. Nevertheless it is developing rapidly and warrants a comprehensive treatment.

10.2 EYE PHYSIOLOGY

Let us recall some facts about human vision (see Chapter 4) and its impact on near-eye display design.

1) Our eyes can see sharply only at the center of view. We don't normally notice it, but any time we want to see anything clearly, we will direct our eyes to it. Larger scenes are perceived by quick eye movements (saccades) between certain points of interest. Other details may simply be overlooked this way.

A perfectly sharp display would need 3600×3600 pixels for $60° \times 60°$ field of view. Outside the very center of view, eye resolution becomes extremely blurry in comparison. For the design of near-eye displays, the most interesting consequence is that clarity is necessary at the center of view only. Anything else can be unsharp. If we could adjust focus dynamically and quickly, according to viewing direction, we could use a display with "bad'" optics that would never have to be sharp over its entire area.

Tracking the eye position is necessary for this, and a dynamic adaptation of focus and geometry correction of the displayed image. This effort gives many degrees of freedom with display design. A display that is never overall crisp, nor free of geometrical distortions, could actually be a very smart solution.

Eye movements can be very fast, so a fast eye tracker is necessary to follow them, faster than a usual camera. Eye tracker cameras don't need high resolution, but should have frame rates between 200 and 1000 Hz. An eye tracker could also be used to reduce bandwidth in communications, or computing effort with image synthesis as in games or object oriented 3D image synthesis, by rendering optimally only those image parts that are currently being viewed.

2) An important feature of the human eye is its very large field of view, over $180°$ horizontally (see Section 4.4.1 at page 109). We won't need to achieve a span this wide for a near-eye display construction, but with smart optics or an adaptive system, a very wide field of view may be covered.

3) We can see over a tremendous range of light intensity, from about 1/1000 lux (starlight) up to 100,000 lux (sunlight). While video applications are quite modest in brightness

requirements, displays for integrating objects into reality have to provide them with due brightness. Fortunately near-eye displays are small, so power consumption is not a big problem.

We can summarize that although the human eye is quite good at seeing, from the point of view of a classical optics design, it's a mess. All the exceptional viewing ability we have is actually accomplished primarily in the brain, and it would be impossible to achieve even a fraction of our brain/eye capabilities with a conventional camera design.

The major challenge with today's display goggles is the attempt to perfect optical design. This doesn't work well. The device gets heavy, the field of view remains small, and the optics literally have to be screwed to the head, mainly to match the exit pupils.

For full-fledged AR applications, dynamic focusing is a requirement. Most 3D systems cause headache because the apparent stereoscopic distance seen does not match the required eye-focus adaptation. A dynamic focusing system should solve this problem by changing focus according to the distances of objects seen virtually. We will address this in Section 10.11 at page 452. The system also has to compensate for image-size changes related to dynamic focusing and for image position changes caused by eye movements and position changes of the glasses toward the head. No fixtures should be necessary anymore. As we can see sharply only in a little area around the center of view, a display with eye trackers would not require an optical design delivering a crisp image at all points. It could be dynamically focused on the area being looked at, and only this area would have to be crisply rendered. Optical distortion should be compensated electronically, resulting in simpler, lighter, and more affordable optics.

For applications aimed mainly at information display and distant objects, the optics could be designed for infinite focus distance and for a very large exit pupil (see Sections 10.7.1, 10.7.2 at page 434. This does not enable full AR but at least offers all capabilities of current smartphone applications, with improved usability.

Finally, display glasses should not disturb normal sight at all, yet offer the capability to project virtual images over the entire field of view. This sounds ambitious but is already close to being achieved with quite conventional optics, by placing the displays to the side or over the eyebrows, out of view, and mirroring the picture before the eyes.

10.3 BRIGHTNESS AND POWER CONSUMPTION

For virtual displays (e.g., optical display images that are produced by near-eye displays), similar measures apply as for real (i.e., physical) displays. The brightness induced on the retina may, however, be a better suited parameter.

We may compare the radiant density of a given scene and the brightness (illuminance) of its image on the retina. For a given natural scene covering the entire viewing area, the average energy density at the surface of the scene exactly equals the energy density at the pupil. Hence we can simply calculate the energy reaching the retina by the area relation between pupil and retina (Figure 10.4). The illuminance (in lux) on the retina can be compared directly to results from real displays.

The light power required for a near-eye display follows straightforwardly from the fact that bright sunlight has about 1 kW/m^2 and that our pupil has less than 2 mm of diameter

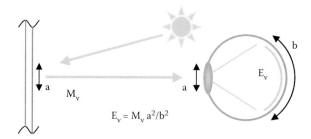

FIGURE 10.4 Brightness of virtual displays.

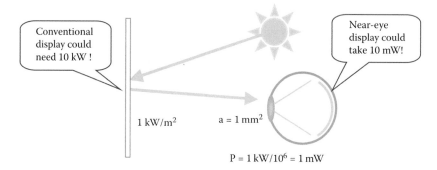

FIGURE 10.5 Calculation of light intensity on the retina.

in this situation, hence an area of approximately 1 mm². In an evenly illuminated scene, this obviously casts about 1 mW of light power into the eye (Figure 10.5). The brightness corresponding to 1 kW/m² is about 100,000 lux.

Given the fact that virtual objects cover only part of the viewing area, we need between 0.05 mW and 0.5 mW of actual light power entering the eye, even in daylight situations, A large flat-panel screen would need kilowatts for this. Indoors, we have to deal with 100 or 1000 times less brightness.

The ratio between electrical power and light output can vary between 5% and 30%, and depending on display type, between 1% and >50% of the light would then actually enter the eye, which gives a wide variation of possible results. We could nevertheless conclude that an average electrical power in the milliwatt range would be sufficient for the display, even in relatively bright environments.

We see that near-eye displays can not only be 1000 times lighter, but they can also draw several thousand times less energy than any classical large screen or even a hand-held screen display.

In addition, fast changing technology obsoletes equipment every two to five years. Throwing away some 30 g of display glasses is much more economical and ecologically sound than dumping a 30 kg large-screen display. A single well-designed AR device can also replace hundreds of conventional screens and other hardware objects; these considerations make near-eye displays a real progress.

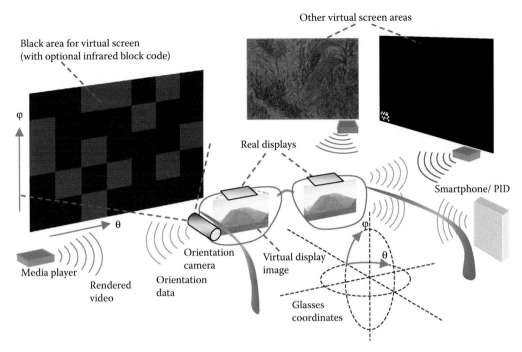

FIGURE 10.6   Simulation and registration of virtual display screens with distributed content sources.

Figure 10.6 illustrates how an NED could replace several large screen displays, without interfering with the user's direct view (because the displays are fixed to real locations). The displays can be freely positioned on several types of real object or surfaces, provided these are not too bright. The content displayed can be supplied by the NED device, but also by several external sources.

10.4 DISPLAY TECHNOLOGIES FOR NEAR-EYE DISPLAYS

Near-eye displays require display solutions with small pixel sizes (in contrast to spatial displays), light weight and low power drain. The following overview is a partial list of favorable display types and their specific properties. The individual SLM technology has been discussed in detail in Chapter 7.

LCD (Liquid Crystal Displays): Very small pixels are difficult to achieve (the minimum thickness of the LC fluid, necessary for polarization turn, sets some limits). They may be a first solution for mask displays, which will be discussed in Section 10.17.3 at page 487.

LCoS (Liquid Crystal on Silicon), need an LC layer only half as thick as LCD (because they work on a reflective basis), allowing for smaller pixels. They are already favored in many projection and beam-forming applications and therefore are available in small sizes.

F-LCoS (Ferroelectric LCoS) have a fast switching speed, allowing for digital modulation, otherwise they offer the same usability as LCoS. Phase-shifting LCoS with pixel sizes of 8 țm are already available (4 țm or smaller are reportedly possible).

Micromechanical displays could actually perform better with smaller pixels, because their elements become faster. Current technology allows for structure sizes below 45 nm already, so pixels smaller than light wavelength will become possible. This enables holographic applications as well.

DMD (digital mirror device or digital light processing, DLP) displays with LED or laser illumination behave a great deal like normal screen displays. New miniature versions for mobile phone projectors, with mirror sizes down to 8 μm, offer new perspectives for vision glasses.

PISTON-type micromirror or MLM (Moving Liquid Mirror) displays can phase modulate light and may be useful for implementing holographic techniques.

Holographic displays are an application, currently conceivable with F-LCoS or piston-type moving micromirror technology for example, that could present little computer-generated holograms. Because the patterns to be displayed require resolutions in the micrometer range, these displays can be made only in small dimensions, and would involve enlargement optics. All modes realistically conceivable to date would use Fourier holograms (Section 9.6.3 at page 402), delivering light field images.

LED on CMOS: Light-emitting diodes are an efficient source and allow for very small pixels, but are difficult to produce because of the necessary use of GaAs or other exotic semiconductors. Currently, all products of this kind have been abandoned in favor of OLED on CMOS.

OLED (organic or polymer light-emitting diodes) can be applied for miniature displays. Samples of large-screen displays have been demonstrated with polymer-based OLEDs. For near-eye displays, an interesting aspect of polymer designs is the possibility of building convex or concave displays. Classical manufacturing processes (wafer technology, vacuum deployment) like OLED on CMOS are the most usual option for microdisplays, but print technology may also enter the field.

OLED on CMOS allows for very small structures directly grown on a CMOS chip. The CMOS chip may contain complex driver circuits and, a special advantage, light sensitive structures integrating a camera right into a display structure, such as for a retina tracker (see Section 10.16.3 at page 480) .

LASER scanning is a very promising technology for application in retinal displays. Practical implementations are low- or medium-resolution raster or vector displays for tactical information in combat (helmet displays for pilots and also for infantry soldiers). Laser scanners present some difficulties, especially as the beam origins have to get thicker (up to 2 mm) to allow focusing for high resolution, and the deflection has to become faster at the same time. The aspects of laser scanning with near-eye displays will be discussed later in this chapter. We will see that with an advanced optical design, these could have specific advantages.

The best efficiency is achieved with laser sources, as nearly 100% of the light produced may be concentrated onto the pupil. Pupil diameters can be as small as 1 mm, and eye movements require a sophisticated and quick adaptation mechanism in order to adjust the laser beam to the pupil continuously.

10.5 EXAMPLES OF NEAR-EYE DISPLAYS

In the following sections, we will first present several examples of existing near-eye display devices and concepts. Later, we will discuss possible future optical designs in more detail.

10.5.1 View-Covering Displays

The simplest kind of near-eye-displays present an image by means of optics positioned in front of the eye, covering up most or all of the field of view (as in Figure 10.1 on page 418). They may even include optical blinds, shielding any outside view from the user. These displays are used for *virtual reality* (VR) applications, where the user is fully immersed into a virtual world (e.g., with computer games, Figure 10.8), and they can also be used for personal TV viewing, simulating a large display screen.

Figure 10.7 shows a basic configuration of a VR display, consisting of two lenses and a screen that can either be one large display panel or two smaller panels side by side. A larger smartphone can be used as a display, delivering both the required screen size approx. 12 cm wide and a high resolution. Cheap head mounts with lenses and a phone holder are commonly used for simpler VR applications and gaming. Smartphones usually have acceleration sensors, as well as sufficient processing power for these applications.

A more powerful implementation of the principle is the **Oculus Rift** (Figure 10.8). It has two 1080 × 1200 pixel displays, advanced optics and motion sensing, and special software to provide a solid VR without causing headaches or vertigo. A main application shall be VR video games. The announced FOV is 110°. The angular resolution resulting with this and the display resolution given does not allow to fully replace a TV or movie screen. For action games, however, mainly relying on 3D and fast motion, resolution is less of an issue. Here, the device's quick and accurate motion response results in a good user experience.

Note that these kind of displays can also be used for AR applications when presenting a live video stream of the real environment that is captured from (at least roughly) the eyes' perspectives. This is called *video see-through* (more on this in Section 10.17.2 at page 485).

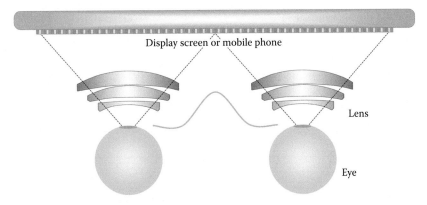

FIGURE 10.7 Closed head-attached display for VR.

FIGURE 10.8 **Oculus Rift** immersive NED. (Images courtesy of **Oculus VR**, LLC.)

10.5.2 Semicovering Displays

Another form of near-eye-displays positions a virtual image in front of the user's eyes (or one eye only), but covering only part of the natural field of view. It appears as a smaller display screen that remains at a fixed position in front of the eye(s), at a constant distance that is defined by the optics. The display can either be mounted in front of the eye, or mirrored into the field of view by a fixed, nontransparent mirror (Figure 10.9). The user can turn or tilt his head and look beneath the virtual screen if desired. Thus, this type of near-eye display may also be used outdoors, for entertainment and for professional applications where context-sensitive data (e.g., manuals or repair-procedures) have to be presented. Video see-through applications are, in principle, also supported; such displays can be very light and can also as be used as add-ons for normal eyeglasses (Figure 10.10).

An extreme example is the Olympus EyeTrek display, which is just 3.2 × 2.4 mm and is positioned at the lower corner of the field of view with a lens allowing it to appear approximately 4 inch diagonal at a distance of 20 inches. As long as the user's pupil is large enough, the display will not cover up any background scene object entirely, which may be a safety advantage in everyday use. The field of view, however, is extremely small (approximately 7° × 9°).

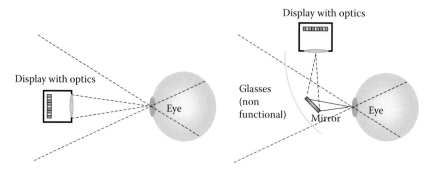

FIGURE 10.9 Semicovering head-attached display principle: these displays allow a view around the optics if necessary. The small image is either shown directly on a microdisplay (left), or is mirrored into the field of view (right).

FIGURE 10.10 Semi-immersive head-attached display example: **Vuzix Tac-Eye LT**, monocular, SVGA+(852 × 600) Color AMOLED, 30° horizontal field of view. Image courtesy: **Vuzix** Corporation.

The **Google Glass** (first generation) is another example of this principle.

10.5.3 Optical See-Through Displays

Optical see-through displays mirror the images of microdisplays into the field of view, without occluding it completely. They are the ideal choice for general use and the most versatile type, enabling applications such as AR, or location-aware information displays. What remains difficult is shaping the mirror and positioning the microdisplay to achieve an optimal optical design. Let's take a closer look at basic considerations for an appropriate optical design.

A natural dead angle in the human field of view is at the eyebrow and above. A microdisplay can be positioned there, because it covers almost no direct sight and allows for a relatively wide projection image (Figure 10.11-1).

The same optical assembly, but with a conventional micro display at the side (Figure 10.11-2), could cause some obstruction and has a smaller projection angle sideways (where humans actually have a large viewing range, over 180°).

In the first two designs, we applied curved mirror beam combiners to cover a large field of view. Many commercial display assemblies apply planar mirror beam combiners instead of curved (Figure 10.11-3), to the disadvantage of increased obstruction and a smaller field of view.

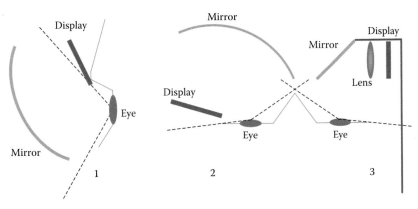

FIGURE 10.11 Basic optical see-through designs.

10.5.4 Additional Components

There are yet a few more issues we have to consider with near-eye displays than simply the basic optical path.

Current designs either rely on head fixtures or use collimated displays (see Section 10.7.1 at page 434), which restricts applications to displaying remote objects. If these restrictions can be overcome, it will open up many new areas of application.

Dynamic image pre-distortions and display adaptations – with help from an eye tracker – could provide for proper perspective and focus. A mechanical lateral displacement could compensate for an incorrect fit and for image shifts resulting from eye movements as well, but it may be more practical to use a larger microdisplay and do this by shifting the image electronically, if the exit pupil of the optics is large enough.

Another design issue is the combiner mirror. If the display uses narrow band primary colors, a dichroic mirror coating, for example, could improve both transparency and reflection to almost 100%.

A few additional elements are necessary as we think of augmented reality applications. A mask display (Section 10.17.3 at page 487), an eye tracker (Section 10.16.2 at page 476), and position sensing elements, cameras, for example, whose pictures are analyzed to determine their own position relative to the surrounding scenery.

Figure 10.12 gives an overview of such a full-fledged AR device, greatly exceeding the basic concept of a simple near-eye display.

10.6 COMBINER MIRRORS

The most common method of combining real and virtual images in augmented reality is based on "half transparent" mirrors, as shown in Figure 10.13. Using thin silver coatings which allow one part of the light to pass while reflecting the other, is an approach still used but is far from optimal. With spectrally selective (dichroic) or spectrally as well as directionally selective (holographic) mirrors, nearly 100% of the display light could be utilized, while ambient light would be attenuated by only a few percent. Here we would exploit the fact that a perfect color picture can be produced in the eye by only three very narrow banded color sources.

10.6.1 Dichroic Combiners

Dichroic filters/mirrors are produced by applying very thin dielectric coatings (usually 20…40 layers) on glass. The resulting filters can have a very narrow bandwidth, down to about 1 nm, compared to the entire visible spectrum (about 300 nm). Contrary to dye filters, they do not absorb (transmissivity >90%), but selectively reflect parts of the spectrum. There are high-pass, low-pass, band-pass and notch filters. Basically, for our purpose we need notch filters, reflecting just one color, hence, narrow band-pass mirrors. Hence, dichroic mirrors can be used as very efficient combiner mirrors for display glasses. There is no problem (except for cost) to use multiple filters stacked upon each other, reflecting several narrow color bands concurrently (Figure 10.14).

Dichroic filters/mirrors have extreme frequency selectivity but unlike HOEs, they have no directional component.

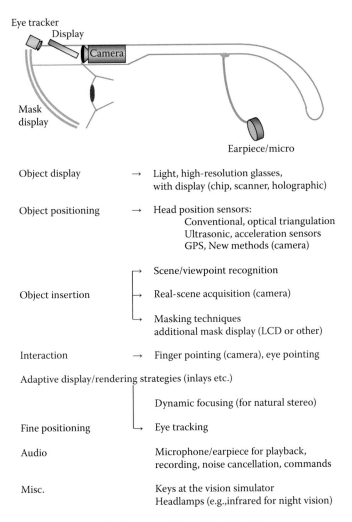

| Object display | → | Light, high-resolution glasses, with display (chip, scanner, holographic) |

FIGURE 10.12 Basic AR near-eye display assembly and its functions.

In principle, the characteristics of dichroic filters can be calculated similarly to electrical filters, but the approach becomes complicated because there are forward- as well as backward-moving waves (refraction index changes in both ways always reflect part of the light).

Because the filter characteristics are defined by the thickness of coating layers, they also vary with the angle of incident light. With most actual optics layouts, light does not always hit the mirror vertically, therefore the filter frequencies would deviate. There is no problem with adjusting the thickness of the coatings for this, or even producing coatings with a gliding thickness change.

With a laser scanner display, reflection angles vary only a little, and the light is perfectly monochrome, so we could use very narrow-banded mirrors, resulting in an almost 100% transparency of the glasses. This would not be a "half-transparent" mirror anymore; it would

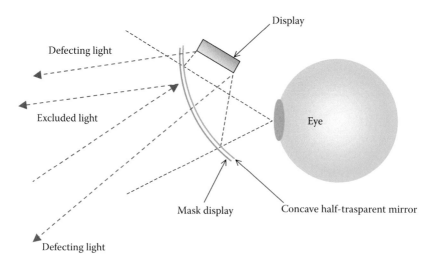

FIGURE 10.13 Front combiner mirror for near-eye displays.

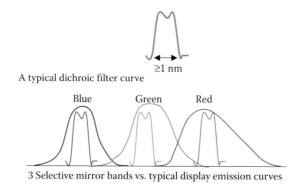

FIGURE 10.14 Principle dichroic filter curves.

not visually absorb any light at all. Likewise, hardly any of the laser light would be transmitted outside the mirror.

Dichroic mirrors may be relatively expensive to manufacture, but the advantages are convincing. With mass production, they could certainly be affordable. Meanwhile, it is possible to apply vacuum coatings, and therefore produce dichroic mirrors, on plastic glasses as well.

Holographic mirrors or combiners, the main alternative, can be produced spectrally as well as directionally selective, and they may perhaps be even less expensive to manufacture. Usually they tend to have a slightly milky appearance however, while dichroic mirrors appear faintly colored but are optically perfectly clear.

10.6.2 Holographic Combiners

Given what we have learned in the holography chapter (Chapter 5), the principle of holographic beam combiners is obvious, and as simple as it gets: many layers of faint refraction index changes form partial reflecting mirrors inside a holographic element (Figure 10.15). If we use light of the right wavelength, and within a certain angular range, all reflections from

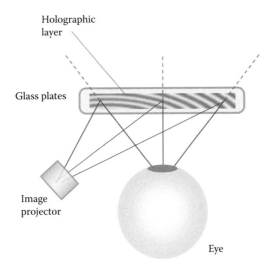

FIGURE 10.15   Working principle of a holographic combiner.

these layers will add up as if they came from a single solid mirror surface. Light of an incorrect wavelength or angle may be partly affected as well (Section 5.4.9 at page 152), but apart from a faint fogging or coloring effect, the holographic layer is almost entirely transparent. Color mirrors can be achieved by multiple exposures during the manufacturing process, or by stacking three layers for different, monochromatic light sources: red, green and blue.

Although extreme reflection angles are possible with holographic mirrors, this may result in some difficulties with surface reflections of the carrier glass. These could, in principle, be reduced if curved substrates are used. Manufacturing HOEs on these is not a problem. Planar HOE mirrors, however, would also allow for planar mask displays, greatly simplifying their construction.

10.6.3 Diffractive Combiners

Using surface instead of volume holograms for a combiner mirror is possible in theory, but there is a problem with low efficiency at steep angles. According to [248], alternative surface structures on a glass plate can be designed to reflect parts of incident light and thereby forming diffractive patterns directing or focusing the light. The reflecting structure elements can be microscopic wedge or step structures, and they have gaps between them to allow direct sight through the plate. The patterns are developed using a Gerchberg–Saxton iterative optimization algorithm [95] quite similar to the one shown in Figure 9.54 on page 404 (see [248] for more detail). This should result in an improved diffraction pattern, directing as well as focusing light from light engines (projectors or scanners) located beneath the eyes. Variations of diffraction gratings using dichroic filter or reflector elements are also described.

10.7 OPTICS DESIGN

The optics of an NED should be light and compact, deliver high resolution, and a wide FOV. We will first cover approaches with spatial displays and classical optics. There are a number of other approaches sharing certain properties with the classic designs but also including

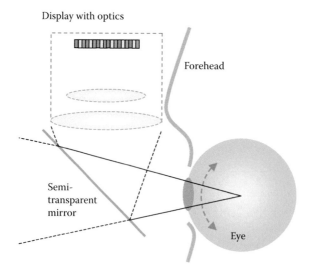

FIGURE 10.16 Optical design principle of many current products. Display and optics may be positioned as shown, or beneath or below the eye.

features even more "exotic" than HOEs. We will address these after laser displays, which share still more details with the classic spatial display designs.

Figure 10.16 shows an approach found in current products, with numerous variations. The straight mirror obviously limits the field of view, or the display lens would be overly large.

A concave (magnifying) mirror would improve this, as we will see later. Many military displays use concave mirrors since long, but with complicated multilens assemblies, too heavy and large for civil applications (examples are shown in Figure 10.2 on page 418 and in Figure 10.17). Overviews with many examples of head-worn displays optics can be found in [50,134].

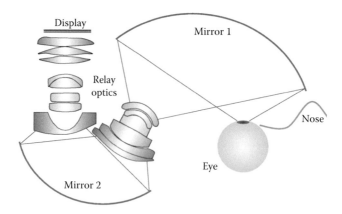

FIGURE 10.17 HMD optics design with dual ellipsoid mirrors and asymmetric free-form correction lenses (top view). Image according to [300].

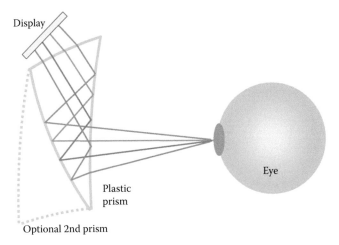

Display

Eye

Plastic
prism

Optional 2nd prism

FIGURE 10.18 Optical design with a prism and an optional 2nd prism claimed to reinstate see-through (US patent 6,049,429, **Canon** 1996).

While civil NED are used in a very limited number of research and industrial applications, military versions are standard equipment for pilots already and some lighter (monocular) versions are used partly as tactical displays in the infantry.

None of the current civil products are intended for permanent use; the lightest are those designed for gaming or TV viewing and these either fully or partially cover the natural view.

An interesting approach with two optical surfaces (actually three, because there is a surface in front of the display that acts as a lens) was presented in a product (**eMagin z-800**) in 2006 (Figure 10.18). This optical system has strong magnification and a decent viewing angle. The prism is quite light (about 11 g).

Obviously a single prism doesn't allow transparency, because the prism would heavily distort any direct view. The original patent mentions a second prism reinstating an optical see-through path, but geometrical issues would have to be expected in this case, at least insofar as a change in the origin of view. Looking through very thick glass always induces such issues. A major problem here is the border of the field of view covered by the glasses, and the merging of the peripheral field of view with the part seen through the glasses.

If we replace the prism surfaces by thin glasses with partially reflective mirror coatings, this could work more effectively. With two surfaces in the line of direct sight, advanced mirror technology will be required to keep light absorption in an acceptable range.

Figure 10.19 (from [111]) shows the basic concave mirror approach. The display is positioned above the eye. This layout could largely resemble normal sunglasses and would be very light. A design without lenses saves weight and avoids chromatic aberrations. We should note that displays beneath the eyes would be a possible approach as well.

The spherical mirror shape (1) has a curved focus area, or *field curvature* (4). This indicates possible advantages with a curved display or some additional optics. Changing the mirror curvature toward the end (2) may reinstate a straight focus field, corresponding to a flat display (3).

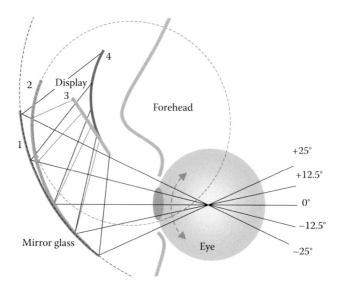

FIGURE 10.19 Design study for a single-mirror display.

The design would also have to be extended into the third dimension. Following the considerations about the spherical aberration of concave mirrors in Section 3.4.3.4 at page 78, the mirror could best be a section of a long ellipsoid or a paraboloid, with the horizontal radii smaller than the vertical. A minimal lens assembly (a thin lens covering the display) can also be used, without adding too much weight. We will say more about this in Section 10.7.4 at page 439.

10.7.1 Self-Adaptation (Collimated Near-Eye Display)

NED can be designed as collimated displays, showing their image content at virtual infinity (Sections 5.4.1 and 7.10.13). Indeed, this should be the default configuration; providing the proper focus for nearby objects can be achieved in various ways (e.g., mechanical display shifting).

An image at virtual infinity means pixel positions on the display are converted to angles (Figure 10.20). Any lateral displacement of the display unit does not change the angular positions of the image (this is the same effect that makes the moon appear to follow us as we

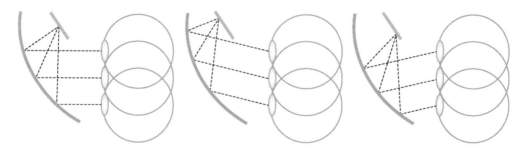

FIGURE 10.20 Collimated NED: object positions at infinity are independent of display position.

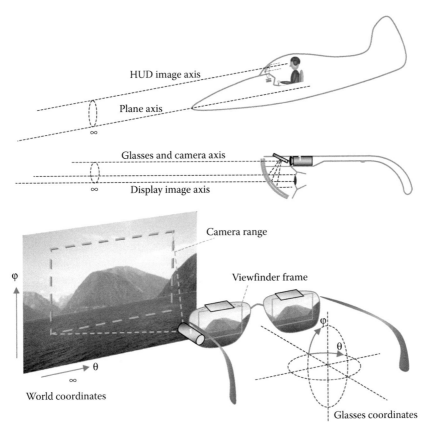

FIGURE 10.21 Automatic alignment of virtual images with collimated displays (HUD of a fighter jet, collimated NED, and virtual viewfinder frame).

drive in a car). Distance changes between the eye and the display also have little effect; only tilting of the display would have to be taken care of in this case.

Figure 10.21 illustrates the general principle and the advantages of collimated optics in AR applications.

In a fighter jet or a car, the vehicle is the reference system, and the HUD is fixed to it. The image in the HUD always stays aligned to the environment if the virtual image is at infinity. Hence, a fighter pilot can aim at a distant object, while his own head position against the HUD does not matter.

The same applies for an NED showing virtual images at infinity. Assuming that we know the display's position and angle in space, a certain pixel could likewise be mapped to a certain angle that originates from the display. Hence, a certain position in the surrounding landscape could be overlaid, independent of any incorrect fitting to the viewer's head. Here, the display itself becomes the reference to the environment, just as the fighter jet in the case of the HUD.

If a camera is attached to the display, for instance, a viewfinder frame can be presented without any necessity for dynamic adjustments. The viewfinder frame will always exactly match the camera frame (regardless of the fit of the glasses) because the camera is rigidly fixed to the glasses.

Therefore, collimated near-eye displays can replace a HUD in a car or an airplane: only the angle between display and vehicle has to be compensated for, by rotating the displayed scene.

For close objects, additional corrections have to be applied. These could be kept simple, as long the object doesn't get too close. This could result in a very economic system for general purposes.

Such an approach has other difficulties: it requires very linear optics with a large exit pupil (see next section). A single mirror may work, but is not ideal. Active geometric corrections by the display will most likely be required.

This simple approach would also not allow for a correct dynamic adjustment of focus as would be necessary if we wanted to provide for a natural eye accommodation to nearby virtual objects. The proper application of object masking with a mask display (Section 10.17.3 at page 487) also requires a great deal more effort – scene cameras and eye tracking at least – because the mask display is not at virtual infinity but on the glasses themselves.

In many applications this approach may nevertheless be sufficient, especially where close-up objects aren't present. Still then, a certain intelligent adaptation of the display assembly should be considered, even if it may only be for a static adjustment.

Display engines with small exit pupils, such as virtual retinal displays (laser scanners, Section 10.9 at page 445) in most cases, need more adaptation technology but could become much smaller and lighter.

10.7.2 Exit Pupil

One major challenge building the ideal NED concerns the exit pupil of the optics. As explained in Chapter 3, the exit pupil is the useful lateral area behind a lens (or a more complicated optical system). If we want to utilize all light provided by the system (saving power with an NED), the eye's entrance pupil should match with the display's exit pupil. But if the user moves his eyes, or the display moves relative to the eyes, these pupils become easily unaligned and the displayed image may deteriorate or vanish.

With classic optics, large magnifications result in a small exit pupil. This is the case with binoculars, for example. The larger the magnification (and the less expensive the make), the more difficult it gets to align eyes with the exit pupils of the device.

Because an eye tracker will be needed in order to show virtual objects correctly aligned with the real surroundings, we could compensate for eye movements by moving the microdisplay (or, in case, a laser projection unit) with the pupil (also suggested in [273]).

Figure 10.22 shows a simplified display design (collimated mode, distant objects only). With a relatively large display and accordingly small mirror magnification and curvature, this device apparently has a large exit pupil.

This exit pupil, however, cannot be used in its full extent. The reason for this can be understood if we dig deeper into the optical design of a single mirror display. In particular, each part of the mirror curvature must be designed for a certain incident and exit angle, for minimum astigmatism. Shifting the eye or the display lets another area on the mirror be effective for the image formation with a particular eye position, and this area has a deviating

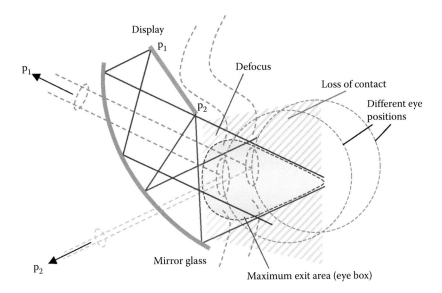

FIGURE 10.22   NED in a collimated mode (image at infinity), with the exit pupil shown.

curvature, not compensating astigmatism in an optimal way. This limits the useful exit pupil, especially with off-axis designs.

With NED, a central topic to be regarded is the image acquisition functionality of the human eye. As the eye can only see sharp within a small central area, larger FOV have to be assembled virtually in the brain, from multiple images acquired by relentless eye movements. Traditional optical instruments typically have a relatively small FOV, and are optimized for an eye pointing toward its center. Eye rotations remain small, and require a small exit pupil. NED, on the contrary, tend to have a large FOV, requiring considerable eye rotations. With NED, the range of allowable eye positions for a complete image perception is also referred to as the *eyebox*. Eye rotations will also affect the linearity of the image in certain configurations, especially for displays with a very large FOV. We will say more on this in Section 10.16.4 at page 482.

Figure 10.23 shows the image formation with a concave mirror [118]. For any single eye rotation angle, only a tiny part of that mirror, just about the size of the eye pupil, is involved in the formation of any single image pixel. This differs substantially from conventional optics designs in that the real exit pupil of the collimated system is in the center of the eyeball, and not in front of the eye pupil.

10.7.3   Free-Form Optics

Any of the small mirror elements effective for different angles as shown in Figure 10.23, could be optimized for the particular incident beam angle on the mirror and the focus distance to the corresponding point on the display. The ideal shape for any such limited area on the mirror would be a properly chosen section of a properly chosen paraboloid. Then we should get an ideally crisp focus point. Alas, the curvature of the entire mirror is not simply the sum of small paraboloids, nor is it a paraboloid itself. We have to find a balance between the local and the general shape. The general shape of the mirror would have to be optimized to have

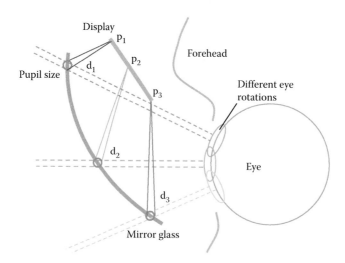

FIGURE 10.23 Image formation in an NED.

all focus points on the display plane, while retaining the best possible approximation to the aforementioned paraboloid shape for any single pupil-sized region on the mirror.

Free-form mirrors therefore are a key technology for the construction of light and compact NED. Finding an optimal shape, however, can be a difficult optimization task. Various optimization methods are common in optical design, with a usual objective of achieving a minimum *least mean square* value for focus deviation and aberrations. These methods approach an optimum by numerous small iterations, guided by an algorithm. Very powerful candidates for this are genetic algorithms or evolutionary [237] strategies. Given the many parameters involved, implementing an optimization for NED is a challenge. An example for such an approach is found in [49]. We will say more about this on page 439. We will also show a very straightforward mirror synthesis method, in Section 10.7.5 at page 440.

10.7.4 Free-Form Displays

The central problem with off-axis designs is astigmatism, as shown in Figure 3.29 on page 78. This can be addressed by using an elliptic mirror (cf. Figure 3.30 on page 79).

The single mirror concept may also work a lot better with a display having a convex shape itself, as indicated in Figure 10.19 on page 434. This also leads to some fundamental solutions, requiring no general free-form optimization approach.

A basic configuration with an elliptic mirror is shown in Figure 10.24 [118]. The eye center is located at one focal point of a rotation ellipsoid defining the mirror. An ideal ellipsoid, however, grants astigmatism free focusing only for its very focal points. If the eye is focused to infinity, we have parallel light beams that do not converge at the other focal point, but on a surface area determined by the lens formula $f = 1/(1/f_1 + 1/f_2)$. It turns out that this surface is closely (not exactly) approximate to another, smaller ellipsoid, sharing the same focal points with the mirror ellipsoid.

The center resolution with this layout is very high, up to the maximum eye resolution of 1 arcmin. The lens equation, however, here only holds for very narrow beams, because of the

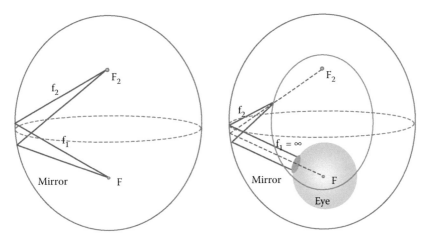

FIGURE 10.24 Principle of an ellipsoid mirror and display configuration [118].

angle and curvature change of the mirror, and indeed this results in a significant aberration for larger and even for normal pupil sizes (Figure 10.25). This turns out to be a generic problem with simple off-axis designs, even with an elliptic mirror and not only with planar, but even with convex displays. Moreover, a convex display shape is difficult to manufacture, if at all (we should however mention that instead of a convex display, also a microprojector with a convex screen could be conceived).

Currently, more realistic constructions can be conceived with a planar display, or a display curved in only one direction (which is already feasible with certain display types).

One of the first performance explorations of single mirror approaches (such as in Figure 10.11 on page 427), has been carried out in [49]. It included designs with a naked flat display, and also with a flat display covered with a thin correction lens. The angular resolution achieved was about 1.5 arcmin for a design including a lens. For the design without

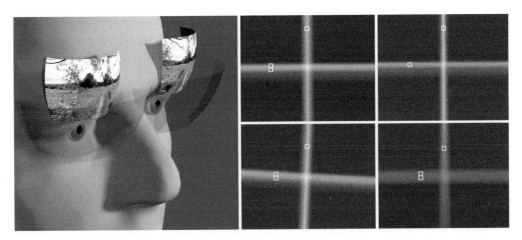

FIGURE 10.25 Left: ellipsoid design, cropped to the useful area for maximum vertical FOV. Right: resolution evaluation (top left: center; top right: 20° upward; bottom left: 20° left; and bottom right: 20° down). The overlaid rectangles are 1 × 1 arcmin [118].

a lens, the contrast curves given indicate a resolution of about 3…4 arcmin. The FOV provided were about ±10° (20° total). The problem with resolution as well as the small FOV, can be overcome by inserting entire lens systems in front of a planar display. This can be stacks of 10 or more lenses, as found in military display helmets [48], and in a recent design for extremely large FOV [300] (Figure 10.17 on page 432), not viable for everyday use due to size and weight.

10.7.5 A Straightforward Mirror Synthesis

A straightforward synthesis approach for mirrors for arbitrary display shapes has been proposed in [118]. The approach relies on the fact that the effective beam width for point formation is small (pupil sized). Figure 10.26 shows the pupil size greatly extended for better illustration. The active mirror section can be approximated, at its edges, by two little planar mirrors (m_1, m_2). The optical effect of said section, focusing a beam of light, can completely be modeled by the two mirrors, reflecting the edge rays of the beam. The curve between these mirrors will always be very well approximated by a circle sector (with center point f_1), provided the section is chosen to be small enough. The initial angles of m_1, m_2, chosen to start with, are known. The point where they meet on the display (image point p_1), is then easily constructed. Now we rotate the eye by one pupil or beam width. The mirror m_2, now at the other edge of the beam, gives us the location of a next image point on the display, p_2, and this, in turn, dictates the angle of a next mirror element, m_3, at the other side of the pupil beam. The spatial position of that next element (its distance from the eye) can perfectly be determined by the sphere sector shape that we expect between the mirrors (with the center at f_2). Iterating this method, we get a number of elements approximating a curve, which should turn out to be the ideal mirror shape (and it does, at least in one dimension). We should note that the principle of the algorithm can also be inverted, to calculate a display shape for a given mirror shape.

Repeating the procedure for an eye rotation from the center upward, completes the vertical center line of the mirror. Note that the iteration process may also be run with smaller pupil sizes, in order to increase the number of coordinate points obtained.

Next, the same procedure can be applied in other directions, in order to develop the entire mirror shape in two dimensions. Trying to combine steps in the horizontal and vertical,

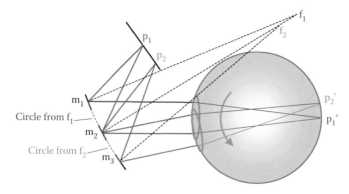

FIGURE 10.26 Algorithm for incremental mirror synthesis [118].

however, we will most certainly result in conflicting values, requiring additional algorithms to combine them into a suitable result. Using the initial algorithm from the center in any directions will result in a star pattern defining a mirror shape, without conflicts. This still has the disadvantage of neglecting the lateral curvature and therefore tolerating an increasing astigmatism toward the edges. The dome mirror shown in Figure 10.30 on page 443, is an example for this.

The straightforward mirror synthesis shown here will always provide a perfect resolution at the center. Trying to achieve a better edge resolution will require to sacrifice some of that center resolution. If we are willing to allow this, one of the before-mentioned general optimization methods can be applied. But how much compromise can be tolerated? At this point, a well-defined quality parameter is needed to indicate progress. This is a central issue with any optimization method. For NED, such a parameter is not easily obtained, because the individual regions of a generally large FOV are of different importance, influenced by physiological factors and also by the particular application.

10.8 ON-AXIS NED

A central difficulty in terms of NED resolution turns out to be the off-axis principle (at least if we deal with classical mirror optics and want a compact and light solution). If we try to avoid this, the display gets into the optical path, which is apparently not a good idea at a first glance. But with a display that is transparent from the back and emits at its front side only, things look different. Displays with such properties have already been built. The working principle involves a display with transparent panel circuitry, or one with gaps through which light can pass, and a pixel raster also with gaps in between (Figure 10.27). Several manufacturers have been presenting large transparent AMOLED displays for showcases and other applications since years. Small, flexible, and transparent varieties for mobile phone and smart clothing applications (e.g., [317]) have also been shown. See Section 10.15.1 at page 473 and Section 10.12 at page 457 for other projected applications.

With such a display, the ellipsoid mirror could, as an ideal example, be replaced with a spherical mirror around the eye, accompanied by an inscribed spherical display (of 1/2 the size, according to the sphere's focus length), as shown in Figure 10.27 [118,119].

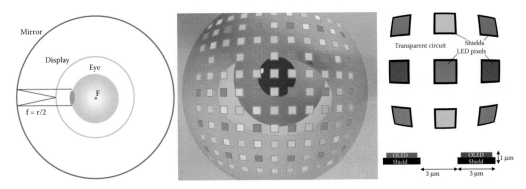

FIGURE 10.27 Principle of a spherical mirror and display configuration, using a transmissive display: schematic (left), greatly enlarged pixels (middle), matrix, and layer detail (right) [118].

The display in this configuration would require a pixel raster of approx. 6 μm for a resolution of 1 arcmin. Considering that OLED typically are 0.1 . . . 0.3 μm thin, this is physically achievable. The optical quality of this spherically concentric design, according to simulations, exceeds that of the eye, and the FOV achievable is extremely large, with no quality degradation toward the edges at all.

A design study of this principle is shown in Figure 10.28. Figure 10.29 shows the resolution of the spherical display (being equally good for all eye rotations), the peripheral resolution (with the eye looking straight ahead), and the influence of a possible displacement of the glasses. The distance to the eye has literally no influence on the resolution (even for the peripheral FOV). An upward or downward shifting of the glasses results in a slight astigmatism. The useful – static – exit pupil turns out to be about 6 mm, for a maximum resolution degradation to about 1.5 arcmin (note that the exit pupil here only refers to the displacement tolerance of the glasses; the eyebox is a lot larger).

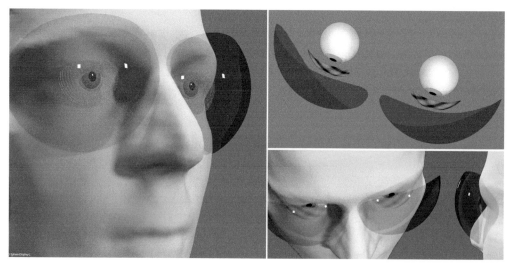

FIGURE 10.28   Design study of a spherical concentric NED display [118].

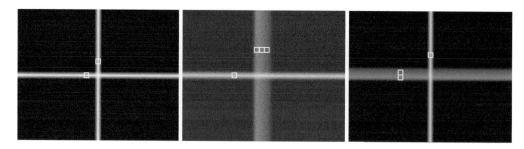

FIGURE 10.29   Resolution of the concentric sphere design: center (left), *peripheral resolution* at 20° (the eye pointing straight ahead), and center resolution for a glasses displacement both 3 mm downward and forward (right). The markers are 1 × 1 arcmin wide.

In conclusion, this approach is the only one known so far that could deliver the full eye resolution and a very large FOV concurrently, without becoming bulky.

Following from our initial considerations, an on-axis design should also have advantages with less ideal display shapes, such as a planar display, or a display curved only in the horizontal.

Remarkably, an on-axis NED with a planar transparent display was proposed as early as 1992, for a camera viewfinder [316]. The display envisioned, however, was a simple transparent LCD, and the principal optical advantages of on-axis configurations were not being considered.

Appropriate mirror shapes for such displays are not derived as easily as with the elliptic or spherical displays. In Section 10.7.5 at page 440, we have shown a straightforward mirror synthesis approach suitable for these applications.

Figure 10.30 shows a resulting design for a planar display. It turns out to be as small as a pair of conventional glasses, but nevertheless it has an FOV of more than 40°, with a very high center resolution and an acceptable edge resolution. Figure 10.31 shows the radial resolution to be perfect for all angles (verifying the synthesis algorithm), while the axial resolution degrades toward the edges, because the radial curvature inevitably lags behind the – optimized – axial one.

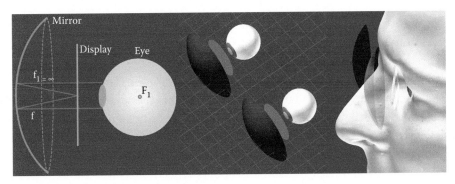

FIGURE 10.30 Schematic and simulation of a planar transmissive NED display with dome-shaped mirrors [118].

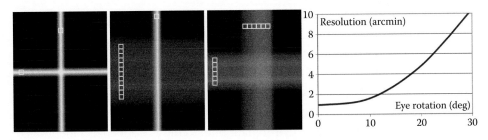

FIGURE 10.31 Planar/dome display. From left to right: center resolution; astigmatism at 20° eye rotation; astigmatism compensated by focus change; and resulting resolution versus eye rotation [118].

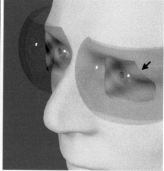

FIGURE 10.32 Simulation of a cylindrical transmissive NED display with barrel-shaped mirrors; left-eye image of a 60 × 120° FOV section (limited by the nose) [118].

Increasing the axial curvature will not help to solve this, because the lateral curvature would then grow even faster. The astigmatism can however be turned into a symmetric blur by changing the eye accommodation, here to a distance value of about 1.25 m. Alternatively, a display displacement of about 1/4 mm can be used for the same result. The display displacement can be a dynamic one realized with a focus mechanism required for a complete NED anyway. The same effect can also be accomplished by introducing some – very small – display curvature. The overlaid rectangles in Figure 10.31 are 1 × 1 arcmin. The ray-tracing simulation shows the resulting blur of a line pattern provided by the display. The edge resolution turns out to be about 5 arcmin at the edges of a 40° FOV, and <1.5 arcmin for 20° FOV (Figure 10.31 (right)).

Figure 10.32 shows the application of the above-shown optimal mirror profile to a cylindrical display with a barrel-shaped mirror. This shape was generated by spinning the mirror curve of the planar display design around the vertical eye center axis.

While the edge astigmatism in the vertical here becomes a bit larger than with the dome mirror and flat display design, the horizontal resolution remains perfect for an arbitrarily large FOV, similar to the spherical example. The apparent conflicts with the eye surrounding physiognomy (the arrow in Figure 10.32) can be avoided by giving the glasses and displays some edge shaping. Less curved displays with more eye clearance – and accordingly adapted mirrors – would be another option. According to Figure 4.7 on page 98, a resulting additional blur at the outer edges could be tolerated to a certain degree.

We should note that with any of the above-described concentric designs, the mirror also reflects light from the eye and its surroundings back to the eye, resulting in a (dim and very blurred) image of the user's eye, overlaid to the display image. Moreover, the display image itself would be visible to other persons and might hide the user's eyes from them. Yet, in AR applications, this would also mean that the image would cover up the user's sight, which would not be a common situation, because virtual images will normally be provided in a sparse manner, taking the real environment into account. Both effects mentioned can effectively be canceled out with displays emitting only narrow-banded spectral colors (e.g., quantum dot-enhanced LED, cf. Section 2.5.6 at page 47) and highly selective mirrors (e.g., dichroic mirrors), which would also be highly efficient and very transparent.

The optical and design simulations shown have been done with the open-source 3D modeling environment **Blender**. It allows for a simulation of the general appearance and fit – being central topics for NED – as well as a precision ray-tracing assessment of the mirror optics, including special aspects such as eye rotation and accommodation. The models used and a guide can be obtained from the book website.

10.9 LASER DISPLAYS

The basic idea of a laser near-eye display (also called a *retinal display* or virtual retinal display) is to deflect a laser beam in a manner that it forms a raster image right on the retina. A naive idea that often arises in this context assumes that a laser beam is very narrow and could be directed right though the pupil by means of a tiny deflection mirror, even ignoring the eye's lens. As we learned in Section 3.5.2 at page 85, this would not work, because laser beams cannot be arbitrarily narrow and they are also affected by lenses. So we need an optical assembly delivering a relatively wide, parallel beam, which would then be focused by the pupil, forming a focus spot on the retina. The deflection assembly must be able to deliver beams from different directions, always through the pupil, because this is the only way of landing them on different parts of the retina.

Placing a deflection mirror directly in front of the eye, as shown in Figure 10.33, would not be useful, as it would require almost zero distance and the mirror would have to be almost as big as the pupil, which would occlude direct sight.

10.9.1 A Classical Laser Scanner Design

We will first review an early laser scanner design, which has been thoroughly analyzed in [273]. It serves as a see-through data display, monochrome red at 640 × 480 resolution. An image is displayed at a fixed position in the user's field of view. The high brightness, which is typical for a laser display, allows it to be used in sunlight, which is mandatory in military applications. If the user moves his eyes, the laser beam may miss the pupil, especially when the latter is very small (adapted to bright sunlight, for example). A measure against this is a special assembly that splits the laser beam (respectively, displaces it sideways in steps). If the pupil moves, at least one ray bundle is always there to enter the eye. For details of this technique, see [273].

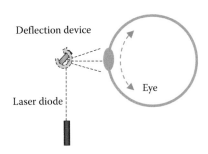

FIGURE 10.33 Basic (non-functional) concept of a retinal laser scanner.

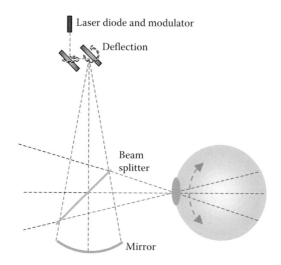

FIGURE 10.34   An early laser scanner design (virtual retinal display).

FIGURE 10.35   Virtual retina laser displays, VGA resolution. Image courtesy: **Microvision** Inc.

This design (Figure 10.34) comprises a laser source, horizontal and vertical deflection mirrors in MEMS (micro electro-mechanical systems) technology, and a beam combiner/mirror assembly. This is a simple optical arrangement with hardly any geometry errors, yet, it is not the small, convenient design that one would like for general use.

Later designs omit the lower mirror. The complete optics is located at the forehead and only a half-transparent mirror is left in front of the eye (Figure 10.35).

10.9.2   Laser Display with Curved Mirror

Let us now apply some of the basic optical design considerations that we made for optical see-through displays in Section 10.5.3 at page 427.

Instead of a planar-mirror beam combiner, we can apply a concave one, as explained above (Figure 10.36). We could also, for instance, conceive a concave scanning mirror instead, or a combination of both.

For a crisp spot at the retina with the eye focused to infinity, the beam would have to arrive as a parallel bundle. The deflection mirror has to be placed at a location where the beam is at least as wide as the pupil. Otherwise the deflected beam would diverge too much and could not be properly focused any longer.

Note that the off-axis configuration will cause astigmatism and aberration effects related to those considered for spatial displays in Section 10.8 at page 441 (but quite different in

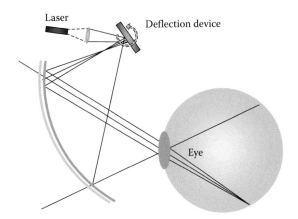

Laser

Deflection device

Eye

FIGURE 10.36 Basic adaptation of a laser unit.

detail). We will consider this again in Section 10.11 at page 452. But first, we will look upon some laser-specific topics.

The mirror size as well as the beam diameter at the pupil would at least have to be 0.25 mm even for VGA resolution (640 × 480), and about 1 mm for some good resolution (≥1600 × 1200).[*] This is sufficient to generate virtual computer or HDTV screens with some margins for surroundings and perspective. At this resolution, we need ≈100 kHz deflection frequency for an acceptable frame rate. Moving a mirror so fast, however, is very difficult. The mirror deflection has to be done in a way that avoids fast accelerations, as was discussed in Section 7.10.15 at page 301.

The angular resolution in this case however, albeit satisfactory in most cases, would still be half as good as our eye resolution. For the perfect resolution of 1 arcmin. (1/60 degree), a mirror of 2 mm diameter would be necessary.

A laser beam, although not entirely parallel, is usually less sensitive to focus changes than a classical assembly, because the effective eye pupil opening in this case is the beam diameter. For a low resolution, this could, for example, mean 0.4 mm vs. 3 mm, giving eight times the focus tolerance of a classical display.

At the highest useful resolution of 1/60° however, the beam diameter has to be about 2 mm, so there is no advantage any longer.

Laser scanners can be built very small; laser diodes are tiny, so the entire laser unit, including deflection, could be shrunk almost to the size of a sand grain, so it would be the smallest and lightest display conceivable.

Laser diodes are rather nonlinear and work only above a certain power threshold; it is therefore not possible to simply modulate their intensity by changes of supply current. Regarding their very fast switching times, digital pulse width modulation is an alternative.

For eye protection, precautions have to be taken against deflection failure. The beam should never be allowed to rest, because it could burn holes into the retina if all its power were to remain concentrated on a single spot.

---

[*] This follows from the considerations about laser beam divergence, as given in Section 3.5.2 at page 85.

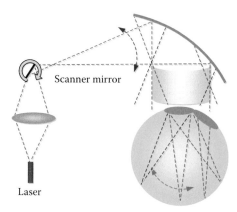

FIGURE 10.37 Example of generating a large exit pupil with a laser scanner.

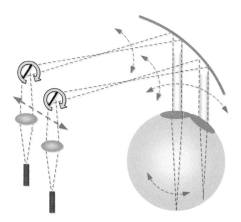

FIGURE 10.38 Keeping pupil contact by moving the scanner unit.

10.9.3 Exit Pupil with Laser Scanners

With laser scanners, a wide beam aperture can be designed if desired (Figure 10.37). This would result in a wide range of tolerable eye movements and could be beneficial for an adjustment-free display for distant images. The drawback to this possibility is that the ability of the laser display to concentrate all its light into the eye is lost.

With a narrow laser beam, the pupil will be missed in case of eye movements. By mechanically moving the entire laser unit (Figure 10.38) this can be avoided. Because the laser scanner unit could become extremely small, it could save more power, in terms of light generation, than has to be expended for the micro servo motors. There would be a considerable construction effort with eye tracking and mechanics, however.

10.9.4 Multi Resolution Scanners

As we have learned, higher resolution requires a larger scanning mirror, but it also requires faster scanning in order to write more raster pixels per unit of time. So the degree to which resolution can be increased is very limited. Achieving just more than VGA (640 × 480) resolution becomes extremely difficult.

A solution could be to use a large-scale image with low resolution, enhanced with high-resolution inlays that dynamically follow the eye's center of view [116]. Although this is speculative so far, we will attempt to calculate the constraints and possible outcome of such an approach.

With laser scanners, this is much easier to achieve than with other display types, because the beam deflection can follow the eye instantly instead of experiencing a delay of up to one frame duration waiting for the image to appear.

One could arrange two small MEMS deflectors for the main image and the inlay side by side, near enough so all rays could still enter the pupil. Aligning such images precisely is difficult but manageable, because the transition area is outside the crisp center of view.

But the human pupil can become very small, almost down to 1 mm, and special optics may be necessary to merge two or three beams advantageously. A holographic 3-way beam combiner (i.e., a HOE, as discussed in Section 5.4 at page 144) could be a solution.

We could think of yet another way to solve the problem: concentric ring mirrors of different sizes. Such mirrors could be etched from a silicon wafer in the same manner as a single mirror.

Section 4.2.5 at page 95 already discussed the average eye resolution with respect to the visual field. Figure 10.39 shows the eye resolution from Section 4.2.5 at page 95 together with the resolution ranges of three mirrors producing an image with 1/2 and 1/4-sized inlays, designed for a center resolution of 2 arcmin and off-center resolutions almost always better than those of the eye.

Each mirror would deliver about VGA resolution (640 × 480), combining for a total resolution of 2560 × 1920.

The reduction in the total number of pixels to be rendered is 10/64 of the high-resolution full frame.

An outer ring mirror of about 1 mm in diameter could draw the innermost picture inlay, with its small viewing angle and very small excitations. The eye is less flicker sensitive at its center of view (see Section 4.2.3 at page 93); so, this mirror could be relatively slow and, with interlacing, have a deflection rate below 10 kHz. A better agility is needed for the outer picture areas, but the mirrors serving them also get smaller. The next ring would be about

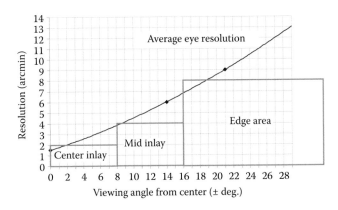

FIGURE 10.39 Eye resolution with respect to the visual field, and possible picture inlay sizes.

0.5 mm large and the center mirror about 0.25 mm, delivering the largest focus spot and drawing the outermost parts of the image. The mechanical construction of such a concentric mirror assembly would of course be quite demanding.

Laser beam deflection can be done in many other ways. For example, by abandoning the rectangular raster scheme and deflecting the beam in a circular spiral movement. Only harmonic, sinusoidal movements would be necessary for this (two sinus motions with 90° phase shift result in a circle being drawn). If the spiral starts at the center of vision, it can be made progressively wider toward the outside, naturally and smoothly adapting to the decreasing crispness of vision.

Varying the spot size and brightness of the scanner accordingly, an evenly illuminated, continuous image could be generated. Moreover, drawing a denser pattern at the center would imply faster movements but at a smaller amplitude, and would be easier to achieve.

The usefulness of most of these concepts has not been tested in practice thus far. What has been tested, is a single scanner used for changing focus spot sizes and resolutions in the same image [254]. Not very recent are high-resolution inlays; glasses with conventional displays such as the FOHMD (Figure 10.2 on page 418) used them. We see, however, that there are quite a number of new approaches at hand for future laser scanners.

10.10 SMART NED

Integrating additional circuitry into the panel can give planar displays additional and very useful features, as discussed in Section 6.5.5 at page 223. A recent example presented by **Ostendo Technologies** is a light field display, a lenticular light field display with dedicated processors for each lenticular element, rendering the according subpixel areas.

For NED, integrated processing can be particularly useful for quick motion response and multi resolution inlays, which are features previously thought to be exclusive for laser scanners.

10.10.1 Smart Displays for Fast Motion Response

One problem with head-mounted displays is the performance with fast head motion (especially turning the head), with displayed virtual objects registered to the environment.

Consider a user turning his head, while keeping his eyes directed onto a virtual object. This requires shifting the entire image of the virtual object, across the glasses' display area. Even at high frame rates, this may give rise to smearing, and the effect becomes progressively more apparent with higher display resolutions. The same principle topic has also been discussed in Section 6.2.4 at page 186, for large panel displays.

Flashing the display light may work to eliminate smear effects in simple head-turning-while-fixating-an-object situations in augmented reality. Nevertheless, a problem remaining in AR applications is the display's inherent delay time – the frame duration. Although the detection of head motion by inertia sensors is very fast, this delay time makes it necessary to "predict" the correct position one frame ahead, or the position of displayed objects will always lag behind the user motion. The inherent inertia of a human head allows motion anticipation algorithms to work for this, to a certain degree. Even small remaining errors may however be disturbing, especially with a high display resolution.

Using higher frame rates could be a solution, but Figure 6.8 on page 187 shows that they would have to be extremely high. This in turn requires higher processing power or – in case of external image generation – higher transmission bandwidth and/or better compression, the latter one also requiring more processing – and electrical – power. In conclusion, providing higher frame rates requires larger batteries, which is very undesirable for display glasses.

An additional CCD circuitry between the display cells would solve the problem, by allowing to move an image across the entire display, in single, horizontal, or vertical pixel steps [117]. For a smooth motion impression, these elementary shifting operations have to be distributed properly over time (cf. Figure 6.39 on page 224). This can be achieved using two separate counters for the lateral and vertical directions (x and y), each running at a clock rate proportional to the desired motion speed in that direction. The counters should have several extra bits at the low end, and they should increment several times faster than the actual shifting operations. If an actual pixel shift is initiated only when a certain higher bit of the counter changes, the result is an average shifting speed with an accuracy given by the number of extra bits implemented. If pixel shifts in x and y happen to occur simultaneously, a short delay should be applied to one of them, to avoid conflicts between charges arriving at a pixel from x and y directions.

Such a time-dithered pixel-by-pixel motion of the entire image will appear to be smooth as long as the pixels are small enough – which should be the case for HD displays. While writing or refreshing a full image at usual video frame rates takes 17…20 ms, a pixel shift can be carried out in a matter of microseconds, resulting in a reaction speed way beyond anything achievable by increased frame rates.

A complete design like this includes a second storage layer where the next frame can be written to in the background, while the displayed (foreground) image is shifted. The complete background image is then transferred to the foreground and the shifting process is seamlessly continued with it.

Loading an image in the background also takes time and hence induces some latency. This could be compensated for by rendering the image with some additional shift according to a motion prediction, risking inaccuracies. Another possibility would be shifting the image with additional circuitry already while loading (a difficult endeavor). A third method would be shifting the image into position after transferring it to the foreground, by some very fast shift operations, while blanking the entire display.

We should also note that image shifting will leave empty edge pixels behind at one side. This can be compensated for by various techniques already known from image stabilization or resizing, but the easiest way would be not to display pixels close to the edges, so that these initially invisible edge pixels would automatically fill the visible edge area during shifting operations.

Rotation or zoom operations would also be possible by pixel shifting, but would involve more complex shifting schemes These could be carried out by providing an appropriate set of motion vectors and proceeding as discussed in Section 6.5.5 at page 223. Tilting or forth/back motions of the human head occur at far slower paces than just turning, hence, these would probably not require such an approach. There may however be another topic requiring it: If distortions of the optics are to be compensated by an inverse distortion of the display image – a feature to be expected in almost any advanced design – the shift operations within the display matrix will not be perceived as entirely parallel. This may result in some remaining motion effects in the peripheral FOV. One method to deal with this would be a nonlinear arrangement of the display matrix, providing a "hard-wired" geometric pre-compensation. The other method would be the aforementioned motion vector-based shifting.

10.10.2 Multi Resolution Smart Displays

The possible savings of processing power for image rendering by peripheral resolution reduction, as discussed in Section 10.9.4 at page 448 also apply to planar displays – theoretically. Simply rendering parts of the image at a lower resolution, however, would not yield any advantage: the rendering processor would have to calculate less actual image pixels, but would then have to fill the pixels between them and smoothen the result. Also, the bandwidth of the image data to be transported to the display would remain the same. Hence, this would save about nothing. If we could accomplish the pixel filling and the smoothing right inside the display chip itself, and perhaps other "smart" features as well [117], this in turn would make a huge difference.

Consider a random addressable CMOS display chip. Consider writing to single pixels, for example, every 2nd, 3rd, and 4th of the actual display pixels. Charge transfer (CCD) functions implemented within the display chip could then be used to fill several adjacent pixels (e.g., a block of 4, 9, or 16 display pixels) with that information (note that in this case it has to duplicate charges, rather than just shifting them).

Subsequently, an appropriate chip circuitry could provide for a smoothing of the resulting coarse image raster, by averaging pixels (charges) at block edges with adjacent ones from neighboring blocks.

Figure 10.40 shows a two-step duplication operation designed to avoid target pixel conflicts. An averaging of incoming charges from two or more directions is also conceivable, depending on circuit design. This would especially be useful for the second step, the deblocking. It could also be used to avoid lateral half-pixel offsets for schemes with even-numbered reductions (every 2nd, 4th, etc. pixel), if it matters.

10.11 FOCUS AND ACCOMMODATION

With spatial displays, it has always been difficult to deliver image content at a virtual distance other than the actual display location. With stereo displays, this results in the well-known disparities between eye convergence and accommodation. In Section 9.5.3 at page 392, we have seen light field-based approaches to focus synthesis. With NED based on classical optics, several other options are available.

A simple focus simulation can be achieved by moving a display or a laser scanning unit relative to the optics (Figure 10.41). Within certain limits, this results in a different virtual distance seen through the optics.

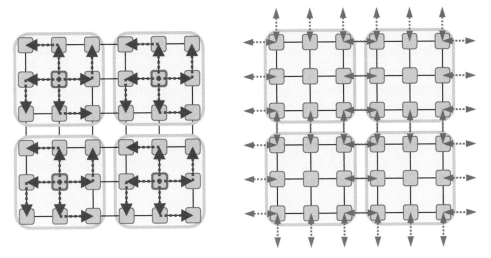

FIGURE 10.40 Sub-resolution scheme for spatial displays. Left: block filling (here: in two steps). Right: deblocking.

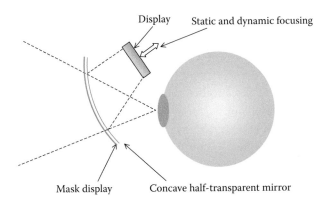

FIGURE 10.41 Basic focus simulation.

As we see clearly only at our center of view, the focus delivered could be dynamically adjusted according to the image content and the actual part of it currently being viewed. The latter information can be obtained by eye tracking.

Because our eyes can't adapt to sudden movements and focus quickly, a dynamic focus adaptation of the display unit itself could be made fast enough to avoid irritating delays.

For this to work seamlessly, it is necessary to exactly determine the actual part of the virtual scene or object viewed, and to dynamically render surrounding scene or object parts of different intended distances with a certain blur, according to the perception of a natural viewing situation. Ideally, this method should be able to deliver an entirely natural impression.

Moving an entire display chip or laser scanning unit continuously and fast enough to follow eye motion may appear difficult, but the difficulty decreases with decreasing sizes and weights of these units. For possibilities of implementation, see Section 10.16.5 at page 482.

Using several transparent display layers at different distances is another approach found in the literature. This does not deliver a continuous focus range but crisp images for discrete focus accommodation distances, with less-defined ranges in between. An example for this is found in [129].

Laser scanners offer yet another possibility for focus adaptation. A varifocal mirror in series with the scanning mirror can modulate the beam focusing very quickly and quite effortlessly (Figure 10.42).

Note that this could also be used to compensate for astigmatism and aberration effects caused by the off-axis optical configuration (considered for spatial displays in Section 10.8 at page 441), especially if the varifocal mirror would allow for different variable foci in x and y directions.

In [254], a varifocal mirror is used to create multiple focus planes sequentially. The initial idea was to modulate focus fast enough to assign any single image point its proper distance. This would require the varifocal mirror to operate at many megahertz, which is hardly possible.

Another approach is to create sequential images at different foci fast enough for them to appear simultaneously. Because of the depth of field range of the eye, this may give a continuous focus range impression, within a limited range. Another possibility mentioned in [254] is delivering several laser beams with different focus adjustments, combining them into one beam, and switching between them while the image is scanned. This can be done fast enough to allow a different focus for any single image pixel. Again, the selection of individual focus steps is limited. Yet another method proposed is to produce multiple focus points, or a continuum of focus points, for a single image point. This can be done using several of the mentioned beams at once, or by using complex focusing elements as we show in Figure 10.43. It illustrates a multi segment lens having several focus points (bi-focal contact lenses, e.g., use this principle). The same can of course be obtained with a mirror, and any number of foci, up to a continuous distribution, are possible.

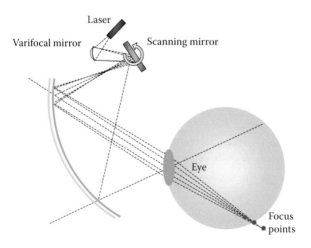

FIGURE 10.42 Laser scanning display with a focus steering mirror.

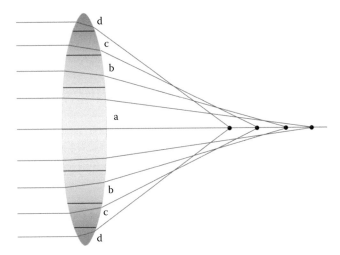

FIGURE 10.43   A lens with segments of stepwise increasing curvature (a–d), resulting in multiple focus points.

The method could be perfected with a diffractive (holographic) display element. We will discuss advanced possibilities of this kind in Section 10.13.1 at page 461.

In [176] and [177], fast focus multiplexing as well as adaptive focus rendering has been researched using a varifocal lens of the liquid type (see Section 3.4.2.5 at page 71), that allows focus changes within approximately 9 ms. In the multi-focal mode, three individual focus planes at 16, 33 and 100 cm were generated, resulting in a relatively natural image impression. In the adaptive mode, the lens was steered according to the viewer's current region of interest, i.e., the objects he looked at within the virtual image.

The generation of multiple foci may produce a natural 3D impression with complex scenes containing haze or fog. This may also be an issue with spatial multiviewer displays. A single user however, which is the given condition with any near-eye displays, can always only focus to a single distance. Any other focus points he would not notice, therefore a dynamic focusing controlled by an eye tracker can result in a comparable level of realism if it works fast enough and if depth-of-field effects are rendered properly.

There may be feedback effects between a focus adaptation mechanism and the user's eye accommodation, especially if a time lag is involved. This leads us to the next topic.

10.11.1   Ghost Objects

This is an entirely new concept [115], expanding the possibilities of virtual objects far beyond those known or imagined from real ones. Consider what would happen if we could actively use our eye accommodation to pick out spots in 3D point clouds. Raw tomography data, for example, is fairly huge by the number of pixels and therefore hard to rotate in real time. Calculating features and surfaces for a solid modeling is even more difficult. If we are looking at nothing but rotating, transparent, raw data pixel clouds, our brain gives us a perfect 3D impression even on a 2D screen. Unfortunately with this simple approach, many features are just occluded by others, even if we render for optimum transparency and actively look at features from all sides.

In order to reduce calculations, confining the rendering process to the center of view, steered by eye tracking, has been tried. What if we also use depth accommodation (focus and eye parallax that is) to render just one depth level that we are accommodating, denser and crisper than others? It would save a lot of computing power as well, because we have to render each pixel only for a small area of main interest, 1/1000 of the volume for example, and anything else at far lower resolution.

Actively confining rendering efforts to area and depth has almost exclusively been addressed to computation reductions for solid modeling as mentioned above (except for [179], covering manipulations of pixel-cloud rendering with eye gestures).

In VR and AR, entirely new things could be created by exploiting active accommodation. This new approach (Figure 10.44) would use the eye parallax or accommodation, giving the actual distance of the point of interest, to render crisp only things at this distance, and others before and after it progressively blurred. Concurrently, foreground components could be made more transparent.

All of these are new, unreal features. Real objects can also be transparent, but even despite parallax and focus effects, we will always have difficulties seeing details within them. With virtual objects reacting to eye directions and parallax, uncovering the detail being viewed, this will be entirely different.

We could build virtual devices that are transparent, have features distributed in 3D space rather than on surfaces, and can be accessed throughout all their physical volume; an entirely new world of designs to explore. So a genuinely 3D device could have controls placed

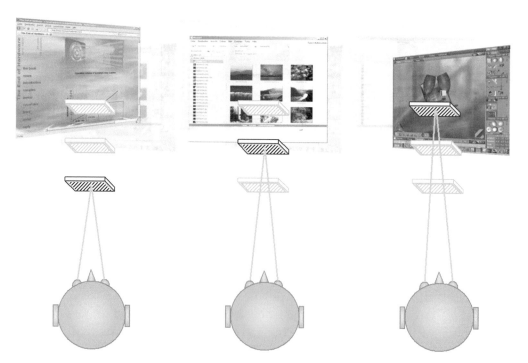

FIGURE 10.44 Active selection and transparency rendering of layered virtual window elements by active accommodation steering.

throughout all of its volume, in many different layers. As with 2D and $2^1/_2$D devices (any real machine is $2^1/_2$D, because its interface consists just of its surface), the combination of eye peering with finger pointing delivers an entirely unambiguous signal of intent.

There are many more possibilities: imagine virtual objects being like faint vapor when not in use, staying in place, just hinting at their existence, but becoming solid all of a sudden when you accommodate to their proper distance. Or, for example, looking through a wall (of course if the picture behind is available) by intentionally accommodating beyond it.

Several layers of windows on a computer screen (to mention the most familiar concepts), could simply be transparent but also change their transparency and crispness according to the depth accommodation of the user. Other than the transparency of current window managers, which is hardly useful at all, this could really work.

Then it would not only be possible to see a window quite well through another transparent one, we could also operate controls on the background window, by eye as well as by finger pointing, without mistaking the action as being meant for the foreground window. This means actual operation in 3D, something not even possible with physical 3D objects.

This computer screen would however have to be a virtual one, provided by a near-eye display. Although some of this may be considered for real displays as well, in that case it would be very difficult to accommodate by parallax on a screen that cannot deliver the appropriate focus as well, and even more so to grasp **into** the screen for the background window.

10.12 LIGHT FIELD NED

Applying light field principles for NED has specific implications. Auto stereoscopic rendering is not a topic here, because each eye has its own display anyway, and the eyes are in a fixed position toward the displays. The only obvious application for light field techniques in NED is focus synthesis. A lenslet arrangement as discussed in Section 9.5.3 at page 392 may be tried to realize a focus-synthesizing NED. In this case, the lenslets will be too close to the eye to be seen separately. They will also replace the one lens usually necessary for a close-up view of a small display. The screen area contributing to point formation here is approximately in the same order as the size of the pupil (the same principle as for a hologram, see Figure 5.35 on page 156). For a focus simulation, several divergent light rays must be able to hit the pupil from the display area through which a certain scenery pixel is seen (Figure 10.45). This requires several, or at best many, lenslets in a pupil-sized area, which may be about 3 mm^2. The "rays" emitted by the lenses, however, have a divergence $\Phi = \lambda/d$, caused by the diffraction limit (cf. Equation 3.34 on page 80).

These lenslets could deliver a better focus resolution than would follow from Equation 9.18 at page 393, but with possible effects from the focus forming only from a few light rays, and at the cost of lower image resolution due to their diffraction limit. An according approach is described in [171], also pointing out the diffraction limit issue. Moreover, the display used may require a very high pixel density, for the same considerations as described in Section 10.12.2.

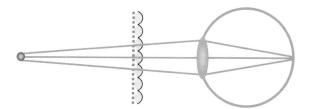

FIGURE 10.45 Reproducing focus by light fields requires multiple divergent beams approaching the pupil area.

10.12.1 Parallax Barrier NED

Using parallax barriers may appear to be even more problematic at a first glance. But this turns out to become a viable alternative with the introduction of advanced barrier patterns as mentioned in Section 9.4.1.2 at page 375 and their generation with a light valve display. Moreover, multiple active barriers as described in Section 9.4.1.4 at page 375 can provide even more complex light fields. The physical configuration necessary can be quite simple, requiring a minimum of just two stacked high-resolution LCD displays, according to a prototype concept presented in [129] (Figure 10.46).

The demanding part of the design, however, remains to be the dynamic real-time generation of the display patterns. These have to be content adaptive (as the entire approach is about providing different focus cues for different displayed objects), and likely they also have to be adaptive to eye rotation. This is done with two state-of-the-art graphics processors located behind the displays.

Using more parallax barriers, as for example in [182], allows for an even more complex beam forming. Theoretically, a sufficiently large number of display layers together with a sophisticated pattern generation could provide an optical impression close to that of a hologram.

10.12.2 Bragg Mirror Array NED

The lens array principle can be a basis for other design approaches. Any lenslet together with the display pixels in its area may be laid out as a separate magnifying box similar to

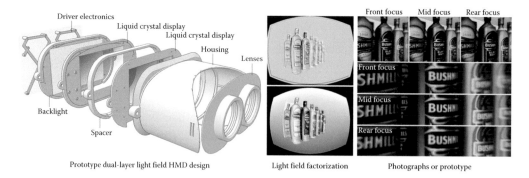

FIGURE 10.46 Light field stereoscope with two stacked LCD panels. Source: [129]. Image Courtesy: Gordon Wetzstein, Stanford University).

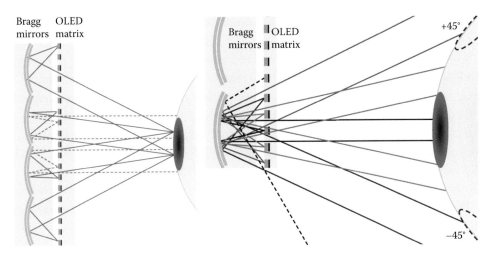

FIGURE 10.47   NED with a Bragg mirror array.

Figure 10.1 on page 418 and Figure 10.9 on page 426. These magnifying boxes then cover the display area, with some possible overlapping. An advantage of this approach, would be that it integrates display and optics into a single, thin plate.

Replacing the lenslets with holographic mirror elements leads to an approach presented in [244] (see Figure 10.47). The display in this case consists of LED pixels emitting away from the eye, with transparent gaps between them (similar display panel technology as in Figure 10.27 on page 441). An array of small concave mirrors, embodied as Bragg structures (cf. Section 5.4 at page 144 and Figure 5.15 on page 138), reflects the display image sections back toward the eye. The holographic mirrors with their according display areas work similar to the magnifying boxes of a lenticular display array. Like with a classical magnifying glass, the individual display areas are seen to be upright, the pixel sequence being preserved. Adjacent mirrors can therefore jointly contribute to delivering the same image pixel (dashed rays in Figure 10.47(left)), and the mirror cells can provide a complete image quite seamlessly.

In an NED application, the physical mirror boundaries should not be visible, as they are too near to focus upon. How well the cells will merge into a complete image, however, remains to be explored with real implementations.

The holographic mirrors are wavelength selective and if they consist of many individual Bragg layers, they will hardly be visible at wavelengths outside their very narrow action range. Therefore, this design can be used for transparent displays, suitable for augmented reality applications.

Several mirror structures can be merged in the same volume hologram, allowing for three reflection bands for the three primary colors. Moreover, neighboring mirror structures may overlap, which may be useful in terms of reducing aliasing effects and increasing resolution. Such overlapping will even inevitably occur, if the Bragg structures are produced similar to Figure 5.24 on page 146, with an array of point light sources (one for each mirror) and a planar or spherical reference beam. This should not result in conflicts between adjacent sections, as rays hitting the "wrong" mirror would be reflected away from the eye area (cf. Figure 10.47(right)), dashed ray).

A limiting factor for this approach is the directional selectivity of the Bragg mirror structures (cf. Section 5.4.3 at page 148); the angular range of the mirrors is therefore limited, and this may cause problems because eye rotation leads to a wide range of pupil positions.

With the maximum eye rotation of $\pm 45°$, causing a pupil displacement of $\approx \pm 8$ mm, each magnifying box also has to support a large angular range, or the peripheral view will be limited, causing a sort of a tunnel view (cf. Figure 10.47(right)). The mirrors may also have an edge astigmatism affecting the angular resolution for peripheral view.

Another difficulty arises from the required resolution of the transmissive display layer itself. The light field generated should ideally provide the same angular resolution as the eye, which is typically 1 arcmin. While a mirror size of, for example, 2 mm diameter is sufficient for this, the appropriate display pixel raster would then have to be smaller than 1 µm; which is not a very difficult issue for a standard display, but hard to achieve for a transmissive display. Making the mirrors larger may cause the mirror raster to become visible. The resolution of the entire display array would therefore have to be very high, as the full pixel count would have to be provided for each and any mirror element. Although the image content would be identical and repeated for each mirror area, this is anything but trivial. The patent [244] deals with several methods to overcome this, up to the extent of proposing an array of small LED points laterally oscillating to provide the impression of a denser pixel array in a time-multiplexed way.

A first-announced approach to holographic mirror array displays is the **Lisplay** by **LusoVu**. Details about it are not yet available. Working prototypes have been announced for 2016.

10.12.3 The Pinlight Display

Another interesting approach has been demonstrated in [183]. It uses the principle of inverted pinhole cameras (i.e., pinhole projectors). A very small light source (pinlight), together with a light valve display (SLM) near the eye, can provide an image of an approximately pupil-sized display area on the retina. With an array of pinlights, many pupil-sized sections of a display can together deliver a larger image.

Figure 10.48 shows the principle. The eye in this case is assumed to be accommodated to infinity. Light rays originating from a point before the eye, at a distance about equal to the eyeball diameter, then become approximately parallel after passing the pupil, and provide an image of a display area between the light source and the eye, in the manner of a shadow cast. A challenge arising from the principle is also illustrated: adjacent display areas won't overlap seamlessly (p_x, dashed ray). This is because the pixel sequence in the individual fields is inverse to the field sequence. The display areas assigned to any of the individual pinlights must therefore be adapted to pupil size and position.

With an always entirely lit array of pinlights, as used in the demonstrator, areas without any displayed objects will be the brightest, overlaying the real world behind the display with a considerable light fog. Where objects are displayed, there will be less brightness, a local dimming of the environment, and a transparent appearance of the objects.

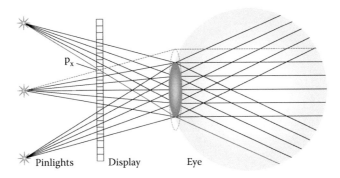

FIGURE 10.48 Pinlight display: image formation and sub-image combination.

A pinlight array allowing for an individual dimming of the pinlights could avoid the background light fog. Using bright pinlights, the display could be adjusted to be very dark for the active areas, providing a mask display function together with the image formation.

A problem of the pinlight concept becomes obvious when regarding a single bright pixel in the light valve display: the wavefront originating from one of the pinlights widens, as the pixel area becomes a new origin (cf. Figure 3.1 on page 54 and 3.2 on page 55). The divergence of the new wavefront is given by Equation 3.39 on page 86 (Figure 3.38 on page 86). This produces a crosstalk—or blur—between adjacent display pixels. If we regard a pinlight display with light valve in 12-mm distance from the eye, and a pixel size of 80 μm, the visual pixel size (measured from the eye center) would be approx. 10 arcmin and the additional beam divergence would be approx. 20 arcmin (λ assumed as 500 nm). The effect could perhaps be reduced a bit by changing the distance to the pinlights, but even if we allow a contrast falloff to the usual $1/e$, the resolution achieved would only be about 10 arcmin in the end. The original paper [183] claims even less. We may wait and see if this can be improved.

10.13 HOLOGRAPHIC IMAGE GENERATION FOR NED

10.13.1 Holographic Scanners

Instead of a moving mirror, the deflection of a laser beam could also be effected by a variable grating pattern [112]. Although the following is almost entirely theoretical at the current state of technology, advances in micro displays are making applications such as this quite likely.

We have demonstrated this principle in Chapter 5. A tiny display with very high resolution could form such a grating, allowing for enough modulation flexibility to grant precise deflection angles. Feeding entire grating images into the display for any tiny change in deflection angle is of course not possible. The patterns required would best be stored or calculated within the chip.

With Figure 10.49 we want to recall the grating equation (see Section 5.3.1 at page 129). If we change the line distances d of a grating, we get different deflection angles β. If we calculate this more thoroughly, we see that an incident angle of $\alpha = 60°$, for example, could

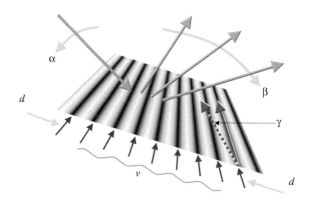

FIGURE 10.49 Grating deflection mirror principle.

theoretically be altered to an exit angle (β) from about 10° to >80°, without any unwanted modes (*n* > 1) showing up.

With sufficiently small mirrors, allowing for a good sine shape approximation (Figure 10.50), higher modes would be suppressed anyway, and the modulation and angles could also be optimized to minimize the zero mode.

The main limitations of this approach are lack of diffraction efficiency, the inferior definition for small angles due to large *d* values, and the smaller apparent mirror area for large angles (which can be partly compensated by a larger mirror area).

The efficiency resulting will be inferior compared to a scanning mirror, but this is not a really critical issue for near-eye displays, because we would never need more than 1 mW of effective light power entering the eye.

The straight line grating in one direction could be produced by generating a sine pattern in the other direction (for gray values), and in just one dimension. The values *v* can be fed into the chip from the side, steering all pixel elements in a line at once.

By changing the line angle γ as well, we could use the grating to deflect in two dimensions at once. Generating such slanted line patterns is complicated, as the lines have to appear at very precise angles. With some dedicated calculation circuitry however, excellent phase

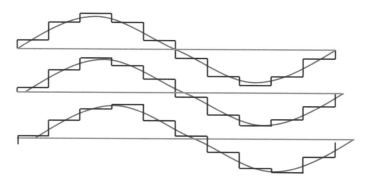

FIGURE 10.50 Generating approximated phase values with raster displays.

accuracy could in principle be achieved for any pixel in a raster display. So this is just a matter of finding an appropriate design.

As the chip would essentially be 1…2 mm small, we could also just tilt or rotate it for the slower deflection axis. We would not need more than about 100 Hz, so this would not be too difficult.

Several other operation modes are possible, for holographic elements. A small hologram could produce parts of the viewing area sequentially, serving each with its own partial image, staged inlays for example, as we have discussed with laser displays.

The deflection chip could even write an image with different resolution parts in just one sweep, switching line frequencies even within lines, without alignment errors. It could also address the edges more often, where the eyes are more flicker sensitive.

A very interesting application would be focusing. A zone plate-like diffraction pattern could simulate a concave mirror, with the possibility of changing its focus quickly, and of generating multiple foci as desired. This would be an interesting approach combined with those in [254] (Section 10.11 at page 452). Combining up to three diffraction displays (for horizontal and vertical deflection and focus), could deliver degrees of freedom similar to a fully holographic display.

Finally we should note that the basic fringe patterns could likely be improved for better efficiency. See Section 10.6.3 at page 431 for a possible approach that could also be applied here.

But what kind of display technology would actually be the right one here?

Some digital holography approaches use DMD devices [132]. It is quite obvious that DMD pixels could be made even smaller than F-LCoS. Sufficiently small structures don't even have to be exact mirrors, because a sub-wavelength mirror will reflect anything as a spherical wave front anyway. For a hologram without artifacts though, we need to produce patterns with gray levels, and pulse-width modulation won't work in this case because interference occurs only between photons emitted at the same time. So the existing attempts to produce even simple Fourier holograms (Section 9.6.3 at page 402) with these devices yield unacceptably noisy results.

What could be effective would be to switch structures way below light wavelength, using the dithering approach. With silicon chip structures below 45 nm (1/10 of blue light wavelength) in mass production already, this may not be unrealistic at all, and the individual switching elements could be an entirely different and much simpler construction than current DMDs.

The piston approach (cf. Section 7.3.5 at page 254)or index modulated LCoS (cf. Section 7.3.13 at page 260 seem likely to be a much better solution so far, because they are analog and natively produce phase shifts (hence, good efficiency). A problem will be mechanical constraints of pixel size vs. required phase shift. A piston display may well need excitations of $\leq$ 80 nm at pixel sizes below 1 μm, which is a great deal. We may also expect effects from pixel boundaries, etc.

Another solution one could consider are MLMs (Moving Liquid Mirror displays) [294], but these have not yet left the laboratory at all. The problem with these MLMs is modulation speed, some milliseconds typically, making this technology interesting for holographic displays perhaps, but not for holographic scanner mirrors.

10.13.2 Holographic Near-Eye Displays

Holographic modulators and laser scanners are extreme varieties of a general wave function modulator for laser beams. The development of current high resolution LCoS SLMs with extremely small pixel sizes had actually been motivated by laser beam shaping.

Integrating not only driver but also signal-processing structures into a holographic display chip could make sense if a real-time synthesis of patterns is required. While achieving full CGH in real time may take 10...15 more years of development, Fourier holograms (Section 9.6.3 at page 402) may nevertheless be accomplished quite soon. We have already treated an existing projection display of this type (Section 7.10.9 at page 294).

Could fully holographic displays (or Fourier based ones) be useful for near-eye displays? The answer may be yes. With a normal hologram, thousands of different viewing angles are contained in the wave front. The larger the display area, the more there are. If we examine a small hologram piece, as if through a keyhole, as we have discussed already, we get more or less a 2D image. In contrast to an ordinary 2D image, however, it still may support different focusing for different objects as a little remainder of the 3D content. If the piece gets even smaller, it acts like a pinhole camera and focus is the same over the entire image (i.e., then it's really 2D). Clipping out even still smaller pieces, the image would get more and more blurred because there won't remain enough fringes to sufficiently define points.

With near-eye displays, there is only one viewer position; no other perspectives must be generated. Hence, in principle we have a keyhole hologram, essentially small enough that the number of required pixels won't need to be much larger than with a conventional display.

As pattern-line sizes are always dictated by wavelength, a very small micro display will in any case not need an astronomical number of pixels even for holographic purposes. Its image has to be enlarged by optics. The objects must be generated in such a way that they appear in their actual size after the magnification.

With the optics reviewed so far, we have seen that it is very difficult to get large magnification together with overall accurate focus and low distortion. With a display chip showing a hologram, we have the option to add some 3D properties; in other words, we could assign any virtual distance to any displayed pixel.

This procedure behaves a bit as if we were simulating lenses. Lenses recorded in a hologram look and behave like real lenses. With a CGH, we could simulate not only lenses but a fairly complex and dynamic optical behavior. So the virtual image pixels are not confined to the display plane but form a 3D point cloud (Figure 10.51), with the ability to simulate object distance (focus) as well as a compensation for different positions of the pupil within the exit pupil volume.

10.14 ADVANCED HOE DESIGNS

10.14.1 Wave Guides

Wave guides in the context of NED optics are slabs or rods of transparent material, inside of which light is propagating with multiple total reflections at the inner surfaces. Diffractive or

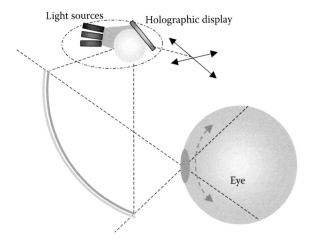

FIGURE 10.51   Raw scheme with CGH display (imaginary pixel positions visualized by sphere).

holographic structures (HOE) are often used to couple light into or out of the wave guide. This technology has led to a variety of new NED designs. It offers high design flexibility and compact optical assemblies. There is, however, a principal limit to the FOV, as this corresponds to the angular range of the light bundle propagating in the wave guide (the *light cone*) [181], for example, states about 45°.

10.14.1.1 Lumus
The extreme characteristics possible with HOEs enable very unconventional designs. In a recently launched product by **Lumus** Inc. (Figure 10.52), for example, light beams from a display are turned into an almost flat bundle by a first HOE (also referred to as a diffractive element), then are totally reflected several times from the inner front and back surfaces of carrier glasses constituting a *wave guide*, and are finally reflected into the eye by a second

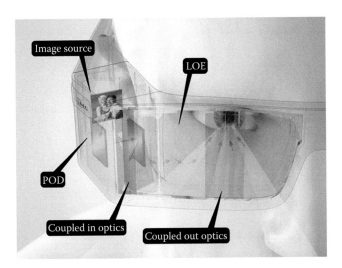

FIGURE 10.52   Display module using a wave guide and holographic (diffractive) optical elements. See-through, viewing angle are design adjustable. Image courtesy: **Lumus** Inc.

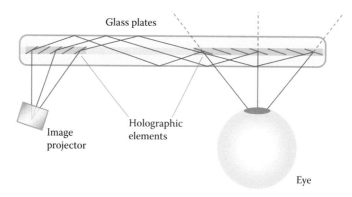

FIGURE 10.53   HOE based flat near-eye display optics (Lumus).

HOE (Figure 10.53). The two HOEs can be designed independent of each other, to almost any desired aperture size and focus length.

10.14.1.2 WaveOptics

WaveOptics, Ltd. recently announced lightweight glasses technology for mass applications. Details are not yet released, but patents indicate that it might in principle be a slab-type wave guide with input and output diffractive elements, resembling the above-mentioned Lumus display.

10.14.1.3 Microsoft Hololens

Another recent example of a wave guide display is the **Microsoft Hololens**. The device has three separate layers for red, green, and blue. Optical detail is not yet available. Figure 10.54 shows an exploded view of the device, revealing the display. The light engine of the display is positioned in the middle, between the light-guiding slabs. Figure 10.3 on page 419 shows the complete device.

FIGURE 10.54   **Microsoft Hololens** display, exploded view. (Used with permission from **Microsoft** [https://news.microsoft.com/videos/b-roll-hololens/]).

10.14.2 The Quantum Display

A quite different solution using diffraction gratings and wave guides is the **Quantum Display** (Figure 10.55), as dubbed by its inventor **BAE Systems**. This may remind one of the wedge display at a first glance, but unlike that, they use a straight glass slab (Figure 10.56). A diffraction foil at the front side lets light leak out at each reflection and converts the exit beam angles to a range around the perpendicular, the desired viewing range. The exit angles

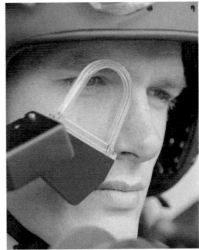

FIGURE 10.55 **Q-Sight** display, helmet mounted. Image courtesy: **BAE Systems**.

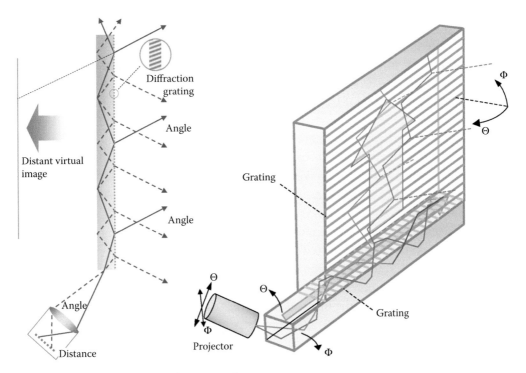

FIGURE 10.56 **Quantum Display**, principle.

depend on the reflection angles of the beams in the slab, which are given by a projection lens and correspond to positions on the projector's display.

Beams from certain display positions leave the projection screen anywhere, but all at the same angle. This results in a virtual image at infinity. Hence, the quantum display is a collimated display.

The right part of Figure 10.56 shows the transformation of projector output angles into two-dimensional display output angles (Φ, Θ). The light beams are deflected several times between walls and top and bottom of a thin, rectangular input wave guide rod, while preserving their angular vector components in the horizontal and vertical. A grating at the top side of the rod resolves the horizontal coordinate (actually an angle, here dubbed Θ). This grating works similarly to the one on the front of the display, a slab type wave guide. Then the rays enter the display slab and behave as shown in the left part of the illustration, but already have their Θ component, and also the preserved second component, which is resolved into the vertical output component (here Φ) when hitting the slab's front grating.

Being clearly transparent for perpendicular light, quantum display technology is used in head-up displays and also in military head mounted displays (e.g., q-sight and q-hud by BAE Systems).

The display is very compact, has a very large exit pupil of, for example, 35 mm, and a field of view of, for example, 30° (up to 40° available). It is monochrome, but the principle behind it allows for expansion to color as with any holography based technology. Current military HMDs are available in monocular or binocular versions and also with integrated eye trackers. Specific advantages are high brightness, the extremely large exit pupil, and the perfectly collimated image, reducing registering efforts (Figure 10.20 on page 434).

10.14.3 A Multiple Depth Plane Display

Magic Leap, Inc. are working on a slab display with the ability to produce image content at different virtual distances. A description of the underlying principles can be found in an according patent application [181]. Our analysis is based on this patent text; actual products may deviate from this.

Light rays from a microprojector are injected into one end of a rectangular wave guide rod and are totally reflected inside of it, bouncing forth and back between the guide walls. Their angular distribution, corresponding to the position distribution of pixels in the image, is preserved in two dimensions throughout multiple reflections (as illustrated in Figure 10.57(left)). By introducing several weak reflecting mirror surfaces inside the wave guide, small parts of the light can be redirected out of the guide, producing a virtual image. The angular distribution of the injected light (also referred to as the light cone), is translated into a point distribution (a virtual image) at infinity, if the mirror elements are all flat and parallel (Figure 10.57(center left)). The light cone may also be back reflected at the ends of the waveguide and reused for the image formation, if this is supported by additional bragg structures for the backward direction. A complete display slab is made from a number of parallel wave guides (Figure 10.57(right)). Each of the wave guides in a displays slab must be supplied with the projected light cone. This is accomplished by using another wave guide ("distributor") with one planar mirror for each of the display wave guides.

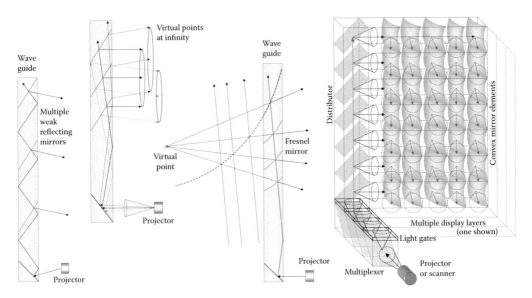

FIGURE 10.57   Left: principle of a rod-type wave guide with straight mirrors, preserving the entrance angle. Center left: translating input angles to image point angles. Center right: defining image point distance by convex mirrors (example of an optional Fresnel mirror). Right: an array combining multiple layers of wave guides with multiple 2D curved mirrors and a multiplexer wave guide.

Producing virtual image points at distances other than infinity, a key feature of the **MagicLeap** display, is accomplished by introducing convex mirrors (cf. Figure 3.17 on page 67).

Within the wave guide, there is no space for a large mirror surface (dashed curve in Figure 10.57(center right)). If necessary, the mirror surface can be split into segments, resulting in a Fresnel mirror (similar to the Fresnel lens in Figure 3.23 on page 72). Figure 10.57(center right), shows the beam reflections on the curved surface as well as on the Fresnel segments within the wave guide, both having identical angles, and the formation of an image point. Note that a parallel displacement of the beams would still result in the same image point. Changing the incident beam angle would result in a different image point but at the same virtual distance. The Fresnel mirror group must be repeated throughout the length of the wave guide. The mirror elements in several parallel wave guides forming a display slab must then be formed according to a 2D convex Fresnel mirror shape, otherwise the point formation would not work correctly. As only about pupil-sized regions on the display contribute to point formation (cf. Figure 10.23 on page 438), the useful size of the Fresnel groups is very limited and they should be considered just an interesting option.

Using mirrors with a certain curvature results in a display rendering an image at just one virtual distance. For a perceptually continuous range of distances, several display layers have to be stacked upon each other. An additional wave guide ("multiplexer"), with a planar mirror and a sequentially switched light gate for each display layer, may distribute the light cone of a single projector into the separate display layers. Alternatively, separate micro projectors can be used for each of the display layers.

The angular distribution of rays is preserved throughout all these steps (see Figure 10.57(right), symbolized by the light cones).

The patent states that the mirror surfaces should be highly angular selective (to cancel out unwanted modes), which indicates that Bragg mirrors might be a preferred implementation. The image source or projector is described to consist of red, green, and blue light sources feeding a single-mode fiber and a scanner. The favored scanning principle according to publications is the scanning fiber projector (see Section 7.10.15.1 at page 303).

As scanning projectors are too slow for a multiplexing of the display layers, a dedicated projector for each layer is used in this case. Principally, a conventional microprojector with a spatial display should also be possible, if it produces narrow-banded light.

For a workable display thickness, up to 10 layers with 1-mm-wide wave guides could be tolerated. The width of the wave guides limits the resolution achievable to about 2 arcmin (diffraction limit for 1-mm aperture). With this, 5...10 display layers are required to provide a sufficient and continuous depth range (cf. Figure 4.31 on page 115). The angular range (FOV) achievable is principally limited to 45°, according to the patent publication.

How the wave guides are manufactured is not yet published. Bragg mirror structures could perhaps be produced similar to HOEs (see Section 5.4.2 at page 146). The display works quite similar to a lenslet light field display. Fresnel mirrors would likely repeat about every 2...3 mm, and there may be possible effects caused by the area boundaries. This may also be an issue if only single, equal mirrors are used. Replacing the mirror segments with Bragg reflector structures produced with a holographic method, allowing for overlapping or interleaved mirror structures, could reduce the effect.

10.15 CONTACT LENS DISPLAYS

The quest for the most minimal near-eye display hardware caused speculations about integrating displays into contact lenses, and research projects, some sponsored by defense funds, have been started to explore the possibilities. This is in a very early stage, however, and some recent reports about actual "contact lens displays" were greatly exaggerated.

A major effort toward future contact lens displays comes from researchers at the University of Washington ([126], Figure 10.58), where the embedding of circuits into a contact lens was demonstrated. The lens shown contained no light sources. A later design mainly focused on power transfer ([216]) has a receiving antenna ring around the lens edge and a single micro LED. An effective energy transfer of about 125μ W could be demonstrated.

Given the many problems contact lenses currently have in everyday applications, it is hard to conceive how this could work, in the battlefield at least. First, contacts aren't supposed to be worn for more than 12 hours for various reasons. Then, although you may even swim with open eyes wearing contacts at least in fresh-water, this is risky as long as the contact lens is still in tear liquid. A sudden, unexpected splash could then wash it out.

If you drink too little, you dehydrate and the contacts may simply fall out of your eyes. Imagine a soldier fumbling around with liquid, trying to clean and reinsert his contact lens.

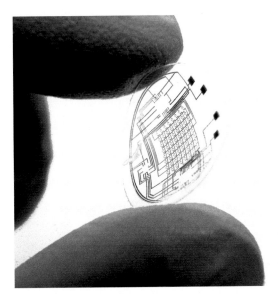

FIGURE 10.58 Contact Lens With Integrated Inorganic Semiconductor Devices. Image courtesy: Babak Parviz, University of Washington.

Dust and sand would also create problems. Dirt in the eye is much more difficult to flush out if contacts are involved.

Apart from this, it is not only a technical but also a major physical problem to design anything that would generate an image in the eye while it sits right on the pupil. Nevertheless, let's try an unbiased look at the options there are.

A naive approach would be a sort of display with many little light sources. In order to form an image on the retina, the light has to come in approximately parallel as it gets focused by the eye's lens. Small light sources, however, do not emit anything parallel. Any single source, the smaller it gets, emits a more or less spherical wave. This wouldn't produce anything like an image inside the eye, or at best it would just be a very blurred agglomerate of a few pixels.

We also have to consider that anything able to focus a light beam sufficiently to form a crisp pixel has to be 2 mm in diameter, or at least 1mm if we allow for a just still acceptable, lower resolution of 2 arcmin. So the image forming element, of whatsoever technology, of a display sitting directly on the pupil would have to comply to these size requirements. Hence, we face the problem how to avoid this element form occluding the sight of the user.

One option would be an array consisting of many coherent sources. If they were all in phase, they could all together form a beam able to create an image. Just using many tiny laser diodes however, would not deliver any global phase relation. We would need a single laser light source, whose light is then phase modulated by many single elements distributed right in front of the pupil. Phase modulation could, for example, be accomplished by liquid crystals changing their refractive index, or by movable micromirrors (Figure 10.59). Then we could think about directing the light beam as a scanner, or forming a Fourier hologram (Section 9.6.3 at page 402), delivering images appearing at infinity, and affordable to calculate. Modifying this for different image distances would still be possible with limited effort. The modulating elements could, however, also affect direct sight, which is of course not intended.

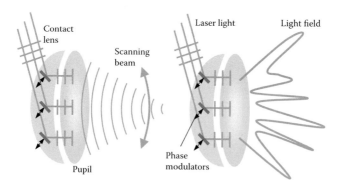

FIGURE 10.59 Hypothetical contact lens displays with a moving mirror phased array scanner (left) or a Fourier Hologram (right), using a single coherent light source.

A conventional approach could use a tiny projector, which would have to be about 1mm, just small enough to fit into a (thick) contact lens (Figure 10.60(left)). What becomes obvious if we evaluate this with a realistic, geometric eye model: the iris sits several millimeters behind the contact lens and strong vignetting occurs with small iris diameters, limiting the angle of view that can be addressed. Moreover, even a 1 mm projector will cause severe view occlusions. Spectrally selective optical assemblies with mirrors or HOEs, perhaps combined with transparent OLED, could be conceived for less occlusive solutions. Another approach could be an array of several even smaller projectors, combining their relatively blurred pictures for a crisper one (super resolution as discussed in Section 8.6.2 at page 334). Yet, this requires a perfect alignment of all projectors. While such an approach could solve the vignetting problem, the super resolution principle would fail for small pupil sizes because only beams from a fraction of all projectors could then reach any specific part of the retina. Implanting a display/projection assembly into an artificial eye lens or into the eyeball itself (Figure 10.60(right)) could avoid the main disadvantages – maybe an option for

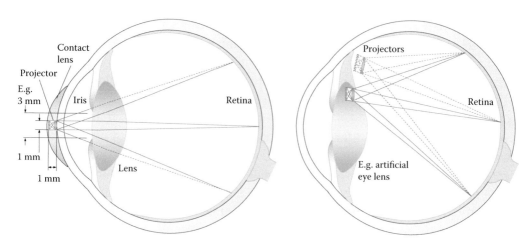

FIGURE 10.60 Left: a collimated micro projector embedded in a contact lens, being a close trade-off between size and resolution and also suffering from vignetting by the iris. Right: a display embedded into an artificial eye lens or implanted into the eyeball would have less restrictions.

future cyborg soldiers? A different approach would be an adaptation of the aforementioned quantum display. Nevertheless, we would again need a 1 mm projector lens for a decent resolution.

Finally, we could think of a holographic optical assembly close to the Lumus approach, with a display chip directly at the image injection plane, keeping the entire construction more flat.

What we have not considered to this point: a contact lens could rotate, or be displaced a little, so its position against the iris would have to be traced, detectable perhaps by tiny cameras or light sensors inside the lens border, looking toward the retina.

We may also need eye trackers to know what the lens bearer views. In theory, microscopic cameras inside the contact lens could do this, by looking just where the eye looks, and they could also concurrently deliver orientation data.

Quantum displays and similar designs as discussed here can also work bidirectional; however, they would deliver images from the eye rather than from outside, just adequate for iris detection. A second light path integrated into the assembly, pointing outward and operating at a different wavelength (infrared) that would not disturb the normal optical path, could perhaps be used for alignment with outside scenery.

The Lisplay (cf. Figure 10.47 on page 459) has been claimed to allow integrating into contact lenses. Apart from the problem of designing an appropriate hologram structure, there are also remaining problems of power supply, signal transmission, etc.

Another item to be discussed is a mask display. Some considerations including this topic can be found in [116].

Shaping of light is not the only challenge with a contact lens display. We have to provide power, not only for the display, but also for signal processing, and this can be quite heavy (pun intended). Yet nobody would want a wire going to the lens.

One possibility could be solar cells, powered by environmental light or by infrared emitters close to the eye, or by an external laser source that could concurrently deliver an in-phase illumination for image forming elements. Another possibility discussed is radio frequency (similar to RFID devices) as in the above-mentioned article [216]. For the mere light output required (order of 1 mW) this is conceivable, but in a real application it would require a problematic amount of RF power, or a transmitting antenna close by, in a glasses frame perhaps.

Thus, even with the latter approaches, we would still need some frame, helmet, or glasses construction to hold the energy source or emitter. It may be questioned what the advantage over classical display glasses would then really be.

10.15.1 Contact Lens-Supported Displays

While building a display as such into a contact lens is difficult, contact lenses can also be used as optical components supporting separate displays. The **iOptik** concept proposed by **Innovega** has a contact lens with a small central lens area focusing that part of the eye pupil to a display positioned close before the eye (principle shown in Figure 10.61). The optical path for the central lens is closely similar to the hypothetical projector inside the lens, as depicted in Figure 10.60(left). It may therefore suffer from the same potential vignetting of the FOV for small iris openings.

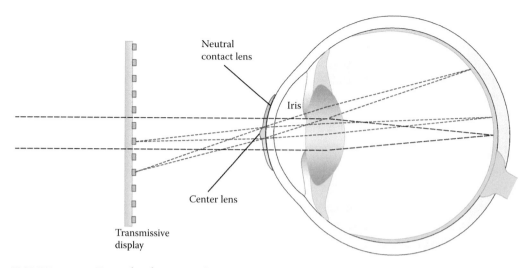

FIGURE 10.61 Example of a contact lens-supported display.

That NED itself may consist of an LED array with transparent gaps (transmissive display), only emitting toward the eye.

The iOptik is claimed to use some sort of filtering to avoid environment light passing the central lens and display light passing the remaining contact lens area. This may be circular polarizers or spectral filters. Details are not yet available.

An advantage of the concept is the ability to shape the contact lens as a prescription-correctional lens. A disadvantage is the restriction to people willing or able to wear contact lenses.

Another restriction originates from the size of the central lens. It has to be below 1 mm to avoid complete coverage of the pupil in bright environments. This limits the resolution obtained to about half the maximum eye resolution of 1 arcmin (cf. Section 3.4.3.6 at page 79).

10.16 ADAPTIVE DISPLAYS AND EYE TRACKING

As stated above, many different effects demand for information about the movements and positions of the viewer's eye pupils. This is necessary in order to compensate for exit pupil restrictions and eye-position-dependent distortions due to the optical construction, and to achieve the accurate and artifact-free positioning of virtual display objects and a proper alignment of mask display content (Section 10.17.3 at page 487), to mention only the most important issues.

A very important application of an eye-tracking system would also be eye pointing, in an advanced user interface.

Therefore, an eye- tracking system is of great advantage. Such systems, in principle, are state of the art. They simply use a camera and image-processing software to track the user's pupil.

10.16.1 Adaptation Requirements

Let us have a look at the positioning problems that occur and the measures to be taken.

Figure 10.62 shows possible position changes of display glasses relative to the eye. The eye tracker, possibly some extra sensors (measuring distance and tilt), and the image-synthesizer software may have to compensate for all of this dynamically.

In an assembly other than the ideal solution of large exit pupil and objects at infinity only, the displayed image will have to undergo various adaptations such as resizing, shifting, tilting, trapezoid distortion, and so forth, in order to constantly appear geometrically perfect to the observer. A first work on this type of image compensation can be found in [252].

It is important to remember that the eye is not steady, as a camera, but is in permanent motion, focusing on details. Even by just looking around in a virtual scene, different parts of the exit pupil are addressed and some subtle perspective changes may occur, which could affect orientation in virtual space. Anything from an unreal impression up to headache or vertigo may result from this.

Image generation, and usually the display as well, will have a delay of at least one frame (e.g., 20 ms), which can result in a significant displacement, with fast movements. This is an issue with head movements and the registration of virtual and real image parts as well; yet, as the head has a certain inertia, a motion prediction algorithm can amend this. For reactions to eye movements, we can rely only on display speed and the fact that small geometry changes may be more forgiving in the case of delays persisting.

Displays building the image pixel by pixel, such as CRT and laser scanners, offer the principal possibility of changing their beam deflection in real time, hence they could react to motion-sensor input directly, within microseconds. This would allow for a very stable image impression.

Other displays, such as LCD, build up an entire picture at a time. Inevitably with these displays, fast movements may result in blur or stroboscopic effects; only a fast frame rate can help to avoid this.

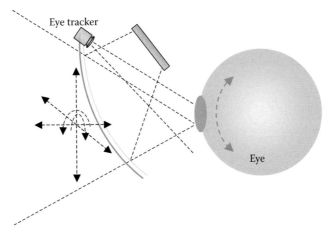

FIGURE 10.62 Example assembly of near-eye display with an eye tracker.

10.16.2 Eye Tracking

Although eye trackers are not anything new, we will consider some design aspects in conjunction with near-eye displays. We will also encounter a relatively new variety, the retina tracker.

Though still expensive for professional use, cheap eye trackers have already been built into cameras and camcorders, guiding the autofocus, for example (**Canon EOS5**, 1992, and **Movieboy E1**, 1994). Eye trackers for display glasses (example in Figure 10.63) have to be much faster and more accurate, but this is simply a matter of chip complexity.

Today, the use of eye trackers is still confined to a few applications, so they are correspondingly expensive. Nevertheless, current models are very small and would fit a much wider range of applications (Figures 10.64 through 10.67).

An eye tracker basically consists of a micro camera and some image analysis software or hardware. Locating the pupil and the iris in an image is just basic image processing (usually based on the Hough transform). There are many options for integrating an eye tracker. The micro camera could, for example, use the main mirror of glasses optics as part of its lens, a camera could be integrated into the display, and possibilities of that nature.

An eye-tracker camera does not require high resolution, but a faster image frequency than the normal video rate of 50 or 60 frames is necessary.

FIGURE 10.63 **Viewpoint PC-60** eye tracker, mounted on glasses. Image courtesy: **Arrington Research**.

FIGURE 10.64 Sensing eye distance by iris diameter.

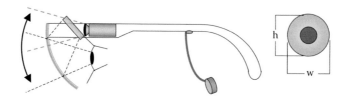

FIGURE 10.65 Detecting tilt by width/height comparison of the iris or pupil.

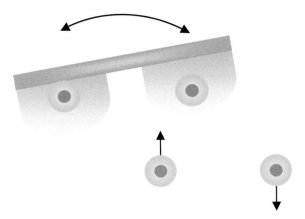

FIGURE 10.66 Lateral tilt detection can be achieved by comparing the vertical eye positions. Here we exploit the fact that eyes usually don't move in opposite vertical directions.

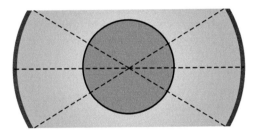

FIGURE 10.67 Finding the center of partially occluded iris or pupil from visible edge arcs.

"One-chip" eye trackers integrating the Hough transform in a low-power, parallel processing CMOS chip are already available, even with 800 Hz image rate (**FhG-IDMT**). One could also conceive a completely integrated CMOS light detector array with an integrated pupil-recognition circuit, that would be ultimately fast. It could even be made just slightly larger than the pupil image and be moved physically, actually tracking the pupil image.

A new method suggested in [115] would be the detection of pattern motion (*visual flow*), a method adapted from optical computer mice (Figure 10.68). This would detect iris motion

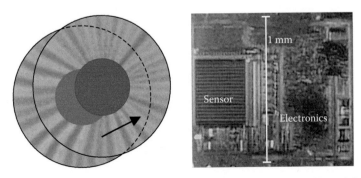

FIGURE 10.68 Detecting very fast motion from simple pattern shifting (left), and the actual motion sensor chip of an optical mouse (right).

robust and efficiently within milliseconds, with minimum effort. With help of visual flow, the actual eye tracker could work with a much lower frame rate, would be much simpler to implement.

Eye trackers are currently not common in near-eye displays, but will be indispensable in the future. Most applications that we are presenting here would include eye tracking.

10.16.2.1 Optical Constructions with Eye Trackers

DMD elements deflect light in off position as well. Thus, we could place an eye tracker camera to receive light from the eye just in this position (Figure 10.69). This would result in a good eye-tracker image with little space required. Rays from the eye will also approach the eye tracker parallel, as required for a camera.

A quite similar approach may be used with other SLM types as well. Because an eye-tracker camera needs some light to see, we would probably use infrared light in order to avoid conflicts with other requirements. Using surface reflection or a dichroic mirror for infrared (one that would have to be transparent to visible light), at the surface of a LED or similar display, we could have the eye tracker camera looking directly into the optical path (Figure 10.70).

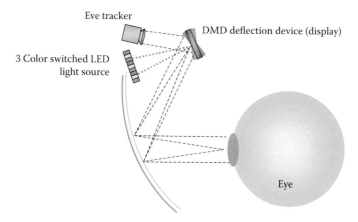

FIGURE 10.69 Eye tracking in a DMD design.

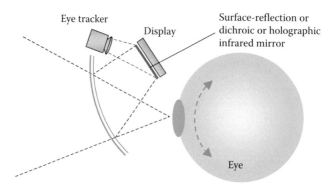

FIGURE 10.70 Coupling example of an eye tracking camera with a near-eye display.

Conversely, we could also place the eye tracker first (with a different main mirror curvature) and use it as a reflector to pass the remaining light to additional optics and the display.

10.16.2.2 Combining Eye Tracking with SLMs

In Figure 10.71), we have combined an eye-tracker chip (left, magnified) and a laser unit (shown right) in the same optical path. The tiny laser-scanner mirror is integrated in the center of the eye-tracker chip (hardly affecting its function). Just a single, small dichroic or holographic mirror, over 90% transparent, brings the picture into the eye.

The entire tracker/scanner unit could be moved to compensate for eye movements, which would also allow the use of a very small tracker camera chip, hardly more sizable than the pupil.

Other variations would use a conventional display. The eye tracker in Figure 10.72 (left, shown enlarged) uses infrared light, which enables the two different light paths to be integrated.

A display chip with integrated light sensitive pixels could work as a retina tracker (Figure 10.72 (right), see Section 10.16.3).

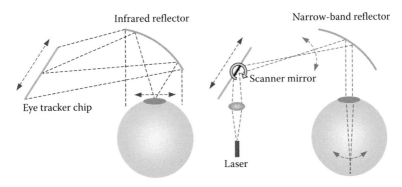

FIGURE 10.71 Eye tracker chip with integrated laser scanning mirror.

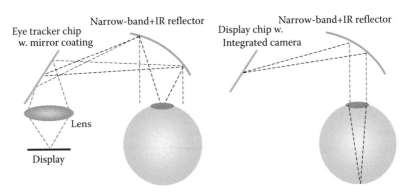

FIGURE 10.72 Dual optical path eye tracker assembly (left) and retina tracker (right).

10.16.3 Retina Tracking

Without lenses, an eye tracker would not see the pupil because it is way out of focus. There is, however, something automatically in focus, which is the retina, seen through the eye pupil. Because the optics and the user's accommodation will always automatically adapt to render a sharp image of the display on the retina, the same will apply for the opposite direction as well.

The retina carries a network of capillary blood vessels, characteristic for each individual (Figure 10.73). Movements of this pattern and even its absolute position can be determined as easily as that of a pupil; therefore this can replace conventional eye tracking. Retina tracking is currently used in eye surgery and has also been explored for military applications, but there has been no application yet in connection with AR.

Retina tracking has specific advantages over conventional eye tracking: Some people tend to squeeze their eyes, which can be a problem with conventional eye trackers, because an insufficient number of arc structures of the pupil or iris borders are visible. Retina patterns can also be used to identify a person, and therefore replace the iris pattern for this purpose.

The retina has to be illuminated for this, and sufficient light from it has to reach the display/sensor chip. Ambient light from the scene will also be on the retina, and it will form an image there. The image sensor in the display will see both on the retina – the environmental scene image and the image from the display – enabling a direct control of proper alignment. Separating the overlaid images of display content and retina structure can be done by subtracting the display image from the camera image, because the image coming back from the retina will hit the very display pixels it originated from.

The mask display's occlusion area may also be adjusted using the display camera image. We could do calibrations on-the-fly, by darkening the mask display and the normal projection for a very short time and projecting markers during that time, too short for the user to perceive. It has already been demonstrated, with studio illuminations by projectors instead of the usual beamers, that marks can be flashed invisibly if the mark projection is followed by a negative of it immediately. For example, add 50% light for 10 ms and subtract 50% for the next 10 ms, and nobody will notice anything, though an electronic camera would see it. Dedicated calibration procedures and continuous refinements of the calibration from differences

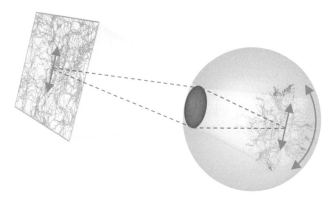

FIGURE 10.73 Retina tracking principle.

measured during normal use may serve as a dynamic adaptation for displacements of the display glasses.

This technology, if it works, could be a formidable simplification for AR applications, also with respect to the other requirements of fitting the virtual to the real. For example, positioning a virtual TV at a wall would require only some unique pattern on that wall, which could be recognized by conventional image processing and would then directly deliver the corner coordinates of the virtual screen with perfect accuracy. Much simpler approaches are possible here as well: hanging a black painting on the wall can deliver a perfect alignment and rendering area for a virtual TV, even for AR glasses not having a mask display. The rendering for such applications is so simple that it can be implemented with inexpensive, low-power hardware.

Recently, displays have been demonstrated (FhG-IPMS) that could implement most of the described variants. The technology used is OLED-on-CMOS. CMOS is ideal because it integrates high-performance electronics. It also allows for integrating light sensing and signal processing on one chip. Organic LED material can be printed or vacuum deployed (preferred here) directly onto the chip. Hence, sophisticated chip assemblies are possible, and integrating camera pixels is no problem (Figure 10.74).

There are challenges that we shouldn't neglect however.

The greatest difficulty will be the light loss because apertures: With a large exit pupil of the display optics (that we may want to have, because otherwise it would be necessary to move the entire display with any single eye movement), only a small fraction of the display light enters the eye. In the other direction, light coming back from the retina has to pass the eye pupil again, is further attenuated and is also overlaid by much stray light from various directions, when reaching the display's image sensors. Hence, separating the image from the retina from the noise of other sources may become quite difficult.

A simple calculation may show this: assume an ambient light of 100 lux (typical indoor scene) and an eye pupil aperture of 2 mm. On the retina (assume 20 × 20 mm retina area) we get only about 1 lux. This 1 lux image then is picked up by the light sensitive display, through the pupil. With an assumed distance of 4 cm, this would resemble a camera at

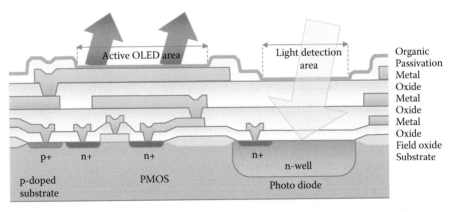

FIGURE 10.74 Bi-directional display with OLED-on-CMOS technology (semiconductor structure cross-section).

approximately f-stop 22. Nobody would try to shoot a photo at 1 lux with f-stop 22. Even if the image sensor is sensitive enough, it may also be affected by stray light from the closely adjacent display pixels. So here we have a challenge. Particularly in the dark, we may need extra lighting, perhaps an infrared emitter, inside the display, together with frequency filtering. Even if this would be infrared, hence invisible, the question remains if and how much this might interfere with night vision.

With a small display and optical aperture (an advantage in terms of weight, energy efficiency, and light collection for the tracking), the retina sensor will only get a picture if the eye's pupil stays within the exit pupil of the optics (i.e., if either this exit pupil is large enough or display and optics properly follow all eye movements). If optical contact is lost, it may be difficult to find the pupil again. As long as the tracking mechanism is faster than the eye (as is desirable), this won't happen very often, but nevertheless the topic has to be addressed. A light field approach (Section 3.6 at page 87) could enable the display camera to provide hints if tracking is lost, by refocusing it for pupil or iris localization, for example. This could also enable several other features.

The distance between eye and display will change the size of the retina pattern, hence, distance will be detectable. A retina tracker should, however, detect intentional accommodation changes as well, to work with ghost objects, for example (Section 10.11.1 at page 455). Without further measures, a willful change of accommodation will just blur the retina picture at the sensor side, without any hint about direction. A light field camera could help here as well. A light field camera, however, could deliver different depth of field or even focus adjustments from the same picture. So we could immediately tell if focus is going forth or back by simply comparing contrast for several different sub-pixel combinations, simultaneously and instantly.

10.16.4 Dynamic Image Linearization

The imaging linearity of the optical system should not be considered a central issue, as it can be compensated for by a pre-distortion of the display image. Nearly all electronic cameras today use electronic linearization, it is a common technology.

An appropriate pre-distortion of the display image leaves more design freedom to the optics. This can either be achieved by electronic pixel-shifting, or by a display with an already distorted pixel raster.

With NED, however, distortions will most often also change with eye rotation. Hence, a dynamic compensation, steered by an eye tracker, has to be considered.

Moving the display to provide exact focus just for the part of the image currently being viewed, is another important ability for a near-eye display because it provides for a realistic distance impression. It lowers the requirements for optical precision as well, but any mechanical or electronic movements must also be accompanied by a dynamic image pre-distortion, of course.

10.16.5 Micromotors

Dynamic focus adaptations, as well as dynamic mechanical adaptations of display and optical geometry, are a central issue with many types of NED, in particular those used for augmented reality. How can this be accomplished in an acceptable and reliable way? The answer may be micromotors. We will therefore have a closer look at these.

10.16.5.1 Piezo Motors

Piezo motors have made rapid progress recently and are now a technology promising to provide several variations of perfect static and dynamic adaptation for the optics of near-eye displays, at stunningly low weight and power consumption.

Electromagnetic motors are good at high-power applications (several kilowatts) where they can be almost 100% efficient, making possible train drives or car engines of magnificent performance. At low power, however, their effectiveness drops limitlessly.

Piezo electric motors are quite different. They don't deliver the almost 100% of large dynamo machines, only about 30% actually, but they continue to do so if we get down to milliwatts or even microwatts (see Figure 10.75).

As piezo elements usually are hard materials or crystals, they deliver very small excitations and require high voltages (but small currents). Manufacturing a motor with this principle is a challenge, but we could get thousands of small movements per second and only need to combine them to one large motion.

The most obvious way of building a piezo motor is to create something that acts like a caterpillar. Climbing microstep by microstep, several thousands of them per second, can result in a speed of many millimeters per second, fast enough for mechanical adjustments of near-eye displays, or even for following eye movements.

A somewhat less obvious principle works like a nut on a thread. The nut is being bent in two directions perpendicular to each other, phase-shifted, resulting in a spiral motion moving it along the thread (or the thread through it) by friction (Figure 10.76). This structure is simple to miniaturize.

Piezo motors such as this one are already found in autofocus systems of pocket cameras, not confined to laboratories anymore, this technology is readily available.

It may be a little confusing to think of a near-eye display unit wiggling around all the time, compensating for eye motion. It may appear primitive at a first glance, even wasteful of energy. Realize, however, that this display unit itself could be as small and fragile as a fly's

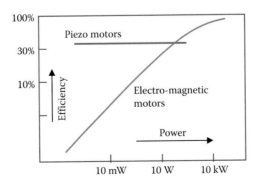

FIGURE 10.75 Efficiency of piezo vs. electromagnetic motors.

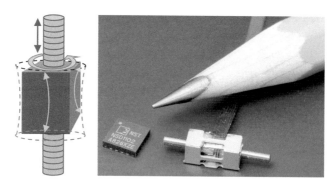

FIGURE 10.76 **Squiggle** piezo electric motor: principle (left), motor and driver chip (right). Image courtesy: **New Scale Technologies**.

wing, and how fast, violently, and continuously such a wing can move with how little energy. Think about micromirror displays, whose tiny mirror elements can execute thousands of movements per second, for decades without tiring, because of an effect called *hyperelasticity*. Hence, mechanics today aren't necessarily what they used to be – wear and tear – as we enter the world of micro- and nanosystems.

10.16.5.2 Artificial Muscles

Other micro motor technologies, often referred to as *"artificial muscles"*, have made considerable progress. The first experiments with this date as early as 1880, when Conrad Roentgen could move a weight by applying voltage to a rubber band. Many electroactive materials have been discovered since, and the greatest progress has been made since 1990, leading to numerous, yet little-known applications. A good overview is found in [198]. The most interesting material for near-eye displays is electroactive polymer. Example figures for an elastic polymer lens with polymer actuators of this type are 10 mm opening diameter, 10 ms response time, and 0...2 W operating power (**Optotune** AG). This may give an impression of what is possible. Most interesting, however, is the specified lifetime of over 10,000,000 cycles. This is an entire year at approximately 3 seconds per cycle, or many years if we consider normal duty times and applications like focus or fit adaptation in a near-eye-display. Driving the electroactive polymer requires only simple electronics, and even though the power consumption appears a bit high at first glance, it is a very interesting technology in this context.

10.17 IMAGE INTEGRATION

It is obvious that the use of beam combiners this far simply combines (equally) light from the surrounding environment (e.g., being transmitted) with light from the microdisplay (e.g., being reflected). This also holds true for laser displays. An important aspect for the application of near-eye displays with respect to the realistic integration of images into the natural sight is to ensure correct occlusion between virtual and real scenery (at least from a classical AR point of view).

This involves either the dimming of certain parts of the field of view by masks or the like (mask display), or the replacement of the entire natural view by camera sight (video-see-through or VST display).

Another possibility for optical see-through would be to compensate the image of the real scene optically by displaying an inverse image.

10.17.1 Optical Compensation

If a natural scene is not too bright, an inverse image of it can be displayed to compensate part of the natural view optically.

For this to be achieved, we first need an image of the real scene from the perspective of the eye (R). This could be taken directly through a beam combiner, but also by stereo cameras and an intelligent perspective synthesis. Given a working dynamic image generation with full compensation of display fit and eye motion, this image could be placed perfectly over the natural sight.

Assume that D is the desired image we expect to see. It consists of R overlaid with an image (V) that contains any virtual scene element that we wish to augment. Then displaying $D - R$ instead of V on the microdisplay will compensate the natural view of the real scene optically while overlaying the virtual scene.

It is clear that this kind of compensation has limitations. As beam combining is additive, it will fail as soon as $R > D$. Note, that this is similar in spirit to the radiometric compensation for projector-camera systems (see Section 8.4 at page 314), although this is multiplicative rather than additive.

At first this appears quite simple, but with the limited color range of any camera or display, it may in cases be difficult to fully achieve. The task therefore requires the sort of optimization that yields the best possible result from the limited reproduction capabilities of the display.

10.17.2 Eyetaps and Video See-Through

An eyetap is defined as a visual interface that intercepts the optical path to the eye, places a camera in the altered light-path instead, and synthesizes the very same visual impression from a display, where additional (virtual) image elements can be inserted. This is also referred to as *video see-through* (VST).

This NED type does not allow a direct view of the real scene any longer, but it has the ability to overlay virtual objects for augmented reality without any transparency, and without requiring an additional mask display.

The classical eyetap assembly (Figure 10.77) uses a double-sided full mirror (instead of a half-silvered beam combiner), delivering to a camera the same perspective the eye would receive.

The other part of the assembly should reproduce exactly the same rays that the camera has usurped, with a display that obviously needs a concentrating lens to produce this reverse light bundle. The assembly is called an *aremac* (camera spelled backwards).

It's obvious that the example shown here conflicts with anatomy, because of insufficient space. Working designs of this type can only deliver a much smaller viewing angle. With

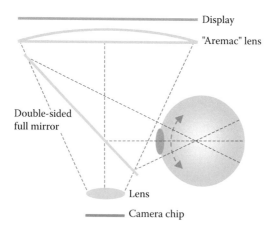

Display
"Aremac" lens
Double-sided full mirror
Lens
Camera chip

FIGURE 10.77   Principle of an eyetap display.

holographic optics, design constraints may be partially overcome, but there still remains the principle difficulty that the eye is not a camera and does not acquire pictures from a fixed position, so a camera view may not replace its sight properly.

The more general VST approach (Figure 10.78) allows for various geometries and combinations of display and camera types (e.g., [52]). An advantage is the possibility of placing, before the eyes, cameras that actually follow eye turning and allow for a larger viewing angle and better alignment to real vision geometry. There is a position difference between the cameras and the user's eyes, however. Issues concerning the imperfection of camera and display images also apply.

There are applications, however, for which VST displays may be the best choice. Think of a minimally invasive surgical operation: direct sight here is of minor importance, only needed for orientation. More significant are images from instrument cameras and perhaps from radiological imaging, projected into the body for best ergonomic performance. This and similar professional applications may be predestined for VST displays. A study of medical applications can be found in [246].

The VST here can also be combined with magnifying functions, as are required for many surgical procedures.

The FOV that a VST display can usefully cover depends on its resolution. While VGA (640 × 480 pixels) translates into 1280 × 960 arcmin or 22 × 16° at 2 arcmin per pixel, yet

FIGURE 10.78   Video-See-Through HMD: **Vuzix-Wrap920AR** with stereo color VGA resolution screens and cameras, 31° diagonal field of view. Image courtesy: **Vuzix** Corporation.

half-eye resolution, HD displays allow up to 60° at the same resolution. While such a resolution and even less is suitable for data or diagnostic image presentation in many cases, it may not always be sufficient for replacing the direct sight. If we require a large FOV and also full resolution, the camera and display resolution required quickly surpasses UHD.

Even the 60° mentioned above are a lot less than we need for orientation in normal life, because the limited FOV can be dangerous as we may overlook the important things happening around us. Hence, many applications require even a VST display to be open at the edges, which in turn requires a certain fit between the displayed and the real scene. A certain geometric fit should be required anyway, or the VST image would be unnatural and irritating. Certain distortions can however be tolerated, as any normal eyeglasses also have them and getting used to this does not take too long.

Brightness matching between displayed and real sight may be a more difficult issue, especially if a display is to be used at day and night likewise. Current cameras can cover an extremely large brightness range, but a single display able to provide brightness levels from at least 10^{-2} to 10^4 lux constitutes a major challenge.

If a VST display is used for close-up activities, another problem arising is the focusing of the cameras. How do the cameras know what to focus upon? We see that eye trackers may be a necessity in this case. They could serve to adjust camera focus by simply measuring the eye convergence.

The color and contrast rendition of current cameras and displays is good enough for most requirements that could arise in practical VST display applications. Cameras can even extend the user's visual abilities as, depending on their quality, they can be a lot less sensitive to blinding lights.

Night vision is another application. Night vision goggles are in fact VST displays, although they are not suitable for general use and in most cases are hampered by poor peripheral vision. But the borders are floating. At the one end of the spectrum, there are simple light-amplifying binoculars, and at the other end, we find fairly advanced vision systems.

10.17.3 Mask Displays

Real masking of objects in the field of view is, in principle, not so difficult to achieve. An inexpensive black-and-white transparent LCD display panel could dim light from the real scene at locations of virtual objects.

Such a mask display, however, would always be out of focus (e.g., appears with blurred edges), which made it a nonpossibility to most people. Quite complicated optical assemblies have been built to achieve a crisp masking for research purposes (Figure 10.79).

On closer examination, however, this challenge might be less significant than anticipated [116].

Mask displays without optics had been suggested several years ago (e.g., in [110] or in Japan patent application 5-328260). Realizing it however required transparent electronics, and these weren't available until more recently. A treatment of the actual performance to be expected has been undertaken in [111].

Demonstrating the principle of such an "unsharp" or out-of-focus mask display is simple: just use a black chip (your thumb may also suffice for a first try) and move it about two

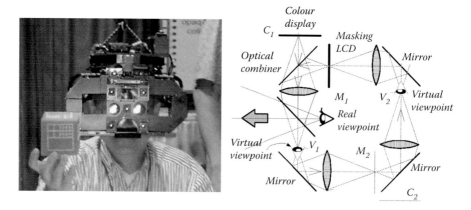

FIGURE 10.79 Optics layout and assembly of an experimental masking display [155]. Image courtesy: Kiyoshi Kiyokawa, Osaka University.

centimeters in front of one of your eyes (close the other one), so that it just exactly covers up the edge of some distant object (Figure 10.80).

It may be surprising that this results in a rather sharp edge of total obstruction, even though an area of half transparent shadow remains beneath it. Use some thin masking object to verify that even tiny distant objects could be cut out quite selectively. The proper size of the mask depends on the pupil diameter. A mask smaller than the pupil can cover nothing completely. A real mask display would have to be corrected for this.

Generating the correct masking shapes also requires a complete knowledge of the real scenery, hence cameras, taking images from approximately the location of the user's eyes.

Figure 10.81 shows virtual screen windows inserted in a background, and a blurred black rim around it as could be caused by a masking process. This demonstrates that out-of-focus masking won't look too disturbing. If the background texture is known (by cameras for example), we could also modify the edges of the displayed image to compensate for the blur of the mask.

We will now discover the real dimension and, most important, the visual impression of the mask blur.

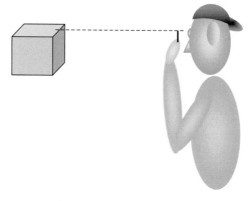

FIGURE 10.80 Simple experiment demonstrating properties of an out-of-focus mask display.

FIGURE 10.81 Original view of images inserted into sections covered by a mask, with typical unsharp borders (white and natural background).

Edge diffraction would have an effect in an area beneath the mask in the order of a few wavelengths at most, hence less than 10 μm. Consider a mask 3 cm before the eye, covering an object 3 m away. A 10 μm diffraction area, projected to the distant object, would then be 1 mm wide, hard to perceive indeed. So edge diffraction should be negligible in a typical case.

Most of the perceived edge bordering will actually result from the size of the observer's pupil. The mask covers an object entirely, if its shape is large enough to cover it from any point on the pupil. It covers its border just partially, if parts of the pupil area can still see around the mask border.

10.17.3.1 Pupil Size

Human pupil sizes can vary over a wide range. Statistics show maximum values from almost 9 mm down to about 3 mm [178]. This maximum possible size degrades with age (the eye tissue becomes less flexible, allowing for less iris expansion). Average maximum values are about 7 mm for young people and 4.5 mm for older people. These maxima are reached only in pitch darkness, or with help of eye drops as in ophthalmologic exams. Under normal lighting, including indoor conditions, more than 3...4 mm of actual pupil size are seldom achieved. In sunlight, the pupil diameter may lower to about 1 mm.

Applications of near-eye displays in extreme darkness will be less common, and in this case it's questionable if mask shadowing would be perceived at all, or if masking will be used at all. Hence, we may assume a pupil diameter of 2..3 mm as a worst case for our considerations.

The pupil diameter p can be thought of as being projected onto objects, turning p into a maximum edge shadow width s (Figure 10.82(right)). The relation obviously is $s = pd/m$. The mask display must cover the object shape plus pupil diameter projected to the mask.

The coverage function is therefore just a simple integral over the pupil area, from one side to the projected mask edge line.

To solve this, we need to have the circle equation in Cartesian coordinates (Figure 10.82(left)), simply given by Pythagoras' theorem, which is $(x-1)^2 + y^2 = 1$ ($r = 1$).

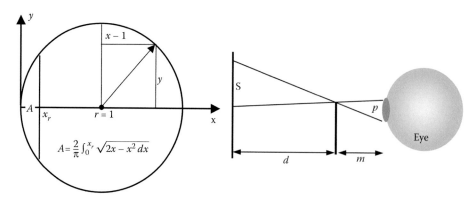

FIGURE 10.82 Left: circle in Cartesian coordinates (normalized for a circle area of one). Right: projected pupil area resulting in edge blurring.

This simple problem leads to a surprisingly complicated mathematical solution (more easily solved numerically):

$$\int \sqrt{2x - x^2}\,dx = \frac{\sqrt{-(x-2)x}(\sqrt{x-2}(x-1)\sqrt{x} - 2\log(2(\sqrt{x-2} + \sqrt{x})))}{2\sqrt{x-2}\sqrt{x}} \quad (10.1)$$

But we are not yet finished: our eye has by no means a linear perception of brightness (see Chapter 4). JND however gives no hint which brightness ratio is subjectively perceived as twice, ten times, and so on, as bright. Because this really is extremely subjective, the only reliable measure (also in literature) is that of *middle gray,* used in painting and photography. It is considered subjectively half-as-bright as white, but objectively it reflects only 1/5 as much light. The renowned Kodak white/gray card set, commonly used in photography, implements this in a white card reflecting 90% and a gray card reflecting 18% of the light.

Assuming a logarithmic brightness perception for the eye, we can resort to the 2/5 relation between perceived and real middle gray to the steepness of a straight line in logarithmic space and get

$$perceived\ attenuation\ A_p = A^{\ln 2/\ln 5} \quad (10.2)$$

This is by the way equivalent to a gamma (see Section 6.2.7 at page 189) of 0.4. Although this certainly won't hold for an arbitrary large brightness range, it also fits the middle part of the sensory experience curve shown in Section 4.2.4 at page 94, and can hence be used for a qualified estimate of the perceived border shadowing of a mask display.

The diagram in Figure 10.83 shows the calculated and the perceived background attenuation around an object, in terms of maximum shadow width, using the above relation.

The difference is significant: at 80% occlusion, the perceived mask shadow is five times smaller than the numerical one. At 50% occlusion it is still two times smaller.

Examples: Pupil 1.5 mm, mask distance 30 mm, object distance 30 cm (e.g., a PC screen), mask shadow 25% of 15 mm or just less than 4 mm.

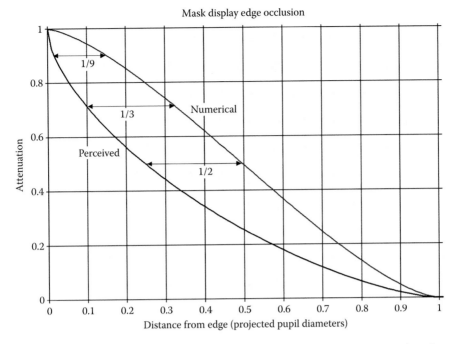

FIGURE 10.83 Calculated edge occlusion of a mask display: linear (Equation 10.1) and perceived (Equation 10.2) attenuations and resulting perceived vs. real border widths for selected attenuation levels.

Same pupil and mask, object distance 3 m (virtual TV), mask shadow for 50% occlusion 40 mm, for 80% = 8 mm.

Close to the object border, the perceived background light rises extremely fast. This explains why the simple experiment mentioned above, covering a distant object with a piece of black cardboard, reveals a very sudden and crisp, 100% coverage as soon as we arrive at a certain point, the point where the pupil is covered entirely.

Quite obviously, the out-of-focus mask display works far more effectively than one would at first anticipate.

Figure 10.84 shows a test pattern (left) and the resulting image when masking the central area with a black stripe approximately 3 mm wide. A simple camera – replacing the eye in the experiment – was used to photograph the right image. The camera aperture was set to approximately 3 mm and the mask distance to approximately 2 cm. This very simple experiment demonstrates how easy it is to mask even small objects and areas quite selectively. It is, however, difficult to generate a perfectly correct impression with such an experiment, as the gamma in this case has to be simulated by image processing.

Finally, we will show an example of how a mask provided by a mask display should be constructed.

The object area to be covered has to be expanded by half of the projected pupil diameter (Figure 10.85). The outer edge of the perceived mask shadow is one projected pupil diameter outside the object border (the perceived shadow size is much smaller of course). The

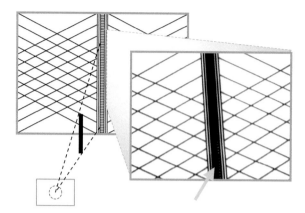

FIGURE 10.84 Real occlusion experiment using a black rod in front of a test pattern. Test pattern (left). Photo with central area covered by a slim stripe (right).

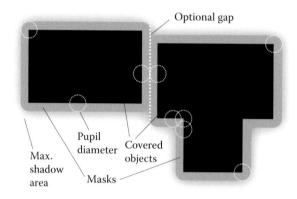

FIGURE 10.85 Construction of a mask image.

narrow gaps between adjacent masked objects may optionally be left open if this appears more natural.

10.17.3.2 Technologies for Mask Displays

With the results shown so far, it is obvious that a mask display, although seen out of focus, will need a relatively high resolution, achievable only with an active-matrix-driven SLM, which is a challenge, because the pixels should be completely adjacent to each other, being able to cover an area entirely, but not leaving a nontransparent grid when not activated. Hence, we need a transparent, active driver circuit.

We should note that a mask display would not always need to attenuate light by 100%. Retaining a little transparency may be a security advantage, because it could enable some minimum vision in case the display shuts off sight when it shouldn't.

As a partial list, we may currently consider the following technological approaches for mask displays (see Chapter 7 for details on individual SLM technologies):

LCD: See-through LCDs are the most apparent choice for mask displays. Transparency will always remain below 50% because of the polarizers. Yet, 50% appear like 80% to the human eye, because of its gamma curve. Simple displays, as those on desktop clocks, will not be sufficient because they use passive matrix driving. Hence, entirely new developments, with transparent driver structures, will be necessary.

Electrowetting displays with dark drops could be considered but aren't really likely to be effective here, because scattering effects by their background structure.

Phototropic glasses, as known from self-tinting eyeglasses, could lead to yet another solution. These glasses contain silver halide, darkening when exposed to light, rather like a photographic film. If this process could also be started by electric fields, and a lot faster of course, it could be a candidate for a mask display.

Electrochromic polymers currently would require at least two absorber layers to cover the entire spectrum, and transmissivity is not yet ideal either. Switching speed is good. A prevalent problem is durability.

Cholesteric LCDs are more suited for color displays. The dyed guest host approach may be able to improve contrast. Disadvantages are that it needs two layers, it loses light due to polarization, and it is slow. An interesting fact is that typical cholesteric LCs turn totally black at about 90°C. This is reversible. Using this effect though would require a lot of energy.

PDLC may be a good approach, as they are simple, fast, non-polarizing, yielding very good transparency. Their habit of turning to an opaque white in the off state is not ideal. Adding a slight tint could make this state appear gray, which may be acceptable for the purpose.

Note that polymer-based SMLs could in principle also be manufactured in spherical shapes, a design advantage for a mask display that is to be integrated into glasses.

In conclusion, there is no ideal technology so far for the mask display, but there are several promising candidates.

10.18 SUMMARY

Near-eye displays have been under development for about two decades at least, but convenient and affordable products that bring advantages for everyday use are far off.

This may be attributed to the fact that many aspects of the technology proved more difficult than anticipated. Progress in several related fields, however, is promising.

The recent interest in AR, fueled by very simple applications using smart-phones, has revived interest in developing alternative technology to overcome the restrictions of small screens.

In this chapter, we have seen that near-eye displays with the potential of replacing current smart-phone screens can be built, at least in theory. A collimated NED already offers a very simple way of overlaying information to real objects, rather than to their image on a mobile phone screen.

Thus, smart-phones may be the first mass-market product implementing essential aspects of AR technology in general.

They might also serve as computing platforms for more sophisticated near-eye displays; eye-tracking and eye-steering particularly might enable new forms of user interaction such as gaze-driven dialing or web-link selection.

Text of web pages, for example, could well be displayed as luminous characters floating in free space, hardly occluding the real environment. A dimming of too bright sunlight could, for example, be achieved with phototropic glass. With a plastic front mirror and a totally integrated eye-tracker chip, this could all be affordable and simple. It would weigh a few grams and would essentially need just a few milliwatts of power.

CHAPTER 11

Discussion and Outlook

11.1 INTRODUCTION

So far, we have focused mainly on today's display technology, with a short glimpse back into the past and an evaluation of some technologies that are at our doorstep. The interesting question certainly is: What can we expect in the future? Making short-term predictions based on new findings in physics, optics, mechanics, and electronics is relatively straightforward. Many novel display technologies already exist as prototypes in laboratories, but simply haven't made their way to the market yet. Thus, an outlook for the next five to ten years is certainly feasible, but predictions of what displays will look like in ten to twenty years from now, or even later, would be presumptuous.

In Section 11.2 at page 496, we will explain what, most likely, the next steps of display technology will be in the foreseeable future. We refrain from any predictions about displays in decades to come. We would like to reflect on the main purpose of display technology throughout the last centuries: as a tool for communication (Section 11.3 at page 498). Direct communication between humans is limited to speech (or acoustic signals in a more general sense). Although visual communication (via optical signals) can be more efficient, it is indirect and requires external tools, such as print media or electronic displays. The efficiency of visual communication depends on the capabilities of these tools. Electronic displays might offer a higher information transport than print media, because displayed images can cognitively be read and interpreted more easily than abstract visuals, such as text. In both cases, our eyes and the human visual system act as a band-limited interface. If this interface is bypassed, displays as we know them might become obsolete. We will provide some facts regarding the state of the art in brain-computer interfaces (especially those that support visual communication, such as retinal implants and neural implants) in Section 11.4 at page 498, and leave speculations on their impact with respect to display technology to the reader's imagination.

11.2 NEXT STEPS IN DISPLAY TECHNOLOGY

We have seen that display technology is developing rapidly with no sudden end in sight. Numerous options are available for display construction, and their number is increasing rapidly. Which of the many will prevail and in which applications is difficult to predict for more than about five years ahead.

One trend foreseen in the first edition of this book and still under way is *OLED displays*. For mobile phones and other small devices, OLED (or AMOLED, as all OLED displays are active matrix displays) screens are now quite common, but large panel devices are lagging behind, in spite of huge investments in production facilities during the last few years. The culprit, as with any new technology, is production yield, which is decisive for a competitive price. LED-lighted LCD displays have become very mature, are energy efficient, and have also improved in color quality, with the introduction of quantum dot-enhanced phosphors (another prediction that became true a bit faster than expected). Nevertheless, OLED also improved substantially, and can be expected to become cheaper than LCD at some point, because they need fewer components.

Microprojectors were trendy when the first edition appeared, but in the end they had less impact than expected. The technologies involved have gone into several niche applications and a number of small home or mobile projection products. Home projection in general experienced a decline, because ever larger displays became ever more affordable.

This also led to an accelerated trend toward ultra-high-resolution displays. In Section 6.2.3.2 on page 185, we have seen that UHD is anything but a necessity (except for media production). It is however an innovation that comes at very low cost: as long as production yield remains high, there is no difference on the number of pixels per square inch. So this is a profitable marketing novelty.

Another trend we discussed in the first edition was *3D TV*. As predicted, it remained a niche application once more. But as also foreseen, it is still a built-in option with many devices, although almost the only content available are movie BluRays. In cinemas, where the 3D effect can be most natural and impressive, it is now a standard at least for action movies that are produced with a lot of computer animation (where 3D output comes as a free lunch).

Near-eye displays have seen the most rapid development during the recent years. This was not really a surprise, but the way it went surely was. In [111], it was pointed out that mobile phones already had the capacity of fully developed VR devices. This was 10 years ago. Presented as sort of a joke there – gluing phones to one's head – it came true when someone used a cardboard box and slide viewer optics to convert a smartphone into a kind of VR goggles.

Meanwhile, this is a major trend, and smartphones are sold with plastic viewer frames already. As this is dirt cheap – the phones have everything necessary, from computing power to motion sensors and even cameras for orientation – this will become everybody's favorite gaming gear. More ambitious users can resort to dedicated devices like the **Oculus Rift**, with better image stability and motion response.

There are drawbacks – the user being isolated from the environment, comfort issues, and so on – but the devices are at least opening up a possibility for new trends in "3D" media, "holodeck"-like experiences surpassing the limits of conventional 3D. This involves a comprehensive scene recording, beyond the capabilities even of holograms, converting real as well as synthetic scenes into *descriptions*, similar to those used in game engines – something dubbed as *virtual media* in [111]. For real scenes, this requires placing cameras in about every single corner, and then assembling a 3D model from their images. For movie production, the current computer vision technology widely used already offers most of the capabilities required, so this will be different but not a complete transformation. We may see if all of this really comes true, and when.

In spite of the rapid development in VR, augmented reality (AR) displays still are a complex challenge. In Chapter 10, we have seen many promising new technologies. Given the breakthrough with VR applications and the fact that all of the big IT companies are investing huge amounts into new AR devices, we may hope for affordable AR anytime soon. But we must admit that this is still a difficult technology; even latest devices leave lots to desire about optical quality and usability, and there are several other issues involved, like the acceptance of orientation cameras in the public. So this is still unpredictable.

Printable displays made substantial progress, together with organic and flexible electronics. Perhaps someday, product packaging will actually yell at us from the shelves in the supermarket and display the very TV commercial that we successfully clicked away the evening before! Newspapers (if they still exist in this form in future) may come with an animated photo for their cover story. This is still a bit uncertain, although some companies are boldly predicting this – *disposable displays*.

E-paper is another variety whose future is certainly bright, but about which we cannot predict everything for sure. E-books are one application, but we also think that E-paper will find many more applications in the long run. E-books can and will replace printed materials in many cases, depending on display quality and convenience. The culprit here are ancient distribution and pricing structures, rather than technical restrictions. Nevertheless, the printed version will remain in use for an unpredictably long time.

In general, with new techniques and methods invented at an apparently increasing pace, we cannot predict which technologies will be there in – say – 20 years from now, or even just in 10.

Although technical solutions in detail may greatly change with time, the principal types of displays we will have are predicted more easily, because for many of them, more than one implementation option already exists – or will surely be existing within the next 5 years.

One day, we will certainly have near-eye displays with stunning capabilities, weighing as little as ordinary eyeglasses. Large flat screens will be prevalent unless or until they are abandoned for near-eye displays, printed displays with built-in printed batteries and electronics will be glued to a multitude of surfaces, even on clothing, and adaptive 3D screens of whatever kind will be able to deliver personalized and perfectly rendered 3D experiences – although this may all take a while.

What we cannot really predict at all are these many new and unforeseen application ideas that arise with the availability of any new technology; these will probably yield more surprises than technology itself.

11.3 A SHORT REFLECTION ON DISPLAYS

In this book we have treated many technologies providing images. We have not concentrated on considering their usefulness; in other words, what is the general reason why we are so fascinated with display technology?

If we look at the common use of displays, we see that most often they are a means of communication. In this aspect, they are unrivaled. Compared with our main communication tool, speech, images can be orders of magnitude more efficient, just as our eyes can pick up a lot more information than our ears.

We as human beings have no comparable output device, no organ that could display the images we are producing in our minds. We need to speak, or to draw sketches as a crutch for optical communication, and all this goes at the speed of Morse code, literally.

If our ancestors had been chameleons or octopuses, perhaps we could display thoughts on our skin and communicate optically with high speed and efficiency. Alas, we don't have such abilities. We need to create drawings or paintings to express our imaginations, or we may create videos or animations, with the right technology at hand. Although this is extremely cumbersome, it has nevertheless revolutionized communications, and the key to it is a device capable of producing images from information – the display.

Developing display technology to the extreme however, does not solve the initial communication bottleneck – our inability to directly express our thoughts through pictures as easily as we can do with speech.

As we have no display device built into our own physiology, we must use a technical one. Currently, we use display technology in a most inefficient way, because we have no means of transferring our thoughts directly to that device. Computer technology could perhaps help to directly pick up and interpret our thoughts from neural signals, transform them to images and send them to a display – or directly to the brains of others. Apart from giving us chameleon-like skin by genetic engineering, this currently is the only apparent way of resolving the output bottleneck of our communication abilities.

Although the common paradigm with such considerations is human-computer interfaces, the real objective has always been improved human-to-human interfacing, or communications.

11.4 BRAIN-COMPUTER INTERFACES – THE ULTIMATE SOLUTION?

Today, *human-computer interfaces* (HCIs) are rather physical in nature. The communication of information from and to computers is limited to the capabilities of individual input and output devices. With a typing speed of less than 50 words per minute and a reading rate of less than 300 words per minute, my transmission rate to and from my laptop is far lower than the communication bandwidth of most computer-to-computer interfaces. Advanced HCI approaches, such as speech recognition, are clearly widening this communication bottleneck. A direct link to the brain, however, would avoid most physiological activities. Ignoring all the required processing tasks for a moment, in the future we might progress to the speed of thought when communicating with computers. These links are called *brain-computer interfaces* (BCI).

In addition to more efficient communication, such BCIs will introduce completely new possibilities. For instance, they will support people with physical disabilities to control prostheses and other interfaces mentally. BCIs also offer promising new approaches in neurological rehabilitation and even in computer games.

Futurists predict that, by the mid-21st century, it will be possible to download human brain content onto a supercomputer. Replicating and changing consciousness can be implied from such capabilities, total recall becomes reality. An example is the Soul Catcher 2025 project of the British Telecom that strives to attach a computer chip directly to the optical nerve and store all sensory impulses that can be downloaded and implanted in someone else's memory. It is estimated that a human's life-time experience can be stored in about ten terabytes. This, however, depends on a large number of assumptions.

Our brain has about 100 billion (10^{11}) neurons. They connect by electrical signals, which lead to the conclusion that information processing in the brain is mainly done by neurons, working similar to a computer, only with a different architecture. But neurons are only 10%–15% of our brain cells. Almost 90 percent are glial cells (named for the assumptions that they only had structural functions). Later research has revealed glial cells to contribute a lot to the brain's functionality [86]. Neurons have extensions called ganglia and axons (nerves). The latter can be up to 1 m long, making these neurons the largest cells in the body. The dendrites have lots of synapses serving as connection points to other dendrites or neurons. Synapses have individual inhibition levels (connection strengths), greatly determining the behavior of the neuronal network. Learning is thought to be connected to the wiring of neurons by synapses (at least for long-term memory). Here, glial cells play a key role. Microglia are roaming the brain, connecting and disconnecting synapses. Other glial cells, oligodendrocytes and Schwann cells, are important for speed: they insulate axonal segments with myelin and speed up the neural signal transmission by a factor of 50 (up to 200 m/s). These cells are only found in vertebrates, and they are decisive for the formation of a central brain (slugs and worms do not have them). Other glial cells, formerly thought to just fill the space between neurons, have proven to be important for information processing. They can be connected to thousands of synapses and are currently suspected to orchestrate large synapse activities. They communicate chemically. Interestingly, Einstein's brain, according to the examination by Marian Diamond in the 1980s, did not have more neurons than an average brain, but a lot more glial cells, especially large ones connecting many synapses. Children's neurons have >10,000 synapses, declining to <10,000 with adults. This is attributed to more selected and specialized synapse structuring due to learning. A human brain hence contains about 10^{15} synapses. If we consider that any synapse can represent several digital bits, due to its analog inhibition value, synapses alone can hold about 10^{18} bits of information (assuming 3 bits per synapse). Not counted here are the glial cells, and possible other forms of information storage (e.g., which could be molecules stored in cells). The total information content of the human brain may therefore be a lot larger.

Currently, two projects (in the United States and EU) are aiming at a full modeling of the human brain in a computer. They only include neuronal structures and are scheduled to completion by about 2025. Considering glial cells, etc., this will not yet be a complete modeling.

Nevertheless, achieving a complete brain model will be but a matter of time.

Considering the three-dimensional structure of the human brain, modeling it in a silicon chip may lead to wiring problems. There are billions of nerves crossing throughout the brain. But there are options to solve this, such as fiber optics (SiO_2 light guides integrated in a silicon chip) that could in theory transport up to 10^{15} bits in just 1 s.

The computer aspect of these developments won't be the problem: current semiconductor structures down to 22 nm are made with 193 nm (UV light) lithography, but extreme UV (EUV) lithography at 13.5 nm wavelength is in the test phase and has been announced that it will be in production by 2015. Although many hurdles still have to be crossed until the required structures of just a few nm can be produced, Moore's law of ten-folding complexity every ten years still seems to be intact, and might prevail until logical elements consist of just a few atoms.

Leading semiconductor manufacturers think computer chips will approach the capacity of the human brain in less than 20 years. In terms of "complexity" it may take considerably longer due to the above considerations, but a silicon chip will also run a lot faster than neuron "hardware".

One question remains entirely open: How long will it take to understand the brain's architecture? Without knowing this, reconstructing the human brain will remain theory: this task is extremely complicated and may take a lot longer than just making super complex chips.

On the way to digital immortality and mental control, there are still many hurdles to overcome. BCI technology, therefore, is not only an exciting but also a very challenging topic.

Current efforts most often focus on "thought control" of computers, machines and prostheses: how can brain signals be sensed both noninvasively and efficiently, how can we process and interpret these signals?

For the topic of our book however, the output side of BCI is less relevant than the input side of it. The question here is: can BCI replace display technology entirely some day? Having a direct interface between brain and computer would make external display technology superfluous.

Such technology does not yet exist, but investigating the state of the art in retinal and neural implants suggests that it might well become feasible in future. The two subsections below briefly explain how retinal implants and neural implants function, and how they can be related to augmenting vision.

11.4.1 Retinal Implants

We learned in Chapter 4 that the photoreceptors (i.e., the rod and cone cells) on the human retina convert light that they receive from the lens into electrical and chemical signals that are transmitted through the optical nerve to the brain. The brain translates these signals to what we actually see.

In the case of many eye diseases, the photoreceptors are damaged while the deeper layers of the retina that transmit the signals to the brain are intact. Retinitis pigmentosa and macular degeneration are classical eye diseases. Although for the former, peripheral vision gradually decreases and eventually is lost, the latter causes the loss of central vision.

A *retinal implant* is an intraocular retinal prosthesis that basically takes over the job of the photoreceptors by stimulating the inner retina cells in deeper layers. This can restore the vision of blind people [312].

Two general approaches to retinal implants currently exist: *subretinal implants* and *epiretinal implants* (Figure 11.1).

Subretinal implants are computer chips that sit directly inside the photoreceptor layer of the retina, and basically replace the rod and cone cells. Light-sensitive micro photo diodes inside the chip modulate the incident light into a current that is injected into the retina via stimulation electrodes to excite retinal cells in the inner retinal layer. The neural cells relay the signals to the brain, through the optical nerve.

An example for a subretinal implant is the device by **Retina Implant AG** (Figure 11.2). This is a three mm wide and 50 μm thick microelectronic chip that consists of 1,500 photodiodes, amplifiers and electrodes. It is implanted in the retina's macular region, provides a field of view of 12° and operates at 0 lux to 100,000 lux.

Epiretinal implants are computer chips placed on top of the retina. In contrast to subretinal implant, they do not directly modulate the light that is naturally falling into the eye. Instead, they apply an external video camera that records the surrounding environment. The video is processed, and then transmitted to the implant via an IR or RF signal. The camera and the transmitter are normally attached to glasses that users must wear.

Figure 11.3 illustrates an example of an epiretinal implant of the **IMI** Intelligent Medical Implants GmbH with 7 × 7 electrodes.

The advantage of subretinal implants over epiretinal ones is that they convert incident light directly into an electrical signal, without the need for an external video source (i.e., a

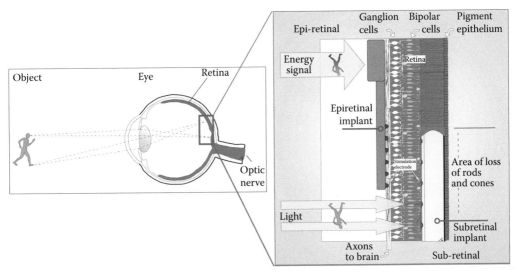

FIGURE 11.1 Locations of subretinal and epiretinal implants within the retina. Image courtesy: Alfred Stett, NMI Universität Tübingen and Eberhart Zrenner, Center for Ophthalmology, University of Tübingen [311].

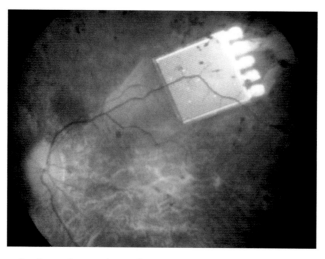

FIGURE 11.2 Example for subretinal implant. Image courtesy: Walter Wrobel, Universitäts-Augenklinik Tübingen.

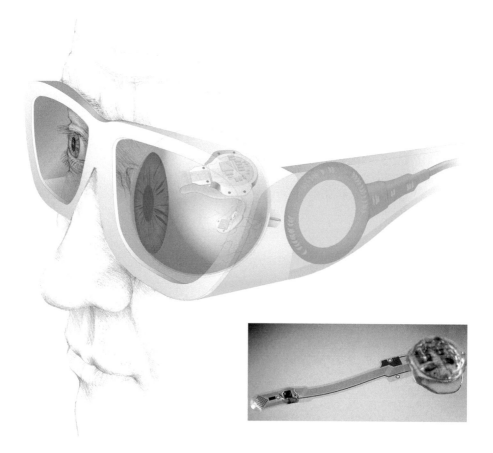

FIGURE 11.3 Example for epiretinal implant. Image courtesy: **IMI** Intelligent Medical Implants GmbH.

head-worn camera). But these signals are faint and therefore have to be amplified. The power supply of subretinal and epiretinal implants is realized either through wires, or wireless.

One option is energy transfer via magnetic coils (same technology as with a cochlea implant). Another option is using infrared light sent into the eye, and receiving cells integrated into the camera chip. The **Bio-Retina** by **Nano Retina Inc.** works on this principle.

Today, the quality of retinal implants does not nearly reach the quality that can be achieved with natural vision. But there is rapid progress. A main disadvantage with early approaches was to take the retina as similar to a camera chip. But the retina contains an information processing layer, converting pixel data into a representation of geometrical primitives (line segments, corners) and speed vectors. Only these can be easily recognized by the brain through the optical nerves. Ignoring this fact leads to blurred images far below the physical resolution of the photoreceptor chip. Recent developments are aiming at chips emulating the required neural structures [213]. The first results from implantations showed dramatically improved resolution and, for the first time, real object recognition.

If it reaches (or even exceeds) the level of retinal photoreceptors, then retinal implants might have the potential to directly serve as effective visual HCI, much like spatial or near-eye displays do today, and not only for the visually impaired. We just want to make sure that we don't run out of power.

11.4.2 Neural Implants

Electrical signal transmission is the fundamental from of communicating in computers and in brains. Research on *neural implants* investigates the possibility of realizing direct interfaces between silicon chips and nerve cells (e.g., by connecting directly to the brain surface or the brain's cortex).

As neurons communicate by pulse series, capacitive coupling is a viable method of interfacing, especially supported by the very thin SiO_2 insulation layers possible with silicon chips. Conversely, *metal-oxide-semiconductor field-effect transistor* (MOS FET) gates can sense neuron pulses capacitive.

Capacitive coupling avoids any unwanted effects as could arise from DC current (e.g., polarization or electrolysis). The transmission of signals from neurons to a chip based on a field-effect transistor first became possible in the early nineties. The reverse process succeeded in the mid-nineties by stimulating neurons electronically from a voltage pulse applied to a capacitor. CMOS is a technology especially suited for neuronal interfacing. Early CMOS experiments were carried out with single neurons from the medicinal leech grown on a silicon chip. Later, larger neural networks could be interfaced with, and CMOS chips (Figure 11.4) with a sensor pitch of 7.8 μm (approaching the width of vertebrate neurons) enabled recording neural activities at high resolution (16 kilopixels) and high speed (2000 fps) [81,165].

Current applications not only record neural or brain activities for research purposes, but also support *deep brain stimulation* and *vagus nerve stimulation* for patients with Parkinson's disease and clinical depression, respectively.

A much more interesting application for neural implants with respect to display technology is the concept of *cortically-based artificial vision*. Experiments in the early twentieth

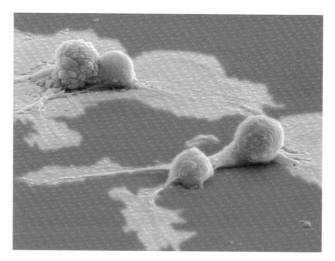

FIGURE 11.4 Snail neuron grown on a CMOS chip with 128 × 128 transistors. The electrical activity of the neuron is recorded by the chip (chip fabricated by Infineon Technologies). Image courtesy: Max Planck Institute of Biochemistry.

century already revealed that electrical stimulation of various regions of the visual cortex leads to the perception of points of light (called *phosphenes*) at specific places in space. The appearance of the phosphenes is correlated deterministically to a stimulated region on the visual cortex.

This observation has led to various research projects investigating visual cortex stimulation with neural implants (i.e., arrays of electrodes (Figure 11.5) implanted over the surface of the visual cortex). Currents in the microampere range are used to evoke individual phosphenes. Simple patterns such as lines can already be perceived by blind humans through current stimulation via small groups of implanted microelectrodes [253]. The resolution

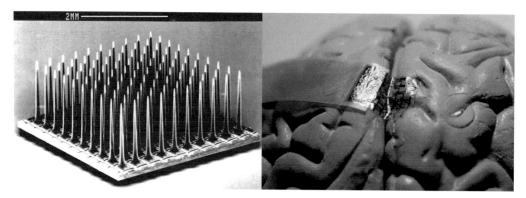

FIGURE 11.5 The Utah Electrode Array (UEA) – 100 1.5 mm electrodes (separated by 0.4 mm) on a 0.2 mm thin carrier substrate (left). Thin and flexible electrode arrays printed onto silk films for recording brain activity (right). Image courtesy: Richard A. Normann, University of Utah, John Rogers, University of Illinois.

of the applied electrode arrays is still relatively sparse. The reason for this is that currents passing through electrodes that are too close cause highly nonlinear interaction between character and location of appearing phosphenes. Therefore, much of the ongoing research in cortically based artificial vision is concerned with improving electrode array designs, in other words, increasing resolution and reducing size (Figure 11.5). If this can be achieved, then it is imaginable that such an approach does not only enable vision prostheses for the blind, but can also augment natural vision for the non-blind without external display technology. The advantage over retinal implants would be that intact photoreceptors could still be used for natural vision, while visual augmentations are created through the stimulation of the visual cortex.

One might argue that the resolution of retinal implants and neural implants is currently too low to be a serious competitor for displays, but be reminded that the resolution of the first Nipkow disks was in the order of 40-50 lines; consider where we are now, just 100 years later. Another argument could be that the invasiveness of a surgical procedure will not be tolerated for the sake of enhanced visual communication. Be reminded that today, however, implants exist for almost every part of the body – and many of them are accepted for purely aesthetic reasons.

11.4.3 Nanobots

A hypothetical but interesting approach to brain interfacing are nano machines (nanobots or nano sondes, known from science fiction). We might think of them as an artificial variety of Microglia. They could infiltrate the brain, connect to synapses, and gather information or stimulate synapses for information transfer into the brain.

Apart from the mere manufacturing, there are several problems with this approach: the nanobots need energy; possibly they could draw on chemical energy, like cells, which indicates that a biological approach based on modified Microglia may be adequate. But they also need navigation and communications, and in this area, technological approaches offer more powerful solutions.

Wireless does not appear an option at this scale. Both navigation and communications could possibly be achieved if the nanobots connect to neighboring nanobots and form a three-dimensional communication web throughout the entire brain. This could be used for relative position sensing, and in some cases for energy transfer as well. Synthetic nanobots could use wire connections, transporting signals way faster than nerves, and also able to transport energy. Organic nanobots might perhaps use optical fiber communications, for example, employing electroluminescence and organic fibers. A hybrid approach using the best of both worlds may be necessary.

Obviously, this would require up to several trillions of nanobots, involving sophisticated applications of bio- and nanotechnologies yet to be developed. This is probably not physically impossible, but something for the more distant future.

11.5 CONCLUSION

Treating this complex and interdisciplinary technology in a single book was a challenge, but we also saw a necessity to provide a basis of knowledge and further reading for anybody interested in this really amazing field. Displays are core components of modern technology. They do not only deliver us any kind of information, they also connect us to what has already become sort of a mind extension – computers and the web. This will remain of major importance, and it will be thrilling to see which transformations this technology may undergo in the future.

Appendix A: Perceptual Display Calibration*

A GOOD DISPLAY DESIGN SHOULD MAKE the inaccuracies and limitations of a display technology invisible to the human eye. However, this requires a good understanding of what is and what is not visible to the human eye. For that reason, display engineering is tightly linked to the understanding and modeling of visual perception.

Chapter 4 of this book introduced the basic limitations of visual perception that are commonly considered in display design. In this chapter we will take a closer look at selected perceptual models and present a few examples where they are used in practice.

As visual models operate on physical units of light, we first need to know how to convert the digital signals driving a display into photometric and colorimetric units. The display models used for such conversion are discussed in Section A.1. The parameters for such display models can be found either by measuring display characteristics with a colorimeter, or with the help of visual calibration procedures if no measurmenet instruments are available, with the help of visual calibration procedures, discussed in Section A.2. Once a displayed image is represented in photometric units, it is possible to predict visibility of small contrast patterns using a contrast sensitivity function (CSF). Section A.3 explains when the CSF is the right visual model for the task and what its limitations are. The last section demonstrates how the CSF can be used to test for and reduce banding artefacts due to limited color channel bit-depth.

A.1 DISPLAY MODELS

Whenever visual perception needs to be modeled for a display application, it is necessary to convert the displayed images or video into the right units. While displays operate in the digital signal domain, with pixels represented as triples of integers, most visual models expect an image to be represented in physical, photometric or colorimetric units. This is illustrated in Figure A.1: the display is driven by digital images to produce light, which is sensed by the human visual system. To simulate how the display transforms digital images into physical units of light, we need a forward display model. A forward display model is often referred as a display model without the word "forward". To find the opposite transformation, from

---

* By Rafał K. Mantiuk.

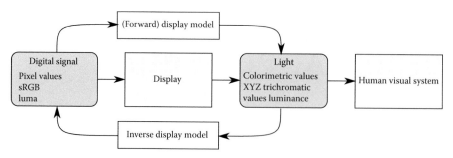

FIGURE A.1 Forward display model simulates the process of transforming digital pixel values into physical light on a display. An inverse display model provides the inverse mapping — it can determine what combination of pixel values is needed to produce a certain color.

physical units into digital values, we need an inverse display model. This section discusses different variants of display models and how they account for display processing.

A.1.1 Gamma and sRGB

The simplest forward display model, explaining the relation between digital and physical units, can be modeled with a so-called *gamma correction* function (refer to Section 6.2.7 at page 189). For color images, the gamma transformation has the form:

$$R = R'^{\gamma}, \quad G = G'^{\gamma}, \quad B = B'^{\gamma} , \tag{A.1}$$

where R' is a red pixel value in the range 0–1, and R is the corresponding red component in the physical space. The gamma value varies from 1.8 to 2.4 and its value is usually close to 2.2.

The R, G and B values in Equation A.1 are sometimes referred as *linear* RGB values because they are linearly related to colorimetric values and to luminance. This is to distinguish them from "gamma corrected" R', G' and B', which are the pixel values driving a display.

The gamma correction function is a reasonable approximation of a display model, especially for CRT monitors, but it tends to be inaccurate for low digital signal values. The sRGB standard refines the gamma correction function to better model a typical monitor's response and is used for most computer monitors. The sRGB non-linearity is given by:

$$R = \begin{cases} \dfrac{R'}{12.92} & \text{if } R' \le 0.04045 \\[2ex] \left(\dfrac{R' + 0.055}{1.055}\right)^{2.4} & \text{otherwise} \end{cases} . \tag{A.2}$$

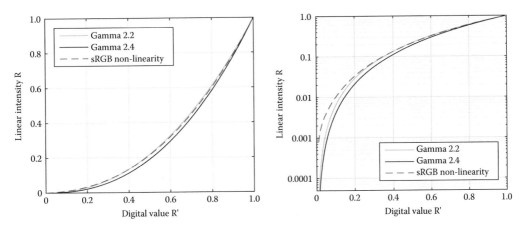

FIGURE A.2 Comparison of gamma function with the sRGB non-linearity. The intensities are plotted using the linear scale on the left and the logarithmic scale on the right. The logarithmic scale is often used for plotting luminance as it better reflects perceived intensity of light.

The equations for blue and green color components are analogous. Though the equation for the sRGB non-linearity seems very different from the gamma correction function in Equation A.1, both functions are in fact quite similar as shown in Figure A.2. Note that the sRGB follows more closely the shape of gamma 2.2, even though the sRGB equation contains exponent 2.4. The main difference between the gamma 2.2 and the sRGB non-linearity is best seen in the plot on the right, which uses the logarithmic scale for linear intensity: the intensities modeled by the sRGB non-linearity are larger. The difference between luminance values 0.001 and 0.0001 may seem negligible, however, the human eye can easily detect such small differences.

The gamma correction (Equation A.1) and sRGB (Equation A.2) functions are known as transfer functions, or more specifically electro-optical transfer functions (EOTFs). The name EOTF has historical roots in analog television, where the function described the relation between electrical signal used to drive a cathode ray tube (CRT) display and the light intensity produced by screen's phosphors. The display technologies used today, such as liquid crystal displays (LCD) or organic light-emitting diode (OLED) displays, have a different response to electrical current than CRT displays. Yet, the display driving electronics of LCD or OLED emulates the behavior of a CRT display not only to remain backward compatible, but also because the gamma correction function well approximates the perceived brightness of light; the digital R', G' and B' values result in more uniform perceived differences between different intensities of color than their linear counterparts, R, G and B.

A.1.2 Color Transformation

A transfer function, discussed in the previous section, is only the first part of a display model. The second part, discussed in this section, explains rendering of colors in terms of device independent CIE XYZ color values (refer to Section 4.3 at page 97).

Most display models assume a linear relationship between the linear RGB values and absolute CIE XYZ trichromatic values:

$$\begin{bmatrix} X \\ Y \\ Z \end{bmatrix} = L_{peak} \cdot M_{RGB \rightarrow XYZ} \cdot \begin{bmatrix} R \\ G \\ B \end{bmatrix},$$ (A.3)

where L_{peak} is the peak luminance of a display given in cd/m^2, and $M_{RGB \rightarrow XYZ}$ is a 3×3 color transformation matrix.

To create the color transformation matrix it is enough to know display primaries: CIE XYZ coordinates for pure red, green and blue colors emitted by a disply. The matrix is constructed by concatenating XYZ values of the display primaries as columns of that matrix. This way the RGB triplet [1 0 0] will result in the XYZ triplet corresponding to the red primary, and green and blue colors will be mapped similarly. For example, any HDTV display should have its primary colors closely matching ITU-R recommendation BT.709 and the chromacity coordinates:

Chromaticity	Red	Green	Blue
x	0.6400	0.3000	0.1500
y	0.3300	0.6000	0.0600
Y	0.2126	0.7152	0.0722

The chromacity coordinates can be transformed into XYZ trichromatic values using the formulas:

$$X = \frac{x}{y} \cdot Y, \quad Z = \frac{1 - x - y}{y} \cdot Y$$ (A.4)

From that, we get that the color transformation matrix for a BT.709-compliant display is:

$$M_{RGB \rightarrow XYZ} = \begin{bmatrix} X_{red} & X_{green} & X_{blue} \\ Y_{red} & Y_{green} & Y_{blue} \\ Z_{red} & Z_{green} & Z_{blue} \end{bmatrix} = \begin{bmatrix} 0.412424 & 0.357579 & 0.180464 \\ 0.212656 & 0.715158 & 0.072186 \\ 0.019332 & 0.119193 & 0.950444 \end{bmatrix}.$$ (A.5)

The matrix for inverse transformation, $M_{XYZ \rightarrow RGB}$, can be obtained by inverting the matrix $M_{RGB \rightarrow XYZ}$.

A.1.3 Gamma-Offset-Gain Model

Both the gamma function and the sRGB non-linearity serve as good inverse display models (for driving the displays), but are not ideal as forward display models (for predicting display performance). This is because hardly any display can achieve intensity values as low as predicted by both models. For example, for pixel value 0, both sRGB and gamma transfer functions predict intensity 0. However, most display technologies emit some small amount of light even if the pixel values are set to 0. Furthermore, unless a display is viewed in a pitch-dark room, some ambient light will be reflected from the screen thus elevating the amount of light that the user senses.

This inaccuracy of both transfer functions is not just an engineering approximation but it is an intentional part of the design. The primary role of the transfer functions is to specify how to drive the display given digital input. When the pixel value is 0, the display should emit the smallest possible amount of light, regardless of what that smallest amount is for a particular display. If a transfer function assumed a certain minimum quantity of light, no display would be allowed to produce deeper black level than specified by the transfer function.

To predict the light emitted by a display, better accuracy is offered by a gamma-offset-gain (GOG) display model [19] or one of its variations: GGO (gain, gamma, offset), or GOGO (gain, offset, gamma, offset) [69]. Those variations describe the same functional form of a model but using different parameters. The GOG model for gray-scale images is the relation between luma (gray-scale pixel) value and emitted luminance, and is modeled as

$$L = (L_{peak} - L_{black})\, V^{\gamma} + L_{black} + L_{refl}, \tag{A.6}$$

where L is luminance and V is luma, where luma varies between 0 and 1 (as opposed to 0–255). For color images, L and V could be replaced by linear R, G or B component and V by R', G', or B' pixel values. L_{peak} is the peak luminance of a display in a completely dark room, L_{black} is the luminance emitted from black pixels (*black level*), and L_{refl} is the ambient light that is reflected from the surface of a display, sometimes known as ambient flare. γ is a parameter that controls non-linearity of a display. For LCD displays L_{black} varies in the range from 0.1 to 1 cd/m² depending on the display brightness and contrast. L_{refl} depends on the ambient light in an environment and can be approximated in the case of non-glossy screens with:

$$L_{refl} = \frac{k}{2\pi} E_{amb}, \tag{A.7}$$

where E_{amb} is the ambient illuminance in lux and k is the reflectivity for a display panel. The reflectivity is below 1% for modern LCD displays and can be slightly larger for OLEDs.

The inverse of the model takes the form:

$$V = \left[\left(\frac{L - L_{black} - L_{refl}}{L_{peak} - L_{black}} \right)^{\frac{1}{\gamma}} \right]_0^1, \tag{A.8}$$

where the square brackets are used to denote clamping values to the range 0–1 (the values greater than 1 become 1, and less than 0 become 0).

Figure A.3 shows some examples of displays modeled by Equation A.6. Note that ambient light can strongly reduce the effective dynamic range of the display (top-left plot). The gamma parameter has no impact on the effective dynamic range, but higher γ values will increase image contrast and make the image appear darker (top-right plot). Lowering the black level increases effective dynamic range to a certain level, then has no effect (bottom-left). This is because the black in most situations will be "polluted" by ambient light reflected from the screen. Brighter display can offer higher dynamic range, provided that the black level of a display remains the same (bottom-right).

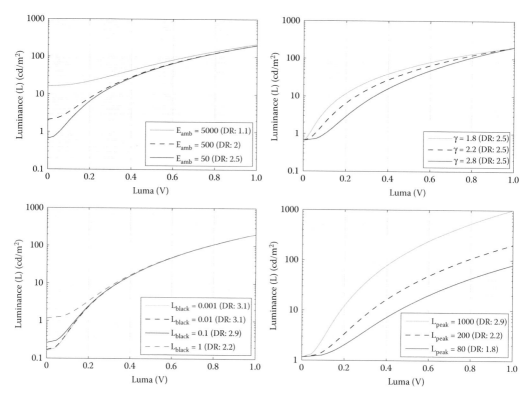

FIGURE A.3 The relation between pixel values (luma — V) and emitted light (luminance — L) for several displays, as predicted by the GOG model from Equation A.6. The corresponding plots show the variation in ambient light, gamma, black level and peak luminance in the row-by-row order. The DR value in parenthesis is the display dynamic range as log-10 contrast ratio (equal to $\log_{10}(L_{max}/L_{min})$). The parameters not listed in the legend are as follows: $L_{peak} = 200\,\text{cd/m}^2$, $L_{black} = 0.5\,\text{cd/m}^2$, $\gamma = 2.2$, $E_{amb} = 50\,\text{lux}$, $k = 1\%$.

A.1.4 Other Display Models

GOG is a relatively simple display model, which was found to be adequate for CRT displays [270]. It can be classified as a physical model because it models the physical process of transforming a digital signal (or voltage) into light emitted from a CRT display [59]. The GOG model is also a good approximation for LCDs, as most LCDs try to emulate CRT displays. However, for some LCDs the GOG model introduces inaccuracy due to color channel interactions [270,287], known as cross-talk. Cross-talk is caused by the driving signal of one channel affecting the other color channel as the electrical charge is applied.

Several display models address the issue of cross-talk between color channels in LCDs. One of them is known as a *masking model* [270]. The model relies on additivity of colors in the CIE XYZ color space. The method requires that a look-up table (LUT), mapping from digital values to XYZ, is stored for red, green, blue, cyan, magenta, yellow and white colors. The idea behind the model is best demonstrated in an example. Let us consider a mapping of an RGB triplet value [1 0.5 0.1] to CIE XYZ color values. First, the gray contribution of the color is extracted by looking up [0.1 0.1 0.1] value in the white LUT. Second, the yellow contribution is estimated by computing the difference in XYZ colors between pixel values [0.5 0.5 0] (*yellow* table) and [0.1 0.1 0.1] (*white* table). Then, the red contribution is computed as a difference between [1 0 0] (*red* table) and [0.5 0.5 0] (*yellow* table) XYZ values. Finally the gray, yellow and red contributions are added together in the XYZ space, resulting in the XYZ coordinates for the RGB pixel [1 0.5 0.1]. Although the procedure is relatively straightforward for the forward display model, it is much more difficult to apply in an inverse model as each step is conditional on the input RGB pixel values.

The physical display models, such as GOG or a masking model, need to make certain assumptions and thus are restricted to "well-behaved" displays, which adhere to those assumptions. If a display violates those assumption, it can be still modelled a 3D look-up table, mapping from RGB pixel values to CIE XYZ color values. This approach, however, requires large amounts of measurements and memory. For example, a relatively sparse grid of $10 \times 10 \times 10$ points, requires 1000 measurements. The accuracy of 3D LUT approach will depend on the interpolation method. For example, the accuracy is usually higher if the interpolation is performed in a uniform color space, such as CIE Lab [59]. The inverse display model usually requires a separate LUT, which cannot be directly measured with a photospectrometer or colorimeter. Such an inverse 3D LUT, from CIE XYZ to digital values, is usually obtained by extracting data from the forward display model.

If the cost of storing 3D LUT in memory is too high, the mapping can be approximated an analytic function. Such function may take a form of a polynomial [287], or a linear combination of radial basis functions [59]. Such representations are more compact than a 3D look-up table, offers higher flexibility than physical models, such as GOG, but can be more computationally demanding than the other two approaches.

The display models discussed so far can be used for a basic colorimetric or photometric calibration, however, they do not account for many other factors that affect the colors of displayed images. For example, the black level of a display is elevated by the luminance of neighboring pixels due to internal glare. Also, some display technologies (e.g. plasma displays, some HDR displays) need to manage a limited power budget and vary peak brightness with image content. In that case, a small white patch shown on a dark background can have much higher luminance than the same patch shown on a large bright-gray background. The models discussed above, however, account for most effects and are relatively accurate for modern LCD displays, which is the dominant display technology at the moment.

A.2 VISUAL DISPLAY CALIBRATION

Displays are normally calibrated by collecting sample colors using color measuring instruments, such as colorimeters or photospectrometers, and then fitting the collected data to one of the display models. A detailed description of display characterization procedures can be found in a freely available standard [264]*. If, however, a measuring instrument is not available, there are several visual procedures that can help estimate the parameters of a display. Such procedures are discussed in this section.

---

* The standard documents and the test patterns can be downloaded from http://www.icdm-sid.org/.

A.2.1 Gamma Calibration

A simple way to visually assess the value of a display gamma exponent is to match the brightness of a black and white pattern, containing the same amount of white and black pixels, with a uniform gray level. An example of a gamma chart for such matching is shown in Figure A.4. Gamma matching charts can be often found in software, in the display calibration settings of an operating system or a graphics card driver, but very few users know how to use those charts effectively. The goal is to see a blend of the white and black pattern so that it is possible to make a match with a uniform gray level. If the pattern appears sharp, most users are not able to make a brightness match. Therefore, it is advisable to look at those charts with defocused vision — without glasses, from a long distance, or by focusing the eye on a point in the front of a display instead of the display plane.

When the white and black pattern is blended in the eye, it produces the luminance that is arithmetic mean of the luminance of black and white pixels. From the GOG display model (Section A.1.3) we have that the luminance of a white pixel is:

$$L(1) = L_{peak} + L_{refl}, \tag{A.9}$$

and the luminance of a black pixel is:

$$L(0) = L_{black} + L_{refl}. \tag{A.10}$$

Now, we need to make the average luminance for the mixture of while and black lines equal to the luminance of the matching gray-level pixel value V_{match}, so that:

$$\frac{L(0) + L(1)}{2} = L(V_{match})$$

$$\frac{1}{2}(L_{peak} + L_{black}) + L_{refl} = (L_{peak} - L_{black}) V_{match}^{\gamma} + L_{black} + L_{refl} \tag{A.11}$$

$$\gamma = \log(0.5 - V_{match}).$$

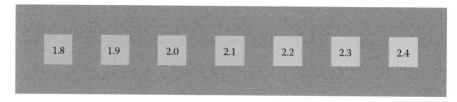

FIGURE A.4   A chart that can be used to visually estimate the gamma exponent of a monitor. The task is to match the brightness of the patterned background to one of the uniform color patches with numbers. The numbers indicate the corresponding gamma values. The match is easier to make when a chart is seen from a large distance or when vision is not in focus (e.g. when looking on the thumb in front of a display plane instead of a display). Note that the chart needs to be enlarged so that the pixels in the pattern match the pixels on the screen, otherwise aliasing artefacts could make the match impossible.

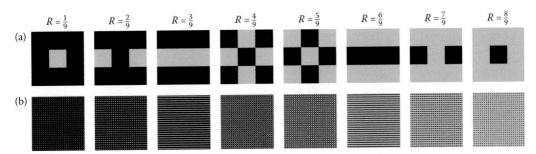

FIGURE A.5 Half-tone patterns that could be used to recover the shape of a display transfer function. R is the ratio of "on" pixels to all pixels in a pattern. Row (a) shows the pattern design and row (b) shows how the pattern appears on a screen. The same pattern can be produced for red, green and blue primaries to recover individual transfer functions.

Therefore, having the pixel gray-value V_{match} that matches in brightness alternating white and bright lines let us easily estimate the value of the display gamma, even if we do not know anything else about the display, including black level, peak luminance and environment in which it is seen.

The same procedure may be used not only to find a single gamma parameter, but also to determine an arbitrary complex shape of a transfer function [209,298] if it is substantially different from the GOG model. The matching must be done for 8–10 half-tone patterns, each containing different ratio of on and off pixels. An example of such half-tone patterns from [298] is shown in Figure A.5. If the ratio of "on" pixels to the total number of pixels is R, the perceived luminance of the pattern is R times the display peak luminance. The actual transfer function can be recovered by fitting a parametric display model [298], or by solving an optimization problem with a smoothness regularization term [209].

A.2.2 Color Calibration

The previous section explained how the first part of a physical display model, the transfer function, can be visually measured. This section explains the procedure for measured the second part of the model, a color transformation matrix.

Most human observers can adjust a color patch so it appears neither red nor green, or neither yellow nor blue. This ability to find unique hues can be used to color-calibrate the display without a measuring device [147].

A schematics of an experiment that could be used to find unique hues is shown in Figure A.6. The user is given a task to indicate a colored circle that has the least amount of blue or yellow tint. The colors are sampled from the HSV (hue-saturation-value) color space by varying hue component and keeping saturation and value fixed. The selection procedure can be repeated several times for the same color, each time narrowing the variation in hue to improve accuracy. The same procedure is run for red, green, blue and yellow colors, and also for the neutral gray point.

The experiment gives the RGB pixel values for four unique hues and the color of neutral gray. Those can be used to find a color transformation matrix from the measured display to another display, for which unique hues are already known [147]. The difficulty here is that

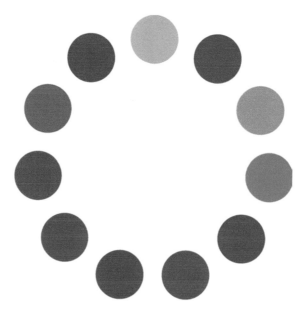

FIGURE A.6 A single step from a unique-hue selection task, used to color-calibrate a display without measuring instruments. The task for the user is to select one color that has the least amount of yellow or blue tint. A sequence of such selections will indicate the unique red color.

the experiment reveals only the position of the unique hue planes but it does not indicate what was saturation or value (brightness) of the selected colors. Because of that, additional regularization terms and constraints are needed to find the transformation matrix.

A.3 CONTRAST SENSITIVITY

The previous sections explained how to map digital pixel values into physical quantities of light, which can be used in visual models. This section will explain in more detail one particular visual model — a Contrast Sensitivity Function (CSF), which was briefly introduced in Section 4.2.4 at page 94.

Contrast sensitivity explains how well a human observer can detect patterns of certain frequency on a uniform background. Such patterns could be for example sinusoidal waves modulated by a Gaussian envelope, so called Gabor patches, shown in Figure A.7. The sensitivity S is defined as the inverse of the detection threshold:

$$S = \left(\frac{\Delta L}{L}\right)^{-1} = \frac{L}{\Delta L}, \tag{A.12}$$

where L is the luminance of the background, and ΔL is the amplitude of the pattern (the difference between the maximum and mean luminance). The sensitivity predicted by the CSF, depends on the number of parameters, such as spatial frequency, temporal frequency, luminance of the background, orientation of the pattern, size of the pattern, and distance from the fovea. In this section we focus on the two parameters that influence sensitivity the most: spatial frequency ρ and the luminance of the background L: $S = CSF(\rho, L)$.

FIGURE A.7   Gabor patches of different spatial frequency, typically used in detection experiments.

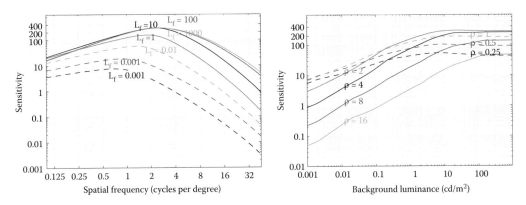

FIGURE A.8   Contrast Sensitivity Function (CSF) plotted as the function of frequency (left) and luminance (right). Different line colors denote different background luminance (L_f), or spatial frequency (ρ). The plots are based on the model from [186] and data from [151].

The plot of the CSF as the function of those two parameters is shown in Figure A.8. The plot reveals that we are not very sensitive to low and high frequency patterns, and we are most sensitive to spatial frequencies between 1 and 5 cycles per visual degree (cpd) for high luminance. The peak sensitivity gradually shifts to about 1 cpd for low luminance. The CSF shows that the drop of sensitivity with luminance is more rapid for high frequencies. Indeed, small high frequency details become invisible at night when the visual system needs to rely on rod vision.

A large number of CSF measurements and models can be found in the literature [11, 12,151,201,277,278]. Most of the historical data was collected in order to gain insights into the visual system rather than provide practical models. Such data was often collected for artificial stimuli and conditions: monochromatic light (single wavelength) [278], corrected for aberrations [201], artificial pupils and monocular viewing. Consequently, such data may not explain how we perceive spatial patterns on actual displays seen in natural conditions. Therefore, it is important to ensure that the CSF models and data represent similar stimuli to those used in a particular application. For example, the data from [277] was collected for a white broadband light and the data from [151] was measured using side-by-side rather than sequential presentation of patterns, which is more relevant for the applications involing static images.

Barten derived a physically plausible model of the CSF [11], which is one of the most comprehensive works in this area, shown to well predict numerous sensitivity datasets. The original work was limited to photopic (daylight) vision but it was later extended to much lower luminance levels in [12]. Another comprehensive CSF model can be found in [64]. Those models were created by fitting analytical formulas to multiple datasets. In contrast to those, the model from [186] relies on a single dataset [151], measured using side-by-side comparisons.

It is important to recognize that the actual shape of the CSF can vary substantially between different models and measurements. This is due to multiple factors, such as differences in experimental procedures, stimuli and its presentation. Therefore, CSF should not be regarded as a rigid ground-truth model of the visual system sensitivity, but rather as a relative characteristic that often needs to adapted to a particular application. The simplest form of such adaptation is a global change of sensitivity. The CSF curves, shown in Figure A.8 can be shifted along the vertical axis to account for different detection tasks. For example, detecting banding artefacts on a display can be more difficult and result in lower sensitivity than detecting Gabor patches in a well-controlled experiment. The peak sensitivity values varies between 300 and 500 for well controlled experiments, which correspond to the smallest detectable contrast between 0.2% and 0.33%. In most practical applications a suitable sensitivity is closer to 100 or less, which translates into detection contrast of 1% or higher.

A.3.1 Contrast Constancy

The CSF plotted as a function of frequency, such as the one on the left in Figure A.8, may resemble a modulation transfer function (MTF). An MTF is often used to describe the loss of resolution in optical systems as the function of spatial frequency. If we were to create a simplistic visual model, we could be tempted to use the CSF as a linear filter and weight each spatial frequency band in an input image by the values from the CSF to simulate a "perceived" image. This, however, would produce false results because the CSF is not a linear filter and it is valid only for very small, barely visible contrast.

The pattern shown in Figure A.9 demonstrates the CSF (also shown in Figure 4.4 on page 95) but also its limitations. The perceived magnitude of contrast in the top rows varies with the frequency. This produces an illusory boundary between visible and invisible contrast, which defines the shape of the CSF. However, the perceived magnitude of contrast remains the same for the bottom rows, in which the physical contrast magnitude is much larger. Those rows do not contain the same variation in perceived contrast as the top rows. This demonstrates *contrast constancy*, which is the ability of the visual system to perceive the same magnitude of contrast regardless of spatial frequency [94]. If the visual system could be explained by a linear filter, we would be able to see the same reduction of perceived contrast magnitude in top and bottom rows. An important consequence of contrast constancy is that CSF is applicable only to patterns of very low contrast, close to the detection thresholds, or close to the illusory CSF line in Figure A.9. If the contrast magnitude is much different

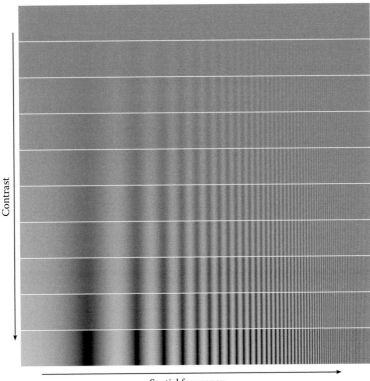

Spatial frequency

FIGURE A.9 The spatial contrast appearance chart. For very low contrast in the top rows, the perceived magnitude of contrast varies with spatial frequency. But the perceived contrast magnitude remains mostly the same for bottom rows containing large contrast.

from the detection contrast, the CSF should not be used to predict how perceived contrast changes.

Since the CSF only applies to a barely visible contrast, its usefulness may seem limited. In practice, however, many visual distortions found in display applications consists of contrast of low amplitudes, for which the CSF prediction are valid. Some examples of those distortions are display non-uniformity or banding due to quantization, discussed in Section A.4. The CSF is also an important component of many supra-threshold[*] contrast perception models, such as models of contrast masking [173], or perceived contrast across the luminance range [280]. Therefore, CSF is a fundamental building block for modeling human vision.

A.3.2 Thresholds across the Luminance Range

Many visual artifacts, such as banding due to quantization discussed in the next section, can reveal themselves across a range of spatial frequencies, so it is impossible to select a single frequency that would be suitable for all cases. Instead, it is better to rely on a conservative

---

[*] Supra-threshold refers to the stimuli whose contrast is much above the detection threshold.

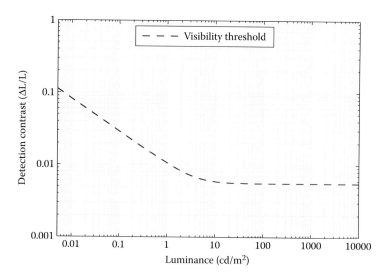

FIGURE A.10 The smallest detectable difference in luminance across the luminance range. The plot is based on the data from [151].

estimate of the detection threshold T by selecting the peak of the CSF at a given background luminance L:

$$T(L) = \frac{L}{\max_\rho \ CSF(\rho, L)} \ . \tag{A.13}$$

The function $T(L)$ predicts the smallest detectable contrast at luminance L and it is plotted in Figure A.10. The contrast that is less than the function $T(L)$ (below the dashed line) is assumed to be invisible to the human eye. The plot shows that it is more difficult to see small contrast differences at low luminance levels.

The function $T(L)$ gives a conservative estimate, which means that actual visibility thresholds in images could be higher than predicted by the function. In rare cases they could be also lower because of the contrast masking phenomenon known as facilitation [173].

A.4 QUANTIZATION AND BIT-DEPTH

The display models presented in Section A.1 were missing an important processing step present in any digital display — quantization due to limited bit-depth. If the number of bits representing color is insufficient, a displayed image can reveal banding artifacts, such as those shown in Figure A.11. Such artifacts can be masked at lower bit-depths by introducing dithering — the use of patterns that are the mixture of two consecutive pixel values, which give an illusion of intermediate intensity levels. And example of banding artifacts that has been masked by dithering is shown in the bottom of Figure A.11.

Dithering is so effective that many displays employ it to deliver smooth gradation of gray levels on low-bit-depth panels. For example, a display could be driven by a 8-bit signal from a PC but have only a 6-bit liquid crystal (LC) panel. In this case, the display control board converts input into a 6-bit driving signal for the LC panel and uses the remaining least

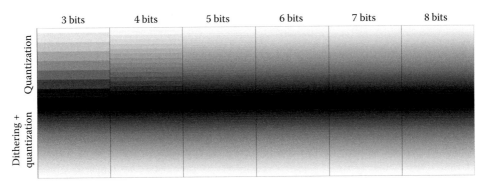

FIGURE A.11 The effect of quantization on a gradient of pixel values. Each column contains an image of different bit-depth, from 3 to 8 bits. The lower part of the gradient was generated using dithering to simulate higher bit-depth.

significant bits to introduce dithering. The dithering can be added in both spatial and temporal domains. Temporal domain dithering is introduced by rapidly switching between pixel values in consecutive frames.

Bit-stealing is another technique for improving bit-depth resolution [274]. The technique involves a small adjustment between the three color components so that intermediate luminance levels are produced at the cost of a small error in color. For example, a pixel color [11 10 10] (using 0–255 range) results in luminance that is higher than for pixel [10 10 10], but lower than for pixel [11 11 11]. As the red component contributes about 21% to luminance, the pixel [11 10 10] with elevated red component produces about 0.21 fractional step in luminance between [10 10 10] and [11 11 11]. In practice, an optimum pixel combinations can be found for every intermediate luminance level so that the distortion in chroma is minimized. The technique works well, especially for gray-scale images, because the visual system is more sensitive to luminance than to chroma variations.

Although both techniques can help extend the perceived bit-depth of a display, the display still requires an input signal of sufficient accuracy to generate dithering patterns or to jitter pixel values for bit-stealing. This raises the question of what bit-depth is sufficient to represent digital images so that no banding artifacts are visible.

A.4.1 Quantization Errors

In this section we combine the display models introduced in Section A.1 and the visibility threshold function from Section A.3.2 to analyze the visibility of banding artefacts.

Figure A.12 shows the maximum quantization errors for a relatively bright display with the peak luminance of 500 cd/m^2 and the black level of 0.1 cd/m^2. The maximum quantization errors are computed as:

$$Q_e(L) = \frac{1}{L} \cdot \left(D \left(D^{-1}(L) + \frac{0.5}{2^b - 1} \right) - L \right), \tag{A.14}$$

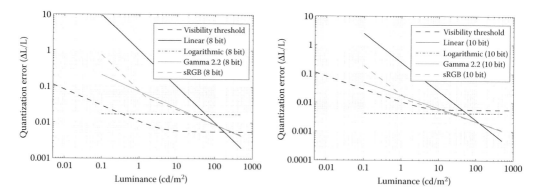

FIGURE A.12 Quantization errors on low dynamic range display ($L_{peak} = 500\,\text{cd/m}^2$, $L_{black} = 0.1\,\text{cd/m}^2$) for selected transfer functions. The errors are shown for 8-bit encoding in the plot on the left and for 10-bit encoding in the plot on the right.

where D is the transfer function transforming luma (0–1) into luminance (in cd/m^2), and D^{-1} is the inverse transfer function transforming luminance into luma. The formula computes the difference between luminance affected by maximum quantization error (0.5 in the luma domain), and accurate luminance, L. The multiplication by $\frac{1}{L}$ brings the values into the same relative contrast units as used for the visibility thresholds in Figure A.10.

Figure A.12 compares four transfer functions: linear scaling into the 0–1 range (effectively no transfer function), the logarithmic function, the gamma 2.2 power function and the sRGB non-linearity. All transfer functions result in visible quantization errors for 8-bit encoding (plot on the left) and only logarithmic encoding brings errors below the visibility thresholds when 10-bit encoding is used (plot on the right). This result is consistent with everyday experience, where quantization errors are easily noticeable on regular 8-bit displays. The plots show that gamma and sRGB are well-aligned with the visibility thresholds for darker colors but they waste bits when encoding brighter colors. The logarithmic curve results in the opposite behavior — it allocates too many bits for darker colors. The lack of any transfer function (*Linear* label in Figure A.12) is the worst choice, with the most visible quantization errors.

Quantization errors are even more visible on a high dynamic range display, producing luminance in the range from 0.005 cd/m^2 to 10 000 cd/m^2, as shown in Figure A.13. 10-bit logarithmic encoding results in banding at higher luminance levels and 2.2 gamma is clearly inadequate for all except the brightest pixels. The floating point encoding (black line) results in very small quantization errors but at the cost of high bit-depth.

A.4.2 Perceptual Transfer Functions

To make the best use of available bit-rate, the transfer function should be aligned with the visibility threshold function $T(L)$. This idea is widely used in medical imaging where certified medical clinical displays have a transfer function scaled in just-noticeable-differences, so called DICOM gray-scale standard display function [1]. Such perceptual transfer function was later extended to high dynamic range (HDR) color images and used for video compression [187,188]. A modified version of such encoding, derived from Barten's CSF model [12]

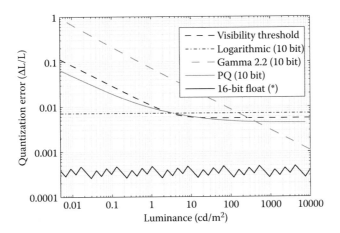

FIGURE A.13   Quantization errors on high dynamic range display ($L_{peak} = 10\,000$ cd/m², $L_{black} = 0.005$ cd/m²) for selected transfer functions and 10-bit encoding.

and known as Perceptual Quantizer (PQ), was proposed as a transfer function for HDR content with a convenient analytical formula [197].

Perceptual transfer functions are straghtfoward to derive from the visibility threshold function $T(L)$. The goal is to find a function mapping luminance into an abstract response so that the increase in the response by 1 corresponds to the increase of luminance by the just-noticeable-difference ΔL. This condition is met when the derivative of the unknown response function R is specified as:

$$\frac{dR}{dL}(L) = \frac{1}{\Delta L(L)} \, . \tag{A.15}$$

Note that the detection threshold $\Delta L(L)$ is the function of luminance L. From Equation A.13 we get that $\Delta L(L) = T(L) \cdot L$ and hence the response function is:

$$R(L_x) = \int_{L_{min}}^{L_x} \frac{1}{T(L)\, L} \, dL \, , \tag{A.16}$$

where L_{min} is the lowest luminance encoded, mapped to the response value 0. The detailed derivation can be found in [189, sec. 2.4]. The resulting trasfer function is shown in Figure A.14 and also in Figure 4.5 on page 96.

Figure A.13 includes the quantization errors for the PQ perceptual transfer function [197]. Although different psychophysical data was used to derive the PQ function and to plot the dashed visibility threshold curve, both curves are relatively similar to each other. The study in [42] showed a slight advantage of the PQ over other perceptual transfer functions in terms of uniformity of banding artifacts across the luminance range.

Figure A.14 shows an interesting property of the perceptual transfer function. The shape of the transfer function is relatively close to the relation between luminance and perceived

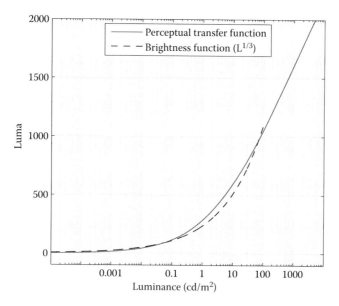

FIGURE A.14 Perceptual transfer function compared with the brightness function (Stevens' law for brightness).

brightness (Steven's law). This demonstrates, that the perceptual transfer function not only reduces visibility of quantization errors, but it also improves perceptual uniformity of the resulting luma values. Note that Steven's power brightness function was demonstrated to hold only for lower luminance levels [97, p.101] and therefore the brightness function is plotted up to $100 \, \text{cd/m}^2$.

A.5 SUMMARY

The quality of any display technology is ultimately judged by the human eye. Therefore, it is essential that visual perception is considered in any display-related application. This chapter introduced models and methods that help to characterize a display and its performance in perceptual terms.

First, we showed how most displays can be modelled using a gain-offset-gamma model (Section A.1). A display model provides a link between digital signal driving a display and light emitted from the screen, which is eventually perceived by the display user. Selected parameters of such display model can be found using visual calibration procedures, discussed in Section A.2. The contrast sensitivity function (CSF) is one of the most commonly used visual models when investigating perceptual aspects of a display design. Such function, however, is applicable only to very small contrast distortions, as discussed in Section A.3. One successful application of CSF is testing for the visibility of banding artefacts, caused by limited bit-depth of the pixels (Section A.4). The same visual characteristic can be also used to drive a perceptual transfer function, which minimizes the visibility of banding artefacts for a given bit-depth.

This chapter provided insight into a small portion of the wider field of perceptual display design and calibration. A general overview of perceptual considerations in display design can be found in Chapter 4 of this book and also in the survey paper [191]. The visibility of more complex spatial distortion, such as display non-uniformity, can be tested using perceptual image difference metrics, such as VDP [64] or HDR-VDP [186]. The code for the latter metric is freely available.[*] When considering video, it is important to account for spatio-temporal contrast sensitivity of the visual system [285] and the temporal aspects of a display [120]. If assessment of color artefacts is important, some level of perceptual scaling can be achieved using uniform color spaces or color appearance models [79,82]. Testing for distortions in binocular stereo displays may require disparity difference metrics [73]. This diversity of visual models, specialized in different aspects of vision, demonstrates the challenge of visual modeling. While specialized visual models, focused on a particular kind of distortion, have been successful used in many areas, there is no single general visual model, which could account for all aspects of vision and could be applicable to a wide range of problems.

---

[*] HDR-VDP-2 can be downloaded from http://hdrvdp.sourceforge.net/

Bibliography

1. PS 3.14-2003. DICOM Part 14: Grayscale Standard Display Function. Technical report, National Electrical Manufacturers Association, 2003.
2. Manoj Aggarwal and Narendra Ahuja. Split Aperture Imaging for High Dynamic Range. In *Proc. of IEEE International Conference on Computer Vision (ICCV)*, volume 2, pages 10–17, 2001.
3. Maneesh Agrawala, Andrew C. Beers, Ian McDowall, Bernd Froehlich, Mark Bolas, and Pat Hanrahan. The two-user responsive workbench: Support for collaboration through individual views of a shared space. In *SIGGRAPH '97: Proceedings of the 24th Annual Conference on Computer Graphics and Interactive Techniques*, pages 327–332, New York, NY, USA, 1997. ACM Press/Addison-Wesley Publishing Co.
4. Will Allen and Robert Ulichney. Wobulation: Doubling the Addressed Resolution of Projection Displays. In *Proc. of SID Symposium Digest of Technical Papers*, volume 36, pages 1514–1517, 2005.
5. T. Amano and H. Kato. Real world dynamic appearance enhancement with procam feedback. Intl. Workshop on Projector-Camera (poster), 2008.
6. K. Arthur, T. Preston, R. Taylor, F. Brooks, M. Whitton, and W. Wright. Designing and building the pit: a head-tracked stereo workspace for two users. In *Proc. of 2nd International Immersive Projection Tecnology Workshop*, 1998.
7. Mark Ashdown, Takahiro Okabe, Imari Sato, and Yoichi Sato. Robust Content-Dependent Photometric Projector Compensation. In *Proc. of IEEE International Workshop on Projector-Camera Systems (ProCams)*, 2006.
8. Mark Ashdown, Imari Sato, Takahiro Okabe, and Yoichi Sato. Perceptual Photometric Compensation for Projected Images. *IEICE Transaction on Information and Systems*, J90-D(8):2115–2125, 2007. in Japanese.
9. Tibor Balogh, Tamas Forgacs, Olivier Balet, Eric Bouvier, Fabio Bettio, Enrico Gobbetti, and Gianluigi Zanetti. A scalable holographic display for interactive graphics applications. In *Proc. IEEE VR 2005 Workshop on Emerging Display Technologies*, Conference Held in Bonn, Germany, March 2005.
10. René de la Barré, Siegmund Pastoor, and Hans Röder. Verfahren und vorrichtung zur autostereoskopischen darstellung von bildinformationen. German Patent, No. DE102007055026, 11 2009.
11. Peter G. J. Barten. *Contrast sensitivity of the human eye and its effects on image quality*. SPIE Press, 1999.
12. Peter G. J. Barten. Formula for the contrast sensitivity of the human eye. In Yoichi Miyake and D. Rene Rasmussen, editors, *Proc. SPIE 5294, Image Quality and System Performance*, pages 231–238, dec 2004.
13. Olivier Bau, Ivan Poupyrev, Ali Israr, and Chris Harrison. Teslatouch: Electrovibration for touch surfaces. In *UIST '10: Proceedings of the 23nd Annual ACM Symposium on User Interface Software and Technology*, pages 283–292, 2010.

14. K. Bazargan. *Techniques in Display Holography*. PhD thesis, Physics Dept., Imperial College, London University, April 1986.

15. K. S. Beev, K.N. Beeva, and S. H. Sainov. Materials for holographic 3dtv display applications. In *Three-Dimensional Television*, pages 557–598. Springer, 2008.

16. J. S. Bell. On the einstein podolsky rosen paradox. *Physics*, 1:195–200, 1964.

17. S.A. Benton. Survey of holographic stereograms. In *Proc. of SPIE'82*, volume 367, pages 15–19, 1982.

18. E. P. Berlin. A three-dimensional display. US Patent 4160973, 1979.

19. Roy S Berns. Methods for characterizing CRT displays. *Displays*, 16(4):173–182, 1996.

20. K. Betsui, F. Namiki, Kanazawa Y, and H. Inoue. High resolution plasma display panel (pdp). *Fujitsu Sci. Tech. J.*, 35(2):229–239, 1999.

21. Ezekiel Bhasker and Aditi Majumder. Geometric Modeling and Calibration of Planar Multi-Projector Displays using Rational Bezier Patches. In *Proc. of IEEE International Workshop on Projector-Camera Systems (ProCams)*, 2007.

22. W. Biehling, C. Deter, S. Dube, B. Hill, S. Helling, K. Isakovic, S. Klose, and M. Schiewe. Laser-Cave - Some Building Blocks for Immersive Screens. In *Proc. of International Status Conference Virtual and Augmented Reality*, 2004.

23. O. Bimber, D. Klöck, T. Amano, A. Grundhöfer, and D. Kurz. Closed-loop feedback illumination for optical inverse tone-mapping in light microscopy. *IEEE Transactions on Visualization and Computer Graphics*, 2010.

24. Oliver Bimber. Projector-Based Augmentation. In Michael Haller, Mark Billinghurst, and Bruce Thomas, editors, *Emerging Technologies of Augmented Reality: Interfaces and Design*, pages 64–89. Idea Group, 2006.

25. Oliver Bimber, Franz Coriand, Alexander Kleppe, Erich Bruns, Stefanie Zollmann, and Tobias Langlotz. Superimposing Pictorial Artwork with Projected Imagery. *IEEE MultiMedia*, 12(1):16–26, 2005.

26. Oliver Bimber and Andreas Emmerling. Multifocal Projection: A Multiprojector Technique for Increasing Focal Depth. *IEEE Transactions on Visualization and Computer Graphics (TVCG)*, 12(4):658–667, 2006.

27. Oliver Bimber, Andreas Emmerling, and Thomas Klemmer. Embedded Entertainment with Smart Projectors. *IEEE Computer*, 38(1):56–63, 2005.

28. Oliver Bimber, Bernd Froehlich, Dieter Schmalstieg, and L. Miguel Encarnacao. The virtual showcase. *IEEE Comput. Graph. Appl.*, 21(6):48–55, 2001.

29. Oliver Bimber, Anselm Grundhoefer, Thomas Zeidler, Daniel Danch, and Pedro Kapakos. Compensating Indirect Scattering for Immersive and Semi-Immersive Projection Displays. In *Proc. of IEEE Virtual Reality (IEEE VR)*, pages 151–158, 2006.

30. Oliver Bimber and Daisuke Iwai. Superimposing dynamic range. *ACM Trans. Graph.*, 27(5):1–8, 2008.

31. Oliver Bimber, Daisuke Iwai, Gordon Wetzstein, and Anselm Grundhoefer. The visual computing of projector-camera systems. In *Proc. of EUROGRAPHICS (STAR)*, pages 23–46, 2007.

32. Oliver Bimber, Daisuke Iwai, Gordon Wetzstein, and Anselm Grundhoefer. The visual computing of projector-camera systems. *Computer Graphics Forum*, 27(8):2219–2245, 2008.

33. Oliver Bimber, Gordon Wetzstein, Andreas Emmerling, and Christian Nitschke. Enabling View-Dependent Stereoscopic Projection in Real Environments. In *Proc. of IEEE/ACM International Symposium on Mixed and Augmented Reality (ISMAR)*, pages 14–23, 2005.

34. Oliver Bimber, Thomas Zeidler, Anselm Grundhoefer, Gordon Wetzstein, Mathias Moehring, Sebastian Knoedel, and Uwe Hahne. Interacting with augmented holograms. In *Proc. of SPIE'05, Practical Holography XIX: Materials and Applications*, pages 41–54, 2005.

35. R. Blach, M. Bues, J.Hochstrate, J. Springer, and Bernd Froehlich. Experiences with multi-viewer stereo displays based on lc-shutters and polarization. In *Proc. of. IEEE VR: Workshop Emerging Display Technologies*, 2005.

36. R. Blache, J. Krumm, and W. Fix. Organic cmos circuits for rfid applications. White Paper, ISSCC Dig. Tech. Papers, February 2009.

37. P.A. Blanche, A. Bablumian, R. Voorakaranam, C. Christenson, W. Lin, T. Gu, D. Flores, P. Wang, W.Y. Hsieh, M. Kathaperumal, B. Rachwal, O. Siddiqui, J. Thomas, R. A. Norwood, M. Yamamoto, and N. Peyghambarian. Holographic three-dimensional telepresence using large-area photorefractive polymer. *Nature*, 468:80–83, 2010.

38. B. Blundell and A.J. Schwarz. The classification of volumetric display systems: Characteristics and predictability of the image space. *IEEE Trans. on Visualization and Computer Graphics*, 8(1):66–76, 2002.

39. B.G. Blundell and A. J. Schwarz. *Volumetric Three-Dimensional Display Systems*. Wiley-IEEE Press, New York, 2000.

40. Lars Boennen. Fohmd: The fiber-optic helmet mounted display and its applications. In *Proc. International Worlshop on Integrative 3D Visualization*, 1994.

41. J. P. Boeuf. Plasma display panels: physics, recent developments and key issues. *J. Phys. D: Appl. Phys.*, 36:R53–R79, 2003.

42. Ronan Boitard, Rafał K. Mantiuk, and Tania Pouli. Evaluation of color encodings for high dynamic range pixels. In *Human Vision and Electronic Imaging*, page 93941K, 2015.

43. J. Bongartz, D. Giel, and P. Hering. Fast 3d topometry in medicine using pulsed holography. In *SPIE '02*, volume 4659, 2002.

44. Matthew S. Brennesholtz and Edward H. Stupp. *Projection Displays*. Wiley, Hoboken, NJ, 2008.

45. Dominique Brosteaux, Fabrice Axisa, Jan Vanfleteren, Nadine Carchon, and Mario Gonzalez. Elastic interconnects for stretchable electronic circuits using mid (moulded interconnect device) technology. In S.P. Lacour J.P. Conde, B. Morrison III, editor, *MRS Proceedings*, volume 926E, pages 82–89, 2006.

46. Michael Brown, Aditi Majumder, and Ruigang Yang. Camera Based Calibration Techniques for Seamless Multi-Projector Displays. *IEEE Transactions on Visualization and Computer Graphics (TVCG)*, 11(2):193–206, 2005.

47. Michael S. Brown, Peng Song, and Tat-Jen Cham. Image Pre-Conditioning for Out-of-Focus Projector Blur. In *Proc. of IEEE Conference on Computer Vision and Pattern Recognition (CVPR)*, volume II, pages 1956–1963, 2006.

48. O. Cakmakci and Jannick Rolland. Head-worn displays: a review. *Display Technology, Journal of*, 2(3):199–216, September 2006.

49. O. Cakmakci, S. Vo, S. Vogl, R. Spindelbalker, A. Ferscha, and J. P. Rolland. Optical free-form surfaces in off-axis head-worn display design. In *Proceedings of The 7th IEEE and ACM International Symposium on Mixed and Augmented reality, ISMAR*, pages 29–32, New York, 2008. Springer.

50. Ozan Cakmakci and Jannick Rolland. Head-worn displays: A review. *Journal of Display Technology*, 2(3):199–216, September 2006.

51. Daniel Carl, Markus Fratz, Andreas Hofmann, and Holger Kock. Dreidimensionale bilder auf einen blick. *QZ*, 55(5):36–39, 2010.

52. Giandomenico Caruso and Umberto Cugini. Augmented reality video see-through hmd oriented to product design assessment. In R. Shumaker, editor, *Virtual and Mixed Reality*, pages 532–541. Springer Verlag, 2009.

53. Dalit Caspi, Nahum Kiryati, and Joseph Shamir. Range Imaging With Adaptive Color Structured Light. *IEEE Transaction on Pattern Analysis and Machine Intelligence*, 20(5):470–480, 1998.

54. E.B. Champagne. Nonparaxial imaging, magnification, and aberration properties in holography. *Journal of the Optical Society of America*, 57(1):51–55, 1967.

55. C. Chiang, S. Wang, Y. Chen, and S. Lai. Fast jnd-based video carving with gpu acceleration for real-time video retargeting. *IEEE Trans. Cir. and Sys. for Video Technol.*, 19(11):1588–1597, 2009.

56. H. Q. Chiang, J. F. Wager, R. L. Hoffman, J. Jeong, and D. A. Keszler. High mobility transparent thin film transistors with amorphous zinc tin oxide channel layer. *Applied Physics Letters*, 86(1):id: 013503, 2005.

57. Myungjin Cho, Mehdi Daneshpanah, Inkyu Moon, and Bahram Javidi. Three-dimensional optical sensing and visualization using integral imaging. *Proceedings of the IEEE*, 99(4):556–575, 4 2011.

58. CIE1931. Rgb color matching functions. In *Commission internationale de l'Eclairage proceedings, 1931*, Cambridge, 1932. Cambridge University Press.

59. Philippe Colantoni, Jean-baptiste Thomas, and Jon Y Hardeberg. High-end colorimetric display characterization using an adaptive training set. *Journal of the Society for Information Display*, 19(8):520, 2011.

60. E. Collett. *Field Guide to Polarization*, volume SPIE Field Guides vol. FG05. SPIE, 2005.

61. Daniel Cotting, Martin Näf, Markus H. Gross, and Henry Fuchs. Embedding Imperceptible Patterns into Projected Images for Simultaneous Acquisition and Display. In *Proc. of IEEE/ACM International Symposium on Mixed and Augmented Reality (ISMAR)*, pages 100–109, 2004.

62. Daniel Cotting, Remo Ziegler, Markus H. Gross, and Henry Fuchs. Adaptive Instant Displays: Continuously Calibrated Projections Using Per-Pixel Light Control. In *Proc. of Eurographics*, pages 705–714, 2005.

63. C. Cruz-Neira, D. Sandin, Tom DeFanti, R. Kenyon, and J. Hart. The cave: Audio visual experience automatic virtual environment. In *Proc. of ACM Siggraph'92*, pages 65–72, 1992.

64. S.J. Daly. Visible differences predictor: an algorithm for the assessment of image fidelity. In Andrew B. Watson, editor, *Digital Images and Human Vision*, volume 1666, pages 179–206. MIT Press, 1993.

65. Gerwin Damberg, Helge Seetzen, Greg Ward, Wolfgang Heidrich, and Lorne Whitehead. High-Dynamic-Range Projection Systems. In *Proc. of SID Symposium Digest of Technical Papers*, volume 38, pages 4–7, 2007.

66. N. Damera-Venkata and N. L. Chang. Display supersampling. *ACM Transactions on Graphics*, 28(1):Article 9, 2009.

67. Niranjan Damera-Venkata and Nelson L. Chang. Realizing Super-Resolution with Superimposed Projection. In *Proc. of IEEE International Workshop on Projector-Camera Systems (ProCams)*, 2007.

68. H. Davson. *Physiology of the Eye*. Macmillan Academic and Professional Ltd., 5th edition, 1990.

69. Ellen A. Day, Lawrence Taplin, and Roy S. Berns. Colorimetric characterization of a computer-controlled liquid crystal display. *Color Research and Application*, 29(5):365–373, 2004.

70. Paul Debevec, Erik Reinhard, Greg Ward, Karol Myszkowski, Helge Seetzen, Habib Zargarpour, Gary McTaggart, and Drew Hess. High Dynamic Range Imaging: Theory and Applications. In *Proc. of ACM SIGGRAPH (Courses)*, 2006.

71. Paul E. Debevec and Jitendra Malik. Recovering High Dynamic Range Radiance Maps from Photographs. In *Proc. of ACM SIGGRAPH*, pages 369–378, 1997.

72. D.J. DeBitetto. Holographic panoramic stereograms synthesized from white light recordings. *Applied Optics*, 8(8):1740–1741, 1969.

73. Piotr Didyk, Tobias Ritschel, Elmar Eisemann, Karol Myszkowski, Hans-Peter Seidel, and Wojciech Matusik. A luminance-contrast-aware disparity model and applications. *ACM Transactions on Graphics*, 31(6):1, nov 2012.

74. E.A. Downing. A three-color, solid-state, three-dimensional display. *Science*, 273:1185–1189, 1996.

75. Dana Dudley, Walter M. Duncan, and John Slaughter. Emerging digital micromirror device (dmd) applications. In *Proc. of SPIE*, volume 4985, pages 14–25, 2003.

76. G. H. Dunteman. *Principal Component Analysis*. Sage Publications, 1989.

77. Jochen Ehnes, Koichi Hirota, and Michitaka Hirose. Projected Augmentation - Augmented Reality using Rotatable Video Projectors. In *Proc. of IEEE/ACM International Symposium on Mixed and Augmented Reality (ISMAR)*, pages 26–35, 2004.

78. Tomohiro Endo, Makoto Sato, Yoshihiro Kajiki, and Toshio Honda. Cylindrical 3d video display observable from all directions. In *Proceedings of the 8th Pacific Conference on Computer Graphics and Applications*, pages 300–306. IEEE Computer Society, 2000.

79. Garrett Johnson Erik Reinhard, Erum Arif Khan, Ahmet Oguz Akyuz. *Color Imaging: Fundamentals and Applications*. CRC Press, 2008.

80. Peter T. Erslev, Hai Q. Chiang, David Hong, John F. Wager, and J. David Cohen. Electronic properties of amorphous zinc tin oxide films by junction capacitance methods. *Journal of Non-Crystalline Solids*, 354:2801–2804, 2008.

81. Björn Eversmann, Martin Jenkner, Franz Hofmann, Christian Paulus, Ralf Brederlow, Birgit Holzapfl, Peter Fromherz, Matthias Merz, Markus Brenner, Matthias Schreiter, Reinhard Gabl, Kurt Plehnert, Michael Steinhauser, Gerald Eckstein, Doris Schmitt-Landsiedel, and Roland Thewes. A 128 x 128 cmos biosensor array for extracellular recording of neural activity. *IEEE Journal of Solid-State Circuits*, 38:2306–2317, 2003.

82. Mark D. Fairchild. *Color Appearance Models*. John Wiley & Sons, second edition, 2005.

83. G. Favalora, R. K. Dorval, D. M. Hall, M. Giovinco, and J. Napoli. Volumetric three-dimensional display system with rasterization hardware. In *Stereoscopic Displays and Virtual Reality Systems VIII, Proceedings of SPIE*, volume 4297A, pages 227–235, 2001.

84. J. L. Fergason. Polymer encapsulated nematic liquid crystals for display and light control applications. *SID Int. Symp.Dig. Technol.*, 16:68–70, 1985.

85. Richard P. Feynman, Robert B. Leighton, and Matthew Sands. *The Feynman Lectures on Physics, The Definitive Edition Volume 3*. Addison Wesley, Reading, MA, 2005.

86. R.D. Fields. *The Other Brain: From Dementia to Schizophrenia, How New Discoveries about the Brain Are Revolutionizing Medicine and Science*. Simon & Schuster, 2009.

87. Matthew Flagg and James M. Rehg. Projector-Guided Painting. In *Proc. of ACM Symposium on User Interface Software and Technology (UIST)*, pages 235–244, 2006.

88. G. Freedman and R. Fattal. Real-time gpu-based video upscaling from local self examples. In *ACM SIGGRAPH 2010 Talks*, 2010.

89. H. Frenzel, A. Lajn, M. Brandt, H. von Wenckstern, G. Biehne, H. Hochmuth, M. Lorenz, and M. Grundmann. Zno metal-semiconductor field-effect transistors with ag-schottky gates. *Applied Physics Letters*, 92, 2008.

90. S. Frey, J. Bongartz, D. Giel, A. Thelen, and P. Hering. Ultrafast holographic technique for 3d in situ documentation of cultural heritage. In *Proceedings of SPIE'03, Optical Metrology for Arts and Multimedia*, volume 5146, pages 194–201, 2003.

91. H. Fuchs, S. M. Pizer, L. C. Tsai, and S. H. Bloomberg. Adding a true 3-d display to a raster graphics system. *IEEE Computer Graphics and Applications*, 2(7):73–78, September 1982.

92. K. Fujii, M.D. Grossberg, and S.K. Nayar. A Projector-Camera System with Real-Time Photometric Adaptation for Dynamic Environments. In *Proc. of IEEE Conference on Computer Vision and Pattern Recognition (CVPR)*, volume I, pages 814–821, 2005.

93. Osterberg G. Topography of the layer of rods and cones in the human retina. *Acta Ophthalmol Suppl.*, 6:1–103, 1935.

94. M A Georgeson and G D Sullivan. Contrast constancy: deblurring in human vision by spatial frequency channels. *J. Physiol.*, 252(3):627–656, nov 1975.

95. R. W. Gerchberg and W. O. Saxton. A practical algorithm for the determination of phase from image and diffraction plane pictures. *Optik*, 35:237–246, 1972.

96. A. Gershun. The light field. *Journal of Mathematics and Physics*, 18(1):51–151, 1936. Translated by E. Moon and G. Timoshenko.

97. Alan Gilchrist. *Seeing Black and White*. Oxford University Press, 2006.

98. Stephen R. Gottesman and E. E. Fenimore. New family of binary arrays for coded aperture imaging. *Applied Optics*, 28(20):4344–4352, 1989.

99. Simon Groeblacher, Tomasz Paterek, Rainer Kaltenbaek, Caslav Brukner, Marek Zukowski, Markus Aspelmeyer, and Anton Zeilinger. An experimental test of non-local realism. *Nature*, 446:871–875, 2007.

100. M. Gross, S. Wurmlin, M. Naf, E. Lamboray, C. Spagno, A. Kunz ad A.V. Moere, K. Strehlke, S. Lang, T. Svoboda, E. Koller-Meier, L.V. Gool, and O. Staadt. blue-c: A spatially immersive display and 3d video portal for telepresence. In *Proc. of ACM Siggraph'03*, pages 819–827, 2003.

101. M.D. Grossberg, H. Peri, S.K. Nayar, and P.N. Belhumeur. Making One Object Look Like Another: Controlling Appearance using a Projector-Camera System. In *Proc. of IEEE Conference on Computer Vision and Pattern Recognition (CVPR)*, volume I, pages 452–459, June 2004.

102. Max Grosse and Oliver Bimber. Coded aperture projection. In *Proc. of Emerging Display Technologies and Immersive Projection Technologies 2008 (EDT IPT08)*, 2008.

103. Max Grosse, Gordon Wetzstein, Anselm Grundhoefer, and Oliver Bimber. Coded aperture projection. *ACM Transactions on Graphics*, 29(3):Article 22, 2010.

104. A. Grundhoefer, M. Seeger, F. Haentsch, and O. Bimber. Dynamic Adaptation of Projected Imperceptible Codes. In *Proc. of IEEE International Symposium on Mixed and Augmented Reality*, pages 1–10, 2007.

105. Anselm Grundhoefer and Oliver Bimber. Real-Time Adaptive Radiometric Compensation. *IEEE Transactions on Visualization and Computer Graphics (TVCG)*, 14(14):97–108, January 2008.

106. John Guild. The colorimetric properties of the spectrum. *Philosophical Transactions of the Royal Society of London*, A230:149–187, 1931.

107. Hitoshi Habe, Nobuo Saeki, and Takashi Matsuyama. Inter-Reflection Compensation for Immersive Projection Display. In *Proc. of IEEE International Workshop on Projector-Camera Systems (ProCams) (poster)*, 2007.

108. R. N. Haber and M. Hershenson. *The psychology of visual perception*. Holt, Rinehart and Winston, New York, 1973.

109. R. Haeussler, A. Schwerdtner, and N. Leister. Large holographic displays as an alternative to stereoscopic displays. In *SPIE Conference Proceedings Stereoscopic Displays and Applications XIX*, volume 6803, 2008.

110. Rolf R. Hainich. Integrative 3d visualization. In *Proc. International Workshop on Integrative 3D Visualization*, 1994.

111. Rolf R. Hainich. *The End of Hardware - A Novel Approach to Augmented Reality*. Booksurge Inc., 2006.

112. Rolf R. Hainich. *The End of Hardware - A Novel Approach to Augmented Reality, 2nd Ed.* Booksurge Inc., 2006.

113. Rolf R. Hainich. Roadmap holography - an essay, September 2006.

114. Rolf R. Hainich. New approaches to 3d displays, invited talk at weimar university, October 2007.

115. Rolf R. Hainich. Near-eye displays - a look into the christmas ball. In *IEEE / ACM International Symposium on Mixed and Augmented Reality*, page xv, Cambridge, UK, 2008. IEEE Computer Society.

116. Rolf R. Hainich. *The End of Hardware, 3rd Ed.: Augmented Reality and Beyond*. Booksurge Inc, 2009.

117. Rolf R. Hainich. 3d vision and displays - basics, spatial display technology and augmented reality - bits conference, May 2012.

118. Rolf R. Hainich. Approaches to ideal freeform mirror and display shapes for augmented reality, January 2015.

119. Rolf R. Hainich. Device and method for the near-eye display of computer generated images. US 2016-0077336-A1, 09 2015.

120. Hao Pan, Xiao-Fan Feng, and S. Daly. LCD motion blur modeling and analysis. In *IEEE International Conference on Image Processing 2005*, pages II–21. IEEE, jul 2005.

121. S.J. Hart and M.N. Dalton. Display holography for medical tomography. In *Proc. of SPIE'90, Practical Holography IV*, volume 1212, pages 116–135, 1990.

122. E. Hecht. *Optics*. Addison-Wesley, Reading, MA, 1987.

123. J. Heikenfeld, K. Zhou, E. Kreit, B. Raj, S. Yang, B. Sun, A. Milarcik, L. Clapp, and R. Schwartz. Electrofluidic displays using young-laplace transposition of brilliant pigment dispersions. *Nature Photonics*, 3:292–296, 2009.

124. G.H. Heilmeier and L.A. Zanoni. Guest-host interactions in nematic liquid crystals. a new electrooptic effect. *Appllied Physics Letters*, 13:91, 1968.

125. R. Herzog, E. Eisemann, K. Myszkowski, and H. Seidel. Spatio-temporal upsampling on the gpu. In *ACM SIGGRAPH Symposium on interactive 3D Graphics and Games*, pages 91–98, 2010.

126. Harvey Ho, Ehsan Saeedi, Samuel S. Kim, Tueng Shen, and Babak A. Parviz. Contact lens with integrated inorganic semiconductor devices. In *Proc. 21st IEEE Intl. Conf. on MicroElectroMechanical Systems (MEMS) 403-406*, pages 13–17, 2008.

127. I.P. Howard and B.J. Rogers. *Seeing in Depth*. Oxford University Press, Oxford, UK, 2008.

128. H. Hua, C. Gao, L. Brown, N. Ahuja, and J. P. Rolland. Using a head-mounted projective display in interactive augmented environments. In *Proc. of IEEE and ACM International Symposium on Augmented Reality'01*, pages 217–223, 2001.

129. F. Huang, K. Chen, and G. Wetzstein. The Light Field Stereoscope: Immersive Computer Graphics via Factored Near-Eye Light Field Displays with Focus Cues. *ACM Trans. Graph. (SIGGRAPH)*, (4), 2015.

130. Fu-Chung Huang, Douglas Lanman, Brian A. Barsky, and Ramesh Raskar. Correcting for optical aberrations using multilayer displays. *ACM Transaction on Graphics*, 31:185:1–185:12, 2012.

131. Fu-Chung Huang, Gordon Wetzstein, Brian A. Barsky, and Ramesh Raskar. Eyeglasses-free display: Towards correcting visual aberrations with computational light field displays. *ACM Transaction on Graphics*, xx, August 2014.

132. Michael Huebschman, Bala Munjuluri, and Harold Garner. Dynamic holographic 3-d image projection. *Opt. Express*, 11(5):437–445, 2003.

133. M. Inami, N. Kawakami, D. Sekiguchi, Y. Yanagida, T. Maeda, and S. Tachi. Visuo-haptic display using head-mounted projector. In *Proc. of IEEE Virtual Reality'00*, pages 217–240, 2000.

134. Ori Inbar. Smart glasses market 2015, augmentedreality.org, 2015.

135. F. N. Ishikawa, H. K. Chang, K. Ryu, P. Chen, A. Badmaev, L. De Arco Gomez, G. Z.Shen, and C. Zhou. Transparent electronics based on transfer printed aligned carbon nanotubes on rigid and flexible substrates. *ACS Nano*, 3(1):73–79, 2008.

136. C. Jaynes, S. Webb, and R. M. Steele. Camera-Based Detection and Removal of Shadows from Interactive Multiprojector Displays. *IEEE Transactions on Visualization and Computer Graphics (TVCG)*, 10(3):290–301, 2004.

137. C. Jaynes, S. Webb, R.M. Steele, M. Brown, and W.B. Seales. Dynamic Shadow Removal from Front Projection Displays. In *Proc. of IEEE Visualization*, pages 175–555, 2001.

138. Christopher Jaynes and Divya Ramakrishnan. Super-Resolution Composition in Multi-Projector Displays. In *Proc. of IEEE International Workshop on Projector-Camera Systems (ProCams)*, 2003.

139. Tyler Johnson and Henry Fuchs. Real-Time Projector Tracking on Complex Geometry using Ordinary Imagery. In *Proc. of IEEE International Workshop on Projector-Camera Systems (ProCams)*, 2007.

140. Andrew Jones, Andrew Gardner, Mark Bolas, Ian McDowall, and Paul Debevec. Simulating Spatially Varying Lighting on a Live Performance. In *Proc. of European Conference on Visual Media Production (CVMP)*, pages 127–133, 2006.

141. Andrew Jones, Ian McDowall, Hideshi Yamada, Mark Bolas, and Paul Debevec. Rendering for an Interactive 360°Light Field Display. *ACM Transactions on Graphics (TOG) - Proceedings of ACM SIGGRAPH 2007*, 26(3):Article 40, July 2007.

142. Claus Jönsson. Elektroneninterferenzen an mehreren künstlich hergestellten feinspalten. *Zeitschrift für Physik*, 161:454–474, 1961.

143. Ray Juang and Aditi Majumder. Photometric Self-Calibration of a Projector-Camera System. In *Proc. of IEEE International Workshop on Projector-Camera Systems (ProCams)*, 2007.

144. Yoshikawa K., Kanazawa Y.and Wakitani W., Shinoda T., and Ohtsuka A. In *Japan. Display 92*, page 605, 1992.

145. Yasuaki Kakehi, Makoto Iida, Takeshi Naemura, Yoshinari Shirai, Mitsunori Matsushita, and Takeshi Ohguro. Lumisight table: An interactive view-dependent tabletop display. *IEEE Comput. Graph. Appl.*, 25(1):48–53, 2005.

146. David Kane, Robin T. Held, and Martin S. Banks. Visual discomfort from stereo 3d displays when the head is not upright. In *Conf. Stereoscopic Displays and Applications*, 2012.

147. D Karatzas and S M Wuerger. A Hardware-Independent Colour Calibration Technique. *Annals of the British Machine Vision Association*, 2007(3):1–10, 2007.

148. R. D. Ketchpel. Direct-view three-dimensional display tube. *IEEE Transactions on Electron Devices*, 10(5):324–328, September 1963.

149. Dongjo Kim, Youngmin Jeong, Keunkyu Song, Seong-Kee Park, Guozhong Cao, and Jooho Moon. Inkjet-printed zinc tin oxide thin-film transistor. *Langmuir*, 25(18):11149–11154, 2009.

150. Felix Sunjoo Kim, Xugang Guo, Mark D. Watson, and Samson A. Jenekhe. High-mobility ambipolar transistors and high-gain inverters from a donor-acceptor copolymer semiconductors. *Advanced Materials*, 22(4):478–482, January 2010.

151. Kil Joong Kim, Rafał Mantiuk, and Kyoung Ho Lee. Measurements of achromatic and chromatic contrast sensitivity functions for an extended range of adaptation luminance. In Bernice E. Rogowitz, Thrasyvoulos N. Pappas, and Huib de Ridder, editors, *Human Vision and Electronic Imaging*, page 86511A, mar 2013.

152. Sang Gyun Kim, Sung Min Kim, Youn Sik Kim, Hee Kyu Lee, Seung Hee Lee, Gi-Dong Lee, Jae-Jin Lyu, and Kyeong Hyeon Kim. Stabilization of the liquid crystal director in the patterned vertical alignment mode through formation of pretilt angle by reactive mesogen. *Applied Physics Letters*, 90, 2007.

153. Masahiko Kitamura and Takeshi Naemura. A Study on Position-Dependent Visible Light Communication using DMD for ProCam. In *IPSJ SIG Notes. CVIM-156*, pages 17–24, 2006. in Japanese.

154. Y. Kitamura, T. Konishi, S. Yamamoto, and F. Kishino. Interactive stereoscopic display for three or more users. In *Proc. of ACM SIGGRAPH'01*, pages 231–239, 2001.

155. Kiyoshi Kiyokawa, Mark Billinghurst, Bruce Campbell, and Eric Woods. An occlusion-capable optical see-through head mount display for supporting co-located collaboration. In *Proc. of IEEE/ACM International Symposium on Mixed and Augmented Reality (ISMAR)*, pages 133–141, 2003.

156. S. Klimenko, P. Frolov, L. Nikitina, and I. Nikitin. Crosstalk reduction in passive stereo-projection systems. In *Proc. of Eurographics'03 (Industrial Project Presentations)*, pages 235–240, 2003.

157. M.A. Klug, A. Klein, W. Plesniak, W. Kropp, and B. Chen. Optics for full-parallax holographic stereograms. In *Proc. of SPIE'97*, volume 3011, pages 78–88, 1997.

158. Sebastian Knorr, Matthias Kunter, and Thomas Sikora. Stereoscopic 3d from 2d video with super-resolution capability. *Image Commun.*, 23(9):665–676, 2008.

159. J. Konrad, B. Lacotte, and E. Dubois. Cancellation of image crosstalk in time-sequential displays of stereoscopic video. *IEEE Transactions on Image Processing*, 9(5):897–908, May 2000.

160. Philipp Krähenbühl, Manuel Lang, Alexander Hornung, and Markus Gross. A system for retargeting of streaming video. In *SIGGRAPH Asia '09: ACM SIGGRAPH Asia 2009 papers*, pages 1–10, New York, NY, USA, 2009. ACM.

161. Franz Kreupl. Dicke stroeme durch duenne roehrchen. *Elektronik*, 11:38–42, 2004.

162. W. Kruger, C.-A. Bohn, B. Froehlich, H. Schuth, W. Strauss, and G. Wesche. The responsive workbench: a virtual work environment. *IEEE Computer*, 28(7):42–48, 1995.

163. Yutaka Kunita, Naoko Ogawa, Atsushi Sakuma, Masahiko Inami, Taro Maeda, and Susumu Tachi. Immersive autostereoscopic display for mutual telexistence. In *Proceedings of the 3D Image Conference 2000*, pages 111–114, 2000.

164. Y. Kusakabe, M. Kanazawa, Y. Nojiri, M. Furuya, and M. Yoshimura. YC-separation Type Projector with Double Modulation. In *Proc. of International Display Workshop (IDW)*, pages 1959–1962, 2006.

165. A. Lambacher, M. Jenkner, M. Merz, B. Eversmann, R.A. Kaul, F. Hofmann, R. Thewes, and P. Fromherz. Electrical imaging of neuronal activity by multi-transistor-array (mta) recording at 7.8 micrometer resolution. *Applied Physics*, A(79):1607–1611, 2004.

166. Manuel Lang, Alexander Hornung, Oliver Wang, Steven Poulakos, Aljoscha Smolic, and Markus Gross. Nonlinear disparity mapping for stereoscopic 3d. *ACM Trans. Graph.*, 29(3):10, 2010.

167. K. Langhans and D. Bahr. Science education in action: Germany's felix project. *Journal of Laser Applications*, 8(5):221–224, 1996.

168. D. Lanman, G. Wetzstein, M. Hirsch, W. Heidrich, and R. Raskar. Polarization fields: Dynamic light field display using multi-layer LCDs. *ACM Trans. Graph.*, 30(6), 2011.

169. Douglas Lanman. *Mask-based Light Field Capture and Display*. PhD thesis, Brown University, School of Engineering, July 2010.

170. Douglas Lanman, Matthew Hirsch, Yunhee Kim, and Ramesh Raskar. Content-adaptive parallax barriers: optimizing dual-layer 3d displays using low-rank light field factorization. *ACM Trans. Graph.*, 29(6):163:1–163:10, 2010.

171. Douglas Lanman and David Luebke. Near-eye light field displays. *ACM Trans. Graph.*, 32(6):220:1–220:10, November 2013.

172. Pak Heng Lau, Kuniharu Takei, Chuan Wang, Yeonkyeong Ju, Junseok Kim, Zhibin Yu, Toshitake Takahashi, Gyoujin Cho, , and Ali Javey. Fully printed, high performance carbon nanotube thin-film transistors on flexible substrates. *Nano Letters*, 13:3864–3869, 2013.

173. G. E. Legge and J. M. Foley. Contrast masking in human vision. *Journal of the Optical Society of America*, 70(12):1458–71, dec 1980.

174. Marc Levoy and Pat Hanrahan. Light field rendering. In *SIGGRAPH '96: Proceedings of the 23rd Annual Conference on Computer Graphics and Interactive Techniques*, pages 31–42, New York, NY, USA, 1996. ACM.

175. J.S. Lipscomb and W.L. Wooten. Reducing crosstalk between stereoscopic views. In *Proc. of SPIE'95 (Stereoscopic Displays and Virtual reality)*, volume 2409, pages 31–40, 1995.

176. Sheng Liu and Hong Hua. Time-multiplexed dual-focal plane head-mounted display with a liquid lens. *Optics Letters*, 34(11):1642–1644, June 2009.

177. Sheng Liu, Hong Hua, and Dewen Cheng. A novel prototype for an optical see-through head-mounted display with addressable focus cues. *IEEE Transactions on Visualization and Computer Graphics (TVCG)*, 16(3):381–393, May / June 2010.

178. I. E. Loewenfeld. Pupillary changes related to age. In H.S.Thomson et al., editor, *Topics in Neuro-Ophthalmology*, pages 124–150. Baltimore, 1979.

179. A. Lu, R. Maciejewski, and D.S. Ebert. Volume composition using eye tracking data. In *IEEE-VGTC Symposium on Visualization*, pages 115–122, 2006.

180. Mark Lucente. *Diffraction-Specific Fringe Computation for Electro-Holography*. PhD thesis, MIT Dept. of Electrical Engineering and Computer Science, 1994. Doctoral Thesis Dissertation.

181. John Graham Macnamara. Multiple depht plane three-dimensional display using a wave guide reflector array projector. US Patent Appl. 2014/0003762 A1, 06 2014.

182. Andrew Maimone and Henry Fuchs. Computational augmented reality eyeglasses. In *Proc. of IEEE/ACM International Symposium on Mixed and Augmented Reality (ISMAR)*, pages 29–38. IEEE, 2013.

183. Andrew Maimone, Douglas Lanman, Kishore Rathinavel, Kurtis Keller, David Luebke, and Henry Fuchs. Pinlight displays: Wide field of view augmented reality eyeglasses using defocused point light sources. *ACM Trans. Graph.*, 33(4):89:1–89:11, July 2014.

184. A. Majumder and G. Welch. COMPUTER GRAPHICS OPTIQUE: Optical Superposition of Projected Computer Graphics. In *Proc. of Immersive Projection Technology - Eurographics Workshop on Virtual Environment (IPT-EGVE)*, 2001.

185. Aditi Majumder and Michael S. Brown. *Practical Multi-Projector Display Design*. A K Peters, Mattick, MA, 2007.

186. Rafał Mantiuk, Kil Joong Kim, Allan G. Rempel, and Wolfgang Heidrich. HDR-VDP-2: A calibrated visual metric for visibility and quality predictions in all luminance conditions. *ACM Transactions on Graphics*, 30(4):40:1—-40:14, jul 2011.

187. Rafał Mantiuk, Grzegorz Krawczyk, Karol Myszkowski, and Hans-Peter Seidel. Perception-motivated high dynamic range video encoding. *ACM Transactions on Graphics (Proc. of SIGGRAPH)*, 23(3):733, aug 2004.

188. Rafal Mantiuk, Karol Myszkowski, and Hans-Peter Seidel. Lossy Compression of High Dynamic Range Images and Video. In *Human Vision and Electronic Imaging*, page 60570V, 2006.

189. Rafał K. Mantiuk, Karol Myszkowski, and Hans-peter Seidel. High Dynamic Range Imaging. In *Wiley Encyclopedia of Electrical and Electronics Engineering*, pages 1–81. Wiley, 2015.

190. Raúl Martínez-Cuenca, Genaro Saavedra, Manuel Martínez-Corral, and Bahram Javidi. Progress in 3-d multiperspective display by integral imaging. *Proceedings of the IEEE*, 97(6):1067–1077, 2009.

191. Belen Masia, Gordon Wetzstein, Piotr Didyk, and Diego Gutierrez. A survey on computational displays: Pushing the boundaries of optics, computation, and perception. *Computers & Graphics*, 37(8):1012–1038, dec 2013.

192. Ian E. McDowall and Mark Bolas. Fast Light for Display, Sensing and Control Applications. In *Proc. of IEEE VR 2005 Workshop on Emerging Display Technologies (EDT)*, pages 35–36, 2005.

193. Ian E. McDowall, Mark T. Bolas, Perry Hoberman, and Scott S. Fisher. Snared Illumination. In *Proc. of ACM SIGGRAPH (Emerging Technologies)*, page 24, 2004.

194. S. McKay, S. Mason, L. S. Mair, P. Waddell, and M. Fraser. Stereoscopic display using a 1.2-m diameter stretchable membrane mirror. In *SPIE '99*, volume 3639, pages 122–131, 1999.

195. P. Merkle, K. Muller, A. Smolic, and T. Wiegand. Effcient compression of multi-view video exploiting inter-view dependencies based on h.264/mpeg4-avc. In *Proc. IEEE Int'l Conf. Multimedia and Expo*, pages 1717–1720, 2006.

196. W. Mildner. *Optimizing Processes with RFID and Auto ID*, chapter RFID - printed on a roll, pages 210–216. Wiley, 2009.

197. S. Miller, M. Nezamabadi, and S. Daly. Perceptual Signal Coding for More Efficient Usage of Bit Codes. *SMPTE Motion Imaging Journal*, 122(4):52–59, may 2013.

198. Tissaphern Mirfakhrai, John D. W. Madden, and Ray H. Baughman. Polymer artificial muscles. *Materials Today*, 10(4):30–38, April 2007.

199. M. Moeller, N. Leyland, G. Copeland, and M. Cassidy. Self-powered electrochromic display as an example for integrated modules in printed electronics applications. *Eur. Phys. J. Appl. Phys*, 51(3), September 2010.

200. Yasuhiro Mukaigawa, Takayuki Kakinuma, and Yuichi Ohta. Analytical Compensation of Inter-reflection for Pattern Projection. In *Proc. of ACM Symposium on Virtual Reality Software and Technology (VRST) (short paper)*, pages 265–268, 2006.

201. Kathy T Mullen. The contrast sensitivity of human colour vision to red-green and blue-yellow chromatic gratings. *The Journal of Physiology*, 359(1):381–400, feb 1985.

202. T. Nagata, I. Takemoto, T. Miyazawa, A. Asano, K. Yanagawa, S. Nakamura, H. Nakagawa, K. Saitou, N. Okabe, K. Matsumoto, and A. Iguchi. Silicon chip based reflective pdlc light valve for projection display. *SID Symposium Digest*, 29(1):37–40, May 1998.

203. Joshua Napoli, Sourav R. Dey, Sandy Stutsman, Oliver S. Cossairt, Thomas J. Purtell II, Samuel L. Hill, and Gregg E. Favalora. Imaging artifact precompensation for spatially multiplexed 3-d displays. In Andrew J. Woods, Nicolas S. Holliman, and John O. Merritt, editors, *Proceedings of the SPIE Stereoscopic Displays and Applications XIX*, volume 6803, 2008.

204. A. Nashel and H. Fuchs. Random hole display: A non-uniform barrier autostereoscopic display. In *Proc. of 3DTV Conference: The True Vision - Capture, Transmission and Display of 3D Video*, pages 1–4, 2009.

205. S. K. Nayar and V. Branzoi. Adaptive Dynamic Range Imaging: Optical Control of Pixel Exposures over Space and Time. In *Proc. of IEEE International Conference on Computer Vision (ICCV)*, volume 2, pages 1168–1175, 2003.

206. S. K. Nayar, V. Branzoi, and T. E. Boult. Programmable Imaging using a Digital Micromirror Array. In *Proc. of IEEE Conference on Computer Vision and Pattern Recognition (CVPR)*, volume I, pages 436–443, 2004.

207. S. K. Nayar, G. Krishnan, M. D. Grossberg, and R. Raskar. Fast Separation of Direct and Global Components of a Scene using High Frequency Illumination. In *Proc. of ACM SIGGRAPH*, pages 935–944, 2006.

208. S. K. Nayar, H. Peri, M. D. Grossberg, and P. N. Belhumeur. A Projection System with Radiometric Compensation for Screen Imperfections. In *Proc. of IEEE International Workshop on Projector-Camera Systems (ProCams)*, 2003.

209. Attila Neumann, Alessandro Artusi, Georg Zotti, Laszlo Neumann, and Werner Purgathofer. An interactive perception-based model for characterization of display devices. *Proceedings of SPIE*, 5293:232–241, 2003.

210. R. Ng, M. Levoy, M. Bredif, G. Duval, M. Horowitz, and P. Hanrahan. Light field photography with a hand-held plenoptic camera. Technical Report CTSR 2005-02, Stanford Tech Report CTSR, 2005.

211. Michael A. Nielsen and Isaac L. Chuang. *Quantum Computation and Quantum Information*. Cambridge University Press, Cambridge, UK, 2000.

212. Hideki Nii, Maki Sugimoto, and Masahiko Inami. Smart Light-Ultra High Speed Projector for Spatial Multiplexing Optical Transmission. In *Proc. of IEEE International Workshop on Projector-Camera Systems (ProCams)*, 2005.

213. Sheila Nirenberg and Chethan Pandarinath. Retinal prosthetic strategy with the capacity to restore normal vision. *PNAS*, 2012.

214. Kenji Nomura, Hiromichi Ohta, Akihiro Takagi, Toshio Kamiya, Masahiro Hiranao, and Hideo Hosono. Room-temperature fabrication of transparent flexible thin-film transistors using amorphous oxide semiconductors. *Nature*, 432:488–492, 2004.

215. Yuji Oyamada and Hideo Saito. Focal Pre-Correction of Projected Image for Deblurring Screen Image. In *Proc. of IEEE International Workshop on Projector-Camera Systems (ProCams)*, 2007.

216. Jagdish Pandey, Yu-Te Liao, Andrew Lingley, Ramin Mirjalili, Babak Parviz, and Brian P. Otis. A fully integrated rf-powered contact lens with a single element display. *IEEE Transactions on Biomedical Circuits and Systems*, 4(6):454–461, 2010.

217. H. Park, M.-H. Lee, S.-J. Kim, and J.-Il Park. Contrast Enhancement in Direct-Projected Augmented Reality. In *Proc. of IEEE International Conference on Multimedia and Expo (ICME)*, pages 1313–1316, 2006.

218. Hanhoon Park, Moon-Hyun Lee, Byung-Kuk Seoand Yoonjong Jin, and Jong-Il Park. Content adaptive embedding of complementary patterns for nonintrusive direct-projected augmented reality. In *HCI International 2007*, volume LNCS 4563, pages 132–141, 2007.

219. Hanhoon Park, Moon-Hyun Lee, Sang-Jun Kim, and Jong-Il Park. Specularity-Free Projection on Nonplanar Surface. In *Proc. of Pacific-Rim Conference on Multimedia (PCM)*, pages 606–616, 2005.

220. Hanhoon Park, Moon-Hyun Lee, Byung-Kuk Seo, Hong-Chang Shin, and Jong-Il Park. Radiometrically-Compensated Projection onto Non-Lambertian Surface using Multiple Overlapping Projectors. In *Proc. of Pacific-Rim Symposium on Image and Video Technology (PSIVT)*, pages 534–544, 2006.

221. Sung C. Park, Min K. Park, and Moon G. Kang. Super-Resolution Image Reconstruction: A Technical Overview. *IEEE Signal Processing Magazine*, 20(3):21–36, 2003.

222. J. Parsons and J. P. Rolland. A non-intrusive display technique for providing real-time data within a surgeons critical area of interest. *Studies in Health Technologies and Informatics*, 50:246–251, 1998.

223. A. Pavlovych and W. Stuerzlinger. A High-Dynamic Range Projection System. In *Proc. of SPIE*, volume 5969, 2005.

224. Ken Perlin, Salvatore Paxia, and Joel S. Kollin. An autostereoscopic display. In *SIGGRAPH '00: Proceedings of the 27th annual conference on Computer graphics and interactive techniques*, pages 319–326, New York, NY, USA, 2000. ACM Press/Addison-Wesley Publishing Co.

225. Hal Philipp. Touchscreens der naechsten dimension. *Elektronik*, special issue Semiconductors:22–26, 2008.

226. Tony Philips. The mathematical uncertainty principle, 2010.

227. Claudio Pinhanez. Using a Steerable Projector and a Camera to Transform Surfaces into Interactive Displays. In *Proc. of CHI (extended abstracts)*, pages 369–370, 2001.

228. Max Planck. 1. ueber das gesetz der energieverteilung im normalspektrum, 2. ueber die elementarquanta der materie und der elektrizitaet. *Verhandlungen der Deutschen Physikalischen Gesellschaft*, 2:237–246, 1900.

229. I. Rakkolainen and K. Palovuori. Wave - a walk-thru virtual environment. In *Proceedings of Immersive Projection Technology Symposium*, 2002.

230. Mahesh Ramasubramanian, Sumanta N. Pattanaik, and Donald P. Greenberg. A Perceptually Based Physical Error Metric for Realistic Image Synthesis. In *Proc. of ACM SIGGRAPH*, pages 73–82, 1999.

231. R. Raskar. Oblique Projector Rendering on Planar Surfaces for a Tracked User. In *Proc. of ACM SIGGRAPH (Sketches and Applications)*, page 260, 1999.

232. R. Raskar, M.S. Brown, R. Yang, W. Chen, G. Welch, H. Towles, B. Seales, and H. Fuchs. Multi-Projector Displays using Camera-Based Registration. In *Proc. of IEEE Visualization*, pages 161–168, 1999.

233. Ramesh Raskar, Paul Beardsley, Jeroen van Baar, Yao Wang, Paul Dietz, Johnny Lee, Darren Leigh, and Thomas Willwacher. RFIG Lamps: Interacting with a Self-Describing World via Photosensing Wireless Tags and Projectors. In *Proc. of ACM SIGGRAPH*, pages 406–415, 2004.

234. Ramesh Raskar, Hideaki Nii, Bert de Decker, Yuki Hashimoto, Jay Summet, Dylan Moore, Yong Zhao, Jonathan Westhues, Paul Dietz, Masahiko Inami, Shree K. Nayar, John Barnwell, Michael Noland, Philippe Bekaert, Vlad Branzoi, and Erich Bruns. Prakash: Lighting Aware Motion Capture using Photosensing Markers and Multiplexed Illuminators. In *Proc. of ACM SIGGRAPH*, page Article 36, 2007.

235. Ramesh Raskar, Jeroen van Baar, and Thomas Willwacher. Quadric transfer for immersive curved display. Technical Report TR2004-034, Mistubishi Eelectric Research Laboratories, January 2004.

236. Ramesh Raskar, Greg Welch, Matt Cutts, Adam Lake, Lev Stesin, and Henry Fuchs. The Office of the Future: A Unified Approach to Image-Based Modeling and Spatially Immersive Displays. In *Proc. of ACM SIGGRAPH*, pages 179–188, 1998.

237. I. Rechenberg. *Evolutionsstrategie '94*. Werkstatt Bionik und Evolutionstechnik. Frommann-Holzboog, 1994.

238. Stephan Reichelt, Hagen Sahm, Norbert Leister, and Armin Schwerdtner. Capabilities of diffractive optical elements for real-time holographic displays. In *Proceedings of SPIE, Vol. 6912, Practical Holography XXII*, volume 6912, 2008.

239. Udo Reinert. *Holographie - Medium der Zukunft*. Holtronic GmbH, 1986.

240. Erik Reinhard, Greg Ward, Sumanta Pattanaik, and Paul Debevec. *High Dynamic Range Imaging - Acquisition, Display and Image-Based Lighting*. Morgan Kaufmann, San Francisco, CA, 2006.

241. Erik Reinhard, Greg Ward, Sumanta Pattanaik, Paul Debevec, Wolfgang Heidrich, and Karol Myszkowski. *High Dynamic Range Imaging: Acquisition, Display, and Image-Based Lighting, Second Edition*. Morgan Kaufmann, San Francisco, CA, 2010.

242. Eleanor G. Rieffel and Wolfgang Polak. An introduction to quantum computing for non-physicists. *ACM Comput. Surv.*, 32(3):300–335, 2000.

243. DisplayăDeviceăConsultantsăLLC. RobertăDonofrio. Update on display aging. In *SPIEăDefenseă&ăSecurityăSymposiumă28ăMarchꞑă1ăAprilă2005*, 2005.

244. John G. Bennet Rod G. Fleck, Andreas G. Nowatzyk. Direct view augmented reality eyeglass-type display. US Patent appl. 20130286053, 2013.

245. Jannick P. Rolland. The past, present and future of freeform optics. In *Renewable Energy and the Environment*, OSA Technical Digest (online). Optical Society of America, 2013.

246. Jannick P. Rolland and Henry Fuchs. Optical versus video see-through head-mounted displays in medical visualization. *Presence: Teleoper. Virtual Environ.*, 9(3):287–309, 2000.

247. K. Ryu, A. Badmaev, C. Wang, A. Lin, N. Patil, L. Gomez, A. Kumar, S. Mitra, H. Wong, and C. Zhou. Cmos-analogous wafer-scale nanotube-on-insulator approach for submicrometer devices and integrated circuits using aligned nanotubes. *Nano Letters*, 9(1):189–197, December 2009.

248. Ehsan Saeedi, Babak Amirparviz, and Xiaoyu Miao. Near-to-eye display with diffraction gratings that bends and focuses light. US patent appl. 2013/0100362 A1, 2013.

249. H. Saito, H. Kimura, S. Shimada, T. Naemura, J. Kayahara, S. Jarusirisawad, V. Nozick, H. Ishikawa, T. Murakami, J. Aoki, A. Asano, T. Kimura, M. Kakehata, F. Sasaki, H. Yashiro, M. Mori, K. Torizuka, and K. Ino. Laser-plasma scanning 3d display for putting digital contents in free space. In *Stereoscopic Displays and Applications XIX, Proceedings of SPIE*, volume 6803, 2008.

250. Joaquim Salvi, Jordi Pagès, and Joan Batlle. Pattern Codification Strategies in Structured Light Systems. *Pattern Recognition*, 37(4):827–849, 2004.

251. Graham Saxby. *Practical Holography*. IOP Publishing, 2004.

252. Henning Schaefer. Kalibrierungen fuer augmented reality. Master's thesis, Technical University of Berlin, 2003.

253. E.M. Schmidt, M..J. Bak, F. T. Hambrecht, C. V. Kufta, D. K. O'Rourke, and P. Vallabhanath. Feasibility of a Visual Prosthesis for the Blind Based on Intracortical Microstiimulation of the Visual Cortex. *Brain*, 119:507–522, 1996.

254. B.T. Schowengerdt and E.J. Seibel. True 3d scanned voxel displays using single and multiple light sources. *Journal of the Society for Information Display*, 14(2):135–143, 2006.

255. Ulrike Schulz, Norbert Kaiser, Peter Munzert, Michael Scheler, and Hein Uhlig. Verfahren zur reduzierung der grenzflaechenreflexion von kunststoffsubstraten sowie derart

modifiziertes substrat und dessen verwendung. German Patent, No. DE10241708.3, 09 2005.

256. Helge Seetzen, Wolfgang Heidrich, Wolfgang Stuerzlinger, Greg Ward, Lorne Whitehead, Matthew Trentacoste, Abhijeet Ghosh, and Andrejs Vorozcovs. High Dynamic Range Display Systems. In *Proc. of ACM SIGGRAPH*, pages 760–768, 2004.

257. Steven M. Seitz, Yasuyuki Matsushita, and Kiriakos N. Kutulakos. A Theory of Inverse Light Transport. In *Proc. of IEEE International Conference on Computer Vision (ICCV)*, volume 2, pages 1440–1447, 2005.

258. M. Selbrede and B. Yost. Time multiplexed optical shutter (tmos) display technology for avionics platforms. *Proc. SPIE*, 6225, 2006.

259. Pradeep Sen, Billy Chen, Gaurav Garg, Stephen R. Marschner, Mark Horowitz, Marc Levoy, and Hendrik P. A. Lensch. Dual Photography. In *Proc. of ACM SIGGRAPH*, pages 745–755, 2005.

260. Romi Shamai, David Andelman, Bruno Berge, and Rob Hayes. Water, electricity, and between... on electrowetting and its applications. *Soft Matter*, 4:38–45, 2008.

261. Claude Shannon. Communication in the presence of noise (reprint). *Proceedings of the IEEE*, 86(2):477–457, February 1998.

262. Yoshinari Shirai, Mitsunori Matsushita, and Takeshi Ohguro. HIEI Projector: Augmenting a Real Environment with Invisible Information. In *Proc. of Workshop on Interactive Systems and Software (WISS)*, pages 115–122, 2003. in Japanese.

263. A.E. Shortt, T.J. Naughton, and B. Javindi. A companding approach for nonuniform quantization of digital holograms of three-dimensional objects. *Opt. Express*, 14(12):5129–5134, 2006.

264. SID. *Information Display Measurement Standard*. Society for Information Display, 1.03b edition, 2012.

265. A. Smolic and P. Kauff. Interactive 3-d video representation and coding technologies. *Proceedings of the IEEE*, 93(1):98–110, 2005.

266. Raymond Spottiswoode and Nigel Spottiswoode. *The Theory of Stereoscopic Transmission and its adaptatopn to the motion picture*. University of California Press, Berkeley and Los Angeles, 1953.

267. Hagen Stolle, Jean-Christophe Olaya, Steffen Buschbeck, Hagen Sahm, and Dr. Armin Schwerdtner. Technical solutions for a full-resolution auto-stereoscopic 2d/3d display technology. In *SPIE Conference Proceedings Stereoscopic Displays and Applications XIX*, volume 6803, 2008.

268. R. Sukthankar, C. Tat-Jen, and G. Sukthankar. Dynamic Shadow Elimination for Multi-Projector Displays. In *Proc. of IEEE Conference on Computer Vision and Pattern Recognition (CVPR)*, volume II, pages 151–157, 2001.

269. Joji Takei, Shingo Kagami, and Koichi Hashimoto. 3,000-fps 3-D Shape Measurement Using a High-Speed Camera-Projector System. In *Proc. of IEEE/RSJ International Conference on Intelligent Robots and Systems (IROS)*, pages 3211–3216, 2007.

270. Nobuhiko Tamura, Norimichi Tsumura, and Yoichi Miyake. Masking model for accurate colorimetric characterization of LCD. *Journal of the Society for Information Display*, 11(2):333, 2003.

271. K. Teunissen, S. Qin, and IEJR Heynderickx. A perceptually based metric to characterize the viewing-angle range of matrix displays. *JSID*, 16(1):27–36, 2008.

272. A.C Traub. Stereoscopic display using varifocal mirror oscillations. *Applied Optics*, 6(6):1085–1087, 1967.

273. Stuart L. Turner. *Coupling Retinal Scanning Displays to the Human Vision System: Visual Response and Engineering Considerations*. PhD thesis, University of Washington, 2000.

274. Christopher W. Tyler. Colour bit-stealing to enhance the luminance resolution of digital displays on a single pixel basis. *Spatial Vision*, 10(4):369–377, jan 1997.

275. T. Uchida, H. Seki, C. Shishido, and M. Wada. Bright dichroic guest-host lcds without a polarizer. *Proceedings of the SID*, 22(1):41–46, 1981.

276. Eden Ashley Umble. Making it real: the future of stereoscopic 3d film technology. *SIGGRAPH Comput. Graph.*, 40(1):3, 2006.

277. A. van Meeteren and J.J. Vos. Resolution and contrast sensitivity at low luminances. *Vision Research*, 12(5):825–IN2, may 1972.

278. Floris L. van Nes and Maarten A. Bouman. Spatial Modulation Transfer in the Human Eye. *Journal of the Optical Society of America*, 57(3):401, mar 1967.

279. Marcelo Bernardes Vieira, Luiz Velho, Asla Sa, and Paulo Cezar Carvalho. A Camera-Projector System for Real-Time 3D Video. In *Proc. of IEEE International Workshop on Projector-Camera Systems (ProCams)*, 2005.

280. Robert Wanat and Rafał K. Mantiuk. Simulating and compensating changes in appearance between day and night vision. *ACM Transactions on Graphics*, 33(4):147, 2014.

281. Dong Wang, Imari Sato, Takahiro Okabe, and Yoichi Sato. Radiometric Compensation in a Projector-Camera System Based on the Properties of Human Vision System. In *Proc. of IEEE International Workshop on Projector-Camera Systems (ProCams)*, 2005.

282. Yu-Shuen Wang, Hongbo Fu, Olga Sorkine, Tong-Yee Lee, and Hans-Peter Seidel. Motion-aware temporal coherence for video resizing. *ACM Trans. Graph. (Proceedings of ACM SIGGRAPH ASIA)*, 28(5):Article 127, December 2009.

283. Yu-Shuen Wang, Hui-Chih Lin, Olga Sorkine, and Tong-Yee Lee. Motion-based video retargeting with optimized crop-and-warp. In *SIGGRAPH '10: ACM SIGGRAPH 2010 papers*, pages 1–9, New York, NY, USA, 2010. ACM.

284. Michael Waschbüsch, Stephan Würmlin, Daniel Cotting, Filip Sadlo, and Markus H. Gross. Scalable 3D Video of Dynamic Scenes. *The Visual Computer*, 21(8-10):629–638, 2005.

285. A. B. Watson. High Frame Rates and Human Vision: A View Through the Window of Visibility. *SMPTE Motion Imaging Journal*, 122(2):18–32, mar 2013.

286. Simon J. Watt, Kurt Akeley, Marc O. Ernst, and Martin S. Banks. Focus cues affect perceived depth. *J Vis*, 5(10):Article 7, 2005.

287. Senfar Wen and Royce Wu. Two-primary crosstalk model for characterizing liquid crystal displays. *Color Research and Application*, 31(2):102–108, 2006.

288. G. Wetzstein, D. Lanman, W. Heidrich, and R. Raskar. Layered 3D: Tomographic image synthesis for attenuation-based light field and high dynamic range displays. *ACM Trans. Graph.*, 30(4), 2011.

289. G. Wetzstein, D. Lanman, M. Hirsch, and R. Raskar. Tensor Displays: Compressive Light Field Synthesis using Multilayer Displays with Directional Backlighting. *ACM Trans. Graph. (Proc. SIGGRAPH)*, 31(4):1–11, 2012.

290. Gordon Wetzstein and Oliver Bimber. Radiometric Compensation through Inverse Light Transport. In *PG '07 Proceedings of the 15th Pacific Conference on Computer Graphics and Applications*, pages 391–399, 2007.

291. D.L. White and G.N. Taylor. New absorptive mode reflective liquid-crystal display device. *Journal of Applied Physics*, 45(11):4718–4723, 1974.

292. B. Wilburn, N. Joshi, V. Vaish, M. Levoy, and M. Horowitz. High-Speed Videography Using a Dense Camera Array. In *Proc. of IEEE Conference on Computer Vision and Pattern Recognition (CVPR)*, volume II, pages 294–301, 2004.

293. Bennett Wilburn, Neel Joshi, Vaibhav Vaish, Eino-Ville Talvala, Emilio Antunez, Adam Barth, Andrew Adams, Mark Horowitz, and Marc Levoy. High Performance Imaging Using Large Camera Arrays. In *Proc. of ACM SIGGRAPH*, pages 765–776, 2005.

294. Alexander Wolter. *Untersuchungen zu einem hochaufloesenden Flaechenlichtmodulator mit einstellbarem Profil einer Fluessigkeitsoberflaeche zur optischen Musterwiedergabe*. PhD thesis, Fachbereich Elektrotechnik der Gerhard-Mercator-Universitaet-Gesamthochschule Duisburg, 2001.

295. Thilo Womelsdorf, Katharina Anton-Erxleben, Florian Pieper, and Stefan Treue. Dynamic shifts of visual receptive fields in cortical area mt by spatial attention. *Nature Neuroscience*, 9:1156–1160, 2006.

296. W. D. Wright. A re-determination of the trichromatic coefficients of the spectral colours. *Transactions of the Optical Society*, 30(4):141–164, 1928.

297. St. Wuttke, S. M. Coman, G. Scholz, H. Kirmse, A. Vimont, M. Daturi, S. L .M. Schroeder, and E. Kemnitz. Novel sol-gel synthesis of acidic mgf2-x(oh)x materials. *Chem. Eur. J.*, 14(36):11488–11499, 2008.

298. Kaida Xiao, Chenyang Fu, Dimosthenis Karatzas, and Sophie Wuerger. Visual gamma correction for LCD displays. *Displays*, 32(1):17–23, 2011.

299. Deng-Ke Yang, Xiao-Yang Huang, and Yang-Ming Zhu. Bistable cholesteric reflective displays: Materials and drive schemes. *Annu. Rev. Mater. Sci.*, 27:117–146, August 1997.

300. Jianming Yang, Weiqi Liu, Weizhen Lv, Daliang Zhang, Fei He, Zhonglun Wei, and Yusi Kang. Method of achieving a wide field-of-view head-mounted display with small distortion. *OPTICS LETTERS*, 38(12):2035–2037, 2013.

301. Ruigang Yang and Greg Welch. Automatic and Continuous Projector Display Surface Calibration using Every-Day Imagery. In *Proc. of International Conference in Central Europe on Computer Graphics, Visualization and Computer Vision (WSCG)*, 2001.

302. T. Yendo, T. Fujii, M. Tanimoto, and M. P. Tehrani. The seelinder: Cylindrical 3d display viewable from 360 degrees. *Journal of Visual Communication and Image Representation*, 21(5-6):586–594, 2010.

303. Takenobu Yoshida, Chinatsu Horii, and Kosuke Sato. A Virtual Color Reconstruction System for Real Heritage with Light Projection. In *Proc. of International Conference on Virtual Systems and Multimedia (VSMM)*, pages 161–168, 2003.

304. L. Zhang and S. K. Nayar. Projection Defocus Analysis for Scene Capture and Image Display. In *Proc. of ACM SIGGRAPH*, pages 907–915, 2006.

305. Qiaohui Zhang, L. V. Saraf, and Feng Hua. Transparent thin-film transistor with self-assembled nanocrystals. *Nanotechnology*, 18(19), 2007.

306. Ziegler, Bucheli, Ahrenberg, Magnor, and Gross. A bidirectional light field - hologram transform. *Computer Graphics Forum*, 26(3):435–446, September 2007.

307. R. Ziegler, P. Kaufmann, and M. Gross. A framework for holographic scene representation and image synthesis. In *ACM SIGGRAPH 2006*, Boston, USA, 2006. ACM.

308. D. Zipperer. Roll-to-roll printed electronics. In *Digital Fabrication*, pages 734–736, 2010.

309. S. Zollmann and O. Bimber. Imperceptible Calibration for Radiometric Compensation. In *Proc. of Eurographics (short paper)*, pages 61–64, 2007.

310. Stefanie Zollmann, Tobias Langlotz, and Oliver Bimber. Passive-Active Geometric Calibration for View-Dependent Projections onto Arbitrary Surfaces. *Proc. of Workshop on Virtual and Augmented Reality of the GI-Fachgruppe AR/VR 2006 (re-print in Journal of Virtual Reality and Broadcasting 2007)*, 2006.

311. Eberhart Zrenner. Will retinal implants restore vision? *Science*, 295:1022–1025, 2002.

312. Eberhart Zrenner, Karl Ulrich Bartz-Schmidt, Heval Benav, Dorothea Besch, Anna Bruckmann, Veit-Peter Gabel, Florian Gekeler, Udo Greppmaier, Alex Harscher, Steffen Kibbel, Johannes Koch, Akos Kusnyerik, Tobias Peters, Katarina Stingl, Helmut Sachs, Alfred Stett, Peter Szurman, Barbara Wilhelm, and Robert Wilke. Subretinal electronic chips allow blind patients to read letters and combine them to words. *Proceedings of the Royal Society B*, 2010.

313. Brian T. Schowengerdt, Cameron M. Lee, Richard S. Johnston, C. David Melville, and Eric J. Seibel. 1-mm diameter, full-color scanning fiber pico projector. *SID 09 DIGEST*, pages 522–525, 2009.

314. Sharon J. Miller, Cameron M. Lee, Bishnu P. Joshi, Adam Gaustad, Eric J. Seibel, and Thomas D. Wang. Targeted detection of murine colonic dysplasia in vivo with flexible multispectral scanning fiber endoscopy. *Journal of Biomedical Optics*, 17(2):021103–1–021103–11, 2012.

315. B.T. Schowengerdt and M.D. WATSON. Ultra-high resolution scanning fiber display. WO 2014113506 A1, 2014.

316. Masakazu Kawada. Combined display and viewing system. EP0580261A1, 1994.

317. Tomoyuki Yokota, Peter Zalar, Martin Kaltenbrunner, Hiroaki Jinno, Naoji Matsuhisa, Hiroki Kitanosako, Yutaro Tachibana, Wakako Yukita, Mari Koizumi, and Takao Someya. Ultraflexible organic photonic skin. *Science Advances*, 2(4):e1501856, 2016.

Index